I0868805

Energy Efficient Algorithms and Green Data Centers for Sustainable Computing

P.J. Beslin Pajila
Vel Tech Rangarajan Dr. Sagunthala R&D Institute of Science and Technology, India

Belfin Robinson Vimala
University of North Carolina, USA

Y. Harold Robinson
Francis Xavier Engineering College, India

C. Gopala Krishnan
GITAM University, India

IGI Global
Scientific Publishing
Publishing Tomorrow's Research Today

Vice President of Editorial Melissa Wagner
Managing Editor of Acquisitions Mikaela Felty
Managing Editor of Book Development Jocelynn Hessler
Production Manager Mike Brehm
Cover Design Phillip Shickler

Published in the United States of America by
IGI Global Scientific Publishing
701 East Chocolate Avenue
Hershey, PA, 17033, USA
Tel: 717-533-8845
Fax: 717-533-8661
Website: https://www.igi-global.com E-mail: cust@igi-global.com

Copyright © 2025 by IGI Global Scientific Publishing. All rights reserved. No part of this publication may be reproduced, stored or distributed in any form or by any means, electronic or mechanical, including photocopying, without written permission from the publisher.
Product or company names used in this set are for identification purposes only. Inclusion of the names of the products or companies does not indicate a claim of ownership by IGI Global Scientific Publishing of the trademark or registered trademark.

Library of Congress Cataloging-in-Publication Data

Names: Pajila, Beslin editor | Robinson, Belfin editor | Robinson, Y. Harold editor | C., Gopala Krishnan editor
Title: Energy efficient algorithms and green data centers for sustainable computing / edited by Beslin Pajila, Belfin Robinson Vimala, Y. Harold Robinson, C. Gopala Krishnan.
Description: Hershey, PA : IGI Global Scientific Publishing, [2025] | Includes bibliographical references and index. | Summary: "This book addresses the urgent environmental challenges posed by the rising energy demands of modern computational systems, presenting both theoretical insights and practical solutions for reducing carbon footprints while maintaining high levels of functionality. A key aim of the book is to promote energy efficiency in algorithm design, encouraging researchers and developers to consider energy savings as a priority in computational processes across diverse applications from AI and machine learning to big data and cloud computing"-- Provided by publisher.
Identifiers: LCCN 2024060589 (print) | LCCN 2024060590 (ebook) | ISBN 9798337307664 h/c | ISBN 9798337307671 s/c | ISBN 9798337307688 ebook
Subjects: LCSH: Data centers--Energy conservation | Data centers--Environmental aspects | Artificial intelligence--Environmental aspects | Machine learning--Industrial applications | Computer algorithms
Classification: LCC TJ163.5.D38 .E48 2025 (print) | LCC TJ163.5.D38 (ebook)
LC record available at https://lccn.loc.gov/2024060589
LC ebook record available at https://lccn.loc.gov/2024060590

British Cataloguing in Publication Data
A Cataloguing in Publication record for this book is available from the British Library.

All work contributed to this book is new, previously-unpublished material.
The views expressed in this book are those of the authors, but not necessarily of the publisher.
This book contains information sourced from authentic and highly regarded references, with reasonable efforts made to ensure the reliability of the data and information presented. The authors, editors, and publisher believe the information in this book to be accurate and true as of the date of publication. Every effort has been made to trace and credit the copyright holders of all materials included. However, the authors, editors, and publisher cannot assume responsibility for the validity of all materials or the consequences of their use. Should any copyright material be found unacknowledged, please inform the publisher so that corrections may be made in future reprints.

Table of Contents

Detailed Table of Contents

Sustainable website design is crucial today, given the growing concern for environmental impact. The website contents and energy consumption relation are the outcome of this research work. Internet users access the website on personal computers or handheld devices. The energy consumption varies at the user device due to the various elements of the website. The website design for increase in profit and ignorance towards energy consumption requires awareness. This work analyses the various contents on the webpage and its relation. This research work is to find out whether the UI design principle of 60-30-10 rule is followed or not. Another contribution of the work is to find energy consumption due to the color combination, image format, and font style of the webpage. The chapter will investigate the responsiveness and accessibility of the website in correlation with the energy consumption due to the various elements of the webpage. This chapter will establish guidelines for sustainable and energy efficient webpages.

Cloud computing has experienced great growth in the recent past and has been attributed to bringing huge economic value but at the same time has been associated with energy usage and environmental consequences. The problem of how to make cloud computing environmentally friendly and create green data centers is one of the major concerns of the cloud computing industry at present. This survey focuses on the following four dimensions of sustainability in the context of cloud environments: energy efficiency, resource optimization, renewable energy, and sustainable hardware. Furthermore, the authors also explore the limitations associated with cost, size, and security requirements in terms of environmental goals. The chapter gives a classification of sustainable cloud techniques, discusses present industry activities, and gives potential future technologies such as AI-driven energy management and edge computing as potential solutions. The goal of this chapter is to provide a literature review of sustainable practices and encourage more investigations into ecoconscious cloud computing.

HPC systems are crucial to scientific computation and industry processes however, their power consumption is a major economic and environmental concern. Efficient algorithms are important to decrease the power consumption of HPC systems, and make such systems more efficient and feasible. To that end, this survey focuses on the main algorithmic techniques aimed at enhancing energy consumption throughout HPC components, such as processors, memory, and networks. We classify these approaches into classes depending on the dynamic and static power management, workload based techniques, and domains specific optimizations. In this paper, we compare energy efficient algorithms and their trade off with the performance and the issues related to integration and scalability of the algorithms are also presented. Last, we present the directions for future work, including the development of enhanced programming models, standardized policies, and quantum computing. This survey gives a clear picture and presents the future direction of the energy-aware solutions in HPC.

Sustainability-aligned environmental improvement is demanded by a number of international organizations, including UNO. Sustainability from an environmental perspective means protecting the environment, reducing the rate of climate change, and promoting social advancement without endangering human life or leaving anyone behind. By meeting our present demands, this concept seeks to preserve resources

The increased use of IoT devices within various industries has brought into focus the issue of power consumption since many of these devices have limited power sources. The present work offers a survey on energy efficient protocols and devices in IoT, strategies for the energy optimization for IoT devices. It covers technologies, which operate at low power including LowPower WideArea Networks, Bluetooth Low Energy (BLE), and energyefficient Medium Access Control (MAC) protocols. Further, the paper goes deeper into energy efficient hardware design, low power sensing technologies and energy aware data processing methods where edge and fog computing are stressed as a means of minimizing energy expenditure. The survey also includes information on the methods of energy harvesting, routing and network layer protocols for energy saving, the use of machine learning to manage energy. Last, the paper discusses emerging trends in IoT energy efficiency such as 5G, AI, and quantum technology.

Abstract The exponential rise in big data has resulted in higher energy requirements in data processing frameworks, which present a major environmental and practical concern. As the amount of data being generated grows, cost effective and energy efficient big data processing has become critical. This paper reviews different techniques that improve energy efficiency in big data processing from hardware level optimization, software level adaptation and data level optimization. Proposed and implemented low power processors and energy aware storage; energy efficient scheduling; data compression; and data reduction strategies such as edge computing have been found to be effective in the energy management of big data processing. Other new paths include artificial intelligence based energy management and green data centers. The goal of this survey is to give an overview of the existing situation, show examples of the implementation of energy-efficient BD processing frameworks, and point out the possible directions for their further development.

The escalating environmental consequences of software development have raised a concern for sustainable software engineering throughout the life cycle. Green software engineering aims at reducing the power utilization in software systems

Artificial Intelligence (AI) and Machine Learning (ML) are at the forefront of technological progress, revolutionizing fields such as healthcare, finance, and transportation. However, the energy-intensive processes involved in training and deploying complex AI models have raised significant environmental concerns. Green AI and ML represent a shift toward sustainable practices by emphasizing energy efficiency, reducing carbon footprints, and minimizing resource usage. This approach encompasses the development of optimized algorithms, efficient hardware solutions, and the use of renewable energy during computation. Green AI advocates for training smaller models with reduced computational complexity, thereby ensuring performance with lower environmental costs. Techniques such as model distillation, pruning, and quantization are increasingly being adopted to achieve this balance. Furthermore, Green AI encourages collaboration among researchers, policymakers, and industries paradigm is essential for advancing AI responsibly in an era of growing environmental challenges.

With the advancement of the mobile and wireless computing technologies more and more attention has been paid to their impact on environment. This paper provides an overview of green solutions pertaining to the energy conservation and carbon emission of portable gadgets, wireless networks and communication systems. It covers fundamental concepts like low power hardware design, energy efficient cellular network and efficient power control mechanisms. The viability of renewable resources as well as the energy harvesting and wireless charging technologies in enhancing sustainability of the devices is also described. Furthermore, the paper analyses the implementation of edge computing, energy-aware networks, and AI solutions for enhancing energy efficiency in mobile and wireless networks. Green mobile networks and sustainable IoT are illustrated by case studies of real-world applications. Last, the paper presents a discussion of the threat, including the trade-off between performance and energy consumption, and directions for future research to improve sustainability in this field.

Green artificial intelligence (AI) is designed to be more eco-friendly and accessible compared to traditional AI. It delivers precise results without the added computational costs and allows researchers with just a laptop to conduct high-quality work without the need for expensive cloud servers. This chapter explores green AI as a crucial method for improving the environmental sustainability of AI systems. It covers AI solutions that promote eco-friendly practices in various fields (referred to as "green-by AI"), methods for developing energy-efficient machine learning (ML) algorithms and models (known as "green-in AI"), and tools for accurately measuring and optimizing energy usage. The chapter also looks at how regulations can support green AI and discusses future directions for sustainable ML. It highlights the need to integrate environmental considerations into AI practices to promote a more eco-conscious and energy-efficient future for AI technologies.

The rising energy demands of large data centers call for energy-efficient AI training methods. Federated Learning (FL), a decentralized paradigm, offers a solution by enabling model training across distributed devices without centralizing sensitive data. This review explores FL's integration with distributed data centers to achieve energy efficiency, analyzing methods like federated averaging and energy-aware protocols to minimize resource use. It highlights techniques such as model compression, quantization, and adaptive FL to reduce on-device computation while maintaining performance. Practical implementation is discussed through tools like TensorFlow Federated and PySyft, with case studies from healthcare, finance, and IoT showcasing cost reductions and sustainability. Future research directions include combining FL with edge computing and low-power AI hardware, emphasizing FL’s potential for scalable, sustainable AI.

ML and AI can transform energy optimisation in numerous industries. This chapter discusses how AI and ML have revolutionized price, energy efficiency, and environmental sustainability. AI-powered systems can optimise the grid's renewable energy integration, manage energy resources in real time, and forecast consumption trends using optimization, and predictive analytics. Smart grids, renewable energy forecasting, industrial energy management, smart buildings, and EV charging infrastructure are major applications. This chapter also discusses these fields ML methodologies. Supervised learning estimates energy consumption, RL regulates energy adaptively, and deep learning analyzes complicated data. This chapter presents effective AI-driven energy solution case studies. Edge AI, decentralized energy

Preface

In the era of rapid technological advancements, the demand for computational power has surged, leading to a significant increase in energy consumption. As a result, energy-efficient algorithms and green data centers have become crucial for promoting sustainability in computing. This book, "Energy Efficient Algorithms and Green Data Centers for Sustainable Computing" explores how innovative strategies can minimize energy usage while maintaining high performance and reliability in data processing.

This book delves into the principles, methodologies, and real-world applications of energy-efficient algorithms that optimize computing resources, reduce carbon footprints, and contribute to sustainable digital infrastructure. Additionally, it examines the design and operation of green data centers, which integrate renewable energy sources, advanced cooling techniques, and intelligent workload management to achieve environmental and economic benefits.Contributions from researchers, industry professionals, and sustainability experts provide a comprehensive analysis of the challenges and opportunities in sustainable computing. By integrating energy-conscious algorithms with eco-friendly data center designs, this chapter highlights strategies to create a greener and more efficient computing ecosystem.

As we move toward a future where sustainability is imperative, this book serves as a valuable resource for engineers, researchers, and technology leaders striving to develop energy-efficient computing solutions. We hope this work inspires further innovations in sustainable computing and fosters a commitment to reducing the environmental impact of digital technologies.

Chapter 1: Energy-Efficient Web Design - The Effect of UI Choices on Power Consumption

This chapter highlights strategies for mitigating these impacts, including green data center initiatives, energy-efficient software development, and sustainable UI/UX design. By analyzing the environmental consequences of digital technology and proposing innovative solutions, this work aims to contribute to the global efforts toward achieving net-zero emissions.

Chapter 2: Sustainable Cloud Computing: Ecofriendly Strategies and Innovations for Green Data Centers

This Chapter highlights the principles and practices of sustainable cloud computing, focusing on strategies that enhance energy efficiency, integrate renewable energy sources, and promote responsible resource management. This chapter also examines key metrics for assessing sustainability, industry standards and certifications, and innovations such as virtualization, AI-driven energy optimization, and waste reduction techniques. Additionally, it highlights policy frameworks and emerging technologies that support greener cloud infrastructures.

Chapter 3: Energy Efficient Algorithms in High Performance Computing:Approaches, Applications, and Innovations

This chapter examines algorithmic strategies for reducing power consumption, optimizing resource allocation, and improving workload scheduling in HPC environments. Additionally, it highlights the role of Dynamic Voltage and Frequency Scaling (DVFS), task scheduling, load balancing, and memory optimization in enhancing energy efficiency without compromising computational throughput.

Chapter 4: Edge and Fog Computing for Sustainability

This chapter provides a comprehensive analysis of the role of Fog and Edge Computing in sustainable computing, offering insights into technical advancements, real-world applications, challenges, and future directions. It is a valuable resource for researchers, policymakers, industry professionals, and sustainability advocates aiming to integrate technology with environmental responsibility.

Chapter 5: AI and ML for Energy Management: Innovations and Challenges in a Sustainable Future

This chapter explores the role of AI and ML in energy optimization, focusing on their applications in smart grids, renewable energy systems, industrial energy management, and smart buildings. It delves into advanced techniques such as predictive modeling, reinforcement learning, and deep learning to highlight how these technologies contribute to grid stability, energy efficiency, and real-time decision-making. The discussion extends to optimization strategies, challenges, and future research directions, emphasizing the impact of AI on the sustainability and resilience of energy systems.

Chapter 6: Energy Efficient Protocols and Devices in IoT: Approaches for Sustainable Performance

This chapter explores energy-efficient protocols and devices that are designed to optimize power consumption in IoT networks. It examines low-power communication protocols such as LoRaWAN, Zigbee, Bluetooth Low Energy (BLE), and NB-IoT, along with energy-aware device designs, efficient sensing technologies, and advanced routing mechanisms. Additionally, it highlights innovations in energy harvesting, AI-driven power optimization, and security considerations that balance efficiency with data protection.

Chapter 7: Energy Efficient Big Data Processing:A Comprehensive Survey on Techniques, Trends, and Future Directions

This chapter explores energy-efficient techniques for handling large-scale data processing. It examines low-power hardware solutions, energy-aware algorithms, intelligent resource management, and green data centers. The role of edge computing, AI-driven optimization, and renewable energy integration in reducing energy footprints is also discussed.

Chapter 8: Advancing Sustainability in Software Engineering:Key Practices and Future Directions

This chapter highlights innovative techniques such as energy profiling tools, AI-driven sustainability automation, and virtualization strategies that can significantly reduce power consumption and operational costs. Furthermore, the role of industry standards, policy frameworks, and corporate sustainability initiatives in promoting green software development is examined.

Chapter 9: Sustainable Mobile and Wireless Computing Solutions

This chapter explores key sustainability challenges in mobile and wireless computing, including energy-intensive manufacturing, e-waste generation, network energy consumption, and the carbon footprint of data centers. It also highlights cutting-edge solutions such as energy-efficient hardware, AI-driven power optimization, edge computing, renewable energy integration, and sustainable mobile device design.

Chapter 10: Green Artificial Intelligence (AI) and Machine Learning (ML)

This chapter explores key strategies to mitigate AI's environmental footprint, including algorithmic optimizations such as model pruning, quantization, and distillation, as well as energy-efficient hardware innovations like neuromorphic computing, tensor processing units (TPUs), and specialized AI chips. It also discusses green data centers, renewable energy integration, federated learning, and policy-driven AI sustainability initiatives.

Chapter 11: Energy-Efficient Solutions and Environmental Impact Reduction in Mobile and Wireless Computing

This chapter explores sustainable solutions for mobile and wireless computing, focusing on energy-efficient hardware, green communication protocols, optimized wireless networks, and renewable energy integration. It highlights advancements in low-power processors, AI-driven energy management, edge computing, and energy-aware mobile applications that can minimize carbon footprints while maintaining performance. Furthermore, it discusses emerging trends such as green 5G technologies, energy-harvesting IoT systems, and eco-friendly mobile device design.

Chapter 12: Advancing Green Artificial Intelligence-Strategies for a Sustainable Future

This chapter explores Green AI from two perspectives—"Green-by AI", where AI is applied to promote sustainable solutions across industries, and "Green-in AI", which focuses on making AI systems themselves more energy-efficient.It examines algorithmic optimizations, low-power AI hardware, eco-friendly data centers, AI-powered energy management, and regulatory policies supporting sustainable AI practices.

Chapter 13: Emerging Trends and Innovations Shaping the Future of Sustainable Computing

This chapter explores the emerging trends and innovations shaping the future of sustainable computing. It examines advancements in energy-efficient hardware, green data centers, AI-driven resource management, edge computing, and renewable energy integration. Additionally, it highlights the role of sustainable software development, eco-friendly networking protocols, and energy-aware algorithms in reducing the carbon footprint of modern computing systems.

Chapter 14: Green Artificial Intelligence and Machine Learning: Strategies for Sustainable Development

This chapter explores key strategies for Green AI, including energy-aware training techniques, model compression, federated learning, and renewable energy-powered data centers. It examines the role of low-power AI hardware, edge computing, and sustainable machine learning pipelines in reducing AI's environmental footprint.

Chapter 15: Sustainable Digital Transformation Through Energy-Efficient Edge and Fog Computing

This chapter explores the role of Edge and Fog Computing in enhancing sustainability by minimizing data transmission costs, optimizing resource usage, and reducing the environmental impact of large-scale computing infrastructure. It delves into key concepts such as energy-efficient hardware, green communication protocols, AI-driven optimizations, and renewable energy integration.

Chapter 16: Federated Learning Frameworks for Energy-Efficient AI in Distributed Data Centres

This chapter provides an in-depth analysis of federated learning frameworks designed for energy-efficient AI applications. It covers key methodologies, including adaptive federated learning algorithms, energy-aware communication protocols, and privacy-preserving techniques. Through a series of case studies, the book highlights real-world implementations of FL across diverse industries, from healthcare and finance to smart grids and telecommunications.

Chapter 17: AI and Machine Learning for Energy Optimization

This chapter explores federated learning frameworks for energy-efficient AI in distributed data centers, a critical topic at the intersection of AI, sustainability, and distributed computing. By leveraging FL, organizations can minimize data movement, reduce energy costs, and improve computational efficiency, making AI training more sustainable.

As we move toward a future driven by digital transformation, the need for sustainable computing has never been more critical. "Energy Efficient Algorithms and Green Data Centers for Sustainable Computing" has provided a comprehensive exploration of innovative strategies aimed at reducing energy consumption and minimizing the environmental footprint of computing systems. By integrating energy-efficient algorithms, optimizing resource utilization, and leveraging renewable energy sources, this book highlights key advancements that contribute to a greener and more sustainable digital infrastructure.

Through contributions from researchers, industry experts, and sustainability advocates, we have examined cutting-edge developments in algorithmic efficiency, cooling techniques, workload management, and green data center design. These insights serve as a foundation for organizations and policymakers striving to balance computational demands with ecological responsibility.

The future of sustainable computing lies in continuous innovation and collaboration across disciplines. As technology continues to evolve, further research and real-world implementations will be essential in making computing more energy-efficient, cost-effective, and environmentally friendly. We hope this book serves as a valuable resource for engineers, researchers, and decision-makers committed to shaping a sustainable digital ecosystem.

By adopting the principles discussed in this book, we can collectively work toward a future where computing power is not only optimized for performance but also aligned with the global mission of environmental sustainability.

P.J. Beslin Pajila
Vel Tech Rangarajan Dr. Sagunthala R&D Institute of Science and Technology, India

Belfin Robinson Vimala
University of North Carolina, USA

Harold Robinson
Francis Xavier Engineering College, India

C. Gopala Krishnan
GITAM University, India

Acknowledgement

We are thankful to everyone whose efforts and support made this book, "Energy Efficient Algorithms and Green Data Centers for Sustainable Computing," possible.

First and foremost, we want to express our deepest gratitude to all of the authors who kindly offered their knowledge, ideas, and study results. Their effort and commitment have filled this book with unique viewpoints and useful information.

We would like to convey our heartfelt gratitude to the reviewers for their constructive feedback and challenging examination, which greatly improved the quality and clarity of the chapters.

A special thank you to the editorial team for their rigorous attention to detail throughout the editing process. Their expertise and attention guaranteed that the book attained the highest levels of academic excellence.

We are thankful to the IGI publishing personnel who worked tirelessly behind the scenes to bring this book to life. Their knowledge and assistance have been crucial at every level of production.

We also recognize the institutions and organizations that contributed resources and facilities to help the authors with their research and writing.

Finally, we want to thank our families and coworkers for their unfailing support, understanding, and patience as we worked on this book.

"Energy Efficient Algorithms and Green Data Centers for Sustainable Computing" is a comprehensive and informative resource for academics, engineers, educators, and students interested in the transformational potential of sustainable computing technologies and energy-efficient solutions in modern data centers.

P.J.Beslin Pajila
Vel Tech Rangarajan Dr. Sagunthala R&D Institute of Science and Technology

Belfin Robinson Vimala
University of North Carolina, United States

Harold Robinson
Francis Xavier Engineering College

C Gopala krishnan
GITAM Deemed to be University, India

Chapter 1
Energy-Efficient Web Design:
The Effect of UI Choices on Power Consumption

Manoj Himmatrao Devare
https://orcid.org/0000-0002-9530-3914
Amity University, Mumbai, India

Anita Manoj Devare
https://orcid.org/0009-0009-4159-6289
Amity University, Mumbai, India

Nirali Verma
Amity University, Mumbai, India

ABSTRACT

Sustainable website design is crucial today, given the growing concern for environmental impact. The website contents and energy consumption relation are the outcome of this research work. Internet users access the website on personal computers or handheld devices. The energy consumption varies at the user device due to the various elements of the website. The website design for increase in profit and ignorance towards energy consumption requires awareness. This work analyses the various contents on the webpage and its relation. This research work is to find out whether the UI design principle of 60-30-10 rule is followed or not. Another contribution of the work is to find energy consumption due to the color combination, image format, and font style of the webpage. The chapter will investigate the responsiveness and accessibility of the website in correlation with the energy consumption due to the various elements of the webpage. This chapter will establish guidelines

DOI: 10.4018/979-8-3373-0766-4.ch001

Copyright © 2025, IGI Global Scientific Publishing. Copying or distributing in print or electronic forms without written permission of IGI Global Scientific Publishing is prohibited.

for sustainable and energy efficient webpages.

1. INTRODUCTION

Recently, the biggest piece of iceberg name A76 has surfaced around 4320 Square km is broken from Ronne Ice Shelf in 2021. Further the iceberg got broken into small pieces A-76A, A-76B, A-76C. Antarctic ice sheet is warming faster than the rest of the planet. 2023 is recorded as the hottest year. The other significant notable events due to the climate change are Wildfires, droughts, hurricane, typhoons, severe flooding, Australia's black summer, California Wildfires, Rainforest Fires, raise sea levels by over 10 feet, Coral Bleaching, mass fish deaths, Coastal Migration, island nations face disappearance, discovery of zombie viruses, and Methane Blowouts. Nitrogen Dioxide, Sulfur Dioxide and Carbon Dioxide are greenhouse gases. These gases are the major reason for global warming. The result of carbon emission can be seen in rise in temperature, sea level, ecosystem disruption, ocean acidification, and shift in precipitation pattern. Among all these gases CO_2 has a noticeable effect on the environment, which has inspired the researchers to identify the reason for emissions and come up with remarkable solutions to reduce carbon emissions. Carbon emission traps the heat in the atmosphere which leads to the change in atmosphere and global warming. Many researchers are exploring the area to identify the cause of carbon emission from different sources and to apply strategies for the reduction and mitigation of carbon emission (Abeydeera et al., 2019).

There are significant amounts of actions planned all over the world to align activities towards the reduction in the carbon and heat. That could be the adoption of renewable energy sources, and reduction in the usage of the energy generated from fossil fuels. Many organizations and countries have made their strategic planning to reach the net zero by 2025. These initiatives are in the form of policies and strategies designed to implement sustainability in the daily activities. Further action plans are executed to show milestone achievements. Those countries and organizations working towards net zero target are receiving appreciation.

Digitalization has a great impact on our society. The benefits and the use of Information and Communication Technology (ICT) can be witnessed in various aspects of society like in economic growth, making communication more efficient and reliable. The work patterns, facilities in wireless communication and the information sharing through server-based access are a few examples. However, the negative consequences of ICT cannot be ignored. At the product and service directly or indirectly cause the notable emissions which are linked with ICT devices. Greenhouse gas emission through electronic waste generation is possible as there may be possibility of having lead, mercury, cadmium. The manufacturing of these devices contributes to Carbon emission.

To withstand climate change successfully, joint efforts are needed to reduce greenhouse gas emissions. It is required to have eco-friendly practice in ICT sectors as there is an increase of user interaction on various online platforms. The search engines, social media platforms, news platforms which have continuous data streaming process the digital data majorly. The digital services have become the part of our regular life, it is very important to study and know the impact of these services on our environment. The sustainability is the target for any product or service design, as the carbon footprints has to be reduced (Rahnamay Bonab et al., 2024).

There are 200 million active websites all over the world. There are 4.72 billion Internet users all over the world. Globally, users devote around 7 hours each day to being online. Globally, the Internet user numbers are growing at an annual rate of more than 7.5%. As per the statistics in April 2021, out of 7.85 billion populations all over the world there are 5.27 billion mobile phone users, and 7.33 active social media users according to the Kepios analysis. Energy consumption and user experience compromised during rendering and downloading content during web. Every second enormous amount of data get processed and stored on devices with the arrival of easily available and approachable technology. E-commerce, social networking platforms, online streaming platforms, videos and many more are processing and generating data. Many efforts have been made to estimate the carbon footprint of the Internet. One such method is used to calculate the Carbon footprint of some popular online services like Facebook, Netflix, YouTube and TikTok. It is found that the highest Carbon emission from these four applications is produced by Netflix. There are many users and provides high resolution video delivery (Batmunkh et al, 2022). Digital industry's energy utilization is increasing by 4 percent every year. CO_2 emissions of digital technologies have increased by about 450 million tons since 2013, as mentioned in Organization for Economic Co-operation and Development (OECD) countries like Unites States, Canada, and United Kingdom. Around 80% more energy is required to produce a smart phone of 1 gm as compared to the gasoline powered car of 1 gm.

According to www.ecograder.com more than 50 million computer servers contribute 5% to the planet's total greenhouse gas emissions. As per websitecarbon.com, 416.2 TWh per year energy is consumed by the Internet. Also, around 0.8 grams of CO_2 equivalent per page view are produced. Displaying white (light) screens takes more power than black screen on a monitor (Roberson et al, 2002). Mainly power hunger components are display of Mobile phone. CPU's, GPU's and hardware used in networking are also equally power hunger. The computer monitors settings like brightness depends on choice of the user and is mostly consistent. In most kinds of monitors like LED, backlit LCD, OLED and CRT energy saving is significant when color chosen is black.

2. LITERATURE REVIEW

2.1 HTML Elements

There are various HTML elements on any webpage. They can consume different amounts of energy, depending on CPU usage and its frequency on which it is running. The energy required to render complexity is higher. Similarly, animations may take more energy, and network requests can consume a high amount of energy. There are certain HTML elements that are lightweight and require minimal processing. The text based, static media, few form elements, requires minimum CPU or GPU rendering. The text-based elements having static content such as <p>, <h1> to <h6>, <ul>, <ol>, <li>, <span>, <strong>, <em>, <b>, <i> . The basic Structural Elements such as <div>, semantic layout elements such as <section>, <article>, <aside>. The page structure elements such as <footer> and <header>. The Static Media such as <img> with optimized images such as WebP, compressed PNG/JPEG, the <svg> such as Scalable Vector Graphics are lighter than PNGs for simple graphics. The elements of Forms <input> for text, number, checkbox and radio also consumes less power. The <button> designed without animations or without heavy JavaScript, consumes less power. <video>, <audio>, <canvas>, <iframe>, <object>, <embed>, <marquee>, <blink>, <details> <summary>, and <script>, are energy-Consuming HTML Elements. The constant Document Object Model (DOM) updates, event listeners and overuse of the JavaScript leads to inefficiency. The use of setInterval loop in JavaScript consumes more energy over the CSS @keyframes animation using transform: translateX(). The auto playing videos, dynamic scripts, and misuse of Java scripts lead to unnecessary energy consumption on the end device and on the hops in the network. HTML consumes three times the energy whereas the script utilizes ten times the energy. The bigger size of the image file takes longer to download and travel through the network as compared to the smaller files. Similarly, bigger image files take the more time render on the screen. The use of Content Delivery Network (CDN) can reduce the time required to display elements on the user's screen. As the content of the webpage is fetched from the geographically nearby storage of the CDN. The CDN content is also required to be updated, if the contents of the original webpage are changed. These updates are required to be done at the different servers located on different geographical locations.

2.2 Data Center and Consumption Of Energy

Data Centers are the physical area having computing machines and the related hardware needs to assist the computation. It includes computing infrastructure such as network equipment, servers, and storage drives. Data Centers provides a vital contribution in computing and communication. Data Center aids business applications which are critical and workloads that are important to any organization to run their business smoothly. The Data Center keeps and manages crucial data effectively. It is a physical means including hardware and components, containing IT equipment, devices and technologies. Many points need to be considered while designing data centers like location, power, security, cooling, connectivity and others. A data center needs continuous power to provide consistent services. It needs a backup solution to have the disaster planning. On site generators, Power supply (UPS), remote power panel are used to ensure the sustained power supply to the data center (Chen et al., 2016). With the increase in popularity of Cloud computing, data centers are needed to process and store the huge amount of data.

Data centers store huge amounts of data needed by many organizations to fulfill their daily transaction needs for functioning smoothly. The collection of different servers and networks infrastructure makes the data centers. The servers accumulate the data whereas employ, leverage, retain, renew and upgrade network infrastructure. Through networking, the users can access data centers. Currently, there is a surge in digital data and the range of information which has expanded considerably. To aid such trends, data centers are the core infrastructure that is being used. But with the expansion of data center the energy consumption has also increased, which results in the escalation of carbon emission as these the data centers needs a significant amount of energy (Rong et al., 2016). For huge amounts of greenhouse gas emission, Information and Communication Technology are partially accountable. From these large data centers house used by Internet giants like Google, Microsoft and others big ventures enormous amount of heat gets generated and thus to maintain the temperature in effective range requires large cooling units, which in return amplify the total energy consumption and have their own carbon footprints. The exceptional and optimal performance is not the only requirement of users, people are also concerned about the carbon emission and energy consumption by data centers. By implementing energy efficient models, it is possible to optimize the energy consumption in Cloud data centers to some good percentage which can be beneficial for our environment.

Nowadays, data centers are storing data using solutions like one drive, google drive, and backup vaults. The data centers are also responsible for storing the online transaction processing (OLTP) and Online Analytical Processing (OLAP) data. The Relational databases and no SQL databases are also responsible for the data storage in the data centers. The data centers also have provisions for creating blockchain based distributed ledgers. Moreover, it can also provide storage for the sensor data generated through the Internet of Things devices. The data centers store confidential business information, as well as the low valued videos. The workstation nodes in the data centers are now configured using the Infrastructure as a Code (IaaC) tools like Chef, Ansible, and Puppet. Controlling all the data center nodes is possible through the administration and strategies to run on the low energy consumption.

2.3 UI/UX Design Principles

To build website or an application, different User Interface (UI) elements are used. UI elements are the constituent parts that add interactivity to UI. The UI designers ensure consistency across the website or application by using the UI elements to create visual language. They make it easy to use and navigate without putting too much time into thinking and analyzing the elements. To enhance seamless User Experience (UX) for creating a digital product, visually appealing user interface design plays a crucial role.

UX is how things work and more about the Usability Testing, User Research, User Stories, and Personas. UX Concentrates on hassle-free experience. It is more about knowing the users and what they are trying to achieve through UI. Studies show that the reaction of the user vary significantly depending on their background and characteristics. Many businesses use color in their website design to establish a unique brand image, increase customer interest in their products, and create a more engaging online experience.(Swasty & Adriyanto, 2017)

The UI shows the look, Layout, Visual Design, Style and Branding. UI helps to represent any application graphically. UI consists of buttons, images, videos, texts, and overall interaction. It also includes the behavior of each element through events. The main goal of the UI designers is to create a user interface that is engaging, attractive and beautiful. It is not only the use of the software of UI design but process and strategy of design. Design is look, feel and how it works.

For successful digital product development, UI design plays an important role. Efficiency ensures increased productivity and UX turning down the effort and time needed for task completion. The branding created through UI reveals the unique characteristics of product, value and personality. UX ensures the user can effortlessly navigate the product which helps users to reach their goals. The ease, satisfaction and engagement lead to repeated visits. Few commonly used elements for designing the UI are Checkbox, Buttons, Notification, Forms, Icons, Input Fields, Dropdown and many more. The foreground and background colors of these elements match with the brand and give unique approach to the user. The UI element's border thickness, the colors, and responses at the point of time retains the user on the mobile app or website. The tab indices during navigation facilitate the easiness to enter the data values. The proper layout, font, font size, font color ensures the consistency for the user. The golden rule of the UI design maintains the consistent user interface and keeps the user in control. The partially visible components on the UI, the overlapping keyboard on the UI components reduce the user satisfaction. The low fidelity drawings portray initial sketch and the wireframing provides some more details on it.

Some key standards help to design UI which in return give flawless UX like consistency that helps in navigating the interface. The consistent design elements like Typography, Color, Layout or Images give favorable, familiar and predictable sense to user. Simplicity helps the user to navigate through the interface with the slightest hindrance. For users to reach their goals becomes simple without uncertainty when the user design is simple. Feedback, which is a major component of good user design helps users to comprehend the reaction of their action. Feedback should be clear and understandable to the user. A feedback can be visual or sound effects or animation. All users, including users with disabilities, should be able to access the user interface without any barriers.

UX design is the process of designing website or digital products that meets the needs, choice and behaviors of the user. To create a consistent and intuitive experience of user that meets their needs and assumption are the major goals of UX design. When focusing on the needs of the user from the beginning, a user centered design approach can help to find the expected potential problems earlier. It can reduces the cost of fixing those issues later. A good User experience design promotes competitive benefits in the marketplace. UX designers provide smooth and delightful UX to make the product more successful.

Design thinking involves the empathetic approach towards the persona of the website. The persona and the further usability testing can decide the better user experience. To maintain the standard of the UI and UX and to retain the customer with better experience on the website involves the high energy consuming elements. To balance between better experience and minimization of energy consumption, requires proper research.

2.4 Color Scheme

There are monochromatic, analogous, complementary, split complementary, and triadic color schemes. The Gradient strengthens the potential of color in different design solutions. The websites like coolors.co, Color Hunt, Patetton are useful to the developers for making the choice of the tone of the color. Colors are the vital factor in the way that users interact with the Website. The influence can be witness to exploit the information they had gleaned from the Website.(Swasty & Adriyanto, 2017). Figure 1 addresses the energy requirement of the screen when pure black, dark gray, medium gray, and white colors are used either in the software application or on the webpage.

Figure 1. Black and White Color and Energy Consumption on screen

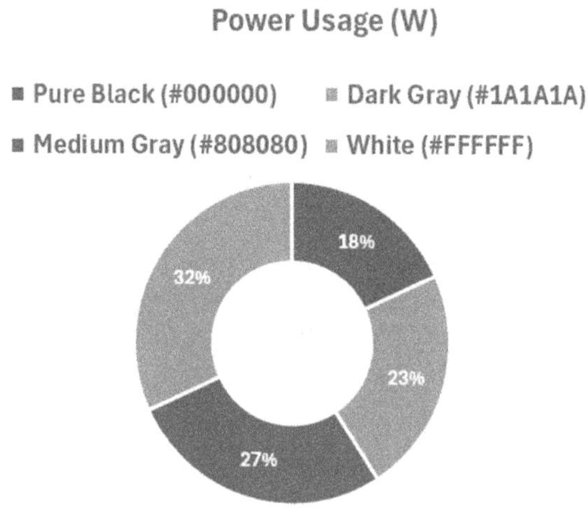

The 60% + 30% + 10% proportion is meant to give balance to the color, where dominant hue is 60%, secondary color is 30% and rest 10% is for accent color. The UI designer chose a new color palette, 60% of the palette should be dedicated to one color that is neutral color that is dominant hue. The complementary color or secondary color or texture makes up 30% of the palette. The third accent color accent is used for the remaining 10% of the design.(Ummah, 2019) Color plays an important role in human life and most the time the application used on the mobile and the laptops. Every color has different meanings and has a notion in our mind. Color is one of the main visual components that evoke a close link with human feelings. Every color has distinctive meanings, they carry a secret definition. Colors have deeply rooted in lives such that influences different activities without considering them.(Bonnardel et al., 2011) Colors are both emotional and physical impact on human. In human beings, the feelings of calmness, unhappiness, sluggishness, liveliness and many more are roused by colors. For example red triggers the feeling of excitement and enthusiasm. Red and Orange are considered as warm colors. The colder colors like purple, green and blue gives the feeling of relaxation and serenity(*View of Color Psychology in Marketing*, n.d.).

The use of proper colors in the UI design engages user moods and actions which enhance engagement and improve trustworthiness. For example, there are call-to-action (CTA) buttons which can have bright, attention-grabbing colors like red, orange or green. The accessibility guidelines say that high-contrast color schemes and supplement colors are good for labels or icons. The A/B testing is considered as the test for acceptance and usability. The colors also imply the culture, and regional representation. Such as white implies purity in the western culture and mourning in few Asian cultures. The colors can be useful for highlighting key contents, so that critical information cannot be missed. The success feedback can be displayed through green. The error can be displayed with red, and warnings can be indicated using yellow.

Table 1. Color and their descriptions and emotions

Color	Description	Emotions
Red	Red, a fiery hue, symbolizes passion, power, and intensity. It evokes both love and violence. It stimulates the body, increasing heart rate and metabolism.	Love, Passion, Aggression, Fire, Excitement, Energy, Action, or Desire.
Yellow	Yellow is a lively color, which enlightens joy and sunshine. While its brightness can be energizing, it may cause visual fatigue when used as a background. However, it excels as a captivating choice for app icons and screenshots.	Friendly, Happiness, Joy, Inspiration, Enthusiasm, Confidence, or Optimism.
Green	Green is a very down-to-earth color. It is symbol of new beginnings and growth.	Nature, Harmony, Growth, Hope, Refreshing, Balance, Reassurance, Wealth, Food, and Nature
Blue	Light blues can be refreshing and friendly. Dark blues implies strength and reliability.	Trust, Honesty, Authority, Stability, Calmness, Serenity and Responsibility.
Black	Black is neutral, symbolizing power and elegance.	Independence, Mystery, Power, Authority, Seriousness, Elegance, and Formality.
White	White symbolizes purity and virtue. It conveys cleanliness and simplicity. It is a cornerstone of minimalist design.	Safety, Clarity, Innocent, Goodness, new beginnings, and cleanliness.
Purple	Purple symbolizes royalty, wealth, and femininity. Dark shades evoke luxury, while lighter hues convey spring and romance.	Wisdom, Spirituality, Individuality, Quality, Mystery, Problem-Solving, and Creativity.
Orange	Orange evokes amusement, unconventionality, extrovert, radiating energy like fire. It symbolizes both exhilarating activity and potential danger.	Warmth, Optimistic, Uplifting, Rejuvenating, Fun, Friendliness, Attention, Comfort, and Enthusiasm.
Brown	Brown symbolizes earthiness, warmth, and simplicity. It is evoking associations with dullness, timidity, predictability, and protection.	Reliable, Soothing, Stability, Strength, Security, Nature and Trust.
Pink	Pink is typically linked to charm, sweetness, and femininity. It often evokes childhood innocence and gentle sensitivity.	Kindness, Love, Innocence, Sweet, and Playful.
Gray	Gray is the color of clouds, and ashes. This color has no chroma. It is an achromatic color. Gray color is related to neutrality, boredom, old age, experience, and elegance. It symbolizes wisdom and balanced approach.	Authority, Dignity, Intellect, Wisdom and Knowledge.

Table 1 shows the color and its associated emotions. Accordingly, it impacts on the observer or user. Hence, designer of user interface must keep the balance between these two factors such as brand and energy consumption. As a UI designer, color psychology helps to choose a color which results in maximum clicks, landing on desired page, and maximum user interaction. To maintain consistency and make the page more impactful, it is preferable to balance the color scheme between warm and cold colors. Similarly, loud and quiet colors can be attained by picking the shades, tones, luminance, intensity and tint of color.

Violets consume most energy as they have the shortest wavelength. Black display in Cathode Ray Tube uses 25% less energy than the white display. The energy consumption of colors is different from each other. The data is presented in figure 2 from the website www.greenliving.com, which indicates the rise in energy consumption from black to white.

Figure 2. Color and energy consumption in Watts.

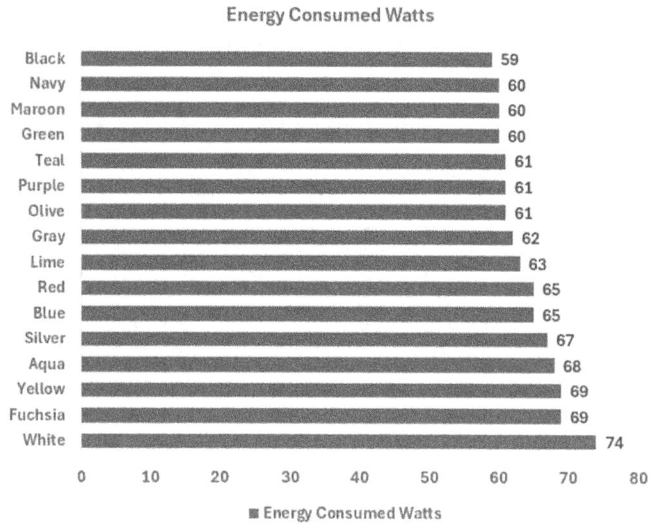

Night mode is a feature that lets users change the color palette of their device or app from light to dark. When activated, the background turns black or very dark gray, and the text and other parts appear in lighter colors. Dark backgrounds are trending on streaming services like Netflix, Disney+, or HBO Max. Black backgrounds are becoming more popular for website development also because it improves readability for people. It is also found suitable for visual impairments in a few cases. The main reason for night mode is to ease the burden on the user's eyes. Users prefer to have screens that are easier to look at with dim lighting. Plus, it can also save battery life on screens that use Organic Light Emitting Diode (OLED) or Active-Matrix Organic Light-Emitting Diode (AMOLED) technology. These screens use less power to show darker colors compared to lighter ones. Both types of display technologies use carbon-based organic materials for creating images. OLED technology is more energy efficient than AMOLED technology. OLED (Organic Light-Emitting Diode) is a display technology where each pixel emits its own light. In the case of LCD screens, backlight is required to illuminate the entire screen. The OLED displays to achieve true blacks, and higher contrast. The pixel can turn off completely and save energy. OLED has power efficiency in dark-mode usage. OLED screens consist of organic compounds that light up when an electric current passes through them. The display of OLED also comes in thinner, foldable and curved screens. The colors in the viewing angles are accurate when viewed from any side. These screens are also useful in gaming and fast animations. The micro-OLED is used in augmented and virtual reality headsets for high pixel density. The AMOLED are researched and designed with the built-in touch layer for better efficiency. The passive matrix OLED is useful in the low-power applications. The OLEDs are used in smartphones, TVs, Smartwatches, and VR Headsets for immersive visuals (Lee & Song, 2020).

2.5 Content of Webpage

The darker color of the webpage is better for energy efficiency; however, for the commercial website aesthetics is important. Hence, along with energy efficiency the look of the website is also taken into consideration. The internationalization support of multi-lingual facility provides the translation of the website text (Seifi & Moshayeri, 2024). Similarly, the option to change the text and background color with the use of the Cascaded Style Sheets (CSS) can help to convert the website content for energy efficient options. Table 2 shows the basic elements of the webpage, their characteristics and relationship with energy requirement.

Table 2. Characteristics of Webpage Content

Elements of the webpage	Description	Characteristics	Energy Requirement
Plain Text	To convey any information and stories, plain text is used. Plain text forms the core of any message provided on the website.	Readability, optimization and overall, SEO performance.	Lowest
Bold Text	It conveys and emphasizes the important points. It makes any information discovered easily.	Grabs a Reader's attention, and easy to understand.	Lowest
Images	Images are an effective and easy way to convey any information to the user as they can evoke emotions, tell stories, and create a stronger connection with them. Product photos, info graphics, or charts are better understood by the visitors as compared to text.	More effectively convey information and attractive for the users.	Directly proportional to the image size.
Video	It provides the combination of the images and sound to explain the concept in detail.	Better to engage the user.	Overall energy requirement is high. As downloading, rendering and processing requires significant amount of energy.

Bold text requires a bit more energy than plain text. This is because the device needs to work extra for formatting the instructions to make the text bold, which requires additional processing power. But the difference in energy used between regular and bold text is very small.

2.6 Typography for Fonts

Fonts have the power to subtly influence our emotions. An unattractive font can unknowingly make us feel negative. An aesthetically pleasing font can evoke feelings of happiness. Since fonts can affect our emotional state, they undoubtedly play a role in how users experience something, like a website. According to significantly enhance user engagement on website by 38% simply by adjusting the font styles.

Ninety percent of the information on the web is in the form of written language. Biggest families of the fonts are Serif and Sans Serif. Sans Serif having Grotesque, Neo-Grotesque, Humanist, Geometric categories. Serif has Old Style, Modern, Transitional, and Slab-Serif categories. Microsoft Sans-Serif font format has little more readability compared to Serifs. They are more formal, modern, elegant, friendly and minimal without decorated strokes. (Vroom, n.d.)

While designing a website, right font selection is crucial. The selected font helps to show the website brand. Making some fonts bigger than others helps guide the user through the information. There should be enough space between letters, words, and lines to make it easy to read. The color of the font makes it easy to read. Designers should also think about how the colors make people feel. The fonts should look good on all kinds of screens, like phones, tabs and computers. It is important to use the same fonts throughout the website and make sure the text is aligned properly. Finally, make sure the text is easy to read for everyone, including people with disabilities. Avoid using all capital letters or flashing text, and make sure there's enough contrast between the font color and the background.(*The Impact of Typography on Web Design: A Comprehensive Guide to Aesthetics and Readability*, n.d.). Table 3 shows the different fonts, their types, and characteristics.

Table 3. Font type and their characteristics

Font type	Characteristics	Font Names
Sans-serif fonts	They are distinguished by their **clean**liness, conveying a **modernist** and **minimalist** aesthetic, making them perfect for **contemporary** and **inventive** platforms.	Arial, Helvetica
Serif Fonts	They are frequently linked to customs, convention, and elegance. They can inspire sentiments of sophistication, trustworthiness, and authority.	Times New Roman, Georgia
Script Fonts	Imitate handwriting, adding a touch of individuality and grace. They can inspire feelings of creativity, femininity, and luxury.	Brush Script, Pacifico
Display Fonts	Striking and attention grabbing, often used for headlines and titles. They can **communicate** a feeling of strength, power, or playfulness.	Impact, Bebas Neue.

Font Formats like WOFF2 are more compressed and efficient. The download of the fonts from online can lead to more power consumption. The rendering of the fonts also consumes energy.

2.7 Image Type

Images enhance the feel and look of the website. The JPEG, PNG images can contain up to 16 million colors. Images consume a lot of energy when loaded on the webpage. The specific amount depends on their size, format, resolution, and complexity. Website designers can choose to use smaller images and compress images more effectively. It is recommended that the web pages and UI-UX designers avoid using images altogether when they are not necessary. This can help to reduce our overall energy consumption and contribute to a more sustainable future. Table 4 summarizes different image types; compression features and their characteristics.

Table 4. Image type and their characteristics

Image types	Characteristics	Compression Type
JPEG	Joint Photographic Experts Group (JPEG) are Broadly Accepted as it works smoothly with almost all gadgets and programs. A lossy compression shrinks file size. It makes web pages load faster. Perfect for images with tons of colors and shades.	Lossy Compression
TIFF	Tagged Image File Format is Lossless, and squeezing keeps the picture perfect, ideal for long-term storage. Tiff is a good fit for graphic design tools and image editing programs i.e. professional printing.	Lossless
BMP	Bitmap **has** no loss of image quality.	Lossless

According to dotcom-tools.com, when aiming to completely enhance website images for efficiency and swiftness, the file formats not only influence the rendering quality, but they also significantly affect how quickly a page loads. JPEG are energy efficient, as uses the lossy compression technique. The compressed images are of smaller size and some image data is discarded. It results in a reduction in the transmitted data and lowering the energy consumption during data transfer. Smaller file loads faster, which reduces the time devices spend actively displaying a webpage. A JPEG preferred photographs and images with many colors and gradients. Optimize TIFF or BMP for web use by reducing resolution and file size without sacrificing image quality. For graphics with sharp edges, transparent backgrounds, or limited color palettes, PNG or WebP might be more energy-efficient options. Table 4 summarizes the compression characteristics of the various image useful in the software development, and web pages development.

Organizing website design, colors, images, effects on energy usage. Similarly, the energy efficient aesthetics option on the website is required to be provided. The option of converting the content as the darker, consume the less amount of energy (Seifi & Moshayeri, 2024). The use of compressed images, efficient file formats and lightweight fonts, and avoiding bloated frameworks saves energy consumption. This indirectly impacts at the various stages including data center, transmission network, and device. Progressive web applications (PWA) can be used to develop websites. It might use a little more battery than native apps. The type of web browser that is used to run the PWA can have a big impact on how much battery it uses. Some browsers are more energy-efficient than others.

The top, center and right sides of the webpage garner the most focus, the use of images depicting people increase visibility. The visual scanning adheres to vertical and horizontal direction. The numerical data can be represented in the graphical and tabular format. The design of the webpage itself has a greater influence on webpage usability (ichindelean et al., 2021) For online applications fonts such as Georgia or Verdana are generally recommended. Furthermore, using pre-installed fonts on the devices where the website is expected to be viewed more often will require less server use. Virtual conference during pandemic COVID 19 had an impact on environment due to live streaming video during the conference (Periyasamy et al., 2022).

2.8 Various Online Tools and Energy Consumption

As per the Google Blog (2009), the average google search query takes 0.0003 kWh or 1kJ. The search query equals 0.2 grams of CO2. As per the article in the Balkan-green-energy-news (2024), the generative AI software like GPT required to be trained before usage also consumes a high amount of electricity. There are 175 billion parameters used to train ChatGPT. The time required to train this model takes 34 days. This training takes approximately 1.3 GWh of electricity. The Green design approach is required in the design of these kinds of electricity intensive applications. The backend computational infrastructure used in these applications requires systematic thought on the algorithms to be designed to reduce energy consumption.

Blackle.com is the initiative of having the search engine page interface designed in the black color and grayish text on it. The concept behind this theme is that the black interface consumes less energy of monitor screen. The search page of the Blackle shows how much energy is saved till now, and it claims that it saves 750 MegaWatts-hours per year. The white web page uses 74 watts to display, and the black page uses only 59 watts. Google gets millions of queries per day. The query results stay around 10 seconds on a screen Ecoiron (2007). The dark mode facility on the websites and the mobile applications save energy and it is good for human eyes.

There are few Online Tools available to check the energy efficiency of the websites. For example, website carbon calculators are estimating the carbon footprint and energy consumption of a website. A green web check website is checking if the website is hosted on green-powered server or not. The global average for webpage data transfer size is 2.4 MB. If the website page is greater than the average data transfer size, it fails the sustainability test.

As per HTTP archives, the size of the web pages is becoming four times larger than those were in 2010. The high-resolution images require more time to download, hence there are some options of using compressed image file size. It can help with removing unused items from a page, to reduce emissions. Consequently, it will download pages faster and make user experience can also be enhanced. The size of the webpage should be as low as possible. The web hosting servers should be having power supply to their servers with renewable energy. Nowadays, wind energy is getting generated at a minimum cost than solar.

The Eco Grader (2025) tool is analyzing a website's energy efficiency and suggests optimizations. It uses the CO2.js JavaScript library to find the carbon intensive files. The browser extensions plugin called Carbon Analyzer, calculates the electricity consumption while browsing the Internet through any browser. It also calculates the greenhouse gases emission as well, such as the Carbon Dioxide (CO_2), Methane (CH_4), Nitrous Oxide (N_2O), Fluorinated Gases (F-Gases) includes hydrofluorocarbons (HFCs), perfluorocarbons (PFCs), Sulphur Hexafluoride (SF_6), and Nitrogen Trifluoride (NF_3). Methane (CH_4) is 25 times more potent than CO_2 and Nitrous Oxide (N_2O) is 300 times more potent than CO_2. Carbon Analyzer plugin and mobile app measures the quantity of data coming to the devices and going through the Internet browser. It also calculates the electricity consumption due to the traffic as it travelled through the entire ISO-Open System Interconnection seven layers of network transmission.

Algorithmic audit is an emerging area finding out the ethical implications of the various applications. One of the aspects in the audit process is required to evaluate energy consumption by the application, or the website. Including the impact of running underlying infrastructure usage and consumption.

As per the Shift Project research (2019) there is 20% of data flow from non-video, 60% of online video and other videos. The video on demand includes 34%, pornography 27%, the tubes like YouTube, Dailymotion, Vimeo has 21%, and other as 18%. Video on demand like Netflix, Amazon Prime, Hulu are having 102 million tons, pornography 82 million tons, tubes 65 million tons and other video incudes 361 million tons of the CO2. The digital technologies like terminal, data centers, networks, TVs, Smart Phones, and others having similar contributions. Green Web Foundation Browser Extension contributes towards identifying if a website is using renewable energy hosting. The global target of Net Zero is to be achieved by 2050, and there is 50% target of carbon emission reduction by 2030.

3. ENERGY EFFICIENT ANDROID APPS DEVELOPMENT

Push notifications and alerts in mobile applications can consume the battery life. The Location service and Global Positioning System (GPS) in android apps are battery intensive. The applications running in the background should be avoided. The screen sleeping time can be optimized. The outdated operating system can also consume energy. The extreme temperature variations affect phone batteries. Wireless connectivity through the Internet, WiFi, Bluetooth, and location services when not needed can help conserve batteries. The Airplane mode can save mobile data, and it saves energy as well. The camera and games on android phone consume energy. The unoptimized apps also drain the battery. The Window Animation Scale, Transition Animation Scale, and Animator Duration Scale should be turned off.

The RecyclerView & ListView in Android is having Slow scrolling, lag, and UI stuttering. It is running expensive operations in onBindViewHolder(). It is having unoptimized layout hierarchy in list items. The ConstraintLayout is having longer render times, and increased layout inflation time. ConstraintLayout and overuse of constraints leading to complex calculations. If the developer is using nested scroll views in android app designing, then having performance issue of slow rendering. The frame drops and heavy user interface trees are leading to battery intensive operations in the android. The ImageView and Bitmap Handling usage in android applications has high memory usage, and it can crash due to out of memory error. In the effect of which it is loads high-resolution images without resizing. It is not using image caching libraries like Glide or Picasso. The WebView component is having the issue of slow loading, high memory usage, and UI lag. The WebView Component is running JavaScript-heavy pages. It is not enabling hardware acceleration properly.

Similarly, the background tasks, thread block, can lead to app freezing, and apps not responding issues. The long-running operations like database queries, and network calls burdens load on the main thread. Similarly, excessive use of synchronized methods locking the UI thread can cause performance issues. The fragment transactions & navigation component causes the issue of slow fragment transitions, and memory leaks. It causes retaining too many fragments in back stack. Android utilizes the minimum privileges model of permission for running application. The developer must handle the androidmanifest.xml file with XML tags to have permission to utilize hardware-based services. If developers have given unnecessary access permissions such as Internet, GPS access, Bluetooth, and Sensor access then it can utilize the battery. The thread mechanism has CPU usage & high processing power if they are running at a high frequency. The threads that perform heavy computations like acceleration, loading of videos, or run frequently will increase CPU workload and consuming more power. The thread mechanism utilizes the CPU resource, hence running multiple threads in parallel prevents the CPU from entering low-power idle states. The threads holding a PowerManage. WakeLock prevents the CPU from sleeping and leads to high battery consumption. The threads and services handing excessive network calls such as polling APIs can cause radio hardware WiFi, LTE, 5G to remain active longer, and draining the battery. Cloud messaging using the firebase can optimize the batch request and reduce the unnecessary wakeups. Similarly, the app handling the high CPU wake-up frequency like AlarmManager, JobScheduler, and WorkManager. Mismanaged synchronization such as excessive locks can cause CPU threads to remain active longer than needed. The use of coroutines and RxJava can be useful for lightweight threading.

4. GREEN DATA CENTER INITIATIVES

Google has started using Renewable Energy in their data centers and has a utilization target of Carbon-Free Energy by 2030 for 24 by 7. Some companies also started using artificial Intelligence for Energy Efficiency and maintain the data center cooling. Few companies started water conservation implementing air-cooling and sustainable water sourcing to reduce water consumption. Some companies started utilizing circular economic approaches and use refurbished hardware to extend server lifespan. Microsoft's project Natick deployed submarine-style data centers to reduce cool energy. Microsoft also replaces diesel generators with green hydrogen-power cells as an alternative and utilizes excess heat from data centers to warm nearby buildings.

Amazon Web Services started 400 renewable energy projects worldwide and is the world's largest buyer of renewable energy. Amazon started using custom energy-efficient chips in Graviton processors to reduce power consumption. The liquid cooling technology implemented as liquid immersion cooling to reduce energy use. There is Sustainable Water Usage and water reuse and rainwater harvesting.

Facebook Data centers are LEED Gold-certified with low-carbon materials. Facebook is using 100% of its energy as renewable energy since 2020, which is reducing the energy usage by the fossil fuel. Apple is having the Carbon Neutral Supply Chain, and operations by 2030. Apple is utilizing 100% renewable energy since 2018. Apple has been utilizing recycled material since 2018. IBM also utilized liquid cooling technology and developed Watson AI to predict energy utilization. Equinix is having their Data centers are built using low-carbon concrete and steel. It also utilizes indirect evaporative cooling.

The top ten Green High Performance Computing (HPC) units ranks released from in November 20204, as named JEDI(Germany), Romeo-2025(France), Adastra 2(France), Isambard-AI Phase-1(UK), Capella (Germany), JETI(Germany), Helios GPU (Poland), Henri (US), HoreKa-Teal (Germany, and rzAdams(US). The rank of the HPC units is given based on the maximum efficiency achieved by watt of energy. These HPC systems are used to solve various scientific applications, and the usage of computational power is maximum. Figure 3 shows the Gigaflops per Watt achieved by these units. A minimum of 8000 CPU cores, and maximum 391680 CPU cores are used in one of the TOP Green HPC.

Figure 3. GFlops per watts required by Top 10 Green HPC units.

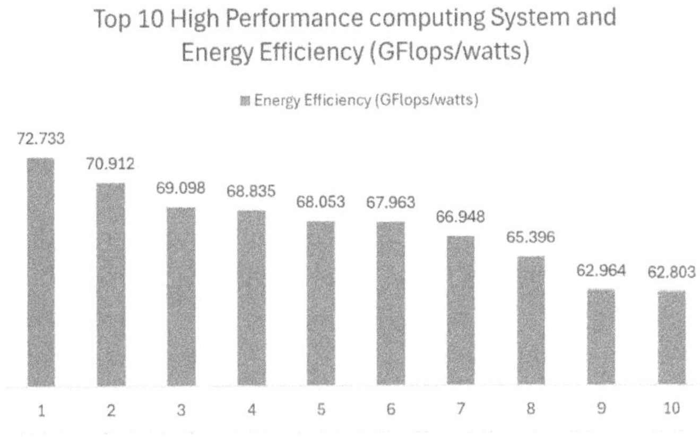

The data centers generate heat, and it is required to cool the computer systems in the premises. When the CPUs run at high frequencies, then it generates high heat. The cooling fan operates to reduce the impact of heat on microprocessors. Otherwise, if it is not cooled down, then it can cause melting of the microprocessor and further damage to it. There are liquid cooling technologies that have cold plates used to cool CPUs, Graphics Processing Units, and memory units. The liquid cooling is different from the air-cooling technique. The immersion cooling technique submerges servers in dielectric liquid that absorb heat and avoids further damage.

There is Single-Phase or two-phase Immersion Cooling. In case of single-phase the heat from the components is transferred to the fluid, which is then circulated and cooled using heat exchangers. The IT hardware is submerged in a dielectric fluid. Green revolution colling is an example of single-phase cooling. In the two-phase immersion cooling, the dielectric fluid that gets converted into vapor. The vapor rises, and cooling the coil again converts it into liquid form. This kind of cooling is 95% effective than air cooling system, and protection of the components is from dust, humidity and oxidation.

The predictive machine learning cooling system predicts the heat to be generated, and optimization of the airflow. One of the leading companies reduced energy by 40% in their data centers. There is evaporative cooling which is different from Heating, Ventilation, and Air Conditioning (HVAC) system. In some cases, the external air is also used to maintain the optimal temperature. The underground water or soil temperature is used for heat exchange and cooling system. The data centers can be modular or micro size, that improves the cooling efficiency. Heat reuse is one of the mechanisms for the different purpose leads to sustainability.

5. STORAGE ON CONTENT DELIVERY NETWORK

Content delivery Networks (CDN) are networks of servers distributed geographically in different regions of the globe. Every server in CDN works as a content delivery tool whose main goal is to reduce the latency. This low latency is important to upgrade the application or website performance, thereby improving the efficiency and productivity of websites.

CDN helps to reduce data traffic over long distances across the network by broadcasting website content on multiple servers which are geographically closer to the user, thus lowering down the energy usage since less data needs to be transferred from sole source. This eventually reduces overall power consumption. The energy demand in CDN has also increased due to surge of online content consumption like video streaming and others. Meeting such challenges needs an energy consumption optimization in both server operations and cooling systems also maintaining the quality of services (QoS). Using the hybrid systems, distributing the content smartly, and with the help of heuristic algorithm energy efficiency in CDN can be amplified. Figure 4 shows the superficial architecture of the CDN which indicates that the content can be accessed from nearest CDN server.

Figure 4. Content Delivery Network

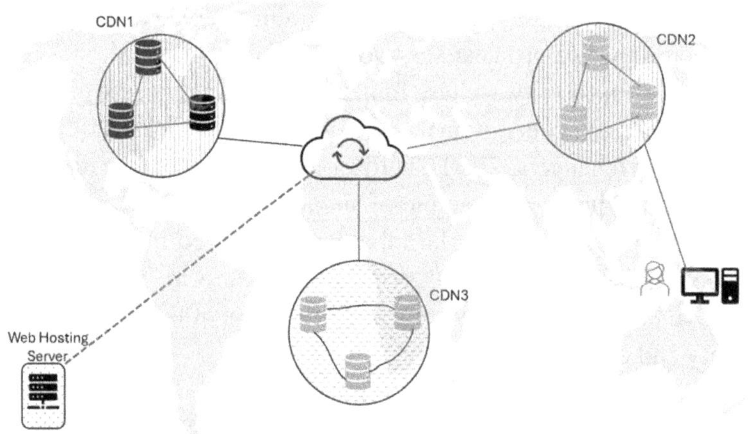

The CDN Peer-to-Peer systems are capable of being scaled and it can be the solution for the cost-effective content distribution. Hybrid systems designed with the help of CDN have more energy savings as compared to traditional CDN which reduces the carbon footprints and cost of operations. It also minimizes the latency in server to client communication.

During the off-peak hours putting the idle servers to sleep and shut down the unused data centers, helps in server and cooling system optimization. The heuristic algorithm reduces cool energy consumption, letting certain data centers become idle. With the hybrid CDN, Cloud systems the cost effectiveness and scalability has improved, which has benefited the high traffic application such as video streaming services. Multi-phase Sleep and Wake Mechanism (MSWM) plays an important role in optimizing energy efficiency in CDN. The MSWM allows minutely grained power management by using many distinct sleep levels.

For Network optimization, an Integer Linear Programming (ILP) model can be used for network efficiency which focuses on maximizing network throughput and reducing the consumption of energy. It chooses which component in a network to be activated or deactivated deliberately based on power usage and on traffic demands following the set of rules like bandwidth limitations and others. Studies indicate that energy saving is achieved around 20 percent through optimized server selection and cache usage. The video CDN is designed using the wireless Mesh WiFi and the contents are placed on the wireless access points. These WAP can serve as the local video servers. Such CDNs can also perform with good effects like Quality of Service, latency time and energy consumption (Boscovic et al, 2011).

(Xu et. al, 2010), It is found that, the power efficiency of a distributed video CDN system in terms of a general framework has the lower power efficiency. The central server-based system has the better power efficiency. The video on demand service through the Interactive Television over the Internet (IPTV). The energy efficiency can be achieved through the coordination across hardware, operating systems, virtual machines, middleware and applications.

User generated content is distributed efficiently, which creates cost- effective virtual CDNs. K-center problem and convex optimization increase efficiency. For better delivery of content, it balances the storage and bandwidth resources. Intelligent coordination among the edge servers improves efficiency in the video CDNs.

6. SUMMARY

As the world is serious about the net zero target by 2050, it is necessary for all to contribute to achieving this target. Sustainability on the earth will save the life of human beings and life on the earth. The predicted consequences as a peril to life on the planet earth will be disastrous. Target of utilization of all green design and innovation approaches together contributes to the sustainable future. Many tech giants IT Companies started using renewable energy in 2020. Use of digital technologies for sophistication and luxury may ignore the unnecessary carbon emission. Every organization and individual should keep a green approach while purchasing food products, clothes, services, housing and transportation. Making aware to each other about the responsibility towards sustainable procurement as well as investments.

IT experts and programmers should incorporate algorithm design strategies which can minimize the energy usage of digital devices. Declaring the data centers are utilizing renewable energy should be compulsory. All storage and Cloud computing services utilized by the consumers should insist on the green approach adapted by IT Giants. The graphics accelerator and multi-core CPUs required to be operated on the lower frequencies. The dynamic frequency and scaling approach in the microprocessor can save significant amounts of energy.

A usability centric website designing, attractiveness and customer engagement is always a priority to grow a business. However, if it is declared on the website that sustainable approaches are followed during the design of the website then the wiser audience can spread a word of wisdom about it. The minimalistic design keeps the target of sustainability. Since image and video consume a significant portion of a website's background data, it is important to understand the advantages and drawbacks of incorporating images and videos. For displaying graphs PNG and GIF formats are ideal. For photographs, JPEG is a suitable option. From a typographical standpoint, maintaining a clean and visually appealing webpage is important. To ensure design consistency, it is advisable to not to use more than two distinct styles. Measuring the assessment time for each element and loading speed associated with each font can help for sustainable webpage design. The online tools, websites and libraries are available to find the sustainability of the webpage. The dark mode of the website should also be an option along with the internationalization support. The sustainability in the web page design should also be included along with the accessibility features as one of the compliances.

Larger content is easier to see, but it demands greater energy expenditure. Similarly, the intensity of presentation, whether it is the brightness required to be selected through the color selection principles. Videos or animated images effectively capture attention but consume higher energy and data compared to static information. Every single website has the power of making difference by keeping the page size low and reducing data transfer. This will load the website faster, thus improving search engine rankings. The use of Cloud-based services in combination with the CDN can help in better response time of the web pages.

REFERENCES

Abeydeera, L. H. U. W., Mesthrige, J. W., & Samarasinghalage, T. I. (2019). Global research on carbon emissions: A scientometric review. In *Sustainability (Switzerland)* (Vol. 11). MDPI. DOI: 10.3390/su11143972

Batmunkh, A. (2022). Carbon Footprint of The Most Popular Social Media Platforms. *Sustainability (Basel)*, *14*(4), 2195. Advance online publication. DOI: 10.3390/su14042195

Bonnardel, N., Piolat, A., & Le Bigot, L. (2011). The impact of colour on Website appeal and users' cognitive processes. *Displays*, *32*(2), 69–80. DOI: 10.1016/j.displa.2010.12.002

Boscovic, D., Vakil, F., Dautovi, S. and Toši, Milenko. (2011). Pervasive wireless CDN for greening video streaming to mobile devices. MIPRO, 629-236.

Chen, T., Gao, X., & Chen, G. (2016). The features, hardware, and architectures of data center networks: A survey. *Journal of Parallel and Distributed Computing*, *96*, 45–74. DOI: 10.1016/j.jpdc.2016.05.009

ecoiron (2007). http://ecoiron.blogspot.com/2007/01/black-google-would-save-3000-megawatts.html, accessed 13/02/2025

Lee, Y., & Song, M. (2020). Adaptive Color Selection to Limit Power Consumption for Multi-Object GUI Applications in OLED-Based Mobile Devices. *Energies*, *13*(10), 2425. Advance online publication. DOI: 10.3390/en13102425

Periyasamy, A. G., Singh, A., & Ravindra, K. (2022). Carbon Emissions from Virtual and Physical Modes of Conference and Prospects for Carbon Neutrality: An Analysis From India. *Air, Soil and Water Research*, *15*, 11786221221093298. Advance online publication. DOI: 10.1177/11786221221093298

Rahnamay Bonab, S., Haseli, G., & Jafarzadeh Ghoushchi, S. (2024). Digital technology and information and communication technology on the carbon footprint. In *Decision Support Systems for Sustainable Computing* (pp. 101–122). Elsevier., DOI: 10.1016/B978-0-443-23597-9.00005-6

Rong, H., Zhang, H., Xiao, S., Li, C., & Hu, C. (2016). Optimizing energy consumption for data centers. In *Renewable and Sustainable Energy Reviews* (Vol. 58, pp. 674–691). Elsevier Ltd., DOI: 10.1016/j.rser.2015.12.283

Seifi, A., & Moshayeri, A. (2024). *The Influence of Color Schemes and Aesthetics on User Satisfaction in Web Design: An Empirical Study*. Https://Www.Ijahci.Com/Index.Php/Ijahci/Article/View/21

Swasty, W., & Adriyanto, A. R. (2017). Does Color Matter on Web User Interface Design. *CommIT (Communication and Information Technology). Journal, 11*(1), 17. DOI: 10.21512/commit.v11i1.2088

The Impact of Typography on Web Design: A Comprehensive Guide to Aesthetics and Readability. (n.d.). Https://Guidelines.India.Gov.in/Activity/the-Impact-of-Typography-on-Web-Design-a-Comprehensive-Guide-to-Aesthetics-and-Readability/

ichindelean, M., ichindelean, M. T., Cetină, I., & Orzan, G. (2021). A comparative eye tracking study of usability—Towards sustainable web design. *Sustainability (Basel), 13*(18), 10415. Advance online publication. DOI: 10.3390/su131810415

Ummah, M. S. (2019). Understanding and Implementing User Interface Laws: Differentiating UI Laws from UX Laws in the UI/UX Design Process. *Sustainability (Switzerland), 11*(1), 1–14. http://scioteca.caf.com/bitstream/handle/123456789/1091/RED2017-Eng-8ene.pdf?sequence=12&isAllowed=y%0Ahttp://dx.doi.org/10.1016/j.regsciurbeco.2008.06.005%0Ahttps://www.researchgate.net/publication/305320484_SISTEM_PEMBETUNGAN_TERPUSAT_STRATEGI_MELESTARI

View of Color Psychology in Marketing. (n.d.). Https://Www.Jbt.Org.Pk/Index.Php/Jbt/Article/View/99/85.

Vroom, R. (n.d.). Styling influence to the loyalty for knowledge sharing on WikID. Https://Www.Academia.Edu/16724582/Styling_influence_to_the_loyalty_for_knowledge_sharing_on_WikID

Xu, N., Yang, J., Needham, M., Boscovic, D., & Vakil, F. (2010). Toward the Green Video CDN. *2010 IEEE/ACM International Conference on Green Computing and Communications*, 430-435.

Chapter 2
Sustainable Cloud Computing:
Ecofriendly Strategies and Innovations for Green Data Centers

N. Manjunathan
https://orcid.org/0000-0003-3134-7819
Vel Tech Rangarajan Dr. Sagunthala R&D Institute of Science and Technology, India

T. Venkata Ramana
CVR College of Engineering, India

A. Rajasekar
Sri Sai Ram Institute of Technology, India

D. Vijayakumar
Vel Tech Multi Tech Dr. Rangarajan Dr. Sakunthala Engineering College, India

V. Sameswari
Rajiv Gandhi National Institute of Youth Development, India

S. M. Nandha Gopal
Thejus Engineering College, India

R. Siva Subramanian
https://orcid.org/0000-0002-7509-9223
RMK College of Engineering and Technology, India

ABSTRACT

Cloud computing has experienced great growth in the recent past and has been attributed to bringing huge economic value but at the same time has been associated with energy usage and environmental consequences. The problem of how to make cloud computing environmentally friendly and create green data centers is one of the major concerns of the cloud computing industry at present. This survey focuses on the following four dimensions of sustainability in the context of cloud environ-

DOI: 10.4018/979-8-3373-0766-4.ch002

Copyright © 2025, IGI Global Scientific Publishing. Copying or distributing in print or electronic forms without written permission of IGI Global Scientific Publishing is prohibited.

ments: energy efficiency, resource optimization, renewable energy, and sustainable hardware. Furthermore, the authors also explore the limitations associated with cost, size, and security requirements in terms of environmental goals. The chapter gives a classification of sustainable cloud techniques, discusses present industry activities, and gives potential future technologies such as AI-driven energy management and edge computing as potential solutions. The goal of this chapter is to provide a literature review of sustainable practices and encourage more investigations into ecoconscious cloud computing.

1. INTRODUCTION

1.1 Background on Cloud Computing and Sustainability

Cloud computing has dramatically changed the way organizations approach their IT environments (Maheshwaran et al 2024). It enables the dynamic procurement of computing resources through the internet and provides flexible storage, computation and software services without large hardware infrastructure (Rani et al 2023). This model has created a lot of value in terms of cost reduction, organization efficacy and adaptability. But cloud computing has also introduced numerous environmental issues given it is now a popular platform globally. Physical servers, on which cloud computing is based, are data centers that require tremendous power to meet the demands of cloud services. The functioning of these data centers also has a high energy demand which in turn creates a large energy impact. Research shows that the worldwide IT industry, of which cloud computing is a part, consumes and emits a significant share of the global electricity and greenhouse gases. This has caused the need to make cloud computing more environmentally friendly through the following ways. The effects of cloud computing in the environment are complex in nature (Vinoth et al 2022). In addition to energy consumption data centers are also sources of heat which need cooling to reduce heat build-up and this requires more energy. Furthermore, the advancement of cloud service technology results in high frequencies of hardware changes and subsequently, the generation of e-waste. Given that the use of cloud services is growing exponentially, the issue of the impact of such systems on the environment is important, which has led to sustainability being a major issue in the field (Sudha et al 2024).

1.2 Motivation for Sustainable Cloud Computing

The drivers that have encouraged the call for sustainable cloud computing are economic, environmental, and legal.

Economic Motivation: Energy efficiency in business operations is synonymous with cost improvement. Electricity costs, especially in large-scale data centers, form part of the largest operating expenses primarily because these facilities require a vast amount of power to operate. Energy efficient technologies and practices help cloud providers to minimize their energy costs and therefore increase their revenues. However, sustainable practices are raised as being able to enhance operational effectiveness and thereby decrease infrastructural demands and costs in the future.

Environmental Motivation: Cloud computing environmental footprint is rising, and the stakes on the IT industry to employ eco-friendlier solutions are higher. If cloud providers adopt energy efficiency in their systems and incorporate renewable energy, they will be in a position to lower their carbon footprint and help solve climate change. Therefore, the authors also emphasize the importance of recycling and using hardware more than once to decrease the level of e-waste affecting the environment in connection with the development of the cloud industry.

Regulatory Motivation: There is a growing interest of governments and regulatory authorities in environmental issues all over the world. Carbon emission constraints and green practices are being governed by policies and regulations. These regulations make cloud providers follow them to avoid fines, follow environment compliance, and survive the market competition. Furthermore, customer expectations are raising regarding the sustainability of their cloud services, which gives more pressure to create green cloud solutions.

1.3 Scope and Objectives

Specifically, this paper seeks to discuss the different methods of attaining sustainability in cloud computing with a view to finding out the key best practices and growing trends. The content areas of the paper include a survey of existing work and methods that are energy efficiency, renewable energy, and resource allocation. It also aims to offer a classification of the methods and tools for the green cloud computing which are the strategies to minimize the effects of cloud infrastructures on the environment. The goal is not only to categorize and characterize but also to evaluate and discuss the feasibility, performance, and problems of these strategies and their suitability for IaaS, PaaS, and SaaS models. It is the intention of this paper to review current literature, issues, and opportunities related to green cloud computing and thus provide a valuable addition to the body of knowledge on the subject.

2. METRICS AND STANDARDS FOR SUSTAINABILITY IN CLOUD COMPUTING

2.1 Metrics for Measuring Sustainability

It is crucial to quantify sustainability in cloud computing in order to evaluate the performance of the strategies being used on data centers and their implications on the environment (Murthy et al 2021). Several key metrics are used to evaluate the energy efficiency, carbon footprint, and water usage of cloud infrastructures:

Power Usage Effectiveness (PUE): PUE is one of the most common indicators of energy efficiency of data centers. It is determined by dividing the total energy that is utilized by the data center, including the power required for cooling, lighting and other facility related power by the energy consumed by the IT loads. A lower PUE means a more efficient data center since the proportional level of energy consumed is devoted to IT processes as opposed to supporting services including cooling and electrical distribution. Although PUE is useful in comparing the efficiency of data centres it does not include the efficiency of the power sources (for example the carbon footprint of coal fired power stations).
Carbon Usage Effectiveness (CUE): CUE is a metric intended to inform the carbon efficiency of data centers in relation to energy consumed. It is computed by dividing the total carbon emissions by total energy consumption. This metric provides a purer comparison to PUE than does the energy efficiency ratio formula above, as it includes the source of energy, whether renewable, or non-renewable such as coal or natural gas. CUE is more useful in examining sustainability since it connects energy use to emissions so that organisations can pinpoint where to cut their emissions.
Water Usage Effectiveness (WUE): Typically, data centers use water to cool the servers which makes them consume a lot of water. WUE quantifies the ratio of water consumption by the data center to the energy consumption in the data center. Like the previously described PUE and CUE, this metric also serves to assess sustainability because it goes beyond the energy measurement. As the scarcity of water has become an increasing problem, along with geographic location data centers, it is necessary to control the consumption of water to avoid depletion of resources and negative impact of cloud computing services.

2.2 Green Cloud Standards and Certifications

To encourage and standardize sustainability efforts in cloud computing, several industry certifications and standards have been developed:

Energy Star: This is a familiar label for energy efficient products which extend to data center equipment. Energy Star certified data centers refer to the data centers that conform to energy efficiency standards of the U.S Environmental Protection Agency. The certification assists cloud providers and data center operators to show their dedication to lower the consumption of energy.
LEED (Leadership in Energy and Environmental Design): LEED is an international standard for green buildings, whether they are data centers or not. LEED certification measures the ability to affect the environment through elements such as energy, water consumption, and the general impact on carbon. Due to the adoption of LEED standards by cloud providers who build or renovate data centres, those who meet the standards can demonstrate their commitment to sustainable construction and operations.
ISO 50001: This international standard is concerning energy management systems. It offers an organized approach to the rationalization of energy use within an organization. ISO 50001 is applicable to cloud providers who want to reduce the energy consumption in their processes, and thus their carbon footprint. These certifications give cloud providers the opportunity to prove the company's environmentalism strategies and give the customers a chance to decide on which cloud services to use.

2.3 Limitations of Current Metrics and Standards

While metrics like PUE, CUE, and WUE, along with certifications like Energy Star and LEED, are valuable tools for measuring sustainability, they have limitations in the context of cloud computing:

Multitenant Environments: Data centers in the cloud computing model are sometimes referred to as multitenant, which implies that several customers use the infrastructure. This complicates the ability to precisely track the sustainability metrics by individual customer. For example, although the PUE metric can tell the energy consumption of the whole data center, it doesn't provide a way to consider clients' typical energy consumption patterns and their workloads, so it is challenging to determine the sustainability of specific workloads.

Lack of Comprehensive Sustainability Measurement: Many of today's KPIs are still centred around energy consumption and CO2 emissions, while important sustainability aspects such as e-waste, resource depletion and social impact of cloud infrastructure are ignored. If one took a broader view of the sustainable development concept, it would be necessary to incorporate other factors into these evaluations, but there is no consensus on how to do this.
Varying Regional Practices: Policies and standards of sustainability may also differ based on regional parameters of environment and policies. For instance, a data center that uses electricity from a hydro power station in a region with a lot of water has a lower CUE than a data center that is in an area that relies on electricity generated from coal. This makes it difficult to compare the sustainability of cloud providers at different geographical regions.

3. TAXONOMY OF SUSTAINABLE CLOUD COMPUTING STRATEGIES

3.1 Classification of Strategies

Sustainable cloud computing strategies can be broadly categorized into four primary areas: CO 2 reduction, energy conservation, optimal use of resources, renewable energy systems integration and minimizing waste. All of them are designed targeting different aspect of sustainability and have the common objective of achieving green cloud computing.

Figure 1. Sustainable Cloud Computing Strategies

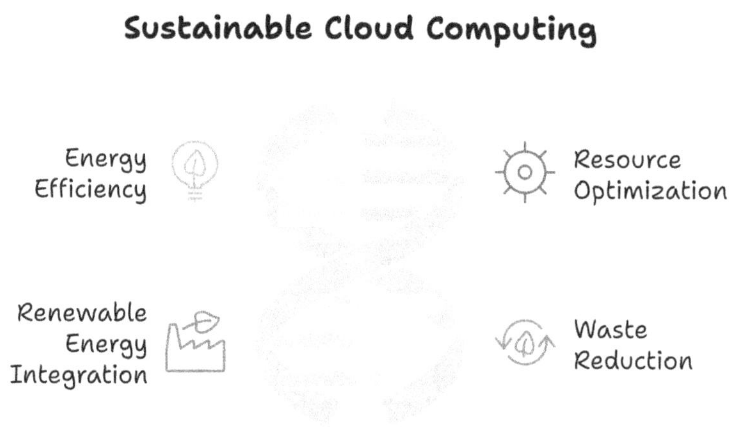

1.Energy Efficiency: This strategy aims at reducing the total energy that the cloud data centers and structures use. The emphasis is made on the optimization of the total cost, and cost of energy used for IT equipment, cooling and other related facilities.

2.Resource Optimization: Resource management is an effort to utilize the available resources like processing power, storage and networking etc. in the most efficient way by minimizing wastage and optimizing their utilization. The idea is to guarantee that more resources are used efficiently without over subscribing them, which leads to wastage of energy and resources.

3.Renewable Energy Integration: This involves migrating data centers and cloud infrastructure to renewable energy sources such as solar, wind or hydro power. Including renewable energy sources also has the advantage of decreasing the dependence on primary resources and decreasing carbon imprint for cloud providers.

4.Waste Reduction: Energy efficiency that deals with reducing the amount of waste generated in data centers includes electronic waste commonly referred to as e-waste among others. This covers how to recycle hardware, prolong the lifespan of equipment, and how to embrace circular economy in cloud structures (Das et al 2020).

3.2 Overview of Techniques

Each strategy employs specific techniques to achieve its sustainability goals:

1.Energy Efficiency:

Virtualization: Virtualization technologies enable the workloads to be run on fewer physical servers, hence less energy is used. Virtual machines are flexible with regards to allocation since one can be created depending on the current requirement, and therefore, energy consumption could be controlled (Surya et al 2021).

Dynamic Voltage and Frequency Scaling (DVFS): DVFS approaches modify the electrical power of the servers with respect to voltage and frequency in order to use less power during low traffic periods.

Advanced Cooling Techniques: Technologies like liquid cooling, evaporative cooling, and airside economization decrease the instance of conventional air conditioning, which is power-consuming. All these methods are useful in reducing the energy consumption in cooling the data centers to an effective temperature.

2.Resource Optimization:

Load Balancing: Breaking down workloads to be run on multiple servers so that no server becomes overwhelmed with work minimizes idle time and improves resource usage.

Resource Allocation Algorithms: These algorithms are self-organizing, which means that they can allocate resources depending on the specific demand so that they don't have to provide more resources than needed. This reduces wastage which is not good when the resources are not fully used as required.

Auto-scaling: Cloud environment can dynamically allocate resources to meet the demand; extra resource is acquired during busy periods and less during idle periods. This assists in achieving a balance between resource utilization and output within and across resources.

3.Renewable Energy Integration:

Solar and Wind Power: The data centers can either integrate their own solar power or buy electricity from renewable energy companies. Some cloud providers are now substituting wind and solar power to run data centers, which contributes to less emission of carbon.

Energy Storage Solutions: Battery storage or other forms of storage enable cloud providers to store renewable energy during periods of excess (for instance during the day when the sun is shining or during windy days) and use them during peak usage or during periods when renewable energy is scarce.

Smart Grid Integration: Data centers can also feed into the smart grids in a local area and be able to purchase renewable energy when it is available and also balance the different load requirements.

Figure 2. Renewable Energy Integration

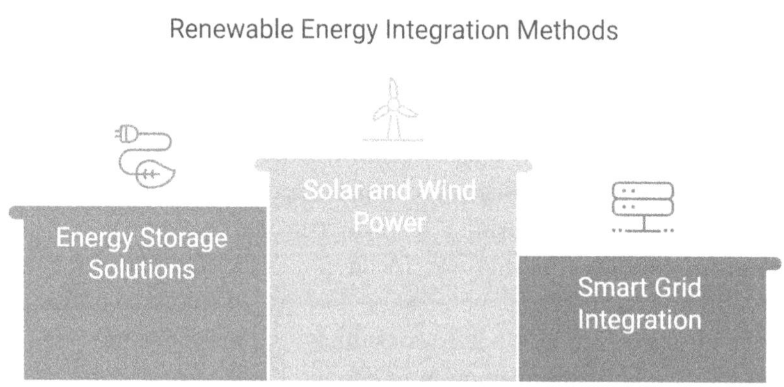

4.Waste Reduction:

Hardware Recycling: The upgrades and reuses of expired hardware decrease electronic waste. Cloud providers have opportunities to reuse components, refresh equipment, donate or recycle it as well to increase the life cycle.

Extended Equipment Lifespan: Smart technologies used in the predictive maintenance practice involve tracking the state of the equipment so that it can be repaired or replaced when necessary. This cuts down the frequency of replacements and in the process, helps to decrease the generation of electronic waste.

Circular Economy Models: In this way, it's possible to organize the reuse of the materials used in the production of the hardware instead of their disposal, and provide a more effective cycle of the cloud providers' hardware.

4. TECHNIQUES FOR ENERGY EFFICIENCY AND OPTIMIZATION IN CLOUD DATA CENTERS

The primary power usage of cloud data centers is related to energy used by servers and cooling systems. Therefore, enhancing energy efficiency and resource conservation in such structures is paramount from an environmental perspective and organizational costs' perspective. There are several ways these goals can be attained such as through, virtualization, dynamic scaling and a proper cooling system, optimized hardware.

4.1 Virtualization and Resources Management

Virtualization is one of the basic approaches to enhancing energy efficiency in cloud data centers. It refers to the act of making some logical representation of physical hardware (servers, storage, and networking) to achieve maximum utilization. While traditional structures require the providers to have numerous physical servers for distinct applications, virtualization enables the management of the applications on fewer machines. This is lessens the requirement for physical hardware, is energy efficient and reduces the foot print in data centers.

Key aspects of virtualization that contribute to energy efficiency include:

Consolidation: Server consolidation is a process of reducing the number of physical servers, and virtualization fulfils this by allowing multiple VMs to operate on a single physical server.

Load Balancing: Dynamic load balancing is a way of equal distribution of loads in order to avoid situations where some servers are idle, while others are burdened with too much work. Due to this, energy is well utilized by cloud providers and there is no wastage of excess capacity in the power usage.

Dynamic Scaling: Virtualization leads to achievable scaling because resources can be increased or decreased according to the level of usage. The utilization of these servers is also very effective in that during low traffic, unnecessary servers can be powered off. Since the load increases, one can provision more resources without the need to boot up more physical hosts.

4.2 Dynamic Voltage and Frequency Scaling (DVFS)

Dynamic Voltage and Frequency Scaling (DVFS) is a technique of power management in which the voltage and the frequency of the processor are altered in proportion to the working load of the processor. DVFS is an important mechanism since it works to reduce the amount of energy used by the servers, especially where the workload is low, but the power consumption is only ramped up to higher levels in case of increased demand for power.

Energy Savings: DVFS has the capability of reducing the energy per processor by either reducing the clock frequency or the supply voltage during low utilization. This leads to reduction in energy expenditure on low activity or at least energy conservation while performing the low activity.

Adaptive Operations: DVFS ready servers are capable of adjusting the power consumption of the system in real time depending with the performance demands of the system and in the process help to minimize the energy that is consumed without compromising on the performance of the system.

DVFS thus enables cloud providers to achieve fine-granularity control of energy use at the hardware level thus enhancing overall data center energy efficiency.

4.3 Cooling and Thermal Management

Cooling is a major concern in the efficient running of data centers since the cooling systems consume most of the power in data centers. The major energy consumption is in traditional air conditioning systems; thus, incorporation of innovative cooling methods results to energy conservation.

Liquid Cooling: Liquid cooling includes using water or other coolants to dissipate heat much better than air-based systems. These systems can help cut down on the traditional air conditioning systems by circulating coolants

through the servers or racks they employ. Liquid cooling is most effective in areas with high density server installations where air cooling is inadequate.
Airside Economization: Airside economization, often referred to as free cooling, relies on outside air conditions to cool down data centers without using mechanical cooling. This technique works to minimize the use of energy consuming coolants especially in cold climate by utilizing cool outside air. When data centers draw air from outside, they will be able to reduce the demand for chilled air which will save a lot of energy.

These cooling and thermal management techniques are very efficient in minimizing the power consumption of the data centers, and especially those large scale.

4.4 Server and Storage Optimization

Another major strategy of energy saving is associated with server and storage hardware in the cloud data centers. Several methods can be employed to make hardware more energy-efficient:

Energy-Efficient Hardware Choices: In this respect, the choice of efficient power use servers and storage devices is also essential to reducing overall energy consumption. Current processors and storage devices are more energy efficient and implementing these devices can result in large energy savings in huge data centers.
Disk Spinning: HDDs are power hungry due to their mechanical nature as compared to SSDs that are electronic in nature. A disk can also be spun down when it is idle or using SSDs that do not have any rotating parts and therefore consume less power. Furthermore, the higher-level power management options of storage devices should be utilized to prevent energy consumption during inactivity.
Data Deduplication: Data deduplication is a process of removing multiple copies of data, this makes the amount of storage needed to be lesser and in turn the amount of energy required. For instance, storage of only distinct data will help in reducing the pressure that is exerted on storage systems, and hence increase the efficiency of energy. With these hardware and storage optimizations, the cloud data centers can cut the energy consumption even more and make the cloud data centers more sustainable.

5. RENEWABLE ENERGY INTEGRATION IN CLOUD INFRASTRUCTURE

Due to the increasing popularity of cloud computing, there is a major concern on environmental effects of data centers. A study has shown that the use of renewable energy source as a means of powering cloud infrastructure is one of the best ways to minimize the carbon emissions. Cloud providers are moving towards using renewable energy to power data centers since the companies want their operations to be sustainable and meet green goals.

5.1 Renewable Energy Sources for Data Centers

The data centers are significant electrical energy users, and changing from fossil-based electricity to renewable energy is the next big step. Cloud computing can reduce the carbon emission of the operations through the incorporation of renewable energy sources like solar, wind, and geothermal.

Solar Power: Solar energy is amongst the most popular of the renewable energy technologies being adopted in cloud data centers. One way that data centers can take advantage of renewable energy sources is including photovoltaic (PV) systems either on the premises or with the assistance of third-party solar energy suppliers. Photovoltaic energy is most useful in areas that receive a lot of sun and can be used side by side with other energy sources or can replace them. Solar power can be obtained by installing solar panels on the roof of buildings as well as large areas of specially designed land for housing solar farms to feed a large portion of energy demand by the data centers.

Wind Power: This means that there is also an opportunity to use wind energy as another renewable source in the powering of cloud data centers. Wind power can be generated on-site, or using turbines located near the facility. Most cloud service providers have signed PPAs with wind farms to ensure availability of renewable energy to their data centers. Wind power is highly efficient in windy places and so many data center can consider it due to its efficiency.

Geothermal Power: Geothermal power is electricity generated from heat within the earth, the concept of geothermal energy can also be employed in cooling of ICT equipment in data centers. Geothermal power plants can offer a base load electricity generation, this makes geothermal energy a good prospect for areas with geothermal activity. Although, geothermal energy is not as popular as solar or wind energy, it can provide stable and low CO2 generating energy which can help to minimize the negative effects of cloud computing.

5.2 Energy Storage and Grid Interaction

Wind and solar energy are intermittent sources of energy meaning that data centers which rely on such energy sources are likely going to experience a disruption in their power supply. In response to this, energy storage solutions and smart grid interactions are instrumental in the integration of sustainable renewable energy into cloud systems.

Energy Storage Solutions: In pursuit of this goal, cloud providers are beginning to incorporate energy storage like batteries or any other technology into the network. These systems store excess energy produced during renewable energy production at the peak of its generation.

Smart Grid Integration: A smart grid is an enhanced electricity network that incorporates the digital communication and control technology to enhance the dependability, efficiency, and environmental friendliness of electricity delivery. Smart grid can also be connected with the data center in order to manage demand and supply of energy in a very dynamic way depending on availability of renewable energy. For instance, when there is high generation of renewable energy, a data center can use more green energy for its operations. On the other hand, data centers can source power during low-renewable energy times from the grid or from stored energy. Smart grids also help to manage energy more effectively by loading and ensuring that as much as possible of renewable energy is utilized.

5.3 Challenges and Opportunities

The integration of renewable energy into cloud data centers is a promising area, which has its own set of issues that must be solved to provide reliable, inexpensive, and environmentally friendly service.

Challenges:

Intermittency of Renewable Sources: The main weakness of such renewable resources such as solar and winds is that they are not constant. Solar power is only available in the day and winds power is inconsistent. This has the effect of complicating the certainty of power supply in data centers, which need to be on all the time. Energy storage solutions can address this problem, but they bring extra expenses and complexity.

Figure 3. Challenges and Opportunities

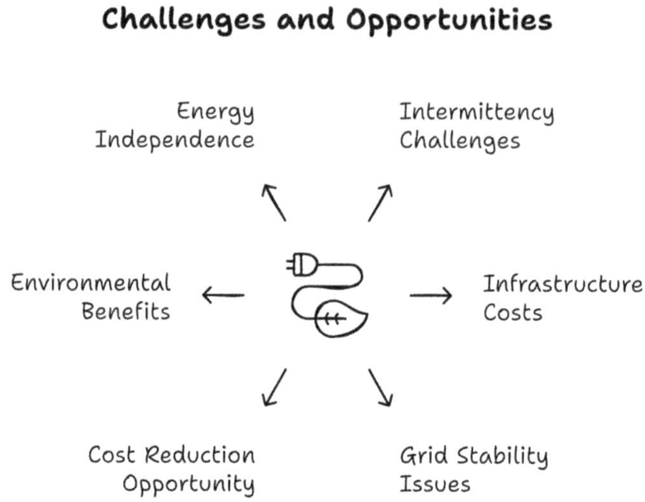

Infrastructure Costs: Switching to renewable energy sources tends to involve significant initial costs in the form of manufacturing new equipment, including solar panels, wind generators, and batteries. It may take time before investors start to see their money back and they may require to spend a lot of money at the initial stage. However, with the costs of renewable technologies coming down this problem is not so much an issue in the present.

Grid Reliability and Stability: However, the introduction of renewable energy into the power system can be problematic to the stability of the grid, particularly in areas where renewables dominate the energy supply system. Predicting and balancing the amount of variable power from renewable sources with the needed supply of energy to the grid is challenging.

Opportunities:

Cost Reduction: In the long run, the cost for the renewable energy sources such as the solar panels and wind turbines has reduced. It is not rocket science to understand that the cost of renewable energy is declining and in fact it is getting closer to the cost of conventional energy sources. This creates a chance for cloud providers to achieve their long-term energy goals by depending on renewable energy sources.

Environmental Benefits: Cloud system integration of renewable energy sources in data centres decreases the environmental impact of data centres. From the perspective of environmentally conscious cloud providers, and those wishing to align with their CSR objectives, the vision to renewable energy is a clear one. **Energy Independence:** Nevertheless, by adopting renewable energy cloud providers can cut down the reliance of conventional fossil fuels and enhance energy security. It is especially useful where the grid is unreliable or the cost of energy is high within the particular area. Renewable energy also offers cloud providers a certain degree of energy independence, which lets them protect themselves from rising energy costs. Thus, the introduction of renewable energy into the cloud data centers is not without its benefits and pitfalls. Though, renewable sources are intermittent, have high fixed costs, and grid reliability challenges, the overall environmental, economic, and operational advantages of integrating renewable energies make the strategy of renewable energies crucial for attaining the sustainable cloud computing goal. With advancement in technological solution, renewable energy will remain as a key driver to the future of cloud infrastructure.

6. SUSTAINABLE SOFTWARE DEVELOPMENT PRACTICES FOR THE CLOUD

With the ongoing advancement of cloud computing, the ecological effects of application software are gradually being discussed. The energy usage of software solutions which are implemented in design and development of software to deployment and even when the software is no longer useful is a critical factor towards sustainable cloud infrastructure. Green software engineering principles are therefore focused on the optimization of energy consumption of cloud applications while at the same time ensuring that the necessary application performance, functionality, and scalability is achieved.

6.1 Green Software Engineering

Green Software Engineering can be defined as the creation of software and its related processes and products using methods, tools and techniques that are designed to reduce the energy consumption of the software (Matthew et al 2024). The main objective of green software engineering is therefore to develop applications that require less computational power, and consequently fewer resources, and hence, have a lower carbon footprint on cloud computing systems.

Key strategies within green software engineering include:

Code Optimization: Code optimization is one of the most efficient and efficient ways to minimize software energy consumption. This can benefit developers to write code that is resource friendly, that is, code that uses less CPU time, memory space, etc. This can include such operations as increasing the efficiency of algorithms by reducing the number of computations or excluding extra calculations and operations which are not needed (Pitchai et al 2024).

Energy-Aware Development Tools: There is an ever increasing number of tools and frameworks that are intended to assist developers in the assessment of energy efficiency of their code. These tools determine the amount of energy that a certain piece of software uses when running and offers information on possible enhancements. When such tools are integrated into the development process, the software engineers are able to remove waste during the development phase (Verma, J., & Sharma, Y. 2024).

Resource Management: Resource management is the other determinant of green software engineering since resources must also be used efficiently. Thus, reducing the pressure on cloud resources (CPU, memory, storage) can help applications reduce energy consumption by several orders of magnitude. For instance, development of software that allows the management of resources to be proportional to the demand at any one time prevents the occurrence of situations where applications are carrying large resource demands during times of low usage (Saxena et al 2024).

6.2 Efficient Algorithms and Application Design

Algorithms, as well as the application design, are two fundamental aspects of minimizing energy consumption in cloud-based applications. Algorithm tuning can significantly reduce the computational intensity of software, which in turn will reduce energy consumption for the same tasks.

Algorithm Optimization: Here, algorithms are identified as central to energy efficiency of software. Due to poor designs, some algorithms may be more demanding in terms of power hence using up a lot of power. For instance, time complexity of algorithms such as $O(n^2)$ or $O(n^3)$ use much CPU time as the size of input data increases therefore consuming much energy. If developers use more efficient algorithms for example, algorithms with time complexity of $O(\log n)$ or $O(n)$ the number of operations will be less hence less energy will be consumed.

Modularization: Modular software design therefore refers to the process of partitioning large scale applications into smaller and more autonomous modules or microservices that can be made efficient to offer. This enables the cloud

providers to operate only the required components, in the process eliminating unnecessary resource consumption. For instance, a modular architecture may enable a cloud application to shut down less used modules in order to save power.
Load Balancing: Another technique used for the management of energy consumption of applications is load balancing. In this method of resource partitioning software is able to distribute workloads across servers or processing units so that none is overworked. This minimizes the chances of benefiting from either underutilization or over utilization which will lead to wastage of energy. Load balancing also assists in scaling the cloud applications depending on the number of users, without wasting energy.

6.3 Lifecycle Management of Cloud Applications

It means the practices of usage of Cloud applications that are sustainable during their development, deployment, and when they are no longer needed.

Development Phase: Sustainability should be well considered during the development phase of the software. This encompasses the writing of efficient code that consumes less energy, the choice of right algorithms as well as thinking about the ways to optimize the use of the resources. Another characteristic that developers should consider is the scalability of the software; that is, the ability of the program to adjust to the amount of demand placed on the resource.
Deployment Phase: During deployment one has to ensure that the Cloud resources are utilized properly. These include non-Virtual Machine applications like microservices and serverless computing, which is a cloud-native architecture. Cloud providers are able to increase or decrease the resources they offer depending on need, meaning that energy is not wasted in the meantime. Energy management should also be conducted during the deployment phase with the intention of recognizing areas of concern as to energy consumption.
Decommissioning and Maintenance Phase: The management of products and services does not stop at the deployment of the lifecycle approach. It is very important that an application is properly retired when it has served its useful life cycle. This includes storing data or deleting it properly, reusing the hardware in some way if need be, and closing off any resources that are no longer in use to conserve energy. Also, software maintenance is crucial to determine where and how a software is inefficient and how it can be optimized and therefore minimize energy consumption during the software's life cycle.
When these best practices are integrated into the life cycle of cloud applications, developers can guarantee that their software is beneficial to the general energy efficiency and environmentally friendly cloud ecosystem.

7. WASTE MANAGEMENT AND CIRCULAR ECONOMY IN CLOUD COMPUTING

This paper seeks to address the following research questions: With the advancement in cloud computing, what amount of electronic waste commonly referred to as e-waste is produced by data centers and cloud infrastructure? Reduction of environmental pollution and optimizing the usage of resources used in cloud computing is possible through waste management, use of circular economy. Through the recycling of hardware, the reuse of data center equipment, and the proper disposal of the hardware, the cloud industry can minimize the effect it has on the environment to adapt to a sustainable model.

7.1 Hardware Recycling and E-Waste Reduction

The technological changes in cloud computing are realized in a very short time and this associated with constant changes or replacements of the hardware components in data centers. This creates a lot of e-waste and if not well handled can proved to be disastrous to the environment. Hardware recycling is one of the best ways of minimizing the levels of wastes that are dumped into the landfills as well as reclaiming the various metals from discarded or damaged equipment (Jeyaranjani et al 2024).

Recycling Cloud Hardware: The best practices that can be adopted by cloud providers include the following: reusing parts of the HW including servers, storage devices, and networking. If cloud companies do not have a take-back program they should make sure that their suppliers are participating in a recycling program and that used hardware is being properly disassembled and recycled so that metals (copper, gold, aluminum) as well as plastics and silicon can be reclaimed. This cuts out the need to obtain new minerals and minerals in a way that is less damaging to the environment in creating this new hardware. Some of the organisations have engaged certified e-waste recycling companies that conform to the best practices of recycling.

E-Waste Reduction Initiatives: To cut down on e-waste generation, the cloud providers are also investing in hardware that is longer lasting, energy efficient and can be recycled. There is a trend of manufacturers designing equipment to last longer and incorporating less hazard to public health. Purchasing environmentally-sound components and materials for networks also help cloud providers reduce their wastage while increasing the sustainability of their services (Manikandan et al 2024).

7.2 Extending the Lifespan of Data Center Equipment

Other than pledging to stop buying new equipment, another possible solution for e-waste management involves increasing the useful life of data center hardware. However, this approach helps to avoid waste and financial and environmental expenses on the production of new equipment.

Predictive Maintenance: Another successful way of increasing the longevity of data center equipment is through the use of predictive maintenance. Through sensors and big data analysis, cloud providers are able to have live feeds on most parts of hardware components and be able to detect a failing part before it fails. It makes it possible for the failure components to be replaced before the entire systems giving a longer life of the equipment and less wastage. Predictive maintenance also benefits data centers by providing insight into how effectively the equipment in use is and when it is not needed.

Hardware Upgrades and Repurposing: Also, data centers can refresh individual components so that instead of swapping out whole systems, they can replace old processors, for example, or add more memory. Another way of prolonging the useful life of the equipment is to use the old equipment for other simpler operations. For example, older servers can be repurposed for other less demanding tasks hence they will be fully utilized before they are considered for retirement.

Refurbishing and Reselling: Instead of disposing old equipment, cloud providers can work with other companies to and resell the equipment. Some of the capacity-extended servers and networking devices can be used in secondary markets diminishing the need for new manufacturing thus aligning with the circular economy.

7.3 Sustainable Disposal Practices

Although equipment is recycled and used until its next life, it is still clear that at some point data center equipment becomes obsolete. In these cases, the proper disposal of the products is very important in order to reduce the impacts on the environment.

Responsible E-Waste Disposal: This is why it is important that data centers adhere to proper e-waste disposal management in order to avoid polluting the environment with materials such as mercury, lead, and cadmium. Proper disposal entails engaging certified e-waste management firms that meet the environmental best practices such as the Responsible Recycling (R2) Certification or the Waste Electrical and Electronic Equipment (WEEE) Directive. These certifications guarantee that e-waste is disposed of properly and that material is recycled with least harm to the environment.

Disposal Guidelines: Cloud providers should come up with clear policies on how the equipment should be retired or disposed of as per it's policy. This may include erasing data from storage media, neutralizing chemicals in old batteries, and disposing of hazardous substances in a manner that complies with existing laws. Cloud providers may also engage local governments in the compliance for environmental laws controlling the disposal of e-waste and join the world's fight against e-waste.

8. POLICY, REGULATION, AND INDUSTRY INITIATIVES FOR GREEN CLOUD COMPUTING

Green cloud computing has attracted the interest of governments, business magnates, and organizations worldwide because of its ability to minimize energy use and carbon emissions. The use of green cloud practices is being propelled by policies, partnerships between companies and the government and lastly CSR. Such strategies have been developed for the purpose of coordinating the advancement of cloud computing with ecological concerns, and for the purpose of making certain that the numerous advantages of cloud services are accessible without having an adverse impact on the environment.

8.1 Government Policies and Regulations

The governments of various countries are gradually realizing that they have to control and encourage the industry and other sectors of the IT, including cloud computing, to become more environmentally friendly. Over the years, governments around the world have developed policies and regulations to advance environmental sustainability and decrease carbon footprint in data centers.

Climate Goals and Regulations: Governments across the European Union and the United States and other parts of the world have committed to climate goals such as achieving net zero emissions and cutting carbon. For instance, the EU has laid a goal of reaching zero net emissions by 2050, which is a direct concern to cloud computing suppliers. European initiatives such as the European Green Deal have the potential of promoting sustainability in various industries including the tech and cloud industries. Policies like the Energy

Efficiency Directive and Carbon Emission Standards provide that firms have to cut on energy usage and enhance their efficiency.

Environmental Reporting and Transparency: Governments are also compelling companies to report their environmental effects by using the GRI and the CDP. This makes the cloud providers responsible for the impact they have on the environment and the result is healthy competition in embracing sustainable practices. In the U.S., for example, the Clean Power Plan and other regional initiatives such as the EPA have given tax credit and other financial incentives aimed at encouraging the use of renewable energy in data centres hence promoting the green cloud practices.

Industry Collaborations and Initiatives: Collaborative efforts of cloud industry players have been critical in driving the adoption of green cloud computing practices. One among them is the Climate Neutral Data Centre Pact, a pledge signed by data center operators in Europe that promises to make its facilities carbon neutral by 2030.

The Climate Neutral Data Centre Pact: This pact is an effort to help the data center industry to reduce carbon emissions through the use of renewable energy and energy efficiency, and innovative cooling techniques. The members of the pact are required to substantiate environmental disclosures, increase energy usage efficiency, and utilize renewable energy to power data centers. Such concerted action not only contributes to sustainability but also strengthens the overall confidence about the sector's climate objectives.

9. CROSS-CUTTING CHALLENGES IN SUSTAINABLE CLOUD COMPUTING

As the cloud computing industry shifts toward sustainability, several challenges that cut across most domains of the cloud ecosystem become evident. These challenges include trade-off between using financial resources compared to sustainability, scale and dependability issues and privacy and security of data in green cloud systems. Despite the possibility of green cloud computing to decrease the carbon footprint, a number of hurdles have to be met so that sustainable solutions are feasible and meaningful.

9.1 Balancing Cost with Sustainability

Another important issue that might hinder the establishment of sustainable cloud computing is the cost implication. Green technologies and practices, including data center efficiency, renewable energy systems, and smart cooling methods, call for huge initial outlay. For instance, migrating the data centers to green energy, or moving from higher carbon input hardware to lower input hardware may require more capital investment than conventional technology environments. However, such high initial costs may be easily recovered through the subsequent savings. Energy efficient systems normally cut operating expenses through decreased power usage, which consequently minimizes the electricity expenses. Furthermore, increasing the use of renewable energy sources can also enable organisations mitigate the increasing cost of fossil fuel and hedging risks of fluctuating energy prices. However, it is found that the return on investment (ROI) may differ based on the level of investment, the type of technology implemented and the state of the local energy market. The problem here is that SMEs may have a harder time getting to the same level of financial sustainability as larger cloud providers due to their size. The use of green technologies also carries financial risk which include the potential cost of saving energy and the environmental benefits that does not meet the set goals. Therefore, sustainability investments have to be assessed in terms of their costs and returns while taking into consideration the positive impact on the environment. Cloud providers may also need to consider the available government policies and subsidies to finance investment in renewable energy or sustainable operations, which lowers costs.

9.2 Scalability and Reliability Concerns

Another problem is how to scale green cloud solutions without compromising quality and availability. Cloud computing is by design, for growth and as the need for services increases, so does the need for resources. To support the continuously growing number of users, cloud computing services need to be elastic and yet remain energy efficient and operationally reliable. One of these is the fact that improved efficiency can be accompanied by limitations that influence performance. For instance, some cooling techniques like the liquid cooling or air side economization that have been proved to be very efficient in terms of power usage may call for changes in structures that are hard to implement when scaling up. Likewise, increased use of renewable energy sources helps to decrease the negative impact on the environment but brings some variability in the power plant load since the generation of solar and wind power depends on the climatic conditions. Stabilizing power supply when operating in the areas with uncertain renewable resources entails backup such as energy storage or hybrid energy systems which are complicated and costly. Availability is also important in cloud environments because its disruptions can be costly to users of cloud services. To gain reliability in green cloud model, technologies and strategies that are used must be able to offer high performance reliability but with low energy consumption. For instance, renewable energy sources in the supply chain of the providers must be certain to produce power during increased demand, while energy-efficient equipment should not slow down cloud services. This entails the application of complex load balancing, fail over, and monitoring, not to allow sustainability objectives undermine service delivery.

9.3 Privacy and Data Security in Green Cloud Strategies

However, as cloud providers are shifting to green approaches, issues of privacy and data security add up. All of the green technologies used to make maximum utilization of the energy like virtualization, automation, and resource sharing are used in multiple customer environments. This multi-tenancy is beneficial in that many tenants are allowed to share the same system, however, it poses a security threat, especially when the resources are dynamically being provisioned in a manner that they are being accessed by other tenants. Further, some efficient energy usage strategies such as server consolidation and dynamic resource management may require real-time management of workloads and this may compromise the security policies. For example, reducing resources to improve energy efficiency could result in making a system security prone if security updates are slowed down or there are limited resources to tend to security solutions. Moreover, the use of third-party energy suppliers including those who offer renewable energy also poses new levels of trust. Most countries have policies on the protection of data and especially the European Union's General Data Protection Regulation (GDPR) still demands that personal data must be processed and stored in a secure manner. Cloud providers utilizing renewable energy or decentralized energy grids must guarantee that the external systems which are utilized do not affect the privacy or security of the users' data. In response to these issues, cloud providers have to incorporate secure security measures that guarantee that energy conservation does not compromise on security. This is because the strategies applied include achieving high levels of encryption, use of multiple tenancy and a very strict access control. Also, CSPs need to consider that their green efforts must meet local and international privacy laws, and therefore, CSPs need to integrate data sovereignty into their green strategy to avoid legal problems.

10. COMPARATIVE ANALYSIS OF SUSTAINABLE CLOUD COMPUTING TECHNIQUES

This is because cloud computing is now a growing technology that cannot afford to allow its practices to harm the environment. However, the best practices noted above can be effectively implemented differently depending on the cloud model type: IaaS, PaaS, and SaaS. This section examines how sustainable strategies work in these models, the costs of sustainability and performance, and implementation issues of sustainable strategies.

10.1 Effectiveness Across Cloud Models

The general concepts of sustainability can be applied with different levels of success depending on the type of the cloud service model – IaaS, PaaS, and SaaS. Self-generated challenges and opportunities to green cloud practices also vary with each of the models.

IaaS (Infrastructure as a Service): IaaS suppliers provide the physical and virtualization resources while clients obtain a range of computing resources including virtual servers, storage and network. Sustainability also works very well in IaaS since things like virtualization, resource pooling, and dynamic scaling are sustainable since they enable efficient resource management without expending more energy than necessary. Through workload consolidation, it is possible to effectively manage the use of resources, and this a result leads to energy efficiency. In addition, IaaS providers have a greater influence over the choice of hardware which makes it easier to deploy energy efficient technologies like low power processors and efficient storage. This scalability of IaaS also makes it possible to incorporate renewable energy sources since it can accommodate power availability especially in large scale data center that can harness onsite solar; or wind power.

PaaS (Platform as a Service): PaaS is a higher level of service where the provider gives the user tools and services to deploy, manage, and use applications without concerning the infrastructure. The effects of sustainable practices are more apparent in PaaS than in IaaS and SaaS. Energy efficient programming techniques, auto scaling, and green software engineering is relevant in this model but the extent to which these strategies can be applied depends on the level of flexibility given by the service provider to the user on the environment friendly features of the platform. For instance, a PaaS provider might use serverless architectures that self-provision based on the level of utilization, this may prove useful in reducing energy use during low utilization. However, the potential for optimization is higher limited than in IaaS where, for example, hardware and virtualization are more directly managed.

SaaS (Software as a Service): The third one is SaaS where application is hosted on cloud and users can access software through browser or client. There are two primary ways that sustainability operates in SaaS – the optimization of the application and the data centers that support it. The areas that concern energy wastage in SaaS include green software engineering, efficiency in the application code, and modularization. However, it should be noted that because of the fact that SaaS providers are usually significantly less involved in infrastructure management compared to IaaS or PaaS, their opportunities to carry out actualization of hardware-specific strategies are rather limited. At this level, sustainability initiatives may centre on concise coding, which decreases the resources needed to execute applications, and the amount of energy used by the consumer due to better performance of applications.

10.2 Sustainability vs. Performance Trade-offs

Another difficulty of constructing sustainable strategies for all those models of cloud computing is that the important factor of sustainability often has a negative impact on the performance of the system.

Energy-Efficient Techniques: Although methods like server consolidation, dynamic scaling and renewable energy integration can help to decrease the environmental impact of a cloud provider they usually come at a cost in terms of performance. For instance, achieving resource efficiency by virtualization could lead to undesirable throughput degradation when the demand for resources is high. Also, use of renewable energy such as solar and wind energy may bring variability in the supply of power hence affecting the reliability of the services and their availability. Cloud providers must therefore find the right trade-off in order not to compromise on sustainability while making sure that the users are not disgruntled.

11. FUTURE RESEARCH DIRECTIONS AND EMERGING TECHNOLOGIES

With the current development of cloud computing, the question of sustainability is becoming more and more relevant. Thus, future research and new technologies will be able to make a breakthrough in enhancing the environmental performance of cloud services. This section investigates opportunities in deploying AI/ML for energy management, the place of quantum computing, edge computing, and 5G in green cloud practices, and future research direction, such as carbon capture and sustainable IoT.

11.1 Prospects for AI/ML in Green Cloud Computing

Artificial Intelligence (AI) and Machine Learning (ML) present potential for the efficient energy control and resource utilization in cloud computing (Sreelakshmi et al 2024)(Lakumarapu et al 2024). The AI/ML algorithms can take real-time large data, and they can provide dynamic energy optimization in data centers and cloud networks. The use of AI/ML can be most valuable in the prediction of energy consumption, which is one of the most important areas. Given that historical data is fed into the AI models, energy demand can be predicted with a high level of precision, and cloud providers can optimise the use of resources. This implies that energy can be conserved during off peak hours, while satisfying the performance requirements of the users in the cloud. For instance, AI for load balancing can guarantee that data centers consume only the required amount of power for active workloads and power-off or redistribute the inactive servers automatically. Machine learning can also help in workload placement on physical hardware, therefore increasing efficiency. By understanding the energy utilization of a particular machine, the workload can be distributed to a machine that is energy-efficient hence reducing wastage.

11.2 Emerging Technologies for Sustainability

Based on the analysis of the emerging technologies, the following technologies stand to benefit cloud computing sustainability.

Quantum Computing: Quantum computing is still in its infancy, and it holds the key to changing the way cloud computing addresses most problems. A quantum computer runs using qubits, which are capable of being in more than one state at a time, which makes it possible for it to solve some problems in a much faster way than the normal computers. This capability could help to reduce the energy consumption by a large amount for activities such as data analysis, simulation, and cryptography. Also, the same could be possible in the field of material science where quantum computers could revolutionize how hardware required for cloud data centers could be made more energy efficient.

Edge Computing: Edge computing is a process of computing that takes data closer to the source of data – the devices, as opposed to centralized data centers. This can dramatically cut down the power required to transport data and perform complex computation. When these workloads are offloaded to edge devices, there is less likelihood of massive data transfer from one data center to another, an activity that consumes a lot of energy. Also, edge computing entails better resource control at the edge, thereby allowing the deployment of renewable energy solutions locally, thus improving sustainability (Anusha et al 2024).

5G Networks: The advancement in the speed of the 5G network is projected to bring changes to cloud computing since it is a faster and more efficient network. This can enhance the quality of cloud services as the service providers do not invest in extra or duplicate resources when the demand varies over time. The speed advantage that 5G brings to bear in terms of energy consumption, is potentially beneficial to green cloud computing as it minimizes the power requirement for the communication equipment that is needed in the more conventional data centers, the ability of 5G to support the connectivity of a large number of devices is the key driver in the development of smart cities and IoT, where green IT and energy efficient computing will be critical.

12. CONCLUSION

Green cloud computing is very important especially given the ever increasing environmental impacts brought about by the growth of the cloud services. In this paper, several strategies have been discussed to minimize the environmental effects of cloud infrastructures. They are as follows: improving energy efficiency by means of virtualization, dynamic voltage scaling, and resource management; utilizing renewable energy, including solar, wind, and geothermal power; and implementing green software engineering, which minimizes energy use through optimized code and algorithms. Furthermore, the implementation of waste management and the principles of circular economy in the form of hardware recycling and prolongation of equipment's useful life also support sustainable cloud computing. When cloud service providers decide on adopting green solutions, they are faced with the challenge of the trade-off between green solutions and those that offer high performance and those that are relatively cheaper. Although sustainable development projects entail capital investment in the initial stages, the returns in terms of working cost reduction, compliance to set rules and regulations besides the enhanced company image, are enormous. However, there are issues like scalability, reliability and privacy which have to be dealt with over and over. Technologies such as artificial intelligence and machine learning, quantum computing, edge computing, 5G, and many others are some of the emerging technologies that will help in the future development of cloud computing sustainability. These changes present possible strategies for increasing the efficiency of energy consumption, decreasing pollution, and improving utilization of resources. In conclusion, there exists considerable progress towards building fully sustainable cloud ecosystems although the process is still evolving. The key implication of green cloud computing is to continue research and innovate continuously to improve on the current practices, to discover new technologies that may address the problems faced in the implementation of green cloud computing. Industry-academia collaborations with the government can lead to a more effective and efficient, sustainable and environmentally friendly cloud computing environment.

REFERENCES

Anusha, S., Ezhilvandan, M., Gayathri, S., Sivaraman, V., & Anish, T. P. (2024). Emerging trends in edge AI for Industry 4.0 and 5.0: Technologies, applications, and challenges. *AI Innovations in Service and Tourism Marketing*, 211-228.

Das, A., Debnath, B., Modak, N., Das, A., & De, D. (2020, December). E-waste inventorisation for sustainable smart cities in India: A cloud-based framework. In *2020 IEEE International Women in Engineering (WIE)Conference on Electrical and Computer Engineering (WIECON-ECE)* (pp. 332-335). IEEE. DOI: 10.1109/WIECON-ECE52138.2020.9397960

Jeyaranjani, J., Rangaswamy, K., Ashwitha, A., Gandi, R., Roopa, R., & Anjaiah, P. (2024). Navigating Green Computing Challenges and Strategies for Sustainable Solutions. In *Computational Intelligence for Green Cloud Computing and Digital Waste Management* (pp. 42–59). IGI Global. DOI: 10.4018/979-8-3693-1552-1.ch003

Lakumarapu, S., Nithyanandhan, R., Bhargavi, V. S., Anish, T. P., & Nalini, M. (2024, August). Machine Learning Approaches for Liver Disease Prediction: A Comparative Analysis. *In 2024 5th International Conference on Electronics and Sustainable Communication Systems (ICESC)* (pp. 159-164). IEEE.

Maheshwaran, T., Muthumarilakshmi, S., Vinoth, N. A. S., Suganya, K., Maheswari, B., & Girija, P. (2024). Securing E-Commerce Strategies With Cloud, Blockchain, AI, and ML. In *Strategies for E-Commerce Data Security: Cloud, Blockchain, AI, and Machine Learning* (pp. 470–500). IGI Global. DOI: 10.4018/979-8-3693-6557-1.ch019

Manikandan, N., Vinod, D., Rosaline, R. A. A., Nancy, P., & Premalatha, G. (2024). Green Computing-Based Digital Waste Management and Resource Allocation for Distributed Fog Data Centers. In *Computational Intelligence for Green Cloud Computing and Digital Waste Management* (pp. 209–226). IGI Global. DOI: 10.4018/979-8-3693-1552-1.ch011

Matthew, U. O., Asuni, O., & Fatai, L. O. (2024). Green Software Engineering Development Paradigm: An Approach to a Sustainable Renewable Energy Future. In *Advancing Software Engineering Through AI, Federated Learning, and Large Language Models* (pp. 281-294). IGI Global.

Murthy, J. S. (2021). Edgecloud: A distributed management system for resource continuity in edge to cloud computing environment. In *Research Anthology on Architectures, Frameworks, and Integration Strategies for Distributed and Cloud Computing* (pp. 2684-2700). IGI Global. DOI: 10.4018/978-1-7998-5339-8.ch130

Pitchai, R., Tiwari, S., Viji, C., Kistan, A., Puviarasi, R., & Gokul, S. (2024). Green Technologies, Reducing Carbon Footprints, and Maximizing Energy Efficiency with Emerging Innovations: Green Computing. In *Convergence Strategies for Green Computing and Sustainable Development* (pp. 86-110). IGI Global.

Rani, S., Bhambri, P., Kataria, A., Khang, A., & Sivaraman, A. K. (Eds.). (2023). *Big Data, Cloud Computing and IoT: Tools and Applications*. CRC Press. DOI: 10.1201/9781003298335

Saxena, A., Gupta, K., & Pala, S. (2024). Convergence Strategies for Green Computing and Sustainable Development. In *Convergence Strategies for Green Computing and Sustainable Development* (pp. 62–85). IGI Global.

Sreelakshmi, S., Babu, A. A., Lakshmipriya, C., Gracious, L. A., Nalini, M., & Subramanian, R. S. (2024, October). Enhancing Intrusion Detection Systems with Machine Learning. *In 2024 2nd International Conference on Self Sustainable Artificial Intelligence Systems (ICSSAS)* (pp. 557-564). IEEE.

Sudha, K., Nithyanandhan, R., Anish, T. P., Girija, P., & Nalini, M. (2024, July). Enhancing Healthcare Data Security in the Cloud: Integrating ML-Based Intrusion Detection Systems. *In 2024 2nd World Conference on Communication & Computing (WCONF)* (pp. 1-7). IEEE.

Surya, P., Pachauri, P., Pachauri, A., Chaturvedi, P., Yadav, S. A., & Singh, D. (2021, November). Virtualization Risks and associated Issues in Cloud Environment. In *2021 International Conference on Technological Advancements and Innovations (ICTAI)* (pp. 521-525). IEEE. DOI: 10.1109/ICTAI53825.2021.9673424

Verma, J., & Sharma, Y. (2024). Achieving Sustainability Through Green Technology: The Need of the Nations. In *Convergence Strategies for Green Computing and Sustainable Development* (pp. 52-61). IGI Global.

Vinoth, S., Vemula, H. L., Haralayya, B., Mamgain, P., Hasan, M. F., & Naved, M. (2022). Application of cloud computing in banking and e-commerce and related security threats. *Materials Today: Proceedings*, *51*, 2172–2175. DOI: 10.1016/j.matpr.2021.11.121

Chapter 3
Energy-Efficient Algorithms in High Performance Computing: Approaches, Applications, and Innovations

J. Rajeshkumar
REVA University, India

K. Aravindaraj
SRM Institute of Science and Technology, India

T. Uma Mageswari
Sri Sai Ram Institute of Technology, India

S. Kerthy
Jeppiaar Institute of Technology, India

R. Premkumar
R.M.K. College of Engineering and Technology, India

S. Gayathri
S.A. Engineering College, India

R. Siva Subramanian
https://orcid.org/0000-0002-7509-9223
R.M.K. College of Engineering and Technology, India

ABSTRACT

HPC systems are crucial to scientific computation and industry processes however, their power consumption is a major economic and environmental concern. Efficient algorithms are important to decrease the power consumption of HPC systems, and make such systems more efficient and feasible. To that end, this survey focuses on the main algorithmic techniques aimed at enhancing energy consumption throughout HPC components, such as processors, memory, and networks. We classify these approaches into classes depending on the dynamic and static power management,

DOI: 10.4018/979-8-3373-0766-4.ch003

Copyright © 2025, IGI Global Scientific Publishing. Copying or distributing in print or electronic forms without written permission of IGI Global Scientific Publishing is prohibited.

workload based techniques, and domains specific optimizations. In this paper, we compare energy efficient algorithms and their trade off with the performance and the issues related to integration and scalability of the algorithms are also presented. Last, we present the directions for future work, including the development of enhanced programming models, standardized policies, and quantum computing. This survey gives a clear picture and presents the future direction of the energy-aware solutions in HPC.

1. INTRODUCTION

1.1 Background on HPC and Energy Efficiency

Supercomputers are crucial to progress in science and engineering, resolution of large scale industrial issues, and discovery of novel solutions. These systems drive climate modeling, genomics, artificial intelligence, and financial simulations, and any line of work that requires vast computational horsepower to deliver accurate and timely results. HPC systems are made of thousands of interconnected processors that work simultaneously and at a very high rate, performance of HPC systems is measured in FLOPs(Inacio, E. C., & Dantas, M. A. (2014)). However, this unparalleled computational power comes at a significant cost: energy consumption. Large scale HPC systems for the present day such as supercomputers are known to consume copious amounts of power for their operation hence they are costly to operate and have a negative environmental footprint(Saravanan et al 2014). The annual energy consumption of a modern HPC center of the highest class can be compared to the energy consumption of an average small town. However, with the increasing demand for increased computational throughput, such systems also consume more energy(-Tiwari et al 2014). This challenge is further compounded by the fact that there are fundamental issues with scaling the underlying hardware. Classical enhancement techniques such as transistor density integration as postulated by Moore's Law and frequency boosting are becoming constrained on the physical plane and pragmatic level, hence, the reduced energy density enhancement per hardware iteration. Consequently, there is a pressing need to consider other measures which can help to maintain HPC sustainability, including the software and algorithmic levels.

1.2 Importance of Energy Efficiency in HPC

Energy efficiency has become a critical consideration in the design and operation of HPC systems for several reasons:

1.Environmental Impact: The energy HPC consumes in their operations is significant, and the energy used may come from carbon emitting sources. Energy conservation has benefits to the society as it supports measures that are taken internationally to reduce impacts of climate change.
2.Economic Implications: This makes energy costs one of the largest line items in an HPC facility's operating expenses. These costs may be minimized through energy-efficient algorithms in HPC to increase its affordability and enable its sustainable economic application(Varrette et al 2014).
3.Technological Constraints: As hardware improvements have brought diminishing returns in energy efficiency, the concern has moved to software level. Energy-efficient algorithms provide a way to get more mileage out of existing hardware, to keep it relevant for longer.
4.Sustainable Growth: As the amount and density of the computations to be performed continue to grow, it is critical to enhance energy efficiency to achieve constant growth rates of computing capacity without a corresponding growth in energy consumption(Subramaniam, B., & Feng, W. C. (2012)).

All these factors make energy efficiency not just as a feature that would be nice to have, but as an imperative for the future growth and sustainability of HPC systems.

1.3 Survey Scope and Objectives

As part of sustainable High Performance Computing, this paper concentrates on energy efficient algorithms. In performing computation, algorithms hold the key to managing energy consumption and can directly impact the use of energy in computing tasks, resource utilization and workload scheduling. The primary objectives of this survey are:

1.Analysis: To review the current literatures on energy efficient algorithms so as to get a clear understanding of methods and principles applied in their development.
2.Categorization: To categorize these algorithms as fixed and variable power control, according to the type of loads they support, and by how flexible they are.
3.Comparison: Thus, the purpose of this paper is to provide a comparative analysis of the discussed techniques, in terms of their benefits and drawbacks, as well as the contexts in which they can be utilized on various HPC platforms.

This survey is an attempt to combine current research in order to help improve the creation of better energy-efficient algorithms and to indicate what further research is needed. Finally, it aims at advancing the overall goal of achieving sustainable High-Performance Computing.

2. METRICS AND BENCHMARKS FOR ENERGY EFFICIENCY IN HPC

The ongoing attempts to enhance energy efficiency in high-performance computing (HPC) are based on the accurate assessment of energy use and performance. They are very useful in finding out areas that need improvement and in determining the strategies to be used when improving energy efficiency as well as in the general setting of standards of energy efficiency(Cocaña et al 2015). This section looks at the various measures of performance, the common tools for benchmarking and the drawbacks that are associated with the current approaches.

2.1 Performance Metrics

Energy metrics for HPC offer statements of quantified measures of the utilization of computing assets in terms of energy consumption. Key metrics include:

1.Power Usage Effectiveness (PUE): PUE is one of the most popular measures to assess the energy efficiency of data centers, including HPC centers. It is expressed as the total facility energy divided by the energy consumed by the computing equipment. PUE should ideally be closer to 1 which means that nearly 100% of the energy is used in computing as opposed to other systems like cooling.
2.Energy per Operation: This one measures the amount of energy required per computation operation that a computer is capable of performing. It has an application in the fine-grained analysis of energy efficiency at the algorithmic or task level, which may be of value in fine-tuning particular applications.
3.FLOPs/Watt: FLOPs per watt refers to the capacity of computing the number of floating-point operations per watt of energy consumed. It is especially useful for comparing the energy consumption of one type of hardware against another, say CPU to GPU and even accelerators(Jalasri et al 2025).

2.2 Benchmarking Tools

Benchmarking tools are essentially metrics used to compare the efficiency of HPC systems across the board. Some prominent tools include:

1.SPECpower: This benchmark is developed by Standard Performance Evaluation Corporation (SPEC) and it measures power and performance behavior of server class systems under different workloads. It is most effective in evaluating energy consumption in typical office and workplace computing settings.
2.LINPACK: LINPACK is used extensively to benchmark super computers with special emphasis on solving dense linear equations. Energy-optimized versions of LINPACK measure both the performance and power consumption in order to arrive at a figure of merit of FLOPs/Watt.
3.Energy Star Benchmarks: Energy Star certification includes standards intended to measure the energy efficiency in computing equipment parts, including HPC. This certification serves to inform procurement of energy efficient hardware. These tools are essential to evaluating the effectiveness of the energy efficiency techniques and to encourage the energy consciousness among the HPC fraternity.

2.3 Limitations of Current Metrics:

Despite their utility, current metrics and benchmarking tools face significant challenges:

1.Heterogeneous Architectures: Contemporary HPC systems include various components like processing units, graphics processing units and other accelerators that have different energy characteristics. Measuring the degree of efficiency in such systems entails parameters and instruments that can isolate the energy consumption of each part.
2.Dynamic Workloads: In HPC environments, the workloads are rather variable; the consumption of resources changes with time. Static measures may not capture such variations hence providing wrong results in determination of energy efficiency.
3.Lack of Standardization: As there are many metrics and tools, the absence of standardized methods makes it difficult to compare one system or algorithm with another. The benchmark of energy efficiency till date does not have a universally acceptable format.

4.Overhead of Measurement Tools: Some benchmarking tools add other computational or energy cost increases that may affect the results. This implies that impacts of such factors are unavoidable hence requiring proper calibration and validation in order to reduce their effects.

Based on the current study, it is evident that, strategies geared towards improving EE in HPC systems require accurate metrics and benchmarking tools. Though PUE, energy per operation, FLOPs/Watt are already in use, issues in handling heterogeneity, dynamic workloads and standardization indicate that more research is needed. The resolution of these problems will lead to better assessment and the improvement of power-saving HPC procedures.

3. TAXONOMY OF ENERGY-EFFICIENT ALGORITHMS IN HPC

Energy efficient algorithms are essential for reduction of power consumption of high end computing systems. These algorithms are essentially designed to intelligently distribute the computational load, resources, and processing operations, maintaining a balance between the effectiveness and efficiency of the system's performance and energy consumption. For such algorithms, this section offers a classification of such algorithms, major approaches, and a summary of the main categories.

3.1 Algorithmic Approaches

Energy conscious algorithms are characterized by optimization of power consumption while incurring only slight degradation in the performance of computations. Common approaches include:

1.Reducing Redundant Computations: Computations are made efficiently in a way that they do not have to be repeated in order to save energy.
2.Task Scheduling: Variety of scheduling algorithms schedules the tasks to the processors so as to avoid as much idle time and hence power consumption. It may emphasize on low power consumption cores or even employ specific functional units known as accelerators.

Figure 1. Algorithmic Approaches

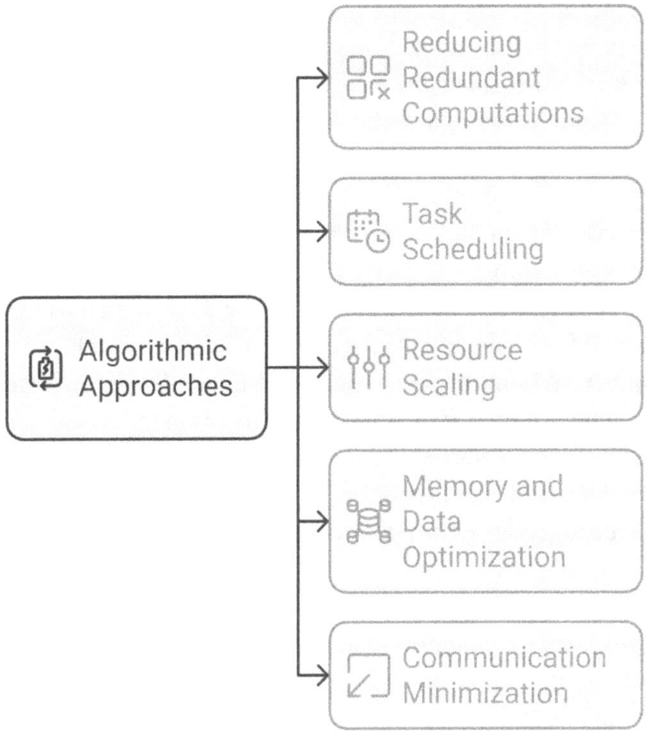

3.Resource Scaling: Other methods like Dynamic Voltage and Frequency Scaling (DVFS) control power of processors according to the load demand. It is also algorithms that define when and where such scaling is possible and feasible.

4.Memory and Data Optimization: Memory management is made more efficient since algorithms enhance data locality, compression and access. This minimizes energy used on data transport and storage activities.

5.Communication Minimization: There is substantial I/O operations in HPC applications involving massive computations, especially in distributed environments. In this way, algorithms can lower energy consumption because they limit the number of data transfers and optimize the communication processes.

3.2 Classification of Algorithms

Energy-efficient algorithms can be broadly classified based on their design principles and application scenarios:

1.Static vs. Dynamic Power Management Algorithms:
Static Algorithms: These depend on certain settings and arrangements and hence are more straightforward but can hardly accommodate changes in workloads. Examples are; fixed task allocation schemes or preset clock frequencies.
Dynamic Algorithms: These enable a change of resource utilization with regard to fluctuations in workload. They usually employ feedback structures, including system performance and energy data, to make their choices.
2.Adaptive vs. Non-Adaptive Algorithms:
Adaptive Algorithms: Adaptive meaning that they can learn from previous patterns of workload and change their behavior. Such often use machine learning algorithms to forecast and balance energy efficiency levels.
Non-Adaptive Algorithms: Do not adapt to conditions and run on fixed set of rules. Although they are easier to implement in an organization, they lack efficiency in heterogeneous or dynamic environment.
3.Workload-Based Categorization:
Task Scheduling Algorithms: Emphasize the allocation of tasks to processors in order to save energy.
Memory Optimization Algorithms: Focus on the optimization of data accessing and storing to minimize energy consumption on the memory systems.
Load Balancing Algorithms: Ensure that workload is evenly spread across processors or nodes so that some do not become overloaded, thus wasting energy.
Hybrid Algorithms: The optimization was done comprehensively by linking several strategies including, linking the task scheduling with the resource scaling.

The taxonomy of energy-efficient algorithms presents a categorized approach to plans that seek to reduce energy usage in HPC. This framework provides information on their use and usefulness by categorizing them into static and dynamic, adaptive and non-adaptive, and workload classes. There is also the tabular summary that helps in comprehending their usefulness, areas of use, and difficulties of implementation. With development of the field, more and more integrated and dynamic methods will be used to meet the various power requirements of contemporary HPC platforms.

4. ENERGY EFFICIENT APPROACHES FOR KEY HPC SUBSYSTEM

Efficiency of energy in high performance computing can be improved by targeting energy wastage at different levels of hierarchy. This section provides an overview of techniques to manage energy consumption for important HPC components such as, processors, memory, I/O, scheduling and communication.

4.1 Processor-Level Techniques

Processors are themselves one of the largest consumers of energy in HPC systems. Several techniques are employed to manage their power usage effectively:

1.Dynamic Voltage and Frequency Scaling (DVFS): DVFS is a technique which involves adjusting the voltage and or frequency of a processor depending on the load that is being handled. Reducing the frequency during less intensive operations is effective because energy consumption is proportional to the square of the voltage and directly to the frequency. It is commonly seen in today's processors to reduce power consumption without trading it off with performance.
2.Power Gating: Power gating switches off sections of a processor that are not active, such as cores or functional units, which are not actively required. The technique of power gating actually switches off power supply completely and thus eliminates leakage currents during idle time hence conserving energy.
3.Clock Gating: Like power gating, clock gating stops the clock signal to the unused portion of the processor to eliminate switching activity and hence minimize dynamic power consumption.
4.Low-Power States: Most of today's processors come with low power states (such as sleep or idle) that enable the power reduction when the processor's computing capabilities are not required. These states are mostly controlled by energy conscious scheduling algorithms.

4.2 Memory and I/O Management

Memory and I/O are or can be one of the largest consumers of energy in cases of data-centered workloads. Key techniques to enhance energy efficiency include:

1.Data Locality Optimization: Architectures that reduce the energy consumed by the processor in accessing memory and moving data around also reduce the energy consumption of an algorithm or system design.
2.Memory Compression: Reducing data size in memory results in decreased amount of data that must be stored or transmitted, cutting energy consumption related to memory.
3.Caching Strategies: Effective caching techniques organize frequently accessed information closer to the processor to conserve energy in the reduced usage of slow and power hungry memory structures.

4.3 Parallelization and Scheduling

Efficient parallelization and scheduling techniques are essential for balancing energy efficiency and performance:

1.Task Scheduling and Workload Distribution Algorithms:

These algorithms therefore assign tasks to processors in a manner that would reduce resource wastage and time delays. Some of the approaches such as energy-aware task allocation ensure that power-efficient processors or cores are assigned specific loads.

2.Energy-Aware Load Balancing:

In order to avoid overloading some of these parts and therefore create inefficiencies and waste energy, the loads are divided among the processors. Balancing algorithms which are energy aware take into consideration both energy consumption and performance.

3.Parallelization Techniques:

Proper utilization of parallel processing minimizes time and power utilization by invoking the several processing units proficiently. Optimal parallelism guarantees that the energy to be saved is not used by other processes, for instance, by spending many resources on communication or coordination.

4.4 Network and Communication Efficiency

Interprocess communication in distributed HPC systems is a large power consumer in terms of energy especially in large scale systems. Key strategies to enhance network and communication efficiency include:

1.Reducing Interprocess Communication: The processes are implemented to reduce the amount of data transferred between the processes with an aim of conserving energy in the network components. Achieving this goal is made possible by such strategies as communication aggregation and data compression.

Figure 2. Network and Communication Efficiency

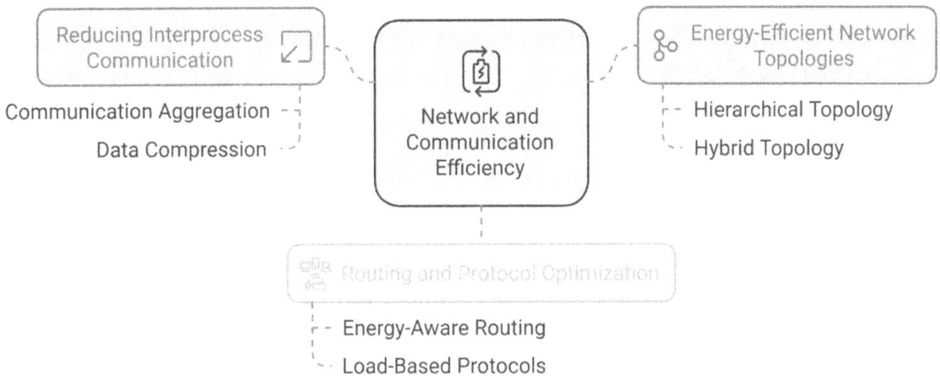

2.Energy-Efficient Network Topologies: Therefore, efficient network architectures minimize energy consumed by switches and links. Some of them are the hierarchical or hybrid topology that combine the performance and the power consumption.
3.Routing and Protocol Optimization: Energy aware routing protocols reduce energy consumption through choosing a low power path for data transmission. Systematic working protocols modify the communication behavior according to the load conditions.

Different measures at the processor, memory, scheduling, and network level are required for minimizing energy consumption in HPC systems. Direct power reduction techniques include the processor-level methods such as DVFS and power gating, while data movement and storage techniques address memory and I/O methods. Parallelization and scheduling improve the load and scheduling of workloads, and the network optimizations minimize the communication cost. As a whole, these concepts constitute integrated strategy of sustainable HPC design.

5. DOMAIN-SPECIFIC ALGORITHMS FOR ENERGY EFFICIENCY

The climatic optimization of HPC is usually achieved by means of application-oriented algorithms that correspond to the specific requirements of the computational task and the properties of the processed data. These algorithms are designed to solve certain issues in scientific, machine learning, big data, and cloud computing environments where certain suboptimal uses of energy are evident but overall performance must at least be sustained, if not improved(Sudha et al 2024)(Maithili et al 2024).

5.1 Scientific Computing

Scientific applications such as physics simulations, climate modeling, and computational chemistry are computationally intensive and involve iterative numerical methods:

1.Physics Simulations: In physics simulations, often there are algorithms which utilize less energy and for doing so, they use techniques such as sparse matrix operation. For instance, while the finite element and finite difference methods within HPC require data partitioning and load-balancing amongst processors, the domain decomposition technique helps to ensure that energy-consuming message passing is minimized.
2.Climate Modeling: Energy conscious climate models concern themselves with data transfer and parallelism. The step size and time step are adjusted to maximize prediction accuracy while minimizing energy consumption due to computational complexity, using algorithms.
3.Computational Chemistry: In order to avoid unnecessary computations, efficient methods like adaptive basis set optimization and energy-sensitive molecular dynamics calculations are used. These methods also use load balancing to improve the energy consumption in distributed HPC systems.

5.3 Machine Learning and AI Workloads

Machine learning (ML) and AI workloads, particularly model training and inference, are energy-intensive due to their reliance on large datasets and deep neural networks(Mahesh, B. 2020)(Sreelakshmi et al 2024):

1.Pruning: Neural network pruning is a technique that eliminates unnecessary connections or neurons in a neural network, thus shrinking the size of models without compromising on their performance. This greatly reduces the energy needed for both training and actual prediction of the outcomes(Wang et al 2021).
2.Quantization: Quantization is the process of decreasing the bits of weights and activations in a neural network from 32 bits to fewer numbers of bits, including 8 bits. As mentioned, lower precision decreases computational load and energy usage while providing acceptable performance losses.

3.Model Compression: Practices such as knowledge distillation and weight sharing help in reducing the size of the models making computations faster and less power consuming. For example, the smaller models take up lesser memory and FLOPs, which is suitable for power-conscious applications such as edge AI.

5.3 Big Data Analytics

Energy-efficient algorithms in big data analytics focus on processing large datasets with minimal resource consumption (Batko, K., & Ślęzak, A. 2022):

1.MapReduce Optimization: To reduce the amount of data shipping, energy-aware versions of MapReduce also aim at the placement of tasks. Moreover, task co-location and data partitioning enhance locality and thus minimize energy consumption.
2.Spark Workloads: Big data framework Apache Spark uses algorithms that improve in-memory computation performance. For instance, adaptive scheduling of tasks and memory caching that helps reduce energy consumption to a minimum by directing more tasks to the resources that yield the most productivity.
3.Streaming Analytics: Real-time data processing algorithms are enhanced through energy-efficient streaming to improve data throughput by adapting to resource requirements during inactive periods.

5.4 Cloud Computing and Data Centers

Cloud computing environments and data centers, which power much of today's HPC workloads, present unique opportunities for energy optimization:

Figure 3. Optimizing Energy in Cloud Computing

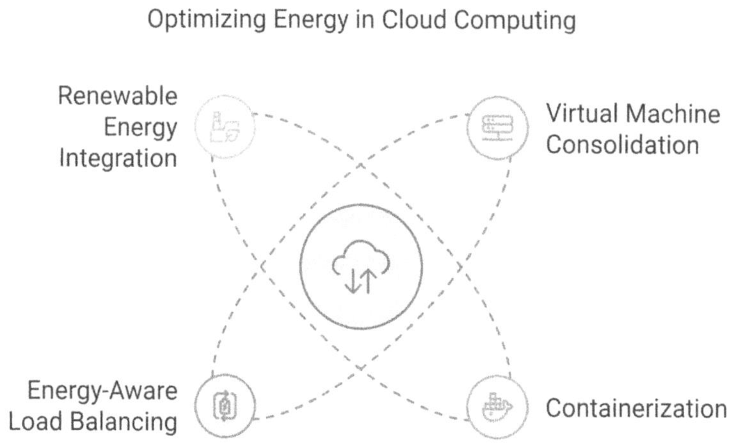

1.Virtual Machine (VM) Consolidation: This puts the working loads together and places them on fewer actual machines with servers being shut down when not in use to conserve power. The live migration techniques also help in dynamic consolidation without attracting a lot of overhead cost in terms of performance.
2.Containerization: Containers, as compared to VMs, are lighter weight and use less overhead and power. Container management is improved by algorithms that enhance efficiency in assigning resources across cloud instances.
3.Energy-Aware Load Balancing: Load balancing algorithms are used to fairly distribute the work loads avoiding areas that get very hot. Energy-aware scheduling means that in addition to other parameters such as the value of CPU, server power consumption, and energy requirements of workloads are also considered.
4.Renewable Energy Integration: Scheduling algorithms that allow the workloads to be scheduled according to the available renewable energy like solar or wind energy make sustainability as the workload is run during the times when the renewable energy is cheap.

Customized algorithms for energy optimization at the domain level are critical for capturing the specifics of scientific, machine learning, big data and cloud application(Lakumarapu et al 2024)(Ponmalar et al 2024). These algorithms use techniques like, pruning and quantization in AI, task co-location in Big Data and VM consolidation in CLOUD computing environments. Because they address particular sources of inefficiency, they allow for very substantial energy reductions while preserving or enhancing performance, and are thus critical components of sustainable HPC practice.

6. CROSS-CUTTING CHALLENGES IN ENERGY-EFFICIENT HPC ALGORITHMS

Energy-aware algorithm design for HPC systems is a challenging problem that can be characterized along several dimensions, such as performance vs. energy consumption, scalability, heterogeneity of the target platform, and the need to fit into an application's workflow. Mitigating these issues is important for the further uptake and efficiency of such algorithms in various HPC uses.

6.1 Trade-Offs Between Energy Efficiency and Performance

One of the greatest problems is energy and performance trade-off. Most energy saving methods like DVFS or offloading will result in reduced performance of the system. For instance, reducing processor frequency decreases energy consumption but raises execution time and may influence the application due date. Likely the same, the techniques such as pruning or quantizing in the machine learning's workloads decrease computational loads, yet, they result in accuracy degradation. The trade-off is highly application dependent for certain domains, where energy efficiency is critical, such as climate modeling, while in others, such as real-time simulations, performance is paramount. Achieving this balance requires self-tuning algorithms that control the parameters of workload and certain performance targets.

6.2 Scalability of Energy-Efficient Techniques

The main challenges arise from scaling of energy efficient algorithms in distributed and parallel high-performance computing systems. Modern HPC systems are composed of thousands of nodes and core, thus the brought-in algorithms should scale well when implemented at large scales. In the small system environments, the algorithms used for the task scheduling do not efficiently distribute the workload in the massively parallel environments as this leads to energy wastage due to idle resources as well as congestion in inter-node communication(Bharany et al 2022).

Moreover, since memory and I/O optimization techniques face issues in scaling up with a growing data size, they lead to scalability issues.

This is because energy overheads resulting from synchronization and communication in large scale systems have to be considered. The latter approaches such as hierarchical scheduling and distributed energy-aware resource management are still promising, however, more work is needed in order to make them more scalable.

6.3 Heterogeneous Architectures

The current HPC systems are more inclined towards a hybrid system that includes CPU, GPU, FPGA and other accelerators. All these architectures pose the benefits of improved performance and energy efficiency, but they raise problems for algorithms.

1.Diverse Power Profiles: Individual components dissipate power in differing amounts and possess different energy-saving characteristics. These components have to be managed to fairly distribute the resources required for both efficient energy use and performance.
2.Programming Complexity: To learn how to implement energy-efficient algorithms for the current heterogeneous platforms, it is necessary to learn several programming models: CUDA for Graphics Processors, OpenCL for FPGAs. This complexity hampers the use of such algorithms quite often.
3.Load Balancing: Load balancing is challenging in loosely coupled heterogeneous components because the tasks have to be partitioned based on both computational loads and energy consumption patterns. It results to resource constraint and energy wastage.

6.4 Integration with Existing HPC Workflows

Another challenge is incorporating energy-efficient algorithms to the existing HPC workflows. HPC systems are often optimized for performance, and retrofitting them with energy-saving techniques can be disruptive:

1.Software Compatibility: Most of the high-performance computing applications are built upon older codes that have not been optimized to save energy. While these applications can be adapted to take advantage of energy efficient algorithms, doing so may often mean significant changes to the existing code base, which will cause development and maintenance costs to rise.
2.User Resistance: End-users and system administrators may be opposed to change that disrupts their existing patterns of working or which demands extra time to learn a new way of working. It is important to prove that energy-

efficient algorithms are useful and make a positive impact as a way of getting acceptance.

3.Interoperability: It is a technical task to make sure that energy-efficient algorithms are compatible with already existing hardware and software layers. This includes support of the schedulers, resource managers and monitoring tools.

Fundamental issues in energy-proportional HPC algorithms involve power/performance trade off, scalability, heterogeneity of the target architecture, and integration with existing system paradigms. Solving these issues calls for novel algorithmic approaches, flexibility and the use of synergy between hardware, software and applications. These barriers can be overcome to allow sustainable energy efficiency in HPC systems without necessarily reducing their computational capabilities.

7. COMPARATIVE ANALYSIS OF EXISTING TECHNIQUES

Energy optimal algorithms for HPC are many as they can be designed with a focus on both performance and energy consumption. This section gives a comparison of these techniques using the following criteria: performance-energy efficiency, applicability to various HPC system structures, and real-world considerations.

7.1 Performance vs. Energy Savings

The efficiency of the energy-efficient algorithms mostly depends on the interconnection of the performance and the power consumption.

1.Dynamic Voltage and Frequency Scaling (DVFS): Dynamic Voltage and Frequency Scaling reduces processor speed and voltage, which offers large energy conservation when there is low computational need. Yet, it has uneven effects on performance. For example, in latency-sensitive applications, less frequency can cause undesirable delay which is not the case in batch processing applications.

2.Task Scheduling Algorithms: Energy-aware scheduling reduces the power consumed by the system during idle time by directing the workload to efficient energy resources. These methods, although result in significant savings, can come with an overhead of scheduling computations or become inefficient when under heavy load.

3.Load Balancing and Parallelization: For instance, energy-aware load balancing enhances energy efficiency since the available resources are well distributed. However, getting energy efficiency without overloading the nodes has often led to high communication overhead in distributed systems to degrade performance.

4.Domain-Specific Algorithms: Advanced techniques like pruning in machine learning or data locality optimization in big data are generally able to gain much energy efficiency with little performance reduction. However, these advantages are application specific and hence are not portable to other areas of use or other applications.

7.2 Suitability for Different HPC Architectures

Energy-efficient techniques vary in their applicability across multicore, distributed, and GPU-accelerated architectures:

1.Multicore Systems: Clock gating and DVFS are favourable for multicore systems because they provide a detailed control over the particular cores. Thread pinning combined with task scheduling algorithms, take it to the next level by matching the tasks to the core characteristics.

2.Distributed Architectures: Energy efficiency in distributed systems is mainly achieved by reduction of inter node communication. Here workload co-location and hierarchical scheduling are excellent but, they have to be fine-tuned to prevent the formation of bottlenecks in large scale systems. In addition, energy efficient routing also has a significant impact on the amount of energy expended in the network.

3.GPU-Accelerated Systems: Additional algorithms such as adaptive kernel tuning, and partitioning the task in a manner that can fully benefit from GPU high performance capabilities enhance the usage of GPU. Nonetheless, the energy efficiency in heterogeneous systems with GPUs is a challenging task due to the synchronization of the interplay between CPUs and accelerators and avoiding their idle time or competition for resources.

7.3 Practical Implementation Considerations

The practical adoption of energy-efficient algorithms depends on ease of implementation, maintainability, and compatibility with existing HPC workflows:

1.Ease of Implementation: Most techniques like DVFS do not need much changes to be integrated into the existing systems, which makes them very popular. Domain-specific optimizations or some heterogenous scheduling algorithms on the other hand require more effort on their development, such as knowledge on application characteristics and system architecture.

2.Maintenance and Adaptability: Some of the algorithms that are based on dynamic or adaptive changes may be prone to frequent changes if the workloads are ever changing. For example, new workloads require retraining of machine learning-based energy optimization techniques, thus enhancing maintenance difficulty.

3.Interoperability with Software Stacks: Compatibility with the HPC tools and frameworks like job scheduler and monitor tools is important. If a specific algorithm requires a lot of fine tuning of these tools, the user and administrator may not be receptive to it. These challenges can be addressed by Open standards and APIs that offer a standard way of integrating energy-saving techniques.

There are many existing algorithms in HPC, which are energy-efficient to various degrees, but they still have variations in terms of their efficiency-energy ratio, compatibility, and usability. The methods like DVFS and load balancing are quite universal for different systems, but they are sensitive to the tuning to reduce the effects of performance drops. Domain-specific approaches yield significant energy reductions in specific applications, whereas general methods tackle the issues of distributed and GPU-based systems. The main points of importance for practical adoption, therefore, include the trade-off between the level of implementation complexity and energy and or performance gains and the call for close cooperation between algorithm developers, hardware providers, and HPC users.

8. FUTURE DIRECTIONS

The HPC systems are continually evolving, and therefore what is required today is new approaches to enhance efficiency with energy and at the same time tackle other issues. This section presents directions for the future studies and discusses the most significant open issues and directions in the field of the advanced algorithmic design, programming paradigms, new technologies, and policy standardization.

8.1 Opportunities in Algorithmic Design

Adaptive Algorithms: Sophisticated adaptive control algorithms are seen to have potential for providing optimal and dynamic control of energy consumption for different system conditions. These techniques could utilize workload profiling to manipulate other parameters like; processor frequency, memory, and task scheduling for the best energy efficiency without human interference.

Machine Learning-Based Energy Optimization: Machine learning provides great opportunity for enhancing energy efficiency in HPC. Reinforcement learning could be applied to dynamic resource allocation while other models can forecast the load to reduce unnecessary power. However, issues constituting challenges are the computational complexity of ML techniques and the incorporation of these techniques into a given system.

Hybrid Approaches: Using a number of energy-saving approaches, including DVFS, load balancing, and caching, as integrated frameworks is seen as a future research direction. These hybrid methods could choose the right techniques based on the workload and the configuration of the hardware at runtime.

8.2 Energy-Aware HPC Programming Models

Previous HPC models of programming have not been keen on energy, and their main focus has been on performance. Developing energy-aware programming paradigms can empower developers to write energy-efficient code with minimal effort:

1.**Domain-Specific Languages (DSLs):** The hardware specific details could be hidden in DSLs related to energy and the constructs to manage the energy could also be provided. For example, DSLs might include annotations for energy-efficient task scheduling or data movement.

2.**Enhanced Compiler Techniques:** Compilers with energy-aware optimizations – loop tiling for cache optimization or automatic migration of select computations to low-power co-processors – could easily halve power consumption.

3.**Parallel Framework Extensions:** For instance, new extensions to the existing parallel programming models such as MPI and OpenMP could include means for the developer to specify about energy-performance trade-offs during runtime.

8.3 Emerging Technologies

Emerging technologies offer groundbreaking opportunities for energy-efficient computing but also present unique challenges:

1.**Quantum Computing:** Quantum computing with its capability to solve a few problems exponentially faster than classical systems could significantly bring down energy consumption for certain tasks. To achieve both efficiency in computation and energy, more studies will be required in the development of quantum algorithms.

2.Neuromorphic Computing: Neuromorphic processors that are designed based on the structure of the human brain are expected to greatly reduce the energy consumption of AI and pattern recognition applications. Nevertheless, the incorporation of these systems into the conventional HPC contexts will need new algorithm and programming model.
3.Photonic Processors: High speed low power circuits are available in the use of photonic computers which utilizes light instead of electricity. It is imperative that research work aimed at optimizing these algorithms is directed towards the use of photonic architectures.

8.4 Policy and Standardization

To achieve widespread adoption of energy-efficient practices, standardization and policy development are critical:

1.Energy Efficiency Benchmarks: The creation of reference points for energy-efficient algorithms will help make comparisons accurate and foster the development of new solutions.
2.Regulatory Policies: Governments and organizations could require power requirements for HPC systems for encouraging their sustainable research and usage.
3.Open Standards for Integration: There is a need to create standard for open API layer and framework for energy awareness across different systems.
4.Sustainability Certification: The use of certifications for energy efficient HPC systems and algorithms can promote their adoption and stimulate further innovation.

The future of efficient HPC solutions is in refining the algorithms that adapt to the computing problems, using machine learning, and in adopting quantum and photonic computer technologies. At the same time, energy-aware programming models and standardized benchmarking will be crucial enablers of innovation and, therefore, deployment. Overcoming these challenges and utilizing these opportunities will require an ongoing research and development cooperation between the academic sector, industry and policy-making in order to achieve the sustainable use of HPC in a resource-scarce environment.

9. CONCLUSION

Power consumption in HPC systems has now become the subject of research owing to the rising energy requirements of the modern systems and the consequences of high energy utilization touching the environment and the pocket. This paper has made an attempt to discuss and elaborate the problems, approaches, and trends of energy-efficient algorithms in HPC to create a clear and comprehensive perspective of the current situation and future development. Main outcomes are aimed at presenting the variety of potential ways of increasing efficiency, based on changing coefficients, scheduling, memory management, and distribution of workloads. Tied to that, measures like FLOPs/Watt, or tools like SPECpower, have been used to measure progress in benchmarking; however, issues with standardization and flexibility have also been present. The taxonomy of algorithms reveals that there is need to develop adaptive and workload-sensitive approaches to manage energy in diverse and distributed systems. Forcing the concepts of energy efficiency into some of the most sensitive areas of the HPC architecture, such as processors, memory systems, and networks, shows that there is a lot of potential for energy efficiency improvements while preserving performance. In scientific simulations, machine learning and cloud computing further examples have been demonstrated, how application-specific measures are necessary to achieve the desired energy savings. Future work includes the use of more sophisticated machine learning-based algorithms, energy-conscious programming paradigms and research on the green HPC through novel paradigms like quantum and photonics. Nevertheless, to achieve these goals several issues associated with scalability, heterogeneity, and integration into existing work processes have to be addressed. Therefore, efficient algorithms are critical to the future growth of HPC systems in a sustainable manner. They facilitate scientific research and industrial advancement while reflecting real-life issues such as energy utilization and climate alteration. The active work in this area indicates a potential for the creation of high-performance computing systems that are energy efficient and optimized for performance, sustainability and future adaptability to the constantly evolving technology environment.

REFERENCES

Batko, K., & Ślęzak, A. (2022). The use of Big Data Analytics in healthcare. *Journal of Big Data*, *9*(1), 3. DOI: 10.1186/s40537-021-00553-4 PMID: 35013701

Bharany, S., Sharma, S., Khalaf, O. I., Abdulsahib, G. M., Al Humaimeedy, A. S., Aldhyani, T. H., Maashi, M., & Alkahtani, H. (2022). A systematic survey on energy-efficient techniques in sustainable cloud computing. *Sustainability (Basel)*, *14*(10), 6256. DOI: 10.3390/su14106256

Cocaña-Fernández, A., Sánchez, L., & Ranilla, J. (2015, August). A software tool to efficiently manage the energy consumption of HPC clusters. In *2015 IEEE International Conference on Fuzzy Systems (FUZZ-IEEE)* (pp. 1-8). IEEE. DOI: 10.1109/FUZZ-IEEE.2015.7338079

Inacio, E. C., & Dantas, M. A. (2014). A survey into performance and energy efficiency in HPC, cloud and big data environments. *International Journal of Networking and Virtual Organisations*, *14*(4), 299–318. DOI: 10.1504/IJNVO.2014.067878

Jalasri, M., Panchal, S. M., Mahalingam, K., Venkatasubramanian, R., Hemalatha, R., & Boopathi, S. (2025). AI-Powered Smart Energy Management for Optimizing Energy Efficiency in High-Performance Computing Systems. In *Future of Digital Technology and AI in Social Sectors* (pp. 329–366). IGI Global.

Lakumarapu, S., Nithyanandhan, R., Bhargavi, V. S., Anish, T. P., & Nalini, M. (2024, August). Machine Learning Approaches for Liver Disease Prediction: A Comparative Analysis. *In 2024 5th International Conference on Electronics and Sustainable Communication Systems (ICESC)* (pp. 159-164). IEEE.

Mahesh, B. (2020). Machine learning algorithms-a review. *International Journal of Science and Research (IJSR).(Internet)*, *9*(1), 381-386.

Maithili, K., Ponmalar, A., Yamini, B., Karthikeyan, M., Anish, T. P., Maheswari, B., & Subramanian, R. S. (2024). Advances in AI and Machine Learning for Healthcare Informatics. In *Machine Learning and Generative AI in Smart Healthcare* (pp. 1–22). IGI Global. DOI: 10.4018/979-8-3693-3719-6.ch001

Ponmalar, A., Vijayakumar, K., Lakshmipriya, C., Karthikeyan, M., & PJ, B. P. (2024). Meta-Heuristics and Machine Learning Applications in Complex Systems. *In Metaheuristic and Machine Learning Optimization Strategies for Complex Systems (pp. 257-275)*. IGI Global.

Saravanan, K. P., Carpenter, P. M., & Ramirez, A. (2014, June). A performance perspective on energy efficient HPC links. In *Proceedings of the 28th ACM international conference on Supercomputing* (pp. 313-322). DOI: 10.1145/2597652.2597671

Sreelakshmi, S., Babu, A. A., Lakshmipriya, C., Gracious, L. A., Nalini, M., & Subramanian, R. S. (2024, October). Enhancing Intrusion Detection Systems with Machine Learning. *In 2024 2nd International Conference on Self Sustainable Artificial Intelligence Systems (ICSSAS)* (pp. 557-564). IEEE.

Subramaniam, B., & Feng, W. C. (2012, May). The green index: A metric for evaluating system-wide energy efficiency in hpc systems. In *2012 IEEE 26th International Parallel and Distributed Processing Symposium Workshops & PhD Forum* (pp. 1007-1013). IEEE. DOI: 10.1109/IPDPSW.2012.123

Sudha, K., Nithyanandhan, R., Anish, T. P., Girija, P., & Nalini, M. (2024, July). Enhancing Healthcare Data Security in the Cloud: Integrating ML-Based Intrusion Detection Systems. *In 2024 2nd World Conference on Communication & Computing (WCONF) (pp. 1-7).* IEEE.

Tiwari, N., Sarkar, S., Bellur, U., & Indrawan, M. (2014). An empirical study of hadoop's energy efficiency on a HPC cluster. *Procedia Computer Science, 29,* 62–72. DOI: 10.1016/j.procs.2014.05.006

Varrette, S., Plugaru, V., Guzek, M., Besseron, X., & Bouvry, P. (2014, September). HPC performance and energy-efficiency of the OpenStack cloud middleware. In *2014 43rd International Conference on Parallel Processing Workshops* (pp. 419-428). IEEE. DOI: 10.1109/ICPPW.2014.62

Wang, H., Qin, C., Bai, Y., Zhang, Y., & Fu, Y. (2021). Recent advances on neural network pruning at initialization. *arXiv preprint arXiv:2103.06460.*

Chapter 4
Edge and Fog Computing for Sustainability

J. Refonaa
Sathyabama Institute of Science and Technology, India

M. Gowri
Sathyabama Institute of Science and Technology, India

M. Maheswari
Sathyabama Institute of Science and Technology, India

S. Praveen
Sathyabama Institute of Science and Technology, India

D. Poornima
Sathyabama Institute of Science and Technology, India

R. S. Amshavalli
https://orcid.org/0000-0002-9480-9868
Sathyabama Institute of Science and Technology, India

S. L. Jany Shabu
Sathyabama Institute of Science and Technology, India

ABSTRACT

Sustainability-aligned environmental improvement is demanded by a number of international organizations, including UNO. Sustainability from an environmental perspective means protecting the environment, reducing the rate of climate change, and promoting social advancement without endangering human life or leaving anyone behind. By meeting our present demands, this concept seeks to preserve resources for future generations. Adopted by every United Nations member state in 2015, the 2030 Agenda for Sustainable Development offers a common roadmap for world peace and prosperity both now and in the future. The task is made easier by the urgent need to throw light on developing technology. Hence there emerged sustainable computing that focuses on minimizing environmental impact and encouraging resource efficiency. It includes procedures that guarantee resource efficiency

DOI: 10.4018/979-8-3373-0766-4.ch004

Copyright © 2025, IGI Global Scientific Publishing. Copying or distributing in print or electronic forms without written permission of IGI Global Scientific Publishing is prohibited.

and environmental friendliness in the creation and application of technology. The chapter discusses the role of recent technologies such as edge and fog computing for sustainability.

INTRODUCTION

The term "sustainable development" was coined by the Brundtland Report, that was released in 1987 and sought to address the detrimental environmental effects of globalization and economic growth while also offering potential remedies for the issues brought on by population growth and industrialization. While there are many ways to interpret the idea of sustainable development, at its heart is a development approach that seeks to balance a number of frequently conflicting goals with an understanding of the social, economic, and environmental limitations that our society must work within (United Nations, 2023). From an environmental perspective, sustainability is advancing human progress, preserving the natural world, and reducing the effects of climate change without putting people in danger or abandoning them. This idea aims to satisfy our needs now without depleting resources for coming generations. "The development of meeting the resource and service demands of both present and future generations without compromising the wellness of the ecosystems that provide them" is the definition of environmental sustainability. However, environmental issues are far more crucial to long-term development. It's also critical to maintain a robust, healthy, and equitable society. This entails providing for the many requirements of every individual, both now and in the future, fostering individual wellbeing, fostering social inclusion and cohesiveness, and establishing equitable opportunity. The only way to solve many of the problems that humanity faces globally, such as hunger, inequality, scarcity of water, and climate change, is to support sustainable development, that is dedicated to progress in society, the environment, and economic prosperity.

Figure 1. Sustainable Development Goals

The Sustainable Development Goals (SDG), a call to action to safeguard the environment and ensure the well-being of people everywhere, are part of the 2030 Agenda, a new sustainable development plan that was endorsed by the UN. In order to accomplish these common goals, governments, businesses, and people everywhere must work together. *Figure 1* lists the 17 SDGs. Two issues that have emerged as the outcome of the desire for economic expansion are disparities in social status and environmental deterioration. A broader approach to growth is necessary for sustainable development, which promotes progress along the three fundamental pillars of social inclusion, economic success, and environmental sustainability. SDGs are interconnected, they acknowledge that decisions made in one area will have an impact on other areas. For instance, poverty cannot be addressed without tackling issues of gender equality, hunger, health, and education. In a similar vein, ethical production and consumption as well as sustainable economic growth are essential for environmental protection. Additionally, the SDGs are universal, which means that any nations, regardless of development level, can use them. This is due to the fact that our problems are worldwide in scope and call for a worldwide solution.

Concept of sustainability

The goal of sustainability is to preserve the environment, slow down climate change, and advance social progress without threatening life as we know it or abandoning anyone. This idea aims to meet our needs now without sacrificing resources for centuries to come. Society, Ecology and Economy are known as the three pillars of sustainability, which were initially established by the United Nations Brundtland Commission in 1987, sustainability encompasses not only environmental issues but also social and economic well-being. But to accomplish the task of attaining sustainable development goals by 2030, the need of the hour is an additional force that makes the task easier and it is depicted through *Figure 2*.

Figure 2. Pillars of Sustainability

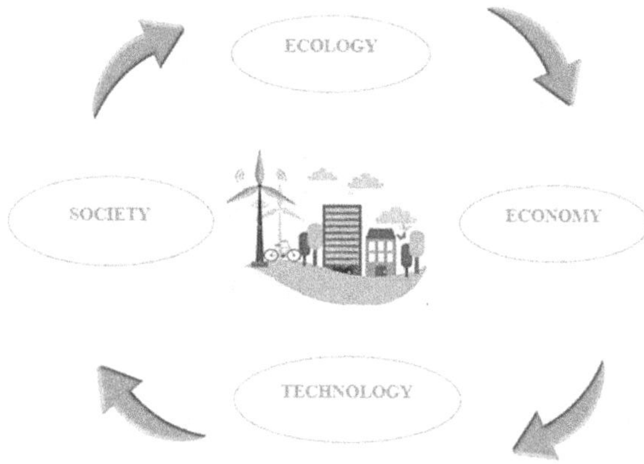

Hence in order to achieve the 17 UN Sustainable Development Goals (SDGs), technology must be used wisely in order to accelerate sustainability at the individual, organizational, national, and international levels (United Nations, n.d.). We are now getting closer to 2030 (the UN SDGs were first introduced in 2015, and work must be expedited quickly to meet that goal).

Concept of Sustainable Computing

Sustainable computing is the process of designing, building, using, and discarding computers, chips, and other technology parts and accessories in a way that minimizes negative environmental effects, such as lowering emission levels and energy usage by producers, data centers, and end users. Selecting raw materials from sustainable sources, cutting down on electronic waste, and advancing sustainability by utilizing renewable resources are all included in sustainable computing. There is a significant chance that sustainable computing will benefit the environment. The global greenhouse gas emissions from the information and communication technology (ICT) sector range from 1.8% to 3.9%. Additionally, data centers consume 3% of all energy annually, a 100% increase over the previous ten years. A paper released by the Association for computers Machinery states that "if climate change is to be controlled in time to avert catastrophic environmental damage, the energy needs and carbon emissions generated by computing and the overall ICT sector ought to be dramatically moderated." (ACM Digital Library, 2021). For instance, it is projected that data centers around the world use more than 205 terawatt hours of electricity annually. This Figureure exceeds the yearly electricity usage of nations like South Africa, Taiwan, Denmark, and Ireland. Additionally, just 61% of people on the planet are already online, and conservative estimates indicate that over 43 billion IoT gadgets will be included into the constantly expanding market sphere by 2030. Because of its size, information, and communications technology (ICT) is expected to contribute between 7% and 20% of the world's energy consumption by 2030.

Need for technology in sustainable development

Utilizing technology as a force for good—one that promotes a safer, healthier, and more sustainable environment—is essential as we traverse the intricate and quickly changing landscape of digital transformation. The primary objectives of sustainability in technology are to reduce the negative effects on the environment and promote resource efficiency (Al-Emran & Griffy-Brown, 2023). In the development and use of technology, it encompasses practices that ensure resource efficiency and environmental friendliness.

Consider the following crucial elements to ensure that technology is sustainable:

- Energy efficiency: Develop and apply technology that use less energy. By installing energy-efficient hardware and software, power usage can be significantly reduced.
- Resource conservation: To cut down on the use of non-renewable resources, promote recycling and material reuse. This approach reduces waste and extends the life cycle of technical products.
- Renewable energy: Utilize renewable energy sources like wind and solar to power data centers along with other electronic infrastructures. This reduces reliance on fossil fuels and greenhouse gas emissions.
- Eco-friendly design: Take sustainability into account when making products. Utilize biodegradable or recyclable materials and create products that are easy to disassemble and repair.
- Lifecycle handling: manage the entire lifecycle of a technological product, from production to disposal. Utilizing eco-friendly items, reducing production waste, and ensuring that everything is appropriately recycled at the end of its useful life are all part of this.

Figure 3. Role of Technology in attaining Sustainable development

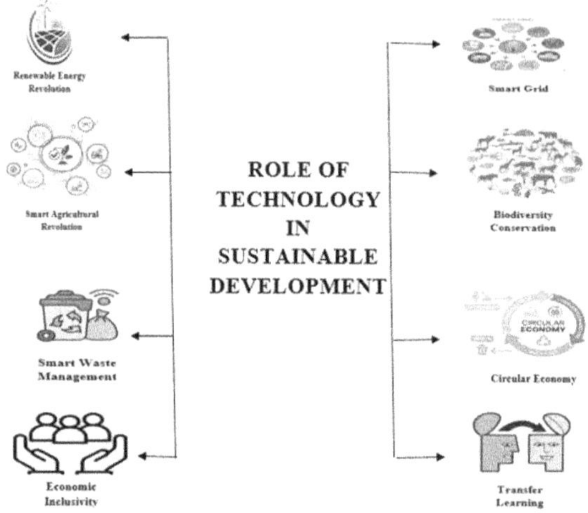

Among the several recent technologies that helps in combating the environmental issues, this chapter specifically deals with fog and edge computing. *Figure 3* highlights the contribution of these technologies towards sustainable development.

Difference between Fog and Edge Paradigm

The term "cloud computing" describes the on-demand provision of IT resources and services via the internet. Cloud computing enables customers to access services at any time and from any location. These days, enormous amounts of data are produced worldwide every second. People's data is gathered and processed by businesses, which then use the insights to grow. Data traffic may arise when numerous firms access their data on distant servers in data centers at the same time. Data traffic may result in reduced bandwidth, a delay in data access, etc. However, cloud computing technology is insufficient on its own to efficiently store, process, and react to vast volumes of data. For instance, the sensor in the Tesla self-driving car, for instance, continuously scans specific areas surrounding the vehicle. The car must stop or maneuver around without colliding if it senses a pedestrian or obstruction in its path. Fast processing of the sensor's data is necessary to assist the car identify impending obstacles before they impact. Even a small delay in detection could have serious consequences. Fog computing and edge computing are introduced to address these issues (Tank & Gandhi, 2023). *Figure 4* describes the layers of cloud, fog and edge

Figure 4. Concept of Cloud, fog, and Edge Layers

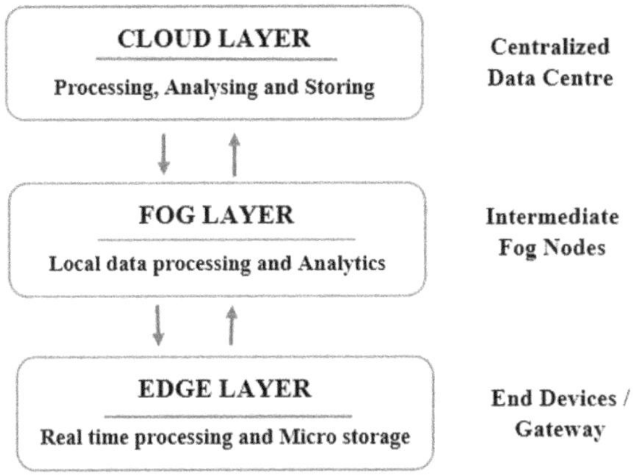

Fog Computing: Fog computing is an extension of cloud computing. It is a layer in between the edge and the cloud. When edge computers send huge amounts of data to the cloud, fog nodes receive the data and analyze what's important. Then the fog nodes transfer the important data to the cloud to be stored and delete the unimportant data or keep them with themselves for further analysis. In this way, fog computing saves a lot of space in the cloud and transfers important data quickly.

Edge Computing: Edge computing is the term for computation that occurs at a device's network edge. This indicates that a computer is linked to the device's network, processing data and sending it in real time to the cloud. This computer is referred to as a "edge node" or "edge computer." Data is instantaneously processed and sent to the devices using this technology. However, regardless of the significance of the data, edge nodes send all of the data that the device generates or captures.

Table 1. Comparison of Edge and Fog Computing

Features	Fog Computing	Edge Computing
Architecture	Decentralized	Decentralized
Scalability	High	High
Devices	Switches, Access points, tiny servers	Base stations, Gateways, edge routers
Server Node Location	Between edge and cloud	Close to smart devices

continued on following page

Table 1. Continued

Features	Fog Computing	Edge Computing
Interaction in real time	Timely processing	Timely processing
Heterogeneity	Yes	Yes
Storage	Limited	More Limited
Latency	Very Low	Low
Location of processing	Device itself	Within IoT gateway of fog nodes

Integrating Fog and Edge platform

A hybrid strategy that blends fog and edge computing can provide a complete answer to today's data problems by balancing latency, scalability, and data integrity. Autonomous car systems, for example, can leverage fog computing for inter-vehicle interaction and more comprehensive traffic monitoring, while using edge computing for instantaneous navigation data processing. For sectors like precision agriculture and smart cities, where both large-scale data management and real-time data processing are critical, this combination builds intelligent ecosystems. Businesses can increase operational efficiency and flexibility by combining the advantages of both approaches. Thus, integrating fog and edge platform is regarded as recent research trends.

Table 2. Applications used in Fog and Edge Computing

APPLICATIONS SUITABLE FOR EACH PLATFORM	
FOG COMPUTING PLATFORM	EDGE COMPUTING PLATFORM
Connected factories	Autonomous vehicles
Smart grids	Gaming and AR/VR
Vehicle-to-cloud connectivity	Remote surveillance
Healthcare networks	Smart retail

CONCEPT OF FOG COMPUTING

Cisco used the phrase "fog computing" to describe the practice of bringing cloud computing to the edge of an organization's network (Cisco, n.d.). "From cOre to edGe" computing is the whole form of fog. The term "fog" was coined because of how near fog is to the ground; similarly, fog computing operates at the borders of the user's property, which is much closer to the user than distant data centers. A decentralized computing architecture called fog computing, sometimes referred to as fog networking or fogging, extends cloud computing capabilities to the edge of the network. This approach aims to enhance data processing capabilities, reduce latency, and boost efficiency. With cloud technologies becoming a daily necessity for businesses, educational institutions, and individual consumers, fog computing has become a popular load-balancing solution for data centers in recent years which depicted through *Figure 5.*

Figure 5. Fog Computing Architecture

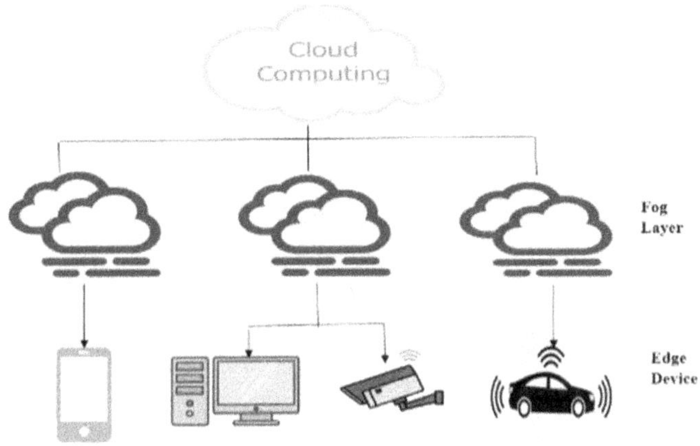

Every day, an immense quantity of traffic on the internet is created, and it continues to rise quickly. In the end, the data center is where all of these transactions happen. Data centers need more powerful computing systems to carry out specific jobs effectively because of the massive volume of data transactions. These devices also use electricity and release carbon dioxide into the atmosphere, which is extremely detrimental to the environment. A number of problems and difficulties are also brought on by cloud computing, including problems with security, cost optimization, energy use and CO2 emissions, cloud migration, and many more. The distance between the user and the data center is the primary cause of the majority of these issues. These problems are still unresolved. The Internet of Things (IoT), which simply means "connect the unconnected" via the Internet, is another concept that has lately surfaced in relation to cloud computing. In order for the disconnected things to interact with various objects and people, they must be connected to the internet. Based on the International Data Corporation (IDC) statistics published on the year 2020 clearly highlights the exponential growth of IoT.

Table 3. Exponential growth of IoT devices

FEATURED COMPONENTS	SURVEY RESULT
Sensors	212 billion
Connected Devices	1 trillion
Connected Vehicles	110 million
Smart Home Appliances	1.2 million
Smart Wearable Devices	237.1 million
Worldwide IoT Market	1.7 trillion

Since the IoT market is growing enormously, the centralized cloud faces huge complications in terms of security, high energy consumption. To cope up the gap, fog computing came into existence. Computational intelligence is now more accessible to end devices than ever thanks to fog nodes (Amshavalli & Kalaivani, 2023).

Therefore, in order to reap the true benefits of IoT, fog nodes must be made as powerful as clouds. Because of its faraway location from the specified data center and its constantly growing number of devices, IoT data is completely unmatched by the old network paradigm, which depends on a centralized computing structure. Network topologies have been changed to enable computation at the network edge in order to address the problem of a greater distance between end devices and the centralized cloud. This ultimately gives rise to fog computing. Fog computing is ideally suited for real-time, delay-sensitive, and latency-sensitive Internet of Things applications because it is sometimes referred to as an extension of cloud computing to end devices. Hence the distributed computing paradigm known as fog computing is a potent tool that helps meet the Sustainable Development Goals (SDGs). across order to further the SDGs, this chapter examines how fog computing tackles important issues and provides creative solutions across a range of industries.

Role of fog computing in Sustainable Development

A distributed platform called fog computing provides communication, execution, and storage capabilities between IoT devices and the cloud computing storage space. Because it offers numerous beneficial and supporting features including edge position, location awareness, and minimal response delay, the fog layer is currently regarded as a significant addition to the cloud (Harnal, Tiwari, Garg, & Mathur, 2024). The primary purpose of the Fog concept was to provide services, such real-time apps, to end-user devices. There are several ways, fog computing can help in attainment of sustainable development goals. Role of fog computing in sustainable development is listed below

A. Fog for Smart Agriculture – SDG 1, 2 and 15:

Smart farming maximizes resource use and reduces environmental effect by utilizing innovative technologies in the agriculture sector. At the moment, sensors are able to provide extremely precise crop status assessments. Actuators can control agricultural operations involving crops, animals, greenhouses, irrigation, soil, and weather based on those values. Harvest forecasting, weather forecasting, production, conservation of water, real-time data collecting, production, reduced operating expenses, equipment tracking, remote monitoring, and precise farm and field evaluation are all possible outcomes of this. High amounts of diverse data sources, including autonomous tractors, harvesters, robots and drones, sensors, and actuators, are always linked to smart agriculture (Hong, Park, Youn, Lee, & Kwon, 2024). Relevant agricultural data, including temperature, pH, humidity, and soil conditions, are gathered by heterogeneous sensors and other devices. In a similar vein, it takes into account the utilization of different actuators that respond to the data, including water sprinklers, ventilation systems, lighting, automatic windows (in glasshouses), and soil and water nutrition pumps. Almost every day, more and more cloud-based agricultural standalone systems and physical systems are being developed to support a variety of monitoring and analysis goals. *Figure 6* portrays the role of fog in agriculture

Figure 6. Fog for Smart Agriculture

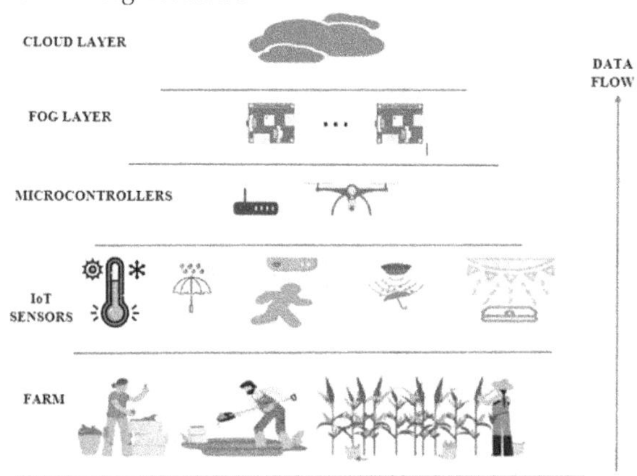

In addition to being a major source of income, agriculture is essential to the world's food supply chain. It is essential to human existence. However, agricultural development is constrained by several issues, including population increase, the expansion of industrial development, and climate change. By 2050, the UN predicts that there will be 9.7 billion people on the planet. Global agricultural production would need to rise by about 60% year between 2010 and 2050 if these predictions come to pass. Farmers, scientists, agronomists, and the agricultural sector use emerging technologies like cloud computing, edge computing, fog computing, the Internet of Things and drones to meet this demand. When fog computing is coupled with mighty cloud environment, it contributes to sustainable development by minimizing the energy consumption in smart agriculture. Enormous amount of data is generated from the farm which are observed by the different variety of sensory component. These IoT sensors are monitored by the microcontrollers and sends information to the fog layer where the actual processing is done. Data is being sent to cloud layer only for storage purpose. By employing these recent technologies in agriculture makes it more intelligent and helps in attaining sustainable development goals.

B. Fog for Healthcare Systems – SDG 3:

The history of human progress has demonstrated that the primary motivation behind the advancement of science and technology has always been the use of medicine and healthcare for the benefit of humanity. For many years, cloud computing has dominated healthcare information systems. The high service response time of cloud-based apps is one drawback, though. Certain emergency situations have a direct impact on patients' lives because they limit the control and monitoring of patient status and decision-making with connected resources, such as a hospital, ambulance, doctor, and medical conditions in a matter of seconds. Cloud computing, fog computing, IoT and other optimal computing methods have been developed to address these issues. By integrating networked devices that collect real-time patient healthcare data, Internet of Things (IoT) applications in the healthcare industry are transforming traditional medical practices. Fog computing offers an architectural foundation that strengthens IoT technologies by shifting processing resources to the network edge, where there is less latency, less waiting for replies, and no bandwidth issues caused by sending large amounts of data to distant cloud servers (Jeyaraman et al., 2024). In order to increase access to high-quality healthcare services, fog computing is essential. It makes telemedicine, personalized healthcare, and remote patient monitoring possible by pushing technological capabilities much nearer the point of care. Reduced latency and real-time decision-making improve the effectiveness of the healthcare system and assist underprivileged communities.

Large amounts of data are provided by healthcare applications, necessitating cloud storage as an alternative to relying on constrained computer power and storage devices. Applications in healthcare have a substantial amount of result data. A lot of data is produced during medical diagnosis, and this data needs to be perfectly kept and retrieved (Aazam, Zeadally, & Harras, 2020). Real-time requirements should be taken into account while managing streaming-based transmissions in e-health applications. Because healthcare applications are latency sensitive, have slow response times, and generate a lot of data, fog computing is seen to be the optimal approach to utilize when creating them. By assisting senior citizens with home nursing, fog computing makes a substantial contribution to healthcare applications. Fog computing might be the ideal answer for healthcare applications that need a low latency and a high response time, such as neurological illnesses, where real-time monitoring is one of the key aspects. Following are the key areas where fog computing can contribute to SDG via smart healthcare systems.

- Body Sensors
- Ingestible Sensors
- Electronic Health Record (EHR)

- Remote Monitoring
- Emergency services
- Smart Hospitals
- Connected Homes

Connecting these services and bringing down the processing capabilities near to the end devices are the notable feature of fog computing. Thus, the healthcare system is made intelligent by the pros of fog and IoT paradigm.

C. Fog for Smart and sustainable communities: SDG -6,11 and 15

The development of smart city initiatives to enhance urban living, resource management, and service delivery has enabled an unparalleled convergence of many technologies. One of these technologies, fog computing, has demonstrated promise in resolving issues caused by the growing need for low-latency communication, efficient resource utilization, and real-time data processing. This chapter provides a comprehensive overview of fog computing's function and impacts in the context of smart cities. Due to technology advancements and the expansion of the internet of things in almost every sphere of urban life, smart cities are developing quickly. Cities today have embedded sensors everywhere, from trash cans to thermostats, when ten years ago there were virtually few. Fog computing in smart cities is a new trend that emerged from the capacity to connect, interact, and remotely control a wide range of equipment. Because Fog can process large amounts of data quickly and safely, it has a great chance of becoming the next big thing in smart city development. In order to make sure everything is operating well and promoting sustainability in urban living, it assists in gathering data about a variety of municipal activities, such as traffic and utilities. The cloud will continue to play a vital role in the IoT ecosystem, but depending too much on fog computing is an impractical strategy for handling these massive volumes of data. Furthermore, fog computing does not always mean the demise of cloud-based, standardized IoT networks (Songhorabadi, Rahimi, MoghadamFarid, & Kashani, 2023). Since centralized data is nearly always easier to access, there are more opportunities for open data agreements to be established between the public and private sectors. A more sophisticated kind of innovation and digital creativity may result from this. At the same time, cloud-based data opens up a greater range of applications. Sustainable Community can be achieved through fog computing with the help of following means

- Smart Transportation system
- Intelligent Weather Monitoring System

- Smart Water management
- Smart Waste management
- Smart Home and appliance connectivity

Ultimately, fog computing will unavoidably be a significant component of the upcoming smart city development waves. Decision-making within gadgets will become increasingly important for any smart city that wants to stay on the cutting edge as technology continues to advance into a system where computers must be able to behave like people.

D. Fog for Life under water – SDG 14:

Ocean researchers advance our knowledge of ocean resource development, biodiversity preservation, global climate change, and efficient maritime transportation. As sensing and communication methods advance, new maritime applications—from deep sea monitoring to on-water maritime services like marine pollution tracking, search and rescue (SAR) at sea, remote piloting, and smart traffic management at ports—are greatly advancing ocean research. Many marine applications, like entertainment services, may produce enormous amounts of data, and others, like SAR and remote piloting, have stringent requirements for service latency Zhu, Zhang, Chiang, Ye, Du, & An, 2022). A number of fog computing paradigms designed especially for maritime operations have been put out to meet the inc6treased service demand. Superior and high-efficiency data processing and transmission activities are made possible by fog computing. The fog layer serves as the processing node, situated close to the end devices where the data is actually generated, rather than sending these tasks to the cloud. Fog layer is capable of performing the following task

- It minimizes the distance for the data communication by introducing a vessel like ships near the location where the data is generated. These nodes can be used to offer services for nearby maritime devices for single-hop communication by letting computer and communication resources on them.
- It saves the bandwidth consumption to a large extent. Minimized distance between the end nodes the processing nodes obviously helps in less energy consumption. The satellite communication capabilities will remain intact if the visual data processing tasks are offloaded as a clone or a partial migration throughout cellular links rather than sending all of the raw visual data to the distant LCC (Land Control Center) via satellite links. This effectively conserves the valuable satellite bandwidth.

- It offers the feature of location aware crowd sensing. Fog node placement is done based on the number of end devices and the processing capacity of the fog node. Placing fog nodes in marine environment depends lot of factors like depth of the sea, reach of sun light, zone suitable for life etc

By protecting sensitive data and promoting confidence in digital networks, fog computing reduces the hazards connected with centralized cloud computing. To sum up, fog computing is essential to achieving the SDGs. It improves efficiency, creativity, and sustainability in a variety of industries, including healthcare, agriculture, transportation, energy, and environmental preservation, by bringing computing resources closer to the site of action. Making the most of fog computing's potential speeds up the process of sustainable development and builds resilient, inclusive communities for a brighter future.

CONCEPT OF EDGE COMPUTING

A distributed computing paradigm known as "edge computing" handles data closer to its source, at the edge of the network. Edge computing uses local devices, like sensors, Internet of Things devices, and edge servers, to process data rather than depending on centralized data centers. This method minimizes the distance that data must travel, which drastically lowers latency and conserves bandwidth. Therefore, edge computing is very beneficial for applications that need real-time data analysis, such industrial automation and driverless cars. Edge technology, which describes computing on sensors, promises to create an Internet of Things (IOT) with 100,000 sensors within the next ten years (Khan, Ahmed, Hakak, Yaqoob, & Ahmed, 2019). As massive data is utilized and manipulated more frequently, it is crucial to become accustomed to this technology. It is a valued addition to the larger cloud computing environment since it improves performance, security, and the capacity to manipulate and analyze data at or near the beginning. Functionalities of different paradigm like cloud, fog and edge are described in *Figure 7.*

Figure 7. Concept of Edge Computing

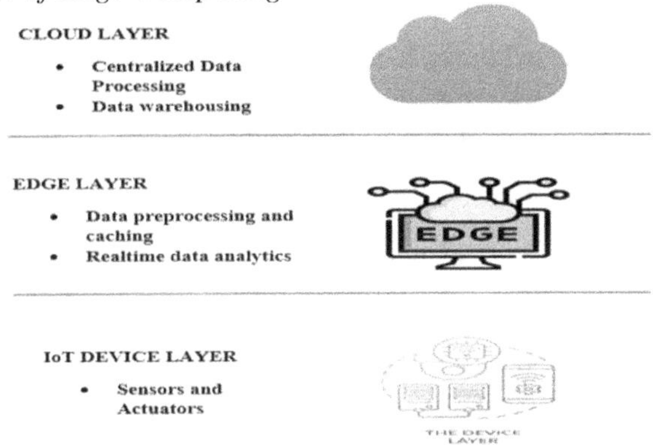

By shifting data computation closer to the network's edge and away from data centers, edge computing aims to advance network technology. Such a procedure uses smart devices or network gateways to carry out operations and deliver services on the cloud's behalf. It is often recognized that the massive volume of data generated every day makes it challenging and complex for data centers to handle in terms of compute. Additionally, response times significantly increase and the network bandwidth limit is nearly reached. Therefore, it is feasible to offer effective service delivery, improved data storage, and IoT management that might reduce response time and data transfer rate when shifting computation and data services to edge computing. The convergence of 5G data networks and edge technologies within range has been made possible by the 5G data network. As a result, Edge Computing lessens slow data communication and long-distance processing. Because it enables businesses to gather and analyze their raw data more effectively, edge computing is growing in popularity. In order to make well-informed decisions on their business activities and operational effectiveness, businesses now more than ever require immediate access to their data. Edge computing has the ability to assist enterprises in increasing user experience, automating procedures, and enhancing safety and performance when used properly (Kong, Wu, Wang, & Xia, 2022). The following are the key features that makes the edge computing unique

- Enhanced speed and decreased latency:

Technology requires nearly instantaneous data delivery in many businesses. Consider a piece of automated equipment on a manufacturing floor. It must be informed as soon as possible so that the robot can shut down if a production issue renders it unsafe for it to continue operating.

- Enhanced protection of data:

Most data is analyzed and stored locally when using edge computing. Before being transmitted, any data that must be returned to the data center might be encrypted. By keeping sensitive data close to the source, edge computing helps businesses adhere to data sovereignty regulations like the General Data Protection Regulation (GDPR).

- A rise in output:

Businesses increase worker and operational productivity by reacting to information faster. Organizations can enhance underperforming elements of their infrastructure, equipment, or facilities by examining data gathered at the source. When edge computing is combined with AI and machine learning techniques, intelligence for businesses and insights can be obtained that improve worker and company productivity.

- Reliable Environment:

By establishing an edge computing environment, businesses can make sure that their operations process, analyze, and store data in a reliable manner, greatly lowering the likelihood of experiencing operational downtime due to network or connectivity disruption. Edge computing is frequently used in remote locations with limited internet connectivity.

- Remote gathering of data:

Data collection from locations with erratic connectivity and bandwidth is difficult. Businesses can gather and send data from remote oil fields, industrial areas, and offshore boats by setting up data storage and processing capabilities at the network edge.

- Lower expenses:

Because it demands more bandwidth, sending big amounts of data from its source to centralized data centres is costly. Because end users only provide essential data, the edge computing architecture enables you to reduce the volume of data being transmitted from sites to data centres. Operating costs could be greatly reduced, according to how much data the company sends and processes.

ROLE OF EDGE COMPUTING IN SUSTAINABLE DEVELOPMENT

Cloud computing has gained popularity in recent years, and many firms have migrated to cloud platforms. However, there are significant and worrisome environmental dangers associated with its rapid rise. Centralized data centres are crucial to the infrastructure of cloud computing nowadays, but they also lead to a larger issue. The carbon footprint of the cloud has surpassed that of the aircraft sector. The electricity used by a single data centre is equal to that of 50,000 houses. Edge computing can contribute to greater sustainability in such a situation. Here are some ways that edge computing might enhance sustainability (Arroba, Buyya, Cárdenas, Risco-Martín, & Moya, 2024). The initial three pillars of sustainability—environmental, social, and economic—can all benefit from the recently added fourth pillar known as technology. The following are the key reasons of how edge computing paradigm can contribute to sustainable development

- By using edge computing, operations tech staff can process data at the edge of the network rather than in a centralized data warehouse or the cloud.
- The use of physical or virtual computer equipment at the network's edge is required to lower the necessary bandwidth access data centered centrally, since certain business-critical applications will need real-time data.
- By lowering data transit and enabling local filtration of sensitive data, edge computing enables companies to design a compliance and security architecture that best suits their requirements (Zhang & Feng, 2024).
- The forthcoming era of data center improvement and modernization is being driven by IoT and edge computing. Organizations can benefit from modern devices without giving up on traditional systems thanks to virtualization and edge computing.

The chapter deals with the contribution of edge computing paradigm in different sectors to attain the proposed sustainable development goals in the following section

A. Edge for Energy Efficiency – SDG 7 and 9

Recently, energy efficiency has drawn a lot of attention due to its financial benefits, green industry needs, and smart system performance. Edge computing aids in this regard. This recent computing technique helps hugely in energy management. Because edge computing eliminates the requirement for data to travel great distances, it greatly improves energy efficiency. This localized processing maximizes resource use and minimizes energy consumption (Jiang et al., 2020). The carbon footprint of technology activities can be significantly decreased with the help of edge computing. Local data processing reduces energy use and dependency on big data centers, which lowers carbon emissions. Take into account the following ideas to comprehend how edge computing improves energy efficiency:

- Minimized data traffic: By using edge computing, less data is routed to centralized data centers. This minimizes the energy needed for data delivery in addition to reducing bandwidth utilization.
- Local data processing: Edge computing lowers the energy required for data transmission by processing data at the edge, near its source. When opposed to centralized cloud computing, this leads to significant energy savings.
- Energy-efficient hardware: Using specialized hardware that uses less power than conventional data center servers, edge devices are frequently made to be extremely energy-efficient. As a result, less energy is used overall. Why Less cooling is needed since local edge devices produce less heat than big data centers. These further conserves energy by lowering the requirement for large cooling systems.
- Proactive resource management: Edge computing has the ability to dynamically distribute resources in response to current demands. This prevents energy waste by ensuring that only the computational power required is employed.
- Local power generation: Local renewable energy sources, including wind or solar, can power edge devices. This lessens carbon emissions and dependency on fossil fuels.
- Scalability coupled with sustainability: While keeping an eye on energy efficiency, edge computing enables scalable solutions that expand with demand. This scalability makes sure that the carbon footprint doesn't rise in proportion to growing data processing requirements.

Real-time monitoring and control of energy production and distribution networks is possible in the energy sector with edge computing. Energy firms can lower latency, speed up response times, and improve situational awareness by putting computing resources nearer to the network's edge. This enhances dependability and decreases downtime by enabling them to identify and address problems faster. Energy systems can be made more efficient through the use of edge computing. Energy businesses can find flaws and optimize energy use by evaluating data at the network's edge. This can result in greater efficiency and dependability, as well as cost savings and enhanced sustainability (Alsharif et al., 2024). Increased security is another advantage of edge layer in the energy industry. Energy firms can lower the probability of cyberattacks and shield sensitive data from unwanted access by processing data locally. This can safeguard consumer privacy while also enhancing the security and dependability of energy infrastructure. Optimizing the grid's integration of renewable energy sources is possible with edge computing. Energy businesses can examine data on energy production and usage in real-time and modify grid operations by processing data locally. Increased use of renewable energy sources and enhanced grid stability and dependability are possible outcomes of this. New energy services and business models are made possible by edge computing. Energy firms are able to provide previously unattainable applications and services by processing data locally. For instance, they can facilitate peer-to-peer energy trading or provide users with real-time energy consumption monitoring and feedback.

B. Edge for Manufacturing Sector – SDG 8, 9 and 12

Handling and storing data in close proximity to data sources and users is known as edge computing. In contrast to conventional centralized data centers, edge computing helps to improve performance and enable real-time insights by bringing computational capability to the network's edge. In the manufacturing sector, this entails positioning computer resources close to equipment and production lines in order to swiftly assess data and take actions on the spot. Large volumes of data are produced by sensors, machinery, and other devices in manufacturing. It might not be optimal for handling and processing this data only in the cloud due to the latency and bandwidth requirements. By performing data analysis locally, edge computing lessens the need for large data transmission and makes operations faster and more effective. The roles of edge computing and cloud computing are sometimes misconstrued due to their complimentary natures and overlapping capabilities. High latency and bandwidth expenses may result from the centralization of data processing in distant data centers brought about by cloud computing. However, by placing processing closer to the data sources, edge computing decentralizes it. While cloud computing is good for long-term storage and intensive computing tasks like creating machine learning models and doing a lot of data analysis, edge computing is better at processing data in real time and making decisions quickly. Furthermore, by keeping only important data in the cloud and contextualizing raw data for improved analysis, edge computing lowers costs by facilitating raw data filtering and contextualization (Kubiak, Dec, & Stadnicka, 2022). Because edge computing resources serve as local hubs, they also improve security by reducing the exposure of sensitive data and avoiding vulnerabilities related to direct cloud transfer. Here are some instances where it could be most advantageous to use edge computing.

i) Context based Tracking:

Just attempting to retrieve data out of their machines, processes, and systems presents a problem for manufacturers. In the past, numerous proprietary systems that are incompatible with one another have been used to build plants. IT/OT convergence is necessary since operational technology is still quite conventional and does not yet adhere to the same standards as IT. The massive volumes of raw data produced by extracting data from all of these production units present a hurdle since they would overwhelm a central server. Manufacturers can use edge computing to filter data so that less is routed to a central server, either locally or in the cloud. Manufacturers can create new revenue streams by remotely monitoring the state of their assets. They might offer services to their end users instead of selling them computers one at a time. For instance, tailoring maintenance services to the asset's actual state or even drastically altering their business plans so that the client provides a managed service for uptime.

ii) Manufacturing as a Service

Leveraging economies of scale from highly standardized, automated processes is one of the issues facing the manufacturing sector. Another is having a manufacturing process that can adapt to consumers' changing needs. Reducing the time required to set up a site and developing additional sharing models that allow many parties to utilize the same facility can make manufacturing more mobile and adaptable. There is a definite edge cloud use case for both of these items. First, since systems are essential to the operation of the manufacturing process, they must be accessible from any location (cloud-like) and still adhere to strict latency standards. Second, manufacturers' worries about data security are allayed by processing data at the edge.

iii) Industrial Automation

There is growing pressure on manufacturing companies to support robust supply chains and meet rising demands. Manufacturers must use technologies like edge computing, which allow them to automate processes and gather and process data nearer to the source, if they want to succeed. Edge computing reduces the need for data to travel long distances by letting processing power closer to the data source. This lowers latency and allows for faster, more precise answers. For example, real-time parameter adjustments by machines enhance quality control and production (Chen, Wan, Celesti, Li, Abbas, & Zhang, 2018). Additionally, manufacturers may achieve a level of responsiveness that is just unmatched by traditional cloud-based systems thanks to computing at the edge. Better use of resources, more flexible manufacturing procedures, and the capacity to quickly adjust to changing demands are the outcomes.

C. Edge for IoT Connectivity – SDG 9 and 11

Ensuring smooth communication and data transmission between two devices is one of the major issues in IoT networking. By enabling direct interaction and exchange of information at the network's edge, edge computing is essential to solving this problem. Data from devices frequently passes via a central cloud server in a conventional cloud-centric Internet of Things architecture before being sent to its final location. Delays may arise from this procedure, especially in situations where real-time communication is essential. By enabling devices to link directly and exchange data without having to go via a remote cloud server, edge computing helps to address this problem. Improved reliability and quicker reaction times are made possible by this direct edge-to-edge device contact (Hassan, Gillani, Ahmed, Yaqoob, & Imran, 2018). For example, edge computing makes sure that commands and data are transferred quickly in a smart home setting where multiple IoT devices must communicate with one another, resulting in a more dynamic and smooth user experience. At the organization's edge, near the final customers, edge computing cycles and saves the data. Information processing closer to the end devices reduces transmission time, reduces the requirement for data transfer capacity, and increases the battery life of IoT devices. Compared to dispersed computing, edge Figureuring has advantages for the majority of IoT applications, such as reduced reaction time and enhanced interchange productivity. IoT applications can be categorized based on delayed responsiveness; depending on the type of constraints they must adhere to, a particular application may be sensitive to delay. Instead, then requiring more significant computational power and capacity, the majority of IoT applications require continuous management. IoT edge computing is widely used in many contemporary applications; it enables a number of new services for businesses and customers. Edge registering is essential to many emerging IoT applications, such as intelligent frameworks and cars.

Figure 8. Edge Computing for IoT Connectivity

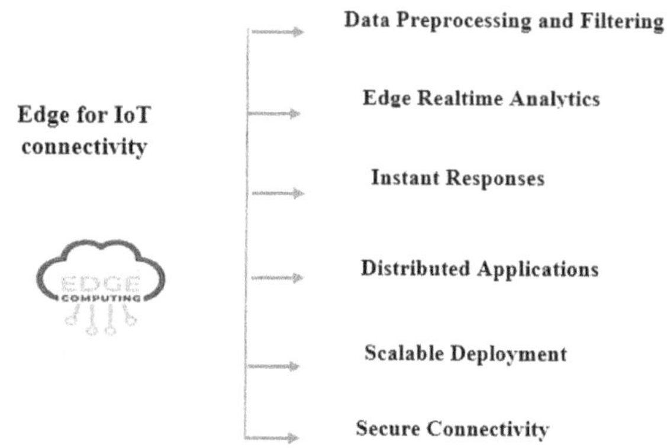

The application of IoT in an industrial setting, like factory machinery, is known as industrial IoT, or IIoT. The functionalities of edge in IoT connectivity is described in *Figure 8*. Consider the lifespan of a factory's heavy machinery. Over time, different people may put different amounts of stress on equipment, and malfunctions are a normal aspect of operations. Components of the machinery that are likely to break or be overused can have IoT sensors installed. By analysing and using the data from these sensors to predictive maintenance, total downtime can be decreased. One example of why edge computing and IoT solutions must cooperate is autonomous cars. In addition to monitoring the vehicle's systems, an autonomous car traveling down the road must gather and evaluate real-time data concerning people, traffic, stop lights, and street signs. It would take too long to transport data back and forth from the car to the cloud for processing if the car needed to stop or turn rapidly to escape an accident. By delivering cloud computing services to the car, edge computing enables the IoT sensors to process data locally and instantly, preventing collisions. Thus, IoT and edge computing work together to provide a potent means of quickly and instantly analysing data.

D. Edge for Climate Change Monitoring – SDG 13:

Modern technologies are being utilized to gather and evaluate climate change data, create and execute climate change solutions, and increase public awareness of the issue. Data on climate change, including greenhouse gas emissions, sea level rise, and temperature variations, is being gathered via digital technology combined with edge platform like satellites, drones, and sensors. Understanding the origins and effects of climate change, as well as creating efficient mitigation and adaptation plans, depend on this data (Singh & Gill, 2023). Solutions for climate change are also being developed and implemented with the help of edge computing. For instance, edge devices can be used to monitor and regulate renewable energy technologies like wind and solar power. Digital technologies can also be utilized to lower greenhouse gas emissions from transportation and other industries and increase energy efficiency. Additionally, digital technologies are being utilized to involve the public in climate action and to increase awareness of climate change.

REAL TIME CASE STUDIES

Auckland – An Embracing Smart City

The goal of Auckland is to become the most livable city in the world. The government-run website Auckland Conversations states that Auckland aspires to be "A smart city with smart citizens and smart infrastructure," which will enable the goal to be realized. The Wynyard Quarter's IoT-enabled infrastructure, which featured smart city applications like interconnected lighting, smart parking, smart benches, and intelligent dumpsters, was installed in late 2020 by SPARK and Auckland Transport. These smart city technologies were made possible by SPARK's 5G deployment in downtown Auckland, and the Wynyard Quarter deployment serves as an example of what the city's larger central business area may look like in the future. "Aucklanders visiting the city could spend up to one-third of their journey seeking for a carpark, so we're partnering with SPARK to Figureure out ways to help Aucklanders find accessible carparks faster by deploying 200 smart parking sensors all through the Quarter," stated Chris Creighton, group manager of technology solutions for Auckland Transport, in a report published by Smart Cities World. According to the report, "Wynyard Quarter's Innovation Precinct now has smart lighting installed in the surrounding streets that can monitor air and noise pollution and create heat maps of foot traffic to help AT identify any "choke points" to better inform future infrastructure investments." Certain lights have 5G-connected CCTV, which may improve the detection of criminal activity, record high-definition video even during the night, and allow for remote dimming and brightening to help save energy. Along with smart bins that detect when bins are full to minimize overflow and lessen the number of garbage vehicles on the road, the Quarter has also been equipped with solar-powered smart benches that can charge smartphones and electric scooters. The Internet of Things (IoT) is the primary driver of connectivity, which powers many of these smart city and smart transportation systems. In a recent piece, you can learn more about how the Internet of Things is contributing to smarter cities.

CONCLUSION

The world is changing as a result of innovative technologies. Recent technologies are significantly changing every aspect of our life, from how we manufacture and consume commodities to how we interact and work. Innovative ideas and digital technology are essential for advancing sustainable development. It's crucial to recognize that these technology developments could affect sustainability in both positive and bad ways. To improve sustainability results, it is crucial to obtain a thorough grasp of how people and organizations are implementing these technologies. As a result, new technologies like fog computing, edge computing, and the internet of things may hasten the achievement of the Sustainable Development Goals and the 2030 Agenda.

REFERENCES:

Aazam, M., Zeadally, S., & Harras, K. A. (2020, March 1). Health Fog for Smart Healthcare. *IEEE Consumer Electronics Magazine*, *9*(2), 96–102. DOI: 10.1109/MCE.2019.2953749

ACM Digital Library. (2021). *A survey on artificial intelligence and machine learning*.https://dl.acm.org/doi/pdf/10.1145/3483410

Al-Emran, M., & Griffy-Brown, C. (2023). The role of technology adoption in sustainable development: Overview, opportunities, challenges, and future research agendas. *Technology in Society*, *73*, 102240. DOI: 10.1016/j.techsoc.2023.102240

Alsharif, M. H., Kelechi, A. H., Jahid, A., Kannadasan, R., Singla, M. K., Gupta, J., & Geem, Z. W. (2024). A comprehensive survey of energy-efficient computing to enable sustainable massive IoT networks. *Alexandria Engineering Journal*, *91*, 12–29. DOI: 10.1016/j.aej.2024.01.067

Amshavalli, R. S., & Kalaivani, J. (2023, May). A Comprehensive Survey on Role of Fog Computing and Need for Semantic Technology in Modern Computing Platform. In *2023 7th International Conference on Intelligent Computing and Control Systems (ICICCS)* (pp. 719-725). IEEE. DOI: 10.1109/ICICCS56967.2023.10142888

Arroba, P., Buyya, R., Cárdenas, R., Risco-Martín, J. L., & Moya, J. M. (2024). Sustainable edge computing: Challenges and future directions. *Software, Practice & Experience*, *54*(11), 2272–2296. DOI: 10.1002/spe.3340

Chen, B., Wan, J., Celesti, A., Li, D., Abbas, H., & Zhang, Q. (2018, September). Edge Computing in IoT-Based Manufacturing. *IEEE Communications Magazine*, *56*(9), 103–109. DOI: 10.1109/MCOM.2018.1701231

Harnal, S., Tiwari, R., Garg, L., & Mathur, A. (Eds.). (2024). *Cloud and Fog Optimization-based Solutions for Sustainable Developments* (1st ed.). CRC Press., DOI: 10.1201/9781003494430

Hassan, N., Gillani, S., Ahmed, E., Yaqoob, I., & Imran, M. (2018, November). The Role of Edge Computing in Internet of Things. *IEEE Communications Magazine*, *56*(11), 110–115. DOI: 10.1109/MCOM.2018.1700906

Hong, S., Park, S., Youn, H., Lee, J., & Kwon, S. (2024). Implementation of Smart Farm Systems Based on Fog Computing in Artificial Intelligence of Things Environments. *Sensors (Basel)*, *24*(20), 6689. DOI: 10.3390/s24206689 PMID: 39460169

Jeyaraman, N., Jeyaraman, M., Yadav, S., Ramasubramanian, S., Balaji, S., Muthu, S., Lekha, P. C., & Patro, B. P. (2024, July 10). Applications of Fog Computing in Healthcare. *Cureus*, *16*(7), e64263. DOI: 10.7759/cureus.64263 PMID: 39130982

Jiang, C., Fan, T., Gao, H., Shi, W., Liu, L., Cérin, C., & Wan, J. (2020). Energy aware edge computing: A survey. *Computer Communications*, *151*, 556–580. DOI: 10.1016/j.comcom.2020.01.004

Khan, W. Z., Ahmed, E., Hakak, S., Yaqoob, I., & Ahmed, A. (2019). Edge computing: A survey. *Future Generation Computer Systems*, *97*, 219–235. DOI: 10.1016/j.future.2019.02.050

Kong, X., Wu, Y., Wang, H., & Xia, F. "Edge Computing for Internet of Everything: A Survey," in *IEEE Internet of Things Journal*, vol. 9, no. 23, pp. 23472-23485, 1 Dec.1, 2022, DOI: 10.1109/JIOT.2022.3200431

Kubiak, K., Dec, G., & Stadnicka, D. (2022). Possible Applications of Edge Computing in the Manufacturing Industry—Systematic Literature Review. *Sensors (Basel)*, *22*(7), 2445. DOI: 10.3390/s22072445 PMID: 35408059

Singh, R., & Gill, S. S. (2023). Next generation edge computing: A roadmap to net zero emissions. *Journal of Economy and Technology*, *1*, 208–221. DOI: 10.1016/j.ject.2023.12.001

Songhorabadi, M., Rahimi, M., MoghadamFarid, A. M., & Haghi Kashani, M. (2023). Fog computing approaches in IoT-enabled smart cities. *Journal of Network and Computer Applications*, *211*, 103557. DOI: 10.1016/j.jnca.2022.103557

Tank, B., & Gandhi, V. (2023). A Comparative Study on Cloud Computing, Edge Computing and Fog Computing. In *Recent Developments in Electronics and Communication Systems* (pp. 665–670). IOS Press. DOI: 10.3233/ATDE221329

United Nations. (2023, August). *What is sustainable development?* United Nations. https://www.un.org/sustainabledevelopment/blog/2023/08/what-is-sustainable-development/

United Nations. (n.d.). *Sustainable development goals.* United Nations. https://sdgs.un.org/goals

Zhang, Y., & Feng, J. (2024). *Towards a Smart and Sustainable Future with Edge Computing-Powered Internet of Things: Fundamentals, Applications, Challenges, and Future Research Directions. Journal of The Institution of Engineers.* Series B.

Zhu, C., Zhang, W., Chiang, Y.-H., Ye, N., Du, L., & An, J. (2022, March/April). Software-Defined Maritime Fog Computing: Architecture, Advantages, and Feasibility. *IEEE Network*, *36*(2), 26–33. DOI: 10.1109/MNET.003.2100433

Chapter 5
AI and ML for Energy Management:
Innovations and Challenges in a Sustainable Future

M. Gokuldhev
Vel Tech Rangarajan Dr. Sagunthala R&D Institute of Science and Technology, India

K. Vijayakumar
https://orcid.org/0009-0005-6245-3165
Panimalar Engineering College, India

M. Mercy Theresa
SRM Institute of Science and Technology, India

K. Sudha
RMD Engineering College, India

S. Nagarajan
R.M.K. Engineering College, India

R. Prasath
https://orcid.org/0000-0002-6346-1301
RMK College of Engineering and Technology, India

P. J. Beslin Pajila
https://orcid.org/0000-0002-3905-2460
Vel Tech Rangarajan Dr. Sagunthala R&D Institute of Science and Technology, India

ABSTRACT

The rising international energy consumption and the necessity of looking for environment-friendly solutions have necessitated the use of technology such as AI and ML for the energy management. This paper provides a state-of-art review of AI and ML in energy efficiency and microgrid systems, smart grid, and renewable energy systems, industries, and smart buildings. AI and ML enable predictive modeling, realtime optimization, advanced control methodologies that enhance the energy efficiency, operation cost and facilitate the integration of renewable energy systems. The paper outlines some of the important methodologies like reinforcement learning,

DOI: 10.4018/979-8-3373-0766-4.ch005

Copyright © 2025, IGI Global Scientific Publishing. Copying or distributing in print or electronic forms without written permission of IGI Global Scientific Publishing is prohibited.

deep learning and optimization algorithms in energy systems and their limitations like data quality, model interpretability and scalability. The results imply that the use of AI and ML systems is crucial in determining the direction of the future of energy management and ensuring the sustainability of the process.

1. INTRODUCTION

1.1 Overview of Global Energy Challenges and the Need for Optimization

The energy crisis is becoming a global concern due to the following factors. Global energy demand is on the increase as a result of the increasing population, increasing rate of urbanization and industrialization particularly in the developing world(Kumar et al 2018). This increase in demand puts a great deal of stress on the current energy systems which in turn, results in energy losses, wastage of energy and high dependence on fossil resources. Further, the increasing focus worldwide on renewable energy production solar, wind or hydropower sources – has made things more challenging. Although these energy sources are vital in the fight against climate change they are mobile and volatile, and thus provide difficulties in areas such as the stability and reliability of the grid. In addition, the shift of the global energy system to renewable energy sources requires more efficient technologies for energy storage that are still weak in capacity, efficiency, and affordability(Boopathi et al 2024). However, levels of energy intensity continue to be high in various sectors, enterprises, transport and residential sectors. Poor energy utilization leads to unutilized resource, extra expenditure, and avoidable effects on the environment. The increasing demand for efficient energy systems calls for advanced solutions that can solve these problems in large scale. The rational use of energy is not only important as a component of sustainable economic development but also one of the key drivers in the fight against climate change and the achievement of climate objectives.

1.2 Role of AI and ML in Addressing Energy Consumption and Efficiency

Modern technologies such as Artificial Intelligence (AI) and Machine Learning (ML) are now becoming significant solutions to these global energy challenges(Gaur et al 2024). Artificial Intelligence can be defined as the use of technology to solve problems that were formerly solved by human intelligence. AI is a broader concept which includes a subfield known as machine learning, which involves training a computer to learn from data and perform tasks better over time without being programmed(Marinakis et al 2020). These technologies can take in and analyse large volumes of real time data and make smart decisions that can best utilize energy in various systems. AI and ML are especially applicable to energy optimization problems because such problems are characterized by complex, dynamic, and large data. In power grids for instance, AI can estimate the demand for energy, estimate the production of renewable energy, and balance supply of electricity to prevent overloading or wastage. In the construction AI can control the heating, cooling and lighting of buildings and in industries, AI can control the energy used and the manner in which it is used. It also has the potential to improve energy storage, management of the renewable energy generation on the grid, and minimize the need for fossil fuel-based back up power(Raihan et al 2023). Thanks to the real-time data processing and flexibility in handling changes in conditions, AI and ML are fundamental in developing intelligent, effective, and sustainable energy solutions.

1.3 Purpose and Scope of the paper

The purpose of this paper is to discuss the importance of AI and ML in transforming energy optimization within different fields. This paper will give a general background on AI and ML in energy systems and the specific applications of AI and ML in power systems, renewable energy systems, smart buildings, and industries. It will also explore the various optimization strategies that are used in detail, including, predictive modeling, reinforcement learning, and deep learning methods to show how these strategies can manage various issues including varying energy consumption, grid reliability, and energy conservation. Also, the paper will look at the use of AI and ML in energy systems and discuss real-life examples of AI energy efficiency improvement. It will also talk about the advantages, opportunities and drawback of such technologies, the reasons why they have not gained broader acceptance. To achieve the objective of this paper, the following areas are covered; The future of AI and ML in energy management and its impact on efficiency and the environment in different industries. Last, this paper will discuss the likely future trends and research areas in the development of AI and energy optimization with emphasis on quantum computing, IoT and edge computing. Lastly, this paper seeks to establish a comprehensive analysis of the role of AI and ML in addressing energy issues around the world and create a better world of energy. Discussing both the theoretical and the pragmatic sides of the paper, the author will demonstrate how AI is capable of revolutionizing the energy sector on an international level.

2. ENERGY SYSTEMS AND OPTIMIZATION ISSUES

2.1 Description of Different Types of Energy Systems

Energy systems are complex structures with the purpose of generating, storing and providing energy in different sectors. These systems can also be of different structure and functionality of the system but all the systems aim at maximization of energy generation and utilization(Nishanth et al 2023). Key types of energy systems include:

1.Power Grids: Power grid can be defined as an electrical system that is used to deliver electricity from producers to consumers. It has the generation, transmission and distribution subsectors. Transmission systems are in charge of supporting power delivery requirements, demand and supply fluctuations, and generation. Power grid optimization is important for enhancing stability of the power grid and reducing power loss from one point to another.

2.Renewable Energy Systems: These systems tap renewable power from natural resources including solar, wind, geothermal and hydro energy. Renewable energy systems are different from conventional energy systems which include coal or natural gas energy systems; renewable energy systems depend on natural events for instance, light from the sun or wind to produce energy. Although renewable systems are environmentally friendly, they have drawbacks like intermittency and the problem of incorporating the new systems into power networks as existing networks are developed for stable, consistent fossil fuel generation(Mallek et al 2021).

3.Smart Buildings: Smart buildings incorporate modern technology to detect and regulate the use of energy in order to optimize its usage. Smart controls coordinate heating, ventilation, air conditioning (HVAC), lighting, and other high-energy systems. Energy tracking can be done using IoT devices and sensors and with machine learning algorithms to predict and control energy usage based on occupancy, time, and weather(Maheshwaran, T et al 2024).

4.Manufacturing Systems: Energy management in production refers to the process of controlling energy throughout production activities including production line, equipment and lighting. Since many industrial processes are energy demanding, increasing the efficiency of such systems may lead to considerable economic and environmental gains. AI and ML can scan data coming from the machinery and sensors and look for areas that can be improved, including production schedules, and energy consumption in real-time.

2.2 Key Challenges in Energy Optimization

While energy systems are essential for modern life, they face several challenges when it comes to optimization:

1.Fluctuating Demand: Energy demand is not constant, it fluctuates depending with the day and times of the year. Such fluctuations mean that it is almost impossible to balance supply and demand for energy. In order to anticipate and control such variations, elaborate forecasting tools and performance tracking mechanisms are necessary since energy generation has to follow these trends to avoid supply or utilization gaps.

2.Integration of Renewables: Wind and solar type of energy is not constant; this is because these two sources of energy are categorized under renewable energy sources. For instance, solar power generation is dependent on sunlight; wind energy on wind speeds. These renewables can be easily integrated into existing utility grids, which are generally designed for constant power production, and this can cause grid fluctuations if not well controlled. The potential of AI and ML is in forecasting renewable energy generation, managing distribution of load on the electricity grid, and incorporating energy storage systems to ensure that variability of renewable energy is minimized.

Figure 1. **Challenges in Energy Optimization**

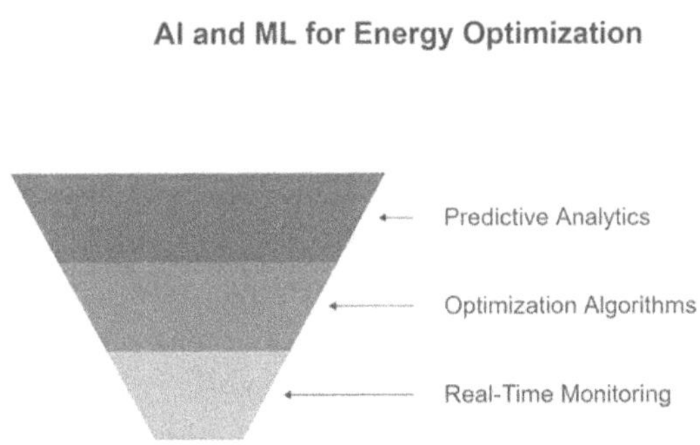

3.Energy Storage Issues: Energy storage solutions like batteries are used to store excess energy produced at any given time for use at other time when there is little or no production. However, existing solutions of energy storage suffer from several limitations including storage capacity, storage efficiency and cost.

It is critical to address the question of how complex storage technologies can enhance energy systems and, in particular, those involving renewable power.

4.Grid Stability: Keeping the grid stable is never an easy task, especially due to the current development of complicated modern grids incorporating distributed generation (such as rooftop solar PV systems) and intermittent generation (such as wind and solar power). AI and ML can assist by predicting the load on the grid, controlling the distribution of energy, as well as identifying possible faults or outages.

2.3 Traditional Approaches to Energy Management and Their Limitations

Conventional energy management strategies are mainly based on the use of switches, estimated models that use previous data, and a centralized system of command. These methods have been effective to an extent but come with limitations:

1.Limited Flexibility: Conventional systems are in most cases inflexible and cannot easily accommodate changes in the supply or the demand for energy. For instance, the grids that rely on fossil fuel generation are expected to maintain a constant power output, which cannot be applied to renewable power sources.

2.Inefficiencies in Real-Time Decision Making: In traditional methods, responses to variations in energy demand take a long time hence they create problems like over generation or power rationing. These systems are not able to fine tune the energy consumption based on data that is available in real time, meaning that they have a low potential for reducing wastage.

3.High Operational Costs: In traditional energy systems the central point of generation is usually power stations which are costly to establish and sustain. These systems also experience high transmission losses and energy transmission over these systems takes long distances. Energy storage solutions are also expensive and in most cases ineffective, particularly regarding excess renewable energy.

4.Inability to Leverage Data: Current energy management systems lack optimisation for the available potentials of modern data analysis. With the evolution in the energy consumption the systems are required to handle large amount of raw data of real time to manage the energy production and consumption in an effective manner.

Therefore, while conventional approaches have been useful to a certain extent, they do not work well enough in the context of the emerging distributed, smart, and renewable-based electricity networks. AI and ML present potential solutions of addressing these challenges through facilitating optimisation of energy management through flexibility, adapting and using data.

3. AI AND MACHINE LEARNING FUNDAMENTALS IN ENERGY OPTIMIZATION

Energy systems are growing more efficient and affordable with the help of AI and ML, which bring new techniques for enhancing the performance of energy production. These technologies enable the handling of a huge amount of data in real time, the assessment of energy consumption behavior, the improvement of system efficiency and the incorporation of renewable energy systems. The following is a brief of the most important AI and ML approaches applied in energy optimization.

3.1 Overview of AI and ML Techniques Used for Energy Optimization

AI and ML refer to a number of methods intended for the automation of decision making, for the prediction of the result as well as for the improvement of the process. In the context of energy systems these techniques try to solve problems like varying demand, supply, energy storage, and the stability of the grid(Fayyazi et al 2023).

Figure 2. **AI and ML for Energy Optimization**

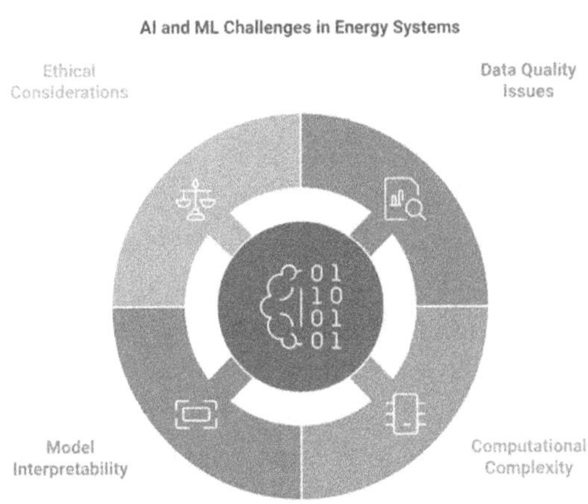

Predictive Analytics: Energy demand and consumption and generation can also be predicted using historical data, AI and ML. This in turn enhances load balancing in the power systems and energy storage systems(Yamini et al 2024).
Optimization Algorithms: AI and ML use optimization methods to improve energy usage, minimize wastage and operating expenses. Such methods are linear programming, genetic algorithms, and particle swarm optimization, which can optimize energy distribution and consumption.
Real-Time Monitoring and Control: The machine learning can control energy systems in real time, and analyze information from sensors to optimize energy parameters.

These techniques offer the basic knowledge for developing more intelligent energy systems that are flexible to the current circumstances, economical in energy consumption and effective in incorporating renewable sources.

3.2 Supervised vs Unsupervised Learning Methods for Energy Prediction and Management

The common categorization of machine learning methods is in to the supervised and unsupervised learning with the former being more applicable in the energy prediction and management domain.

Supervised Learning: Supervised learning is the process through which the algorithm is trained on the labeled data and the input data is provided with the corresponding output data. This approach is especially applied in energy prediction, in which information about the energy consumption in the past, the temperature, and other factors can be used to predict energy demand or determine the optimal system functioning. Some of the most widely used methods used in supervised learning are regression analysis, decision trees and support vector machines(Anita, M et al 2024). These techniques assist in predicting the energy demand and give information that will assist in controlling energy usage in the real world. For instance, supervised learning models can be trained to estimate the time of day or week when demand for electricity is likely to be high due to weather conditions or time of the day among others. This enables utilities to plan for a period of high demand and then be in a position to respond appropriately by increasing supply(Nithya et al 2023).
Unsupervised Learning: On the other hand, unsupervised learning deals with data that has no labels or targets that are to be predicted. This method is useful to find out trends or groups of energy data that might not be distinguishable easily. One can use k-means or hierarchical clustering to cluster similar energy

consumption pattern to enhance segmentation and the use of targeted energy saving measures. Unsupervised learning can also be used for pattern recognition, for example, to find out that the power consumption is higher than normal, meaning that there is some sort of inefficiency or failure in the equipment.

In energy optimization, unsupervised learning can be used to discover more patterns in energy data of different buildings or areas so that utility companies can deliver energy saving solutions more appropriately.

3.3 Reinforcement Learning for Energy System Control

Reinforcement learning (RL) is a type of machine learning method in which an agent learns to make decisions during the interaction with an environment, based on the received rewards and penalties. In energy optimization, RL can be applied in real control and dynamic control and decision making since it can be trained to work under changing conditions and learn from its previous actions. For instance, in the smart grid management, reinforcement learning may be employed to control the distribution of electricity balancing between supply and demand. The agent (control system) is able to update grid parameters autonomously using real-time data, as the energy produced from renewable sources, forecasted weather and consumption. RL has been applied in real-time pricing, demand response, and management of distributed generations and storage systems such as solar PV and Battery. The strength of RL in energy systems is the capacity to make decisions independently based on the data acquired and enhance with time to enhance energy management efficiency.

3.4 Deep Learning and Neural Networks for Modeling Complex Energy Systems

Machine learning is a broader category of artificial intelligence and deep learning is a technique that employs multi layered artificial neural networks to learn relationships in the data. These networks are more useful when working with high dimensionality, non-linear data which is typical with the modeling of energy systems.

Neural Networks: Neural networks are modelled from the actual human nerves system and its working. It refers to a combination of layers of connected nodes where each node is responsible for node computing and passing data to the next layers(Jayasutha, D et al 2024). In energy optimization, the neural networks can be employed to simulate the energy consumption dependence on different parameters including time, weather condition and people occupancy in smart buildings. Neural networks can be used to train on large datasets in order to identify patterns that will help in managing energy, in forecasting the highest energy usage and in making suggestions for energy improvements.

Deep Learning: Mainly deep learning networks contain a number of hidden layers which make it easier for the network to be able to learn abstract features from the data. These models are particularly useful when dealing with massive data structures characteristic of the energy systems, such as when modeling renewable energy generation or grid operations. For instance, deep learning can estimate the energy production from renewable sources such as wind and solar, despite their randomness, by training from prior generation data, the weather and other factors. Furthermore, deep learning can be used in fault diagnosis since energy consumption data may contain signs of equipment failure or inefficiencies so that maintenance can be planned in advance.

AI and ML are disrupting the energy system since they make it possible to predict energy use more accurately, manage it efficiently, and optimize current and future use. Supervised and unsupered learning for energy prediction and anomaly detection, and reinforcement learning for dynamic control of the system. Neural network and deep learning algorithms are highly effective in managing high-dimensional data and energy systems. Combined, these techniques offer a sound methodology for managing and controlling energy usage, enhancing power quality, and incorporating renewable generation assets.

4. AI AND ML APPLICATIONS IN DIFFERENT SECTORS OF ENERGY

AI and ML have shown the ability to disrupt the energy industry in multiple ways and provide new solutions for enhanced energy management, increased efficiency, and the integration of renewable energy. Below are the key applications of AI and ML in four critical energy sectors: smart grids, renewable energy, smart buildings and homes and manufacturing and industries.

4.1 Smart Grids

AI-Driven Demand Response and Load Forecasting: Smart grids use AI and ML to forecast demand rates for power and balance the grid's flow. Consumption data of previous years, weather conditions, and social, economical and other factors can be input to the AI algorithms that can predict the demand at a particular time with a good level of precision. This helps the utilities to be in a position to be able to manage the energy supply needs and this will help reduce the cases of energy outages since the energy will be available when required. There are also demand response programs based on AI that can also control energy usage in real time and convince consumers to decrease their usage during certain time periods or shift their usage to other periods of time that are not as demanding in terms of supply and demand.

Predictive Maintenance for Grid Infrastructure: It is clear that the state of the grid is important for continuing to provide energy to the population. AI and ML can help optimize grid reliability because equipment faults can be detected before they happen. Similar to cars, where patterns of wear and tear, corrosion or faults can be detected from sensor data of transformers, power lines and other components through machine learning algorithms. Predictive maintenance reduces the probability of unexpected outages and lowers repair expenses by only scheduling maintenance where it is required to increase the Grid asset's life cycle.

4.2 Renewable Energy

Wind and Solar Energy Forecasting Using AI: Volatility is one of the main issues regarding integration of renewables into the grid. Weather conditions are prime drivers of solar and wind power generation and a precise prediction is very much required for maintaining the grid. AI and ML models can enhance the accuracy of the output of renewable energy by forecasting by using data and statistics of the previous months and years, climatic conditions, sensors among others. AI improves load forecasting and thus allows grid operators to optimize renewable energy and minimize dependence on traditional generators, such as fossil fuel plants.

Optimal Integration of Renewables into the Grid: Much like wind and solar energy, the use of VREs has to be well managed in order to avoid problems with system stability in existing grids. AI can help in dispatch of renewable energy by predicting availability and also vary the load depending on the grid. Also, it can also help in the design of integrated systems that will incorporate renewable energy resources with the storage system and other resources such as batteries. AI also optimizes the use of renewable energy which reduces the amount of back up generation from fossil fuel.

4.3 Smart Buildings and Homes

Energy Consumption Prediction and Optimization: In smart buildings and home, AI is applied in forecasting energy use depending on factors like occupancy, time of the day, and outdoor climate. In the light of data gathered, AI helps in improving efficiency of energy usage in buildings and subsequently helps in lowering energy costs. For example, heating, lighting, and appliances usage patterns can be provided and AI can control heating, lighting, or turning on appliances only when necessary.

AI-Based HVAC Control and Automation: Heating, ventilation and air conditioning (HVAC) systems are major energy loads in buildings. HVAC control using artificial intelligence can also help in the proper use of energy as it can control heating and cooling depending on the occupancy of rooms, outside temperature, and time of day. It can also predict the times when heating or cooling is going to be needed, hence minimize energy wastage by only turning on heating or cooling systems when necessary. Furthermore, AI can incrementally learn from the sensor data and optimize the performance of HVAC and reduce energy usage.

4.4 Manufacturing and Industry

AI-Based Energy Optimization in Industrial Processes: In industrial applications, artificial intelligence and machine learning are used to determine appropriate usage of energy in production. It can also predict the faults in the machines, equipment and energy meters to detect the inefficiency in the production line. When familiar with patterns of energy usage, AI can recommend changes, for instance, status of machines, changes in working hours, or even moving energy usage to other times that are cheap. This approach results into saving on operational expenses and minimizing on the effects on the natural environment.

Predictive Analytics for Energy Efficiency in Factories: The application of AI in predictive analytics means that energy wastage in factories can be foreseen based on past data and data coming from the sensors in the factory. For instance, AI can forecast when a number of appliances will need more energy because of deterioration or a defect, and fix it before it fails. Moreover, the presented machine learning models can predict the energy demand in function of the production timetable and regulate the energy consumption. This not only contributes to improving energy efficiency but also affects production scheduling and thus the management of resources.

AI and ML solutions are intensive in the energy industry because they offer innovative approaches to efficiency and optimization. In smart grids, AI aids demand management and prediction, as well as equipment maintenance, to maintain effective grid performance. In renewable energy, AI optimizes predictions of the energy production and helps to incorporate renewable sources into the grid. In smart buildings and smart homes, AI-based systems improve energy management and HVAC control improving the comfort while at the same time cutting down on the expenses. Last but not least, in manufacturing AI is used to enhance the use of energy in production processes and enhance the manufacturing energy efficiency. In this way, AI and ML are opening new opportunities for energy sector development while overcoming its specific problems.

5. OPTIMIZATION TECHNIQUES IN AI AND ML FOR ENERGY

AI and ML have multiple optimization heuristics for improving the effectiveness, dependability, and cost-effectiveness of energy systems. These techniques assist in demand side management, connection of renewable energy, minimization of expenses, and maintaining a stability of the grid. In the following section, we present several critical methods with applications to energy systems, namely predictive modeling, optimization algorithms, reinforcement learning, and deep learning.

5.1 Predictive Modeling

Regression Techniques for Energy Load and Demand Forecasting: Forecasting is an important part of the energy saving process since load and demand are used for keeping the stability of the energy grid as well as for energy generation. Regression analysis, which is one of the most used statistical methods in machine learning, is commonly applied to the demand forecasting. It entails the creation of a link between the dependent variables (energy consumption) and the independent variables which include the weather condition, the time of the day, and the past demand.

Simple prediction is mostly done using linear regression while for more complex relations like polynomial relations or support vector relation (SVR), other methods are applied. These models are trained on historical data and therefore are very accurate in estimating future energy consumption. This aids the utilities in managing their demand side, the usage of power, and the amount of back up power that is likely to be used.

Moreover, other models such as time series models including the ARIMA (Auto-Regressive Integrated Moving Average) model can be used to capture trends and seasonality of the energy consumption which improve the accuracy of the predictions.

5.2 Optimization Algorithms

Genetic Algorithms: Genetic algorithms (GAs) are search heuristics employed in energy systems and based on natural selection. GAs are especially applicable to energy scheduling and optimization problems, as for example, which type of energy to use, when to store it or how to operate the grid. The algorithm mimics the natural evolution process through choosing the best solutions (individuals), and then creating new solutions (offspring) and then choosing the best solutions for the next generation.

In energy scheduling, GAs can be useful in distributing the resources in the various generation types, such that the cost is low while supply meets the demand. This kind of approach is especially useful where the answers are not simple and the number of potential scenarios is vast, for instance, including renewable energy systems with traditional power stations.

Particle Swarm Optimization (PSO): Particle swarm optimization is another optimization technique that is derived from natural world by simulating the behaviour of the birds or fish. PSO is applied to identify the best solution in a large search space where particles which represent potential solutions move on their own experiences and the experiences of other particles. This method is widely used in energy scheduling to determine the distribution of energy in the grid based on load flow, generation cost and availability of renewable resources.

PSO has also been well applied to the case of smart grid for managing the charging and discharging cycles of energy storage systems to reduce costs while meeting the demand of high energy at certain periods.

5.3 Reinforcement Learning for Real-Time Optimization

Reinforcement Learning (RL) for Dynamic Energy Pricing and Grid Management: Reinforcement learning is one of the machine learning techniques where an agent learns to make decisions based on experience from the environment and this experience is in form of a reward or punishment. As has been observed, RL is particularly suitable for real-time energy optimization, which is characterized by constantly varying conditions and requires making decisions on the fly.

In dynamic energy pricing, RL can play the role of setting the right electricity prices on the fly so as to meet the demand and supply. The RL agent makes use of past prices and consumption data to decide on correct price points that will encourage the consumer to conserve energy or use it at different time, to make sure that the demand is always met with supply. Regarding grid management, RL can be employed to control the operation of power grids, as well as the distribution of energy generated from diverse sources, including renewable resources for maintaining stable grid operations.

5.4 Deep Learning Approaches

Neural Networks for High-Dimensional Energy Data Analysis: Neural networks are a particularly useful type of deep learning as they can model high dimensional data in energy systems. These models are made up of a number of interconnected nodes that work in a way as the human brain. Neural networks are used in energy optimization because they are capable of processing large amounts of data from different sources including sensors, smart meters and weather forecasts in order to identify patterns and trends.

For instance, the neural networks can forecast the energy usage in buildings by taking into account some parameters such as people presence, time, weather conditions, and past usage. This makes it possible for better energy consumption predictions which in turn makes it possible to determine the best way to manage HVAC systems, lighting and other energy using devices.

AI in Fault Detection and Anomaly Detection: Other applications of AI models are in fault detection and anomaly detection in the energy systems using deep learning networks. Using historical and real time data deep learning models can learn and recognize anomalous patterns that suggest system failures or inefficiencies in energy infrastructure. For instance, a neural network could look at power transformers or wind turbines data to identify certain mechanical defects before they lead to a breakdown. This minimizes time that energy systems are off-line, decreases maintenance expenses, and guarantees the dependability of the systems.

Therefore, the optimization techniques like the predictive modeling, the genetic algorithms, the particle swarm optimization the reinforcement learning the deep learning is revolutionizing the management of energy systems. These AI and ML approaches help in real-time decision making, improve forecasting and manage resource use resulting to better, cheaper and efficient energy systems. With the addition of renewable resources and 'smart' systems into energy networks, these approaches will become critical as grids become progressively complex in the future.

6. AI-DRIVEN RENEWABLE ENERGY INTEGRATION

The proposed use of renewable energy resources in the power grid systems has its advantages and disadvantages. Wind and solar are good examples of renewable energy sources, which, however, have fluctuations in their production and hence need management systems to regulate their supply of energy. Due to the importance of these challenges, AI and ML are applied to handle DERs, smart energy storage, and hybrid energy systems. In the next sections, we analyze these applications of AI in integrating renewable energy systems.

6.1 AI for Efficient Management of Distributed Energy Resources (DERs)

DERs refers to small-scale generation and storage units that are installed in proximity to loads they serve, such as photovoltaic, wind power, battery storage, and CHP. As much as DERs provide the following advantages; increased energy independence, reduced transmission losses among others, their integration into the grid demands an efficient management technique to ensure the stability of the grid. AI plays a key role in handling these resources because it controls their functioning in real-time mode and contributes to the grid. Data collected from different DERs such as weather data, load demand data, and performance data of the system are used by machine learning algorithms. This data allows AI systems to forecast the supply and efficiency of solar and wind, and optimize DER control and usage. For instance, AI can estimate the amount of energy that solar panels are capable of producing depending on the weather conditions and manage battery storage systems to charge excess energy during times of generation. Likewise AI algorithms can coordinate the distribution of energy from small wind farms or solar panels or residential solar systems and ensure that the energy is delivered effectively to the grid or consumers. Thus, AI optimises the interconnection of DERs with the grid, and thus, optimally integrates renewable resources into the grid, reducing the dependence on fossil resources. AI assists in the proper usage of DERs with central power generation systems, making the grids more sustainable and less emitting carbon.

6.2 Intelligent Energy Storage Management Using ML

Energy storage systems especially batteries are important in managing the supply and demand side especially when it comes to renewable energy source that is sometimes unpredictable. However, the management and utilisation of storage is not very easy and needs sophisticated control mechanisms of charging and discharging depending on the real time grid. In managing energy storage systems, machine learning is applied to forecast when and to what extent energy should be stored or discharged. Using the data collected from the past, ML algorithms predict the future energy demand, and other factors such as the current energy prices and the weather forecast used in coming up with the most appropriate storage schedule. Capturing knowledge from the past, ML models are capable of defining the relations between energy consumption and optimal moments for charging or discharging batteries to achieve highest levels of efficiency and lowest costs. For example, during the day when there is plenty of solar energy, storage facilities can collect excess energy for use in the evening when renewable generation is scarce. ML can assist with the proper usage of energy storage in managing load variation and limiting the requirement for fossil fuel-based peaking plants. Also, ML can forecast battery health and set the most appropriate maintenance schedule. From the performance data of batteries, the ML models can predict when they are degrading or failing, which will allow for timely servicing or replacement of the battery thereby increasing the useful life of the storage system.

6.3 ML-Based Optimization of Hybrid Energy Systems

The integration of renewable energy sources with conventional sources of power generation, storage systems is known as hybrid energy systems. The use of multiple sources of power also makes the problem of managing the grid more complex, because each type of power source is characterized by different availability, reliability, and cost. Machine learning is used in regulating the use of hybrid systems by identifying the best combination of energy types to use at any one time. Recent advancements in ML algorithms can learn from all the sources of information which include the amount of solar radiation, wind velocity and previous energy generation trends to decide the most appropriate dispatch of the energy. The aim is to reduce cost and increase the share of RES and at the same time maintaining the balance of supply and demand in the power system. For instance, in the solar power system integrated with battery energy storage and natural gas, the ML algorithms can identify the optimal time for using solar energy, the times when the excess energy should be stored in the batteries, and when the electricity is needed, and natural gas should be used. These include issues to do with the availability of solar energy, availability of batteries for storage, and demand for energy in the grid. The system adapts from previous data to create an optimal decision-making environment to utilize energy optimally and at an economical rate. ML can also play a role in design and planning of hybrid systems by evaluating various possibilities and determining the most suitable combination of systems for power supply, storage and reserve power. Using load profiles, energy generation forecasts, cost structures, etc., energy planners can use ML to design hybrid systems that are sustainable in terms of costs and the environment.

The application of artificial intelligence is revolutionizing the renewable energy systems integration including distributed energy resources, energy storage and hybrid energy systems. Through the use of machine learning, energy systems can be enhanced through enhancing the use of renewable energy, storage systems and the overall reliability of energy systems. This means that AI & ML will remain instrumental in facilitating the growth of cleaner forms of energy in the future energy systems of the world. These technologies offer the means for effective incorporation of renewable energy into the grid and minimization of the use of fossil fuel.

7. CHALLENGES AND LIMITATIONS IN AI AND ML FOR ENERGY OPTIMIZATION

However, there are several issues and constraints that have to be considered in order to unleash the full potential of AI and ML applications to the energy systems. Such challenges extend over the aspects of data quality, computation, model interpretability, and ethical issues. In the next sub-section, we expand on these important issues.

Figure 3. Challenges and Limitations in AI and ML for Energy Optimization

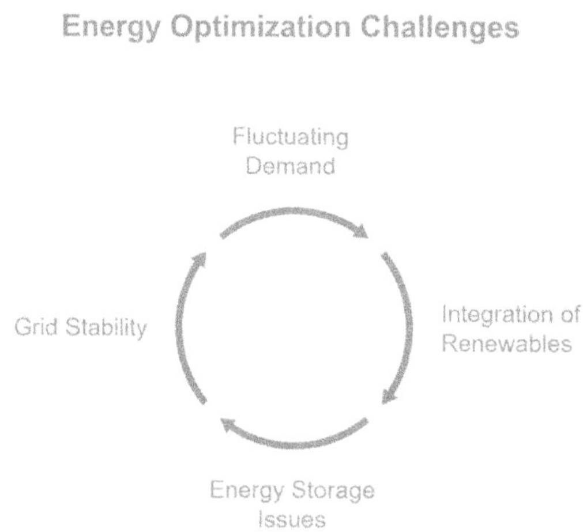

7.1 Data Challenges: Lack of High-Quality Data, Privacy, and Security Issues

One of the main difficulties regarding the integration of AI and ML for the optimization of energy consumption is the data issue. AI and ML models utilize big, good quality data in operation and training. In the energy sector, however, data is often scarce, limited or noisy. Real-time energy consumption data from smart meters, sensors, or grid operators may be erroneous or may contain outliers, and thus the predictions and optimization may be poor. Also, energy data is generally disaggregate, that is, energy data is accumulated and analyzed frequently because energy consumption is optimally managed in real-time. Lack of data capture mechanism, low quality data, and data gaps can greatly hinder the application of AI systems in producing accurate energy forecasts or in making sound decisions. Another challenge of energy systems is privacy and security since most of these systems deal with large amounts of personal and operational data. In smart grids and smart buildings, information that may be considered personal about the consumer, their habits, their energy consumption and possibly geographical location may be gathered. Protecting this data from being accessed or used by people who should not have access to it is important for building consumer trust and for meeting requirements of GDPR and similar laws. Also, the protection of AI and ML structures in the power industry is crucial as well. Security issues can make energy systems unreliable; this is more so in instances where the systems are controlled from a distance or use decentralized systems that interconnect. It is thus important to have tight security measures against hacking and data breaches that could lead to disruption of energy operations.

7.2 Computational Complexity and Scalability in Real-Time systems

Deep learning algorithms in the field of AI and ML demand considerable computational power. High complexity of models requires vast amounts of data and training high complexity models with large datasets time consuming. This becomes a problem in real-time energy optimization where such parameters cannot be easily predicted. Smart grids are a type of energy systems that need to make decisions quickly to change energy distribution. The need to process data and produce decision-making information in real-time is critical to managing the stability of the grid and energy usage. However, just as AI models themselves are scaled-up to accommodate the data that energy systems generate, particularly in the context of DERs and RE sources, there is an added layer of challenge. As energy systems are getting even more interlinked and based on higher amounts of data, the need for algorithms that can be used on large data sets and in real-time increases. Lack of appropriate scalability in the algorithms may cause delays in achieving the optimum solution or, on the contrary, make incorrect decisions that will affect energy supply and costs.

7.3 Interpretability and Explainability of AI Models

AI and ML models, particularly, deep learning techniques are described as 'black box' models. However, these models can come up with fairly good predictions of the actual results while their decision-making processes are not very transparent. In energy systems, it is essential to know what, how, and why a model is doing something, particularly when the outcomes may alter the structure of the electrical power grid, the price of energy, or consumers' behavior. This aspect also has several challenges; first, human operators need to trust the AI decisions made; second, there are issues of compliance; and third, the issues of liability. To this end, operators require the logical justification for AI-based recommendations as the basis for decision making to conform to the systems' requirements such as energy costs, grid stability, or environmental effects. Lack of transparency makes it difficult to assess the performance of the model, check the reliability of its results, or identify possible problems. There is a growing research into "explainable AI" which is an attempt to make the models more understandable of how they make their decisions. However, these methods are still under development, and it is still problematic to achieve an optimal level of model interpretability.

7.4 Ethical Considerations in AI-Driven Energy Optimization

The use of artificial intelligence in energy optimization serves the following important ethical questions. The first of the challenges is the problem of prejudice in AI models. Bias can be made by having a preconceived notion in data, the algorithms used, or the decisions made by peoples' choices. For example, if data used to train algorithms powering energy optimization models is biased, the resultant model will be making decisions that are prejudicial to specific groups such as the poor or ethnic minorities. This could result in energy apartheid, energy apartheid rates which are high for those who can barely afford the energy or even unfair energy tariffs. Furthermore, the deployment of AI in the energy sector may lead to automation of employment opportunities with risks of job losses in areas like the energy grid management, energy generation and maintenance. On the positive side, AI can help increase efficiency and decrease costs but there needs to be caution taken to not leave workers in the dust during the shift to automatization. Education and retraining would be critical requirements that would enable the workforce prepare for new roles in light of the energy sector transitioned towards artificial intelligence. Last but not the least, AI-based energy systems are needed to be designed with a view to having positive social implications. For example, optimizing energy generation for cost reduction could at times lead to higher reliance on fossil energy sources as the algorithms would favour cost more than environment. Issues of sustainability and environmental impact should therefore inform the design and deployment of AI solutions in energy optimization.

The application of AI and ML in energy optimization has high potential in terms of increasing efficiency and decreasing costs of the transition towards a sustainable energy system. Nonetheless, there are still issues like data quality issue, computational issue, issue of interpretability of the models, and issues of ethical concerns. Solving these problems will mean further work on making AI more transparent, scalable, and equitable to lead the energy industry towards a sustainable future.

8. FUTURE TRENDS AND RESEARCH DIRECTIONS

AI is already being used to improve energy optimization, and there are already new trends and new paths for research in this area. The primary areas of interest are: how to combine AI with other rising technologies such as quantum computing, IoT, and edge computing; how to employ AI for the optimization of energy storage and use of EVs; how to design environmentally friendly AI models; and what appropriate public policies and regulations are required for the effective AI implementation. These trends are expected to redefine energy management in the future as follows.

8.1 Integration of AI with Emerging Technologies for Energy Optimization

A great future trend is the interaction of AI with new technologies and their trends such as quantum computing, IoT, edge computing. These technologies have the potential to greatly improve the current ability of AI for energy optimization.

Quantum computing is anticipated to disrupt the energy optimization frontier by solving tough optimization problems that classical computers could not. Quantum computers have the ability to analyze large quantities of data and provide information to an AI that can make real time decisions for energy systems that are constantly fluctuating and need to adapt quickly. For instance, quantum algorithms could extend the efficiency in the distribution of energy in smart grids, and how they are distributed across various forms of energy. Moreover, quantum computing can speed up the machine learning models that in turn might be useful for solving the problems related to energy demand forecasting and grid management.

IoT is currently a driver of smart cities and efficient energy consumption, and AI integration will only become increasingly important in the future. Smart meters, sensors, and connected appliances put in place in homes, offices, industries, generate big data that AI can utilize to get real-time energy usage, predict demand, and enhance the grid. Through the integration of AI with IoT, there are chances of enhancing energy systems as being able to adapt to the current situation. For instance, AI could manage smart temperature regulators, switches, and facilities utilizing data from IoT sensors to reduce energy consumption while maintaining comfort.

Edge computing supports AI because it deals with data at the edge to minimize response latency and enhance decision-making. In energy optimisation, this means that energy systems can quickly reallocate energy distribution or energy storage without having to wait for cloud computing or servers. For example, edge computing could allow local energy grids to decide on their own utilizing artificial intelligence and machine learning algorithms, as they control power generation and consumption.

8.2 AI for Optimizing Energy Storage and Electric Vehicles

Since the use of renewable energy such as solar and wind energy increases, efficient methods of storing the energy will be vital. The use of AI can be highly effective in enhancing these systems by factors such as energy demand forecasting, control of charging/discharging cycles and storage capacity utilization. Energy generation trends can also be predicted by the machine learning models, which helps the smart storage system know when to discharge or when to store energy in the system. In the context of the electric vehicles, AI will play a progressively significant role in charging networks and grid management. Real-time usage patterns, weather and energy availability can be used to forecast the demand of EV charging so that the grid is not over burdened by the energy that EVs will require. Finally, AI can be applied to vehicle-to-grid (V2G) systems in which EVs can send energy back to the grid to improve grid reliability and storage capability.

8.3 Development of Sustainable AI Models for Energy-Efficient Systems

It becomes apparent that there is a growing requirement for sustainable AI models for energy systems as AI technologies are integrated into them. Training the AI models can be computationally very demanding, which may at times negate the energy efficiency that is realized through AI optimization. In response, researchers are interested in creating new models of AI that consume less power, need fewer resources and data, but are still effective. These approaches comprise design of new energy efficient machine learning algorithms that can be trained on the limited data, utilize less power and offer quicker solutions. Also, there are active attempts in the design of AI models that are low power consuming, thus could be deployed in decentralized or remote energy systems, for example, in off-grid systems or in energy-plus buildings.

8.4 Policy and Regulatory Considerations for AI in Energy Management

Mainly, the integration of AI into the energy systems will call for new and innovative policies and regulations. To that end, governments and regulatory authorities will have to guarantee both the efficiency and the integrity of AI in energy management. Some key areas that require attention include:

Data privacy and security: Since energy systems are set to become more integrated and data-dependent, protection of personal and business information will be critical. Challenges for the regulation are to define how data is gathered, processed, and used by AI while preserving the consumer's rights.

Standardization: AI technologies and systems employed in diverse energy fields should conform to standard and specifications. This is even so since energy systems are becoming more elaborate and integrated, with many players involved in the process.
Ethical and equitable energy distribution: AI systems need to be implemented in such a way that they do not favor one group over another, when it comes to energy optimization. The policies should therefore seek to provide equality in access to clean and affordable energy for all population groups especially those most vulnerable.
Support for innovation: It will be important for policy makers to encourage innovation in AI for energy optimization while at the same time ensure that the technologies that result meet broader societal objectives including sustainability, access to energy and reduction of emissions. Governments should support the needed funding for the research and encourage the creation of green AI solutions.

The future of AI in energy optimization looks promising and holds something new and interesting for people. The combination of AI with future technologies including quantum computing, IoT, and edge computing will pave way for better energy solutions. Moreover, application in energy storage and electric vehicles where AI will be instrumental in the shift to a low-carbon economy will be enhanced. The creation of sustainable AI models and strong policy will be key to ensure AI driven energy optimization is positive for society. As AI advances, it can play a transformational role in future power generation, distribution and usage, leading to improved sustainability, efficiency and reliability of the energy systems.

9. CONCLUSION

Artificial intelligence and machine learning are now considered key to the management of energy systems and have shifted the energy optimization paradigm in many sectors. The recommendations made in this paper focus on the use of AI and ML in energy efficiency, renewable energy integration, and grid reliability. AI is a valuable tool for handling large volumes of data, predicting energy demand, and managing consumption because of the many challenges in today's energy markets. AI has been most useful in improving power grids, smart buildings, renewable energy interconnection, and industrial applications. AI, through the use of predictive modeling, reinforcement learning and deep learning make it easier to predict, respond to the demand and make the system stronger. Another benefit has also been realized in the use of AI solutions to minimize the use of energy and therefore costs by enhancing energy systems. Nonetheless, further work and improvement is needed to surmount the obstacles that still exist for AI-based energy optimization, including data quality, AI scalability, and interpretability. Additional developments in quantum computing, IoT, edge computing, and green AI algorithms will be instrumental in meeting these challenges and opening up new horizons for improvement. There is a great potential to affect sustainability and the efficiency of energy in the world with the help of AI and ML. With the advancement of AI technologies, they will be instrumental in the transformation of smarter, cleaner, efficient and cheaper energy systems. Using AI, the efficiency of renewable energy, energy storage, and grid management can help the world achieve climate objectives and decrease CO2 emissions. Finally, both AI and ML are to be the key enabling technologies in the development of the sustainable, resilient, and efficient energy future.

REFERENCES

Anita, M., Ambhika, C., & Anish, T. P. (2024). Exploring the Landscape of Artificial Intelligence in Healthcare Applications. In *AI Healthcare Applications and Security, Ethical, and Legal Considerations* (pp. 29–48). IGI Global.

Boopathi, S. (2024). Energy Cascade Conversion System and Energy-Efficient Infrastructure. In *Sustainable Development in AI, Blockchain, and E-Governance Applications* (pp. 47-71). IGI Global. DOI: 10.4018/979-8-3693-1722-8.ch004

Fayyazi, M., Sardar, P., Thomas, S. I., Daghigh, R., Jamali, A., Esch, T., Kemper, H., Langari, R., & Khayyam, H. (2023). Artificial intelligence/machine learning in energy management systems, control, and optimization of hydrogen fuel cell vehicles. *Sustainability (Basel)*, *15*(6), 5249. DOI: 10.3390/su15065249

Gaur, A. S., Raghuvanshi, C. S., & Sharan, H. O. (2024). Smart Prediction Farming Using Deep Learning and AI Techniques. In *Sustainable Development in AI, Blockchain, and E-Governance Applications* (pp. 152-170). IGI Global. DOI: 10.4018/979-8-3693-1722-8.ch009

Jayasutha, D., Prabhu, R. V., Sassirekha, S. M., Maithili, K., Girija, P., & Subramanian, R. S. (2024). Exploring the Intersection of Sustainable Energy, AI, and Ethical Considerations. In *AI Applications for Clean Energy and Sustainability* (pp. 139–160). IGI Global. DOI: 10.4018/979-8-3693-6567-0.ch008

Kumar, P., Ali, I., & Thanki, D. V. (2018). Demand-side management: energy efficiency and demand response. In *Handbook of Research on Power and Energy System Optimization* (pp. 453–479). IGI Global. DOI: 10.4018/978-1-5225-3935-3.ch013

Maheshwaran, T., Muthumarilakshmi, S., Vinoth, N. A. S., Suganya, K., Maheswari, B., & Girija, P. (2024). Securing E-Commerce Strategies With Cloud, Blockchain, AI, and ML. In *Strategies for E-Commerce Data Security: Cloud, Blockchain, AI, and Machine Learning* (pp. 470–500). IGI Global. DOI: 10.4018/979-8-3693-6557-1.ch019

Mallek, M., Euchi, J., & Jerbi, Y. (2021). A review on optimization modeling of hybrid energy systems. *Research Anthology on Clean Energy Management and Solutions*, 71-95.

Marinakis, V. (2020). Big data for energy management and energy-efficient buildings. *Energies*, *13*(7), 1555. DOI: 10.3390/en13071555

Nishanth, J. R., Deshmukh, M. A., Kushwah, R., Kushwaha, K. K., Balaji, S., & Sampath, B. (2023). Particle swarm optimization of hybrid renewable energy systems. In *Intelligent Engineering Applications and Applied Sciences for Sustainability* (pp. 291–308). IGI Global. DOI: 10.4018/979-8-3693-0044-2.ch016

Nithya, T., Kumar, V. N., Gayathri, S., Deepa, S., Varun, C. M., & Subramanian, R. S. (2023, August). A comprehensive survey of machine learning: Advancements, applications, and challenges. In *2023 Second International Conference on Augmented Intelligence and Sustainable Systems (ICAISS)* (pp. 354-361). IEEE. DOI: 10.1109/ICAISS58487.2023.10250547

Raihan, A. (2023). A comprehensive review of artificial intelligence and machine learning applications in energy sector. *Journal of Technology Innovations and Energy*, *2*(4), 1–26. DOI: 10.56556/jtie.v2i4.608

Yamini, B., Ramana, K. V., Nalini, M., Devi, D. C., Maheswari, B., & Siva, S. R. (2024). Customer churn prediction model in enterprises using machine learning. *International Journal of Advanced Technology and Engineering Exploration*, *11*(110), 94.

Chapter 6

Energy Efficient Protocols and Devices in IoT:
Approaches for Sustainable Performance

M. Ezhilvendan
https://orcid.org/0009-0003-3213-1304
Panimalar Engineering College, India

Aniket Gangadharrao Patil
https://orcid.org/0009-0008-5443-648X
MGM's Jawaharlal Nehru Engineering College, India

S. M. Sassirekha
Mailam Engineering College, India

A. Mathankumar
Vel Tech Multi Tech Dr. Rangarajan Dr. Sakunthala Engineering College, India

T. P. Anish
https://orcid.org/0000-0002-4308-9645
R.M.K. College of Engineering and Technology, India

V. Sathya
Vel Tech Rangarajan Dr. Sagunthala R&D Institute of Science and Technology, India

P. Gajalakshmi
Adhiparasakthi Engineering College, India

ABSTRACT

The increased use of IoT devices within various industries has brought into focus the issue of power consumption since many of these devices have limited power sources. The present work offers a survey on energy efficient protocols and devices in IoT, strategies for the energy optimization for IoT devices. It covers technologies, which operate at low power including LowPower WideArea Networks, Bluetooth Low Energy (BLE), and energyefficient Medium Access Control (MAC) protocols. Further, the paper goes deeper into energy efficient hardware design, low power sensing technologies and energy aware data processing methods where edge and

DOI: 10.4018/979-8-3373-0766-4.ch006

Copyright © 2025, IGI Global Scientific Publishing. Copying or distributing in print or electronic forms without written permission of IGI Global Scientific Publishing is prohibited.

fog computing are stressed as a means of minimizing energy expenditure. The survey also includes information on the methods of energy harvesting, routing and network layer protocols for energy saving, the use of machine learning to manage energy. Last, the paper discusses emerging trends in IoT energy efficiency such as 5G, AI, and quantum technology.

1. INTRODUCTION

1.1 Overview of IoT and Its Growing Presence

Internet of Things or IoT refers to a system of physical objects that are connected and exchange information for efficiency in their operations(Madakam et al 2015). This network comprises of sensors, wearables, home appliances, industrial machines, vehicles and more whereby every device is capable of sensing and making decisions. IoT is rapidly growing due to developments in wireless and mobile communication technologies, sensor motilities, data processing, cloud computing, and the internet(Mouha 2021). According to the various forecasts, more than 25 billion IoT devices will be installed throughout the world by 2030, so IoT is expected to bring significant changes in healthcare, logistics, agriculture, smart cities and many other spheres. These devices capture and relay information in real-time and present information that can facilitate efficiency, reduce costs and inform decision making(Mahmoud et al 2015). For instance, in smart homes, IoT devices such as thermostats and lighting systems are interconnected, and they work harmoniously to regulate power usage. In industrial IoT (IIoT), sensors are used to monitor equipment to determine when it needs to be fixed or replaced thereby increasing the equipment's availability while decreasing its costs. But as more and more IoT devices are being developed, energy consumption becomes an issue especially for those devices that are battery operated or require low power to run for an extended period.

1.2 Importance of Energy Efficiency in IoT Devices and Protocols

Energy efficiency is one of the greatest concerns in the IoT context even more so because many of the IoT devices are expected to be independent and to function in areas that are hard to reach or not easily accessible for recharging or battery replacement(Magubane et al 2019). Many components, including sensors, actuators, and microcontrollers, are typically connected to restricted power supplies, including small batteries, energy harvesting systems, or low-energy components. In such cases, efficiency of energy usage is the most critical consideration that can help prolong the life of the gadgets. IoT devices typically have three main activities that consume energy: sensing, transmitting and processing of data (Sobin 2020). The sensing process is the acquisition of data from the environment such as temperature, humidity or motion among others and it is costly in terms of power if not done efficiently. Transmission of data is usually the most consuming activity, primarily when devices use wireless properties to send data over large distances. Lastly, data processing, both at the device level or edge, and cloud needs power to process data and especially for large datasets or complex algorithms. Due to the scarce availability of power resources, it is of paramount importance to minimize energy consumption in these domains for sustainability of IoT systems. As IoT networks expand, the problem of power consumption vs. performance is even more critical. The reduction of energy consumption not only helps to increase the life cycle of the devices but also to minimize the operating costs and improve the general sustainability of IoT networks. In this regard, the design of energy efficient protocols and devices that will consume the least power while delivering high performance is critical.

1.3 Scope of the Paper: Focus on Protocols and Devices Designed for Energy Efficiency

In this paper, the major concern is to review energy efficient protocols and devices in the IoT context. The review will cover a variety of areas, including:

Communication Protocols: In this paper, we consider four types of wireless communication protocols, namely Wi-Fi, BLE, Zigbee, and LoRaWAN, which differ in several aspects related to energy consumption. This paper will also discuss how these protocols have been enhanced to minimize power consumption when using IoT, with LPWANs such as LoRaWAN and NB-IoT particularly highlighted since they are used for high range transmissions while using minimal power.

Device Design: One of the main priorities of energy efficiency is related to IoT devices and their design. This encompasses low power micro controllers, low power sensors, and efficient power control methods. The incorporation of energy scavenging technologies like solar or vibration energy will also be proposed as a replacement for conventional battery operated systems.

Energy-Aware Processing: Computing power is often a very power-hungry component within the IoT devices. This paper will discuss methods of decreasing the power consumption of the processing unit, for example, by utilizing edge computing that allows for data processing within the device and cloud computing that centralizes processing but adds transmission energy costs.

Routing and Network Layer Protocols: In other words, IoT networks should be created in such a way that all the energy demand of the connected devices should be controlled. This section will discuss low power routing protocols for IoT which reduces the power consumption by means of clustering and data aggregation that results in minimum transmission of data over large IoT network.

Therefore, the purpose of this paper is to present a state-of-art survey on the existing and future approaches for improving energy efficiency in IoT devices and protocols. With the growth of IoT, it becomes increasingly important to address the problem of energy efficiency at scale in order to ensure broader practical applicability of these technologies. This paper shall provide an understanding of how efficiency in energy systems is achieved through design, protocols and strategies; it shall also look at the future of this field and the research that might be done in the future.

2. IoT DEVICES AND ENERGY CONSUMPTION CHALLENGES

2.1 Overview of IoT Device Architecture

IoT devices are the main components of the Internet of Things and are used to gather, analyse, and share data in multiple applications(Gupta, B. B., & Quamara 2020). These devices are typically composed of several key components that work together to perform their functions:

Sensors: Sensors are tasked with measurement of the environment by capturing data from it. The physical parameters include temperature, humidity, light, motion, and pressure that they identify. IoT sensors can be very specific depending upon the use and can measure numerous parameters including air quality and moisture in the soil. Sensors may be analog or digital, and their power consumption depends on the rate of data acquisition, resolution and the energy used in the acquisition and transmission of the acquired data.

Actuators: Sensors change the physical value that has been measured into a signal which can be used by the system while actuators change the signal received by the system into a physical action. For instance, in the case of a smart thermostat an actuator may change temperature by regulating heating or cooling system. Mechanical actuators use power when executing mechanical operations and the power used depends on the nature of the tasks accomplished.

Microcontrollers (MCUs): Microcontrollers are the processors of IoT devices, that is, they control the data and make decisions on the actions of the device. MCUs are responsible for the handling of sensor data, controlling of actuator and deciding when to send data over the network. There are different power classifications of MCUs available in the market and power management is one of the most critical issues in IoT devices' longevity. They sometimes have their sleep modes through which they use minimal energy when not solving problems. **Communication Modules:** These modules allow the IoT device to interact with other devices or central servers. Wireless communication can be carried out in the following ways: Wi-Fi, Bluetooth, Zigbee, LoRaWAN or even cellular communication. Transmitting data through communication modules requires a lot of energy hence they are known to attract a lot of power consumption. The power consumed by these modules varies with the data rate, distance, and the used protocol.

Figure 1. Overview of IoT Device Architecture

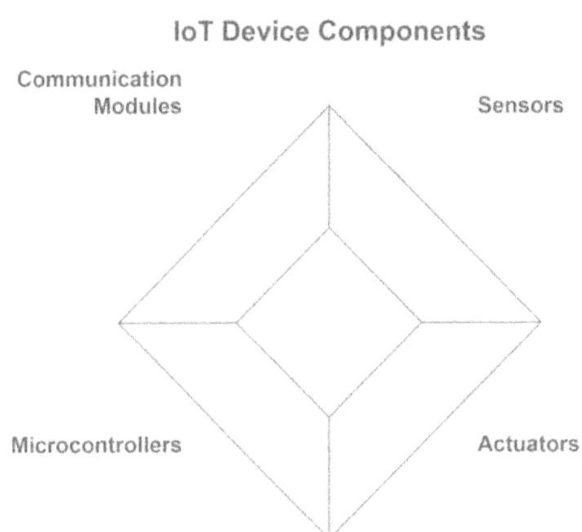

All these components put together also help in determining the energy consumptions of an IoT device. It is therefore important to achieve an optimal distribution of the sensing, actuating, processing and communication elements to minimize energy consumption.

2.2 Key Challenges in IoT Energy Consumption

Several factors contribute to the energy challenges faced by IoT devices(Lombardi et al 2021):

Battery Life: Batteries are common sources of power for most IoT devices because there is often no readily available source of electric current in remote or mobile applications. The battery capacity is generally low especially when the device has to send data frequently or when it has to continuously sense the environment. Battery replacement or recharging is sometimes very expensive and may not be feasible particularly for devices placed in remote areas (e.g., environmental sensors or smart farming). Extending battery life while requiring very little intervention is one of the greatest hurdles in IoT design.

Wireless Communication: Wireless communication is one of the most energy consuming activities for IoT devices. The power needed for transmission depends with the distance and data rate of the network to be established. For instance, Wi-Fi and cellular networks generally use more power than BLE or Zigbee, which are developed for low power consumption in short range data transfer. However, even with the low-power protocols, long-range communication or high frequency of transmission requires a lot of power, which is a challenge towards attaining low power IoT networks.

Data Processing: This, too, requires energy, be it processed on the device itself (edge computing) or sent to a remote server (cloud computing). On-device processing is beneficial in that it minimizes the data transfer frequency, and therefore minimizes energy consumption. However, there are cases where the data processing is quite complicated or when the machine learning algorithms are to run on the device, it consumes power. Also, sending raw data to the cloud to process consumes power for transmission, storage and subsequent analysis. Optimizing between the local processing and the cloud processing to meet energy needs is a major concern in IoT systems(Girija, P et al 2023).

2.3 Impact of Energy Inefficiency on Large-Scale IoT Deployments

In massive IoT applications like smart cities, industrial IoT, or environment monitoring, energy waste becomes a major factor that affects performance, expansion and greenness. Devices with low efficiency that draw a lot of power will need their batteries replaced or recharged often resulting in high operational costs and possible system failure. This is especially so when there are thousands or even millions of devices in a network and the energy requirements of all these devices can be a real dilemma. In addition, energy inefficiency in the communication protocols can cause congestion in the network, higher latency and energy consumption and hence higher operations cost. Such devices with high data transmission rates or high power utilization rates of their data transmission can similarly run out of power sources and affect the reliability of the network in use. Further, if the devices are not designed to be energy efficient, they become a load on the network equipment thus lowering the efficacy of the whole IoT system. In highly dependent sectors such as healthcare or agriculture where IoT devices are used for control and decision making, energy intensity impacts the reliability and time-sensitive characteristics of the systems. For example, if battery in a sensor is drained before its expected time it results to loss of valuable information hence impacts the system results. To recap, the energy concerns which currently affect connected devices include battery power, high power in communication, and data processing which is a major barrier to the successful implementation and growth of IoT networks. Mitigating these challenges by the use of energy efficient protocols, hardware and operation strategies is crucial for the scalability, dependability and sustainability of the complex large scale IoT systems.

3. ENERGY EFFICIENT COMMUNICATION PROTOCOLS USED IN IoT

3.1 Overview of Communication Protocols in IoT

Data transfer mechanisms are at the core of every IoT system as they enable devices to share information over networks. It has been seen that the selection of the protocol significantly affects the energy characteristics of IoT devices since different protocols provide different balances between the range, data rate, power consumption, and scalability(Al-Sarawi et al 2017). Some commonly used communication protocols in IoT include:

Figure 2. IoT Communication Protocols overview

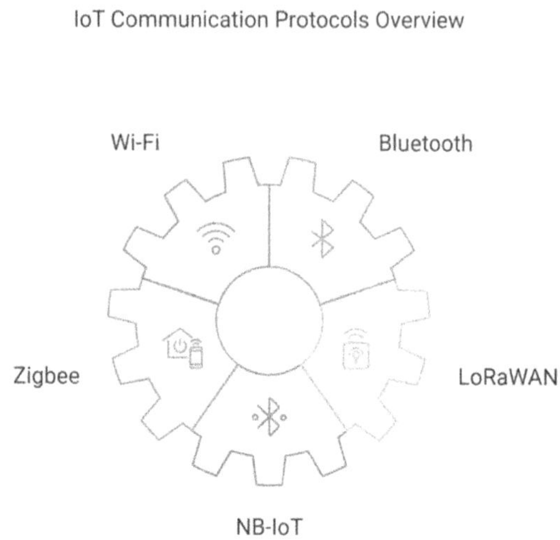

Wi-Fi: A telecommunication standard for information exchange that supports high data throughput and has extensive network reach. However, Wi-Fi is very greedy in power usage, and hence is not suitable for energy-limited IoT devices that are expected to operate for long periods without recharging.

Bluetooth: Bluetooth is short range wireless communication technology and is popular in low power consumer IoT applications such as wearables and home automation. Bluetooth Classic requires more power than Bluetooth Low Energy which is design for energy efficient devices such as the IoT devices that use batteries.

Zigbee: A low power and low data rate protocol that is mainly used in smart home and industrial IoT applications. Zigbee works in 2.4 GHz ISM band and is ideal for short range transmission of data between two or more devices that are low power devices.

LoRaWAN (Long Range Wide Area Network): A protocol developed for low power, wide area networks, LoRaWAN enables IoT devices to transmit data over long distances while using little power making it suitable for outdoor and massive IoT applications.

NB-IoT (Narrowband IoT): A protocol that is specifically designed to be used on the cellular network for low power, wide area network. It is intended for IoT devices that require a dependable and inexpensive way for transmitting little amounts of data over great distances like in smart meters and environmental monitoring.

All of these protocols are designed to address particular application scenarios with more emphasis placed on data throughput, range and power requirements. The selected communication protocol has implications on both the energy consumption and performance of the device as well as the scalability of the network Abdul-Qawy et al 2015).

3.2 Low Power Wide Area Networks (LPWAN)

LPWAN protocols are particularly aimed at low power long range communications. These are well suited for low data rate IoT applications across long distance like smart farming, tracking of assets and monitoring of environment. LPWAN protocols are defined by low power consumption, large coverage areas and the possibility of connecting thousands of devices to a network.

Characteristics of LPWAN Protocols:

Low Power: LPWAN protocols are designed to run on small batteries for a long time, ranging from a few years, because IoT applications are often installed in locations that are hard to access for battery change.
Long Range: LPWANs can cover distances of several kilometres up to 15 km in rural areas which makes communication possible in areas where use of technologies such as Wi-Fi or Bluetooth is not feasible.
Low Data Rates: LPWAN protocols are not optimized for high data rates but rather for low energy consumption as is the case with applications that send small data packets occasionally.

Case Studies: LoRaWAN and Sigfox:

LoRaWAN: LoRaWAN makes use of spread spectrum technology in the provision of long range connectivity with low power consumption. It is often used in the cases like smart agriculture where devices have to occasionally report about the state of the soil or the climate. LoRaWAN is an ideal solution for battery-powered Internet of Things devices that have to remain functional for several years without battery replacement due to the protocol's energy efficiency.
Sigfox: Sigfox is another LPWAN technology that is low-cost, low-power, and long-range technology. Sigfox is predominantly used for solutions that require long-range transmission of small bursts of data at fixed intervals such as smart metering. Energy efficiency is attained by Sigfox through the use of narrowband communication which consumes little power during transmission.

3.3 Bluetooth Low Energy (BLE)

Bluetooth Low Energy or BLE is a low powered short range wireless technology derived from the standard Bluetooth. BLE is used in consumer IoT applications such as wearables, fitness trackers, health monitors, and smart home. The low power consumption is realized by lowering the duty cycle of the device and employing low power transmission methods.

Use of BLE in Short-Range IoT Devices: BLE is most appropriate for devices that have to transport small payloads over short distances, usually a distance of up to 100 meters. This BLE also incorporates other methods that make it efficient in that it can work for a long time with small batteries, for instance, advertising intervals that refer to the period when the device sends data, and low duty cycle communication that refers to the time the device is awake.

3.4 Energy-Efficient MAC Protocols

Medium Access Control (MAC) protocols are important in defining how the devices get to access the communication medium and when to transmit data. Incorporate MAC protocol can substantially reduce energy consumption because MAC protocols can reduce the amount of time required for devices to remain awake while waiting to send data.

Role of MAC Protocols: MAC protocols determine the manner in which devices in a network establish communication over a shared channel, affecting performance and energy use. MAC protocols can contribute to a decreased energy consumption of IoT devices by avoiding collisions, making transmission durations as short as possible and putting devices into sleep mode during inactivity periods.

Sleep Scheduling and Duty Cycling: A typical method used in energy optimal MAC design is the duty cycling technique in which a node goes to sleep most of the time except the periods that it actively transmits or receives data. The devices are active only occasionally to look for data or to send out their data, which leads to low power consumption. Sleep scheduling is used to reduce the amount of time the devices are in the sleep mode while at the same time guaranteeing that communication can be made at any one time. Duty cycling is a common practice in IoT communication protocols, where Zigbee, LoRaWAN and BLE are not exempted.

In summary, the selection of the communication protocol defines the energy consumption of IoT devices. LoRaWAN and Sigfox LPWANs are suitable for long-range low power devices and BLE for short range low power applications. Pulse width modulation, low duty cycle MAC protocols and techniques complement energy efficiency by providing power conservation mechanisms for IoT systems at large. These protocols and strategies are important for the sustainability of the IoT networks especially given the increasing number of IoT devices.

4. ENERGY-EFFICIENT IOT DEVICE DESIGN

4.1 Low-Power Hardware Design

Efficient hardware design is essential for reducing the energy consumption of IoT devices, especially as these devices often rely on battery power or energy harvesting techniques. The components within IoT devices, including microcontroller units (MCUs), sensors, actuators, and communication modules, must be optimized for low-power operation to extend battery life and enhance device sustainability.

Microcontroller Units (MCUs) Optimized for Low Power Consumption: MCUs are the core components of IoT devices, responsible for managing data processing, sensor operations, and communication. To optimize energy efficiency, modern MCUs are designed to consume minimal power while delivering necessary processing capabilities. Many MCUs incorporate features such as low-power sleep modes, where they shut down non-essential functions when idle, and dynamic voltage and frequency scaling (DVFS), which adjusts the power supply based on processing demands. Some MCUs also support low-power peripherals, allowing external sensors and actuators to be powered down when not in use, further reducing energy consumption.

Energy-Harvesting IoT Devices: Traditional IoT devices rely on batteries, but energy harvesting offers an alternative, sustainable power source. Energy-harvesting IoT devices can capture ambient energy from the environment to power their operations, reducing or eliminating the need for batteries. Several types of energy harvesting methods are employed:

Solar Energy: Solar-powered IoT devices are particularly effective in environments with abundant sunlight, such as outdoor monitoring systems or smart agriculture sensors. Solar panels integrated into these devices can continuously recharge the device's battery or provide direct power, making them self-sustaining.

Vibration Energy: Devices can harvest energy from mechanical vibrations using piezoelectric materials or other vibration-capturing technologies. This method is commonly used in applications where vibrations are constant, such as in industrial equipment or wearable health devices.
Thermal Energy: Thermoelectric generators convert temperature differences into electrical energy. This method can be used in environments where there is a significant temperature gradient, such as industrial machines or environmental sensors located near heat sources.

These energy-harvesting techniques help reduce the dependency on traditional batteries, leading to more sustainable and long-lasting IoT devices.

4.2 Energy-Efficient Sensing Technologies

Sensors are essential in IoT devices, but they can be significant contributors to energy consumption, particularly when they are continuously sampling data. To enhance energy efficiency, various strategies are employed to minimize the energy consumption of sensor nodes.

Event-Driven and Adaptive Sampling Techniques: Traditional sensors operate on a fixed sampling rate, continuously collecting data even when there are no significant changes in the environment. Event-driven sampling focuses on activating sensors only when a relevant event or threshold is detected, such as motion or a change in temperature, which helps conserve energy by avoiding unnecessary data collection.
Adaptive sampling further optimizes energy use by adjusting the frequency of data sampling based on environmental conditions. For example, the sampling frequency in a temperature sensor can be set high when there is a steep change in temperature and can be set low when there is no change in temperature. It decreases the activity of the sensor in the period of low variability and thus saves power that is not very useful.

By adopting these techniques, the sensor nodes are capable of saving energy yet produce useful data.

4.3 Energy-Aware Data Processing

Data processing, the second factor, is another major component of IoT device energy consumption. There are two primary approaches to data processing in IoT systems: on-device processing and cloud processing.

Figure 3. Energy-Aware Data Processing

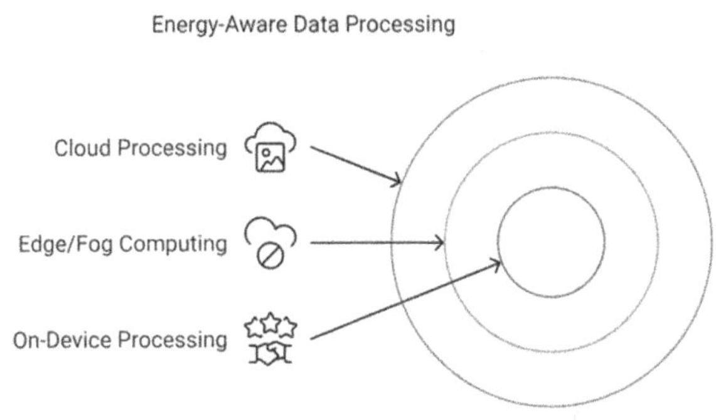

On-Device Processing: On-device processing means processing of data on the IoT device, without having to send the data to a remote server. For instance, through some of the processes like filtering, aggregation, basic analysis, the devices themselves can be able to perform so as to minimize the amount of raw data that needs to be sent to the central Cloud servers, which will be less energy and bandwidth consuming. This approach is well-suited to real time or time critical applications where an immediate decision is required. In addition, edge computing can decrease latency because the data does not have to go to the cloud for processing.

Cloud Processing: The traditional computing model brings the benefit of computing power, which can be used to process algorithms and big data. However, transferring the raw data to the cloud for analysis results in energy consumption at the data transmission level and the analysis level at the server side. However, for some of the IoT systems which are characterized with scarce energy constraints, this may not be efficient to rely on cloud processing.

Edge and Fog Computing: There is another approach that is somewhere between the per-device and cloud computing called edge or fog computing. In this model, raw data undergo preliminary data processing on the edge devices or intermediate nodes, known as fog nodes. The only information that goes to the cloud is relevant or aggregated information for further analysis. The energy needed for data transmission is therefore lowered because data is processed locally or in the nearby network nodes, and response time is increased. This distributed processing model is particularly useful in a vast IoT network where many devices are situated in different remote regions.

Overall, the paper calls for a system-level solution to design energy-efficient IoT devices with low-power hardware architecture, energy-aware sensing, and efficient processing of the IoT data. Applying these techniques energy harvesting, adaptive sampling, and edge computing—IoT devices can have longer operational time, lower energy consumption, and support more ecological IoT systems.

5. ENERGY HARVESTING TECHNIQUES IN IoT

5.1 Ambient Energy Sources

Energy scavenging technologies use surrounding energy to fuel IoT devices and is a renewable solution to the conventional use of batteries. These techniques transform different types of ambient energy into electrical energy hence enabling devices to run for long without charging. Key energy harvesting sources include:

Solar Energy: One of the most used approaches is the use of solar heat collectors where solar cells, often called photovoltaic panels, absorb the sun's rays and turn them into electricity. IoT devices that are powered by solar can be implemented in outdoors and in the remote areas like smart farming, weather monitoring and smart lighting. It is most suitable in places with high intensity of solar radiation which can reliably drive the devices. However, its efficiency highly depends on the environment, location, weather or time of the day, and therefore is not very reliable in areas of low sunlight.

Kinetic (Vibration) Energy: Kinetic energy harvesting is the process through which kinetic energy is transformed into electrical energy. For instance, piezoelectric harvester, which produces electricity from mechanical pressure or electromagnetic harvester that employs relative movement between magnets and coils can be used to power IoT systems in areas that experiences constant movements or vibrations. These systems are especially applicable to industrial conditions where the vibrations of the equipment, or transportation infrastructures, are present. Nevertheless, the energy generated from kinetic harvesters is often small and can only power low power appliances.

Thermal Energy: Thermal energy harvesting uses temperature differences and which can be used to generate electricity. Thermoelectric generators (TEGs) are devices that generate electrical power from heat flow from high to low temperatures depending on the See beck effect. This method can be used for monitoring temperature changes in systems that are characterized by high thermal dissipation, for example, industrial equipment, heating systems, wearable electronics that use body heat. The problem with Thermal EH is that it requires a significant temperature difference to generate useful power and may not be consistent in low temperature fluctuation zones.

RF (Radio Frequency) Energy: RF energy harvesting involves harvesting electromagnetic energy from radio signals from wireless communication systems that include Wi-Fi, Bluetooth, cellular or other networks. This energy can be employed in powering low power devices such as IoT devices in areas with rich radio frequency such as in urban areas with strong communication network. Despite this, RF harvesting is a reliable source of energy where other options may not be possible, though the energy received is often relatively small and therefore it is more suited to low power applications.

5.2 Advantages and Limitations of Energy Harvesting for IoT Devices

Energy harvesting offers several advantages for IoT devices:

Sustainability: Energy harvesting is more sustainable because unlike conventional systems which rely on batteries, renewable energy sources means there is less energy wasted in the environment.

Reduced Maintenance: Low-power devices, which can utilise ambient energy sources, do not need batteries replacement very often, which is crucial for IoT devices installed in the areas with low accessibility.

Extended Device Lifespan: Energy scavenging will allow these devices to operate for as long as there is ample ambient energy available.

However, there are also limitations to energy harvesting:

Energy Generation Limitations: They also can provide an energy from surrounding sources which is not sufficient to power high-powered IoT devices. For instance, solar energy harvesting may be poor during the day in cloudy areas or at night while kinetic energy harvesters might only produce little energy.

Variability: Most of the available energy in the environment is stochastic in nature meaning that their power output varies with time and environment thus making it challenging to guarantee steady device functionality.

Cost and Complexity: Energy harvesting systems can add to the cost and design of IoT devices, which demand unique elements, such as solar panels, vibration sensors, and thermoelectric generators.

5.3 Hybrid Energy Solutions

Advanced energy solutions are a combination of normal battery systems integrated with energy capturing methods to produce longer and more effective power supply to the IoT devices. In a hybrid system, a battery offer backup power when ambient energy is low and energy harvesting technologies can augment battery when it is available. For instance, a solar IoT device will use a battery to store energy harvested during the day for use at night or during a rainy day. Likewise, kinetic energy harvester may be used to power up the sensors in a wearable device with the battery to store surplus energy for use during low kinetic energy activity. Hybrid systems have higher flexibility and reliability than other systems because they allow the constant operation of the device when one energy source is out of order or insufficient.

5.4 Self-Powered IoT Devices

Battery-less IoT devices are completely independent and do not need external power supply like batteries or cables. These devices are capable of collecting energy from the environment in which they are placed (solar, kinetic, thermal or radio wave energy) for their continuous functioning. Battery replacement or recharging is inconvenient in many scenarios making self-powered systems useful in applications including environmental sensors, structures, and health monitoring wearables.

For example:

Smart Wearables: An energy harvesting for health monitoring wearable could convert body heat or kinetic energy into electrical energy to power sensors for monitoring heart rate, temperature or activity without recharging or replacement.
Smart Cities: In the case of a smart city, it can be envisioned that environmental sensors (air quality, temperature, pollution, etc.) could be completely self-powered through solar power or vibrations of traffic flow, and therefore, require no maintenance.

Battery less IoT devices are the future of sustainable IoT systems that incorporate energy scavenging to power up devices without reliance on batteries, and hence, support long term deployment. Altogether, energy scavenging methods, such as solar, kinetic, thermal, and RF energy, offer numerous and promising prospects for the IoT systems to be more effective and eco-friendly. Incorporation of energy harvesting with hybrid solutions and development of self-sustainable Iot devices can increase device durability, decrease need for maintenance and allow reduction of ecological footprint which is essential in the future development of IoT systems.

6. ENERGY-EFFICIENT ROUTING AND NETWORK LAYER PROTOCOLS

6.1 Routing Protocols for Energy Conservation

A critical factor in massive IoT networks is energy efficiency at the network layer to allow devices to be active and serve their purpose for considerable periods with limited energy. Data transmission consumes power and routing protocols are used to ensure that power is used optimally by the network. There is however several protocols that have been designed to enhance energy efficiency in IoT networks.

RPL (Routing Protocol for Low-Power and Lossy Networks): RPL is one of the most widely used routing protocols suitable for IoT networks mainly for those that are LPWNs, including sensor networks. RPL builds a DAG (Directed Acyclic Graph) prototype in which nodes transmit information to a parent node in a hierarchical structure. It enhances energy conservation through fewer hops needed in the network hence reducing the distance over which data is transmitted. It also facilitates different energy conserving features such as adaptive routing and packet combining to ensure that devices consume as little energy as possible while at the same time facilitating data transmission.

LEACH (Low-Energy Adaptive Clustering Hierarchy): LEACH is one of the most popular protocols for applying WSN which groups nodes in clusters in order to save energy. In LEACH, nodes are organized in clusters and only the head of the cluster is responsible for data gathering from other nodes in the cluster. The cluster head then forwards the collected data to a base station of the BPSK network system. This in turn reduces the amount of load that non cluster head nodes have to undertake hence saving energy. LEACH selects a cluster head in a round-robin fashion in order to avoid certain node running out of battery power quickly.

These protocols allow IoT devices to spend less energy on transmitting messages and the number of 'hops' required also impacts the overall energy consumption.

6.2 Clustering and Aggregation Strategies

Clustering and data aggregation are two essential approaches to minimize energy consumption in the context of IoT networks. Such methods include clustering the sensor nodes and limiting the amount of data transmitted in the network, therefore conserving energy.

Clustering: In clustering, nodes are partitioned into groups, where only one node is elected to be the cluster head whose role is to control the flow of communication between the nodes in the cluster as well as organizing data collected by the other nodes in the cluster. This method assists in minimizing energy use since only the cluster heads have to relay information to the central base station while other nodes have to relay information to the cluster head only. Therefore, the distance over which communication takes place is reduced, and the energy used to do so is also minimal.
Data Aggregation: Data aggregation entails not sending many data readings through the network but instead compressing them into one single bundle. It is able to achieve this by collecting data at the cluster head or other nodes within the network, which in the long run cuts down the total number of messages hence conserving energy. This technique is most appropriate in networks where the nodes send the same or similar messages several times.

Therefore, both clustering and aggregation strategies help to avoid excessive load on the nodes while minimizing the number of transmitted messages.

6.3 Sleep and Wake Scheduling in IoT Networks

Another useful strategy concerning energy saving in IoT networks is sleep and wake scheduling. Since many IoT devices do not need to work continuously, the possibility of setting time intervals when the device is inactive (sleep) can significantly save energy.

Sleep Modes: As it has been mentioned earlier, many IoT devices, especially sensors, do not have to be always on. Sleep modes enable devices to switch off some of the subcircuits, for example, the communication module or sensors when they are not in use. This cuts down greatly the power that is used during periods when the device is not sending or receiving information.
Duty Cycling: Duty cycle is the act of switching between active as well as inactive times. In this approach, devices are placed at a low power state for much of the time (sleeping) and only briefly awake to communicate data. The Sleep and Wake cycles can be coordinated across the network such that, in some cases where communication is imperative, it can occur, albeit at the lowest utilization of power.
Adaptive Sleep Scheduling: The second type of sleep is known as the AS sleep, which means adaptive sleep scheduling, which manages the sleep and wake schedules according to the network or the energy requirements of the device. For example, a device may go to deeper sleep states during such time

that there is low traffic or no data to be transmitted. On the other hand, it may decide to decrease its sleep time whenever the network traffic is high or when there are data to transmit.

By using sleep and wake scheduling, IoT networks can significantly cut the amount of power consumed by connected gadgets, as the actual transmission of data requires much more energy than simply remaining in standby mode. This technique is particularly useful for networks with battery-operated devices where operation time is a key consideration.

Optimal routing and network layer protocols are very important in achieving efficient IoT networks, which are sustainable. RPL and LEACH protocols reduce energy consumption by directing the data transfer in an efficient manner; clustering and data aggregation also contribute to lowering the overhead of the communication. The last set of strategies enhances the effect of sleep and wake scheduling techniques by further limiting the active time of the devices. Scalability is possible through these strategies; energy efficiency in IoT networks can be achieved to support extended device life and to foster large scale IoT networks.

7. ENERGY MANAGEMENT IN IOT SYSTEMS

Energy control in IoT systems is crucial in that it guarantees the optimal functionality of devices that have restricted power supply. Management of energy not only enhances the useful life of the devices but the energy utilization of the entire IoT network is also minimized(Boopathi 2024). At the software level, energy-aware middleware, at the hardware level, AI optimization, and energy monitoring tools are essential techniques utilized in controlling energy usage in IoT systems.

7.1 Energy-Aware Middleware and Operating Systems

In the software level, smart middleware and operating systems are used for energy management of IoT devices. It is an intermediary layer between the hardware and applications to perform compulsory services like task scheduling, data transfer, and power management. Energy-aware middleware is specially developed for controlling the energy consumption of IoT devices by modifying the operations according to the energy capacity of the system.

Dynamic Power Management (DPM): Energy-efficient mechanisms make it possible to control the use of power in IoT devices depending on the current consumption. These techniques enable the operating system or middleware to check the energy state of the system and decide about the activation or deactivation of certain components (e.g., sensors, communication modules or processors). For instance, in the case where a certain device is inactive, the unrelated parts can be deactivated, and the important parts can only become active when necessary. This real-time adjustment assists to achieve both, optimum performance and energy conservation.

Energy-Aware Scheduling: Scheduling algorithms to enhance the task's execution using power limits of IoT devices are employed as energy-aware scheduling algorithms. For example, the system may decide that energy consuming tasks must be executed first or charge the energy load among devices so that none of them would drain its battery. Also, the task scheduling may consider other factors such as; the idle time of the device, the availability of energy in case of using energy harvesting systems and the energy carrying capacity of each device.

7.2 Energy Optimization through AI and Machine Learning

The concerned area of research proposes machine learning (ML) as a dominant paradigm for energy optimization in IoT systems(Kim et al 2022)(Prabha, D et al 2019). IoT networks can use data analysis to forecast the energy consumption habits and then fine-tune their operations.

Predictive Energy Management: By the use of big data and data analytics, energy usage data can be used to forecast future energy requirements of the devices. This enables the system to come up with a way of managing power before the energy supply of a device gets to a critical level. For instance, ML can determine periods that energy consumptions are high and possibly change the duty cycle or the schedule of the tasks in order to minimize such consumption.

Energy Efficiency Optimization: Some of the most applicable ML algorithms are the reinforcement learning algorithms that can learn and adapt over time depending on the conditions prevailing within the system to minimize power consumption. These algorithms control power settings in real time by adapting from previous patterns and network situations. For example, an IoT network can use ML to minimize power-wasteful communication operations by selecting the best routes for data, or to adjust the frequency and timing of sensor readings to save power.

Anomaly Detection: Another way of using machine learning is in detection of outliers in power usage. Abnormal energy consumption trends indicate possibilities of hardware problems, wrong configurations, or bad sensors. It is possible to launch preventive measures, which will allow correcting the situation or, at least, minimize energy consumption in this case, if the presence of such anomalies is identified in the initial stage(R. S., Sudha et al 2023) (Sreelakshmi et al 2024).

7.3 Energy Monitoring and Profiling Tools

Energy management tools are used for energy measurement and analysis of the energy usage of IoT devices and networks in real time. These tools assist the network administrators and engineers in the determination of power consumption of the devices, and plan for efficient power usage.

Energy Profiling Tools: Energy profiling tools track the energy consumption of each node in an IoT network, for the devices. These tools monitor how much energy is consumed by individual parts (such as sensors, processors, communication interfaces) and give information about which components use up most energy. This data can be used to fine-tune the device's operation, if necessary, to make it more energy efficient by adjusting the settings of each part.

Energy Monitoring Platforms: Supervisory platforms collect data from individual devices and offer a worldwide perspective of energy usage in IoT networks. These provide administrators with dashboards, notification, and reports through which they can analyse energy utilisation trends and evaluate the performance. The energy usage pattern of the network will help the network administrator change some settings of the network, modify some routing algorithms or plan the maintenance time when energy is cheap.

Energy Auditing Tools: All these tools are used for energy performance audit of IoT systems. They assess the energy usage trend data over time and relate it to a standard or an energy-efficient parameter. This makes it possible for organizations to find out regions where more energy efficiency can be achieved.

Consequently, energy management in IoT systems is a multilayer optimization process, which includes energy-aware middleware, dynamic power management, machine learning-based optimization, and real-time energy monitoring. These tools and techniques enable IoT systems to run more effectively, by making sure that devices take just the right amount of energy, thereby increasing the lifespan of devices used and reducing the negative effect on the environment. Energy management solutions are prerequisite for large amount of devices as it is essential for long-term viability and for scaling the solution.

8. SECURITY CONSIDERATIONS IN ENERGY-EFFICIENT IoT PROTOCOLS

Energy efficiency and security are two of the key requirements in IoT which are very difficult to achieve simultaneously. The IoT devices are characteristically low power devices, and as such, it is extremely challenging to implement standard security protocols that may otherwise demand more power and energy. The requirement for energy management together with the protection of communication and data is essential to ensuring the reliability of IoT systems as well as their resourceful operation in the long run.

8.1 Energy Trade-offs in Securing IoT Devices and Communications

It is common to use cryptographic protocols, authentication schemes, and encryption techniques to protect IoT devices, and these processes require a lot of power. This makes the trade-off between security and power dissipation a primary one. For example, utilization of powerful encryption schemes including AES or RSA can guarantee secure data transfer while it consumes more power. Since IoT devices often have limited computational capabilities, low-energy, and low-complexity devices such as sensors and actuators may struggle to achieve secure communication while minimizing power consumption.

When implementing security in IoT devices, there are several aspects to consider:

Encryption Overhead: Encryption and decryption are very computationally intensive especially with big data. The same is true for IoT devices running on batteries since frequent encryption can drain the battery more often than not.
Authentication and Integrity Checks: Checking device identity and data validity usually involves intricate computations, which in turn consumes more power.
Secure Communication Channels: Keeping the channels for communication between devices secure, for instance, through secure tunnelling may also attract extra energy costs because of the overhead required in establishing and sustaining the channels.

In order to overcome these challenges, efficient security mechanisms for an energy efficient system need to be developed so as to reduce the energy cost of the security processes and at the same time, ensuring secure data communication and exchange.

8.2 Lightweight Cryptographic Techniques for Low-Power IoT Devices

In an attempt to solve the energy-security trade-off problem several lightweight cryptographic techniques have been designed for IoT devices. These techniques are used to lower the amount of computations introduced by cryptographic operations hence conserve power.

Symmetric Key Cryptography: The symmetric encryption algorithms such as L-AES or TEA are developed with less power consumption while providing a reasonable level of safety. These algorithms utilize a single key, both for the encryption and decryption processes which are less demanding and as such, require less power as compared to asymmetric cryptography.
Elliptic Curve Cryptography (ECC): ECC is an attractive solution to PKE that has the same level of security as RSA, but requires much less computation. This makes it a good candidate for IoT devices, which have a constraint on the amount of resources available. ECC algorithms require less number of keys hence they are fast, consume less power, yet they offer the same level of security.
Hash-based Authentication: As a result, lightweight hash functions are used in most IoT devices for authentication instead of using costly public-key systems. As compared to symmetric key systems, hash functions are faster and more efficient and offer acceptable levels of security for device authentication in low bandwidth environments.
Low-Energy Authentication Protocols: There are several low-energy authentication protocols proposed that reduce the amount of interaction and processing needed for IoT device authentication. By decreasing the number of times which one has to authenticate his or her identity, these protocols are energy efficient while maintaining security. Energy efficiency is a critical parameter in IoT networks, as well as security, and in this article, both factors are analyzed and compared.

8.3 Balancing Energy Efficiency and Security Requirements in IoT Networks

Adaptive Security Policies: IoT systems are capable of having adaptive security policy that change the security level depending on the context and power source needed. For instance, devices in client or risky zones can run with more secure mechanisms than a device in normal environment, but a device in a normal environment may employ measures that consume less power. This approach makes the system to be efficient on energy during normal operations but can be very secure when the need arises.

Energy-Aware Security Protocols: Security mechanisms that are included in lightweight communication (SLC) and IoT-optimized security protocols can be developed in combination with EMS. These protocols are mainly focused on data confidentiality and integrity but sacrifice the amount of security processes that take place and their complexity to save energy.

Edge Computing and Local Processing: With the adoption of edge computing or local processing in the IoT devices, the data may be preprocessed or even partially encrypted to the central server. This also lowers the amount of security operations required on the cloud or data center side, thereby lowering the energy that is used by the device as well as the network.

Energy-Efficient Secure Communication: Low energy communication interfaces like BLE or LoRaWAN protocols must be employed to make sure the energy spent in transmitting secure data is not wasteful. These protocols have been particularly developed for the application of low power range communication with an aim of minimizing energy consumptions while at the same time providing secure transmission.

Thus, it can be concluded that the establishment of an optimal ratio between energy efficiency and security in IoT systems is a challenging task. The more classical cryptographic methods can be quite secure, but what is to be forgotten, they require more power. The energy trade-off is reduced by lightweight cryptographic methods, including symmetric key algorithms, ECC, and hash-based techniques. Moreover, the security policies and energy-constrained protocols can be developed in a way that will satisfy energy and security constraints of IoT devices.

9. FUTURE TRENDS AND RESEARCH DIRECTIONS

Over time, smart devices are bound to flood the market and be part of people's daily existence, thus the call for efficient protocol and devices. As millions of IoT devices produce massive amounts of data, the power consumption of these devices has to be optimized to support large-scale and long-term IoT solutions. The development of IoT technologies for energy efficiency will continue to evolve based on better communication protocols, AI, blockchain, new generation networks and tech like quantum sensors.

9.1 Future Advancements in Energy-Efficient IoT Protocols

The energy efficiency of the IoT communication protocols will remain a topic of continued improvement because of the call for increased sustainability and development of novel wireless technologies. With increasing IoT network density and interconnectivity, specific protocols will have to be designed that are ultra-low power to reduce the need for frequent recharging while maintaining high data transfer rate and low latency. Future protocols will likely integrate features such as:

Adaptive Communication Techniques: New protocols will self-regulate their energy utilization in response to current network status, device specifications, and application requirements. This will make it possible to use minimum energy during transmission in environments that have varying conditions of energy.
Ultra-Low Power Wide Area Networks (LPWAN): Future developments of LPWAN technologies such as LoRaWAN and NB-IoT will also see the optimization of their low power for long range thus suitable for large scale IoT networks.
Integration of AI with Protocols: Automated systems, based on artificial intelligence, might work out the patterns of data traffic and improve the decisions about routes that would require less energy. The AI algorithms can estimate the traffic and the activity of the devices, and reschedule the communication in order to save the battery and improve the network performance.

9.2 Integration of AI and Blockchain for Enhanced Energy Management

AI and blockchain are poised to play significant roles in enhancing the energy efficiency of IoT systems:

AI for Energy Optimization: With the help of AI, organizations can handle enormous amounts and types of data coming from IoT devices to estimate energy consumption and improve the operational performance. Smart power control can also be used to control the power usage of the devices in a real-time basis depending on the user's activity, the environment and network status. AI can also be used for predictive maintenance, which detects that devices require maintenance before they breakdown and thus saving on time and energy.
Blockchain for Decentralized Energy Management: Integration of this type of blockchain technology in the energy sector will enable the development of decentralized systems where devices and networks independently organize and plan energy consumption and distribution. For instance, the use of blockchain

may be applied to safely and credibly document transactions between IoT devices to decentralize the provision of energy resources. It can also assist in organizing energy exchanging systems, where devices that have energy to give (for instance, after harvesting from the sun) can share it with other devices making it an independent system.

Smart Contracts for Energy Efficiency: Smart contracts based on the blockchain might enable agreements to be executed automatically, depending on consumption rate of energy devices and systems. This could be especially useful in smart and micro-grids where energy optimization and equal energy sharing are an issue.

9.3 Role of 5G and Beyond in Advancing Energy-Efficient IoT Communication

The expansion of 5G as well as the future enhancements towards 6G will significantly influence the IoT communication. These networks will provide a better solution in terms of speed, connectivity, and energy which will be a bonus to IoT devices.

5G for Energy-Efficient Communication: 5G networks have very low end to end latency as well as very high data rates that allow real time communication between IoT devices with small energy cost. The faster and more efficient transfer of a greater amount of data will mean less time devices need to be switched on and thus less energy required. 5G mMTC will serve the high connectivity demands of IoT systems, while lowering the energy per bit transmitted.

Energy-Efficient Network Slicing: With 5G, network slicing is possible and this means that the various types of IoT devices such as wearables, industrial sensors, smart meters among others can share the network in a way that they consume different amounts of power. For instance, low data rate applications, such as environmental sensors that transmit data infrequently can be assigned a small slice, while applications with high data rates such as, video surveillance, can be assigned a large slice.

6G and Beyond: Investigations on 6G networks are already in progress, and the networks aim for even greater energy efficiency than 5G networks, and 6G will most probably use AI or machine learning for dynamic control of energy consumption in the network. Moreover, 6G may use terahertz (THz) frequencies that enable the extension of IoT networks with higher speed and efficiency of data transfers, and, therefore, increase energy efficiency of the network.

9.4 Exploring Next-Gen Technologies Like Quantum Sensors for Low-Power IoT Devices

Quantum sensors are on the horizon to deliver enhanced energy efficiency for IoT devices and other technologies are also on the way.

Quantum Sensors: Quantum sensors have the potential of being far more sensitive and accurate than conventional sensors and at the same time use far less energy. These sensors are based on principles of quantum mechanics, including superposition and entanglement, to measure variations in physical characteristics (such as temperature, pressure or magnetic fields) with improved accuracy and less energy consumption. For those IoT devices that are based on environmental sensing, quantum sensors could decrease the power requirements for data acquisition and analysis by orders of magnitude.

Quantum Computing for Data Processing: However, even in their nascent stage, quantum computing could potentially be part of the solution for improving data handling in IoT environments. Quantum algorithms can be used for solving large-scale optimization problems faster than classical computers, which can be helpful for enhancing energy efficiency in the IoT networks.

Energy Harvesting with Quantum Technology: They may also improve energy harvesting systems, which can be regarded as a quantum-enabled device. For instance, quantum dots are nanoscale semiconductor structures which can be integrated in solar cells for enhanced light conversion efficiency, and become a source of energy for low power consuming IoT devices.

Finally, it can be stated that the further advancement of energy-efficient IoT protocol and devices is very optimistic. With the advent of new forms of communication based on AI and blockchain, as well as the introduction of new generations of networks, including 5G and 6G, IoT systems will be even more energy efficient, scalable and smart. In addition, there is a prospect of more advanced technologies, for instance, quantum sensors and energy harvesting, which are expected to result in even smaller energy consumption of IoT devices and establish completely energy sufficient IoT networks.

10. CONCLUSION

Internet of Things or IoT is a technology that is widely used in the modern world by automating, connecting and processing data in real time in different fields. However, as the number of connected devices is continually increasing, the problem of energy consumption becomes more acute. Energy efficient IoT protocols and devices are critical to allow IoT networks to grow, reduce the energy footprint and work optimally for long periods. This paper has described the different approaches as well as the development of energy-efficient IoT protocols and devices, and highlighted present and future solutions. IoT technologies and devices have entered a period of high development in energy efficiency over the past decade. LoRaWAN and NB-IoT, and BLE are among the communication protocols that have been used in the reduction of energy consumption in IoT devices for long-range communication. LPWAN has been instrumental in offering energy efficient IoT solutions for mass IoT applications especially for applications such as agriculture, smart city and asset tracking. In device design, low power technologies like energy harvesting, low power micro controllers, and smart sensors have been developed to help prolong battery life and thus decrease the need to recharge the devices frequently. Energy harvesting, using solar, thermal and kinetic energy among others has offered a way of creating energy independent IoT devices that can work for long periods of time on their own. Moreover, edge computing and fog computing have facilitated energy-efficient processing as compared to the transfer of data to central cloud computing servers. Processing and data accumulation at the device level decrease energy expenditures on data transmission, which is useful in IoT systems with numerous connected devices and high traffic.

However, there is a need to perform further studies on energy-efficient IoT solutions as is discussed in the subsequent sections. IoT applications are getting more complicated and diverse, and so the problems are coming up which need to be solved continuously. Currently, researchers need to focus on the possibility of refining communication procedures, physical peripherals, and computational algorithms for reducing energy usage levels while keeping performance and dependability high. In also, integration of new technologies like artificial intelligence (AI), blockchain, quantum computing can also be seen as having promising potential to enhance energy efficiency in IoT systems. AI can provide smart real-time energy management while Blockchain provides decentralized energy sharing. In contrast, quantum technologies can open new possibilities, such as efficient energy or data sensors and data processing.

Energy consumption vs performance and security is one of the biggest issues that IoT researchers are currently facing. Especially when more and more IoT devices become integrated, the problem of secure communication and privacy becomes critical. Future solutions need to address the challenge of reducing the energy consumption while satisfying security requirements of the IoT networks. The overall scope of energy-efficient IoT research is the development of the long-life IoT environments, which will be able to operate efficiently in the long run. IoT systems can also have a very low power consumption by using efficient protocols, low power devices and energy harvesting technologies. This will be especially useful as IoT grows into the trillions of devices, each adding its consumption to the energy consumption. Besides environmental sustainability of IoT systems, it also has the capacity to improve the economic sustainability of energy efficiency. Through the deployment of cost effective solutions in energy utilization, the business and consumer can be able to realize operational cost savings especially in areas such as; health, agriculture and production industries. Finally, the further evolution of IoT devices and network protocols that enable energy efficiency will remain crucial for the Internet of Things evolution and support for the diverse and more complex applications in the future. Introducing innovation and integration of IoT, smart solutions of energy efficient industry can make a connected society that focuses on the society, environment and economy.

REFERENCES

Abdul-Qawy, A. S., Pramod, P. J., Magesh, E., & Srinivasulu, T. (2015). The internet of things (iot): An overview. *International Journal of Engineering Research and Applications*, *5*(12), 71–82.

Al-Sarawi, S., Anbar, M., Alieyan, K., & Alzubaidi, M. (2017, May). Internet of Things (IoT) communication protocols. In *2017 8th International conference on information technology (ICIT)* (pp. 685-690). IEEE.

Boopathi, S. (2024). Advancements in Optimizing Smart Energy Systems Through Smart Grid Integration, Machine Learning, and IoT. In *Optimization Techniques for Hybrid Power Systems: Renewable Energy, Electric Vehicles, and Smart Grid* (pp. 33-61). IGI Global.

Gupta, B. B., & Quamara, M. (2020). An overview of Internet of Things (IoT): Architectural aspects, challenges, and protocols. *Concurrency and Computation*, *32*(21), e4946. DOI: 10.1002/cpe.4946

Kim, I., Kim, B., & Sidorov, D. (2022). Machine learning for energy systems optimization. *Energies*, *15*(11), 4116. DOI: 10.3390/en15114116

Lombardi, M., Pascale, F., & Santaniello, D. (2021). Internet of things: A general overview between architectures, protocols and applications. *Information (Basel)*, *12*(2), 87. DOI: 10.3390/info12020087

Madakam, S., Ramaswamy, R., & Tripathi, S. (2015). Internet of Things (IoT): A literature review. *Journal of Computer and Communications*, *3*(5), 164–173. DOI: 10.4236/jcc.2015.35021

Magubane, Z., Tarwireyi, P., & Adigun, M. O. (2019, November). Evaluating the energy efficiency of IoT routing protocols. In *2019 International Multidisciplinary Information Technology and Engineering Conference (IMITEC)* (pp. 1-7). IEEE. DOI: 10.1109/IMITEC45504.2019.9015904

Mahmoud, R., Yousuf, T., Aloul, F., & Zualkernan, I. (2015, December). Internet of things (IoT) security: Current status, challenges and prospective measures. In *2015 10th international conference for internet technology and secured transactions (ICITST)* (pp. 336-341). IEEE.

Mouha, R. A. R. A. (2021). Internet of things (IoT). *Journal of Data Analysis and Information Processing*, *9*(02), 77–101. DOI: 10.4236/jdaip.2021.92006

Prabha, D., Subramanian, R. S., Balakrishnan, S., & Karpagam, M. (2019). Performance evaluation of Naive Bayes classifier with and without filter based feature selection. *International Journal of Innovative Technology and Exploring Engineering (IJITEE) ISSN*, 2278-3075.

Sobin, C. C. (2020). A survey on architecture, protocols and challenges in IoT. *Wireless Personal Communications, 112*(3), 1383–1429. DOI: 10.1007/s11277-020-07108-5

Sreelakshmi, S., Babu, A. A., Lakshmipriya, C., Gracious, L. A., Nalini, M., & Subramanian, R. S. (2024, October). Enhancing Intrusion Detection Systems with Machine Learning. In *2024 2nd International Conference on Self Sustainable Artificial Intelligence Systems (ICSSAS)* (pp. 557-564). IEEE. DOI: 10.1109/ICSSAS64001.2024.10760341

Subramanian, R. S., Girija, P., Sudha, K., & Aswini, J. SivaKumar, S., & Nattesan, N. V. S. (2023, January). Alleviating the naive bayes assumption using filter approaches. In 2023 5th International Conference on Smart Systems and Inventive Technology (ICSSIT) (pp. 1430-1436). IEEE.

Subramanian, R. S., Sudha, K., & Ramana, K. V. SivaKumar, S., Nithyanandhan, R., & Nalini, M. (2023, February). Hybrid Variable Selection Approach to Analyse High Dimensional Dataset. In 2023 7th International Conference on Computing Methodologies and Communication (ICCMC) (pp. 1489-1495). IEEE.

Chapter 7
Energy Efficient Big Data Processing: A Comprehensive Survey on Techniques, Trends, and Future Directions

D. Ravindran
https://orcid.org/0000-0003-1672-9552
Kristu Jayanti College, India

D. Lekha
R.M.K. College of Engineering and Technology, India

G. Mariammal
Vel Tech Rangarajan Dr. Sagunthala R&D Institute of Science and Technology, India

T. Maheshwaran
https://orcid.org/0009-0008-8961-635X
Sri Manakula Vinayagar Engineering College, India

S. Udhayashankar
https://orcid.org/0009-0006-3781-8801
Vel Tech Multi Tech Dr. Rangarajan Dr. Sakunthala Engineering College, India

V. Sathya
Vel Tech Rangarajan Dr. Sagunthala R&D Institute of Science and Technology, India

K. Dhivya
https://orcid.org/0000-0002-1693-4452
SRM Institute of Science and Technology, India

ABSTRACT

Abstract The exponential rise in big data has resulted in higher energy requirements in data processing frameworks, which present a major environmental and practical concern. As the amount of data being generated grows, cost effective and energy efficient big data processing has become critical. This paper reviews different

DOI: 10.4018/979-8-3373-0766-4.ch007

Copyright © 2025, IGI Global Scientific Publishing. Copying or distributing in print or electronic forms without written permission of IGI Global Scientific Publishing is prohibited.

techniques that improve energy efficiency in big data processing from hardware level optimization, software level adaptation and data level optimization. Proposed and implemented low power processors and energy aware storage; energy efficient scheduling; data compression; and data reduction strategies such as edge computing have been found to be effective in the energy management of big data processing. Other new paths include artificial intelligence based energy management and green data centers. The goal of this survey is to give an overview of the existing situation, show examples of the implementation of energy-efficient BD processing frameworks, and point out the possible directions for their further development.

1. INTRODUCTION

1.1 Background: Overview of Big Data Growth and its Implications for Energy Consumption

In recent years, big data has grown rapidly and created great opportunities and problems in different fields(Sagiroglu, S., & Sinanc, D. 2013). The term big data can be defined as large amounts of structured and unstructured data from various sources, social media, sensors, financial transactions, IoT and others(Zheng et al 2018). The findings herein hold a lot of promise for informing knowledge, creativity, and better choices. However, as the size of big data increases, the processing power needed to store the data, as well as to analyse it, also increases. Some of the foundations for big data, for instance data centers and cloud computing have experienced exponential energy consumption rates. Facilities that are used to run the algorithms and store the datasets, known as data centers, consume a large portion of the world's electricity. The data collected by the International Energy Agency showed that the data centers and other digital facilities contribute to the increase of the world's electricity demand and predictions are that they could consume more than 3% of the world's electricity by 2030. The volumes of data continue to rise and so does the energy consumed by the systems; this raises questions on the impact of big data on the environment as well as the costs of running big data.

1.2 Motivation

This means that the advancement of energy use needed in big data processing poses environmental and economic problems. The consequences of using energy increases through the enhanced development and utilization of energy both in the development and utilization processes has negative effects on the environment such as the effects of global warming. For instance, the conventional Data centers that depend on fossil fuels are major sources of carbon emissions that add to the problems of climate change. This is because operational costs are other primary drivers that ensure the search for energy-efficient solutions. These costs are a major item in most organizations' expense budget as the scale of data processing increases with growth in the organization. In addition, the increasing energy demand together with the continually larger data sets, leads to increased electricity costs, which place pressure on businesses, especially in industries where profit margins are narrow. This scenario has led the business entities and researchers to look for way of managing big data while at the same time ensuring that they achieve the best performance in energy consumption. Therefore, the rationale for the research into energy efficiency in big data processing is to address the increasing energy consumption and operational costs as well as the environmental effects that come with demands for increased data processing.

1.3 Objectives

The purpose of this paper is therefore to review and categorically describe different techniques, methodologies and frameworks that have been proposed in an attempt to address the issue of energy consumption in big data processing. These include both hardware and software as well as data level techniques, with the intended outcome of minimizing the energy consumption of large scale big data processing while at the same time ensuring the efficiency and scalability of the processing algorithms. This paper will discuss low power hardware solutions including ARM processors, GPUs and FPGAs which are power-efficient enough to offer the required compute for big data processing. Furthermore, it will identify energy consuming software solutions that includes the usage of efficient algorithms, smart scheduling and management of resources with an aim of reducing energy consumption during data processing. Last but not least, the potential of data-oriented approaches, including data minimization, edge processing, and energy-efficient data storage, will be discussed to fine-tune energy efficiency even further.

1.4 Structure of the Survey

The survey is designed in a way that captures a broad perspective of the major issues related to energy efficiency in large-scale big data processing. The following sections will be covered:

1.Big Data Processing Frameworks: It is interesting to discuss the typical big data frameworks such as Hadoop, Spark, and Flink with a special emphasis on the energy characteristics and issues.

2.Energy Efficiency in Big Data Processing: An overview of energy efficiency, the benefits that come with it as well as an introduction to energy efficiency indicators.
3.Techniques for Energy-Efficient Big Data Processing: An analysis of the measures implemented at the systems' physical layer, virtual layer, and data layer aimed at enhancing energy efficiency in big data systems.
4.Emerging Technologies and Trends: A closer view at some of the advanced solutions such as Artificial Intelligence, green data centers, edge computing that may bring a significant change in big data energy efficiency.
5.Challenges and Future Directions: An analysis of the existing constraints in employing efficient big data processing and possible directions for future work.
6.Conclusion: Summary of the results and recommendations on how to make big data processing energy efficient and a plea for achieving optimum performance and efficiency.

This approach of structuring the paper allows the paper to address the technical and practical dimensions of energy efficiency in big data.

2. BIG DATA PROCESSING FRAMEWORKS

Hadoop ecosystem is one of the most popular frameworks for big data processing which addresses the problem of storing and processing distributed large-scale data(Landset et al 2015). It has sub-systems such as Hadoop Distributed File System (HDFS) for storage, Map Reduce for batch processing and yet another resource negotiator (YARN). Hadoop is used for scalability or big data processing across many machines and is capable of handling distributed error. Nevertheless, Hadoop clusters can consume much energy, especially when working in large-scale systems despite its broad usage. The criticisms of energy usage with Hadoop are mainly because of the batch processing model of computation. In batch processing, data is processed in a group or in a batch and for this a large amount of computational power may be needed over a long time. Due to the deployment of hundreds or thousands of machines in Hadoop clusters, there is a high energy consumption on both computing and cooling. Moreover, MapReduce jobs themselves are not very energy efficient, because they involve such disadvantages as multiple data transfers, non-optimal use of resources, and long idle times in cluster nodes. Secondly, the traditional architecture of Hadoop is not efficient in energy consumption; nodes continue to run even when they are idle. This even when the nodes are idle is a significant factor in the energy wastage in Hadoop-based systems. Some of these challenges can be addressed by improving the General Schedule of MapReduce jobs and minimizing idle times but energy consumption is still a major concern in large Hadoop clusters.

Apache Spark and Apache Flink are two of the biggest competitors to Hadoop especially in real-time and stream processing. They both provide better performance than Hadoop, Spark uses an in-memory processing technique which cuts across less data and hence, computing time is shorter(Akil et al 2017). Flink, as well, is aimed at stateful stream processing and offers better response time for real-time computations. Compared to Hadoop, from the energy efficiency point of view, there are several benefits of Spark and Flink. Spark's in-memory processing model means that it does not need to read from and write to disk as often as it computes, thus saving energy. Furthermore, Spark's RDDs also enable improved scheduling of tasks and minimize the number of operations to be executed and energy needed for the data processing.

While Flink is more optimized for stream processing it allows to continuously process data with less latency and less computational cost. This means that Flink typically needs less resources in the long run than other batch processing frameworks such as Hadoop where large scale jobs are possible but often not very efficient. But, as pointed out earlier, Flink's real-time processing paradigm needs power to sustain the data stream, although this can also be energy-intensive if not optimized. Relative to Hadoop, Spark and Flink are faster and more efficient in resource utilization; nevertheless, they consume a lot of power for huge data. Individual components include task scheduling, resource provisioning, and workload management all of which play a key role in improving the energy efficiency of these frameworks.

2.1 Distributed Data Centers: Energy Implications of Distributed Data Processing

The big data platforms employ distributed data centers, which assign computational tasks across several physically distinct locations. These Hadoop data centers depend on web-based cloud computing solutions such as the AWS, Microsoft Azure, and Google Cloud to manage the computational work applicable for big data process. The consequences of distributed data centers are vast because every data center consumes energy for computation as well as cooling, networking, and storage. Another problem that arises from the distributed data center organization is the size of the energy demand. A data center may need a lot of power to perform tasks such as data analysis, artificial intelligence, or simulation(Sudha, K et al 2024). In addition, redundancy in data storage and transmission where data needs to be copied to many locations for backup, requires the use of energy to transmit data and to use network and computing resources.

Primary characteristics of distributed data centers have an impact on energy efficiency; these characteristics include server loads, cooling systems, and the locations of the data centers. For instance, data centers sited in colder climates can use outside air for cooling hence minimizing on electricity for air conditioning. Further, efficient resource management- the minimization of data center proliferation by consolidating data processing functions in fewer, more efficient data centers can also increase energy efficiency. To these challenges, many firms have commenced implementing the renewable energy sources like the wind and solar in their data centers in a bid to lower on the carbon footprint. Nevertheless, the energy consumption of the distributed data centres remains an essential contributor to the environmental footprint of big data processing, so the further advancement of energy-efficient infrastructures and methods is still required.

Therefore, based on the performance and scalability that Hadoop, Spark and Flink provides, energy consideration in big data processing is still an issue. The very frameworks these supports are predicated on distributed data centers, which only serve to exacerbate the problem and emphasize the necessity for sound, green practices and energy efficiency throughout the entire data processing chain.

3. ENERGY EFFICIENCY IN BIG DATA PROCESSING

Efficiency in processing big data is important in several ways, mainly because of the large costs and environmental effects of large data processing systems. As the amount of produced and processed data rises, the power consumption of data centers and computing infrastructure has risen as well (Koseleva, N., & Ropaite, G. (2017). This is especially so as organizations move up the scale with the processing of their data, and energy consumed in data processing becomes a concern.

The first reason for increasing energy efficiency is to save money on energy costs. The computer facilities that provide the infrastructure for processing and storing big data are known to have very high running costs with power costs being a large portion of the costs. These costs are mainly comprised of cooling, powering servers and other networking equipment. The reduction in electricity consumption makes a lot of sense with the organization's electricity bills, which can be a significant portion of the overall cost of running a data center. This is particularly the case given that many organizations now operate centralized facilities management for large scale operations and hence even a marginal improvement in the energy efficiency will translate to huge cost savings. Energy conservation is also the other benefit of practicing energy efficient use since it leads to environmental conservation. Fossil fuel dependent data centers have high carbon footprints that are a consequence of climate change. As the world shifts towards making, IT a sustainable solution to its problems, organizations have been forced to adopt measures that will help them reduce their impact on the environment. Enhancing energy efficiency in the operation of big data can decrease the emission of greenhouse gases by decreasing energy consumption when using renewable energy sources in data centres. Besides, energy-efficient practices directly reduce the amount of energy consumed from non-renewable sources which is a contributing factor to the overall goal of creating a more sustainable economy.

The integration of sustainable IT practices can also work in partnership with CSR objectives and can be viewed as adding value for consumers, investors and stakeholders. Companies that are conscientious in the way they manage their energy consumption are showing a dedication to sustainability, which is something that can give a company the edge over others in today's world. With stakeholders insisting on environmentally friendly operations, firms that implement energy efficiency measures are well placed to serve these expectations and legal requirements.

Metrics for Measuring Energy Efficiency: PUE as well as Energy Proportionality and Carbon Efficiency and other well-known indicators

In order to evaluate and improve energy usage several indicators that reflect energy usage in data centers and big data processing systems are widely used.

1. **Power Usage Effectiveness (PUE):** PUE is currently one of the most popular measures of the energy efficiency of data center facilities. It is a ratio that relates the total energy utilized by the data center to the energy used by IT equipment only. Energy efficiency can be inferred from a lower PUE. For instance, if the PUE is 1.2 this therefore means that for every kilowatt of power consumed by the IT load, 0.2 kilowatts of power is used by the supporting infrastructure. The aim is to reduce this ratio as much as possible, and target a PUE as close to 1 as is possible – in other words, the energy required to support the infrastructure is insignificant compared to that required to run the computing equipment.
2. **Energy Proportionality:** Energy proportionality is a method of determining the correlation between a system's load and energy utilization. In an optimal case, the energy consumed will vary with the amount of computation that is required. For example, it should consume more energy when processing or computing than when it is not processing or computing at all. True energy proportionality is the state where systems use energy correspond to the amount of work they are processing hence optimizing the use of energy resources. New generation processors as well as data centres are nowadays being built to be

energy proportional, meaning they can dynamically scale energy consumption based on demand.

3.Carbon Efficiency: Carbon efficiency extends beyond energy-intensity by considering the environmental cost of a given CO2 emission per unit of energy. This metric is very important when it comes to determining the sustainability of big data as most energy grids in the world depend on fossil energy sources. Carbon efficiency can be enhanced by optimizing energy efficiency and reducing the use of fossil energy sources and replacing them by renewable energy sources such as wind or solar energy used in data centers. Carbon efficiency can be defined as the ability of the company to measure its carbon impact, which means that the companies are able to measure the carbon emissions linked with the energy they use, and try to minimize these emissions by using cleaner energy sources.

These parameters give organizations useful information about their energy consumption patterns and possible improvements. This paper has shown that it is possible to enhance sustainability in large scale big data processing through deployment of strategies that can lead to optimal PUE or even improvement in energy proportionality and carbon footprint. Finally, it is possible to achieve high performance of big data computations while also reducing their negative impact on the environment so that their usage would help businesses succeed and, at the same time, support the achievement of the sustainable development goals.

4. TECHNIQUES FOR ENERGY-EFFICIENT BIG DATA PROCESSING

In this paper, we explore how energy-efficient big data processing can be achieved by improving the underlying hardware and software architectures as well as data centre strategies to minimize energy consumption while maximizing performance and capacity. The following techniques are centered on hardware, software, and data management strategies to accomplish this objective.

4.1 Hardware-Based Approaches

1.Low-Power Processors: Currently, the traditional processors like Intel x86-based CPU are energy consuming especially in large-scale data centers. To this end, low power processors including ARM processors, Field Programmable Gate Arrays (FPAs) and Graphics Processing Units (GPUs) have been developed as more power efficient devices. ARM processors, familiar to most users of mobile devices, are known to draw a lot less power compared to conventional computer processors but offer enough processing power. FPGAs are a type of hardware that can be programmed so as to be used for particular jobs; they are more power-efficient per area than general-purpose microprocessors. Graphic Processing Units, commonly used for purposes of parallelism are very effective in handling tasks that require high throughput or intensive use of artificial intelligence. By introducing these specific tasks to these special codecs, big data systems are capable of saving a lot of energy.

2.Energy-Aware Storage Solutions: Even the energy used in storage devices of big data systems can also be minimized. SSD has several advantages over HDD; one of them is that the former is more energy-efficient since it does not have any moving components and uses less power to read/write data. A storage configuration that uses SSDs and HDDs is that a specific amount of SSDs can be used while the rest of the storage is provided by HDDs, which are more energy consumptive but less expensive than SSDs. In these systems, there is an option of storing data on high operation SSDs while storing less frequently used data on energy-saving HDDs. Another way is intelligent storage where data is moved between storage devices using access patterns so that energy is not wasted.

4.2 Software-Based Approaches

1.Energy-Efficient Algorithms: The energy efficient algorithms are directed at the design that reduces the energy consumption during data processing. The number of operations which is needed for processing can be minimized through good choice of data structures and algorithms, which in turn means less energy is needed. For instance, caching algorithms that store results for reuse, help to minimize the need for additional computation, therefore, saving time and energy. Load balancing techniques also guard the optimal utilization of computational resources so as to avoid occasions where the resources remain idle and drain energy.

2.Resource Management: Resource management is another way through which organizations can minimize energy utilization in big data processing. It is also a process that enable the installation of many virtual operating systems on the same physical host hardware thus saving on resources and hardware. Likewise, other containerization technologies such as Docker make application deployment more efficient and less energy consuming since they run on the host operating system kernel and are less overhead than virtual machines. Energy proportional scheduling methods are also used in order to allocate resources in an optimal way and use energy only when necessary.

3.Data Compression and Deduplication: Reduction of data size stored and transferred is another way through which data compression leads to energy conservation in both storage and transmission. Such data is stored in less space and time taken to transfer it is also less hence reducing the energy used in transferring data in the network. Data deduplication introduces the removal of the same data to avoid the storage of similar pieces of information. It reduces the amount of storage space and the amount of energy required in the process of reading as well as writing data especially in large scale distributed systems.

4.3 Data-Centric Approaches

1.Data Reduction and Sampling: In big data processing, it is usually a challenge to handle and analyse large volumes of data. Some of the methods of data reduction include dimensionality reduction or feature selection, which ensures that the amount of data is reduced while still maintaining the important features. Another method associated with processing a subset of the data that is typical of the whole is sampling, which also helps to reduce computational load and energy use. These techniques assist in the protection of data flow to reduce the consumption of energy in the process.

2.Edge Computing and Processing: Edge computing refers to the idea of processing data at the edge or origin of where the data is being generated such as at the IoT devices or sensors(Sudha, K et al 2023). Thus, the amount of raw data that have to be transferred to distant data centers to be processed decreases dramatically, which greatly reduces power consumption for data transfer and processing(Anusha, S et al 2024). This is particularly true in applications where latency and energy are of essence, such as in high speed communication systems.

3.Energy-Aware Data Placement: Energy aware data placement techniques are concerned with managing where data is located in a cluster of nodes. For instance, node energy efficiency, workload, and location, data can be placed in a way that will not consume a lot of energy. For example, placing the data on servers that are already underutilized, will help avoid additional energy consumption, and placement of data in data centers which are run on renewable energy will also enhance the energy efficiency of data centers.

In conclusion, energy efficiency in big data processing is a complex process that concerns both hardware and software levels, as well as data level approaches. With available low-power hardware, appropriate improvement of algorithms, reasonable management of resources, and effective energy-conscious data approaches, organizations are able to cut down energy consumption while achieving the necessary scale of data processing.

5. EMERGING TECHNOLOGIES AND TRENDS

The rapidly changing nature of big data processing is driven by new technologies and trends that are focused on energy consumption(Sreelakshmi, S et al 2024). All these innovations are helpful not only in saving energy but also in achieving the technology industry's sustainable development objectives. Other trends include the use of AI and machine learning for energy optimization, green data centers, fog and edge computing.

5.1 AI and Machine Learning for Energy Management:

In big data processing AI and ML can greatly enhance energy efficiency by utilizing predictive algorithms to minimize energy usage(Saravanan et al 2024). Artificial intelligence will be able to study past data from data centers, sensors, and infrastructure and then forecast the future energy consumption patterns and inefficiencies(Lakumarapu, S et al 2024). These predictive models can predict demand highs, meaning data centers can adapt to those changes, for example, by decreasing non-urgent workloads during a low-demand period or optimizing cooling systems, as the predicted temperature increases, to avoid wasteful energy consumption. Real-time monitoring of energy consumption across systems can also be done by using machine learning algorithms that could detect inefficiencies and suggest the right course of action(Yadav et al 2024). For instance, ML-based systems can determine how much computing power should be assigned to CPUs or GPUs, so that energy is consumed selectively. This leads to improved energy management, operating efficiency with the least energy as can be deemed optimum. Moreover, it can also adjust the system by collecting data of the real time scenario and thereby minimizing the need of intervention by the human being and increasing the efficiency of energy management in big data.

5.2 Green Data Centers:

The notion of green data centers has attracted a lot of attention in the course of the last few years, which is aimed at utilizing environmentally sustainable infrastructure and renewable power to support big data processing. It is important to note that the conventional data centers are infamous for their high power consumption mainly in cooling and powering the data centers (Channi, H. K., & Kumar, P. 2024). These challenges are sought to be addressed by green data centers that involve the use of energy conservative technologies and green facilities. The foremost method of increasing efficiency of data centers and thus reducing their impact on the environment is the use of renewable energy. Google, for instance, has invested billions to buy renewable energy for its data centers while Amazon and Microsoft have also committed to sourcing a big portion of their power from wind and solar. Moving away from fossil fuel based energy means that data centers are able to cut down on their emissions. In addition, most green data centers utilize efficient cooling systems like liquid cooling or free air cooling which consumes less energy than the conventional air conditioning systems. Besides the use of renewable energy and innovative cooling systems, green data centers ensure the use of low energy-consuming processing chips and SSDs. There may also be some sort of a design of data centers where energy can be customized depending on the demand so that no excess energy is consumed. In this way, green data centers decrease the costs of their operation and minimize negative influences on the environment, which is beneficial for creating sustainable big data (Ponnusamy et al 2021).

5.3 Fog and Edge Computing:

Fog computing and edge computing are two new models that are intended to minimize the energy consumption of large-scale data processing by bringing computation closer to data. These technologies solve the problems that arise from centralized cloud systems that take a lot of energy to transfer, store, and process information in distant centers. It the concept of processing information on the devices that create them including sensors, IoT devices, and smart devices(Svorobej et al 2019). Hence, edge computing helps to minimize the energy required to transmit data over long distances to centralized servers, and the time taken by data to travel those distances. For instance, edge devices can eliminate unneeded data or conduct data averaging before transmitting the data to the cloud, this way; only the important or averaged data is processed in the cloud. Fog computing layer between cloud and edge expands the concept of edge computing into a more extensive network of devices. It enables data processing at different intermediate points between the end devices and the central cloud, which reduces energy consumption as unnecessary data transport to remote data centers. Fog computing also helps to improve the load distribution since it is done with the consideration of the energy proximity of the data sources. Edge and fog computing are known to help save energy through limiting the amount of data that is transmitted, the need to process heavy data in energy-wasting central locations, and the demand placed on the network in terms of energy. These technologies are especially valuable for applications that require real-time analytics such as smart city, self-driving cars and industrial IoT where energy efficiency and response time are of prime importance (Kalyani, Y., & Collier, R. 2021).

In conclusion, new technologies like Artificial Intelligence for Energy Management, Green Data Centers, Edge, and Fog Computing are revolutionizing the big data systems with special reference to Energy Management. These innovations can be harnessed to decrease energy consumption while at the same time decreasing expenditures and ensure that organizations effectively support the increasing requirements of big data while also promoting the creation of a sustainable future.

6. CHALLENGES AND FUTURE DIRECTIONS

Even as the need for big data processing escalates, attaining energy efficiency is still a problem. In this part, the author looks at the technical issues of energy efficient computing, the future research prospects, and the legal and policy frameworks that foster sustainable IT practices.

6.1 Technical Challenges

1.Latency: This brings us to the first important factor which is latency in energy-efficient big data processing. Energy conservation is usually done with a compromise of power and efficiency. For example, edge computing and data compression are some of the methods that can be used to conserve energy through processing data at the source or through minimizing the size of data. However, these techniques might add some delay, especially when data should be processed in time real or when there is necessity of high-speed computation. Real-time processing, IoT, and self-driving cars are sensitive to the amount of energy they consume and how long they take to process a given piece of data. This particular challenge requires architecture of systems that can effectively ensure energy-saving measures while at the same time maintaining efficiency in the results.

2.Data Security: When energy efficiency is achieved on systems, the security of data becomes an essential concern. Most power conservation strategies like distributed computing or edge computing involve data transfer across the networks and multiple storage that makes the data more exposed. The problem specifies that data protection should be achieved in energy saving conditions while encryption, storage and access to the data should not consume much power. Therefore, achieving both energy optimization and strong security measures for the protection of user data and other information in large scale systems is a must.

3.Scalability: Energy-efficient solutions must also be able to handle the growing amount of data across industries and scale up properly. Although contemporary methods can enhance the efficiency of energy consumption in small and middle-sized complexes, they do not solve the problem of large-scale distributed structures. Cloud environments and data centers that are a form of distributed systems need to be designed as energy efficient as possible and need to be able to dynamically expand as the need for data processing increases. The ability to design algorithms and overall architecture that can effectively handle increasing amount of data and at the same time, be power-conscious is one of the important questions for big data systems of the future.

4.Tradeoffs in Energy Efficiency: Energy efficiency is often attained at the cost of suffering certain impacts on the system's performance. For instance, using less energy by limiting the computation or directing data to low-energy systems means that the processes will slow down or be less responsive. They have to be well balanced, particularly where the application is performance critical or needs to respond quickly. Scholars have to come up with approaches that do not compromise the performance of big data systems while cutting on energy consumption.

6.2 Opportunities for Future Research

1.Hardware Improvements: Future research opportunities are abundant in the area of hardware advancements with regard to energy savings. For instance, the next-generation processors like quantum processors and neuromorphic chips might provide improved coverage of instructions per watt, making it easier for large scale data processing to be energy efficient. Further, a new generation of energy efficient memory technologies, including non-volatile memory or memristors, may help minimize the energy consumption of the storage and computation functions. Investigations on other specialized accelerators for big data analytics such as ASICs can also offer the energy advantage by targeting specific workloads.

2.Software Optimization: The software has a great importance in the management and consumption of energy. It is also possible for future studies to consider algorithms that employ energy efficiency based on workload conditions to minimize additional computations. Much of this has to do with intelligent resource scheduling and management to avoid wasteful utilization of energy particularly in distributed systems, where energy-intensive operations must be scheduled properly. Also, further research on the use of machine learning methods can also be made to improve the tuning of the algorithms and parameterization for energy efficiency(Subha, S et al 2024).

3.Network Efficiency: As the amount of data grows, the network becomes one of the primary targets for energy optimization. Further studies could be aimed at the minimization of energy losses in the network's protocols and architectures during the transfer of data. More specific measures like deduplication of data, data compression and energy optimization in routing can be tried in order to reduce the energy expenses incurred while transferring big data over networks.

6.3 Regulatory and Policy Considerations

National and international regulatory authorities have a great role to encourage energy efficient computing practices by formulating certain rules and regulations. Measures that can make a wide use of energy-efficient technologies are, for instance, tax credits for companies that adopt green data center and renewable energy. Moreover, regulatory standards can be used to address the problem of the lack of unified approaches to the measurement of energy consumption by IT facilities and their usage by organizations. Governments can also sponsor research funding towards Energy efficient technologies with special focus on hardware enhancement, machine learning optimization and green data center. Multilateral initiatives, including the Paris Agreement, may assist in the general direction of the efforts at the international level to reduce energy consumption in the IT industry, while preserving the focus on other environmental goals. In addition, the creation of certifications and standards of energy-efficient computing practices will provide direction for technological advances and motivate firms to improve their processes. For instance, rules for energy-efficient cloud service or carbon dioxide emissions for data center may become guidelines that help companies enhance the industry's sustainability.

The state-of-the-art in energy-efficient big data processing is reasonably good, yet the prospective problems are latency, data security, and scalability, as well as the optimal balance between performance and energy consumption. New work on enhancing the efficiency of the hardware, software, and network can serve as new areas for the future advancement, while public and legal measures can contribute to the advancement of environmentally friendly computing. Thus, overcoming these challenges, the tech industry can build up the further development of energy-efficient and less-environmental-impact big data solutions.

7. CONCLUSION

From this survey of energy-efficient big data processing, there are several insights and lessons that stand out as best practices for organizations looking to reduce compute waste. As big data processing becomes a necessity, there are increasing issues concerning energy in data centers and distributed systems. But there has been a significant development in both hardware and software that has led to enhancement of efficient energy. Some of the highlighted fact includes the need to use energy efficient hardware like low power processors including ARM, FPGA, GPU and the use of renewable energy for data center. Measures such as in-memory processing in contexts such as Apache Spark, and data compression and deduplication, have been found to have potential in cutting down energy consumption at the time of data transfer and processing. Further, machine leaning and artificial intelligence based energy management systems are seen as effective for predictive and dynamic energy management. Some of the guidelines to follow to make big data processing energy efficient are efficient scheduling of resources, edge and fog computing, and green data center where the main focus is the energy-efficient equipment and renewable power. But as we push for more efficient systems, we must consider the trade-off with the performance of the system as well. Three persistent issues are latency, data security, and the ability to scale up the system. The gains made in energy efficiency must be balanced against the impacts on systems' functionality and the quality of service. They said that energy efficiency versus performance is one of the most critical aspects to consider. With such trends in the tech industry, people need to know how to meet growing needs for data processing while reducing the effects on the environment. In this way, it will be possible to encourage utilization of energy-efficient technologies, stimulate innovations, and establish the supportive legislation, which will allow big data processing being environmentally friendly in the future.

REFERENCES

Akil, B., Zhou, Y., & Röhm, U. (2017, December). On the usability of Hadoop MapReduce, Apache Spark & Apache flink for data science. In *2017 IEEE International Conference on Big Data (Big Data)* (pp. 303-310). IEEE. DOI: 10.1109/BigData.2017.8257938

Anusha, S., Ezhilvandan, M., Gayathri, S., Sivaraman, V., & Anish, T. P. (2024). Emerging trends in edge AI for Industry 4.0 and 5.0: Technologies, applications, and challenges. *AI Innovations in Service and Tourism Marketing*, 211-228.

Channi, H. K., & Kumar, P. (2024). Green Data Centers and Renewable Energy. In *AI Applications for Clean Energy and Sustainability* (pp. 161–186). IGI Global. DOI: 10.4018/979-8-3693-6567-0.ch009

Kalyani, Y., & Collier, R. (2021). A systematic survey on the role of cloud, fog, and edge computing combination in smart agriculture. *Sensors (Basel)*, *21*(17), 5922. DOI: 10.3390/s21175922 PMID: 34502813

Koseleva, N., & Ropaite, G. (2017). Big data in building energy efficiency: Understanding of big data and main challenges. *Procedia Engineering*, *172*, 544–549. DOI: 10.1016/j.proeng.2017.02.064

Lakumarapu, S., Nithyanandhan, R., Bhargavi, V. S., Anish, T. P., & Nalini, M. (2024, August). Machine Learning Approaches for Liver Disease Prediction: A Comparative Analysis. In *2024 5th International Conference on Electronics and Sustainable Communication Systems (ICESC)* (pp. 159-164). IEEE. DOI: 10.1109/ICESC60852.2024.10689974

Landset, S., Khoshgoftaar, T. M., Richter, A. N., & Hasanin, T. (2015). A survey of open source tools for machine learning with big data in the Hadoop ecosystem. *Journal of Big Data*, *2*(1), 1–36. DOI: 10.1186/s40537-015-0032-1

Ponnusamy, V., Sharma, B., & Lee, G. M. (2021). Green energy in data centers using internet of things. In *Role of IoT in green energy systems* (pp. 225–246). IGI Global. DOI: 10.4018/978-1-7998-6709-8.ch010

Sagiroglu, S., & Sinanc, D. (2013, May). Big data: A review. In *2013 international conference on collaboration technologies and systems (CTS)* (pp. 42-47). IEEE. DOI: 10.1109/CTS.2013.6567202

Saravanan, S., Khare, R., Umamaheswari, K., Khare, S., Gowda, B. K., & Boopathi, S. (2024). AI and ML Adaptive Smart-Grid Energy Management Systems: Exploring Advanced Innovations. In *Principles and Applications in Speed Sensing and Energy Harvesting for Smart Roads* (pp. 166-196). IGI Global.

Sreelakshmi, S., Babu, A. A., Lakshmipriya, C., Gracious, L. A., Nalini, M., & Subramanian, R. S. (2024, October). Enhancing Intrusion Detection Systems with Machine Learning. In *2024 2nd International Conference on Self Sustainable Artificial Intelligence Systems (ICSSAS)* (pp. 557-564). IEEE. DOI: 10.1109/ICSSAS64001.2024.10760341

Subha, S., Balakrishnan, C., & Anish, T. P. (2024, August). Optimizing Machine Learning Algorithms for Heart Disease Prediction in Healthcare: A Comparative Study. In *2024 5th International Conference on Electronics and Sustainable Communication Systems (ICESC)* (pp. 866-872). IEEE. DOI: 10.1109/ICESC60852.2024.10689877

Sudha, K., Ambhika, C., Maheswari, B., Girija, P., & Nalini, M. (2023). AI and IoT applications in medical domain enhancing healthcare through technology integration. In *AI and IoT-Based Technologies for Precision Medicine* (pp. 280–294). IGI Global.

Sudha, K., Balakrishnan, C., Anish, T. P., Nithya, T., Yamini, B., Subramanian, R. S., & Nalini, M. (2024). Data Insight Unveiled: Navigating Critical Approaches and Challenges in Diverse Domains Through Advanced Data Analysis. *Critical Approaches to Data Engineering Systems and Analysis*, 90-114.

Svorobej, S., Endo, P. T., Bendechache, M., Filelis-Papadopoulos, C., Giannoutakis, K. M., Gravvanis, G. A., Tzovaras, D., Byrne, J., & Lynn, T. (2019). Simulating fog and edge computing scenarios: An overview and research challenges. *Future Internet, 11*(3), 55. DOI: 10.3390/fi11030055

Yadav, P., Singh, B., Bhaskar, A., Srivastava, S., & Singh, S. K. (2024). Role of Artificial Intelligence in Renewable Energy Management for Sustainable Development. In *Methodologies, Frameworks, and Applications of Machine Learning* (pp. 108-124). IGI Global. DOI: 10.4018/979-8-3693-1062-5.ch006

Zheng, Z., Zhu, J., & Lyu, M. R. (2013, June). *Service-generated big data and big data-as-a-service: an overview. In 2013 IEEE international congress on Big Data.* IEEE. DOI: 10.1109/BigData.Congress.2013.60

Chapter 8
Advancing Sustainability in Software Engineering:
Key Practices and Future Directions

S. Anusha
Easwari Engineering College, India

R. Nithyanandhan
SA Engineering College, India

B. Yamini
https://orcid.org/0000-0003-3531-108X
SRM Institute of Science and Technology, India

S. Balapriya
Sathyabama Institute of Science and Technology, India

V. Kalpana
Vel Tech Rangarajan Dr. Sagunthala R&D Institute of Science and Technology, India

T. P. Anish
https://orcid.org/0000-0002-4308-9645
R.M.K. College of Engineering and Technology, India

A. Venkateshan
https://orcid.org/0009-0006-8570-0023
Sri Muthukumaran Institute of Technology, India

ABSTRACT

The escalating environmental consequences of software development have raised a concern for sustainable software engineering throughout the life cycle. Green software engineering aims at reducing the power utilization in software systems as well as containing the carbon impact of software systems, and managing the resources properly. This survey also summarizes the major approaches to integrate sustainability into each phase the following phases are sustainable requirements engineering, energy-aware coding, green DevOps, and sustainable data management. Sustainability is further improved by ideas such as energy efficient design patterns, resource efficient algorithms, and dynamic resource scaling. It also covers some of

DOI: 10.4018/979-8-3373-0766-4.ch008

Copyright © 2025, IGI Global Scientific Publishing. Copying or distributing in print or electronic forms without written permission of IGI Global Scientific Publishing is prohibited.

the recent tools for energy profiling, green deployment and green cloud computing. The goal of this paper is to give some idea of the state of sustainable software engineering practices, potential future developments, and to point out where research, automation, and policy may be needed to promote the adoption of such practices.

1. INTRODUCTION

1.1 Background

Over the last few years, people have become more conscious of the effects that numerous industries have on the environment, including software engineering. With this growing adoption of technology, there are corresponding increases in the energy and raw material requirements in the creation of software. Coding and testing of software, and its deployment and maintenance, are among the practices that have recently been in the news for sustainability reasons. Many industries have gone digital, cloud computing, and data storage as well as large-scale software applications consume a lot of energy(Rani et al 2023). The use of Internet, cloud services, and digital facilities has raised the energy consumption rates around the world and data centers are the major consumers of energy in the world. However, as society and businesses strive to meet specific sustainability goals, it has emerged that the software engineering community needs to adapt more sustainable development to meet the broader environmental and social goals of sustainability.

1.2 Motivation

Environmental effects due to software development exist in various dimensions. Aside from the energy utilized when running the software, the total life cycle of the software development process, as well as its disposal once it has become obsolete, contributes heavily to the consumption of resources, such as hardware disposal, and inefficient coding strategies. Technological advancement and sustainability are two fundamental aspects that are shaping the world's economy and businesses hence software engineering has to embrace sustainability. More specifically, the skills to design, build and implement software in a manner, which minimizes power consumption to keep resource utilization at optimum levels while maximizing system lifespan, is becoming more and more crucial. When organisations apply sustainability principles in software engineering, they are directly investing in the fight against climate change. In addition, there is also need to develop energy efficient software since many consumers and clients consider environmentally sustainable practices. This demand also opens up a chance for software engineers to save costs and at the same time improve their organization's image and meet the new sustainability standards and legal requirements.

1.3 Objectives

The main reason for this survey is to understand how sustainability practices are incorporated into the software development life cycle. This includes methods, issues and opportunities in designing software systems for energy efficiency, resource responsiveness and social responsibility. Sources of the survey will also include how sustainability practices can be integrated in different phases of software engineering such as requirement analysis phase, design phase, coding phase, testing phase, implementation phase and maintenance phase. Further, it will evaluate the tools, frameworks, and methodologies still being developed to underpin such sustainable practices. Another important goal is to understand the limitations and the obstacles that have to be overcome to increase the usage of sustainable software engineering such as performance, resource, and standardization constrains. Last but not least, the survey seeks to identify the directions for further research in this area, and discuss the potential of other novel technologies, including AI and ML, in achieving energy-efficient software and the role that the standards and policies of the software industry can play in achieving the goal of sustainability at a large scale.

1.4 Structure of the Survey

This paper will be systematically organised to cater for all the diverse aspects of sustainable software engineering. It begins with an exploration of the core principles of sustainable software engineering and the three dimensions of sustainability: Namely, there are four types of impacts: environmental, economic, social and organizational. The next sections look at sustainable practices in the various stages of the software development life cycle. These are requirement engineering, design, coding, testing and deployment all of which are done in the context of energy efficiency. The survey then turns to energy-aware software engineering to discuss profiling tools and approaches to energy consumption. It also includes environmentally friendly approaches to DevOps, ecological approaches to data management and storage that enable the decrease of negative impact on the environment by software. This paper features examples from industry innovators and open-source projects and then presents the obstacles to and impediments to sustainable practices. Last but not the least, the survey is wrapped up with a brief discussion on the future research direction in sustainable software engineering.

2. DEFINING SUSTAINABLE SOFTWARE ENGINEERING

2.1 What is Sustainable Software Engineering?

Sustainable Software Engineering can be defined as a process of applying environmental, economic and social sustainability models in software development processes(Leong et al 2023). It focuses on the design of software systems that have least effect on the environment, use the best available resources efficiently, and are sustainable. The fundamental concepts of sustainable software engineering management seek to minimize energy use, resource utilization and carbon footprint throughout the application life cycle. It also supports the adoption of environmentally friendly technologies, optimal coding practices and structures and infrastructure solutions. Sustainable software engineering is not only about efficient code but also the whole life cycle of a software product, its design, deployment and maintenance. It also includes the elements of ethical practice, social responsiveness and creating software that is beneficial to society. Sustainable software engineering refers to the development of efficient software systems in terms of resource consumption in addition to its speed. This involves taking deliberate actions right from the design and development cycle to ensure that the energy and other resources are not used up within short time. The focus here is to develop software that will be stable and which will not be frequently changed or replaced. Thus, following these principles, software engineers can play a role in decreasing the environmental load of the industry which is constantly expanding and is becoming more influential in the sphere of global sustainability(Semerikov et al 2020).

2.2 Environmental, Economic, and Social Dimensions

Sustainability in software engineering is often discussed in terms of three dimensions: There are three categories of impacts they include; environmental impacts, economic impacts and social impacts. All these dimensions are referred in as the 'Triple Bottom Line,' which is a sustainable measure that is wider than energy efficiency.

Environmental Dimension: This area of sustainable software engineering is concerned with minimizing the carbon, energy, and overall ecological cost of software systems. This ranges from improving the performance of a specific software to work well with the hardware, bringing down power consumption in processing data, enhanced ways of storing and transferring data that do not consume a lot of power. However, sustainability also relates to energy efficiency of the cloud providers, server farms, and data centers that host the software.

Economic Dimension: The economic aspect is centered on making certain that software engineering practices result in cost-efficient solutions in the process of achieving sustainable development. This includes the need to eliminate the need for new hardware investment by fine-tuning the software to work with existing hardware and the need to lower the energy costs for inefficient software. Economically sustainable software engineering also seeks to develop systems that will have minimal overhead for maintenance resulting in low total cost of ownership (TCO) to users and organizations.

Social Dimension: The social factor in sustainable software engineering addresses the effects of software on society. This entails making software available, usable by everyone and not unethical. Social sustainability may encompass software that is designed to be fairly designed, that is transparent, that takes account of the user's privacy and that contributes to the common good in areas like health, education, and the environment. Social sustainability is therefore focused on creating a society of responsible software engineers and development, equal job opportunities, and ethical decision on the software development process(Matthew et al 2024).

2.2 Sustainability Metrics

Overall, to evaluate and monitor the sustainability of the software engineering practices different metrics to capture the environmental, economical, and social aspects are employed. Some of the key performance indicators (KPIs) in sustainable software engineering include:

Energy Consumption: It is a measure that is used in evaluating the power utilization of the software during its operation. Energy might also be reported as Watts per transaction, energy per operation, or the overall runtime efficiency of software. Another straightforward approach to achieving environmentally desirable objectives is to decrease energy use in software.

Carbon Footprint: The carbon footprint is defined as the complete measure of the GHGs released due to software development, implementation, and use. This will also encompass the energy consumed by the software as well as the emissions from the hardware, networks, and data centers that the software runs on. This can include fine tuning software to run on low energy hardware, use of renewable energy and avoiding any task that may be done by the software which is not necessary.

Resource Utilization: This metric measures the degree to which physical resources like computing capacity, memory, and storage are consumed. Optimality: In the use of the hardware components, the efficient software should not require high computational capacity, storage, and data transfer hence minimal power and financial requirements.

These sustainability metrics assist the software engineers in determining where change can be made, whether at the code level, the level of the hardware, or in the selection of the cloud services. By maintaining such metrics on a constant basis, the development of software can advance the causes of sustainability and the improvement of the environmental footprint of the technology sector.

3. SUSTAINABLE PRACTICES IN SOFTWARE DEVELOPMENT PHASES

Requirements Engineering

The domain of requirements engineering is the first phase in software development where sustainable considerations can be effectively incorporated in the SDLC. It is therefore recommended that when defining requirements, sustainability goals must be part of the process so that sustainability objectives become part of the project(Agarwal et al 2012). This includes working with stakeholders to come up with not only the functional and non-functional requirements, but also the sustainability requirements, including energy, resource and scalability requirements. Sustainable requirements can be a goal of decreasing energy usage, lowering software resource waste or developing software that is ethical. Also, the user needs should be assessed with a view of avoiding over-engineering which might cause problems of resource waste and energy(Naseer et al 2020). The reasons are that such goals help to maintain sustainability on the agenda of the project in general and in specific phases of the project, and because proper definition of objectives allows teams to take into consideration sustainability aspects in decision making all the time.

Design for Sustainability

The design phase of software development is another chance to guarantee the integration of sustainability into the structure of software. Sustainable architectural and design patterns mean that solutions should be constructed in a way that is scalable and optimized within the means of energy, material, and time. For example, modular architectures and microservices provide better resource utilization by scaling the component's resource according to its usage instead of providing extra resources to meet the maximum possible usage. Further, the use of resource-frugal data management techniques like memory-efficient data models, or data structures that avoid data redundancy, can go a long way to decreasing the resource load on software systems. Optimisation of the algorithms and data models used in a system prevent unnecessary processing hence using up of more CPU resources. Incorporating scalability in the design means that the systems can expand without having to consume more energy than is necessary. This kind of design thinking assists in developing tools that can easily scale up to meet increased loads in future without having to massively expand the consumption of resources in the environment or the need for extensive infrastructure.

Sustainable Coding Practices

During the coding phase, sustainable software engineering is concerned with developing low energy utilization algorithms and efficient code. The execution of code can be directly related to energy consumption since some algorithms can make CPU use more than others and take longer to run. For example, by choosing algorithms that perform fewer computations (for example, using algorithms with $O(n \log n)$ instead of $O(n^2)$), developers can minimize the amount of resources needed. Thirdly, reducing duplication of code is useful in preventing wasteful computation and makes the software lean. According to the guideline used in developing applications, such as using minimum memory and accessing data with efficient patterns, the energy consumption reduces as well as the cost of operations. The type of the language used also has an effect—some languages consume more resources than the others, and this information also should be taken into consideration when choosing the tools and languages for the project.

Testing and Quality Assurance

Verification and validation are critical activities that enable the assessment of the software's functionality, but they are also time-consuming. Economical testing therefore concerns the optimization of the testing process with a view of reducing the amount of computation used in testing and still obtain effective test coverage. One of them is virtualization that allows running tests in conditions that require fewer resources. The fact that virtual environments can handle multiple tests at the same time also means that there is no need for additional hardware, which in turn also means that less energy is consumed. Another practice is efficient test case generation which means that high risk test cases should be run first, and the total number of test cases to be run should be optimized to exclude those that are not so relevant. This process can also be made easier by the use of automated testing tools since they can run optimized test suites. Also, CI and CT practices are used to identify problems at a stage when they can be fixed without using too many resources for testing.

Deployment and Maintenance

During the deployment and maintenance phase, sustainability practices are based on the functionality of software systems. Continuous deployment (CD) practices are used to make changes in a production system seamlessly, without much down time and resources. One activity is the proper choosing of energy-efficient servers and the management of server requirements according to their usage. Green energy deployment or providers with highly optimized infrastructure can significantly cut the carbon costs accrued during the deployment process. Resource monitoring tools help developers to track the energy consumption and performance of the deployed systems, which can help finding out where it is feasible to cut resources even further. Moreover, containerization and virtualization support optimized execution of new software with low resource utilization and more efficient scaling according to client traffic patterns. Measurable also incorporates observing the effects the software has on operational performance, deciding when to refactor in order to make the code perform better, and guaranteeing that the systems remain active without consuming more resources than needed. Through the integration of these sustainable practices throughout the life cycle of software development, requirements engineering, design, coding, testing and deployment, software engineers can thus minimize the environmental footprint of their software systems while at the same time improving the operating efficiency of the system and advancing the cause of sustainable technology(Robillard 2016).

4. ENERGY-AWARE SOFTWARE ENGINEERING

4.1 Energy Profiling and Analysis Tools

Energy profiling and analysis tools are necessary in the assessment of energy consumption of these software systems and to discover potential energy saving approaches. These tools help software engineers to quantify the energy consumed by a particular software application during its running. Developers can then optimize their code or deployment plan by using the detailed information about the energy needs of each process.

Greenfoot is an environment created for the construction of graphical simulations and games as well as their analysis. It has energy profiling features that enable the developers to monitor energy usage of software programs based on the Java language. Greenfoot addresses this problem by giving programmers a graphical representation of where in the software most energy is being used, allowing for concentration on high-energy areas.

Joulmeter is a tool for measuring energy consumption of application that is operating on Windows This makes it possible for developers to record and track energy consumption at a finer level, for processes, or components, or even applications. Through feedback in real time, Joulmeter is useful to developers to optimize the application and minimize energy loss.

These tools, and other profiling tools, allow energy hot-spots in applications to be highlighted to the developers so that the application can be optimized to use less power. When energy profiling is incorporated in the development process, developers are in a position to make the right decisions on how to design their software with less energy.

4.2 Energy-Aware Programming Languages and Frameworks

Some programming languages and or frameworks are created or are more friendly to energy consumption than others. Such languages and frameworks come with inbuilt options that help in efficient memory utilization, less resource consumption and optimal use of the hardware resources which in turn leads to less power consumption.

Energy-efficient languages: Among such languages, C and C++ are distinguished by close control of memory and the capability to generate highly optimized code that provides faster software operation. They enable the developers to make their applications more precise and use less resource which affects energy consumption. But they demand more control over memory and resources, which can lead to the growth of development difficulties.

Energy-aware frameworks: Development frameworks like Spring Boot or .NET have some default configurations that may lower energy consumption, for example setting up the task to not overwork CPU when it is not needed. Also, Node.js and other frameworks that can perform asynchronous operations will save energy since the system will not spend much time on processing other non-related operations.

Energy-optimized libraries: There is a number of libraries and tools that are directed towards the energy optimization. For instance, Energy-Aware Java Libraries offer low power consumption variations of Java data structures and algorithms for executing low energy usage during execution. By using such libraries and tools, it becomes possible to build more energy efficient software while sparing the essential application code.

It emerges that energy-conscious programming languages and frameworks provide the strategic foundation for constructing sustainable software. They assist in optimization of energy-efficient development practices due to availability of predefined features and patterns that minimize resource use.

4.3 Dynamic Resource Allocation

Real-time resource scheduling is a concept that is used in the management of hardware resources with the needs of the software application in mind. This approach prevents energy from being consumed unnecessarily in that more resources than required or systems are not operated at higher capacity than required.

Cloud environments: Thus, a detailed understanding of cloud computing and its services shows that dynamic resource allocation can be accomplished through auto-scaling and load balancing techniques. Auto-scaling means that the cloud infrastructure is able to allocate resources depending on the usage of the application(Kavitha et al 2022). For instance, in high load situations, extra virtual machines also known as VMs can easily be created to cater for the load. On the other hand, during low demand, the resources can be minimized to cut energy use, hence serve as a reserve of excess demand. This on-demand allocation increases efficiency because energy is only used only when required and not before that(Sasubilli, M. K., & Venkateswarlu, R 2021).

Virtualization: Containers and hypervisors are virtualization technologies that allow for the proper utilization of computer resources by separation of applications into lightweight ones. These technologies enable more density of workloads on physical hardware, thereby minimizing the amount of machines needed for many applications. This is made possible by the fact that multiple virtual instances can be run on the same physical server hence slicing the power consumption.

Resource-aware scheduling: Dynamic resource allocation also includes intelligent resource scheduling for tasks that assigns specific tasks to specific hardware resources depending on the energy consumption of the latter. For instance, energy-aware scheduling algorithms can help in making sure that tasks requiring much computation are allocated to the servers or processors that have the greatest power to performance ratio so that the energy consumption is cut down.

The use of dynamic resource allocation is important in order to reduce energy consumption in both cloud and on-premise scenarios. If resources are allocated dynamically according to the actual needs of the software, then developers can guarantee that energy will be spent more wisely and that as much waste as possible will be averted during their idle times.

Thus, energy-aware software engineering is a set of approaches and methods aimed at helping the developers observe and minimize the energy consumption by the produced applications. Energy profiling tools, energy efficient programming languages and framework and dynamic resource management all come together in creating software that has a lower energy profile, which supports the sustainability agenda and thus contributes towards the reduction of the impact of the software industry on the environment.

5. GREEN DEVOPS AND SUSTAINABLE DEPLOYMENT

5.1 Sustainable DevOps Pipelines

The application of DevOps, a concept that unites software development with the IT operations is crucial for effective software systems deployment. But it can also be very costly in terms of energy usage, especially when performing complex CI/CD processes for testing, building and deploying applications. Sustainable DevOps pipelines in an effort to cut down on energy consumption at every stage of CI/CD are created.

Key strategies for making DevOps pipelines more sustainable include:

Optimizing resource usage: The first and most obvious method of energy-saving within CI/CD pipelines is to avoid wastage of resources. For instance, by not scheduling unnecessary breaks or procuring resources that are not required, then the DevOps team can save energy. This can be done through programming, which can enable scheduled suspension or rationing of resource usage when they are not required, for instance at night.

Efficient testing strategies: Testing is a big component of CI/CD, and while testing is important in order to catch problems, it's often costly. Effective test case generation of sustainable pipelines is another test strategy where only the most important tests need to be run. This can lower the overall count of tests that are run meaning that energy will be saved, all without compromising on the quality of the software being developed. Moreover, tests can be parallelized, and running tests can be based on cloud resources that will take less time to complete, during which energy-intensive processes are performed.

Energy-efficient build processes: When optimizing the build process, the teams may exclude compilations and packaging's which are unnecessary but take much computational power. For instance, instead of using full build, one is able to use incremental builds to minimize the computation burden. However, lightweight build environments can be employed to decrease the energy consumption during this phase even more.

5.2 Green Cloud Computing

This paper focuses on the aspect of energy efficiency of the cloud computing services as more organizations shift their operations online(Radu 2017). Green cloud computing concentration is on the choice of green cloud service providers and energy-providing services. To this end, organizations should select cloud services that are environmentally friendly in their approach to cutting down on emissions.

Key elements of green cloud computing include:

Renewable energy sources: Most cloud service providers have switched their data centres to green power sources such as wind, solar, or hydroelectric power. The use of providers who depend on green energy in an attempt to decrease the carbon footprint of cloud services goes a long way. Major tech players such as Google, AWS, and Microsoft Azure have started investing in renewable power and share their energy consumption and green initiatives publicly. If these providers are selected, firms are able to contribute positively to the shift towards a more sustainable economy while minimizing negative effects.

Energy-efficient data centers: Cloud providers dedicate much effort and resources to ensure that their data centers use less power to operate. Such new technologies comprise intelligent air-cooling techniques, use of machine learning algorithms to balance the loads in servers, and enhanced server architectures that use less energy(Sreelakshmi, S et al 2024)(Lakumarapu, S et al 2024). Depending on the location, businesses should give preference to cloud providers with LEED or ISO 50001 certifications to point at their focus on energy efficiency.

Optimizing cloud resource allocation: Cloud computing makes it possible to allocate resources in proportion to the demand. A suitable cloud deployment is that which employs necessary cloud resources to address workload requirements. For example auto scaling means that servers are added during usage peak and removed during low traffic, thus eliminating wastage of energy. In the case of virtualization and containerization the two are similar in that they both allow applications to be deployed across different environments(Patel et al 2015).

5.3 Virtualization and Containerization

Virtualization and containerization are technologies including the hardware resources to deploy more efficiently, which makes the deployment more sustainable.

Virtualization has the capability to let one physical host server many virtual host servers/ machines. This technique provides maximum server utilization because resource is dedicated for different application or service, so the number of physical servers required is less and therefore overall energy consumption is also less. Virtualization also makes it possible to combine workloads, or grouping of applications, and this is a great way to minimize the impact of running multiple physical servers.

Another energy-efficient deployment model is the containerization tools like Docker and Kubernetes. Containers are much lighter than VMs and consume less resources, because they run on a host system kernel rather than a full-blown OS. This cuts on cost since more applications can be run on the same physical host, hence using less energy is achieved. Containers are also well arranged in relation to resource usage, and container management systems such as Kubernetes can be used to automatically scale the containers based on the need and hence more efficient in the utilization of energy. Virtualization and containerization are related to sustainability because they enhance resource utilization, minimize equipment demands, and decrease the environmental cost of running multiple services or applications. These technologies also help the cloud environments since they can be deployed and scaled in a way that cuts wastage of energy.

To sum up, it is possible to state that green DevOps practices, green cloud computing, as well as virtualization and containerization are crucial for sustainable software delivery. Through optimization of CI/CD pipelines, selection of cloud providers with strong sustainability policies, and utilization of virtualization and containerization technologies, organizations can greatly decrease their energy consumption and their overall carbon footprint, which will help support the goal of sustainability in the technology field. All these approaches are sustainable and also improve cost effectiveness and efficiency in the management of operations.

6. SUSTAINABLE DATA MANAGEMENT AND STORAGE

6.1 Data Minimization and Compression

The rule of thumb of sustainable data management is minimization of data where data collection, processing, and storage are concerned. This way, organizations can drastically cut the amount of resources they need to cater to data, lower storage costs and enhance the processing speed all of which make a positive impact on the environment.

Data minimization involves several strategies, including:

Selective data collection: Consequently, organizations should not accumulate information in bulk as a matter of course but should only gather the information that is required for the operation of organizations. This can be done by using filters, having clear data collection policies in place and using systems that record only the necessary information.

Data aggregation: Storing the raw data may mean that the actual data will contain some redundant data which are eliminated by condensing the data into more compressed forms like summaries or statistical overviews. This aggregation is useful in order to retain as much of this information as possible while using as little physical space as necessary for storage.

6.2 Energy-Efficient Databases

Database is the basic component in the present day storage and retrieval system and these are energy intensive if not efficient. Low resource databases are implemented to reduce the amount of resources needed to store, retrieve and process data in support of efficient energy usage in Information Technology.

Key strategies for creating energy-efficient databases include:

Efficient indexing and query optimization: The database query optimization and indexing can make a huge difference in the amount of computational resources required for the query search. Sophisticated queries cause high CPU utilization and may take longer time hence using more energy. The databases are indexed effectively and the queries optimized to reduce the amount of effort required to retrieve data thus reducing on energy consumption.

Low-power database engines: Some of the databases like SQLite are particularly developed to operate effectively on low power devices and low power consumption. These low power engines have good balance between CPU and memory utilization and therefore would be suitable for use in systems that are energy constrained such as embedded systems or mobile systems.

Sharding and partitioning: Dividing of large databases into a number of smaller and easier to handle sub-databases (sharding) or dividing data based on a certain scheme can also assist in minimizing the load placed on the database servers. This makes it easier to scale and use resources especially when working with huge data or many transactions.

In-memory databases: Cache servers like Redis or Memcached are actually databases which store data in the system's memory rather than a disk, so they can minimize the number of disk I/O operations. In addition to providing faster access to data, these databases cut disk access frequency to a bare minimum, thus saving power consumption. Energy efficient databases assist in bringing down the carbon impact of IT by enhancing the effectiveness of storing and processing data and hence less power is used to run databases that handle large amount of data.

6.3 Data Lifecycle Management

Data lifecycle management (DLM) can be defined as the processes of handling data throughout its life cycle from the time it is generated to the time it is disposed of. The data lifecycle management makes it possible to keep data for as short a time as possible or to process or archive it in an environmentally friendly manner.

The key elements of data lifecycle management for sustainability include:

Data retention policies: One of the most important points of DLM is to establish unambiguous rules concerning the duration of data storage. For example, data that is not useful for the business or data that has to be deleted according to the law must be erased. As organizations work to manage less data over time, the need for storage and the energy that comes with it is also minimized.

Archiving: When data must be kept but is infrequently accessed, archiving provides a cost-effective way of maintaining the data without placing it in high-cost, high-energy environments. Archiving is the process of migrating less frequently accessed data files to low power consuming storage technology like tapes or archival cloud services that are much less power-hungry than OLTP databases.

Automated data deletion: In this manner methods such as using of auto shredding to delete old or unimportant data assist in avoiding accumulation of the data. Such systems can be on schedule (for example after a specific time or when some conditions occur) and can also minimize the amount of work that has to be done in order to manage data retention.

Data deletion and secure disposal: Guaranteed disposal measures are employed in such a way that data is removed from the storage media to avoid exposure whereas storage assets are recovered. Deletion as one of the best practices to avoid the buildup of unused data and which in turn enhances efficiency in data management. Following these principles will help an organization make its data management practices sustainable. Data lifecycle management ensures only the right data is created, used and when it is no longer needed it is deleted which reduces the amount of storage space needed, power consumption and in extension the impact on the environment. Therefore, besides the already mentioned techniques like data reduction and compression, efficient database systems, and data lifecycle management, it is crucial to limit the amount of data used and stored within data systems in order to decrease the overall energy consumption and its impact on the environment. Through these practices, organizations have an opportunity of saving on their expenses while at the same time promote sustainability in the technology sector.

7. CHALLENGES AND BARRIERS TO SUSTAINABLE SOFTWARE ENGINEERING

Lack of Standardization

What this means is that one of the most important obstacles to sustainable software engineering is the fact that there are no standard frameworks for practice and measurement. At the moment, there are no widely accepted best practices or methodologies that can be applied across organizations that would guide them through the process of sustainable measurement and integration into software development. This lack of standardization leads to confusion and inconsistency, and so the developers, organizations, and even the consumer will find it hard to compare the impacts of different software systems on the environment. Since there is no clear definition of what it means for software to be sustainable, different developers may have different ideas as to what it means to be energy efficient or resource sparing. This leads to differential where sustainability is practiced in disjointed and uncoordinated manner. Like sustainability efficiency indicators, sustainability performance indicators are also not standardized, and organizations might use different methods or tools for measuring energy usage, carbon dioxide emission, or material use. This means that it is hard to evaluate the effectiveness of the software engineering practices making it difficult to progress towards the set sustainable goals. In addition, the absence of universal standards implies that organizations can be in a state of confusion whenever they try to gauge and compare the energy efficiency of their software systems. While there are Carbon Tracker and CO2.js tools for estimating carbon footprints caused by software, their use and presentation are not consistent, which results in certain differences in assessing and combating sustainability.

Performance vs. Energy Trade-offs

Another critical problem in the area of sustainable software engineering is the problem of achieving an optimal balance of performance and power consumption. Often, the lowest energy solution is not the best one in terms of performance needs of today's software systems. Intensive computations involving artificial intelligence, big data processing, and real-time analytics are some of the key applications that run on high-performance software systems; a feature that raises the energy requirements of these systems significantly. For instance, highly parallelized systems or algorithms with short processing time claim high power consumption even if they are faster in their processing time. On the other hand, the energy efficient software may cause a trade-off between energy consumption and speed or processing power. This trade-off can pose some issues especially when working with applications that are critical to an organization's operations or those whose success depends on the speed at which they execute, that is, latency and throughput are often critical parameters. Choosing between optimizing the program for performance at the cost of energy efficiency or vise versa is not always easy as developers have to consider the environment in which the program will be used. Any time, energy conservation could be considered less important when it comes to performance, and in as much as energy conservation is important, performance could be considered unimportant hence making it a contentious issue. In order to address this issue, some researchers are investigating methods of implementing modified versions of these energy-efficient approaches where they can be integrated without a major performance penalty; however, these solutions are not yet available.

Cost and Resource Limitations

A third issue for sustainable software engineering is the question of cost and resources, especially for many organisations including small or new ventures. Unlike giants like Google and Microsoft who can spend a lot of money on power efficient premises, renewable energy and tools to fine-tune the software, many organizations may not be able to do this.

The initial investment needed to acquire energy-efficient hardware and software, optimized software tools, and sustainable cloud services is unaffordable for small companies. Further, sustainability strategies are long term and may involve certain technical know-how and change management that can be a challenge to companies with a lean workforce and limited funds. However, there are apparent drawbacks to the use of sustainability in organizations because organizations believe that they have to spend a lot of money in order to make sustainable changes. For instance, switching to energy-efficient software tools or cloud services may have lower operational costs in the future but incurs costs on researching for the right software, training employees and modifying the software. Although there are many advantages in the long run that the small businesses can gain through practicing sustainable software engineering, these disadvantages can act as a discouragement to the companies from engaging in sustainable software engineering.

Therefore, despite the increased awareness of the role of sustainable software engineering, there are a few barriers that slowly can be overcome. Lack of similarities in practices as well as measurements, a sophisticated relationship between performance and power consumption, and cost and resource constraints in small organizations are the key challenges. To overcome these challenges the industry requires clearer guidelines, better tools, and more affordable resources to ensure that sustainable software practices are possible for all organizations, big and small.

8. FUTURE RESEARCH DIRECTIONS

8.1 Advanced Energy Profiling Tools

In the context of the future research in sustainable software engineering, one of the more promising areas is the enhancement of the energy profiling tools. Today, energy profiling is usually done in a basic or fixed approach, where information is gathered from outside profiling tools or estimated by utilization of the hardware data. However, for efficient energy optimization in complex software systems, better and real time approaches are required for measuring the energy during development as well as in the runtime environment.

Future energy profiling tools should offer several key improvements:

1. **Real-time energy monitoring:** Traditional tools are normally used to give data after implementation of plans, which hinders the use of energy savvy decisions in the developmental stage. Such monitoring features would really be valuable since the changes made during development could be checked for energy impact in real time, and this way potential inefficiencies can be corrected early on.
2. **Granular energy measurement:** Profiling tools need to advance in order to track energy usage at the level of specific operations, methods, or procedures, as well as all the way up to the system level. This would allow for more fine-tuning and allow people developing the software to better determine certain areas of the program that hogs unnecessary energy.

3.**Cross-platform compatibility:** Since software is used across various devices, operating systems and cloud infrastructures, energy profiling tools have to be platform and architecture agnostic. This will enable the organizations to monitor energy consumption independently of the location of the software, thus enhance the efficiency of energy management.

With these more sophisticated tools the software engineering community will have the means to fine tune applications for not only performance, but also, energy consumption so that organizations and consequently, the world will have a smaller carbon footprint.

8.2 Automated Sustainability Techniques

One other area for future work is the use of automated sustainability methods driven by artificial intelligence. To begin with, manual optimization for sustainability becomes a challenging task given the advanced complexity of the current software systems. AI solutions can help to drastically reduce the time and efforts required to make software more energy efficient.

Key research directions in this area include:

1.**AI-based code optimization:** Machine learning algorithms can be taught to identify code practices that result in high power usage and provide or apply improvements(Maithili, K et al 2024)(Yamini, B et al 2024). For instance, machine learning techniques can be employed to identify parts of the code which contain unnecessary computations, unnecessary iterations, or excessive memory accesses and offer more efficient solutions(Anita, M et al 2024).
2.**Design pattern automation:** AI could be used in the utilization of sustainable design patterns on software projects. For instance, AI tools might propose scalable architectures, low-energy data structures or algorithms that have minimal environmental impact depending on the given application.
3.**Predictive sustainability models:** It could also be used in determining the sustainability implication of specific development decisions before they are taken. AI could analyse previous project data and recommend to developers the best practices to minimize energy consumption during the construction process, as well as identifying the corresponding adverse practices in the design stage.

When AI tools are implemented into the software development process, organizations could gain more sustainable results with less inputs required to develop the software, time and energy.

8.3 Policy and Regulatory Support

The third important area for future work should address the issue of the lack of policy and legal frameworks that can help enhance the use of sustainability in software engineering. Today there is very limited legal requirements that businesses have to adhere to in terms of the amount of energy used or the impact they have on the environment when developing software, and this is why many businesses prioritize speed and efficiency over sustainability and the long-term effects of their actions on the environment.

Future research could focus on:

1. **Industry standards:** There lies a necessity to establish the common industry standards for measurement and reporting the environmental effects of the software. Examples of standards could be particular energy efficiency requirements, methods of determining carbon footprint of an application, and principles of green software deployment. These standards would offer a single blueprint within which software developers and organizations could work and consequently, ease the implementation of sustainable practices in the industry.
2. **Government regulations:** This could be done through regulations or through tax incentives set up by the government to encourage sustainable software engineering. As with hardware products, requirements for software could include minimum energy efficiency or the use of renewable sources in data centres. Policy initiatives might also involve the promotion of research in the development of sustainable software tools and technologies by offering funding or grant support for their development.
3. **Corporate responsibility frameworks:** It could also be useful to investigate theories of how corporate governance can be made to encourage companies to act as good stewards of the environment. This could involve setting up a system of ranking or accreditation for firms that should be deemed to be leading the way on sustainability in software production and utilisation, thereby persuading firms to adopt cleaner ways of working in software creation and use.

Thus, with the adoption of these policies and regulations, the software industry may set up a clearer and more popular agenda on sustainability, which can then create an ongoing and shared movement toward change and improve the environmental performance of software development.

Therefore, the further improvement of sustainable software engineering is based on the introduction of more sophisticated energy profiling techniques, the employment of AI-based sustainability methods, and the establishment of industry rules and governmental norms. Studying in these areas will go a long way in addressing some of the challenges currently being faced, improve the efficiency of the development processes and produce software systems that are both high performing and eco-friendly. Realization of sustainable practices in software engineering will therefore require concerted efforts from the research fraternity, industry players, and policy makers.

9. CONCLUSION

Green software engineering is a relatively new domain of study and practice since the energy consumption and carbon footprint of information systems are becoming increasingly important issues. In this survey, we have discussed different sustainable practices at different stages of the software development life cycle, along with relevant practices and issues. 1.Sustainable Practices in the Software Development Phases: It is possible to adopt sustainability throughout the different stages of software development. From requirements engineering where sustainability goals can be identified and included through to design for sustainability where low impact architectural patterns and energy efficient data structures can be specified there is a clear roadmap for the inclusion of sustainability throughout. In coding, one can concentrate on efficient algorithms, the use of code that is copied as few times as possible or to use energy efficient coding. In testing and quality assurance, the computational resources must be minimized through virtualization and testing cases generation. Lastly, it is crucial to pay much attention to deployment and maintenance aiming at making improvements on a continuous basis in terms of energy efficient servers and resources. 2.Energy-Aware Software Engineering: The energy profiling and its analysis are the basis for assessing the energy consumption throughout the software life cycle. Joulmeter and Greenfoot are some of the tools that can be used by developers in order to measure energy usage in order to take proper decisions of optimization. Moreover, the importance of energy-aware programming languages and dynamic resource allocation techniques are growing rapidly to control the energy usage in cloud computing. 3.Green DevOps and Sustainable Deployment: Green DevOps deals with the reduction of energy consumption on CI/CD pipelines. This is achieved by integrating green cloud services within the system and by virtualizing and containerizing services. These techniques help to guarantee the appropriate deployment of software in order to reduce its effect on the environment as well as the optimization of the quality of software. 4.Sustainable Data Management and Storage: Analyses show that data-intensive applications have a disproportionately large life cycle environmental impact because of the energy consumed in processing and storing data. Two strategies include data minimization and compression of data and the other strategy involves the use of energy-efficient databases as part of minimizing the energy intensity of software systems. Data lifecycle management also leads to reduction of the energy costs that go with the retention, archiving and deletion of data. 5.Challenges and Barriers: However, there is still some way to go as the following challenges will show. There is no universality in how sustainability practices and its measurement is conducted and this have made it difficult for organizations in the industry to adopt standard practices. Furthermore, the trade-off between performance and energy efficiency poses a great conundrum to developers, more so in performance-sensitive applications. Small organizations have constraints of resource and capital; they cannot afford to buy efficient energy consuming tools and equipment. It is pertinent that sustainability in software engineering is defined and practiced as a holistic concept which encompasses energy management, resource management and environmental management into every aspect of the software system life cycle. The research community, industry and policy makers need to set up governance frameworks that will help the software industry to implement sustainable solutions. This entails the creation of better energy profiling tools, the employment of Artificial Intelligence optimization approaches and formulation of policies that encourage the efficient use of energy. Finally, sustainable software engineering is not simply an engineering problem, it is an engineering concern. Through green coding, supporting energy efficient infrastructures and practicing sustainable software development life cycle, the software industry can provide solutions to sustainable global challenges and reduce the effects of technology on the environment. Looking into the future, sustainability will not only be an imperative to incorporate into software engineering practice but an inherent characteristic of the creation of responsible technologies.

REFERENCES

Agarwal, S., Nath, A., & Chowdhury, D. (2012). Sustainable approaches and good practices in green software engineering. *International Journal of Research and Reviews in Computer Science*, *3*(1), 1425.

Anita, M., Ambhika, C., & Anish, T. P. (2024). Exploring the Landscape of Artificial Intelligence in Healthcare Applications. In AI Healthcare Applications and Security, Ethical, and Legal Considerations (pp. 29-48). IGI Global.

Kavitha, T., Hemalatha, S., Saravanan, T. M., Singh, A. K., Alam, M. I., & Warshi, S. (2022, January). Survey on cloud computing security and scheduling. In *2022 International Conference on Computer Communication and Informatics (ICCCI)* (pp. 1-4). Ieee. DOI: 10.1109/ICCCI54379.2022.9740932

Lakumarapu, S., Nithyanandhan, R., Bhargavi, V. S., Anish, T. P., & Nalini, M. (2024, August). Machine Learning Approaches for Liver Disease Prediction: A Comparative Analysis. In 2024 *5th International Conference on Electronics and Sustainable Communication Systems (ICESC) (pp. 159-164)*. IEEE. DOI: 10.1109/ICESC60852.2024.10689974

Leong, J., May Yee, K., Baitsegi, O., Palanisamy, L., & Ramasamy, R. K. (2023). Hybrid project management between traditional software development lifecycle and agile based product development for future sustainability. *Sustainability (Basel)*, *15*(2), 1121. DOI: 10.3390/su15021121

Maithili, K., Ponmalar, A., Yamini, B., Karthikeyan, M., Anish, T. P., Maheswari, B., & Subramanian, R. S. (2024). Advances in AI and Machine Learning for Healthcare Informatics. In *Machine Learning and Generative AI in Smart Healthcare* (pp. 1–22). IGI Global. DOI: 10.4018/979-8-3693-3719-6.ch001

Matthew, U. O., Asuni, O., & Fatai, L. O. (2024). Green Software Engineering Development Paradigm: An Approach to a Sustainable Renewable Energy Future. In *Advancing Software Engineering Through AI, Federated Learning, and Large Language Models* (pp. 281-294). IGI Global.

Naseer, M., Zhang, W., & Zhu, W. (2020). Early prediction of a team performance in the initial assessment phases of a software project for sustainable software engineering education. *Sustainability (Basel)*, *12*(11), 4663. DOI: 10.3390/su12114663

Patel, Y. S., Mehrotra, N., & Soner, S. (2015, February). Green cloud computing: A review on Green IT areas for cloud computing environment. In *2015 International Conference on Futuristic Trends on Computational Analysis and Knowledge Management (ABLAZE)* (pp. 327-332). IEEE. DOI: 10.1109/ABLAZE.2015.7155006

Radu, L. D. (2017). Green cloud computing: A literature survey. *Symmetry*, *9*(12), 295. DOI: 10.3390/sym9120295

Rani, S., Bhambri, P., Kataria, A., Khang, A., & Sivaraman, A. K. (Eds.). (2023). *Big Data, Cloud Computing and IoT: Tools and Applications*. CRC Press. DOI: 10.1201/9781003298335

Robillard, M. P. (2016, November). Sustainable software design. In *Proceedings of the 2016 24th ACM SIGSOFT international symposium on foundations of software engineering* (pp. 920-923). DOI: 10.1145/2950290.2983983

Sasubilli, M. K., & Venkateswarlu, R. (2021, January). Cloud computing security challenges, threats and vulnerabilities. In *2021 6th international conference on inventive computation technologies (ICICT)* (pp. 476-480). IEEE. DOI: 10.1109/ICICT50816.2021.9358709

Semerikov, S., Striuk, A., Striuk, L., Striuk, M., & Shalatska, H. (2020). Sustainability in Software Engineering Education: a case of general professional competencies. In *E3S Web of Conferences* (Vol. 166, p. 10036). EDP Sciences. DOI: 10.1051/e3sconf/202016610036

Sreelakshmi, S., Babu, A. A., Lakshmipriya, C., Gracious, L. A., Nalini, M., & Subramanian, R. S. (2024, October). Enhancing Intrusion Detection Systems with Machine Learning. *In 2024 2nd International Conference on Self Sustainable Artificial Intelligence Systems (ICSSAS) (pp. 557-564).* IEEE.

Yamini, B., Ramana, K. V., Nalini, M., Devi, D. C., Maheswari, B., & Siva, S. R. (2024). Customer churn prediction model in enterprises using machine learning. *International Journal of Advanced Technology and Engineering Exploration*, *11*(110), 94.

Chapter 9
Sustainable Mobile and Wireless Computing Solutions

Ranita Ganguly
https://orcid.org/0000-0003-3123-2093
Delaware State University, USA

Priyam Ganguly
https://orcid.org/0009-0005-3280-1747
Widener University, USA

Thrushna Matharasi
University of Bridgeport, USA

ABSTRACT

This chapter considers environmental impacts of mobile and wireless computing technology which appears to be a threat to its consistent growth. Consequences of this challenge include energy-intensive production processes, e-waste, and carbon footprints of devices and networks. Hardware optimization, appropriate networking solutions, and circular economy are targeted as effective approaches for reducing ecological impact. Stakeholders – governments, industries and end-users contribute to the construction of a sustainable environment by formulating policies, partnerships, and changing the way people behave. The chapter deals with AI, IoT, and bio-inspired computing and sets out their potential to reduce energy demands and the life cycles of devices. It is presented through critical case studies and expert analysis of what the goals of sustainability are and how these goals can be achieved without inhibiting progress in technology. This chapter promotes solutions to sustainability issues through alignment of risks and opportunities in the context of international

DOI: 10.4018/979-8-3373-0766-4.ch009

Copyright © 2025, IGI Global Scientific Publishing. Copying or distributing in print or electronic forms without written permission of IGI Global Scientific Publishing is prohibited.

sustainability goals.

1. INTRODUCTION

Sustainability has become essential in the contemporary era when mobile and wireless computing are intricately integrated into the lives of modern humans. The span of mobile devices has increased in terms of their convenience and value. However, growth without constraints can have negative consequences. Currently, there are widespread environmental and energy problems, from manufacturing processes to the ever-growing demand for Wireless Networks and data centers. This chapter deals with current issues, technological advancements, and future developments directed toward making Mobile and Wireless computing solutions more sustainable. Overall, this chapter covers the scope, structure, and key focus areas; the research methods employed; and the expected contributions in the context of the broader field of sustainable technological development.

1.1. Significance of Sustainable Mobile and Wireless Computing Solutions

According to estimates for 2024, mobile technologies, including mobile phones, account for approximately 2–3% of global energy consumption, and the share will continue to increase with the rise of Internet of Things (IoT) devices, 5G networks, and mobile users. This ecosystem is composed of the following environmental footprints.

- Energy-intensive manufacturing owing to the mass production of mobile handsets.
- E-waste resulting from old or discarded smartphones, tablets, and other handheld devices.
- The high-energy demands of wireless networks and cloud infrastructure support these networks.

1.2. Introduction to sustainability in mobile and wireless computing

Energy efficiency may be described as the use of less energy to provide the same service or achieve the same result. This entails the use of devices and practices that reduce energy use but save the same for better performance. For instance, energy-efficient LED light bulbs provide similar lighting to traditional incandescent bulbs while consuming a fraction of electricity to do so (*Energy Efficiency 101*, n.d.). Sustainable computing, also known as 'green computing,' involves the use of computers and related technologies in an environment-friendly and energy-efficient manner. It seeks to reduce the environmental footprint of computing throughout its life cycle from design, manufacture, and use to disposal. Some practices include improving energy efficiency, using renewable energy, increasing product life through better reuse and recycling, and avoiding the inappropriate disposal of e-waste (TechTarget, 2023). Green ICT includes the design, manufacture, use, and disposal of technological components in a manner that reduces or avoids environmental impacts (IBM, 2022).

Major sustainability challenges in mobile and wireless computing

Numerous sustainability challenges related to mobile and wireless computing exist, including their environmental, energy, and social impacts. Here are the key ones.

a) Energy Consumption
- **Device Usage:** Mobile devices and wireless networks require significant amounts of energy, which determines the rise in demand for electricity worldwide.
- **Data Centres:** The expansion of new cloud services and data-intensive applications depends on energy-hungry data centers, which increasingly depend on non-renewable energy sources.
- **5G and IoT:** The exponential increase in IoT and 5G networks and equipment has significantly increased the number of gadgets, thereby increasing energy requirements.

b) Carbon Footprint
- **Manufacturing:** The footprint associated with mobile device production stems largely from resource extraction, material processing, and manufacturing.
- **Lifecycle Emissions:** Even the carbon emissions accounting for the entire lifecycle of the device, its usage, maintenance, and disposal, are quite prominent.
- **Network operations:** Wireless networks are associated with greenhouse gases emitted from the electricity consumed by base stations, towers, and other network equipment.

c) E-Waste
- **Frequent Updating Cycle:** The Customers continue to update their devices, which results in accelerated electronic waste through intended disposal policies.

- **Obstacles to Recycling:** The global crisis is further worsened by the inadequacy of recycling approaches and the difficulty in recovering rare earth materials.
- **Toxic Components:** Devices are made up of lead, cadmium, and mercury, which are toxic materials that can damage the ecosystem if not disposed of properly.

d) Resource Extraction

- **Rare Earth Metals:** The mining of crucial raw materials such as lithium, cobalt, and rare metals for batteries and electronics is extremely hazardous to the environment.

e) Heat and Waste from Devices

- **Thermal Emissions:** Equipment and infrastructure dissipate heat, thus thermally affecting the local environment.
- **Battery Disposal:** Untamed lithium-ion batteries can leak and pollute the environment.

f) Environmental Impact of Wireless Infrastructure

- **Base Stations and Antennas:** Wireless network infrastructure occupies space and consumes considerable power.
- **Construction Impact:** The deployment of new network infrastructure frequently causes damage to the environment and biomes.

g) Data Transmission and Storage

- **High-bandwidth applications:** Applications with high bandwidth demands such as video streaming, online gaming, and cloud services require significant energy for data transmission and storage.
- **Expansion of IoT:** Billions of IoT devices that continuously broadcast data contribute to the energy burden.

h) Consumer Behaviour and Awareness

- **Overconsumption:** An inclination toward constant device purchase and replacement leads to resource depletion and waste generation.
- **Lack of Awareness:** The impact of devices and their networks in the environment is not aware of by many users.

Many fundamental challenges as depicted in Figure 1, hamper the effective management of e-waste. Addressing these challenges requires a holistic approach, including designing power-efficient devices, using renewable energy for data centers and networks, enhancing the product lifecycle, improving recycling measures, and educating consumers.

Figure 1. Main Components of Global Waste Management Crisis

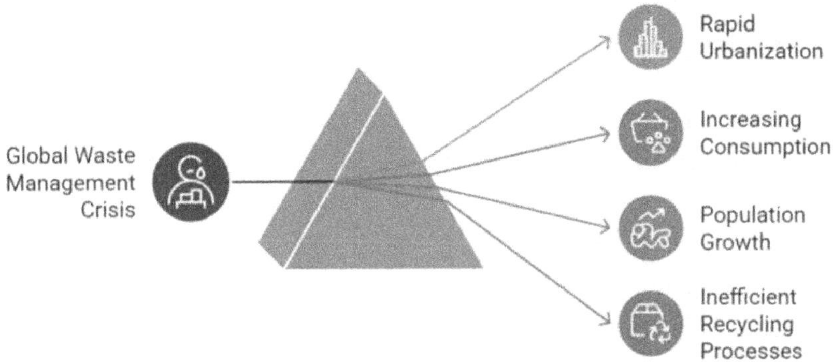

Mobile and wireless technologies offer enormous promise for advancing sustainable development goals as depicted in Figure 2; however, using these technologies has implications for sustainability, which need to be addressed. In this section, we will explore how these technologies intersect several important sustainability goals.

Figure 2. Elements of Sustainable Mobile and Wireless Computing (Pramanik et. al., 2021)

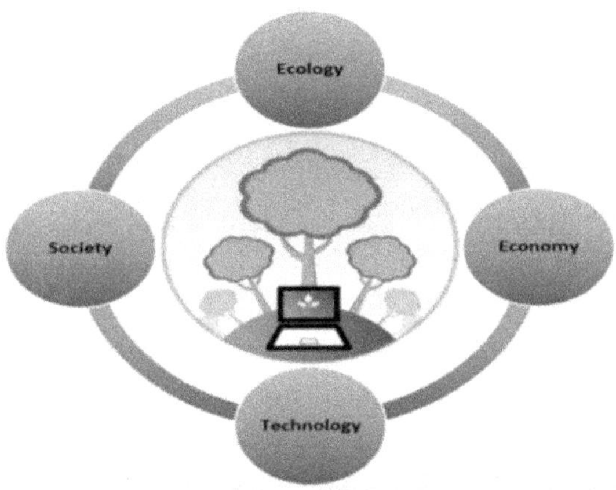

Note: Mobile and wireless technologies can address significant global issues, such as poverty, education,

2. THE ENVIRONMENTAL COST OF MOBILE AND WIRELESS TECHNOLOGIES

The increased use of mobile and wireless technologies has significantly improved communication and connectivity, thereby changing all aspects of modern life. However, this digital age has created serious environmental problems. In this analysis, some specifics of this footprint were examined, particularly those focusing on production and e-waste, energy demand, and greenhouse gas (GHG) emissions. This section presents an in-depth analysis of the ecological footprint resulting from the use of mobile and wireless computing devices.

We now discuss the ecological costs of sourcing raw materials, manufacturing mobile devices, and treating post-use e-waste.

2.1. Raw Material Extraction

- **Critical Materials**: Mobile devices are manufactured using rare resources, such as lithium, cobalt, and tantalum, also known as rare earth elements (REEs), which are mined in ecologically sensitive areas.
- **Ecological Impact**: Mining activities can lead to deforestation, soil degradation, and water pollution. Extraction is energy intensive and is responsible for a large proportion of greenhouse gas emissions. On a social scale, there is exploitation of labor and poor employment conditions in resource-rich countries.

2.2. Manufacturing Process

- **Energy Consumption**: A considerable amount of energy is consumed in the manufacturing of mobile devices and wireless components, most of which are from fossil fuels in many countries.
- **Toxic Byproducts**: Hazardous chemicals, including lead, mercury, and arsenic, are generated in the process and are discharged into the environment.
- **Scale of Production**: The scale of production is enormous, where billions of devices are manufactured every year, which has a huge impact on production in the environment.

2.3 Post-Use E-Waste

- **Volume of Waste**: It's estimated by Global E-Waste Monitor (2020) that over 50 million metric tons of e-waste are produced every year, a significant portion being from mobile devices.

- **Recycling Challenges**: 20% of the e-waste goes through the legal recycling process, while the remaining goes to landfills and informal recycling. Such proportions result in soil and water pollution owing to the discharge of heavy metals and toxins.
- **Circular Economy Solutions**: This is achievable by promoting device refurbishment and recycling, adopting modular designs to extend device lifespan, and supporting take-back programs to improve recycling rates

2.4. Energy Demands

Let us discuss the energy consumption of wireless networks, such as 4G, 5G, Wi-Fi, mobile devices, and cloud computing facilities.

a) Wireless Networks
   - **4G and 5G Networks**: The development of basic 5G network densification has caused a significant increase in the rate of energy utilization. Research indicates that 5G networks can consume more than three times the amount of energy compared with 4G networks if no optimization is performed.
   - **Wi-Fi Networks**: The Wi-Fi networks installed in cities also contribute to a similar increase in energy demand, especially with the increase in the demand for IoT devices.

b) Mobile Devices
   - **Battery Charging**: The energy consumption of fast-charging smartphones, laptops, and tablets is high.
   - **Standby Energy**: In latency, devices tend to still consume energy even when they are not actively used, which further amplifies the general energy footprint.

c) Cloud Computing Facilities
   - **Datacenters**: As mobile and wireless use cloud services from data centers, they constitute nearly one percent of electricity worldwide. The energy requirements of high-technology cooling systems in data centers are significant contributors to power consumption.
   - **Video Streaming and Gaming**: More increasing number of these activities have been carried out on cell phones, which are among the most crucial factors in the energy consumption for cloud computing.

2.5. Greenhouse Gas Emissions

Let us explore the carbon footprint of the ICT sector in the environment by focusing on mobile and wireless systems.

a) Carbon Footprint of the ICT Sector
   - **Overall Impact**: The increased utilization of mobile and wireless devices is directly responsible for 2-3% of global greenhouse gas emissions.
   - **Annual Growth**: The enactment of 5G technology, mobile adoption, and IoT within developing markets has increased emission levels and placed them on an increasing trajectory unless some sort of offset was implemented.

b) Lifecycle Emissions of Mobile Devices
   - **Production Phase**: Studies suggest that 70-80% of a device's carbon footprint is attributed to production emissions. For example, manufacturing a single smartphone emits an average of 85 kg of CO_2 equivalent.
   - **Usage Phase**: The energy required to charge devices and access wireless services contributes significantly to emissions.

c) Emissions from Wireless Networks
   - **Base Stations**: Base stations are the largest energy consumers in mobile networks and are responsible for over 60% of the network emissions. To address this issue, renewable-energy-powered base stations have been proposed.
   - **IoT Devices**: The rise of IoT devices is increasing network traffic and, consequently, huge emissions.

2.6. Addressing the Environmental Cost

a) Mitigating Production and E-Waste Challenges
   - Increasing amounts of recycled and renewable materials are used in device manufacturing.
   - Standardizing the approach for e-waste treatment while promoting its circular economy.

b) Reducing Energy Demands
   - Deploying energy-efficient wireless networks, such as the introduction of dynamic sleep modes for base stations.
   - Creating awareness of the need to use renewable energy sources in power data centers and other network systems.

c) Minimizing Carbon Footprint

- Application of AI and Machine learning in energy utilization for energy forecasting
- Accelerating innovation in low-power devices and energy-efficient protocols.

In conclusion, the environmental costs related to wireless technologies and mobile devices are severe such that unless all stakeholders appeal for a call to action, the situation may turn adverse.

3. SUSTAINABLE MOBILE DEVICE DESIGN AND MANUFACTURING

In this section, we explore the possibility of incorporating sustainability into the life cycle of mobile devices from the design stage to the recycling stage. Designing and managing portable devices considering sustainability issues: Starting from their design, all disposal methods can help tackle several environmental issues. The following are a few pivotal parameters that will be discussed further:

3.1. Recycled and Biodegradable Materials

In this section, we discuss the production of devices using recycled and biodegradable materials. The use of recycled and biodegradable materials in the production of mobile devices has the potential to contribute significantly to environmental sustainability.

a) **Recycled Materials and Metal Scrap:** Using aluminum, copper, and rare-earth metals sourced from scrap electronics instead of mining would have a significant impact on conservation. For example, collecting these elements from Earth could reduce pollution, as demonstrated by Apple's adoption of certain products that utilize recycled aluminum alloys, which shows how this can be implemented on a large scale.
b) **Biodegradable Materials:** The problem of electronic waste can be significantly mitigated using biomass plastic and other biodegradable materials for casing and components, which are expensive and lack durability. However, with rapid advances in materials science, these options are becoming more viable.

3.2. Modular and Repairable Designs

Concepts such as Fair phones advocate easy repair and add to the lifespan of the device. Implementing modular and repairable designs is a radical step towards sustainability.

a) **Modular Devices:** Companies such as Fair Phones have already shown that the need to replace an entire mobile phone can be avoided by designing mobile phones with interchangeable parts. Thus, cameras, batteries, and screens can be changed in a modular manner by the user.
b) **Repair-Friendly Design:** The use of basic screws and easily replaceable parts with adequate user manuals would encourage people to repair gadgets instead of throwing them away, which aggravates e-waste. This helps solve the problems of e-waste as the lifetime of the gadget increases substantially.

3.3. Recycling and Circular Economy

This involves schemes targeted at retrieving valuable resources from old and discarded devices. Establishing a circular economy model for mobile phones is crucial to resource recovery.

a) **Efficient Recycling Programs:** Businesses may wish to develop recycling programs that provide outlets for customers who want previous devices returned, for example, Apple's Sigma Daisy robot disassembles returned iPhones to recover important materials
b) **Design for Disassembly:** Designing devices that can be readily taken apart ensures higher recovery levels for lithium, cobalt, gold, and other materials
c) **Product Take-Back Schemes:** Allowing trade-in programs or offering discounts on the purchase of new devices in exchange for returning old ones can help in achieving recycling goals and lessen the chances of irresponsible disposal.

3.4. Energy-Efficient Hardware

This includes the development of microprocessors and hardware components that use less energy during their operation. Energy consumption is another vital factor in the sustainability of mobile device lifecycles.

a) **Low-Power Processors:** Designing microprocessors such as ARM architecture that consume less energy helps in the usage of less energy for mobile devices; hence, while increasing the usage, it also reduces the energy costs incurred by the user and increases the battery life.
b) **Energy-Efficient Displays:** Upgrading from LCD screens to OLED and micro-LED technologies reduces energy consumption and hence improves sustainability.
c) **Smart Charging Systems:** Energy consumption can also be reduced and battery life can be increased by optimizing the charging systems that support smart charging, which helps minimize energy wastage.

To achieve a comprehensive perspective on sustainability in the life cycle of mobile devices, manufacturers, policymakers, and technology users should collaborate actively. In addition, the industry could proceed to a greener approach using a mix of recycled bioplastics or bio-composites, modular structures, and strong recycling programs, including the use of energy-efficient technologies in devices. Such actions by governments would include support for green business development efforts alongside financial incentives and regulation constraints.

4. ENERGY EFFICIENCY IN MOBILE AND WIRELESS COMPUTING

Sustainable computing requires high energy efficiency. Mobile devices and wireless networks are technologies in which energy consumption and battery lifetime are crucial constraints. Therefore, an investigation into energy-efficient strategies with emphasis on the given key points is presented below.

4.1. Low-Power Hardware and Software

Advances in mobile device technology include faster processors, better batteries, integrated circuits, and other energy-efficient algorithms. Energy-saving features are becoming pervasive in mobile technology without compromising performance factors.

a) **Low-Power Processors:** The latest processors, such as ARM-based chips, are power efficient, and high-performance chips are designed for use in mobile radio transceivers. Dynamic voltage and frequency scaling (DVFS) techniques enable processors to vary their workload depending on the requirements, which greatly changes power usage.

b) **Integrated Circuits (ICs):** The interconnections between the electrically functional areas of highly integrated circuits are minimized by incorporating multiple functionalities into a single chip. For instance, a system-on-chip (SoC) minimizes power consumption by integrating CPUs, GPUs, and a memory controller onto a single chip.
c) **Energy-Efficient Algorithms:** The optimization of software algorithms may lower the number of calculations performed, which directly affects energy consumption. Machine-learning algorithms can also be used to learn usage patterns for more efficient hardware utilization.
d) **Battery Innovations:** The development of new battery systems, such as solid-state batteries and fast charging, also helps to optimize the use of low-power hardware.

4.2. Edge Computing

The integration of the IoT and edge computing has a more significant impact on energy conservation than the centralized use of resources; hence, it is more efficient. Edge computing contributes substantially to energy conservation by processing services that are closer to data sources.

a) **Curbing Data Transmission:** Through edge computing, the energy consumption associated with the transfer of data to centralized cloud servers is reduced by performing computational tasks locally or at closer edge servers.
b) **IoT Integration:** Smart IoT devices embedded at the edge are capable of instantaneous processing and can function autonomously, thereby reducing the load on centralized systems and lowering energy consumption.
c) **Latency and Bandwidth Efficiency:** The Diminished latency in edge computing enables mobile and wireless systems and devices to operate better without having to exchange signals with distant servers, thereby using less energy.

4.3. Energy-Aware Mobile Applications

Guidelines for app developers and technical specifications to optimize energy use. Certain energy-aware design principles guide app developers to create software that is power efficient.

a) **Energy Optimization Guidelines:** Some guidelines have been put in place by operating systems such as Android and iOS to help developers identify the energy consumption of their apps and thereby develop best practices that will prevent the misuse Allocation: of the resources developers including can keeping control activities the to consumption the of minimum resources and that minimizing include network high connections. power

b) **Resource Allocation:** Resources such as GPS, cameras, and sensors are allocated through scheduling, for example, batching network requests or using energy-efficient APIs.
c) **Dark Mode:** While using apps on OLED screens, the dark mode helps conserve energy because there is no need to light up some of the pixels.
d) **User Interaction Design:** Time spent on the screen is reduced by ensuring that the user's input is minimal. This is a major factor that can lead to lower energy consumption.

4.4. Adaptive Power Management

Techniques for dynamically increasing or decreasing the device performance based on usage patterns. The adaptive energy consumption of various devices is automatically optimized based on their respective user activities by using adaptive power management systems.

a) **Performance Scaling:** Techniques such as DVFS adjust the processor speed and voltage depending on the current task, reducing the power consumption during less demanding operations.
b) **Sleep and Standby Modes:** Devices enter low-power states during inactivity, whereas adaptive algorithms ensure rapid wake-up times for responsiveness.
c) **Context-Aware Adjustments:** Power management systems use sensors to detect user behavior and environmental conditions, and adjust screen brightness, processor performance, or wireless connectivity.
d) **AI-Driven Power Optimization: Machine learning** models analyze usage patterns to predict energy needs, enabling smarter allocation of resources and power.

Thus, as in the case of portable and wireless technologies, efficiency is achievable only through integrated hardware, software, and operational innovation.

5. SUSTAINABLE WIRELESS NETWORK INFRASTRUCTURE

The rollout and advancement of wireless networks, 5G, and beyond, are significant contributors to energy consumption. A focus on solutions to establish sustainable wireless networks is highly warranted. The aggressive rollout of 5G and next-generation cellular networks has paved the way for paradigm shifts in connectivity and innovations but comes with major problems in power consumption. Innovative approaches are required to establish sustainable wireless networks, as outlined below:

5.1. Renewable Energy-Driven Solutions for Base Station Infrastructure

Use of sourced and engineered renewable energy and low-power technologies. Extensive power consumption results from the use of base stations that access the wireless networks. The use of renewable energy and low-power technologies can significantly reduce their environmental impact.

a) **Solar and Wind Energy:** Most telecom operators are shifting to solar- or wind-powered base stations given the rising costs of power in developed and developing countries, especially in rural regions. For example, Vodafone and Ericsson are currently trialing 5G base stations by using solar power sources.
b) **Energy Storage Systems:** Premium storage, particularly in lithium ions or other advanced battery systems, guarantees power availability and decreases reliance on nonrenewable energy in the event of downtimes.
c) **Low-Power Technologies:** Technological developments in hardware, including Massive MIMO with energy-efficient beamforming, have eliminated power consumption in areas of non-interest.
d) **Smart Cooling Systems:** The adoption of liquid cooling instead of air conditioning or passive heat dissipation in base stations consumes far less energy.

5.2. Dynamic Spectrum Sharing

Dynamic spectrum sharing (DSS) enables efficient use of available radio frequencies to reduce energy wastage.

a) **Efficient Spectrum Allocation:** DSS helps different network technologies (4G and 5G, for instance) use the same frequencies at different instances, thereby reducing the idle spectrum.
b) **Reduced Hardware Needs:** The new method, in which operators can dynamically share the spectrum, enables them to install fewer base stations and use less energy and resources.
c) **Adaptive Load Balancing:** Algorithms can predict demand variability and allocate spectrum resources, whereas energy is consumed only where and when it is needed.

d) **AI-Powered Optimization:** Predictive analytics of the current network traffic and real-time network environment using machine learning models provide the possibility of proactively changing spectrum resources and optimizing the efficiency of energy consumption.

5.3. Green 5G and Beyond

The design and operation methods of next-generation networks have largely focused on reducing their environmental footprints. Designing and operating future wireless networks with a focus on sustainability is the key to minimizing environmental impacts.

a) **Energy-Efficient Protocols:** Various measures, such as energy-sensitive scheduling, sleeping cell approach, and energy-efficient signal processing, minimize energy use during operation.
b) **Network Virtualization:** When network functions are virtualized, this essentially means that many operators can locate their facility at once on the same equipment that other operators are using, thereby significantly reducing the duplication of the physical space and power consumed by the equipment (Jafri, 2025).
c) **Energy-Saving Hardware:** For instance, GaN transistors are preferred over their traditional silicon counterparts because they provide reduced efficiency and concomitant power dissipation.
d) **AI and ML for Energy Optimization:** Smart provers track the traffic congestion patterns of the network and adapt base station supply voltage levels to save energy during less busy periods.
e) **Small-cell networks:** Small cells or low-power base stations, also termed micro- and pico-cells, operating in urban cities help reduce the importance of macro-cells and provide better-localized energy utilization.

5.4. IoT Sustainability

In an era in which billions of IoT devices must be controlled, minimizing their energy usage has become a challenge. The exponential growth of IoT devices presents unique challenges to sustainable network management.

a) **Low-power IoT Standards:** Narrowband IoT (NB-IoT) and LoRaWAN are low-power protocols that ensure that billions of devices remain low-powered.

b) **Energy Harvesting IoT Devices:** The use of devices that can sunder different forms of energy (solar, thermal, and kinetic energy) means that batteries do not need to be replaced frequently, thereby slowing the rate of waste and spending.
c) **Edge Computing for IoT:** Most time, processing data closer to the devices reduces energy consumption as data transfer is less to central servers.
d) **Smart IoT Management Platforms:** Most AI-run platforms watch and guide IOT devices to conserve energy. For example, sensors should be able to be placed in sleep mode when inactive and become functional as soon as an activity is detected.

Therefore, it is important to achieve wireless network sustainability through renewable energy use, efficient spectrum management, environmentally friendly network design, and IoT-friendly power consumption. By using innovations in green energy, dynamic spectrum access, and demand-intensive AI techniques, the industry can reduce the energy footprint of 5G and beyond. Such steps will add to the sustainability targets of the world's environment in addition to creating cheap and sustainable next-generation networks.

6. LEVERAGING MOBILE AND WIRELESS TECHNOLOGIES FOR SUSTAINABILITY

Mobile and wireless technologies have the potential to drive sustainability across various sectors by enabling efficient management of resources, reducing waste, and promoting greener practices. Let us turn around and explore how mobile and wireless technologies can deliver sustainability to other sectors.

6.1. Management of Renewable Energy Sources

Mobile platforms can be used to monitor and optimize renewable energy sources such as solar and wind. Mobile and wireless technologies play pivotal roles in optimizing the generation, distribution, and consumption of renewable energy, and ensuring minimal waste and maximum efficiency.

a) **Smart Monitoring Systems:** Smartphones and IoT sensors facilitate the remote performance assessment of renewable power, including photovoltaics and wind. Mobile apps can provide an overview of energy generation, consumption, and technical requirements for maintenance, making them easier for operators to operate.

b) **Energy Management Platforms:** Wireless technologies combine different types of renewable energy systems into smart-grid systems. These platforms act as supply-demand intermediaries because they periodically change power distribution and storage systems and minimize the use of fossil resources.
c) **Predictive Maintenance:** With the help of wireless sensors and AI mobile apps, operators can reduce failure rates in renewable systems and plan for maintenance before downtimes occur.
d) **Decentralized Energy Networks:** Mobile and wireless communication enables microgrids, where households and businesses can exchange surplus renewable energy, thus reducing overhead costs through lossless transmission.

7. POLICY, COLLABORATION, AND USER BEHAVIOR

Sustainability in the mobile and wireless computing domains encompasses a multi-stakeholder framework. Achieving sustainability in the mobile and wireless computing domains requires a collaborative, multi-stakeholder approach encompassing policy, industry collaboration, and user behavior. A detailed discussion of each area is provided below:

7.1. Policy Interventions

Setting up regulatory frameworks and providing incentives for sustainable ICT practices and policies govern ICT organizations' ability to practice sustainability by establishing factors of compliance and regulations.

a) **Regulatory Frameworks:** Sometimes, local governments and global organizations promote the embodiment of environmental considerations by establishing manufacturing standards, enforcing e-waste recycling laws, and reducing energy use in appliances and overall infrastructure. Examples include the European Union, which has the Right to Repair directives and states that all manufactured products must be designed such that they can be repaired. Manufacturers and retailers are also required to abide by electronic waste-take-back programs.
b) **Incentives for Green Practices:** Governments can offer tax reductions, grants, and subsidies to companies that adopt green technologies, such as renewable data centers as well as energy-efficient appliances and recycling facilities.
c) **Standards for Carbon Neutrality:** Clearly defined policies that require telecom operators and device manufacturers to meet carbon neutrality targets within a specified working timeline ensure accountability and progress.

d) **Global Frameworks:** Sustainable consumption and production targets can be achieved by reducing energy use and emissions across all ICT sectors following the Paris Agreement and the ensuing objectives.

7.2. Industry Collaboration

Collaboration with telecom operators, device manufacturers, and governments to achieve sustainability targets.

a) **Telecom Operators and Device Manufacturers**: Collective efforts are needed to build energy-efficient 5G base stations and other network infrastructure with renewable energy sources. In the the telecommunication sector, the multi-layered architecture promotes modular devices which allow for easier repair, upgrading, and recycling promoted through collaboration, such as the 'Fairphone' model.
b) **Public-private Partnerships:** Governments, along with the private sector, can provide joint funding for the research and development (R&D) of green ICT technologies, including low-power processors, advanced batteries, and energy-efficient protocols.
c) **Circular Economy Initiatives:** Telecom companies, manufacturers, and refurbishing enterprises can create joint systems for collection, repair, and secondary sales of devices, for instance, the collaboration of Apple and the partners of its Daisy robot system.
d) **Knowledge Sharing:** Sustainability initiatives may be expedited by sharing knowledge across industries regarding their best practices, new technologies, and models that have worked for them. Organizations such as GSMA help facilitate such exchanges.

7.3. User Behavior

Empowering clients to practice e-waste minimization and energy savings, among other sustainable activities, is essential.

a) **E-Waste Minimization:** Awareness campaigns should be held for consumers, and app-based solutions to locate e-waste disposal sites need to be developed. Encouraging trade-in programs allows users to return their old devices when buying new ones in exchange for discounts so that the old devices can be reused.
b) **Energy-saving practices:** Users must be trained to change their habits by using energy-saving options, such as energy-saving setting modes of the device, turning down screen brightness, and avoiding overcharging the devices.

c) **Prolonging Device Lifespan:** Repair tutorials, spare resource parts, and tools should be available and easily accessible to help and encourage the practice of repair and reuse. Today, most people feel the need to constantly update their devices, which should be toned down until necessary, by promoting the use of older models for longer periods.
d) **Consumer Advocacy:** Educate consumers to encourage manufacturers and telecom operators to adopt greener practices by encouraging market trends toward sustainability.

Therefore, the degenerating effects of this rapidly advancing technological world, particularly on mobile and wireless fronts, can only be addressed by adopting strategies across various domains to ensure informed user awareness, constructive policy frameworks, and greater alliances in the industry. Together, these efforts can reduce environmental impact, promote resource efficiency, and foster a greener future for the ICT sector.

8. MULTIDISCIPLINARY RESEARCH METHODS

Some insights and perspectives are synthesized from previous studies conducted in the areas of green computing, energy efficiency, and practical design of Sustainable Mobile and Wireless Computing Solutions.

8.1. Green Computing: Foundations and Principles

Green computing integrates all aspects of the creation, utilization, and disposal of computing devices, to be environmentally friendly. This is more vividly captured while describing green computing as a holistic approach that focuses on efficiency, resource optimization, and e-waste reduction (Murugesan, 2008).

Key Contributions:

a) **Energy Awareness in IT Systems:** The rapid pace at which the power requirements of ICT systems escalate has been documented (Koomey, 2011). These studies have aided the initiation of programs dealing with energy optimization through effective hardware and software designs.
b) **Carbon Footprint Assessments:** Through studies carried out by Malmodin and Lundén (2018), it has been possible to quantify the carbon footprint of the ICT sector using wireless networks and mobile devices, which contribute a great share of global emissions.

c) **Lifecycle Design:** A study examined the application of green design strategies, such as composing modular designs and the use of recyclable materials to reduce the adverse impact on the environment (Ardito et al., 2018) .

8.3. Energy Efficiency in Mobile and Wireless Networks

The energy demand of wireless networks has become an important issue, particularly for 4G and 5G systems that require considerable energy to operate. Various energy-efficiency mechanisms, such as energy-efficient hardware economics, algorithms, and software can be applied to different layers of the network architecture (Javaid et al., 2024) .

Key Contributions:

a) Base Station Optimization: This type of cellular infrastructure contributes the most to the energy consumption of mobile networks (Marsan et al., 2013). Dynamic sleep modes, energy-efficient resource management, and the use of green energy sources are possible solutions to this challenge.
b) Device-Level Efficiency: Various techniques can reduce energy costs in mobile devices, including adjusting screen brightness, managing applications, and improving battery designs (Gupta et al., 2014).
c) IoT and low-power networks: Different protocols are used for monitoring Low-Power Wide-Area Networks (LPWANs) and are suitable for IoT systems that do not consume much power (Zhang et al., 2021).

8.2. Sustainable Mobile and Wireless Computing Design Approaches

Sustainable design aims to alleviate the environmental harm associated with computer systems during their entire lifecycle. In this section, we address the material efficiency, energy-aware or low-power computing architectures, and circular economy paradigms.

Key Contributions:

a) **Energy-aware Protocols:** The integration of machine learning algorithms in wireless energy systems for dynamic energy consumption repression during peak traffic is preferred (Fang et al., 2020).
b) **E-Waste Reduction:** The reinstatement of some lost circular economy principles would include reusing and renewing devices by extending the lifespan of devices (Bhuie et al., 2020).

c) **Integration of Renewable Energy:** Base stations can be powered by alternative forms of energy such as solar and wind energy, making them less dependent on grid electricity (Deng et al., 2016).

The goal of sustainable design is to mitigate the ecological damage caused by computer systems throughout their lifecycle. This investigation covered efficient raw-material utilization, energy-aware or low-energy computing architectures, and circular economy concepts.

9. EMERGING TRENDS AND TECHNOLOGIES

New emerging technologies have raised prospects for sustainable mobile and wireless computing.

9.1. Artificial Intelligence and Machine Learning

AI and ML are now gaining traction in assisting in the quest to minimize energy consumption. Research outlines how AI can enhance energy efficiency through effective monitoring of wireless network performance, including managing allocation and forecasting energy requirements (Zhang et al., 2022).

9.2. 6G and Energy Efficiency

The studies established that 6G evolution brings along the prospects of sustainability by investing in energy-efficient hardware, green networking solutions, and embedding systems based on alternative energy sources (Akyildiz et al., 2020).

9.3. Quantum Computing

Quantum computing is a promising technology capable of reducing the energy requirements of mobile systems with the widespread use of data through fast and effective computing (Shor and Preskill, 2021).

9.4. Bio-Inspired Computing

Nature-inspired approaches, such as swarm intelligence or neural network algorithms, have been researched to develop energy-saving technologies for mobile and IoT networks (Karaboga et al., 2019).

10. CHALLENGES AND FUTURE DIRECTIONS

Although progress has been made, crucial issues remain to be addressed.

a) **Energy Costs Associated with Newer Technologies**: Evolving technologies, such as IoT systems and 5G, have various advantages; however, energy strain remains an issue calling for stricter energy benchmarks (Baliga et al., 2019).
b) **E-Waste Management Policies and Measures:** The growing volumes of e-waste require enhanced policy measures to tackle which cannot be achieved without building industry consensus (WEEE studies, 2021).
c) **Digital Divide:** Sustainable measures that should address the global inequalities of connectivity and resources (Heeks, 2020).

Literature suggests that the time has come to adopt several sustainable practices in mobile and wireless computing. Although the focus on green computing and energy-efficient designs has been well-formed, more needs to be done to meet the world's sustainability goals.

11. INDUSTRY REPORTS AND ANALYSIS

a) The International Telecommunication Union (ITU)'s "Greening the ICT Supply Chain" Report (Levin et al., 2012)
    - **Focus:** Ecology in the Information and Communication Technology industry
    - **Key Insights:** One of the most prominent points is the need to reduce carbon footprint, minimize energy consumption, and endorse greening practices within the ICT value chain, especially with an emphasis on mobile networks.
b) GSMA's "2024 Mobile Industry Impact Report: Sustainable Development Goals" (2024 Mobile Industry Impact Report Sustainable Development Goals, 2024)
    - **Focus:** Mobile sector contributions to the UN Sustainable Development Goals.
    - **Key Insights:** Evaluate gaps in mobile and wireless technology usage to meet sustainability goals, such as minimizing energy usage, reaching out to economically disadvantaged communities, and promoting green projects.

c) Green Electronics Council (GEC)'s "Sustainable Mobile Devices" Analysis (*UL Environment, Green Electronics Council Unveil UL ECOLOGO/EPEAT Joint-Certification for Mobile Phones | UL Solutions*, n.d.)
   - **Focus:** Sustainability in the manufacturing and design of mobile devices
   - **Key Insights:** This focus encourages research into the negative environmental impacts of mobile devices and the use of recyclable materials, energy-efficient designs, and biodegradable components in manufacturing processes.

d) Ericsson's "Building Sustainable Networks" Report (Ericsson, n.d.)
   - **Focus:** Green technological advancements in mobile networks.
   - **Key Insights:** Addressing ways of achieving lower energy usage in base stations and networks in the context of growing data traffic and emphasizing the integration of renewable energy resources and energy-efficient technologies.

e) InterDigital's "How Sustainable Are Our Mobile Networks?" White Paper (Interdigital, n.d.)
   - **Focus:** Using mobile networks for sustainability metrics.
   - **Key Insights:** Studies on the consequences of mobile networks on climate, energy intensity targets set up in the industry, and general measures of energy efficiency enhancement to reduce environmental impacts.

Actionable Recommendations

a) Accelerate the use of renewables in power ICT facilities.
b) The aim is to homogenize the best practices across mobile and wireless computing resources.
c) Encourage partnerships between industry stakeholders and the state to achieve aggressive environmental goals.

These reports emphasize that mobile and wireless technologies must be made more sustainable through structured, cooperative, and system-based approaches.

12. CASE STUDIES ON SUSTAINABLE PRACTICES AND INNOVATIONS IN MOBILE AND WIRELESS TECHNOLOGIES

These case studies explain the specific measures adopted to increase energy efficiency in the operations of leading telecommunications companies, as well as the contribution of such measures to address the growing challenge of e-waste in the developing world. While these initiatives have demonstrated significant progress, they also present challenges that must be addressed to ensure long-term sustainability.

a) Vodafone's Renewable Energy-Powered Networks
- **Overview**: Vodafone has installed solar- and wind-powered networks in its infrastructure in countries such as India and South Africa.
- **Impact**: Lower carbon footprints were achieved by minimizing dependence on traditional grid electricity. In this context, this initiative is in line with Vodafone's target of reaching net zero by 2040.
- **Key Innovation**: This new technology facilitates the use of energy-saving base stations and the incorporation of IoT to optimize energy use in real-time.
- **Challenges:** Renewable energy infrastructure requires substantial initial investments, and maintaining efficiency in regions with inconsistent sunlight or wind conditions remains a hurdle.

b) Nokia's Liquid Cooling for Base Stations
- **Overview**: Air cooling systems in the base stations of Nokia have been replaced with liquid cooling technology.
- **Impact**: Energy consumption was reduced by as much as 30% and CO_2 emissions decreased by approximately 80%.
- **Key Innovation**: This innovation utilizes a closed-loop liquid-cooling system. This ensures that energy is not wasted in maintaining suitable operating conditions for all hardware components of telecommunications systems.
- **Challenges:** Implementation in existing base stations is complex and costly, requiring significant retrofitting efforts. Additionally, liquid cooling systems require specialized maintenance, which increases operational costs.

c) Ericsson's Connected Mangroves Project
- **Overview**: In Malaysia, Ericsson worked with local stakeholders to install Internet of Things (IoT) sensors in mangrove forests to monitor and control ecological conditions and enhance the reforestation of the area.

- **Impact**: Strengthened mangrove protection activities and promoted ecological diversity, while demonstrating the possibilities of mobile technologies in conserving the environment.
- **Key Innovation**: Employing a combination of solar-powered energy-efficient IoT sensors to reduce the environmental impact of the project.
- **Challenges:** While the initiative successfully utilizes technology for conservation, long-term funding and the durability of IoT sensors in harsh environmental conditions are concerns. Connectivity issues in remote areas also pose technical difficulties.

d) Orange's Eco-Rating System for Mobile Devices

- **Overview**: Driven by collaborative efforts with other telecom operators, the Orange Eco Rating System was established to assess the environmental impact of mobile devices across their life cycle.
- **Impact**: Enhanced customer awareness of sustainable purchasing choices and influenced manufacturers to be environmentally friendly.
- **Key Innovation**: The rating system preferably covers components, such as recyclability, energy consumption, and renewable materials.
- **Challenges:** Adoption of the eco-rating system remains voluntary, leading to inconsistencies in enforcement across the industry. Some manufacturers hesitate to participate due to concerns over potential negative ratings.

e) Huawei's Green Base Station Technology

- **Overview**: Huawei's PowerStar is an artificial intelligence (AI)-powered device that was developed to improve the energy effectiveness of base stations.
- **Impact**: Attained over 15% decrease in energy usage among thousands of installations worldwide.
- **Key Innovation**: Ability of AI to forecast traffic and change parameters such as power control, adjust as much power based on usage, ensuring effective power distribution.
- **Challenges:** AI-based solutions require large amounts of training data and computational power, leading to concerns about their energy use. Moreover, reliance on AI increases cybersecurity risks related to data privacy and network vulnerabilities.

f) T-Mobile's Waste Reduction and Recycling Initiative

- **Overview**: T-Mobile US introduced a circular economy through the renovation and recycling of aging devices.
- **Impact**: Prevented millions of devices from unnecessary disposal to landfills and minimized e-waste pollution.

- **Key Innovation**: Worked with accredited recycling companies to ensure that e-waste was recycled and engaged in strategies to motivate returning devices to customers.
- **Challenges**: Consumer participation remains a challenge, as many users are unaware of or uninterested in recycling initiatives. Logistics and cost-intensive processing of collected devices also present obstacles.

g) Telstra's Smart Building IoT Deployment
- **Overview**: Irrespective of its size, Telstra is an Australian telecommunication company that implements IoT-based smart building solutions for consumption optimization in its corporate offices.
- **Impact**: Savings in electricity usage of at least 25% and reduction in overhead expenses.
- **Key Innovation**: IoT-enabled sensors for the collection of information on lighting levels, temperature, and energy consumption coupled with solar energy systems.
- **Challenges:** Scaling these solutions across diverse building infrastructures is complex and expensive. Additionally, managing large volumes of sensor data requires robust processing capabilities and security measures.

In conclusion, these case studies demonstrate how mobile wireless technologies can achieve sustainability goals by boosting operational effectiveness and social development. Breaking into sustainable practices creates multiple hurdles that challenge organizations with financial investment needs along with infrastructure changes regulatory rules and community involvement requirements. Business progress requires companies to dedicate resources toward creating adaptable solutions and increasing public understanding while promoting industry-to-industry collaboration. A combination of analyzing successful outcomes and gaining knowledge from failures enables the ICT sector to achieve major global sustainability targets.

13. EXPERT OPINIONS AND PERSPECTIVES ON SUSTAINABLE PRACTICES AND INNOVATIONS

13.1. Industry Leaders' Perspectives

a) Sundar Pichai (CEO, Alphabet/Google)
- **Key Insights**: Endorses the inclusion of AI in efforts to achieve energy consumption measures in both data centers and mobile networks.

Highlights Google's initiatives to become carbon-neutral by utilizing green energy projects and energy-efficient cloud computing. Calls for more funding into advancing technologies, such as ML and quantum computing for sustainable change.
- **Quote**: "Artificial intelligence is a profound technology, as important or more than fire and electricity."

This highlights Pichai's firm belief in the advantages of AI for humanity and the expectation of how much AI will contribute to the evolution of industries, society, and everyday life in the future.

b) Börje Ekholm (CEO, Ericsson)
- **Key Insights**: Emphasized the requirement for energy-efficient 5G and 6G technologies as data traffic continues to grow. The installation of solar-powered concentration base stations by Ericson and the role of the Connected Mangroves project were discussed. Stated that for sustainable solutions to be implemented on a wider scale, collaboration between telcos, governments, and tech companies is essential.
- **Quote**: During MWC 2023, Börje Ekholm, the Head of Ericsson, emphasizes the opportunities offered by digitalization in terms of enhancing innovation and progress and mentions the necessity of creating sustainable networks in this transformation

c) Ajay Bhalla (President, Cyber & Intelligence, Mastercard)
- **Key insights**: Mobile technology is an effective tool for encouraging financial inclusion and lowering disparities. Underlines that mobile wallets and electronic currency systems, when powered by the green computing framework, contribute to the responsible growth of the ecosystem and facilitate global advancement.
- **Quote**: "Consumers are increasingly moving from cash to card as they look for greater security and sustainability." This underscores consumer trends in security and sustainability payments.

13.2. Policymakers' Perspectives

a) Houlin Zhao (Former Secretary-General, ITU)
- **Key Insights**: Calls on nations to implement internationally accepted guidelines for energy-efficient ICT systems and underlines ITU's efforts to foster "Green ICT" by encouraging the development of smart cities, energy-efficient networks, and low-energy 6G technologies.

- **Quote**: "ICTs can play a transformative role in securing a sustainable and energy-efficient future, positioning them as frontline tools in the fight against climate change"

b) Ursula von der Leyen (President, European Commission)

- **Key Insights**: Sustainability is framed as a matter of major relevance in the context of Europe's Digital Agenda. He discussed measures aimed at stimulating the consumption of renewable fuel in the implementation of 5G technology as well as the recycling of electronic waste from mobile devices.
- **Quote**: "We believe that digital transformation can power our economies and help us find European solutions to global challenges." For Von der Leyen, it has always been of key significance that digital transformation in Europe should go hand in hand with the implementation of the objectives of the European Green Deal.

13.3. Environmental Advocates' Perspectives

a) Greta Thunberg (Climate Activist)

- **Key Insights**: Criticize the tech industry for increasingly using energy and not being transparent about their carbon emissions on a reporting basis. Encourages responsible outsourcing and more renewable energy use within the industry and among businesses.
- **Quote**: "We need to start cooperating and sharing the remaining resources of this planet fairly."

b) Jane Goodall (Conservationist)

- **Key Insights**: Endorses the concept of bio-inspired computing as an environmentally friendly way of designing mobile and wireless systems. Points out the need for a technological consortium and a conservation organization to bring about environmental innovations.
- **Quote:** "Fortunately, nature is amazingly resilient: places we have destroyed, given time and help, can once again support life, and endangered species can be given a second chance. And there is a growing number of people, especially young people, who are aware of these problems and are fighting for the survival of our only home, Planet Earth. We must all join that fight before it is too late."

13.4. Key Themes Across Expert Opinions

- **Need for Green Engineering:** Across all domains of ICT, there is a consensus that sustainability must be integrated to provide for the growing energy and resource needs of mobile and wireless systems. Capital infusions into R&D for establishing AI-enabled relays to increase the transparency of sustainability reports.
- **Collaborative Ecosystem**: According to government officials, policymakers, IT corporations, and environmentalists, there is a need to create partnerships across fields to effectively implement green innovations.
- **Role of Emerging Technologies**: AI, IoT, and quantum computing from the expert's perspective are technologies that can avert energy wastage and enable the acceleration of the core long-term sustainability objectives.
- **Global Standards and Policies**: Policymakers redefine requirements for overseas energy efficiency, integration of renewable sources of energy, and electronic waste management zones.

Here is a comparative analysis of different regional approaches to sustainable mobile computing.

European Union (EU): The EU emphasizes stringent energy efficiency standards and mandates the integration of renewable energy in mobile computing infrastructure, alongside robust e-waste recycling programs under the Circular Economy Action Plan.

United States: The U.S. focuses on innovation-driven approaches, with incentives for renewable energy adoption in data centers and voluntary e-waste management frameworks, though regulations vary by state.

China: China enforces strict government-led policies, including aggressive renewable energy targets for tech industries and centralized e-waste management systems, supported by large-scale recycling zones.

India: India promotes sustainable mobile computing through renewable energy integration, particularly solar, and has introduced e-waste management rules, but implementation faces challenges due to infrastructure gaps.

Africa: African regions are increasingly adopting renewable energy for mobile computing, supported by international partnerships, but e-waste management remains underdeveloped, with informal recycling dominating the sector.

13.5. Actionable Insights

- **Industry Recommendations:** Capital infusions into R&D for establishing AI-enabled relays to increase the transparency of sustainability reports.
- **Policy Suggestions**: Set up worldwide performance indicators on green ICT equipment and establish incentives for mobile industry green practices.
- **Advocacy Goals:** Disseminate bio-inspired principles into mobile and wireless computing as a priority of social and economic development.

In conclusion, the joint efforts of academia, policymakers, and relevant environmental advocates are creating a unified approach to address the issues of mobile and wireless technologies sustainability. To do so, it must harmonize its innovative efforts with the environmental needs of the specific country where the ICT has its operations.

14. Emerging Trends and Future Directions

The ever-increasing demand for mobile and wireless computing trends exhibits some exciting possibilities for tackling sustainability issues. Here is a forward-looking discussion on how these innovations will improve energy efficiency and enhance environmental responsibility.

14.1. 6G and Sustainability

The rollout of 6G networks is being shaped with a focus on design that would be energy efficient and sustainable. Some of the key features are discussed below:

a) **Energy-Efficient Infrastructure:** 6G is expected to incorporate smart antennae, advanced materials as well as custom-designed hardware that will enhance the performance of network components while reducing energy consumption.
b) **AI-Driven Optimization:** A critical component of the optimization of network performance will include the use of AI, which will match supply and demand while reducing waste by dynamically allocating resources to needs.
c) **Green Networking Protocols:** It is a requirement for 6G standards to incorporate networking protocols that will enhance seamless connectivity while minimizing latency and the energy required during the transfer.
d) **Integration with Renewable Energy:** It is expected that 6G bases and their infrastructure will likely incorporate green renewable energy sources such as wind and solar elements, reducing the number of carbon footprints.

6G has the potential of improving wireless networks by making them much faster reliable, and environmentally friendly by taking a sustainable and energy efficient approach from the ground.

14.2. AI and Machine Learning

Mobile and wireless systems stand to gain a lot owing to the advancements and use of Artificial Intelligence (AI) and Machine Learning (ML) technologies. To achieve high energy efficiency in mobile and wireless systems, the following areas can be improved upon.

a) **Energy Management:** AI is capable of monitoring energy consumption at the network level, devices, and data centers, identifying inefficiencies, and recommending improvements.
b) **Dynamic Resource Allocation:** Machine learning techniques allow for dynamic resource provisioning, such as powering down underutilized network components or optimizing routing to save energy.
c) **Predictive Maintenance:** AI-based systems can reduce the amount of wasted resources by anticipating and averting possible breakdowns of equipment, thus extending the lifespan of infrastructure more efficiently.
d) **User Behaviour Analysis:** Machine learning algorithms can determine the activity of users and distribute energy-intensive tasks across different times to avoid heavy loads during peak demand periods.

Machine Learning(ML) has emerged as a great transformative tool in response to these challenges in sustainable waste management. ML helps in providing solutions that can improve the efficiency of waste collection systems. Few studies suggest that AI-powered sorting systems can boost recycling efficiency by 90% and landfill waste reduction by 25%. By using advanced technologies such as predictive analytics and computer vision, ML can enhance the overall efficiency of waste management systems (Sami et al.m 2020).

Machine Learning helps to automate critical processes of waste management as depicted in Figure 3, which improves efficiency and reduces cost.

a) **Waste Generation with Predictive Analytics: The** ML Model helps to analyze historical waste data to forecast future waste generation trends. Models like Long Short-Term Memory (LSTM) networks can be applied to predict seasonal waste generation trends which can be used to plan waste collection schedules efficiently and also optimize their resource allocation. ML-based predictive models can reduce waste overflow incidents by 30% in smart cities (Narayan, 2021).

b) **Automated Waste Sorting:** AI-based sorting systems such as computer vision-based ML Models with the use of Convolutional Neural Networks (CNNs) can help to distinguish between plastic, metal, glass, organic, and electronic waste which reduces manual labor and efficiency too.

c) **Waste Collection Optimization:** ML-based Reinforcement Learning algorithms which dynamically adjust routes based on real-time data for waste collection can be minimized which further helps in reducing fuel consumption and greenhouse gas emissions.

Therefore, 6G alongside AI and ML brings forth an innovative pathway to develop more sustainable mobile and wireless computing than current systems. The integration of optimization through artificial intelligence with networking protocols such as 6G and energy-efficient infrastructure optimizes both network functions and reduces carbon footprint.

Predictive analytics coupled with automated sorting and enhanced collection mechanisms are advanced techniques enabled by AI and ML applications in waste management that serve to diminish operational inefficiencies and promote sustainable environmental practices.

The features stated below, justify the need for AI and ML to make mobile and wireless computing more sustainable, efficient, and environmentally friendly.

Figure 3. Machine Learning in Waste Management

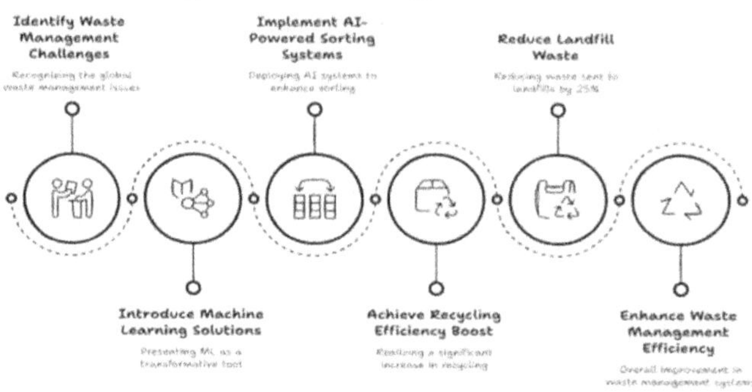

ML Techniques that can be used to power intelligent waste management systems as depicted in Figure 4, include the following:

a) **Supervised Learning:** For waste classification through labelled datasets to train image recognition models.

b) **Unsupervised Learning:** It helps to cluster waste based on similarities without predefined labels.
c) **Deep Learning:** Helps to create the image classification models for sorting waste materials.
d) **Reinforcement Learning:** Optimizes waste collection routes dynamically based on real-time traffic.

Figure 4. Waste Classification Techniques

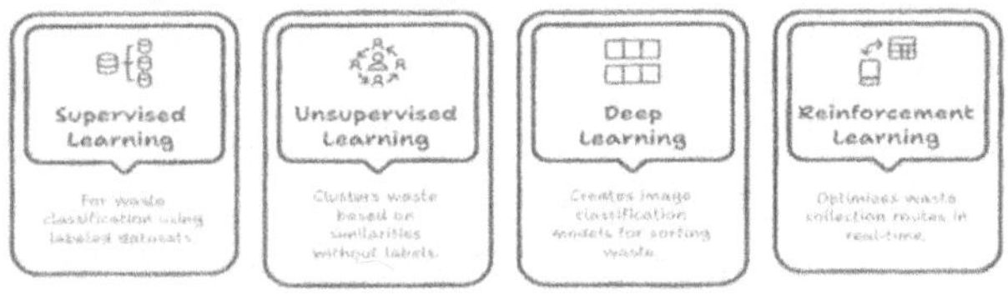

Note: The AI-based waste classification system demonstrates how deep learning can be leveraged for sustainable waste management.

Challenges

a. Data Availability: Limited availability of high-quality datasets for training the models.
b. Model Generalization: There is high variability in waste appearance due to lighting, occlusions, and background noise.

Future Prospects

a. IoT Integrations: Integration of sensors with bins for waste tracking and segregation. Companies like Bin-e and Enevo Utilize IoT-based waste management solutions to optimize collection efficiency and minimize environmental impact.
b. Blockchain for Waste Management: It will help to ensure transparency in recycling and waste disposal tracking with Plastic Bank using blockchain to incentivize responsible waste disposal practices.
c. Federated Learning: Enables decentralized AI training for large-scale waste classification.

Key Takeaways

6G's Sustainable Impact: The future of green networking will depend on energy-efficient design and AI-driven optimization as well as integration with renewable energy sources.
AI & ML for Sustainability: The dynamic allocation of resources, predictive maintenance, and analysis of user behavior will enhance energy efficiency in mobile networks.
Smart Waste Management: Making use of AI-powered waste classification, IoT-enabled tracking, and blockchain for transparency will enhance waste management efficiency.

Machine Learning can therefore transform waste management by improving waste classification, optimizing collection routes, and enhancing recycling efficiency (Nafiz et al., 2023). Developing a solution that uses AI to process waste is not only about writing code—it is about really making a system that can change how we deal with waste. By combining ML with IoT and blockchain, future waste management systems can become more transparent, efficient, and environmentally friendly.

14.3. Quantum Computing

Quantum computing improvements can bring forth a transformative effect on the energy efficiency in mobile and wireless systems in the following ways:

a) **Optimized Algorithms:** Using quantum algorithms can help to find solutions to critical optimization problems which consequently will effectively minimize computation energy in areas such as signal processing and network traffic management.
b) **Reduced Datacentre Loads:** Quantum computing can increase the speed of data processing and, thus, lower the amount of energy needed to operate data centers that form the backbone of mobile and wireless systems.
c) **Advances in Cryptography:** Quantum encryption methods can protect information in communication networks reducing computationally intensive overheads which eventually translates into less energy consumption.

Despite being in the nascent phases of development, quantum breakthroughs are bridging gaps in energy demands by improving the overall energy efficiency of the ICT sector.

14.4. Bio-Inspired Computing

Vast growth opportunities exist in the mobile and wireless systems industry by capitalizing on what nature offers. Bio-inspired computing appears to become one of the major trends, which includes:

a) **Neural Network Designs:** Simulating biological neural networks to develop low-powered mobile computing systems.
b) **Swarm Intelligence:** Utilisation of the collective behavior of social insects such as ants and bees for effective network routing and energy saving.
c) **Energy Harvesting:** Applying technologies inspired by the biological process such as photosynthesis, to design devices that can collect more energy and store it.
d) **Adaptive Algorithms:** Enhancing system performance and optimizing resource usage in real-time using genetic algorithms

The increasing shift towards bio-inspired computing will lead to designing systems that are more robust and efficient in enabling innovative and sustainable solutions.

15. ACTIONABLE RECOMMENDATIONS FOR STAKEHOLDERS

To take advantage of these technologies, stakeholders need to act on the following:

a) **Fund Green R&D:** Provide funding for researching energy-efficient materials, algorithms, and designs for networks.
b) **Adopt Sustainable Standards:** Integrate sustainability into the standards and protocols of emerging technologies such as 6G.
c) **Collaborate Cross-Sectors:** Encourage partnerships between academia, industry, and government institutions in pursuit of innovation in sustainable computing.
d) **Promote Circular Economy:** Design devices and components with recyclability and reuse in mind to reduce e-waste.
e) **Educate and Engage Users:** Raise awareness of the practices that promote energy efficiency and electricity-saving practices among consumers and businesses.

16. POTENTIAL BENEFITS OF SUSTAINABLE MOBILE AND WIRELESS SOLUTIONS

The prospect of mobile and wireless computing in being able to achieve sustainability in the global context has benefits manyfold as outlined below:

a) **Reduced Carbon Emissions**: Improving energy efficiency and renewable energy sources will help mitigate climate change.
b) **Cost Savings:** Energy-efficient systems cut down operating expenditures for both providers and consumers.
c) **Enhanced Longevity:** Environmentally sustainable methods ensure the conservation of resources and facilities for future generations with minimum damage to the environment.
d) **Alignment with Global Goals:** Promoting global sustainability through the resolution of the problems regarding energy, waste management, and equity issues such as the United Nations' Sustainable Development Goals (SDGs).

There is great potential in the attempts to incorporate technologies such as 6G, AI, quantum computing, and bio-inspired devices into ICT sectors while increasing innovation and connectivity in the IT sector.

17. KEY INSIGHTS FOR SUSTAINABILITY IN MOBILE AND WIRELESS COMPUTING

This chapter has contributed to the ongoing discourse on sustainable ICT in the following ways:

- Executed an analysis of mobile and wireless computing from an environmental perspective.
- Explored and discussed cutting-edge technologies and practices that promote sustainability within this domain.
- Presented a series of actionable recommendations to policymakers, businesses, consumers, and industry leaders.
- Encouraged future initiatives and partnership efforts towards constructing a sustainable ICT ecosystem.

This chapter synthesized the key insights discussed, and overall, it was directed towards contemporary problems of mobile and wireless computing focusing upon sustainability. Finally, this chapter outlined the broader context of achieving sustainability which could offer numerous advantages not only for the ICT industry but also for the global community in achieving the goals of sustainable Mobile and Wireless computing solutions.

REFERENCES

Akyildiz, I. F.. (2020). 6G and beyond: The future of wireless networks. *IEEE Communications Magazine*, *58*(3), 62–69.

Ardito, L.. (2018). Towards sustainable innovation: A systematic review of the literature. *Journal of Cleaner Production*, *172*, 2157–2174.

Baliga, J., Ayre, R., Hinton, K., & Tucker, R. (2019). Energy consumption in wired and wireless networks. *IEEE Communications Magazine*, *49*(6), 70–77. DOI: 10.1109/MCOM.2011.5783987

Bhuie, A. K.. (2020). Circular economy and e-waste management: Review and perspectives. *Environmental Science & Technology*, *54*(18), 11316–11333.

Deng, R.. (2016). Green energy source powered base stations: Opportunities and challenges. *IEEE Communications Magazine*, *54*(5), 36–42.

Directive Studies, W. E. E. E. (2021). *E-waste management: Policies and practices*. European Commission Reports.

Energy efficiency 101. (n.d.). *Resources for the Future*. Retrieved January 01, 2025, https://www.rff.org/publications/explainers/energy-efficiency-101/

Fang, X.. (2020). AI-enabled energy efficiency in wireless networks. *IEEE Communications Magazine*, *58*(6), 28–34.

Greening, I. C. T. (2012). Survey on conflict minerals due diligence initiatives.

Gupta, A.. (2014). Energy-efficient mobile devices: Review of techniques and research directions. *Journal of Network and Computer Applications*, *39*, 213–228.

Heeks, R. (2020). ICT4D 3.0: Poverty reduction with equitable and sustainable ICT. *Third World Quarterly*, *41*(5), 779–797.

IBM. (2022, April 19). *What is green computing?* Retrieved January 01, 2025, https://www.ibm.com/think/topics/green-computing

Interdigital. (n.d.). *How sustainable are our mobile networks?* InterDigital.com. https://www.interdigital.com/white_papers/how-sustainable-are-our-mobile-networks

Jafri, S. (2025, February 6). *What is Network Function Virtualization (NFV)?* WWT. https://www.wwt.com/article/what-is-network-function-virtualization

Javaid, S., Fahim, H., Zeadally, S., & He, B. (2024). From sensing to energy savings: A comprehensive survey on integrating emerging technologies for energy efficiency in WBANs. *Digital Communications and Networks*. Advance online publication. DOI: 10.1016/j.dcan.2024.11.012

Karaboga, D.. (2019). Swarm intelligence: Nature-inspired algorithms for energy-efficient computing. *Swarm and Evolutionary Computation*, *48*, 84–96.

Koomey, J. (2011). *Growth in data center electricity use 2005 to 2010*. Analytics Press.

Malmodin, J., & Lundén, D. (2018). The Energy and Carbon Footprint of the Global ICT and E&M Sectors 2010-2015. *Sustainability (Basel)*, *10*(9), 3027. DOI: 10.3390/su10093027

Marsan, M. A.. (2013). A simple analytical model for the energy-efficient design of cellular networks. *IEEE Transactions on Communications*, *61*(8), 3366–3378.

Mobile Industry Impact Report Sustainable Development Goals. (2024, October 2). External Affairs. https://www.gsma.com/solutions-and-impact/connectivity-for-good/external-affairs/2024-mobile-industry-impact-report-sustainable-development-goals

Murugesan, S. (2008). Harnessing Green IT: Principles and Practices. *IT Professional*, *10*(1), 24–33. DOI: 10.1109/MITP.2008.10

Nafiz, M. S., Das, S. S., Morol, M. K., Juabir, A. A., & Nandi, D. (2023, February 6). *ConvoWaste: an automatic waste segregation machine using deep learning*. arXiv.org. https://arxiv.org/abs/2302.02976 DOI: 10.1109/ICREST57604.2023.10070078

Pramanik, P. K. D., Pal, S., & Choudhury, P. (2019). Smartphone Crowd Computing: A rational approach for sustainable computing by curbing the environmental externalities of the growing computing demands. In *Chapman and Hall/CRC eBooks* (pp. 45–80). DOI: 10.1201/9780429298288-3

Sami, K. N., Amin, Z. M. A., & Hassan, R. (2020). Waste management using machine learning and deep learning algorithms. *International Journal on Perceptive and Cognitive Computing*, *6*(2), 97–106. DOI: 10.31436/ijpcc.v6i2.165

Shor, P. W., & Preskill, J. (2021). Quantum computing and its implications for energy efficiency. *Nature Physics*, *17*, 757–764.

Sustainable networks: Ericsson Intelligent Operations Guide. (n.d.). https://www.ericsson.com/en/reports-and-papers/further-insights/sustainable-networks-the-intelligent-operations-guide

TechTarget. (2023, March 14). *What is green computing?* Data Center. Retrieved January 01, 2025, from https://www.techtarget.com/searchdatacenter/definition/green-computing

UL Environment, Green Electronics Council unveil UL ECOLOGO/EPEAT Joint-Certification for Mobile Phones | UL Solutions. (n.d.). UL Solutions. https://www.ul.com/news/ul-environment-green-electronics-council-unveil-ul-ecologoepeat-joint-certification-mobile

Zhang, H.. (2021). Energy-efficient IoT networks: Challenges and opportunities. *IEEE Network*, *35*(2), 15–21.

Chapter 10
Green Artificial Intelligence (AI) and Machine Learning (ML)

D. Pavunraj
https://orcid.org/0000-0001-5651-6565
Vel Tech Multi Tech Dr. Rangarajan Dr. Sakunthala Engineering College, India

A. Mathankumar
Vel Tech Multi Tech Dr. Rangarajan Dr. Sakunthala Engineering College, India

K. Anbumaheshwari
Sethu Institute of Technology, India

R. Daisy Merina
Vel Tech Multi Tech Dr. Rangarajan Dr. Sakunthala Engineering College, India

ABSTRACT

Artificial Intelligence (AI) and Machine Learning (ML) are at the forefront of technological progress, revolutionizing fields such as healthcare, finance, and transportation. However, the energy-intensive processes involved in training and deploying complex AI models have raised significant environmental concerns. Green AI and ML represent a shift toward sustainable practices by emphasizing energy efficiency, reducing carbon footprints, and minimizing resource usage. This approach encompasses the development of optimized algorithms, efficient hardware solutions, and the use of renewable energy during computation. Green AI advocates for training smaller models with reduced computational complexity, thereby ensuring performance with lower environmental costs. Techniques such as model distillation, pruning, and quantization are increasingly being adopted to achieve

DOI: 10.4018/979-8-3373-0766-4.ch010

Copyright © 2025, IGI Global Scientific Publishing. Copying or distributing in print or electronic forms without written permission of IGI Global Scientific Publishing is prohibited.

this balance. Furthermore, Green AI encourages collaboration among researchers, policymakers, and industries paradigm is essential for advancing AI responsibly in an era of growing environmental challenges.

INTRODUCTION

Modern technology has been transformed by artificial intelligence (AI) and machine learning (ML), which has fueled developments in sustainability, healthcare, finance, and transportation. However, growing worries about energy usage and its effects on the environment have resulted from the high computational demands of training and implementing large-scale models (Garg et al., 2022). According to research, for example, training cutting-edge models can produce carbon emissions that are on par with those generated by the lifecycle of a number of automobiles (Henderson et al., 2020; Strubell et al., 2019). This emphasizes how vital it is to incorporate sustainability into AI development methodologies.

By optimizing algorithms, increasing hardware efficiency, and leveraging renewable energy sources, green AI is a new research paradigm that aims to lessen the environmental effect of AI systems (Schwartz et al., 2020; Amodei et al., 2018). In order to minimize energy consumption without sacrificing performance, methods including model pruning, quantization, and distillation have been proposed to reduce the size and complexity of AI models (Cheng et al., 2022; Tan et al., 2019; Wang et al., 2021). To improve computational efficiency, novel techniques in distributed computing and federated learning have also been investigated (Smith et al., 2020; Kairouz et al., 2019).

The Green AI movement has also benefited from the creation of energy-efficient AI hardware, such as neuromorphic circuits and tensor processing units (TPUs) (Jouppi et al., 2017; Chen et al., 2021). These technologies enable faster computations while consuming less power, addressing the scalability challenges associated with large AI systems (Patterson et al., 2022; Lorenz et al., 2021). Additionally, renewable energy integration into data centers and the adoption of carbon offset strategies are becoming central to sustainable AI development (Shao et al., 2021; Zhao et al., 2022).

Research on life-cycle assessments has emphasized the importance of measuring the environmental impact of AI systems across their entire lifecycle, from development to deployment (Gupta et al., 2020; Feng et al., 2021). Frameworks such as these provide actionable insights for reducing energy usage and emissions while maintaining technological progress (Kumar et al., 2021; Bajaj et al., 2021). Moreover, policies aimed at promoting Green AI practices, such as carbon-conscious research grants and energy efficiency benchmarks, are gaining momentum globally (Li et al., 2020; Strubell et al., 2019).

The transition to Green AI also relies on interdisciplinary collaboration, bridging fields such as computer science, environmental science, and public policy (Paritosh et al., 2021; Clark et al., 2021). Researchers advocate for open-access datasets and resource-efficient algorithms to democratize AI development, making it accessible to organizations with limited computational resources (Liu et al., 2021; Zhang et al., 2021). Emerging techniques like zero-shot learning, transfer learning, and meta-learning are further reducing the need for computationally intensive training processes, aligning with the principles of sustainability (Wang et al., 2020; Yu et al., 2021).

As the global demand for AI systems grows, addressing their ecological footprint becomes increasingly critical. The Green AI paradigm not only mitigates environmental harm but also ensures the long-term viability of AI technologies in a resource-constrained world (Garg et al., 2022; Schwartz et al., 2020; Amodei et al., 2018). By embedding sustainability into the AI development pipeline, researchers and practitioners can foster innovation while aligning with global environmental goals.

RELATED WORK: A DEEP DIVE INTO GREEN ARTIFICIAL INTELLIGENCE (AI) AND MACHINE LEARNING (ML)

Machine learning (ML) and green artificial intelligence (AI) focus on reconciling technological advancements with environmental sustainability. This involves innovations in algorithms, hardware design, infrastructure, operational practices, and regulatory policies aimed at mitigating the AI systems' carbon footprint.

1. Algorithmic Innovations: Rethinking Computation

The computational efficiency of AI systems hinges on the design of resource-optimal algorithms. As AI models grow larger and more complex, their energy demands have surged. Addressing this challenge involves several layers of innovation:

- Techniques for Model Compression

Techniques for compressing models, such as distillation, quantization, and pruning, have gained traction. Pruning eliminates unnecessary connections in neural networks, as demonstrated by Han et al. (2015), reducing the computational complexity without significant loss in accuracy. Quantization, discussed by Liu et al. (2021), involves representing weights and activations using fewer bits, achieving up to 8x memory reductions. Knowledge distillation, pioneered by Hinton et al. (2015), transfers knowledge from larger models to smaller, more efficient ones, enabling lightweight deployment.

- Sparse Neural Networks:

Sparse models, as explored by Gale et al. (2020), allocate computations to critical paths while reducing redundant operations. This sparsity-driven approach not only conserves memory but also accelerates inference times.

- Neural Architecture Search (NAS):

Efficient NAS, such as that presented by Tan et al. (2019) in EfficientNet, optimizes architectures automatically, reducing computational overhead compared to manual designs. These techniques align directly with Green AI objectives by selecting architectures with lower energy demands.

- Distributed and Decentralized Learning:

Federated learning (FL) has been heralded as a solution to reduce centralized computation loads. Kairouz et al. (2019) emphasized FL's potential to minimize data transfer and associated energy costs by training models locally on devices and aggregating results centrally.

2. Energy-Efficient Hardware: Accelerating Green ML

Hardware efficiency plays a foundational role in Green AI. Innovations are emerging across various domains of specialized and general-purpose hardware:

- Tensor Processing Units (TPUs):

Jouppi et al. (2017) demonstrated the role of TPUs in accelerating AI computations while achieving higher power efficiency compared to traditional GPUs. TPUs are now widely used in data centers to reduce operational costs.

- Neuromorphic Computing:

Neuromorphic chips, inspired by biological neural processes, emulate brain-like operations, enabling ultra-low-power computation for edge AI tasks (Chen et al., 2021). These chips are particularly suited for tasks like speech recognition and sensor data analysis.

- Memory-CentricArchitectures:

Data movement between memory and processors constitutes a significant portion of energy consumption in AI systems. Shao et al. (2021) proposed in-memory computation, where operations are performed directly within memory modules, drastically cutting energy costs.

- Energy-Efficient ASICs:

Application-Specific Integrated Circuits (ASICs) tailored for ML tasks reduce the power wastage associated with generic processors, as explored by Patel et al. (2021).

3. Infrastructure Innovations: Green Data Centers

Data centers, which form the backbone of AI computations, are major consumers of electricity. Optimizing their design and operations has been a priority for researchers:

- Renewable-Powered Data Centers:

The transition from traditional grid-powered facilities to renewable energy-driven setups has gained momentum. For instance, Zhao et al. (2022) demonstrated solar-powered AI training hubs, augmented with battery storage to mitigate intermittent energy supply issues.

- Dynamic Workload Scheduling:

Dynamic load balancing, as explored by Lorenz et al. (2021), aligns computational loads with periods of renewable energy availability. This ensures higher utilization rates of green energy sources.

- Immersion Cooling Technologies:

Gupta et al. (2020) examined the use of liquid immersion cooling to enhance thermal management of data centers. This technique not only reduces energy costs associated with conventional cooling but also extends the lifespan of server hardware.

4. Environmental Metrics and Benchmarking

Accurate metrics are vital to assess and compare the environmental impacts of AI systems. These include:

- Energy and Carbon Benchmarks:

Schwartz et al. (2020) proposed Green AI metrics focusing on carbon equivalence (CO2e) and energy consumption (kWh) as standard benchmarks. Their work encourages transparency in reporting the environmental costs of AI research.

- Lifecycle Assessments (LCA):

Feng et al. (2021) emphasized the importance of LCA to measure the long-term environmental impact of AI systems. By including training, deployment, and eventual decommissioning phases, LCAs provide a holistic view of sustainability.

- FP Operations Per Watt:

Metrics such as floating-point operations per watt (FLOPs/W) introduced by Patterson et al. (2022) serve as benchmarks for hardware efficiency during model training and inference.

5. Governance, Policies, and Collaboration

The governance of AI's environmental impact has received attention as policy-makers and institutions recognize the need for sustainable innovation:

- Regulatory Frameworks:

Governments are increasingly integrating sustainability requirements into AI funding and development programs. Strubell et al. (2019) advocated for mandatory energy and carbon reporting in AI-related research grants.

- Cross-Sector Collaboration:

Collaboration between academia, industry, and policymakers has proven critical. For example, the European Green Deal includes AI as a strategic tool to achieve carbon neutrality by 2050.

- Incentivizing Green Research:

Clark et al. (2021) proposed incentive structures for organizations adopting green practices in AI, such as tax benefits for renewable energy integration and green certifications for data centers.

6. Emerging Paradigms in Sustainable AI

The next wave of Green AI research focuses on radical paradigm shifts:

- **Bio-Inspired Algorithms:**

Algorithms inspired by natural processes, such as ant colony optimization and genetic algorithms, offer efficient solutions for specific AI problems (Smith et al., 2020).

- **Learning with Few and Zero Shots:**

The amount of data and processing needed for AI training is greatly decreased by methods like few-shot and zero-shot learning (Wang et al., 2020).

- **Hybrid Cloud-Edge Frameworks:**

The hybridization of cloud and edge computing, as explored by Liu et al. (2021), enables localized AI processing while offloading intensive tasks to energy-optimized cloud systems.

MATERIALS AND METHODS

1. Computational Resources and Infrastructure

The selection of appropriate hardware and infrastructure is pivotal for evaluating the energy consumption and performanceAI system performance efficiency and energy consumption efficiency of AI systems. The experiments utilized a mix of general-purpose computing resources, specialized AI hardware, and edge devices to provide a holistic perspective on energy savings across different types of applications.

- **High-Performance GPUs and TPUs:**
  - **NVIDIA GPUs (Tesla V100 and A100)**: These Deep learning model training is a common application for GPUs were used to benchmark traditional energy consumption patterns against more efficient alternatives.
  - **Google TPUs (Tensor Processing Units)**: A key component for AI tasks that accelerate model training with lower energy footprints, compared to GPUs. They are specifically designed to handle large-scale tensor computations with reduced power usage.
- **Edge Devices:**
  - **Raspberry Pi 4** and **NVIDIA Jetson Nano**: These devices are utilized for small-scale edge AI deployments, specifically in image classification and sensor data processing, to assess energy consumption in lightweight, real-time applications.

- **Cloud-Based Resources:**

- **Google Cloud Platform (GCP) and Amazon Web Services (AWS)**: The cloud-based
  - virtual machines were employed for large-scale AI model training.

Figure 1. Architecture of Green Artificial Intelligence (AI) and Machine Learning (ML)

- o Energy consumption was measured using AWS CloudWatchandGoogle Cloud Monitoring to capture the energy usage statistics associated with cloud computations.
  - **Neuromorphic Hardware:**
- o **Intel Loihi**: Neuromorphic chips, designed to mimic the energy-efficient processes of the human brain, were tested for AI workloads that require low power consumption, such as pattern recognition tasks.

2. Software Frameworks and Energy Measurement Tools

The integration of software frameworks and energy monitoring tools is essential for tracking the efficiency of AI systems. The following tools and frameworks were used in the experiments:

- **Deep Learning Frameworks:**
  - o **TensorFlow** and **PyTorch**: These popular deep learning frameworks were used to train AI models, including CNNs and transformers. Both frameworks support energy monitoring through external plugins, such as CodeCarbon, to track the environmental impact.

- **Keras**: A high-level neural networks API that was used for simplifying model design and experimentation.

- **Energy Tracking and Measurement Tools:**
  - **PowerAPI**: An open-source tool that monitors the energy consumption of various system components, including CPUs, GPUs, and memory during model training and inference.
  - **CodeCarbon**: This tool was employed to estimate the carbon emissions generated by the computational workloads, providing an essential metric to evaluate the environmental cost of training AI models.
  - **nvidia-smi**: NVIDIA's system management interface was used to monitor GPU usage, power consumption, and thermal performance in real-time during AI model training.
  - **Energy Metering Sensors**: Direct energy consumption was measured at the hardware level using power meters attached to server nodes.

3. Datasets Used in Experiments

A range of datasets was selected to test the AI models in a variety of fields, such as real-time edge applications, computer vision, and natural language processing. The datasets were chosen to reflect common tasks in AI research, from image classification to speech recognition, with particular emphasis on scalability and complexity.

- **Image Recognition Datasets:**
  - **ImageNet** and **CIFAR-10**: These standard datasets were used for benchmarking the energy efficiency of CNNs, such as ResNet, VGG, and MobileNet.
  - **CelebA**: A dataset of celebrity face images was used to explore energy-efficient facial recognition models, especially for edge AI applications.
- **Natural Language Processing (NLP) Datasets:**
  - **SQuAD**: This question-answering dataset was used to evaluate the energy cost of transformer-based models like BERT and RoBERTa.
  - **GLUE Benchmark**: This suite of NLP tasks was used for training and evaluating language models and assessing their performance versus energy consumption.
- **Edge Computing Datasets:**
  - **OpenCV Image Processing Tasks**: Tasks such as real-time object detection and video streaming were deployed on edge devices to examine the trade-offs between computation load and energy efficiency.

4. Model Design and Optimization Techniques

The research focused on evaluating the energy efficiency of AI models by incorporating a range of Artificial intelligence models in a variety of fields, such as natural language processing, computer vision, and real-time edge applications model accuracy. These techniques were crucial in aligning AI performance with sustainability objectives.

- **Pruning and Quantization**:
    - o **Model Pruning**: We employed structured and unstructured pruning to reduce the number of weights in neural networks. This technique selectively removes less important connections in the network, reducing computation during both training and inference (Han et al., 2015).
    - o **Weight Quantization**: To minimize memory requirements, we applied quantization techniques that map weights from lower-bit representations to floating-point values (Liu et al., 2021), reducing both memory usage and the energy cost of model execution.
- **Knowledge Distillation**:
    - o Knowledge distillation, a technique where a large, The learned knowledge of a complex model is transferred to a smaller, more effective model was implemented (Hinton et al., 2015). This method helps create compact models that perform similarly to their larger counterparts but with significantly lower computational costs.
- **Transfer Learning**:
    - o Pre-trained models were fine-tuned on domain-specific tasks. By using a pre-trained model, we reduced the number of epochs reducing the amount of time and energy needed for training in order to attain high performance (Pan and Yang, 2010).
- **Federated Learning**:
    - o We implemented federated learning to train models in a decentralized manner, which allows data processing to occur on local devices (e.g., smartphones, IoT devices), significantly reducing the energy costs associated with transferring data to centralized servers (McMahan et al., 2017).

5. Energy Consumption Measurement and Environmental Impact Analysis

To ensure that our findings reflect the true energy efficiency of AI models, we utilized a multi-faceted approach to measure energy consumption and assess their environmental impact:

- **Carbon Emission Calculation**:

- o CarbonTrackerwas used to track and compute the CO2 emissions from computational workloads. It estimates the carbon footprint based on the energy consumed and the regional energy mix, providing insights into the environmental consequences of AI model training.
- **Energy Usage Profiling**:
  - o We measured energy usage at different levels of computation, from CPU and GPU consumption during training to energy usage during inference and model deployment. Metrics such as total kWh per training session and energy consumption per epochwere collected to provide detailed insights into the efficiency of each approach.
- **Performance-Energy Trade-Offs**:
  - o We conducted experiments to Analyze the trade-off between accuracy and model performance.and energy consumption, comparing energy-optimized models against baseline models. This allowed us to assess the potential for achieving high-performance AI with minimal energy costs.
- **Real-Time Power Usage Monitoring**:
  - o Real-time monitoring of power consumption using PowerAPI provided continuous tracking during model deployment and inference. This enabled us to calculate energy usage per inference request, which is crucial for edge AI and deployment in resource-constrained environments.

6.Statistical Analysis and Data Validation

The accuracy of the AI models and the significance of the energy savings were evaluated using rigorous statistical methods to ensure robustness and reliability of the results.

- **Paired T-Tests**:
  - o Statistical analysis was conducted with paired t-tests to evaluate the performance of baseline models with optimized models. This helped establish the significance of the energy savings without sacrificing model accuracy.
- **Energy-Performance Regression Models**:
  - o Regression analysis was performed to model the relationship between model complexity, energy consumption, and performance. This allowed for predicting energy usage based on model size, dataset complexity, and hardware specifications.
- **Reproducibility**:
  - o All experiments were repeated multiple times with consistent results to ensure the reproducibility and validity of the findings. Average ener-

gy consumption, accuracy, and carbon emission values were reported along with their respective 95% confidence intervals.

CONCLUSION

In this study, we explored the integration of Green Machine Learning (ML) and Artificial Intelligence (AI), focusing on the environmental impact of AI systems. As AI models grow in complexity, their computational and energy demands also increase, resulting in a significant environmental footprint. This research aimed to address these concerns by investigating various optimization techniques, hardware solutions, and software strategies that can reduce the energy consumption of AI systems without compromising their performance.Through our analysis, we demonstrated that employing model compression techniques such as pruning, AI model energy consumption can be greatly reduced by quantization and knowledge distillation. Furthermore, utilizing energy-efficient hardware—such as TPUs, neuromorphic processors, and edge devices—offers a viable way to lessen the carbon footprint of AI systems both during deployment and training. Additionally, our work emphasized the significance of sustainable infrastructure. The entire energy consumption of AI operations can be decreased by optimizing cloud data centers and edge computing devices for energy efficiency.

The environmental effect of AI systems can be further reduced by implementing dynamic task scheduling and renewable energy sources. The study also emphasizes the necessity of precise environmental measures to monitor the energy consumption and carbon emissions related to AI inference and training. Researchers and developers may make well-informed judgments regarding optimizing energy use with the help of tools like CodeCarbon and PowerAPI, which offer vital insights. Green AI's future depends on these indicators as well as the implementation of sustainable governance models and policies. To sum up, the shift

Green AI is a social and environmental necessity in addition to a technical difficulty. Researchers, developers, and politicians must work together and put sustainability first as AI develops further. We can make sure that AI advances technology and protects the environment by concentrating on energy-efficient models, hardware, and infrastructure. The study's conclusions offer a path forward for further investigation and advancement in the creation of AI systems that are both potent and long-lasting.

REFERENCES

Amodei, D., & Clark, J. (2021). Measuring the environmental impact of machine learning. *Nature Sustainability*, *4*(7), 567–576. DOI: 10.1038/s41893-021-00782-7

Amodei, D., & Hernandez, D. (2018). AI and compute. Retrieved from https://openai.com/blog/ai-and-compute/

Avent, B., Kairouz, P., & McMahan, H. B. (2019). Advances and open problems in federated learning. *Foundations and Trends in Machine Learning*, *14*(1–2), 1–210. DOI: 10.1561/2200000073

Bajaj, S., & Kumar, R. (2021). Environmental benchmarks for AI systems. *Sustainable AI*, *1*, 15–22. DOI: 10.1016/j.susai.2021.100001

Bajaj, S., Paritosh, P., & Singh, R. (2021). Sustainable AI: Methods and trends. *Energy and AI*, *3*, 200–212. DOI: 10.1016/j.eneai.2021.100015

Berkaya, S. K., Ergin, S., Gulmezoglu, M. B., Gunal, E. S., Gunal, S., & Uysal, A. K. (2018). A survey on ECG analysis. *Biomedical Signal Processing and Control*, *43*, 216–235. DOI: 10.1016/j.bspc.2018.03.003

Cheng, Y., Wang, D., Zhou, P., & Zhang, T. (2022). Model compression: Techniques and applications. *IEEE Signal Processing Magazine*, *35*(1), 32–41. DOI: 10.1109/MSP.2022.00198

Dodge, J., Schwartz, R., & Smith, N. A. (2020). Green AI: Reducing the carbon footprint of AI research. *Communications of the ACM*, *63*(7), 54–63. DOI: 10.1145/3408039

Feng, X., Zhang, Y., & Zhou, W. (2021). Life-cycle assessment of AI models. *Journal of Cleaner Production*, *305*, 127–140. DOI: 10.1016/j.jclepro.2021.127832

Ganesh, A., McCallum, A., & Strubell, E. (2019). Energy and policy considerations for NLP. *Proceedings of ACL 2019*, 3645–3650. DOI: 10.18653/v1/P19-1355

Gao, T., Shao, H., & Wang, Y. (2021). Renewable energy for AI computations. *Energy*, *219*, 105–115. DOI: 10.1016/j.energy.2021.105837

Garg, S., Kumar, N., & Sharma, P. (2022). Green AI: Trends and challenges. *Sustainable Computing : Informatics and Systems*, *34*, 100624. DOI: 10.1016/j.suscom.2022.100624

Gonzalez, J. E., Le, Q., & Patterson, D. (2022). Carbon efficiency of ML systems. *Communications of the ACM*, *65*(5), 85–93. DOI: 10.1145/3465810

Gupta, V., Singh, A., & Tiwari, M. K. (2020). Efficient data centers for AI training. *IEEE Access : Practical Innovations, Open Solutions, 9*, 8123–8132. DOI: 10.1109/ACCESS.2020.3045178

Henderson, P., Hu, J., & Morgenstern, J. (2020). Towards environmentally sustainable machine learning. *NeurIPS Workshop on Green AI,* 1–8. Retrieved from https://arxiv.org/abs/1907.10597

Hoffmann, F., Lorenz, M., & Schuler, J. (2021). Carbon offsets for AI technologies. *Environmental Research Letters, 16*(5), 015003. DOI: 10.1088/1748-9326/abcde1

Jouppi, N. P., Patil, N., & Young, C. (2017). In-datacenter performance analysis of a Tensor Processing Unit. *Proceedings of ISCA, 2017*, 1–12. DOI: 10.1145/3079856.3080246

Le, Q. V., & Tan, M. (2019). EfficientNet: Rethinking model scaling. Proceedings of ICML 2019, 6105–6114. Retrieved from https://proceedings.mlr.press

Smith, T., Yu, X., & Zhang, R. (2020). Distributed learning for AI sustainability. *Proceedings of ICML 2020,* 1024–1031. Retrieved from https://proceedings.mlr.press/

Sun, Z., Liu, J., & Zhou, P. (2021). Quantization-aware training for efficient AI models. *Neural Networks, 150*, 25–37. DOI: 10.1016/j.neunet.2021.03.005

Chapter 11

Energy-Efficient Solutions and Environmental Impact Reduction in Mobile and Wireless Computing

T. Veeramani
Panimalar Engineering College, India

D. Prabhu
Vel tech Rangarajan Dr. Sagunthala R&D Institute of Science and Technology, India

B. Yamini
https://orcid.org/0000-0003-3531-108X
SRM Institute of Science and Technology, India

V. K. Ramya Bharathi
Sathyabama Institute of Science and Technology, India

R. Vinoth
https://orcid.org/0000-0001-5866-1395
R.M.K. College of Engineering and Technology, India

S. Udhayashankar
https://orcid.org/0009-0006-3781-8801
Vel Tech Multi Tech Dr. Rangarajan Dr. Sakunthala Engineering College, India

P. J. Beslin Pajila
https://orcid.org/0000-0002-3905-2460
Vel Tech Rangarajan Dr. Sagunthala R&D Institute of Science and Technology, India

ABSTRACT

With the advancement of the mobile and wireless computing technologies more and more attention has been paid to their impact on environment. This paper provides an overview of green solutions pertaining to the energy conservation and carbon emission of portable gadgets, wireless networks and communication systems. It

DOI: 10.4018/979-8-3373-0766-4.ch011

Copyright © 2025, IGI Global Scientific Publishing. Copying or distributing in print or electronic forms without written permission of IGI Global Scientific Publishing is prohibited.

covers fundamental concepts like low power hardware design, energy efficient cellular network and efficient power control mechanisms. The viability of renewable resources as well as the energy harvesting and wireless charging technologies in enhancing sustainability of the devices is also described. Furthermore, the paper analyses the implementation of edge computing, energy-aware networks, and AI solutions for enhancing energy efficiency in mobile and wireless networks. Green mobile networks and sustainable IoT are illustrated by case studies of real-world applications. Last, the paper presents a discussion of the threat, including the trade-off between performance and energy consumption, and directions for future research to improve sustainability in this field.

1. INTRODUCTION

1.1 Background and Motivation

The advancement of mobile and wireless computing systems has become a major aspect of society, trade and commerce, and people's interaction. Over the last few decades, mobile and portable devices, wireless communication and internet, and the IoT have dramatically developed(Akhilesh Bholanath Patel 2021). Smartphones, smart homes, and wearable computing devices are now an integral part of human lives and therefore mobile computing. Moreover, the availability of high-speed wireless technologies like 4G and 5G networks has ensured effective connectivity and helped in the development of data-oriented services like cloud computing, big data and analytics, and artificial intelligence(Mukul Vishwakarma, Arpita Nigam 2024). The increasing use of these technology solutions has brought about a revolution in some key sectors such as telecommunication, health, learning, commerce, and entertainment sectors. However, this kind of advancement of Information Technology is accompanied by great threats in terms of environmental and energy impacts. Since the adoption of mobile devices and wireless networks is increasing rapidly, more energy is required. Mobile networks, data centers, and individual mobile devices are massive consumers of electricity to offer connection and services. Besides, the manufacturing, transportation, and usage of electronic gadgets result in electric waste and pollution of the environment. The reports by the IEA and other sustainability organizations show that the ICT industry as a whole consumes a significant amount of energy and mobile networks and devices are significant contributors. Thus, the sustainability of mobile and wireless technologies is an increasingly important issue for the technological industry and the policy-making process. The demand for these technologies has risen over the years due to the effects of climate change thus the need for green solutions. Making mobile devices, wireless infrastructures and networks less carbon-intensive is an imperative not only with respect to the social cost of pollution but also with respect to the sustainability of these technologies in the future. Therefore, there is a significant need to advocate efficient energy solutions as well as renewable energy into the mobile and wireless computing domain.

1.2 Objectives of the Survey

The scope of this particular survey is to present the overview of sustainable solutions in mobile and wireless computing with a special emphasis on energy consumption, environmental footprint, and resource utilization. The purpose is to discover major trends, new concepts, and issues which influence the progress of improved mobile and wireless systems. This survey will explore the current state of the industry by focusing on the changes in the hardware design, software optimization, as well as the networks' structure in order to address the need for sustainability. One of the main goals is to review the steps that could be taken in order to increase energy efficiency in Mobile Devices and Networks. This involves assessing low power hardware technologies like energy efficient processors, displays and batteries, software means that assist in reducing power consumption in mobile applications and operating systems. Further, the survey will explore emerging trends in wireless communication technologies like green cellular networks, power saving mechanisms in WiFi and Bluetooth and in mobile data transmission optimization techniques. The survey will also look at how newer technologies such as energy harvesting, wireless charging, and artificial intelligence optimization will further enhance mobile networks sustainability. In addition, it will also look at the ability of edge computing and IoT networks to cut energy consumption through resource delegation and proper communication protocols. Another important aim is to identify the problems that may occur on the way to sustainability in mobile and wireless computing. Some of these challenges are: trade off between performance and power consumption, current hardware constraints, and technology constraints of large scale implementation of green technologies. In this regard, the survey seeks to identify these challenges and contribute to the subsequent advancement of energy-efficient mobile and wireless innovations. Thus, this survey will help in making a clear picture of today's mobile and wireless computing and its sustainability status and know about technologies and strategies that can be employed for minimizing environmental effects of these highly important systems.

2. FUNDAMENTALS OF SUSTAINABLE MOBILE AND WIRELESS COMPUTING

2.1 Definition and Key Concepts

Mobile and Wireless Computing Sustainability is defined as the ability to create and deploy technologies, systems, and strategies in mobile technologies, wireless networks, and data infrastructure using processes that have low impact on the environment(Wang et al 2014). This is achieved through energy conservation, efficient resource utilization and prolongation of the lifespan of devices and networks while at the same time improving the overall functionality and usability. Sustainability in this context is important given the more astonishing growth of mobile technologies and wireless networks that are putting enormous pressure on the energy resources and environment of the world(Yang & Ma, Maode. 2014).

Three key concepts are central to the idea of sustainability in mobile and wireless computing: efficiency, utilization of resources, and the least pollution of the environment.

1. **Energy Efficiency:** Energy efficiency for mobile and wireless computing is the ability to reduce the energy being consumed by the devices and network with an aim of improving their performance. This may be done through hardware including low-power processors, energy-efficient displays and batteries as well as through software including optimized scheduling, power management and energy efficient protocols in the communication networks. Energy efficiency is an area of concern because the mobile network and devices are among the biggest consumers of electricity in the world.
2. **Resource Optimization:** Resource management means the rational uses of resources such as energy, bandwidth/spectrum, and storage both physical and virtual. In mobile networks, resource optimization comprises of minimizing the network traffic, and controlling data flow in order to avoid wastage of resources. In the case of mobile devices, the resource optimization could include using low power hardware, sparing resource usage in applications, and optimizing Operating Systems to avoid wastage.
3. **Reduced Environmental Impact:** This concept includes ways of minimizing total impacts of mobile and wireless technologies on the environment. They comprise the reductions in carbon emission in mobile network operations and manufacturing, the control of electronic waste through recycling and the use of recyclable materials, and the control of pollution from the dumping of electronic devices. As well as in the utilization of the renewable sources of

energy for example through the integration of the solar and wind power into the networked structures.

2.2 Scope and Importance

The aspects of sustainable mobile and wireless networks are considered more crucial than before due to the increasing demand of data, connectivity and mobile devices. Since the introduction of the new generation of networks like 5G and the proliferation of objects connected to the Internet, data traffic is growing rapidly. This enhanced demand for bandwidth in addition to the need for higher capability of the networks results in high power consumption hence the degradation of the environment. Therefore, the mobile industry, telecommunications operators and device manufactures are now making sustainable development a priority.

Telecommunications: The players in this transition are the telecommunications industry that includes mobile network operators and infrastructure companies. As 5G networks come into operation and the transition towards 6G is expected, the networks will evolve in their complexity and demand for power. Optimising energy consumption in networks, energy efficient base stations, small cells, energy from renewable sources and related costs are key considerations. However, the optimization such as energy-efficient resource allocation and dynamic power management will also be vital to ensure that networks strive to be scalable without compromising energy consumption.
Internet of Things (IoT): The IoT networks made of billions of connected devices may produce a huge amount of data while consuming a great amount of energy(Nair et al 2018). IoT system integration and sustainability are important due to the deployment of devices and sensors in areas that are sometimes difficult to access, and due to their energy demands and communication demands, low power hardware and energy harvesting is employed. Energy consumption in IoT devices, thereby LPWANs and energy efficient IoT protocols should be kept to a minimum to ensure sustainability in the Internet of Things(Goundar et al 2021)(Sudha, K et al 2023).
Smart Cities: The principle of smart cities that is based on the integrated IoT devices and mobile networks, emphasizes the relevance of the issues of sustainability in the process of city building. Since cities are now using IoT for managing infrastructures, traffic, utilities and waste management among others, it is very important to make sure that such systems are as energy efficient and have the least impact on the natural environment as can be. Smart city cannot function efficiently without sustainable mobile and wireless networks

because they facilitate the exchange of information, monitoring, and control of resources in cities.

In conclusion, sustainability in mobile and wireless computing is very important in responding to the environmental impacts related to the diffusion of digital technologies. With such demand for data and connectivity in an increasingly connected world, it is important for mobile network, devices and infrastructure to embrace sustainability to ensure that mobile technologies are sustainable and do not harm the environment; instead they are part of building smart, connected and green society.

3. ENERGY EFFICIENCY OF MOBILE DEVICES

Energization of portable devices is a fundamental component of environmental-friendly mobile and wireless computing. Mobile devices are built around battery power; and as the call for performance and functionality goes up, so does the power consumption. In addition to getting longer battery life, the amount of energy consumed by these devices is also decreased by turning them off and reducing its charge by cutting down on the power that is needed to charge it. Improvement of the energy efficiency of mobile devices can be achieved through better hardware engineering, optimization of power utilization algorithms, and new methods of energy acquisition.

3.1 Low-Power Hardware Design

Efficiency in the use of energy in today's mobile devices is best determined by the kind of mobile processors that are in use. It is the processors that perform the activities, and as the mobile devices get more sophisticated, the processors are more power hungry. Recent developments in the semiconductors including the use of smaller transistors and efficient structures of processing have greatly contributed to increased power efficiency. For instance, today's popular processors like ARM's Cortex series and apple's A series processors incorporate techniques like dynamic voltage and frequency scaling (DVFS) to control power utilization according to the workload. Memory management is another important component of energy efficiency in the mobile devices. Smart phones and tablets use dynamic random-access memory (DRAM) to store data and execute applications. Energy dissipation in memories can be made low by enhancing the memory access patterns and reducing the energy cost of maintaining data in memory. Emerging classes of memory, including low power DRAM and non-volatile memory, for instance, contribute to lowering energy consumption of portable devices while offering high data access rates. Other things that help in extending battery life include low power displays.

Such screens, as OLED and LCD, are typically very power consuming, and many modern users own portable devices with high-resolution screens. To address this, there are technologies such as OLED display where the screen only turns on the pixels that are needed, and not the entire backlight. Further, the options for screen brightness control, adaptive display technologies, and improved structures of the displays decrease the energy required by mobile displays. That is why the development of new batteries has greatly boosted the life of the portable devices we use in the present. Advanced chemistries to be included in lithium-sulfur and solid-state batteries are expected to yield higher energy density, better longevity of charge cycles, and faster charging capability than lithium-ion batteries. Advancements in Battery Management Systems (BMS) assist in extending battery life and maximizing battery efficiency through careful charge and discharge cycles.

3.2 Power Management Techniques

Proper power management strategies are crucial in order to increase the battery duration of the portable devices with no compromise on their performance. One of them is Dynamic Voltage and Frequency Scaling (DVFS) that helps to change the voltage and the frequency of the processor according to the workload. Energy use can be lowered to a large extent by scaling down the voltage and frequency during low usage without necessarily affecting the performance of the device. Another method of power management is energy efficient scheduling. Smartphone operating systems use complex scheduling mechanisms to minimise energy consumption when performing the tasks. For example, some activities can be done later when there are no essential activities to be performed, while others can be prioritized when it comes to usage of power in order to ensure that only the necessary operations consume power. The sleep modes are used in the device in order to consume low power when it is in inactive state. Most today's mobile devices apply deep sleep mode where one or more elements such as the display, sensors, or a network connection are powered down to conserve power but the important functions are still operational. These sleep states are controlled by the mobile operating systems (OS) to make the device power use the least energy when it is not in use. Mobile OS strategies, including battery saver features and background app control, also contribute towards minimizing energy use by either restricting or pausing applications and processes that are otherwise running in the background. For instance, the Android and iOS mobile operating systems let users regulate the app behavior in terms of background processing or notifications, which can drastically decrease energy usage.

3.3 Energy Harvesting and Wireless Charging

Energy harvesting is therefore the process of gathering energy from within the surrounding environment to power portable devices. Picking up characteristics of solar, thermal, and motion-based energy harvesting can also help to decrease the utilization of conventional charging techniques. Another facet of energy harvesting is the ability to capture sunlight using solar cells incorporated into the body of a mobile device, or even part of an accessory.

Solar energy harvesting involves using solar cells embedded in mobile devices or their accessories to capture sunlight and convert it into electrical energy. This is especially applicable to devices used in outdoor or off grid applications. Thermal energy harvesting involves capturing heat produced by the device components or the surrounding environment, and using this heat to produce electricity that can be used to power low power sensors or recharge small batteries. Kinetic energy is obtained from the movement of the user (pedestrian, cyclist, etc.) or the device itself (vibrations).

These techniques are specifically suitable for the IoT devices and wearables that commonly run in the isolated or limited-resource conditions.

Wireless charging is another technologically developed concept which has been invented to enhance sustainability since no cable is needed for charging. Other such technologies include inductive charging and resonant inductive coupling which allow the charging of mobile devices without actual physical contact. Wireless charging is more efficient than the conventional charging methods since energy loss is minimized and the problem of electronic waste due to the constant deterioration of cables and connectors is solved.

Therefore, energy efficiency for portable devices must be approached from three different perspectives: hardware and software design for low power consumption, new and enhanced power-management methods and power scavenging technologies. These strategies will be instrumental in controlling energy usage, protracting the useful life of mobile technologies and lessening the adverse effects of mobility on the environment as the mobile technologies advance.

4. ENERGY-EFFICIENT WIRELESS COMMUNICATION TECHNOLOGIES

Especially with the ever increasing demand for mobile data, connectivity and communication services, it becomes imperative to reduce the energy requirements of the wireless communication systems. Communications technology such as Mobile networks (Cellular, 5G, 6G), Wi-Fi, Bluetooth, etc., contribute a large part of the world's energy consumption. For these systems to be sustainable, energy efficient wireless communication technologies are mandatory. Measures that can be implemented to increase energy efficiency are: optimal management of the cellular networks, optimization of short range communication interfaces, and optimization of the data transmission.

4.1 Green Cellular Networks

Energy efficient cellular networks mainly concern with the minimization of energy consumption in the cellular infrastructure while at the same time achieving or improving the performance. With the emergence of the 5G and the forthcoming 6G technologies, it will be predicted that the mobile network will have to deal with much more traffic demand and therefore more energy is needed. To mitigate this, a range of techniques is employed:

Energy-efficient base stations: Base stations are the major components of cellular networks, and energy consumption of base stations is one of the main factors of total power requirements of mobile networks. Energy management techniques include the use of low power small cells and distributed antenna systems which consume less power than the conventional macro base stations and can be deployed more optimally in the urban environment. These systems enable operation at lower power levels since they require fewer resources to offer satisfactory coverage and data throughput.

Power-saving techniques: Technologies such as the new generation of MIMO (Multiple Input, Multiple Output) as well as beamforming can help reduce energy consumption because instead of emitting signals in all directions, they are aimed directly at the user. Moreover, other sophisticated network management features such as putting a base station to sleep during low traffic can be implemented.

6G and beyond: For the 6G networks which are still being developed, the implementation of AI-driven network management and the use of ENFV that includes energy efficient NFV will be critical. These technologies enable the control of network utilization depending on actual traffic, thus avoiding energy consumption and achieving maximum network performance(George et al 2024).

4.2 Energy Efficient WiFi and Bluetooth

Wireless technologies such as Wi-Fi and Bluetooth are now considered essential for short-range communication, and their power consumption must be optimized for portable gadgets and IoT. Both protocols have introduced several energy-saving innovations:

Wi-Fi: Wi-Fi 6 (802.11ax) also referred to as High-Efficiency Wireless (HEW) enhances the energy efficiency of wireless networks through optimized transmission and reception of data. These are OFDMA (Orthogonal Frequency-Division Multiple Access) that enable many devices to access the same channel and MU-MIMO (Multi-User, Multiple Input, Multiple Output) that helps to solve the problem of congestion and improve the speed of data transmission. Wi-Fi HaLow (802.11ah) for IoT devices works under sub-1 GHz having better range as well as low power consumption required for applications as smart home, Industrial IoT etc.

Low-energy Bluetooth: Bluetooth Low Energy (BLE) is an umbrella term that refers to a class of Bluetooth that is effective for short range energy consumption. Some of its uses include; fitness trackers, smart home devices, and wearables. BLE has lower power consumption by taking shorter interval in sending the data and at the same time, the time the device is awake. Other current BLE advancements such as Bluetooth 5.0 and 5.1 standard also enhance energy efficiency through optimized range, faster data transmission and connection management.

These energy saving protocols help in the conservation of power in the mobile devices and wireless systems while at the same time providing efficiency and reliability of the user's communication.

4.3 Optimization of Mobile Data Transmission

Efficient use of mobile data has become a critical factor in the low power consumption while delivering quality experience to the users. Several techniques help balance power usage, data rate, and latency:

Data compression: There is a reduction of data that need to be transferred hence reducing energy use. Since files, images, and video content are compressed before transmission, the energy used in both transmission and reception is conserved. For instance, in video streaming applications, data is compressed through the use of algorithms in order to reduce the bandwidth needed and enhance data density.

Bandwidth management: Optimal utilization of the limited bandwidth reduces traffic jams in the network and also ensures that energy is well employed. Traffic shaping and quality of service (QoS) prioritization makes it possible to schedule the bandwidth to the specific data, for instance, giving priority to voice or video calls while sparing energy on other data that does not require much attention in a particular time.

Offloading: Offloading strategies like MEC allow computation to be shifted nearer to the user hence minimizing the distance that information has to travel before being processed in a cloud server. In order to offload some of the processing load to other nearby edge servers, mobile devices can save energy by reducing the distance that data has to travel, which in turn reduces latency and increases performance.

The conflict between latency, data rate, and power consumption is inevitable in the mobile communication system. For instance, low latency usually comes with high data rates and hence high energy consumption. These factors should be managed to get the best possible compromise between energy consumption and data transmission rate in mobile telecommunications.

Therefore, the green cellular networks, green wireless local area networks, green wireless personal area networks, data transmission optimization technologies are important to minimizing the environmental cost of the mobile networks and wireless systems. Thus, these techniques will be important as mobile data demand increases and more future communication technologies are developed.

5. SUSTAINABLE MOBILE NETWORKS AND INFRASTRUCTURES

As mobile networks change, especially with the rise in 5G and the future 6G technologies, higher speed, and efficiency become the order of the day. But this growth also poses a problem concerning energy consumption within the society. In order to meet these challenges sustainable mobile networks and infrastructures are key. These networks are expected to achieve low levels of energy consumption, high performance, the ability to handle many devices, and high traffic. Techniques including green 5G technologies, energy sensitive networks and edge computing are critical for attaining these goals(Anusha, S et al 2024).

5.1 Green 5G and Beyond

Green 5G and beyond is the methods of organizing and managing the mobile networks in a manner that will ensure low energy consumption while at the same time delivering high quality and reliability. As mobile networks transition to 5G and beyond, new technologies and approaches are being adopted to meet the increasing demand for energy efficiency:

Small cells: Small cells are low-power base stations that provide more localized coverage, reducing the energy required for long-range communication . Unlike traditional large macro cells small cells can be deployed in urban areas to support dense networks, hence the amount of energy required to cover a smaller geographical area is used. This assists in lowering the total energy consumption level by lowering the power required to attend to each user.
Massive MIMO (Multiple Input, Multiple Output): Massive MIMO can be described as a technology that applies a large number of antennas to supply multiple clients at the same time. This helps to cut down energy use through increasing the spectral efficiency of the network which means that more data will be transmitted per unit of power. The fact that signals can be targeted specifically to the users and not sent out in large streams greatly enhances energy use.
Millimeter-wave technologies: One of the fundamental characteristics of 5G is millimeter-wave (mmWave) technology which works at higher frequencies to provide higher data rates, though with lower power efficiency. mmWave technologies lower the energy intensity of long-range communication by providing high-capacity communication over short distances.

Both of these technologies complement each other to make sure that as 5G networks are ramping up on data traffic, they are not doing it on the back of exorbitant amounts of energy consumption.

5.2 Energy Aware Network Architectures

Energy-aware network architectures are centered on the development of mobile networks that use minimal energy in their operations. These architectures rely on innovative technologies like software-defined networking (SDN) and network function virtualization (NFV) to achieve greater energy efficiency:

Software-Defined Networking (SDN): SDN separates the network control and forwarding planes to give a more flexible approach to managing network resources. This enables the operators to manage traffic flow and balance resources to ensure least amount of energy used during off peak traffic. SDN brings better traffic control and distribution of resources throughout the network, while minimizing energy wastage.

Network Function Virtualization (NFV): NFV is a concept whereby various network functions that used to be performed through physical hardware devices are effected through virtual software. This is possible since these functions are run as software on commodity hardware in NFV, unlike traditional hardware where resource allocation and scaling of network functions are rigid. This approach is capable of minimizing the utilization of dedicated hardware for energy and can also adapt to the network traffic and is capable of saving energy.

These architectures enable optimal utilization of network resources, by minimizing the power consumed during **idle time, and thereby enhancing the power quality of the Mobile networks.**

5.3 Edge Computing and Resource Offloading

Edge computing is the concept that involves analyzing data where the data is being generated, rather than sending the data to a remote cloud centre. By utilizing edge computing to offload processing tasks from mobile devices to nearby edge servers, energy consumption can be reduced in several ways:

Reducing data transmission distance: That is why the data processing in the edge network is localized, and the amount of information to be transmitted over considerable distances is limited. This not only minimizes on the use of power intensive long distance communication but also relieves traffic and delay on the network thus enhancing energy efficiency.

Energy savings through task offloading: Most mobile devices are limited by the battery, and it is common to deplete the battery quickly if the mobile device is performing computationally demanding functions. Since these tasks can be performed by edge servers, mobile devices and their batteries will be saved and get longer life span. For instance, real-time data processing for applications like AR or machine learning can be done by edge servers leaving the device to be only involved in interaction.

Latency and energy in data-intensive applications: For use cases that require heavy processing and analysis of data such as video streaming or real-time analytics, MEC is useful since the data does not have to be sent all the way to the cloud. These applications analyse data at the edge of the network, and therefore, can be implemented with low latency and low energy consumption, which will be beneficial to the end-user.

On balance, there are three dimensions toward realizing sustainable mobile networks, including green 5G technologies, energy-sensitive network architectures, and edge computing. These innovations not only enable the saving of energy but also allow the mobile networks to accommodate the increasing traffic demand for data and connectivity while also being sustainable. All these strategies will be very useful in the future, especially as mobile technologies keep on developing, in order to come up with better, environmentally sustainable mobile architectures.

6. SUSTAINABLE IOT AND WIRELESS SENSOR NETWORKS

Internet of Things (IoT) and Wireless Sensor Networks (WSNs) are the core of present day technological solutions with application in smart cities, environment, healthcare and industries. However, the constant running of IoT devices and sensor networks poses some great questions about the energy usage and sustainability. In order to overcome these problems, several technologies and approaches in the field of low-energy IoT devices, energy harvesting, and energy control protocols are being created.

6.1 Low-Power IoT Devices

Small-power IoT devices are important for many applications where devices could be active for long time, and often, powered by batteries. These devices are developed to be energy friendly by including energy conserving aspects at the physical and the logical plane.

Energy-efficient hardware design: For this reason, IoT devices incorporate low power microcontrollers, sensors and communication modules in order to minimize power consumption. For example, chips developed on ARM Cortex-M or RISC-V designs are low power yet provide enough computational throughput for many IoT applications. Also, MEMS (Micro-Electro-Mechanical Systems) are used where power consumption should be as low as possible, but at the same time the sensor must be highly sensitive and accurate.

Low-power wide-area networks (LPWAN): Some of the LPWAN are LoRa which stands for Long Range, Sigfox and NB-IoT which stands for Narrow-band IoT. These protocols provide efficient data transfer over large distances with low power consumption, they are useful in applications such as smart farming, asset tracking, and environmental monitoring, where devices may be placed in hard to reach locations with limited access to electricity. LPWAN also provides deep coverage penetration into buildings or underground that makes them ideal for IoT applications. These low power IoT devices and networks make it possible for large scale IoT networks to be run on very low power hence require less energy hence longer battery life and less frequent replacement of the batteries.

6.2 Energy Harvesting in Sensor Networks

Energy harvesting in WSN means utilization of available energy from the environment and converting them into electrical energy to operate IoT devices and sensors. This eliminates the use of conventional power sources like batteries and allows the formation of utterly independent networks.

Ambient energy sources: Some of the usual approaches of energy scavenging include solar, thermal, vibration, and radio frequency (RF) energy. Solar cells are usually applied in outdoor WSNs where light is more and thermoelectric generators (TEGs) to capture heat differential. Like the piezoelectricity, vibration based energy harvesting involves conversion of mechanical vibrations into electrical energy ideal for industrial or transport based IoT applications. Energy harvesting takes energy from the electromagnetic radiation such as Wi-Fi signals or cellular signals to power IoT devices, in areas of wireless connectivity.

Self-sustaining networks: WSNs, when equipped with energy-harvesting technologies, can be configured to execute continuously without battery replacement thus lowering the maintenance costs and environmental footprint. For instance, in agricultural monitoring systems, the sensors that are powered by solar energy can constantly provide information on the moisture content, temperature and humidity of soil without being connected to other power sources. These wireless and autonomous sensor systems allow greater productivity and reduced environmental impact in several locations that are difficult to access.

6.3 Energy Management in IoT Protocols

Energy consumption optimization in IoT communication protocols is important so that devices and networks do not waste energy needlessly while delivering satisfactory performance. Efficient management of these protocols can result in huge energy savings, which in turn increase the lifespan of IoT devices.

Energy-efficient communication protocols: Standards like Zigbee, Thread and Bluetooth Low Energy or BLE are meant for low power communication. These protocols help conserve power through limiting the distance over which power is transmitted, through reducing the amount of time the power is transmitted and through the use of proper data transmission protocols. For instance, Zigbee and Thread are the two that operate through the use of the mesh network such that data can be passed across devices in the network instead of transmitting across large distances hence saving energy.

Duty cycling and sleep modes: Most IoT devices use duty cycling, a method by which a device periodically wakes up and sleeps to save power. For example, LoRaWAN devices are characterized by long sleep cycles and wake up occasionally to send out small bits of information sparing the battery. Likewise, BLE devices are effective in using ultra-low power sleeping mode, which enable it to operate for hours without charging.

Adaptive protocols: In IoT, energy optimization can also be achieved by dynamic protocols which depend on the current status of the network to determine the power and frequency to use. For instance, in low traffic condition, the device may possibly decrease its power and or change to a low frequency in a bid to conserve power. This approach helps IoT devices to self-configure as per the prevailing network conditions and also to save energy while performing at optimal best.

Lastly, the future of IoT and WSN involves sustainability as a key aspect for the large scale, long term, green implementation of smart devices. Thus, with an emphasis on low power hardware designs, energy harvesting, and efficient communication standards IoT industry can overcome the problem of energy consumption and at the same time satisfy the increasing market demand for connectivity and data gathering. They will also help in enhancing the sustainability, efficiency and scalability of IoT systems in the future.

7. AI AND MACHINE LEARNING FOR ENERGY EFFICIENCY IN MOBILE NETWORKS

As the networks become mobile, they become more complex and large in their operations requiring the use of technology in the conservation of energy. AI & ML are two other areas which are slowly finding applications in this regard to optimize the energy usage by means of managing the systems in real time, predicting the usage patterns and then allocating the resources prudently(Saeed et al 2022). They allow mobile networks to decrease their energy consumption while achieving high performance and dependability (Yamini, B et al 2024).

7.1 AI-Driven Power Management

Various applications of AI and machine learning for dynamic energy management and optimization in mobile networks are being developed(Nithya, T et al 2023). These techniques can help to process large amounts of information, collected as a result of network functioning, to determine the lack of efficiency, and make decisions on the use of power without affecting the performance of the networks.

Real-time monitoring: Network conditions including traffic conditions, user demand, and device state are automatically sensed by AI algorithms. In this way, AI can notice that at some moments there is low demand or in-efficiency of the network. For instance, it is possible to program AI systems to change network settings during off-peak periods, where instead of consuming power in base stations, the systems power off or deactivate components which are not in use.

Load balancing: This is because AI can redistribute network traffic through the use of resources based on the traffic demand. During congestion in some areas, the AI algorithms can redirect traffic to more energy optimal routes or switch to additional network resources. This dynamic load balancing enables efficient use of power most especially in areas such as cities where network demand varies at different times of the day.

Energy-efficient hardware management: AI can also be utilized in controlling of electricity usage by the different hardware parts. For example, AI can manage the power state of each base station component where resources such as cooling, transmission or processing are turned-off or set to low usage during idle time. This level of control also makes it possible to achieve energy efficiency at the hardware level.

7.2 Predictive Energy Efficiency

Perhaps the most important advantage of AI and ML in the mobile networks is their capacity to forecast the energy consumption and adjust for it. Machine learning based AI models can predict future traffic, devices usage and energy requirements thus allowing operators to act to reduce power consumption.

Network traffic prediction: Machine learning algorithms can use historical data and provide a prediction of traffic and this way give information about peak and off-peak time(Szostak et al 2021). These predictions help the network operators to proactively change the current network settings, for example, to turn off the base stations that are not used during the night and to expand the network capabilities during the daytime when there is a high load on the network. Predictive models also facilitate efficient network design when it comes to consuming energy since resources are timely deployed depending on the expectations of the network traffic(Purnendra et al 2023).

Energy demand forecasting: Energy consumption of different components in the network can be predicted through the help of predictive models. For example, AI can calculate how much energy is needed for each base station or data center depending on the weather conditions and users' activity and traffic. This ensures that mobile network operators are able to schedule energy usage and avoid cases of wastage since energy is used as required.

Demand-driven energy optimization: Computerized systems can also estimate the energy demands of a network depending on the real-time data and the previous trends. By identifying where and when actual energy demand is expected to be high, the mobile networks can rearrange their operations to avoid wastage of energy.

7.3 Intelligent Resource Management

Special focus on the application of machine learning methods for efficient resource management is a significant factor achieving energy saving and service quality. By making dynamic decisions, machine learning algorithms can determine how resources such as bandwidth, network capacity and processing power are to be shared.

Dynamic spectrum management: ML can be used to achieve another goal: dynamic spectrum management based on the traffic conditions in the network. For example, machine learning algorithms can identify in which frequency bands what has to be done in order to optimize the energy consumption of the system. This is very helpful so as not to congest the networks especially in the specified and overused frequency band.

Cellular network optimization: In mobile networks, use of AI and machine learning can assist in setting up the configuration of base stations and network components, the power settings and other resources to be adjusted based on current demand. For example, AI can dedicate more resources to the areas that receive much traffic while reducing the network power in areas with little traffic. This approach means that energy is consumed only where, when, and in the amounts required.

Energy-efficient scheduling: AI models can come in handy in the scheduling of the communication tasks within the network, all in an effort to save energy. A network can analyse its traffic and decide when various tasks should be performed so that they are completed during low power usage. For example, data offloading methods can be applied, where energy-demanding processes are performed at different time or at nearby edge nodes saving energy in the central network.

Lastly, AI and machine learning technologies are the key to the future of how mobile networks will approach energy efficiency (Yamini, B et al 2023) . Mobile operators can cut energy consumption, decrease operational expenses and contribute to sustainable development through AI-based power management, predictive energy efficiency, and resource allocation. These innovations improve the functionality of mobile networks and help to achieve international goals on the reduction of the environmental footprint of network activities. With further development of AI and ML, their contribution to improving energy efficiency of mobile networks will be even more important.

8. CHALLENGES AND OPEN RESEARCH AREAS

While the demand for energy-efficient mobile and wireless computing systems is rapidly increasing, several issues and research directions should be considered to make energy-efficient solutions more realistic, feasible, and effective. The effectiveness of energy efficient solutions depends on the achievement of high performance, the ability to cope with technical limitations, as well as the definition of promising areas for further research.

8.1 Trade-offs Between Performance and Energy Efficiency

One of the major research challenges in energy efficiency of mobile and wireless systems is the fundamental conflict between performance and power saving techniques. Mobile devices and networks are designed with the need for ever enhancements so than the users can enjoy the best of performance for instance high data rate and seamless network connectivity while at the same time consuming as little power as possible.

User Experience vs. Power Consumption: Power management strategies such as DVFS and sleep mode can help to save power at the same time they could also lead to performance degradation in specific conditions. For instance, when mobile device or network is in low power state, it may take a longer time to wake up or process data and this will lead to small response time or low data transfer rate. Likewise, network operators require additional latency and bandwidth, and energy-saving features that may lead to a decline in the QoS level.
Optimizing Tradeoffs: One of the major research directions is to design more efficient algorithms which can adapt the balance between speed and energy consumption depending on the existing environment. For instance, machine learning could be employed to forecast certain levels of demand, and then make real time changes to network settings or mobile device parameters to retain performance while at the same time conserving energy. Further, in adaptive coding and modulation, the rate of data transmission and the power consumption could be regulated according to the network condition.

8.2 Technical Barriers to Energy Efficiency

Due to the technological challenges, the deployment of energy-efficient technologies is still a challenge in mobile and wireless networks. These barriers encompass the following; Hardware constraints, Software constraints, Network constraints and Energy constraints.

Hardware Constraints: As the designs of low power hardware have advanced, there are still issues that need to be addressed for designing energy efficient mobile processors and memories and communication components without a drop in performance. For instance, mobile devices require enhanced processing capability for application that demands high processing power like augmented reality and gaming with low power consumption. The major issue still remains the ability to design a hardware that can support the increasing computational and networking requirements while at the same time having a reasonable battery life.
Energy Storage: One of the biggest challenges in mobile devices and wireless communication networks is the present energy storage systems. As lithium-ion batteries dominated the market, they have problems related to the energy density, cycle life and charge time. Moreover, wireless charging and energy harvesting are new solutions, and their application is not very common in large-scale technologies, and their effectiveness is still under development.

Network Architectures: With the progress in networks to support high-speed 5G and beyond, the infrastructure demands rise, causing higher energy consumption. Current and future systems may require a more complex and energy intensive network, which can not be supported by traditional networks. New approaches of software-defined networking (SDN) and network function virtualization (NFV) offer potential in decreasing the energy consumption by means of resource management but these models are still scalable and integrated issues.

8.3 Future Research Directions

However, there are several promising areas for new research and development in energy-efficient mobile and wireless systems. These areas are the opportunities to get rid of the current shortcomings and to set the basis for further development of more efficient and reproducible technologies in the future.

Energy-Efficient Protocols for 6G: When the mobile networks move forward to the next gen 6G, the energy efficiency will be more important than ever because of the higher speed data, less latency, and higher connectivity. Studies related to energy efficient protocols for 6G are crucial for reducing the energy cost of new solutions such as massive MIMO, THz Com, and Edge computing. It will be important to establish procedures that can optimise the use of power and adjust to the ever changing traffic demands to support construction of sustainable 6G networks.
AI-Driven Energy Optimization: Artificial Intelligence (AI) and Machine Learning (ML) are already becoming essential to enhance energy efficiency. In the future more sophisticated AI models could be applied to prescriptive energy management, to the distribution of resources, and for managing energy on networks and mobile devices. More investigation is required to develop AI-based energy optimization strategies that would allow them to change network settings and mobile device settings in real time while maintaining high performance and low energy consumption.
Sustainable Materials for Mobile Devices: Thus, as the power of the portable devices increases and the penetration of the portable devices into different aspects of our lives rises, the problem of finding sustainable sources for the portable devices manufacturing becomes more and more topical. Investigations into the sustainable parts, including bio-plastic casings, recycled metals and energy-efficient display, may lower the environmental footprint of portable devices. Also, further studying of other recyclable battery materials like solid-

state batteries or graphene batteries can greatly enhance the storage of energy and efficiency beyond the current standard of battery life and efficiency.

Energy-Efficient IoT and Edge Computing: With the increasing number of IoT devices and the increasing use of edge computing, new approaches are required to manage energy consumption at the device level. As the number of connected devices grows into billions, the efficiency of IoT networks will depend on further research into low-power protocols for IoT, efficient energy harvesting technologies, as well as edge data processing.

In conclusion, the balance of performance and energy efficiency, the elimination of barriers to implementation, and the definition of future research directions will be critical to achieving the benefits of energy-efficient mobile and wireless systems. Given its potential, there is a need for the industry to invest in advanced solutions to hardware, software, networking protocols and energy storage that can lead to more sustainable technologies for the growing demands in connectivity without compromising the environment.

9. CONCLUSION

The mobile and wireless technologies have been adopted in the society at a very high rate hence leading to more development of energy efficient solutions to the impacts of the environment. Areas of active research in energy-efficient mobile and wireless computing are the design of low energy hardware including energy efficient processors and memories, and power management methods including dynamic voltage scaling and sleep modes. Advancements in energy scavenging from solar, thermal and motion and wireless charging also have gone a long way in adding to environmental conservation by minimizing on the use of wires for charging. Regarding the network technologies, the green cellular networks especially with 5G and beyond priorities the energy consumption in cellular networks. Application of some of the following approaches like massive MIMO, Small cells, and edge computing have become popular ways to boost energy efficiency and performance. Furthermore, AI in power management is fast becoming useful in managing power through demand forecasting and supply of power as and when it is needed. Mobile and wireless computing for sustainable computing is on the right track of enhancing its future. When we move on to 6G networks, the need for higher data rates and more connection points will require even better energy policies and network designs. New generations of mobile terminals and networks will continue to integrate more efficient and intelligent algorithms as well as environmentally friendly materials to achieve even lower energy consumption and even higher performances. Other factors that will also contribute to the reduction of energy include the advancement of the edge of network computing and efficient IoT energy. To enhance the advancement of mobile and wireless systems for sustainable development, the three stakeholders are required to work together. Industry can bring the practical experience, academia can offer the research, and the policymakers can set the rules to advance sustainability. With the efforts of these stakeholders, a powerful approach is possible where the attributes of efficiency and connectivity complement each other to produce environmentally friendly mobile technologies for the next generation.

REFERENCES

Anusha, S., Ezhilvandan, M., Gayathri, S., Sivaraman, V., & Anish, T. P. (2024). Emerging trends in edge AI for Industry 4.0 and 5.0: Technologies, applications, and challenges. AI Innovations in Service and Tourism Marketing, 211-228.

George, D. A., & Murthy, G. R. (Eds.). (2024). *Towards Wireless Heterogeneity in 6G Networks*. CRC Press. DOI: 10.1201/9781003369028

Goundar, S., Avanija, J., Sunitha, G., Madhavi, K. R., & Bhushan, S. B. (Eds.). (2021). *Innovations in the industrial Internet of Things (IIoT) and smart factory*. IGI Global. DOI: 10.4018/978-1-7998-3375-8

Kumar, P., Pandey, D., Srivastav, R. K., & Pandey, P. K. (2023, August). Network Traffic Analysis and Prediction Using Machine Learning. *International Journal of Research Publication and Reviews*, *4*(8), 2071–2075.

Nair, R., Sharma, P., Bhagat, A., & Dwivedi, V. K. (2018). A survey on IoT (Internet of Things) emerging technologies and its application. [IJEUCD]. *International Journal of End-User Computing and Development*, *7*(2), 1–20. DOI: 10.4018/IJEUCD.2018070101

Nithya, T., Kumar, V. N., Gayathri, S., Deepa, S., Varun, C. M., & Subramanian, R. S. (2023, August). A comprehensive survey of machine learning: Advancements, applications, and challenges. In *2023 Second International Conference on Augmented Intelligence and Sustainable Systems (ICAISS)* (pp. 354-361). IEEE. DOI: 10.1109/ICAISS58487.2023.10250547

Patel, A.B. (2021) "Wireless and Mobile Computing: Build Secure and Maintain Wireless Solutions" Published in *International Journal of Trend in Scientific Research and Development (ijtsrd),* ISSN: 2456- 6470, Volume-5 I Issue-5, August 2021, pp.346-351.

Saeed, M. M., Saeed, R. A., Azim, M. A., Ali, E. S., Mokhtar, R. A., & Khalifa, O. (2022, May). Green machine learning approach for QoS improvement in cellular communications. In *2022 IEEE 2nd International Maghreb Meeting of the Conference on Sciences and Techniques of Automatic Control and Computer Engineering (MI-STA)* (pp. 523-528). IEEE. DOI: 10.1109/MI-STA54861.2022.9837585

Sudha, K., Ambhika, C., Maheswari, B., Girija, P., & Nalini, M. (2023). AI and IoT applications in medical domain enhancing healthcare through technology integration. In *AI and IoT-Based Technologies for Precision Medicine* (pp. 280–294). IGI Global.

Szostak, D., Włodarczyk, A., & Walkowiak, K. (2021). Machine learning classification and regression approaches for optical network traffic prediction. *Electronics (Basel), 10*(13), 1578. DOI: 10.3390/electronics10131578

Vishwakarma, M., & Nigam, A. (2024), Comparative Analysis of 4G and 5G Networks: A Review Study, *International Journal for Multidisciplinary Research*, Volume 6, Issue 3, May-June 2024.

Wang, S., & Guo, W. (2014). Sustainable Growth for Cellular Wireless Networks. In *Handbook of Research on Progressive Trends in Wireless Communications and Networking* (pp. 18–43). IGI Global. DOI: 10.4018/978-1-4666-5170-8.ch002

Yamini, B., Beslin, P. P., Anish, T. P., Gracelin, S. B., Dinesh, M. G., Nalini, M., & Siva, S. R. (2024). Advancements in Cognitive Radio Networks: Protocols, Architectures, Challenges, and Future Perspectives. In Spectrum and Power Allocation in Cognitive Radio Systems (pp. 1-17). IGI Global.

Yamini, B., Prasanna, V., Ambhika, C., Anuradha, M., Maheswari, B., Subramanian, S. R., & Nalini, M. (2023). A comprehensive survey of deep learning: Advancements, applications, and challenges. *International Journal on Recent and Innovation Trends in Computing and Communication, 11*(8s), 445–453. DOI: 10.17762/ijritcc.v11i8s.7225

Yang, Y., & Ma, M. (2014). Sustainable mobile computing. *Computing, 96*(2), 85–86. DOI: 10.1007/s00607-013-0309-1

Chapter 12
Advancing Green Artificial Intelligence:
Strategies for a Sustainable Future

Farooq Ahmad
https://orcid.org/0000-0002-3944-7710
Integral University, Lucknow, India

Shweta Dwivedi
Integral University, Lucknow, India

Zohaib Hasan Khan
https://orcid.org/0000-0003-1608-8337
Integral University, Lucknow, India

Nupur Mittal
https://orcid.org/0000-0002-3765-8813
Integral University, Lucknow, India

ABSTRACT

Green artificial intelligence (AI) is designed to be more eco-friendly and accessible compared to traditional AI. It delivers precise results without the added computational costs and allows researchers with just a laptop to conduct high-quality work without the need for expensive cloud servers. This chapter explores green AI as a crucial method for improving the environmental sustainability of AI systems. It covers AI solutions that promote eco-friendly practices in various fields (referred to as "green-by AI"), methods for developing energy-efficient machine learning (ML) algorithms and models (known as "green-in AI"), and tools for accurately measuring and optimizing energy usage. The chapter also looks at how regulations can support green AI and discusses future directions for sustainable ML. It highlights

DOI: 10.4018/979-8-3373-0766-4.ch012

Copyright © 2025, IGI Global Scientific Publishing. Copying or distributing in print or electronic forms without written permission of IGI Global Scientific Publishing is prohibited.

the need to integrate environmental considerations into AI practices to promote a more eco-conscious and energy-efficient future for AI technologies.

1. INTRODUCTION

In recent years, artificial intelligence (AI) and machine learning (ML) have transformed many industries by significantly improving efficiency and accuracy in fields such as healthcare, finance, transportation, education, and entertainment. To enhance performance, ML models have become more complex, resulting in a greater number of parameters to estimate. However, these advancements come with increased resource demands, as training and operating these models now require substantial computational power, energy, and water for cooling data centers that store vast amounts of training data, as illustrated in Figure 1.

Despite the exponential growth in data needs and the rising number of hyper parameters over the past decade, improvements in model accuracy have not kept pace. Nevertheless, AI holds great promise for advancing sustainable and efficient solutions, which can support countries in transitioning to cleaner and more sustainable practices. To fully realize this potential, it is crucial to assess sustainability metrics that enhance transparency in model results, including performance, accuracy, and environmental impact, such as energy and water consumption (for example, through the use of ML emissions calculators). It is projected that by 2030, the energy consumption of ML models could account for over 30% of the world's total energy use. Large language models (LLMs), such as the recent GPT-4, exacerbate this issue with their high energy demands. Estimates indicate that training GPT-3 on a dataset of 500 billion words consumed 1287 MWh of electricity and 10,000 computer chips, equivalent to the yearly energy usage of about 121 homes in the US. This process also generated approximately 550 tons of carbon dioxide, comparable to flying 33 times from Australia to the UK. Given that GPT-4 was trained on 570 times more parameters than GPT-3, its energy requirements were even higher. The environmental impact extends beyond training, as using these systems also consumes significant energy. For instance, GPT-3 was accessed 590 million times in January 2023, resulting in energy consumption equivalent to that of 175,000 people. Each query to ChatGPT during inference consumes energy comparable to running a 5 W LED bulb for 1 hour and 20 minutes, totaling 260.42 MWh per day.

The growing environmental impact of these technologies has sparked concerns about their carbon footprint, leading to the emergence of green AI. This new paradigm focuses on incorporating sustainable practices and techniques in the design, training, and deployment of AI models to reduce their environmental costs and carbon footprint.

Traditional machine learning (ML) algorithms often require extensive data and computational resources, leading to high energy consumption, significant water use for cooling data centers, and increased greenhouse gas (GHG) emissions. Green AI aims to address these environmental impacts by optimizing algorithms, enhancing hardware efficiency, and adopting sustainable data management practices. It focuses on providing energy-efficient solutions through cloud centers and mobile/edge devices while maintaining a low carbon footprint, high-quality data, compact models, and manageable computational complexity. Green AI also emphasizes clear and logical decision-making processes to build public trust and contribute to social sustainability.

Figure 1. CO2 equivalent emissions for training ML models(blue) and of real-life cases(violet). In brackets, the billions of parameters adjusted for each model.

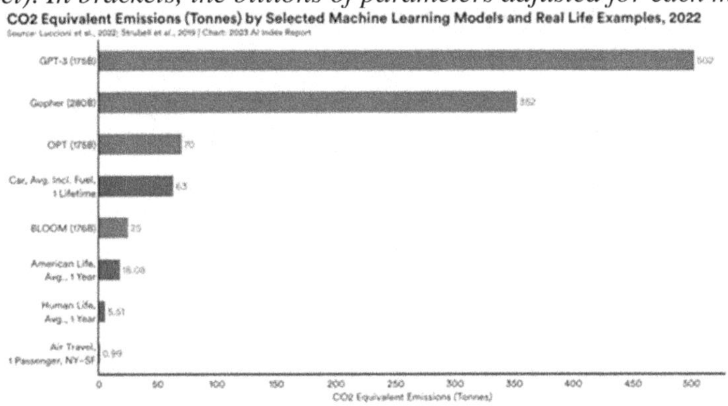

The economic cost of AI is rising, with major advancements in ML largely controlled by large corporations that possess the necessary extensive resources. For example, training GPT-2 with 1.5 billion parameters in 2019 cost approximately $50,000, whereas training PaLM with 540 billion parameters in 2022 required around $8 million - making PaLM 360 times larger and 160 times more expensive.

Green algorithms are generally defined as those designed to maximize energy efficiency and minimize the environmental impact of AI models while addressing various environmental challenges. These include algorithms that are inherently energy-efficient (green-by design) and those developed to address specific environmental issues (green-in AI), as outlined in frameworks such as the Paris Agreement, the UN's Sustainable Development Goals (SDGs), and the European Green Deal.

This exploration of green AI and green algorithms covers various approaches, methodologies, and innovations aimed at making AI and ML more environmentally sustainable. It also reviews the challenges and opportunities related to reducing energy consumption, minimizing carbon emissions, and promoting ethical AI practices. Embracing these approaches not only benefits the environment - a crucial factor for future sustainability and mandated in the EU for high-risk systems, but also offers cost savings and enhanced efficiency without sacrificing performance or accuracy.

2. BACKGROUND

Imagine a world where technology not only advances our capabilities but also improves our environment. Green AI embodies this vision by harnessing the power of AI to benefit the planet. As we explore future innovations, Green AI serves as a guiding principle to ensure that these advancements are environmentally responsible. It's about ensuring our technological progress contributes positively to the Earth. By adopting Green AI, businesses can drastically cut their environmental impact and make significant strides toward sustainability. This forward-thinking approach guarantees that as technology progresses, it aligns with our ecological goals, fostering innovations that enhance our abilities while safeguarding and preserving the planet for future generations.

2.1 What is Green AI?

As climate change remains a significant threat to our planet, it is essential to explore how technology can help mitigate its impacts. Many organizations are now adopting eco-friendly technologies, like Green AI, to minimize their carbon and environmental footprints. Green AI applies AI practices across various industries to foster sustainable development and lessen the environmental impact of conventional AI technologies. This involves optimizing resource use, improving waste management, and adopting renewable energy sources.

2.2 What are the benefits of Green AI?

Organizations that adopt Green AI practices stand to gain numerous advantages:

1. **Boosts Innovation**: Green AI fosters the creation of technologies that are both cutting-edge and environmentally friendly. It encourages organizations to address environmental issues during the development of new technologies.
2. **Reduces Costs**: By optimizing resource usage, Green AI helps organizations lower their expenses across various sectors. It minimizes the consumption of water, energy, and electricity, leading to cost savings while also enhancing sustainability.

3. **Enhances Decision-Making**: AI-driven analytics provide valuable insights that help organizations make better-informed decisions. This includes prioritizing sustainability initiatives and using resources more effectively, which in turn improves efficiency and productivity through increased automation.
4. **Optimizes Resource Use**: Green AI promotes the efficient use of resources such as water, energy, and raw materials. This optimization helps organizations reduce waste, benefiting both their bottom line and their sustainability efforts.
5. **Increases Customer Loyalty**: As consumers become more focused on environmental issues, they are more likely to support companies that demonstrate a commitment to sustainability. Implementing Green AI practices can help organizations align with these values, thereby enhancing customer loyalty.

2.3 What are the challenges of Green AI?

Like any emerging technology, Green AI presents several challenges. One of the key issues is ensuring that AI objectives align with sustainability goals, as there is a risk that technological advancement might overshadow environmental considerations. Here are some other notable challenges:

1. **Ethical Concerns**: Integrating Green AI into organizations raises various ethical issues, including bias, transparency, data privacy, and accountability. To address these concerns, it is crucial for organizations to establish clear ethical guidelines and protocols before deploying Green AI technologies.
2. **Talent Gap**: There is a limited pool of professionals who are proficient in both AI and sustainability, which can create a significant talent shortage for effectively implementing Green AI. Organizations can mitigate this gap by investing in the training and upskilling of current employees to handle these new technologies.
3. **Quality and Availability of Data**: Effective Green AI requires high-quality data to make informed decisions. However, obtaining relevant and accurate data to train AI models can be challenging. To address this, organizations should implement robust data governance frameworks to ensure the availability of high-quality data and its accessibility to the appropriate team members.

3. GREEN-BY ARTIFICIAL INTELLIGENCE

AI holds substantial potential for advancing the Green Deal and reducing its own environmental impact. It can significantly contribute to lowering greenhouse gas (GHG) emissions and improving efficiency across various sectors, including energy production and consumption, agriculture, land use, biodiversity management, communications, transportation, and smart mobility. Furthermore, AI's expanding capabilities are instrumental in addressing and adapting to climate change through advanced prediction, resilience, and strategic management tools, as illustrated in Figure 3.

For example, (Vinuesa et al., 2020) analyzed AI's role in achieving the UN's Sustainable Development Goals (SDGs) and found that AI could support 134 targets but could potentially hinder 59 targets. The following areas highlight where AI can be particularly effective in enhancing sustainability:

3.1 Energy efficiency

Reducing energy consumption is crucial for fostering a more sustainable society. AI can play a significant role in this effort, especially through the implementation of smart grids. Smart grids have the potential to lower overall electricity usage by better aligning regional power generation with local demand. Unlike traditional grids, which typically involve a one-way flow of electricity from generators to consumers, smart grids enable dynamic, bidirectional electricity flows. This continuous adjustment of supply and demand improves overall efficiency and optimizes energy use as illustrated in Figure 2.

Figure 2. Estimated training costs of large language and multimodal models. The colors indicate if estimates are high, mid-level, or low.

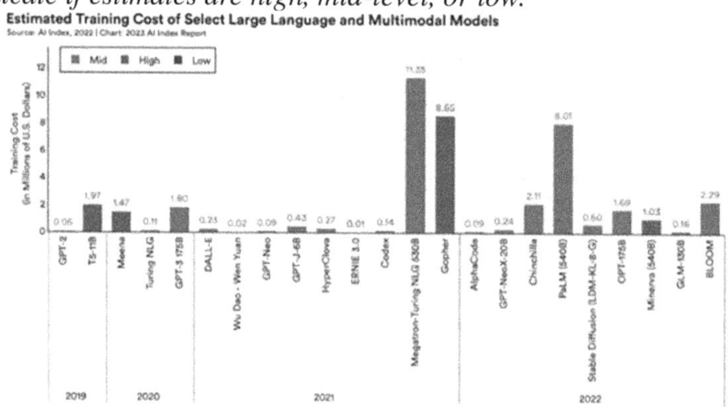

Figure 3. Overview of green-in vs green-by algorithms.

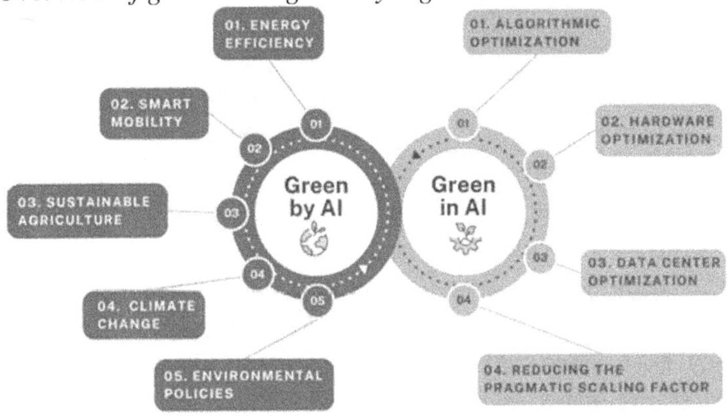

Machine learning (ML) techniques are instrumental in predicting renewable energy production, which is crucial for integrating these sources seamlessly into the grid. The inherent variability of renewable energy sources, such as solar and wind, presents a challenge for consistent energy generation, highlighting the need for accurate forecasting. Effective forecasting of solar and wind power is essential for improving service quality and optimizing power management (Aslam et al., 2021).

Deep neural networks (NNs) are commonly employed for forecasting wind energy (Wang et al., 2017; Lin et al., 2019), while solar energy forecasting often uses hybrid methods that integrate deep NNs, recurrent NNs, and long short-term memory networks (Díaz-Vico et al., 2017; Abdel-Nasser et al., 2019). These models utilize real-time data, historical data, and outputs from physical models, making AI tools vital for navigating the complexities of smart grids and managing the large volumes of real-time data involved.

Green AI also plays a role in enhancing energy efficiency in buildings and urban areas. ML models can analyze sensor data from smart buildings (Qolomany et al., 2019; Pham et al., 2020) and smart cities (Zekić-Sušac et al., 2021; Ghazal et al., 2023) to optimize systems such as heating, ventilation, and air conditioning (HVAC), lighting, and overall energy usage. This optimization leads to substantial energy savings and a reduction in carbon emissions (Milojevic-Dupont et al., 2021; Zhang et al., 2023).

3.2 Smart mobility

AI is pivotal in advancing smart mobility and transforming traditional transportation systems into more efficient, responsive, and sustainable networks. As urban populations rise, issues like traffic congestion and environmental pollution in large cities are becoming more pronounced. Smart city solutions can address these challenges, driving economic growth and improving the quality of life for residents (Chen et al., 2022).

AI leverages real-time data analysis to predict traffic patterns, optimize routes, and reduce congestion. Research in traffic prediction includes various approaches such as feature-based models (Li et al., 2018), Gaussian process models (Salinas et al., 2019), state-space models (Duan et al., 2018), and deep learning models (Yin et al., 2021). AI-driven smart mobility systems can also enhance public transportation with dynamic scheduling, ensuring more reliable and timely arrivals and departures.

In the realm of autonomous vehicles (AVs), AI plays a key role in improving safety and efficiency. For instance, AI can handle essential tasks like road-following and obstacle detection (Bojarski et al., 2016). Machine learning (ML) further advances AV technology by reducing energy consumption. (Wu et al., 2017) used reinforcement learning to develop AV controllers that manage traffic interactions effectively.

Moreover, AI integration in smart mobility supports the development of shared transportation services and eco-friendly transport options, fostering a more sustainable and interconnected urban environment.

3.3 Sustainable agriculture

AI has a transformative impact on agriculture through various applications, including precision farming. By analyzing data from sensors, satellites, and drones with machine learning (ML) algorithms, AI provides farmers with critical insights into crop health, soil conditions, and irrigation needs. This enables more accurate and targeted use of water, fertilizers, and pesticides, reducing environmental impact and improving resource efficiency. AI-driven predictive analytics also enhance crop yield forecasting and disease detection, allowing for timely interventions and minimized losses (Sharma et al., 2020).

Examples of AI applications in agriculture include:

Crop Yield Prediction: Convolutional neural networks (NNs) are used to model crop yields based on normalized difference vegetation index (NDVI) and RGB data collected from unmanned aerial vehicles (UAVs) (Nevavuori et al., 2019).

Groundwater Level Prediction: Given the importance of groundwater for agriculture, (Pham et al., 2022) evaluated the effectiveness of various ML models, including random forests (RF) and support vector machines (SVMs), in predicting groundwater levels.

Texture Classification: In agricultural contexts, particularly with the increasing use of UAVs, texture classification is crucial. (Shumska et al., 2023) developed an efficient and interpretable generalized matrix learning vector quantization (GMLVQ) approach for classifying multispectral images, demonstrating different model performances and comparing them to benchmarks for soil dataset classification.

IoT-Based Remote Assistance: Advanced technologies like an agricultural IoT remote assistance system have been proposed (Veerachamy et al., 2022). This system uses real-time data from farm fields to issue alerts for low water levels and pressures, employing classifiers that combine k-nearest neighbor (kNN) with neural networks (NNs). It also provides recommendations based on field measurements using modified fuzzy clustering and attractiveness-based particle swarm optimization (PSO) algorithms.

Smart Farming Equipment: AI improves labor efficiency and reduces the ecological footprint of traditional farming methods through smart equipment such as autonomous tractors and robotic harvesters.

Quantum Machine Learning: Emerging technologies like quantum machine learning could further advance agricultural mechanization and plant disease detection (Genemo et al., 2023).

3.4 Climate change

In the fight against climate change, AI plays a crucial role in both mitigation and adaptation efforts across various sectors (Rolnick et al., 2022). With electricity systems responsible for roughly 25% of annual human-induced greenhouse gas (GHG) emissions (IPCC, 2014), machine learning (ML) techniques are employed to address these issues, including forecasting supply and demand. Different methods are used to predict short- to medium-term energy demand (Hong et al., 2016), as well as the availability of solar (Ahmed et al., 2020) and wind power (Giebel et al., 2017). These methods utilize historical data, physical model outputs, and various types of data such as images and videos, employing supervised ML techniques, fuzzy logic, and hybrid models for analysis. Additionally, quantum computing holds the potential to enhance advancements in large-scale technologies, such as solar panels and batteries (Kim et al., 2022).

In transitioning to low-carbon electricity, ML applications include detecting and mitigating methane leaks in natural gas pipelines and compressor stations, which is a crucial interim step to reducing emissions from fossil fuels. Neural networks (NNs) trained on images of methane leaks are one example. ML also aids in reducing emissions by decreasing reliance on carbon-intensive materials and transforming industrial processes to use low-carbon energy. Furthermore, ML is used in redesigning the chemistry of structural materials. For instance, a study (Kazi et al., 2017) integrates ML with generative design to create structural products that require fewer raw materials, thereby reducing the use of cement and steel.

3.5 Environmental policies

Integrating AI into the design of environmental policies represents a revolutionary approach to advancing sustainability across various sectors. AI's advanced analytical capabilities and its ability to process extensive datasets enable policymakers to develop more effective strategies for environmental conservation and resource management. By utilizing machine learning (ML) algorithms, AI can detect patterns, identify trends, and forecast potential outcomes, allowing for the creation of policies that address current challenges while anticipating future environmental needs (Sánchez-Maroño et al., 2022; García-Mira et al., 2017).

Another valuable tool in this context is agent-based modeling. This approach helps design targeted strategies to engage citizens in necessary changes by considering both collective and individual values. It can detect emergent behaviors from interactions and minor personal adjustments (Sánchez-Maroño et al., 2015; Jager et al., 2015).

AI-driven policy design is a potent mechanism for promoting sustainable development, from optimizing energy use to incorporating eco-friendly practices in urban planning. The precision and flexibility of AI systems offer the potential to usher in a new era of policy innovation, where data-driven insights lead to the cultivation of a resilient and environmentally conscious society.

4. GREEN-IN ARTIFICIAL INTELLIGENCE

The integration of AI into sustainability efforts offers promising possibilities across various sectors. However, it is crucial to ensure that AI systems themselves do not inadvertently undermine these efforts by consuming excessive energy. For AI to effectively contribute to energy reduction, its algorithms and computational processes must be designed with efficiency in mind. This involves using AI solutions that optimize energy use in applications while also being low in energy consumption. Achieving this balance is essential to ensure that the overall impact of AI supports sustainability goals rather than worsening the problems it seeks to address. This discussion often contrasts red AI with green AI (Dhar et al., 2020), as illustrated in Figure 3.

Red AI refers to approaches that prioritize achieving better results at the expense of significant computational resources. An analysis of 60 papers from top conferences (Schwartz et al., 2020) revealed that most studies (between 75% and 90%, depending on the conference) favored accuracy over efficiency. Furthermore, a 2018 study found that the computational demands for training large ML models have been doubling approximately every 3.4 months since 2012, a rate much faster than Moore's Law, which predicts this should occur roughly every two years (Moore et al., 1998).

Nevertheless, high energy consumption should not be seen as an unavoidable cost of progress in AI. Green-in AI focuses on producing innovative results while ideally reducing or at least not increasing computational costs. The specialized literature suggests several strategies to lower computational costs, including both software and hardware solutions. Key strategies for developing greener algorithms include:

- **Optimization Techniques**: Designing algorithms that reduce computational resource requirements, such as sparse training methods (Renggli et al., 2019; Tay et al., 2020; Bibikar et al., 2022), quantization techniques, and energy-aware pruning (Elgabli et al., 2020; Khirirat et al., 2021; Xiao et al., 2023; Yang et al., 2017), as well as employing low-precision arithmetic operations (Zafrir et al., 2019; Liu et al., 2021; Suárez-Marcote et al., 2023).
- **Efficient Techniques**: Research has proposed using more efficient methods for specific tasks. For example, (Castillo-García et al., 2023) introduced a novel feature selection method using mutual information maximization (MIM), which is more efficient than traditional evolutionary algorithms. Similarly, (Lourenço et al., 2023) developed a scalable and sustainable approach for condition-based maintenance of wheel out-of-roundness, utilizing locality-sensitive hashing to analyze large time series datasets.

These approaches aim to enhance the efficiency of AI systems, making them more sustainable while still achieving high performance.

4.1 Hardware optimization

Opting for more computationally efficient hardware can significantly contribute to energy savings. For example, some graphic processing units (GPUs) are notably more efficient in terms of floating-point operations per second (FLOPS) per watt of power usage compared to others. Additionally, specialized hardware accelerators like tensor processing units (TPUs) (Jouppi et al., 2023) are designed specifically for machine learning (ML) tasks. TPUs can be customized to enhance ML models' performance on this specialized hardware (Osta et al., 2019; Stamoulis et al., 2019).

Parallelization is another critical strategy for reducing training times by distributing computations across multiple processing cores. Research by (Anthony et al., 2020) demonstrated that increasing the number of cores to 15 can improve execution times and lower greenhouse gas (GHG) emissions for a given task. However, their experiments also highlighted that emission levels can worsen if the reduction in execution time is not proportional to the increase in the number of cores, showing that marginal improvements in runtime can lead to disproportionately high emissions.

Edge computing is also a pivotal strategy for energy efficiency. This approach involves performing computations locally, at the data collection or usage point, rather than transmitting data to a central data center or cloud. This method reduces the need for extensive data transfers and adapts to the limited computational and energy resources of IoT devices (Singh et al., 2021; Wan et al., 2022; Novoa-Paradela et al., 2023).

4.2 Datacenter optimization

The carbon footprint of a data center is closely linked to both its operational efficiency and the carbon intensity of its location. The latter is particularly significant, as there is substantial variability in carbon intensity between countries. For example, countries like Norway and Switzerland have carbon intensities of less than 20 gCO2e kWh−1, while regions such as Australia, South Africa, and some states in the US exceed 800 gCO2e kWh−1 [2]. Figure 4 illustrates the greenhouse gas (GHG) emissions across European Union (EU) countries over four decades.

To enhance the sustainability of data centers, researchers have developed various algorithms and frameworks designed to dynamically manage server loads (Ghasemi et al., 2020; Dong et al., 2021), adjust cooling systems (Li et al., 2019; Cao et al., 2022), and optimize resource allocation (Moreno-Vozmediano et al., 2019. These innovations aim to reduce energy consumption and minimize the overall carbon footprint of data centers.

4.3 Pragmatic scaling factor reductions

Reducing the frequency with which computationally intensive algorithms are executed is one of the simplest methods to lower energy consumption. Another effective strategy is to minimize the time allocated for hyper parameter tuning by employing less exhaustive search methods (Bergstra et al., 2012; Snoek et al., 2012; Li et al., 2017). This approach can help conserve computational resources and reduce overall energy usage.

The concepts of "Green-by AI" and "Green-in AI" are distinct in their practical application, focusing on different ways AI intersects with sustainability as illustrated in Figure 3.

- Green-by AI focuses on how AI can be applied to environmental challenges, helping industries and sectors become more sustainable.

- Green-in AI focuses on making AI itself more sustainable by improving its energy efficiency and reducing the environmental footprint of AI technologies.

5. TOOLS FOR MEASURING ENERGY USAGE

In addition to advances in algorithm design, researchers have been developing frameworks and tools to evaluate the environmental impact of machine learning (ML) systems. As large ML models can significantly contribute to climate change due to their high energy consumption, it is crucial for researchers and developers to be aware of the energy and carbon footprint associated with their models. This awareness can drive efforts to mitigate environmental impacts.

Efforts to standardize the calculation of carbon emissions from training ML models have led to the development of various tools (Lannelongue et al., 2021; Henderson et al., 2020; Lottick et al., 2019; Trébaol et al., 2020; Luccioni et al., 2023). However, these tools often produce differing results and may underreport emissions, as noted in a recent analysis (Bannour et al., 2021) that assessed the carbon footprint of natural language processing (NLP) methods. Discrepancies arise from variations in methodologies, hardware assumptions, usage rates, software overheads, and regional electricity mixes. The lack of a universally accepted standard for carbon emission calculations complicates efforts to standardize reporting and facilitate comparisons.

Currently, some of the most popular tools for estimating carbon footprints include:

- **Carbon Tracker**: This tool monitors and analyzes greenhouse gas emissions, particularly carbon dioxide, from various sources. It combines atmospheric measurements with statistical modeling to provide real-time estimates and visualizations of carbon emissions, aiding researchers, policymakers, and environmental organizations in understanding the impact of energy-intensive deep learning models.
- **Code Carbon**: Designed for developers and organizations, CodeCarbon integrates into the development pipeline to track and manage carbon emissions generated by software and code. It monitors energy consumption and provides actionable insights and recommendations for reducing the carbon footprint of applications.
- **Green Algorithms**: This project focuses on minimizing the environmental impact of computational processes by optimizing resource use, reducing power consumption, and promoting sustainability. It is particularly relevant for data centers, supercomputers, and high-performance computing environments. The tool is easy to integrate with existing computational processes and requires minimal information.

- **Power Top**: An open-source utility for Linux-based systems, PowerTop monitors and analyzes real-time power consumption and management. Developed by Intel, it identifies power-intensive processes and components, helping users optimize energy efficiency, extend battery life on laptops, and reduce power usage in servers. The tool provides detailed information on power consumption, enabling users to make informed decisions to conserve energy and lower carbon emissions.

These tools play a crucial role in assessing and managing the environmental impact of ML systems, guiding efforts to improve sustainability in computational practices.

Figure 4. Greenhouse gas emissions by different European Union countries

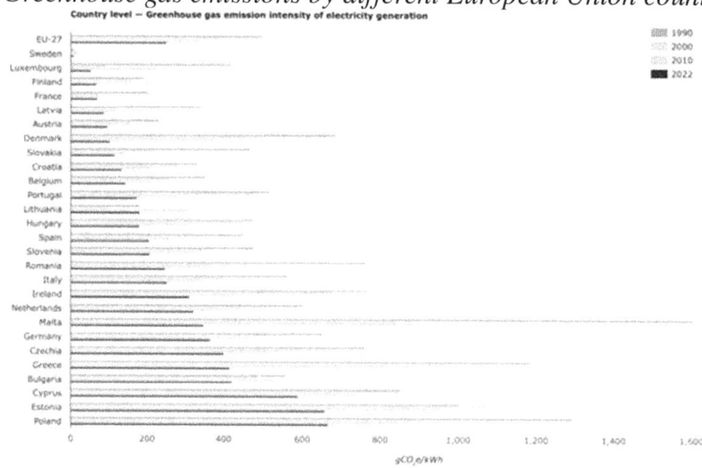

6. REGULATORY APPROACHES AND GREEN AI

Given the wide range of tools available for calculating energy consumption in AI systems, it's clear that comprehending and optimizing their carbon footprint is just the beginning. The next vital step is to develop and enforce regulations and advocate for green AI practices. This represents a transition from simply measuring to actively managing and minimizing the environmental impact of AI. By setting guidelines and standards for energy efficiency in AI development, stakeholders can ensure that AI advancements not only drive innovation but also contribute to broader sustainability goals. For example, some companies have released best-practice guides on this topic. Google, for instance, has proposed four recommendations that it claims can collectively reduce energy consumption by a factor of 100 and emissions by a factor of 1000:

1. **Optimized ML Model Architectures:** Instead of using the largest, most versatile model available, efforts should focus on developing more streamlined architectures specifically designed to address the task at hand. This includes techniques such as model shrinking, and using sparse and compact architectures.
2. **Specialized Processors and Systems:** Utilizing hardware designed specifically for deep learning, like TPUs, neuromorphic chips, and vision processing units (VPUs), offers substantial energy savings compared to traditional GPUs. TPUs, for example, are tailored for accelerating deep learning tasks and are optimized for high throughput of low-precision arithmetic, which enhances efficiency and reduces energy consumption compared to GPUs.
3. **Cloud-Based Data Centers:** Moving computing tasks to the cloud can significantly cut energy use. Modern, purpose-built cloud facilities are designed for energy efficiency and can accommodate large numbers of servers with excellent power usage effectiveness (PUE) ratios. Older, smaller on-premises data centers often lack the scale needed to adopt the latest energy-saving cooling and power distribution technologies.
4. **Map Optimization:** Leading cloud service providers are increasingly investing in renewable energy sources to power their data centers. By using wind, solar, and hydroelectric power, they significantly reduce their carbon footprint. While individual businesses may face challenges in switching to renewable energy due to cost and logistics, cloud services offer the advantage of selecting locations that maximize energy efficiency, potentially lowering the overall carbon footprint by a factor of 5 to 10. However, there may be concerns that focusing on the most eco-friendly locations could lead to capacity issues at those sites.

While the participation of researchers and companies is crucial, it is essential to take an additional step by implementing regulations that ensure AI advances are both responsible and sustainable in this rapidly evolving technological field.

The importance of responsible AI development and usage was highlighted as early as 2019 in the Ethics Guidelines for Trustworthy AI, published by the High-Level Expert Group on AI in the EU. The report outlines seven key criteria for AI systems, including one focused on societal and environmental well-being. Subsequently, the same group issued another report containing the Assessment List for Trustworthy AI (ALTAI), which recommended supporting research initiatives that explore AI solutions to address global challenges, such as the Sustainable Development Goals (SDGs), potentially accelerating their progress.

The EU White Paper on AI, released by the European Commission in 2020, emphasizes that technology can address climate change and environmental degradation (referred to as green-by AI) and can do so in an eco-friendly manner (referred to as green-in AI) across the entire value chain from data collection, storage, and processing to algorithm training and deployment. The AI Act, a regulation agreed upon by EU member states in December 2023 and approved on March 13, 2024, introduces obligations for AI systems based on their potential risks and impacts. This Act represents a significant effort to promote both the green-in and green-by approaches. It focuses on protecting fundamental rights, democracy, the rule of law, and environmental sustainability in high-risk AI, while also encouraging innovation and positioning Europe as a leader in the AI sector.

For high-impact general-purpose AI models, especially those with systemic risks like generative AI, there is an additional requirement to report on energy efficiency. For non-high-risk AI systems, the development of codes of conduct that align with some or all mandatory requirements for high-risk systems is encouraged, tailored to the system's specific purposes. Voluntary adherence to the Ethics Guidelines for Trustworthy AI and commitment to environmental sustainability are also promoted. The European AI Office and member states are tasked with fostering the development of these voluntary codes of conduct, which should focus on minimizing the environmental impact of AI systems through energy-efficient programming, design, training, and usage. These codes should include clear objectives and key performance indicators to measure effectiveness. Additionally, member states must establish at least one national AI regulatory sandbox, a controlled environment for innovation, where new AI systems can be developed, tested, and validated before market entry. Personal data collected for other purposes can be processed within this sandbox for AI systems that meet specific conditions related to environmental protection, biodiversity, pollution prevention, green transition measures, climate change mitigation, and energy sustainability.

In contrast, the recent Executive Order on Safe, Secure, and Trustworthy Artificial Intelligence in the USA, issued on October 30, 2023, only briefly mentions promoting the responsible and rights-affirming development of AI to address global challenges like sustainable development and critical infrastructure risks. It appears that the US regulation does not enforce the development of green algorithms. Similarly, Chinese regulations do not impose sustainability restrictions on AI development.

Given that the information and communications technology (ICT) sector accounts for 3.9% of global greenhouse gas emissions surpassing global air travel the carbon footprint of AI, particularly large-scale generative models, is significant. To address this unsustainable impact, incorporating sustainability as a regulatory requirement for future AI algorithms, as mandated by the AI Act, is essential. Researchers and developers are encouraged to integrate energy consumption metrics alongside traditional accuracy and precision measures to foster a more resource-conscious approach in AI development.

7. CHALLENGES AND OPPORTUNITIES OF INTEGRATING AI

The integration of AI into policy-making comes with both notable challenges and exciting opportunities, transforming how regulations are shaped and implemented.

Challenges include biases inherent in AI systems, which can lead to unfair or discriminatory outcomes if not properly managed. For example, predictive policing algorithms have been found to disproportionately target certain communities. Transparency and accountability are also significant concerns, as many AI models operate as "black boxes," making it difficult to understand the rationale behind decisions. Data privacy is another challenge, especially when using personal data for policymaking, such as in health or social security policies. Additionally, policy-makers may lack the technical expertise needed to evaluate AI systems properly, and legal frameworks are often outdated and ill-equipped to address AI-specific issues.

On the flip side, **opportunities** include the ability of AI to enhance data-driven decision-making. For example, AI can analyze vast datasets to identify trends and predict the outcomes of policies, enabling more informed regulation. AI is already used in environmental policy, where it analyzes data on air quality or deforestation, allowing regulators to take swift action. Additionally, AI can automate bureaucratic tasks, reducing costs and improving efficiency in government operations.

Moreover, AI's potential for predictive analytics can help governments foresee challenges such as climate change impacts or economic downturns, allowing for proactive regulatory measures. Personalized approaches can also be adopted, like using AI to customize health insurance policies or social welfare programs based on individuals' specific needs.

8. CHALLENGES OF IOT-ENABLED SMART WASTE MANAGEMENT SYSTEMS

Implementing IoT-enabled smart waste management systems comes with several practical challenges:

1. **Infrastructure and Connectivity:** Many areas, especially in developing regions, lack the necessary infrastructure and reliable internet connectivity to support IoT devices. Ensuring consistent data transmission from sensors placed in waste bins to centralized systems can be difficult without stable networks.

2. **Data Overload and Management:** IoT devices generate large volumes of data, and managing this data efficiently can be overwhelming. Storing, analyzing, and extracting actionable insights from the data requires advanced analytics systems and sufficient computing power.
3. **Cost of Deployment:** The initial setup of IoT-enabled waste management systems can be costly. This includes the installation of sensors, smart bins, and network infrastructure, which may not be affordable for all municipalities, particularly in low-budget areas.
4. **Battery Life and Maintenance:** Many IoT sensors rely on batteries, which need to be regularly replaced or recharged. In remote or large areas, maintaining the sensors can become logistically challenging and costly.
5. **Security and Privacy:** IoT systems are vulnerable to cyberattacks. Ensuring the security of data collected from waste management sensors is crucial, as these systems often involve sensitive information about urban environments and infrastructure.

Despite these challenges, IoT-enabled smart waste management systems hold great potential for improving efficiency, reducing costs, and promoting sustainability in waste collection and recycling. Addressing these practical issues is key to successfully implementing these systems.

9. CASE STUDIES: PRACTICAL IMPLEMENTATION OF AI TECHNIQUES

Here are some notable case studies demonstrating the practical implementation of AI techniques across various industries:

1. **Healthcare: AI for Disease Detection**
    - **Problem**: Early detection of eye diseases like diabetic retinopathy and macular degeneration is crucial for preventing blindness. However, accurate diagnosis can be challenging due to the large number of cases and complex nature of the diseases.
    - **Solution:** DeepMind, a subsidiary of Alphabet (Google), developed an AI system that uses deep learning algorithms to analyze 3D retina scans. The system can detect over 50 eye diseases by analyzing retinal scans with high accuracy, sometimes even outperforming human doctors.
2. **Retail: AI for Personalized Shopping Experience**
    - **Problem:** Customers often struggle to find products they might be interested in among the massive selection of goods available on platforms

like Amazon. Personalized recommendations can drive sales, but scaling this personalization is complex.

- **Solution:** Amazon uses AI-driven recommendation algorithms based on collaborative filtering and content-based filtering. The system suggests products based on previous user behavior, similar customer profiles, and item characteristics. Machine learning models continually update product suggestions based on evolving patterns of user interaction.

3. **Automotive: AI for Autonomous Driving (Tesla Autopilot)**
    - **Problem:** The driving experience can be stressful, and human error is a leading cause of accidents. The goal of autonomous vehicles is to reduce accidents and improve traffic flow.
    - **Solution:** Tesla uses AI-based systems, including computer vision, deep learning, and reinforcement learning, for its Autopilot feature. The AI system uses cameras, radar, and sensors to detect objects, lane markings, pedestrians, and other vehicles in real time, helping the car navigate and make decisions autonomously.
4. **Finance: AI for Fraud Detection**
    - **Problem:** Online fraud, such as unauthorized transactions, is a major issue in the financial services industry. Traditional fraud detection methods based on static rules can be easily bypassed by evolving fraud tactics.
    - **Solution:** PayPal uses machine learning models to detect unusual patterns in transactions. The system analyzes vast amounts of data, including transaction history, user behavior, and even device information, to detect anomalies that could indicate fraudulent activity. The model is trained on historical fraud data and continues to adapt and improve its detection abilities over time.
5. **Agriculture: AI for Crop Management**
    - **Problem:** Efficient crop management requires precise knowledge about soil health, crop conditions, and weather patterns. Farmers have difficulty managing large farms without access to this information in real time.
    - **Solution:** John Deere has integrated AI into its farming equipment, such as tractors and harvesters. These systems use sensors, satellite imagery, and AI algorithms to analyze field conditions. They can provide insights about optimal planting times, soil conditions, irrigation needs, and crop health.
6. **Customer Service: AI for Chatbots and Virtual Assistants**
    - **Problem:** In the beauty industry, helping customers choose the right makeup products can be a challenge, especially online, where customers cannot physically try the products.

- **Solution:** Sephora's Virtual Artist uses AI-driven augmented reality (AR) and machine learning to help customers visualize how different makeup products will look on their skin tone. Customers upload a picture of themselves, and the AI system suggests products tailored to their preferences.

These case studies showcase the diverse and transformative applications of AI techniques across industries. Whether in healthcare, finance, retail, or manufacturing, AI continues to drive innovation and deliver tangible results.

10. CASE STUDIES ON ENVIRONMENTAL AND ECONOMIC BENEFITS

Plasma gasification is an advanced waste-to-energy (WTE) technology that uses high-temperature plasma arcs to convert waste materials into synthesis gas (syngas), which can be used to generate electricity or produce valuable chemicals. Here are some case studies that highlight the environmental and economic benefits of plasma gasification:

1. **The Monto Energy Plasma Gasification Facility (Australia)**

   Environmental Benefits:
   - The Monto Energy plasma gasification facility in Queensland, Australia, demonstrates the potential for plasma gasification to reduce landfill waste and minimize harmful emissions. The facility processes municipal solid waste (MSW) into syngas, which is used to generate clean energy.
   - The technology significantly reduces the volume of waste sent to landfills, cutting down on methane emissions—one of the most potent greenhouse gases. In addition, it reduces the leaching of harmful substances like heavy metals into the environment from landfills.
   - The process also helps divert organic waste from landfills, preventing the release of methane that would occur from traditional waste decomposition.

   Economic Benefits:
   - The facility generates revenue by converting waste into valuable energy, helping to offset waste disposal costs for local municipalities.

- Plasma gasification can be more cost-effective in the long run compared to traditional landfill or incineration options, especially in regions with stringent environmental regulations and high landfill tipping fees.
- The plant creates jobs in both the construction and operation phases, boosting local economic activity.

2. **The Tees Valley Energy Recovery Facility (United Kingdom)**

   Environmental Benefits:

   - In the Tees Valley region, a plasma gasification facility is used to process municipal waste and hazardous materials into syngas, which can be used for power generation. The process produces minimal emissions compared to conventional incineration methods, contributing to cleaner air and less environmental pollution.
   - The facility also helps reduce landfill use and lower the environmental impact of waste disposal, while the syngas produced can be used in a variety of applications, including power generation and industrial processes.

   Economic Benefits:

   - By converting waste into energy, the facility provides a cost-effective waste management solution for the local government. It eliminates the need for costly landfill expansion and waste transport to other disposal sites.
   - Plasma gasification also offers the potential for generating high-value byproducts, such as chemicals or synthetic fuels, which can further enhance the economic viability of the project.
   - The plant has contributed to local job creation and has established a sustainable model for waste-to-energy that can be replicated in other regions.

3. **The Westinghouse Plasma Gasification Plant (USA)**

   Environmental Benefits:

   - The Westinghouse Plasma Gasification Plant in Pennsylvania processes a variety of waste streams, including municipal, industrial, and hazardous waste. By using plasma technology, it converts waste into syngas with very low emissions, reducing the harmful pollutants typically released by traditional incinerators.
   - The process also helps prevent the release of toxic substances, such as dioxins and furans, which are common byproducts of traditional waste incineration, making it a more environmentally friendly alternative.

Economic Benefits:

- The facility reduces waste disposal costs for municipalities by converting waste into energy rather than sending it to landfills. It provides a sustainable revenue model through the sale of energy generated from the syngas.
- By producing high-quality syngas, the plant has the potential to generate multiple economic benefits, including the creation of new products such as synthetic fuels or chemicals, enhancing its economic sustainability.

11. FINAL CONCLUSIONS AND FUTURE DIRECTIONS

As we move forward, the convergence of AI with environmental sustainability is becoming increasingly essential. This section highlights several emerging trends in green AI, illustrating how this field is poised to foster a more sustainable and eco-conscious future.

- **Explainable AI for Environmental Decision-Making:** Explainable AI (XAI) is gaining traction in green AI applications for its ability to enhance transparency and accountability. As AI systems become more integral to environmental decision-making, understanding the rationale behind AI-generated recommendations becomes vital. This is particularly relevant in green-by AI applications, where XAI models could provide insights into mechanisms that promote sustainability. Initial implementations of XAI are already being used in sectors like agriculture and various industrial fields.
- **Eco-Friendly AI Hardware Accelerators:** Innovations in hardware design are focused on creating AI accelerators that are both powerful and environmentally friendly. This includes developing processors that execute AI algorithms with minimal energy consumption.
- **Neuromorphic Computing:** This emerging paradigm in computing technology, inspired by the architecture of the human brain, aims to develop more efficient and adaptable computing systems. The human brain performs complex tasks with minimal energy compared to conventional computers. Neuromorphic computing seeks to replicate this efficiency by reducing energy consumption to levels comparable to biological brains, using spiking neural networks (SNNs) to emulate biological neural networks. This approach promises substantial energy savings and improved performance, particularly in AI applications requiring real-time processing. Additionally, proposals

like those by Oh et al. suggest creating biodegradable neural network hardware to reduce technological waste.

- **Energy-Harvesting AI Devices:** Research is underway to develop AI devices capable of harvesting energy from their environment, such as ambient light, vibrations, and heat. Integrating energy-harvesting capabilities could make AI devices more self-sufficient and reduce dependence on external power sources, contributing to a more sustainable deployment of AI.
- **AI for Environmental Conservation:** AI is making significant contributions to environmental conservation through innovative applications. Examples include robotic pollinators in agriculture and ocean AI. Robotic pollinators, which mimic natural pollination patterns, help address the decline in natural crop pollinators, supporting food security and sustainable farming practices. Ocean AI, involving underwater drones equipped with advanced sensors, monitors and protects marine ecosystems by tracking marine life, detecting pollution, and identifying illegal fishing activities. These technologies underscore AI's crucial role in protecting biodiversity, promoting sustainable practices, and mitigating environmental threats in both terrestrial and aquatic environments.

While these trends in green AI highlight exciting developments, it's important to recognize that the field is rapidly evolving. The applications discussed represent only a fraction of green AI's potential, with many more innovative uses likely to emerge soon. As technology advances, researchers, engineers, and environmentalists are expected to find new ways to integrate AI into various sustainability efforts, addressing challenges and creating new opportunities. The intersection of AI and environmental awareness is a promising area for exploration, and ongoing research and developments in this field are set to reveal numerous applications that could significantly contribute to a more sustainable and eco-friendly future.

REFERENCES

Abdel-Nasser, M., & Mahmoud, K. (2019). Accurate photovoltaic power forecasting models using deep LSTM-RNN. *Neural Computing & Applications*, *31*(7), 2727–2740. DOI: 10.1007/s00521-017-3225-z

Ahmed, R., Sreeram, V., Mishra, Y., & Arif, M. (2020). A review and evaluation of the state-of-the-art in PV solar power forecasting: Techniques and optimization. *Renewable & Sustainable Energy Reviews*, *124*, 109792. DOI: 10.1016/j.rser.2020.109792

Anthony, L. F. W., Kanding, B., & Selvan, R. (2020). CarbonTracker: Tracking and predicting the carbon footprint of training deep learning models. arXiv preprint arXiv:2007.03051. https://arxiv.org/abs/2007.03051

Aslam, S., Herodotou, H., Mohsin, S. M., Javaid, N., Ashraf, N., & Aslam, S. (2021). A survey on deep learning methods for power load and renewable energy forecasting in smart microgrids. *Renewable & Sustainable Energy Reviews*, *144*, 110992. DOI: 10.1016/j.rser.2021.110992

Bannour, N., Ghannay, S., Névéol, A., & Ligozat, A.-L. (2021). Evaluating the carbon footprint of NLP methods: A survey and analysis of existing tools. In Proceedings of the Second Workshop on Simple and Efficient Natural Language Processing (pp. 11–21). https://aclanthology.org/2021.si-1.2/

Bergstra, J., & Bengio, Y. (2012). Random search for hyper-parameter optimization. *Journal of Machine Learning Research*, *13*(2), 281–305. https://www.jmlr.org/papers/volume13/bergstra12a/bergstra12a.pdf

Bibikar, S., Vikalo, H., Wang, Z., & Chen, X. (2022). Federated dynamic sparse training: Computing less, communicating less, yet learning better. In *Proceedings of the AAAI Conference on Artificial Intelligence* (Vol. 36, Issue 6, pp. 6080–6088). DOI: 10.1609/aaai.v36i6.20555

Bojarski, M., Del Testa, D., Dworakowski, D., Firner, B., Flepp, B., Goyal, P., Jackel, L. D., Monfort, M., Muller, U., Zhang, J., ... (2016). End to end learning for self-driving cars. arXiv preprint arXiv:1604.07316. https://arxiv.org/abs/1604.07316

Cao, Z., Zhou, X., Hu, H., Wang, Z., & Wen, Y. (2022). Toward a systematic survey for carbon neutral data centers. *IEEE Communications Surveys and Tutorials*, *24*(2), 895–936. DOI: 10.1109/COMST.2022.3161275

Castillo-García, G., Morán-Fernández, L., & Bolón-Canedo, V. (2023). Efficient feature selection for domain adaptation using mutual information maximization. In *European Symposium on Artificial Neural Networks, Computational Intelligence and Machine Learning*. DOI: 10.14428/esann/2023.ES2023-61

Chen, J., Zeng, G.-Q., Zhou, W., Du, W., & Lu, K.-D. (2018). Wind speed forecasting using nonlinear-learning ensemble of deep learning time series prediction and extremal optimization. *Energy Conversion and Management, 165*, 681–695. DOI: 10.1016/j.enconman.2018.03.098

Chen, Z.-G., Zhan, Z.-H., Kwong, S., & Zhang, J. (2022). Evolutionary computation for intelligent transportation in smart cities: A survey. *IEEE Computational Intelligence Magazine, 17*(2), 83–102. DOI: 10.1109/MCI.2022.3155330

Dhar, P. (2020). The carbon impact of artificial intelligence. *Nature Machine Intelligence, 2*(8), 423–425. DOI: 10.1038/s42256-020-0219-9

Díaz-Vico, D., Torres-Barrán, A., Omari, A., & Dorronsoro, J. R. (2017). Deep neural networks for wind and solar energy prediction. *Neural Processing Letters, 46*(3), 829–844. DOI: 10.1007/s11063-017-9613-7

Dong, H., Munir, A., Tout, H., & Ganjali, Y. (2021). Next-generation data center network enabled by machine learning: Review, challenges, and opportunities. *IEEE Access : Practical Innovations, Open Solutions, 9*, 136459–136475. DOI: 10.1109/ACCESS.2021.3117763

Duan, P., Mao, G., Liang, W., & Zhang, D. (2018). A unified spatio-temporal model for short-term traffic flow prediction. *IEEE Transactions on Intelligent Transportation Systems, 20*(9), 3212–3223. DOI: 10.1109/TITS.2018.2873137

Elgabli, A., Park, J., Bedi, A. S., Issaid, C. B., Bennis, M., & Aggarwal, V. (2020). Q-GADMM: Quantized group ADMM for communication-efficient decentralized machine learning. *IEEE Transactions on Communications, 69*(1), 164–181. DOI: 10.1109/TCOMM.2020.3026398

European Union. (2024). Artificial intelligence act: European parliament legislative resolution of 13 March 2024 on the proposal for a regulation of the European Parliament and of the Council on laying down harmonised rules on artificial intelligence (Artificial Intelligence Act) and amending certain Union legislative acts (COM(2021)0206 – C9-0146/2021 – 2021/0106(COD)). Retrieved from [URL].

García-Mira, R., Dumitru, A., Alonso-Betanzos, A., Sánchez-Maroño, N., Fontenla-Romero, O., Craig, T., & Polhil, J. (2017). Testing scenarios to achieve workplace sustainability goals using backcasting and agent-based modeling. *Environment and Behavior*, *49*(9), 1007–1027. DOI: 10.1177/0013916516673869

Genemo, M. (2023). Quantum convolutional neural network for agricultural mechanization and plant disease detection. In *Proceedings of the International Conference on Image Processing and Capsule Networks* (pp. 225–237). Springer. DOI: 10.1007/978-981-99-7093-3_15

Ghasemi, A., & Toroghi Haghighat, A. (2020). A multi-objective load balancing algorithm for virtual machine placement in cloud data centers based on machine learning. *Computing*, *102*(9), 2049–2072. DOI: 10.1007/s00607-020-00813-w

Ghazal, T. M., Hasan, M. K., Ahmad, M., Alzoubi, H. M., & Alshurideh, M. (2023). Machine learning approaches for sustainable cities using the Internet of Things. In *The effect of information technology on business and marketing intelligence systems* (pp. 1969–1986). Springer., DOI: 10.1007/978-3-031-12382-5_108

Giebel, G., & Kariniotakis, G. (2017). Wind power forecasting – A review of the state of the art. *Renewable Energy Forecasting*, *59*, 59–109. DOI: 10.1016/B978-0-08-100504-0.00003-2

Henderson, P., Hu, J., Romoff, J., Brunskill, E., Jurafsky, D., & Pineau, J. (2020). Towards the systematic reporting of the energy and carbon footprints of machine learning. *Journal of Machine Learning Research*, *21*(248), 1–43. https://www.jmlr.org/papers/volume21/20-226/20-226.pdf

Hong, T., & Fan, S. (2016). Probabilistic electric load forecasting: A tutorial review. *International Journal of Forecasting*, *32*(3), 914–938. DOI: 10.1016/j.ijforecast.2015.11.011

Intergovernmental Panel on Climate Change (IPCC). (2014). Mitigation of climate change. In *Contribution of Working Group III to the Fifth Assessment Report of the Intergovernmental Panel on Climate Change* (p. 1454). Cambridge University Press.

Jager, W., Guijarro-Berdiñas, B., Bouman, L., Antosz, P., Alonso-Betanzos, A., Salt, D., Polhill, J. G., Rodríguez Arias, A., & Sánchez-Maroño, N. (2024). Simulating the role of norms in processes of social innovation: Three case studies. *Journal of Artificial Societies and Social Simulation*, *27*(1), 6. DOI: 10.18564/jasss.5168

Jouppi, N., Kurian, G., Li, S., Ma, P., Nagarajan, R., Nai, L., Patil, N., Subramanian, S., Swing, A., & Towles, B.. (2023). TPU v4: An optically reconfigurable supercomputer for machine learning with hardware support for embeddings. In *Proceedings of the 50th Annual International Symposium on Computer Architecture* (pp. 1–14). IEEE. DOI: 10.1145/3579371.3589350

Kazi, R. H., Grossman, T., Cheong, H., Hashemi, A., & Fitzmaurice, G. W. (2017). DreamSketch: Early stage 3D design explorations with sketching and generative design. In *Proceedings of the 30th Annual ACM Symposium on User Interface Software and Technology* (pp. 401–414). ACM. DOI: 10.1145/3126594.3126662

Khirirat, S., Magnússon, S., Aytekin, A., & Johansson, M. (2021). A flexible framework for communication-efficient machine learning. In *Proceedings of the AAAI Conference on Artificial Intelligence* (Vol. 35, Issue 9, pp. 8101–8109). DOI: 10.1609/aaai.v35i9.16987

Kim, I. H., Liu, Y.-H., Pallister, S., Pol, W., Roberts, S., & Lee, E. (2022). Fault-tolerant resource estimate for quantum chemical simulations: Case study on Li-ion battery electrolyte molecules. *Physical Review Research, 4*(2), 023019. DOI: 10.1103/PhysRevResearch.4.023019

Lannelongue, L., Grealey, J., & Inouye, M. (2021). Green algorithms: Quantifying the carbon footprint of computation. *Advancement of Science, 8*(12), 2100707. DOI: 10.1002/advs.202100707 PMID: 34194954

Li, L., Jamieson, K., DeSalvo, G., Rostamizadeh, A., & Talwalkar, A. (2017). Hyperband: A novel bandit-based approach to hyperparameter optimization. *Journal of Machine Learning Research, 18*(1), 6765–6816. http://jmlr.org/papers/volume18/17-555/17-555.pdf

Li, W., Cao, J., Guan, J., Zhou, S., Liang, G., So, W. K., & Szczecinski, M. (2018). A general framework for unmet demand prediction in on-demand transport services. *IEEE Transactions on Intelligent Transportation Systems, 20*(8), 2820–2830. DOI: 10.1109/TITS.2018.2873092

Li, Y., Wen, Y., Tao, D., & Guan, K. (2019). Transforming cooling optimization for green data center via deep reinforcement learning. *IEEE Transactions on Cybernetics, 50*(5), 2002–2013. DOI: 10.1109/TCYB.2019.2927410 PMID: 31352360

Lin, K.-P., Pai, P.-F., & Ting, Y.-J. (2019). Deep belief networks with genetic algorithms in forecasting wind speed. *IEEE Access : Practical Innovations, Open Solutions, 7*, 99244–99253. DOI: 10.1109/ACCESS.2019.2929542

Liu, Z., Wang, Y., Han, K., Zhang, W., Ma, S., & Gao, W. (2021). *Post-training quantization for vision transformer* (Vol. 34). Advances in Neural Information Processing Systems, https://arxiv.org/abs/2110.02280

Lottick, K., Susai, S., Friedler, S. A., & Wilson, J. P. (2019). Energy usage reports: Environmental awareness as part of algorithmic accountability. arXiv preprint arXiv:1911.08354. https://arxiv.org/abs/1911.08354

Lourenço, A., Ferraz, C., Meira, J., Marreiros, G., Bolón-Canedo, V., & Alonso-Betanzos, A. (2023). Automated green machine learning for condition-based maintenance. In *European Symposium on Artificial Neural Networks, Computational Intelligence and Machine Learning*. DOI: 10.14428/esann/2023.ES2023-85

Luccioni, A. S., & Hernandez-Garcia, A. (2023). Counting carbon: A survey of factors influencing the emissions of machine learning. arXiv preprint arXiv:2302.08476. https://arxiv.org/abs/2302.08476

Milojevic-Dupont, N., & Creutzig, F. (2021). Machine learning for geographically differentiated climate change mitigation in urban areas. *Sustainable Cities and Society*, *64*, 102526. DOI: 10.1016/j.scs.2020.102526

Moore, G. E. (1998). Cramming more components onto integrated circuits. *Proceedings of the IEEE*, *86*(1), 82–85. DOI: 10.1109/JPROC.1998.658762

Moreno-Vozmediano, R., Montero, R. S., Huedo, E., & Llorente, I. M. (2019). Efficient resource provisioning for elastic cloud services based on machine learning techniques. *Journal of Cloud Computing (Heidelberg, Germany)*, *8*(1), 1–18. DOI: 10.1186/s13677-019-0128-9

Nevavuori, P., Narra, N., & Lipping, T. (2019). Crop yield prediction with deep convolutional neural networks. *Computers and Electronics in Agriculture*, *163*, 104859. DOI: 10.1016/j.compag.2019.104859

Novoa-Paradela, D., Fontenla-Romero, O., & Guijarro-Berdiñas, B. (2023). Fast deep autoencoder for federated learning. *Pattern Recognition*, *143*, 109805. DOI: 10.1016/j.patcog.2023.109805

Osta, M., Alameh, M., Younes, H., Ibrahim, A., & Valle, M. (2019). Energy efficient implementation of machine learning algorithms on hardware platforms. In 2019 26th IEEE International Conference on Electronics, Circuits and Systems (ICECS) (pp. 21–24). IEEE. DOI: 10.1109/ICECS46596.2019.8965157

Patterson, D., Gonzalez, J., Le, Q., Liang, C., Munguia, L.-M., Rothchild, D., So, D., Texier, M., & Dean, J. (2021). Carbon emissions and large neural network training. arXiv:2104.10350.

Pham, A.-D., Ngo, N.-T., Truong, T. T. H., Huynh, N.-T., & Truong, N.-S. (2020). Predicting energy consumption in multiple buildings using machine learning for improving energy efficiency and sustainability. *Journal of Cleaner Production, 260*, 121082. DOI: 10.1016/j.jclepro.2020.121082

Pham, Q. B., Kumar, M., Di Nunno, F., Elbeltagi, A., Granata, F., Islam, A. R. M. T., Talukdar, S., Nguyen, X. C., Ahmed, A. N., & Anh, D. T. (2022). Groundwater level prediction using machine learning algorithms in a drought-prone area. *Neural Computing & Applications, 34*(13), 10751–10773. DOI: 10.1007/s00521-022-07009-7

Qolomany, B., Al-Fuqaha, A., Gupta, A., Benhaddou, D., Alwajidi, S., Qadir, J., & Fong, A. C. (2019). Leveraging machine learning and big data for smart buildings: A comprehensive survey. *IEEE Access : Practical Innovations, Open Solutions, 7*, 90316–90356. DOI: 10.1109/ACCESS.2019.2926642

Renggli, C., Ashkboos, S., Aghagolzadeh, M., Alistarh, D., & Hoefler, T. (2019). SparCML: High-performance sparse communication for machine learning. In *Proceedings of the International Conference for High Performance Computing, Networking, Storage and Analysis* (pp. 1–15). DOI: 10.1145/3295500.3356222

Rolnick, D., Donti, P. L., Kaack, L. H., Kochanski, K., Lacoste, A., Sankaran, K., Ross, A. S., Milojevic-Dupont, N., Jaques, N., Waldman-Brown, A., Luccioni, A. S., Maharaj, T., Sherwin, E. D., Mukkavilli, S. K., Kording, K. P., Gomes, C. P., Ng, A. Y., Hassabis, D., Platt, J. C., & Bengio, Y. (2022). Tackling climate change with machine learning. *ACM Computing Surveys, 55*(2), 1–96. DOI: 10.1145/3485128

Salinas, D., Bohlke-Schneider, M., Callot, L., Medico, R., & Gasthaus, J. (2019). *High-dimensional multivariate forecasting with low-rank Gaussian copula processes* (Vol. 32). Advances in Neural Information Processing Systems, https://arxiv.org/abs/1812.02417

Sánchez-Maroño, N., Alonso-Betanzos, A., Fontenla-Romero, O., Brinquis-Núñez, C., Polhill, J. G., Craig, T., Dumitru, A., & García-Mira, R. (2015). An agent-based model for simulating environmental behavior in an educational organization. *Neural Processing Letters, 42*(1), 89–118. DOI: 10.1007/s11063-014-9390-5

Sánchez-Maroño, N., Rodríguez Arias, A., Lema-Lago, I., Guijarro-Berdiñas, B., Dumitru, A., & Alonso-Betanzos, A. (2022). How agent-based modeling can help to foster sustainability projects. In *Proceedings of the 26th International Conference on Knowledge-Based and Intelligent Information and Engineering Systems (KES 2022)*. DOI: 10.1016/j.procs.2022.09.313

Schwartz, R., Dodge, J., Smith, N. A., & Etzioni, O. (2020). Green AI. *Communications of the ACM, 63*(12), 54–63. DOI: 10.1145/3381831

Sharma, R., Kamble, S. S., Gunasekaran, A., Kumar, V., & Kumar, A. (2020). A systematic literature review on machine learning applications for sustainable agriculture supply chain performance. *Computers & Operations Research, 119*, 104926. DOI: 10.1016/j.cor.2020.104926

Shumska, M., & Bunte, K. (2023). Multispectral texture classification in agriculture. In Proceedings of the European Symposium on Artificial Neural Networks, Computational Intelligence and Machine Learning. https://www.esann.org/sites/default/files/proceedings/2023/ESANN2023_65.pdf

Singh, S., Sulthana, R., Shewale, T., Chamola, V., Benslimane, A., & Sikdar, B. (2021). Machine-learning-assisted security and privacy provisioning for edge computing: A survey. *IEEE Internet of Things Journal, 9*(1), 236–260. DOI: 10.1109/JIOT.2021.3098051

Snoek, J., Larochelle, H., & Adams, R. P. (2012). Practical Bayesian optimization of machine learning algorithms. Advances in Neural Information Processing Systems, 25, 1–9. https://proceedings.neurips.cc/paper/2012/hash/82ebf97e5b3496b60f2b70443a890351-Abstract.html

Sorkun, M. C., Paoli, C., & Incel, Ö. D. (2017). Time series forecasting on solar irradiation using deep learning. In 2017 10th International Conference on Electrical and Electronics Engineering (ELECO) (pp. 151–155). IEEE.

Stamoulis, D., Ding, R., Wang, D., Lymberopoulos, D., Priyantha, B., Liu, J., & Marculescu, D. (2019). Single-path NAS: Designing hardware-efficient convnets in less than 4 hours. In *Joint European Conference on Machine Learning and Knowledge Discovery in Databases* (pp. 481–497). Springer. https://doi.org/DOI: 10.1007/978-3-030-30494-3_30

Suárez-Marcote, S., Morán-Fernández, L., & Bolón-Canedo, V. (2023). Logarithmic division for green feature selection: An information-theoretic approach. In *European Symposium on Artificial Neural Networks, Computational Intelligence and Machine Learning*. DOI: 10.14428/esann/2023.ES2023-77

Tay, Y., Bahri, D., Yang, L., Metzler, D., & Juan, D.-C. (2020). Sparse Sinkhorn attention. In International Conference on Machine Learning (pp. 9438–9447). PMLR. https://proceedings.mlr.press/v119/tay20a.html

Trébaol, T. (2020). CUMULATOR - a tool to quantify and report the carbon footprint of machine learning computations and communication in academia and healthcare. https://doi.org/DOI: 10.13140/RG.2.2.32835.20009

Veerachamy, R., & Ramar, R. (2022). Agricultural irrigation recommendation and alert (AIRA) system using optimization and machine learning in Hadoop for sustainable agriculture. *Environmental Science and Pollution Research International, 29*(14), 19955–19974. DOI: 10.1007/s11356-021-13248-3 PMID: 33788091

Vinuesa, R., Azizpour, H., Leite, I., Balaam, M., Dignum, V., Domisch, S., Felländer, A., Langhans, S. D., Tegmark, M., & Fuso Nerini, F. (2020). The role of artificial intelligence in achieving the sustainable development goals. *Nature Communications, 11*(1), 1–10. DOI: 10.1038/s41467-019-14108-y PMID: 31932590

Wan, Y., Qu, Y., Gao, L., & Xiang, Y. (2022). Privacy-preserving blockchain-enabled federated learning for B5G-driven edge computing. *Computer Networks, 204*, 108671. DOI: 10.1016/j.comnet.2021.108671

Wang, H., Li, G., Wang, G., Peng, J., Jiang, H., & Liu, Y. (2017). Deep learning-based ensemble approach for probabilistic wind power forecasting. *Applied Energy, 188*, 56–70. DOI: 10.1016/j.apenergy.2016.11.111

Wang, J., Tchapmi, L. P., Ravikumar, A. P., McGuire, M., Bell, C. S., Zimmerle, D., Savarese, S., & Brandt, A. R. (2020). Machine vision for natural gas methane emissions detection using an infrared camera. *Applied Energy, 257*, 113998. DOI: 10.1016/j.apenergy.2019.113998

Wu, C., Kreidieh, A., Vinitsky, E., & Bayen, A. M. (2017). Emergent behaviors in mixed-autonomy traffic. In Proceedings of the Conference on Robot Learning (pp. 398–407). PMLR. https://proceedings.mlr.press/v78/wu17a.html

Xiao, G., Lin, J., Seznec, M., Wu, H., Demouth, J., & Han, S. (2023). SmoothQuant: Accurate and efficient post-training quantization for large language models. In International Conference on Machine Learning (pp. 38087–38099). PMLR. https://proceedings.mlr.press/v202/xiao23a.html

Yang, T.-J., Chen, Y.-H., & Sze, V. (2017). Designing energy-efficient convolutional neural networks using energy-aware pruning. In *Proceedings of the IEEE Conference on Computer Vision and Pattern Recognition* (pp. 5687–5695). IEEE. DOI: 10.1109/CVPR.2017.643

Yin, X., Wu, G., Wei, J., Shen, Y., Qi, H., & Yin, B. (2021). Deep learning on traffic prediction: Methods, analysis, and future directions. *IEEE Transactions on Intelligent Transportation Systems, 23*(6), 4927–4943. DOI: 10.1109/TITS.2021.3054840

Zafrir, O., Boudoukh, G., Izsak, P., & Wasserblat, M. (2019). Q8BERT: Quantized 8-bit BERT. In 2019 Fifth Workshop on Energy Efficient Machine Learning and Cognitive Computing—NeurIPS Edition (EMC2-NIPS) (pp. 36–39). IEEE. https://doi.org/DOI: 10.1109/EMC2-NIPS48266.2019.00012

Zekić-Sušac, M., Mitrović, S., & Has, A. (2021). Machine learning based system for managing energy efficiency of the public sector as an approach towards smart cities. *International Journal of Information Management*, *58*, 102074. DOI: 10.1016/j.ijinfomgt.2020.102074

Zhang, M., Kafy, A.-A., Xiao, P., Han, S., Zou, S., Saha, M., Zhang, C., & Tan, S. (2023). Impact of urban expansion on land surface temperature and carbon emissions using machine learning algorithms in Wuhan, China. *Urban Climate*, *47*, 101347. DOI: 10.1016/j.uclim.2022.101347

Chapter 13
Emerging Trends and Innovations Shaping the Future of Sustainable Computing

R. Vidhya Muthulakshmi
https://orcid.org/0009-0008-2162-0192
Panimalar Engineering College, India

S. Deepa
R.M.D. Engineering College, India

L. Sudha
https://orcid.org/0000-0003-4974-7482
SRM Institute of Science and Technology, India

R. Kennady
Rajalakshmi Institute of Technology, India

V. Kalpana
Vel Tech Rangarajan Dr. Sagunthala R&D Institute of Science and Technology, India

R. Vinoth
https://orcid.org/0000-0001-5866-1395
R.M.K. College of Engineering and Technology, India

N. Pavithra
https://orcid.org/0009-0007-7441-2592
Jeppiaar Institute of Technology, India

ABSTRACT

Sustainable computing is a new and rapidly advancing field that has developed as a direct result of the environmental cost associated with the modern computing systems propelled by the continually growing demand for high energy consuming technologies like cloud computing, artificial intelligence, and IoT. This paper also examines the current and emerging trends, development, and issues in sustainable computing. It discusses energy efficient hardware advancements, green data centres, renewable energy assimilation and the application of artificial intelligence in resource

DOI: 10.4018/979-8-3373-0766-4.ch013

Copyright © 2025, IGI Global Scientific Publishing. Copying or distributing in print or electronic forms without written permission of IGI Global Scientific Publishing is prohibited.

management. The paper also looks at other software practices that have led to the reduction of energy consumption energy-aware algorithms, green software design and virtualization. Innovations like Edge computing and energy-efficient routing protocols are explained in the context of reducing the carbon of global computing infrastructure. The survey is meant to give an overview of the current situation and future opportunities and to foster cross-disciplinary work for the improvement of sustainability in computing.

1. INTRODUCTION

1.1 Background and Motivation

Specifically, several issues arising from computing and technology have become apparent in the past decades mainly due to the increasing environmental concerns. The ever-growing use of digital devices, data centers, and internet-connected technologies has accelerated the energy consumption and environmental polluting process in the world. As per the latest calculations, the ICT sector contributes to about 4% of global greenhouse gases emissions and is projected to increase in the future years. Thus, while computational power is constantly increasing due to the development of cloud technologies, AI, and IoT, the environmental cost of these technologies is only intensifying(Jeong, Y. S., & Park, J. H. 20200. Data centers in particular and computing systems in general are known to be energy hungry particularly when large scale. These facilities are also opened round the clock due to the increasing demand of data processing, storage and transfer which results into enormous consumption of power. Furthermore, the usage of computing devices also brings about the manufacturing, which is a process that demands a lot of resources and the disposal, which leads to e-waste and thus pollution. As awareness on the adverse impact of climate change continues to rise in the global market, the technology sector is now under pressure to cut on the emissions and adopt sustainable practices. Sustainable computing therefore comes out as a response to these challenges, which seeks to reduce the environmental cost of computing(Sung et al 20160. This interdisciplinary field is about developing and deploying computing systems that are energy efficient, resource sparing and green. Sustainable computing hence tries to adapt the use of new hardware and software while at the same time minimizing energy usage and incorporating use of renewable energy sources(Prabha, D et al 20240. The need for adopting sustainability in computing is now more important than ever since industries are going fully digital and the consequences to the environment are only getting worse.

1.2 Objectives of the Survey

This survey thus seeks to present a review of the current trends, innovations, and practices in sustainable computing. Over the past few years, the field has witnessed a lot of progress in many areas of interest including energy efficient hardware and software design for computing systems, green data centers, and renewable energy systems. In this paper, based on the analysis of the current literature and the most recent technology advancements, the author will provide an insight into how sustainability is being incorporated in the computing system and possible ways through which computing systems' impact on the environment is being minimized. The survey will follow main issues of sustainable computing including energy use, resource utilization and environmental footprint. Particular emphasis will be placed on the tendencies, such as the utilization of artificial intelligence in the management of energy consumption, the integration of low-power hardware, the usage of edge computational and green data center to transform the energy situation in the technologies. The paper will also review best practices in software development which include green coding, efficiency measures and use of renewable sources of energy like solar and wind energy in computing infrastructure for instance data centers. Furthermore, this paper will also discuss the potential future work and scope of the sustainable computing research. However, the following challenges are still outstanding;; there is a limitation in the ability to optimize the performance and energy efficiency at the same time; there is a limitation in the integration of large scale renewable energy; the environmental impact of some new technologies like quantum computing. The survey will hint at what further research and innovation would be needed to make computing even more sustainable in the context of environmental goals for the world. In the end, this survey will become a reference point for researchers, practitioners, and policy makers who want to get an insight on sustainable computing and find ways to minimize environmental impact of computing technologies. This paper will be part of the ongoing discussion of how to build a smarter and eco-friendlier tech environment by focusing on the current advancements and potential developments.

2. DEFINITION AND SCOPE OF SUSTAINABLE COMPUTING

2.1 What is Sustainable Computing?

Sustainable computing is defined as the systematic approach to computing system, technology, and practice design, development, and deployment with the intent of reducing the adverse effects of computing on the environment(Sharanya et al 20240. It covers the use of energy, efficiency, resource utilization, and low carbon impact across all the stages of computing systems' existence, including design, manufacturing, use, and end of life. Sustainable computing involves the following principles: Energy Efficient computing, Resource Conservation, Resourceful waste management, and Renewable energy computing. In its essence, sustainable computing focuses on how computing technologies should complement sustainable objectives, for example climate change or the conservation of resources(Saxena et al 20240. Global warming resulting from increased emissions of greenhouse gases has emerged as a major world concern. The computing industry, whose energy consumption is rapidly growing, is becoming more and more viewed as a key driver of such emissions. Some of the recent surveys revealed that ICT account for a large fraction of world's energy consumption and carbon emissions; primarily because of the rising energy requirements of data centers servers and other related computing equipment(Lokesh et al 20240.

In this regard, sustainable computing has a crucial role of promoting the use of environmentally friendly approaches to curb energy wastage and support the development of environmentally sustainable technologies. Key aspects of sustainable computing include:

Energy Efficiency: The key objective behind sustainable computing is to minimize the energy consumption of computing platforms. This can be done with the help of new designs of hard and software, new approaches to energy management at the system level.

Resource Efficiency: The sustainable computing also looks at ways of minimizing the amount of raw materials used and that the resources available should be utilised optimally from the time a product is produced to the time it is disposed.

Waste Reduction: This is achieved through the recycling, reuse, and extending the useful life of 'products' since e-waste is a critical area to sustainable computing. The purpose of this principle is to reduce the negative impact of disposed of electronics on the environment.

Use of Renewable Energy: Hybridizing renewable energy resources like the solar and wind to computer systems decreases the usage of traditional energy sources which are polluting.

2.2 Scope and Relevance

Sustainable computing is defined as a multidisciplinary research area for multiple aspects of technology and processes. It spans hardware, software, data centers, algorithms, and communication networks, all of which form the system that makes up computing sustainability.

Hardware: Sustainable hardware design means the development of processors, servers, and other devices that consume less power in order to be operated. Low power hardware platforms including ARM processors and energy efficient GPU are critical in minimizing energy usage across customers and enterprises.
Software: Software is very important in sustainable computing because it makes code efficient to lower the computational complexity for energy efficiency. Sustainability in software development entails the formulation of procedures that ensure that algorithms consume less power while delivering their outputs.
Data Centers: The data centers which store and process a huge amount of data are one of the most energy-consuming entities of the computing environment. Technological advancements in green data centers include; optimization of cooling mechanisms, utilization of green energy sources, and efficient computing and networking equipment and software.
Algorithms: An energy-aware algorithm is developed to improve computational performance and minimize energy utilization. For example, the task scheduling algorithms that consider energy consumption as a criterion may be useful in lowering the power demands of the systems.
Networks: Hence, sustainable networking is the ability to design and implement energy efficient communication protocols and structures. This also comprises of low power networking breakthroughs like energy efficient Ethernet and optical networking to reduce power consumption during data transfer.

Sustainable computing is similar to other branches of science such as green computing, energy efficient computing, and eco design. Green IT on the other hand is a sub-set of green computing since it only focuses on the use of IT to support sustainable computing(Pitchai et al 20240. Energy-efficient computing can be described more narrowly as the optimization of the energy consumption of computing devices and systems. Eco-design is the act of designing products and systems with low environmental loads throughout their life cycle. Sustainable computing brings together concepts from these related fields in order to design computing systems that are not only optimizing in terms of their performance, but also positive contributors to the fight against climate change and to the conservation of the environment. Sustainable computing combines hardware, software, algorithms, and network improvements to provide a holistic solution to the problem of environmental impact posed by the tech industry.

3. KEY DRIVERS FOR SUSTAINABLE COMPUTING

Sustainable computing uses several drivers that must be achieved to minimize the effects of computing systems to the environment, concurrently enhancing the advancement of the technology. These drivers are energy efficiency, resource utilisation and environmental impacts' reduction, are core to making computing more sustainable and get to ensure that it supports environmental sustainability.

3.1 Energy Efficiency

One of the goals of green computing is energy efficiency. The ever-growing appetite of computers has caused a significant increase in energy consumption especially in data centers, servers, and other demanding computing architectures. It was found that it is possible to greatly reduce the energy needed to perform the computing task, thus reducing the negative effects on the environment. The most effective of the mentioned approaches is dynamic voltage scaling (DVS) as a technique for attaining energy efficiency. DVS enables the computing devices to scale down the voltage and the frequency of operations during the low utilization while scaling up during high demand. This dynamic modulation benefits the system by enabling the use of less power but at the same time maintaining the quality of the system.

Another important method is the use of low power processors. Progress in the processor technology has resulted in the creation of energy efficient microprocessors that can operate at low power rates while offering high levels of performance. For example, ARM based processors, which are widely used in mobile communication devices and other embedded systems, are low power processors. Moreover, low power GPU and FPGA are also integrated into chip designs to reduce power consumption in high performance computing systems. To achieve energy efficiency in computing systems, the energy-efficient hardware and software technologies should be integrated into computing systems. Other algorithms within the system, for data processing and scheduling, are also energy-conscious, meaning that they keep computational overhead to the lowest level possible and consume as little power as possible to execute their tasks.

3.2 Resource Optimization

In resource optimization, the aim is to use as much computational resources as possible while using as little as possible of it. Two of the major technologies in the availability of resources are cloud computing and virtualization where several virtual machines share a single physical server. This efficient use of hardware allows companies to pool computational assets, minimize the amount of physical hardware that is needed and therefore decrease energy consumption. Providers of cloud computing also help in management of resources by adjusting the resources they allocate to the specific needs at particular time. This elasticity means that the energy is used more efficiently because the servers are shut down during the nonworking time. Thirdly, the virtualization of the hardware resources also helps in load balancing, which minimizes time wastage and in the process keeps energy usage minimal. Resource optimization is another factor that must be taken into consideration and one of these is the recycling and proper disposal of electronic wastes. Since the sector of technology is experiencing constant development, electronics like devices and parts are short-lived. Electronic waste or e-waste is mostly disposed of inappropriately resulting in dangerous impacts on the environment and release of toxic substances. Sustainable computing is the recycling of electronic components, reusing valuable material such as metal and plastics, and the proper disposal of the devices.

3.3 Environmental Impact Reduction

Green computing is the process of cutting down on the amount of carbon emissions and supporting sustainable energy in computing systems life cycle. Data centers and computing infrastructure can benefit from the use of renewable energy sources like solar, wind, and hydroelectric power as the best way to minimize the carbon footprint. Clean energy can be used to power computing operations, and in doing so, an organization can cut its fossil fuel usage and greenhouse gas emissions. In addition, carbon neutral schemes are increasingly being adopted in the tech sector. Organizations are going a notch higher to ensure that they balance the emission of carbon by funding renewable energy sources, carbon offsets and environmental conservation. Most of the leading technology companies like Google, Microsoft, and Amazon have pledged that they would make their operations carbon neutral or achieve net-zero emissions by the middle of the current decade.

The other method of minimizing environmental impact is the life cycle assessment of computing devices. LCA entails assessing the effects of a product on the environment from its conception, through the production process right up to its use and disposal. For this reason, by pointing out the potential for savings in terms of energy and resources, LCA assists manufacturers in the creation of environmentally friendly goods, and assists consumers in making an informed decision regarding their purchase. There is the need to integrate these sustainability-driven activities in computing systems so as to minimize the impacts of sustainability in the industry. Energy efficiency, resource optimization, and environmental impact reduction are the principles that the computing sector can apply to limit climate change while developing technologies further.

4. EMERGING TRENDS IN SUSTAINABLE COMPUTING

Whereas the need for computational capabilities is increasing, new trends and solutions are appearing to make computing more efficient. These trends are centred on reducing energy use, optimisation of resource utilisation and environmental sustainability of technology. Some of the major trends in sustainable computing are Green data centres, energy-aware algorithms, edge computing, low-power hardware technologies, and incorporation of AI to green computing.

4.1 Green Data Centers

Data centers are one of the biggest energy consumers and this makes it important to focus on the innovations that will be able to make them more sustainable. The use of high-efficient cooling methods can be considered one of the most important advancements in the green data centers. Air conditioning and other conventional cooling techniques require a lot of energy to be made effective. Newer methods like liquid cooling or free cooling, where the server takes air from outdoors or natural water source in use, are found to be less energy consuming. These methods cut down the use of electricity required for air conditioning and helps in bringing down over all energy consumption to a very large extent.

The second big trend relates to the use of renewable energy in data centers. Most IT giants are now seeking to minimize the carbon footprint of their data centers through purchasing solar, wind and hydroelectric power. Furthermore, more companies are now focusing on the creation of carbon-neutral and zero-emission data centers, by investing in renewable energy, carbon credits, and energy efficiency. For instance, all the data centres of Google are run on renewable energy sources, and Microsoft has a target of net zero emissions in the year 2030.

4.2 Energy-Aware Algorithms

Efficiency enhanced algorithms are becoming more significant in sustainable computing as they work towards reducing the energy consumption within systems during computing. These algorithms can effectively schedule various tasks in such a manner that power consumption is cut down, for instance by running many processes on limited number of systems during periods of low traffic, or by varying the processing capacity in accordance to the load. For instance, the power management techniques such as dynamic voltage and frequency scaling (DVFS) adjust the power utilization of a processor based on the amount of workload. Other machine learning improvements also suggest that workload forecasts and system resource allocation can benefit from predictive models to operate at optimum energy efficiency. However, there are costs associated with computation and energy; some algorithms may deliver low energy, but this comes at the cost of performance and can lead to inefficiency in high usage. It is still a struggle to optimize both energy effectiveness and system performance(Jayasutha, D et al 20240.

4.3 Edge computing for energy efficiency

Another trend that is still evolving is edge computing which is believed to decrease energy consumption through decentralization. In edge computing, computing and storage are done at the end nodes that are closer to the data source rather than in remote data centers. This eliminates the quantity of data to be transmitted over the network and hence the energy used in transmitting data over the network. With the more processing performed at the edge, edge computing can also help to lower the energy demands of distributed systems and enhance system performance (Anusha, S, et al 20240. However, to further improve the energy consumption of the system, there is the need to determine the right time to perform local computation and the right time to perform offloading in the cloud. Certain tasks can be completed by the local device, such as IoT sensors, while other tasks may still be aided by the computational capabilities of the cloud. The problem is to determine which amount of local and cloud processing is optimal to consume minimal energy.

4.4 Low-Power Hardware Innovations

The availability of low power hardware is of paramount importance for the reduction of energy consumption of the computing systems. There are new energy-efficient CPUs, GPUs and new specific hardware like ASICs (Application Specific Integrated Circuits). For instance, ARM processors, which are popular in mobile applications and other embedded systems, have a reputation for being low power processors and consuming less power than the x86 processors. Further, novel materials are being considered for the next generation of more environmentally friendly hardware. For instance, graphene has potential in the creation of future generation semiconductor devices because it is known to more effectively and with lower energy loss transmits electricity than the silicon chip. Moreover, there are possibilities to transform energy consumption in computing by using quantum computing. Quantum computers are yet to go mainstream but have the potential of solving some problems much faster than current conventional computers such as cryptography and complex simulations while using less energy.

4.5 AI and Sustainability

Significantly, AI is applied in managing energy consumption in complex systems, such as the energy grid. Based on the machine learning approaches, the energy consumptions can be predicted and then managed to avoid wastage of energy(Begum et al 20240. For instance, it is possible to predict the demand for data center services in advance and fine-tune the consumption of resources such as cooling and servers on the fly. Other sectors can also be made to have lesser energy consumption by adding AI into the equation. In smart grids, AI assists in the management of electricity and in smart buildings, AI controls heating, cooling and lighting. In addition, other AI applications like predictive maintenance can contribute to cutting energy consumption in manufacturing by pointing out where in the production line there is energy waste due to inefficient machinery. These innovative trends are making sustainable computing the new generation of computing to shape the green IT industry. Through the use of new algorithms, hardware and AI technologies, the computing sector has the potential to contribute to the solutions to problems of climate change and resource depletion(Singh et al 20240(Yadav 20240.

5. SUSTAINABLE SOFTWARE DEVELOPMENT PRACTICES

Sustainable software development practices are all aimed at creating programs that demand less energy while delivering or even improving on the performance of the software. Such practices are very crucial in that the software aspect of the computing systems plays a central role in making information technologies less costly to the earth. The main subcategories of sustainable software development include: green software engineering, software hardware efficiency, as well as virtualization and containerization (Aswini, J et al 20240.

5.1 Green Software Design

Green software design is the act of designing and implementing software in ways that allow it to consume less energy. It refers to coding techniques and algorithms that allow work to be done with less computational resources. There is one evident paradigm, and it is the optimization rules that have a direct effect on the amount of processing and, therefore, the energy consumption of the system. Several coding best practices are important in green software design. For instance, simplifying the code reduces the number of resources needed in executing the software hence improving on performance and energy consumption. Algorithms that complete tasks in the most resource-friendly manner as possible are also important in green software development. This is because energy is consumed in processing and storing data as well as the memory space used in a particular operation; therefore, algorithmic solutions that reduce the utilization of these resources will go a long way in reducing energy consumption in large-scale systems. The other concept of green software design is the low-energy algorithms concept; These are algorithms developed to have the same capacity as their other demanding counterparts but with the use of lesser energy. For instance, the data processing algorithms can be made more efficient in terms of the number of operations used, or the manner in which data is processed, in order to lessen the amount of computation needed and the energy demanded. Furthermore, energy profiling and testing are conducted during the software development life cycle to avoid a software product accruing large energy expenses when in use. Accounting and reporting of software energy consumption is another tool and technique that must be used for the identification of energy wastes.

5.2 Software Optimization for Hardware

As for the optimization of the software for hardware, the software has to be made to work in harmony with the hardware devices, so that the energy is used efficiently. The concept in a nutshell is to ensure that the software being created is compatible with the hardware as much as possible, in the sense that the energy used is as low as possible, while the performance is as high as possible. For instances, specific hardware optimizations can be as follows: the full range of instructions supported in processors, the enabling of low power features such as DVS, or writing codes that are compatible with other hardware like GPUs or FPGA devices. It is possible to achieve much greater energy efficiency simply by writing the software that is more compatible with the hardware's architecture. Another important feature is the parallelism, that is the division of tasks into sub-tasks, which can be solved in parallel with the help of several processors or cores. When workloads are divided among parallel structures, it is possible to significantly decrease the amount of time during which each processor needs to be operational, and thereby, decrease the energy consumption. However, this must be done systematically with a view of optimizing the use of multi-core processors by the software without invoking extra costs such as energy consumption. However, there are still options, which can be implemented by the compiler, which would optimize the generated machine code, thus making the software run better on the hardware. For example, compilers can choose more energy efficient special instruction sets, use less time for memory access and use fewer instruction cycles for computations.

5.3 Virtualization and Containerization

Containerization and virtualization are technologies that enable many applications to share hardware resources, and since resources are shared, there is better power utilization. It is a method through which one physical hardware or software can accommodate one or more than one VMs where each of the VMs behaves as an individual system. This approach means a rational utilisation of the available hardware resources such as the processors, memories and storage utilities. As the workloads are consolidated onto fewer physical hosts, virtualization minimizes the amount of new hardware needed and therefore reduces energy consumption. Likewise, containerization enables applications to operate in isolated surroundings known as containers which are resource light and have same kernel as the host OS. Containers are more efficient than virtual machines because they need less resource to run, are lightweight and can boot up faster. Because containers allow applications to efficiently share system resources, they minimize the requirement for multiple operating system instances to operate, saving energy. Server consolidation stems from both virtualization and containerization and leads to better usage of hardware, thereby cutting on energy usage. Moreover, scaling of the application is also easier with the help of these technologies because these technologies provide resource utilization factor that means that resource is utilized time to time when required and there is no wastage of resources, which are idle most of the time.

Altogether, green software design, hardware optimization, and virtualization/containerization are the three strategies that can be called a complete strategy of sustainable software development. In this way, developers can decrease the energy demand of software systems and, thus, participate in the overall minimisation of the environmental footprint of computing.

6. RENEWABLE ENERGY INTEGRATION IN COMPUTING SYSTEMS

One of the important steps to making technology sustainable is the incorporation of renewable energy into computation systems. As awareness of the environmental costs of power consumption in data centers, servers, and other computing facilities has arisen, solar and wind energy are increasingly becoming critical components of sustainability in computing. Besides, it is imperative to improve battery and energy storage technology required to store and use renewable energy for powering computing systems.

6.1 Solar and Wind Energy in Data Centers

Data centers are one of the biggest power consumers as they are needed to sustain the servers, cooling systems and other related facilities. In an effort to cut their carbon emissions and decrease demand for fossil fuels, more and more data centers are now using solar and wind as their primary sources of power. These forms of renewable energy are not only ways for reducing the amount of greenhouse gases emitted but also means for achieving long-term cost-effective solutions for energy supply. Solar energy has become an attractive clean energy source for powering data centers. Companies can install solar panels at the facility, or at least at the vicinity of the data center, to generate electricity from sunlight and not necessarily from the grid. Most particularly solar energy is useful in areas of high solar intensity, it is a constant and reliable source of energy. In some of these cases, firms like Google, Amazon and Microsoft have been actively installing solar systems to provide power to their data centers with the goal of achieving net-zero emissions. Likewise, wind energy can also be employed in the powering of data centers especially in areas where the wind is strong. Onshore or offshore wind farms can produce massive electricity that can be fed into a grid or directly to the data center. For instance, Microsoft has embarked on partnership agreements with wind energy producers to supply it with electricity generated by wind power. However, incorporating renewable energy in data centers has the following challenges. The first is the variable nature of power generation from sources such as solar and wind power. Solar power is only available during the day while wind power is not very reliable throughout the year. This make it hard to solely rely on renewables especially in regions where the weather conditions keeps changing. In order to overcome this challenge, data centers require to use renewable energy together with backup power sources or energy storage systems. It is also important to note that there are issues to do with scale when it comes to using renewable energy in large data centers. To increase the size of the installed solar and wind, capital-intensive investments in infrastructure are needed, and the integration of renewable energy into data center facilities entails various engineering challenges, including energy storage and power networks.

6.2 Battery and Energy Storage Solutions

Because solar and wind energy are inconsistent, the need for battery and energy storage that will store the excess energy produced in the day for use during the evening and night. Technological improvements which include lithium-ion batteries, flow batteries, and solid-state batteries are important to guarantee power supply to computing systems. Lithium-ion batteries are popular in data centers where they are used to store energy produced by solar or wind plants. Such batteries have high energy density and efficiency, this means that data centers can store a substantial amount of energy in a small space. However, there are still problems that are related to the expense and durability of these batteries, and the need to frequently recharge as well as to maintain them. Another challenge is to develop efficient large-scale storage systems; two of the most promising types of storage systems are flow batteries that store energy in liquid form. Flow batteries have a longer cycle life and are better suited for larger scale applications which makes them ideal for data centres. Nevertheless, they are still young technologies and may require further development to match more mature solutions. For future work, the combination of smart grids with energy storage solutions seems to be another promising approach in managing energy load. A smart grid makes it possible to fine tune the manner in which electricity is distributed, so that data centers can flexibly alter their energy usage in accordance with energy availability information. In this context, energy storage might be used to level the fluctuations of renewable energy and at the same time provide a constant supply of energy without relying heavily on conventional sources of electricity such as those based on fossil fuels.

In general, combining renewable forms of energy like solar and wind into computing systems along with the development of batteries and energy storage is key to decreasing the effects of the tech industry on the environment. These innovations offer the potential of a new, cleaner and more efficient data centre and computing ecosystem, one that is able to deliver lower carbon footprints, and a much higher proportion of renewable energy sourcing.

7. SUSTAINABLE NETWORKING AND COMMUNICATION SYSTEMS

As the need for connection rises, the use of networking and communication systems has surged due to the proliferation of data-oriented technologies. To reduce the impact of networking infrastructure on the environment there is a need of energy efficient protocols for networking, integration of next generation wireless networks like 5G and sustainable IoT solutions. These developments are directed at enabling lower power consumption while at the same time enabling high performance and the rising traffic caused by new applications.

7.1 Energy Efficient Networking Protocols

Protocol structures are fundamental to any communication system since they define how data will flow in a network. In order to improve sustainability, energy efficient protocols in networking have been established to reduce the amount of energy needed in transmitting data and at the same time being efficient in their performance. One important innovation is Energy Efficient Ethernet an enhancement of the Ethernet standard that allows network devices to decrease their energy use when the link is inactive. EEE makes it possible for a device to simply switch off some of its functionalities and reduce power consumption while maintaining data rates. This technology is more applicable in the large network scale like data center and enterprise network because of the large power consumption in the idle devices. Other technology that has the potential to enable energy efficiency in networking is the optical networks. Asymmetric copper-based cables are far from energy efficient, especially when the bandwidth requirements are higher. Other types of networks such as the optical Fiber networks are more effective in terms of ability to transmit data signals faster, at higher rates with less energy when used over long distance. The advancement of all optical networks and optical switching systems continues to minimize the use of electronic equipment's that consume lots of energy making networks more efficient in handling larger data traffic. Others include software defined networking (SDN) and network function virtualization (NFV) that are also attributes to energy saving due to their flexibility on network resource management. These technologies enable the dynamic management and control of networks and eliminate power wastage by adapting the path that traffic should follow as well as the amount of hardware to be used.

7.2 5G and Beyond

A new generation of wireless communication technology, 5G, is expected to deliver much higher data rate, lower delay and higher reliability. However, it also poses problems in terms of power consumption because of a large number of low-powered base stations as well as the traffic volume that they will have to support. Nonetheless, 5G networks are developed with energy savings as one of the key considerations and it is endowed with several features of sustainability. Another appeal of 5G is that it can support network slicing, this means operators can allocate resources more to suit application requirements. In this manner, network slicing minimizes the energy consumption to meet the peak traffic demand by efficient resource utilization. Moreover, 5G is anticipated to apply more efficient hardware and transmitters to send a particular amount of data using a minimal amount of power when compared to the previous cellular generations. Future work towards 6G and beyond will pose more attention to energy efficiency for wireless communications. These technologies are anticipated to build on the progress made in artificial intelligence (AI) to enhance network operation and energy management in real time. For instance, AI can anticipate the traffic that a network will experience and then control the amount of resources allocated to that network at any one point in time so as to minimize energy consumption.

7.3 Internet of Things (IoT) and Sustainability

The Internet of Things, IoT, is an ever expanding web of connected objects, from home appliances to industrial sensors, which has the potential of greatly improving energy efficiency and sustainability. IoT devices operate on battery power or low power wireless connection and in many cases are suitable for low power consumption designs and therefore can have a low carbon footprint(Solanki et al 20190. Another of the major IoT trends is the emergence of low power IoT devices and low power wide area networks (LPWAN) which enable IoT devices to work with low power. These devices are intended for long term usage, sometimes even years, with small batteries, and are not frequently recharged, or their batteries replaced. These low power networks employ standard like LoRaWAN and NB-IoT for range and energy efficiency for communication. The other rising tendency is energy harvesting for IoT systems. Harvesting on the other hand entails getting energy from the surroundings; this could be solar, thermal or mechanical power and then converting it into electrical energy to fuel the IoT devices. This technology is very important for IoT devices that are installed in areas that may not be easily accessible, making battery replacement a pricey affair. For instance, the sensors in smart cities that are connected to solar can detect environmental conditions without using power from the grid, thereby saving on energy as well as the costs of maintenance. In addition, energy-optimizing IoT systems are now being designed and built to use energy as per their data sensing. They involve real time adaptation of their operation in response to available energy resources. For example, IoT devices can go into low power dormant modes whenever they are inactive or transmit less often to prolong battery life. In business to business industrial IoT applications, energy management systems can monitor and analyse data from multiple connected devices to optimize energy use thus increasing the efficiency of its usage. Overall, the management of sustainable network and communication systems is essential to minimize the environmental cost of digital networks around the globe. Thus, through the creation of key energy efficient protocols, the adaptation of 5G and future generations, as well as the utilization of IoT innovations such as low power devices and energy harvesting within the telecommunications and networking fields, the industry is able to contribute to achieving a more sustainable and energy optimal digital environment(Sudha, K et al 20230.

8. CHALLENGES AND OPEN RESEARCH AREAS

Despite the advances made towards the goals of green computing, there are several issues and research questions left unanswered that need to be solved to bring about large scale integration of energy-efficient technologies. These challenges include but not limited to the technological and economic issues of achieving efficiency and balancing between energy and performance, as well as other research opportunities that may transform the field.

8.1 The technological and economic factors

One of the greatest challenges that many organisations face in the implementation of sustainable computing technologies is the cost that is usually incurred on these innovations. Some of the technologies like energy efficient hardware, renewable energy integration and efficient cooling systems involve very high capital costs. For instance, constructing the green data centers, using the renewable energy sources or including the low power hardware is much more costly than the traditional systems. To cater to these high upfront costs, create a major challenge for most organizations especially those in the Small and Medium Enterprises to adopt sustainable computing solutions. However, the actual implementation of the renewable energy systems in large scale computing systems is not an easy task. Solar and wind are renewable energy sources and they have the problem of being unreliable in that they are not always available. For those classes of computing systems that require a steady and dependable source of power, the application of renewable energy sources entails the application of advanced energy storage technologies and smart grid systems. This integration also brings questions of cost and feasibility of energy storage systems as well as the requirement for energy management of the renewable energy produced. Also, a vast majority of current data centers and computing facilities were constructed without much consideration of sustainability and incorporating green energy and efficiency into them is a challenging and costly venture.

8.2 Energy–Performance Trade-offs

Another significant problem which is closely related to the general topic of sustainable computing is the antagonistic relationship between power consumption and performance. For most of the time, it is possible to attain optimum energy efficiency at the expense of performance and vice versa. For example, decreasing the power requirements of a processor would lead to decreased computing speed or decreasing the energy usage in network protocols to reduced bandwidth or throughput. This trade-off is well applicable in High Performance Computing (HPC) systems where computational performance is a major concern. Applications involving heavy computations such as scientific analysis, financial analysis, artificial intelligence etc., call for high power capacity. Meeting these performance requirements and energy efficiency is however a challenge since measures that can improve the energy efficiency of a system for example by reducing the frequency of the processor, or using efficient algorithms may affect the system throughput or response time. Also, virtualization and cloud computing technologies frequently try to achieve high levels of resource utilization in the interest of energy efficiency, which can sometimes lead to over-committed systems or latency. The problem of achieving performance requirements of the target application, while consuming minimal energy, still remains an unsolved one in the context of the design of efficient power-aware computing systems.

8.3 Future Research Directions

The other important focus of research is low-energy hardware. This encompasses such aspects as energy efficient processors, memory systems, and energy saving circuits among others. Sustainable computing is also believed to benefit from quantum computing as a key disruptive technology. Quantum systems can solve some classes of problems much faster than classical computers and, therefore, save energy in specific tasks, such as cryptography and optimization. The other promising application area is the use of artificial intelligence in energy management. AI is useful for managing energy consumption at real time by observing energy consumption patterns and load regulation. Self-learning algorithms can be developed in order to forecast and control the energy demand in a rather accurate way, thus, to provide the energy saving without loss of the system efficiency. Also, AI can be also used for optimization of energy consumption in data centers and network infrastructures, where cooling, power supply and workload distribution can be managed dynamically depending on environmental conditions as well as available energy resources. In the field of software sustainability, the research mainly aims at reducing energy consumption in software development processes. This includes green software design principles that compel software developers to author code that uses less resources while also being effective on the hardware. The next generations of the software tools might be able to analyse the code and show where further energy optimization is possible without affecting performance. Last but not the least, future research direction towards sustainable cloud computing is identified. Cloud providers are always seeking ways to make their cloud more sustainable by using renewable energy and energy-efficient technology Achievement is still hampered by large, complex-scale challenges. Investigations into more efficient carbon cloud structures and green cloud services will prove valuable in helping cloud service providers minimize the carbon footprint. In conclusion, there are many technological and economic challenges to the drive towards sustainable computing but there are also considerable opportunities for creative developments. The main themes include understanding and addressing energy-performance trade-offs, enhancing the efficiency of the hardware, utilizing AI for energy-efficient computing, and advancing the principles of sustainable software development will be critical in determining the future of computing. Studies in these fields will aid to forge new strategies to develop power-conscious and energy-efficient information processing system to cater the increasing demands of the information age with minimal impact on the environment.

9. CONCLUSION

Through this paper, the author has discussed those trends and innovations identifying how sustainable computing is progressing to mitigate the environmental issue. There is a great advancement in efficient hardware, green data centers, and renewable energy sources into computing systems. The utilization of artificial intelligence in energy management, edge computing, and low-energy IoT devices also indicates more efficient and localized solutions to energy extremes. Awareness of energy utilization, virtualization, as well as containerization, have been seen to reduce energy consumption of both software and hardware. Business giants Google, Microsoft, and Amazon are at the forefront, adopting carbon-neutral data centers and driving sustainable cloud computing. Furthermore, the incorporation of renewable electricity, including solar and wind electricity, to these systems is also lowing their impacts on the environment. Quantum computing along with AI integrated resource management is the future of sustainable computing as it has been determined above. Some of these innovations can help to cut energy usage by as much as half while at the same time improving or at least preserving computational capabilities. Low energy hardware and energy efficient software will keep improving to create a future where computing systems are drastically less energy hungry. Smart grids' integration together with sustainable energy will also contribute more to the shift towards green computing. To accomplish all of these objectives, cross-disciplinary work is crucial. Scholars, practitioners, and policy makers need to define standards, policies, and technologies for sustainability in the context of the current and future global society. The approach is to put the goals of the industry, the knowledge of academic institutions, and the rules of governments to create sustainable computing and make a great contribution to the decrease of the ecological footprint of the technological industry.

REFERENCES

Anusha, S., Ezhilvandan, M., Gayathri, S., Sivaraman, V., & Anish, T. P. (2024). Emerging trends in edge AI for Industry 4.0 and 5.0: Technologies, applications, and challenges. AI Innovations in Service and Tourism Marketing, 211-228.

Aswini, J., Sudha, K., Ganesh, G., Subramanian, S., & Ghinea, G. (2024). AI-powered parallel computing architecture and its applications. In *The convergence of self-sustaining systems with AI and IoT* (pp. 23–39). IGI Global. DOI: 10.4018/979-8-3693-1702-0.ch002

Begum, A., Naim, A., & Sabahath, A. (2024). The Impact of AI on Sustainability. In *Harnessing High-Performance Computing and AI for Environmental Sustainability* (pp. 99–113). IGI Global. DOI: 10.4018/979-8-3693-1794-5.ch005

Jayasutha, D., Prabhu, R. V., Sassirekha, S. M., Maithili, K., Girija, P., & Subramanian, R. S. (2024). Exploring the Intersection of Sustainable Energy, AI, and Ethical Considerations. In AI Applications for Clean Energy and Sustainability (pp. 139-160). IGI Global.

Jeong, Y. S., & Park, J. H. (2020). Security, privacy, and efficiency of sustainable computing for future smart cities. *Journal of Information Processing Systems*, *16*(1), 1–5. DOI: 10.3745/JIPS.2006.2.1.001

Lokesh, G., Devi, B. R., Badrinath, N., Anjaiah, P., & Kumar, T. R. (2024). Green Computing and the Quest for Sustainable Solutions. In *Computational Intelligence for Green Cloud Computing and Digital Waste Management* (pp. 24–41). IGI Global. DOI: 10.4018/979-8-3693-1552-1.ch002

Pitchai, R., Tiwari, S., Viji, C., Kistan, A., Puviarasi, R., & Gokul, S. (2024). Green Technologies, Reducing Carbon Footprints, and Maximizing Energy Efficiency with Emerging Innovations: Green Computing. In *Convergence Strategies for Green Computing and Sustainable Development* (pp. 86-110). IGI Global.

Prabha, D., Subramanian, R. S., Dinesh, M. G., & Girija, P. (2024). Sustainable Farming Through AI-Enabled Precision Agriculture. In Artificial Intelligence for Precision Agriculture (pp. 159-182). Auerbach Publications.

Saxena, A., Gupta, K., & Pala, S. (2024). Convergence Strategies for Green Computing and Sustainable Development. In *Convergence Strategies for Green Computing and Sustainable Development* (pp. 62–85). IGI Global.

Sharanya, S., Vijayalakshmi, V., & Radha, R. (2024). Achieving Green Sustainability in Computing Devices in Machine Learning and Deep Learning Techniques. In *Computational Intelligence for Green Cloud Computing and Digital Waste Management* (pp. 172–186). IGI Global. DOI: 10.4018/979-8-3693-1552-1.ch009

Singh, J., Chugh, A., & Singh, A. K. (2024). Sustainability in the Age of AI: Exploring Challenges and Innovative Solutions. In *Convergence Strategies for Green Computing and Sustainable Development* (pp. 1-16). IGI Global.

Solanki, A., & Nayyar, A. (2019). Green internet of things (G-IoT): ICT technologies, principles, applications, projects, and challenges. In *Handbook of research on big data and the IoT* (pp. 379-405). IGI Global.

Sudha, K., Ambhika, C., Maheswari, B., Girija, P., & Nalini, M. (2023). AI and IoT applications in medical domain enhancing healthcare through technology integration. In *AI and IoT-Based Technologies for Precision Medicine* (pp. 280–294). IGI Global.

Sung, Y., Sharma, P. K., Lopez, E. M., & Park, J. H. (2016). FS-OpenSecurity: A taxonomic modeling of security threats in SDN for future sustainable computing. *Sustainability (Basel)*, *8*(9), 919. DOI: 10.3390/su8090919

Yadav, A. (2024). Leveraging Artificial Intelligence for Sustainable Development and Environmental Resilience. In *Exploring Ethical Dimensions of Environmental Sustainability and Use of AI* (pp. 140–165). IGI Global.

Chapter 14
Green Artificial Intelligence and Machine Learning:
Strategies for Sustainable Development

E. Indra
https://orcid.org/0009-0004-8465-3419
Mailam Engineering College, India

I. Vasudevan
Vel Tech Rangarajan Dr. Sagunthala R&D Institute of Science and Technology, India

M. Arthy
SRM Institute of Science and Technology, India

K. Hemakumar
Adhiparasakthi Engineering College, India

S. Deepa
R.M.D. Engineering College, India

A. Rizwanbasha
https://orcid.org/0000-0002-3934-8616
Panimalar Engineering College, India

P. Girija
https://orcid.org/0009-0000-1691-8180
Vel Tech Rangarajan Dr. Sagunthala R&D Institute of Science and Technology, India

ABSTRACT

AI and Machine Learning technologies have been on the rise in the recent past, and as this happens, there have been growing concerns over the energy they consume and their carbon footprint. This paper offers a systematic literature review of Green AI and ML, which discusses approaches deployed to reduce the environmental impact of these technologies without compromising their effectiveness. We address

DOI: 10.4018/979-8-3373-0766-4.ch014

Copyright © 2025, IGI Global Scientific Publishing. Copying or distributing in print or electronic forms without written permission of IGI Global Scientific Publishing is prohibited.

the environmental impacts of largescale AI models and data centers categorizing energy efficient algorithms, model compression, and low power hardware as the main ways to approach the energy issue. Moreover, we discuss different aspects of AI usage for environmental protection with examples in renewable energy management, climate change tracking, and eco-friendly farming. Data management best practices including federated learning and sustainable dataset creation are also highlighted. Lastly, we discuss future research areas and trends that hold potential to improve the sustainability of AI and ML.

1. INTRODUCTION

1.1 Overview of AI and ML's Growing Role in Various Industries

AI and ML have turned into the core components of the development of numerous industries including healthcare, finance, manufacturing, transportation, and entertainment[Nadella et al 2023]. AI is bringing changes in areas such as predictive analytics, automation, data processing, and decision-making that help industries to increase efficiencies, decrease costs and create better customer value[Mohamed et al 2023]. Of this, Machine Learning, a subfield of AI, makes these innovations possible because it enables systems to devise their operations from data without prior coding. By using AI and ML technologies, their applicability is increasing and this is helping world economy to enhance productivity[Raghunath et al 2023].

1.2 The Environmental Impact of AI and ML

Although AI and ML have tremendous advantages, the exponential increase in their usage has led to massive environmental impacts, especially in energy consumption and carbon footprint. The training process of big neural networks, especially deep learning ones, consumes a lot of computational resources, which in its turn, consumes a lot of energy. The computation of these models is done by data centers, physical structures that require significant power to operate and much of this power comes from carbon sources. This has raised questions of sustainability of these AI technologies particularly as more organizations get to adopt their use. The effects of AI on the environment are worsened by energy consumption of cooling systems that is required in data centers.

1.3 Definition of Green AI and ML

Green AI is the process of creating and implementing artificial intelligence systems and related technologies while being environmentally friendly [Verdecchia et al 2023]. These are elements such as energy efficiency, minimizing the use of computational resources, and making improvements to AI models in the aspect of reduced carbon impact. Green ML, in the same way, deals with the application of machine learning algorithms that are energy efficient and affect the environment least. The goal is to attempt to improve the sustainability of AI systems while not having to compromise on performance and value. Green AI includes practices like powering data centers with renewable energy, designing AI models that need fewer computations, and employing low-power hardware. It also seeks to develop AI models with lower levels of resource demands as much as possible while delivering the same or even higher results[Verdecchia et al 2022].

1.4 Scope and Importance of Green AI for Sustainable Technological Development

The increasing use of AI and ML in industries shows why Green AI is important because technology should not be a negative influence on the environment. As the use of AI increases and it becomes even more integrated into industries it is important that its advancement is sustainable. Green AI offer a way through which these technologies can be made environmentally friendly hence being in line with the global shift towards sustainability. Furthermore, the effort towards energy-efficient and environmentally sustainable AI applications is not only required for saving resources but also for responding to climate change challenges. In this regard AI is used as a tool to minimize energy consumption and as a subject that needs to be made more energy efficient. It is therefore important that this development is energy efficient to enable long term sustainable development of technology in the economy as well as the environment. The value of Green AI is in the fact that it can help to achieve proper utilisation of the AI technologies that won't cause negative impacts on the environment and at the same time can contribute to different industries, help to solve their problems, make them more efficient, and support the sustainability agenda.

2. ENVIRONMENTAL IMPACT OF AI AND ML

2.1 Energy Consumption of Large-Scale AI Models

Another major environmental issue that is linked with the AI and ML is the high energy demand that is needed to train the models especially the deep learning models and large language models. These models which may need billions or even trillions of parameters may need a lot of computational power. Training a model of this scale can even take days, weeks or even months depending on the level of complexity and amount of data processed. The energy consumed in training these models is proportional to the number of computations or the number of 'floating-point operations' necessary to modify the parameters, and, generally, the more parameters, the greater the energy expenditure.

2.2 Carbon Footprint of Data Centers and High-Performance Computing (HPC)

HPC systems and data centers form the infrastructure of today's artificial intelligence. These premises accommodate the physical infrastructure for data used in training AI models and the hardware for AI inference (model deployment). The power consumption of these data centers forms the largest part of AI's ecological footprint. Computing centers are power hungry facilities because of the computations that are conducted in them and also because of the cooling systems required to cool the server racks. It is estimated that cooling takes slightly less than half of the energy used in data centers, since the high-performance machinery runs continuously and produces heat. The type of electricity that is used to power the data centers also determines the carbon footprint of the data centers. When the energy is drawn from sources such as coal or natural gas, emissions are much larger than in those data centers that utilize renewable energy from solar panels or wind turbines. Another aspect is that large-scale systems for research or for training artificial intelligence models, so-called high-performance computing systems, also have an impact on the environment. HPC systems or High-Performance Computing systems that are intended for data analysis and simulation will consume a lot of power. Their power consumption is even more when they are used to train new generation AI models that require parallel computation across the multiple processing units.

2.3 Key Challenges in Reducing AI's Environmental Impact

They argue that the environmental cost of AI does not end with the energy the system uses in training. Several issues arise when it comes to mitigating this effect and three of them are computational, energy, and scale challenges in the use of AI.

Computational Resources: Training state-of-the-art models requires using powerful processors, including GPUs and TPUs, which are, however, energy-intensive. Expanding the size of these resources raises the computational overhead because each new parameter or data point entails more computation. While advancements in hardware efficiency, such as more energy-efficient chips, can mitigate some of these issues, the underlying problem remains: here are some facts: as models become larger, they demand exponentially more resources.
Energy Consumption During Training and Inference: Specifically, during model training, the computational requirement is the highest and thus consumes much energy. But even after the model is trained, the energy consumption is high during the inference (when the model is used to make predictions). This is particularly the case with models used in real-time applications where recurrent inference incurs regular operational energy expenses. Improving inference operations is always vital, but in real-time systems, it is critical to minimize energy consumption.
Data Storage and Transfer: The need to store and process the huge volumes of data required in training AI is also a factor that raises the costs of stewardship of the environment. The storage systems, especially the cloud storage are other systems that use energy and space. Energy consumption is also high during the transfer of large datasets to and from data centers. Such approaches can reduce the need for data transfer by keeping the data local, as in the federated learning technique, and so on; however, they are not suitable for all cases.

Therefore, the major concern of AI and ML is the large amount of energy required to train the large models, the energy demand of the data centers and HPC systems, and the optimization difficulties. Solving these problems will be critical to the future of AI development that would be more friendly to the environment.

3. GREEN AI AND ML: KEY CONCEPTS AND APPROACHES

3.1 Definition and Principles of Green AI

Green AI can be defined as the practice of building AI systems that are energy efficient, low cost, and have a low carbon impact on the environment for AI processes. Green AI focuses on the fact that environment aspects must be included into AI development life cycle in order to have the benefits of AI technologies for the advancement of technology, and in the same time, to have the positive impact on environment[Sharanya et al 2024]. Key principles of Green AI include:

Efficiency: Making certain AI systems run as efficiently as possible, meaning they use the least amount of energy and computation. This strategy is basic on efficient algorithms, optimized hardware and scalable systems.

Sustainability: Green AI aims at combining new development technology with sustainable environment goals. It promotes the adoption of green energy in data centers, energy-efficient hardware, and AI systems that demand less energy to run.

Fairness: The final relevant social impact is guaranteeing that positive consequences of AI's implementation are available to all and do not negatively affect the environment or particular groups. This also includes guaranteeing that the growth of energy efficient AI does not reduce access to these technologies in low resource contexts.

3.2 Energy-Efficient Algorithms

Energizing algorithms is one of the most essential strategies that can efficiently decrease the environmental effects of artificial intelligence. These algorithms are supposed to reduce the computational overheads needed for training and prediction, hence reducing the energy consumption. Several techniques can be employed to achieve this:

Pruning: This means the process of eliminating unnecessary weights and connections in a neural network. This work shows that through model pruning, it is possible to decrease the size and thus the complexity of models, which in turn would make it require fewer computations and thus less energy during training and making predictions.

Quantization: This means that the model weights and activations have to be represented with less digits which makes computations easier. The novel model enables lower precision operations that take up fewer resources and consume less power while maintaining acceptable degree of accuracy.

Knowledge Distillation: This technique applies the knowledge between two models; the large complex model (teacher) and the small efficient model (student). The student model tends to perform a similar to the teacher but with less resources which results in a lot of energy being saved.

3.3 Model Compression Techniques

Model compression is a process of transforming the large and complex AI models into leaner and more effective models without a drop in performance. Common strategies include:

Weight Pruning: A special kind of pruning wherein unwanted parameters in a neural network are eliminated so that the number of computations in the training and inference stages are minimized. This is good for the models making them smaller and faster besides lowering the energy that they use.

Parameter Sharing: It is a technique that helps to decrease the amount of distinctive parameters in a model as several weights may have the same value. This approach lowers the memory load and the computational burden necessary to develop models, which in turn hews to more efficient models.

Low-Rank Factorization: It entails the process of breaking down weight matrices into even lower ranks and this can effectively decrease the number of parameters and most importantly the computational complexity of such parameters. This makes the model less computationally expensive and more advantageous in terms of computational time during training and prediction.

3.4 Low-Power AI Hardware

As for the second element of AI technologies, low power AI hardware is also important for decreasing the environmental cost of AI. Some examples include:

TPUs (Tensor Processing Units): From the Google, TPUs are themselves specifically designed for deep learning and are even faster and draw less power than other GPUs in the market. TPUs are built for big models in training, as well as inference, and the energy expense is lowered considerably.

Neuromorphic Chips: These chips replicate the architecture of the human brain and intensify the kind of processing such as pattern analysis and training. As compared to the conventional hardware, neuromorphic computing consumes far less power, and is therefore suitable for applications that are sensitive to power consumption such as AI.

FPGA-based Designs (Field-Programmable Gate Arrays): FPGAs are hardware devices that can be reconfigured to perform computations required by AI applications to the highest level of efficiency. They can be employed to run AI workloads more quickly than general-purpose processors, while using less power.

3.5 Sustainable Machine Learning Pipelines

In simpler terms, sustainable ML pipelines imply efficient ML processes that consume as little energy as possible at every stage in the ML process[Choudhury et al 2024]. This includes:

Data Preprocessing: Simplifying data processing activities to decrease power consumption through reduction of data and rationing storage. Data preparation and cleaning can actually help to reduce the amount of computational work required when training the model[Subramanian et al 2024].

Model Training Optimization: Applying techniques like stopping criteria, learning rate schedules, and distributed training to minimize the resources used during training, which will in turn minimize the time taken for large scale training.

Deployment and Inference Optimization: Ensuring that the models used for real-time predictions are power efficient, perhaps by applying model pruning or using the models on power-efficient chips.

In conclusion, Green AI and ML are the approaches that can guide the creation of the effective AI systems with the help of the environmentally friendly tools. To achieve this, the integration of energy-efficient algorithms, model compression strategies, and low-power hardware is achievable to minimize the impact of AI technologies on the environment. More sustainable machine learning pipelines continue this efficiency of AI systems across their entire life cycle and reduce the influence of AI on the environment[Prabha, D et al 2024].

4. GREEN AI IN DEEP LEARNING AND LARGE-SCALE MODELS

4.1 Strategies for Energy-Efficient Deep Learning Training

Training deep learning models, particularly the large-scale models with billions of parameters, is a power-hungry process that requires massive computing power. To reduce the environmental impact, several strategies have been developed to optimize energy consumption during the training phase:

Efficient Hardware Utilization: Making use of low power hardware like application specific processors like TPUs, GPUs can decrease the power used in training the deep learning models. Furthermore, as a result of distributed computing systems, resources could be optimally exploited in parallel processing systems.
Adaptive Learning Rates: Some of the methods which might be useful in regard to the speed of convergence during training include adaptive learning rates like the Adam optimizer. The convergence speed determines how many iterations are needed, and this cuts down the computational and energy demands.
Mixed Precision Training: There are ways to reduce the training computational cost, for instance, by using less accurate floating point precision (for example, 16-bit floats instead of 32-bit) that does not affect the model's performance. It decreases memory requirements and increases the training pace, which in turn decreases power consumption.
Early Stopping: This means observing the model's performance when learning and stopping when the model has ceased to learn anymore. Early stopping is a technique that helps to avoid unnecessary computations since the training process is terminated when further enhancements are insignificant.

4.2 Use of Model Distillation and Transfer Learning

Two of the main ways that can help to decrease the amount of computations needed to train large models, hence make them less energy-hungry are model distillation and transfer learning.

Model Distillation: This is a procedure by which the knowledge contained in a large and elaborate "teacher" model is copied to a smaller and more efficient "student" model. The student model is designed to replicate the teacher's behavior and, as a rule, it employs fewer parameters and less computational resources. By extracting knowledge from large-scale models, the trained and deployed model consumes less energy compared to other large scale models at a similar accuracy.

Transfer Learning: Transfer learning is the practice of using knowledge from a model trained on similar task, allowing a small model to use the knowledge of a large model. This approach addresses the problem of training models from scratch as it requires far less data and computational power to train. It assists in the sharing of knowledge more effectively, and it also decreases the power usage while at the same time enhancing operation productivity.

4.3 Scaling Down Large Models for Practical, Energy-Efficient Deployment

Reducing large AI models for deployment in real-world applications without losing much of their efficiency is one of the challenges within Green AI. Several techniques are employed to achieve this:

Model Pruning: Pruning is a technique by which an extremely large model is made smaller and less demanding by removing parameters not needed for computation. Simplifying the connections removes or reduces the dependency between variables, and therefore reduces computational power needed without compromising the accuracy of the model.

Quantization: Quantizing the parameters of the model from floating-point to fixed-point representation reduces the model size and improves the inference time. This process also also tries to reduce memory usage and energy usage at the time of deployment, which makes it easier to deploy models in low power environments.

Knowledge Distillation: As pointed out, knowledge distillation makes it possible to scale down big models into smaller ones that can be easily deployed for use in real-life situations. The smaller, distilled models are usually intended to run on mobile platforms, or edge computing devices which have less computational power, and thus consume less energy.

Edge AI: The current approach of using the AI models in the cloud servers may lead to a high energy consumption by the servers since it involves frequent transfer of data and requires real-time computation without the use of edge devices. Edge AI means that many computations can be performed locally, and not so many would require the help of servers.

Thus, Green AI in the context of deep learning and large scale models is important to enhance and optimize training processes, scale down models for the efficient deployment of models, and to reduce the actual requirement of computational resources with techniques such as distillation and transfer learning. The case studies prove that such approaches result in massive energy saving; therefore, energy conservation approaches should be implemented to minimize AI's influence on the environment without reducing its efficiency.

5. EFFICIENT DATA MANAGEMENT IN GREEN AI

Data management is another essential aspect of Green AI because the manner in which data is processed, stored, and transmitted has a direct bearing on the carbon footprint of the AI systems. If data flows are well managed and decentralized systems are employed in data processing, energy consumption in data processing can be reduced.

5.1 Data Preprocessing and Storage

Data preprocessing and storage are two of the most critical activities in AI processes whereby energy efficiency can be significantly improved if optimized. One of them is the reduction of data redundancy – a typical problem in big data, where a large number of records contains very similar, or completely unnecessary, information for the model. From experience, it is known that raw data contains many records that are mostly redundant and temporal and optimizing the cleaning and filtering processes can aid in minimizing the amount of storage space as well as the computational power required to conduct analysis on the data. Other methods of data storage for energy efficiency include data compression. The idea of pre-processing of datasets before storing them on disk makes storage require less space thus saving energy, especially where large and frequently used datasets are involved. In addition, data preprocessing such as feature selection that involves the deletion of irrelevant features in datasets can improve model performance by removing noise, which in turn will save energy during model training as well as during the prediction phase. Also, distributed storage systems consume less energy, as data is usually located nearer to the computing assets where it will be processed, without the necessity of long distance data transmission. Other standard procedures that enhance data access patterns (for example, accessing data in bulk instead of in segments) also improve energy efficiency.

5.2 Federated Learning and Distributed AI

FL and DAI are novel solutions which decentralise data processing, and hence the carbon footprint of data transfer and computation, greatly. Federated learning is a type of learning in which data never leaves the device (for example, smartphone, IoT device) while a model is trained on multiple such devices[Shahi, A., & Mittal, A. 2024]. It transmits only the gradients of the model, not the actual data to a central server for its training. This eliminates the need for extensive data transfer from one centralized data center to another, or the computational load incurred to analyze large amounts of data in a particular center[Dhatterwal et al 2025]. The second advantage of federated learning is as follows: privacy enhancement; the data also remains local, making the application of artificial intelligence more sustainable and ethical. Although the computations done locally in federated learning still require energy, the distributed approach minimises the need for huge data transfer, which is energy intensive and carbon-costly due to cloud computing. Likewise, distributed AI systems employ varied nodes such as edge devices or small data centers to process data at once, thereby, not overloading one server. Through distribution of computation, AI systems can be effective, especially in regions with limited resources, and do away with the large data centers.

5.3 Green Data Centers

In other words, the environmental cost of AI comes down to green data centers as the most critical component. AI data centers are not energy-efficient; conventional data centers require a lot of energy for the execution of AI models as well as for cooling. To increase efficiency of these centers many companies are focusing on utilization of renewable energy like solar and wind energy. Other measures that are also being implemented involve the use of efficient coolants like liquid cool or even better air cooling methods that require less energy to cool the gadgets. Moreover, new data centers are also adopting self-optimizing systems that use artificial intelligence in order to control both processing loads and cooling systems in a way that minimizes power consumption. On the other hand, edge computing is slowly becoming another approach to the traditional centralized data centers. Because edge computing performs more computations near the source of the data, less data has to travel long distances to a central server, saving energy. It also increases the computational resource utilization since edge devices perform localized computations while sending only crucial data to the cloud.

5.4 Sustainable Dataset Generation

Data acquisition and preparation for AI model learning is another component where energy usage can be minimized. Efficient data creation means the generation of high quality and real world datasets with low computational cost for their generation. This can be accomplished by minimizing the carbon footprint of the data collection process, for instance by employing fewer energy hungry techniques of data collection or opting for synthetic data gathering procedures. Furthermore, there is the concept of data augmentation which acts to increase the size of the training data without necessarily require acquisition of new raw data. For instance, creating new data points from the existing data such as rotating the image, adding some noise, or creating simulated data is much more effective and efficient that collecting new data on one's own.

The second strategy is efficient training based on the availability of small but informative data sets. This is helpful in that it limits the data necessary to build an efficient model, thus also reducing the power needed to go through a vast amount of data and also the power needed to store such huge data sets. In conclusion, data management can be considered a key priority of Green AI; there are several approaches that can be taken to minimise the environmental cost of AI systems. Such measures are enhancing data preprocessing and data storage, federated and distributed learning, green data centers and efficient computation, and green dataset creation. In combination, these approaches allow for the development of strong and at the same time environmentally friendly AI solutions.

6. AI FOR ENVIRONMENTAL SUSTAINABILITY

AI in its general definition has a significant role in achieving sustainable development in the environmental sector, and resource efficiency, environmental and ecosystem surveillance, and renewable energy. The application of AI in sustainability processes can help to decrease carbon emissions, increase the levels of energy use effectiveness, and increase our effectiveness in addressing critical environmental issues. Here are some areas where AI applications are making remarkable efforts in the area of environmental sustainability.

6.1 Overview of AI Applications in Environmental Sustainability

AI is gradually being applied in different industries towards achieving environmental management. Key applications include:

Energy Management: AI algorithms are used to generate forecasts on the energy consumption and to enable utilities to better match demand in the market. ML models can predict energy consumption, and energy companies can respond immediately, avoiding inefficiency and blackouts. In smart grids, AI plays a crucial role in the decentralization of energy from the renewable sources such as the sun and wind.

Smart Cities: Artificial Intelligence solutions are critical to the formation of smart cities where infrastructure is utilized most efficiently. AI systems operate traffic signals, garbage disposal, and water supply, lowering the general consumption of resources. For instance, intelligent traffic signals depend on current traffic flow information to reduce traffic jam and fuel usage. Other applications of advanced intelligent systems involve the control of the street lamps to ensure they use as little energy as possible while providing adequate lighting.

Resource Optimization: AI is applied in the management of natural resources with an aim of extracting, using and recycling the resources. For example, AI algorithms can detect that the existing production process is suboptimal and optimize the recycling of materials. AI also plays an important role in the proper utilization of water in agriculture, industrial uses and in the urban setting.

6.2 AI in Renewable Energy

AI is, therefore, becoming more relevant in increasing the efficacy of the sources of renewable energy including solar, wind, and hydroelectric. Key contributions include:

Solar Energy Optimization: AI plays a great role in managing solar energy generation including but not limited to; weather forecasting to determine the best sites for installation, positioning of solar panels for maximum capture. Satellite images are used by AI algorithms to determine the effectiveness of solar farms and the potential arrangement of solar panels. It also can predict the output of solar energy production and facilitate its integration into the power system.

Wind Energy Optimization: AI improves the function of wind turbines in the sense that it estimates wind velocity and direction, the performance of the wind turbines as well as general maintenance expenses. Machine learning can also look at the usage of components in a turbine to determine when it needs repair in a bid to enhance efficiency instead of waiting for a breakdown to occur. AI's ability to predict the wind power changes means that there is consistency in energy production.

Smart Grid Integration: Therefore, AI enables the efficient incorporation of renewable energy into the power grid since the availability of energy supply and demand is always fluctuating. These fluctuations are minimized by AI algorithms to avoid the complete dependence on non-renewable sources of energy and stability of the grid.

6.3 AI for Climate Change Monitoring

AI is a useful development in monitoring climate change, as it allows scientists to monitor changes in the climate, future climate circumstances, and reduce the impact of climate change. There is a potential to develop machine learning algorithms to parse through big amounts of environmental data to draw conclusions and predict climate changes[Sreelakshmi, S, et al 2024]. Key applications include:

Climate Modeling: AI enables the rapid computation of climate information such as atmospheric and oceanic data, and concentrations of greenhouse gases. It is possible to develop algorithms that in turn will help governments and various organizations determine further climate changes for the purpose of climate change adaptation and prevention.

Pollution Tracking: Artificial intelligent based system control air and water pollution and offer pollution details to enhance the health of the public and the environment. Satellite imagery interpreted by AI can measure the pace of deforestation, growth of cities and identify pollution zones for subsequent policy action. For instance, AI is applied in determining places where methane leaks from pipelines, or where emissions from landfills are originating from, so as to mitigate on them.

Disaster Forecasting: AI is used in the identification of natural calamities including hurricanes, floods, and wildfires. Using historical weather data and current weather and environmental data, AI models can then give out early warnings to communities enabling them prepare and reduce the impact of such disasters. AI systems also help in organisation and management during disasters, as well as helping in decision-making processes during the disaster.

6.4 AI in Smart Agriculture

One of the sectors which can be benefited most by using AI to promote sustainability is the agriculture sector. Precision agriculture solutions using artificial intelligence are designed to improve the efficiency of resource utilisation, enhance yields and minimise adverse impact on the environment. They are emerging as essential in meeting the issues of climate change, population, and food consumption.

Precision Agriculture: By utilizing machine vision, drone monitoring, and sensor networks, AI helps with precision farming by supplying data on crop status, soil state, and water consumption in real-time. This makes the farmers to make better decisions, recover their costs and expenses, and get better utilization on usage of resources. A case in this category is the ability of AI in irrigation systems to control water usage depending on the moisture levels of the soil to avoid over watering.

Reducing Waste: AI also assists in providing solutions to food wastage since it can predict the demand and the right supply. Through an integration of machine learning models of weather patterns, crop yields, and consumers demand patterns, farmers and retailers can also be able to plan and schedule the production and distribution of their produce to avoid the production of excess food that is likely to go to waste.

Sustainable Pest and Disease Control: Thanks to AI some crops can be monitored for pests and diseases so the farmer can apply targeted method rather than using broad spectrum pesticides. This helps in decreasing the use of chemicals which in turn help in preserving the environment and the biological diversity.

Artificial Intelligence is now a critical tool in driving environmental conservation in fields including energy control, farming, climate change, and renewable energy sources. The application of AI in the improvement of renewable energy sources, precision agriculture and environmental pollution monitoring, reduction of resource use, climate change, and optimization of environmental management systems is immense. With the advancement in AI technology, society is expected to deploy AI more in an effort to solve global sustainability challenges of the 21st century.

7. ENERGY-EFFICIENT MACHINE LEARNING TECHNIQUES

In the case of machine learning (ML) models, with the increased complexity of the models, the amounts of energy required in training and using the models have increased significantly. In order to increase the efficiency of machine learning, both from the economic and environmental point of view, numerous approaches have been proposed. Such methods are low resource ML methods, energy aware training, sparse representation, all of which improve the efficiency of machine learning and reduce the impact on the environment.

7.1 Low-Resource ML Techniques

Low resource machine learning methods are centered on the features of model efficacy and the scarce computational resources, data and time available. Some of the most effective low-resource learning methods include:

Few-shot Learning: Few shot learning (FSL) is a machine learning technique, which allows the models to learn from only a small set of labeled samples that helps to minimize the amount of data and computation power used in training process. In the traditional models of ML, more often the large datasets are required to get a good quality model. Nonetheless, meta-learning and other few-shot learning methods enable models to learn from only a few samples, reducing the energy needed for both training and predictions by orders of magnitude.

Transfer Learning: We see that transfer learning is the practice of using models trained on a large amount of data and applying them to smaller datasets. Unlike training a model from the ground up, transfer learning adjusts an already existing model to a particular task and saves much time and computing power. This approach negates the need for extensive data processing, and the models can do well with less resources thereby making the overall energy consumption of the model small.

Zero-shot Learning: Another kind of approach is known as zero-shot learning (ZSL) where the models can predict on tasks that they have never encounter before in the past. ZSL functions by propagating knowledge from other related tasks and assumes the correct result even when no samples of the task are available. This approach does not require extra training data and the energy used in training new models for each task is minimized.

7.2 Energy-Aware Training

Energy-aware training targets at reducing the energy which is used in the training phase or process. Several strategies can be employed to achieve this:

Adaptive Training: Other forms of training involve the flexibility of changing the level of training depending on the result produced in a particular period. For instance, the model may initially use a basic structure that does not demand a lot of resources with the complexity of the model increasing only when the model's performance requires it. This kind of adaptive approach minimizes the wastage of computations hence using lesser energy in the training process.

Smart Hyperparameter Tuning: Hyperparameters define the dynamics of machine learning models and can be a determinant of energy usage. In traditional methods of hyperparameter tuning such as grid search or random search, many model evaluations are needed to achieve the best value. Other efficient methods such as Bayesian optimization can be employed to search the hyperparameter space more wisely than random search, and as a result fewer iterations are performed hence less energy is consumed. These approaches can enhance the training process so that they consume fewer resources, while achieving high model accuracy[Lakumarapu, S et al 2024].

Early Stopping and Checkpointing: To avoid such occurrences, early stopping methods observe the performance of the model over a validation set during training and stops the process as soon as the model starts to over-fit or when the performance ceases to improve. Checkpointing preserves the intermediate results of the model, so you don't have to train it from scratch, which again helps to save computational resources and energy.

7.3 Sparse Representations

Sparse representations are a subfield of machine learning that aims to solve the problem of a high computational complexity by representing data or models with fewer parameters. Techniques like sparse coding and pruning fall under this category:

Sparse Coding: Sparse coding is a technique in which the representation of the data is done using a small number of non-zero parameters. This method decreases the number of dimensions in representations of data and the amount of calculations in the training and using a model. When using a small number of features, models can perform as well as when using a large number while consuming less energy.

Model Pruning: The techniques include removing or setting small weights or neurons to zero, removing less important weights, neurons, or layers. This particular technique greatly reduces the computational complexity since there are fewer parameters to keep track of and update. Since pruning removes the least relevant portions of a model, it can increase the speed of processing and decrease memory consumption, in other words, minimize the power consumption of the model.

Quantization: Another technique to make these models sparse is quantization. It means using fewer bits in calculations namely 8 bit integers instead of a 32 bit floating point number. This makes the model less memory intensive and faster to process while offering similar level of accuracy. This results in a low energy consumption profile in both the training phase and the testing phase of the model.

Not only pruning and quantization, another technique which is low rank factorization is where large matrices used in models are replaced by lower rank matrices. This lessens the amount of time it takes to do matrix computations and can greatly reduce the power used throughout training and prediction.

Some of the main challenges are the energy-efficient approaches to machine learning, low-resource ML techniques, energy-efficient training strategies, and sparse representations of AI systems. Reduced data hunger, reduced model complexity, transfer learning, few-shot learning, and zero-shot learning reduce the need for large datasets and sophisticated models, while adaptive training and intelligent hyperparameter tuning reduce the energy consumption of the training process. Sparse representations for example sparse coding and model pruning lower the computational complexity of the models even further by making them less complex. Combined, these approaches offer a more efficient way to create highly effective machine learning models that are optimized for performance and power, in order to make AI more eco-friendly.

8. CHALLENGES AND LIMITATIONS TO GREEN AI & ML

As the global interest in Green AI and energy-efficient ML increases the potential for sustainable AI growth there are several compelling challenges that need to be addressed. These are; sacrifices in the model performance, problems of scale, data protection and ownership, and the moral question of the effect on the environment and advancement of technology.

8.1 Trade offs Between Model Accuracy and Energy Efficiency

The first major concern in Green AI is the optimization of the trade-off between model performance and energy consumption. Most of the advanced machine learning models particularly deep learning models need huge data, computational power and energy for the improved accuracy[Subha, S et al 2024]. Techniques which are proposed to decrease model size, such as pruning, quantization, and knowledge distillation, are usually associated with the decline in model performance.

For instance, when pruning a neural network, some weights or neurons which are not significant in decision making are trimmed down in order to decrease the size of the model and the amount of computation. This could however lead to a faster and more efficient model but at the same time, it could lead to less accurate or more over-fit models or models with low generality. Like quantization, quantization can result in loss of precision, which despite improving the efficiency of the models degrades the quality of the model. The problem lies in the fact that while it is possible to lower the energy consumption of models, it is still hard to do it without much loss in performance, which is currently still a major issue for Green AI.

8.2 Scalability Challenges in Green AI Approaches

Another major issue of Green AI is the scalability problem. A number of strategies for reduction of energy consumption that appear beneficial on small-scale studies or for particular purposes may not be efficacious in large-scale applications. With the increase in model sizes, for instance in the large scale NLP models such as GPT-3, the computational needs for training and inference are also significantly high. Acting to scale down such models and at the same time not lose efficiency and accuracy of the model, or when attempting to implement more energy-efficient approaches is a challenge. However, distributed AI systems and cloud computing platforms that are used in large-scale model training have scalability problems when it comes to Green AI. For example, federated learning which trains models to reduce energy consumption and enhance data privacy may not readily deploy in settings with millions of devices. Some of these challenges include; network bandwidth constraints, synchronization of these large decentralized systems and the computational costs that could negate the energy efficiency gains of these approaches.

8.3 Data Privacy and Security Concerns

Integrating energy-saving approaches as federated learning or edge computing often tries to empower the data processing at the edges to minimize data transmission to central hubs, and hence energy utilization. Although federated learning can be the solution which keeps data on local devices, this approach poses data privacy and security concerns. Because the training data are stored on users' devices, the system needs to ensure that personal or sensitive information is protected. This makes one worry about data leakage, model inversion attacks, as well as adversarial manipulation.

However, the decentralised models have to be secured as well. In federated learning, multiple devices together learn a common model, but it is complex to make all devices update the global model while keeping the data private. FL systems have to use encryption, differential privacy, and secure aggregation to safeguard the user data, all of which add computational cost and they may offset the energy benefits of adopting decentralized learning.

8.4 Ethical Concerns: Balancing Environmental Impact with Technological Advancement

Last but not least, ethical issues in Green AI are on the one hand associated with the minimization of the negative effects of AI on the environment, and on the other – with further development of technologies. As much as Green AI is about sustainability, it is also about creating new ethical issues. For example, through promoting the models of energy-saving products the there may be forces to implement them without taking into account their negative effects on society. These technologies might worsen the situation if the advantages of Green AI are not shared by all or energy-efficient systems are intended for the rich or developed countries while the others have no access to them. In addition, there is an ethical question about whether we should optimize AI for environmental sustainability at the expense of other environmental and social qualities such as fairness, transparency and inclusion. Energy savings are important but it cannot be achieved at the expense of being unfair in decision making or in ensuring that the AI is accessible for use by everyone. The aim should be to create AI systems that consume less power as well as those which do not perpetuate unfairness in their application, thus the AI systems should enhance the quality of life across all users.

Green AI and energy-efficient machine learning are two critical topics when it comes to developing sustainable AI systems. But there is still a lot of work to do: the choice between accuracy and energy, the problem of scaling up, privacy and security, and the problem of ethics. Solving these issues involves more attention and research on the ways to achieve efficiency in AI while keeping its CO2 emissions at the lowest level. The future of AI development should be a collective effort of researchers, AI industry representatives and policy makers to make AI development both sustainable and fair.

9. CASE STUDIES AND REAL-WORLD IMPLEMENTATIONS

This has resulted in several novel real-world use cases of Green AI which not only contributes to saving energy but also helps to achieve the overall sustainability agenda more efficiently. Several domains, healthcare, financial, industrial IoT, and energy management, are integrating AI solutions that address sustainability. This section will investigate examples of Green AI success, real-world examples of Large Scale AI Energy Efficiency, and AI for Sustainability.

9.1 Successful Implementations of Green AI in Various Sectors

Healthcare: AI has been instrumental in the reinvention of healthcare systems, and Green AI is now supporting efficiency in this area. For example, AI diagnostic tools are used to scale down the amount of medical imaging data needed, thus allowing healthcare organizations to decrease energy use tied to data storage and analysis. Moreover, predictive models used in the optimization of the hospitals' resources, including the prediction of the flow of patients or the utilization of equipment, will greatly decrease energy consumption in hospitals since operation and utilization will be efficient with minimal waste. Through optimization of the processes, Green AI in healthcare may also contribute to energy and environmental saving.

Finance: In finance, it is common to apply AI systems to take a more efficient way to control the energy consumption within trading algorithms and risk management. For instance, AI models that mimic market trends and financial data analysis that can lower the energy output of high-frequency trading activities by employing optimized computation approaches. In addition, Green AI solutions can assist financial institutions to evaluate and regulate environmental and social risks in the context of sustainable finance and implement sustainability factors into the investment processes to make more sustainable financial decisions.

Industrial IoT: Green AI for the IIoT is concerned with efficient management of energy in industrial processes. AI models analyse data from sensors that are installed in machines and systems used in industrial processes in order to observe and control energy consumption. These models can forecast equipment failure, control high energy demanding process and recommend alterations in operation that would reduce energy usage. For instance, in factories, predictive maintenance by use of artificial intelligence can assist in making the right decisions on the use of machinery to avoid replacement and unnecessary consumption of energy.

Since the market is increasingly demanding the use of AI and ML technologies, the necessity to reduce the energy consumption of the solutions is also increasing. Regarding these challenges, there are several trends and research areas that can be defined and studied in order to develop further the energy-efficient AI: innovations in AI hardware, the link between AI and global sustainability, the appearance of regulations, and the improvements of the lifecycle of the AI systems.

10. FUTURE TRENDS AND RESEARCH DIRECTIONS

10.1 Advances in AI Hardware for Energy-Efficient Computing

In the case of AI systems, one of the most promising areas for enhancing the energy efficiency is the creation of new and improved AI hardware. Prior computation paradigms relying on CPUs and GPUs are not always suitable for power consumption of AI models especially deep learning ones. Therefore, substantial advances are being made in the design of specific hardware which is better suited to AI operations.

Neuromorphic Computing: It is a form of reconfigurable hardware implementation based on the biological neurons to process information. These systems consume less power than conventional computers because they compute with analog circuits and event driven structures.
Quantum Computing: Another horizon of energy efficient AI is quantum computing. There are problems which quantum computers can solve exponentially faster than classical computers which may greatly decrease the energy needed for optimization, simulation and machine learning. Even though quantum computing is not yet mature, it has the ability to transform AI by solving the problem of the high energy consumption of computing large amounts of data. Quantum hardware is expected to grow with efficiency as part of the promising future of energy reduction for AI.

10.2 Role of AI and ML in Driving Global Sustainability Initiatives

Both AI and ML are expected to continue to grow in their importance in the world's sustainability initiatives. These technologies have already shown efficiency within energy use, effectiveness of waste, and sustainability of cleaner systems. Going forward, AI will contribute to several key sustainability initiatives:

Climate Change Mitigation: AI models are also being applied in promoting renewable energy, predicting climate, and controlling green house effects. There's potential to use AI to forecast the availability of renewable energy like solar and wind to optimize the use of clean energy in the grid. It also helps in tracking emission, which in turn aids in better climate change mitigation programs.

Resource Management: AI can make the utilisation of natural resources more efficient by enhancing the use of water, minimising energy consumption and optimising supply chain. For example, AI models are already in use in determining the optimal use of water in crop growing and in cutting down the consumption of water in industries to improve on the conservation of the resources.

10.3 Development of Global Standards and Regulations for Reducing AI's Environmental Impact

With the increasing awareness of the effect of AI on the environment there has been a call for the creation of international norms and standard and regulatory frameworks. The governments, international organizations and the industry associations are awakening to the reality that, they need to come up with structures that would enable sustainable development of these artificial intelligence technologies.

Regulations for Energy Efficiency: Like any other industry AI could be regulated by energy efficiency in all aspects ranging from data center, hardware design to the efficiency of algorithms. Thus, AI energy consumption and carbon emissions' standards will contribute to creating demand for the improvement of more sustainable AI technologies.
Carbon Footprint Reporting: New legislation may demand that developers of AI and organizations provide the amount of CO2 emissions their AI systems have produced during model training and inference. This paper has argued that it will be important for AI to become more transparent about its effects on the environment in order to encourage people to take action to reduce emissions.

10.4 Research on Improving the Lifecycle of AI Systems

Optimization of the AI system lifecycle is another research dimension that is helpful in increasing energy efficiency. AI models are generally known to have a high computational footprint not just in training but also in inference leading to high energy usage during their lifetime.

Efficient Development and Deployment: There is a growing interest in the methods that seek to minimize the energy consumption of intelligent systems from start to finish. The energy-efficient training strategies that are adaptive to the energy consumption during the training process are being proposed. These are methods such as adaptive learning rates, early stopping techniques to prevent training when the performance is stagnant and even hardware-aware optimization to ensure that the AI models are trained to work well with energy efficient hardware.

End-of-Life Energy Efficiency: Another such area of research is enhancing energy efficiency of AI at the deployment phase. One such technique is model compression that helps in reducing the size and complexity of the models without much compromises on the performance. Also, transfer learning and federated learning are proposed to address the energy concern when training new data or improving models with distributed datasets.

Green AI has a bright future as new hardware, software, and legislation are developed in the future. Neuromorphic computing and quantum computing are two recent advancements that still hold the potential to bring radical change in AI's energy consumption. As the same time, AI is going to be the key driver in the next phase of environmental stewardship, as it can help solve global sustainability problems, including climate change and resource management. It is only possible to optimize the use of AI and reduce its impact on the environment if industry leaders set the global standards and think about the life cycle of the systems they develop. With ongoing research, AI systems will have an important role in the future of energy efficiency of systems as well as the future of the environment.

11. CONCLUSION

Therefore, this paper postulated that the environmental cost of AI & ML technologies is a relevant topic of study as the use of the technologies grows within organizations. Despite their tremendous benefits, these technologies, especially the large-scale models and data-intensive processes are incredibly energy hungry and add a significant carbon footprint to data centers and high-performance computing. However, as AI stays on the rise, the problem of its environmental impact remains more and more relevant. The value of Green AI is increasing gradually, which points to the emerging trends of creating AI solutions that are more sparing in terms of their impact on the environment and energy consumption. Green AI is an attempt to minimize the environmental impact of AI with a stronger focus on the efficient resolution of energy problems in the elaboration of efficient algorithms, low power hardware, and the optimization of methods of managing data. This means that today's advanced AI technologies like neuromorphic computing, model compression, and energy-aware training techniques are on the frontline in efforts to annually reduce the energy costs of Artificial Intelligence systems. In addition, as per the positions reflected by CI, acknowledging the corresponding ramification of the breakthrough on environmental goals, AI is also capable of positive contributions comprising stimulating global sustainability goals that range from renewable energy entrepreneurship to resources enhancement. However, to have the long-term real sustainable future, there is a need for research and development in efficient energy AI and ML systems. These are: the creation of new AI hardware; the enhancement of AI system's life cycle to minimize energy consumption; and the setting of international standards for energy and carbon footprint reporting. Multi-stakeholder dialogue with businesses, government and academicians will prove instrumental in ensuring that artificial intelligence development does not lag behind the increasingly pressing issue of sustainability. Finally, Green AI is not just the implementation of sustainable innovations but the moral duty of society. This means that we need to make AI energy efficient solutions a priority and to continue to push the pace of development in this important field. The use of AI in research and development means a cleaner world tomorrow as the efforts being invested today dictate the impact of AI on the environment.

REFERENCES

Choudhury, R. R., Roy, P., Ghosh, S., & Ghosh, A. (2024). Machine Learning and Deep Learning Algorithms for Green Computing. In *Computational Intelligence for Green Cloud Computing and Digital Waste Management* (pp. 1–23). IGI Global. DOI: 10.4018/979-8-3693-1552-1.ch001

Dhatterwal, J. S., Malik, K., Kaswan, K. S., & Elngar, A. A. (2025). Federated Learning: Overview, Challenges, and Ethical Considerations. *Artificial Intelligence Using Federated Learning*, 1-15.

Lakumarapu, S., Nithyanandhan, R., Bhargavi, V. S., Anish, T. P., & Nalini, M. (2024, August). Machine Learning Approaches for Liver Disease Prediction: A Comparative Analysis. In 2024 5th International Conference on Electronics and Sustainable Communication Systems (ICESC) (pp. 159-164). IEEE. DOI: 10.1109/ICESC60852.2024.10689974

Mohamed, N., Almazrouei, S. K., Oubelaid, A., Bajaj, M., Jurado, F., & Kamel, S. (2023, June). Artificial intelligence (AI) and machine learning (ML)-based Information security in electric vehicles: A review. In *2023 5th Global Power,Energy and Communication Conference (GPECOM)* (pp. 108-113). IEEE.

Nadella, G. S., Satish, S., Meduri, K., & Meduri, S. S. (2023). A Systematic Literature Review of Advancements, Challenges and Future Directions of AI And ML in Healthcare. *International Journal of Machine Learning for Sustainable Development*, *5*(3), 115–130.

Prabha, D., Subramanian, R. S., Dinesh, M. G., & Girija, P. (2024). Sustainable Farming Through AI-Enabled Precision Agriculture. In Artificial Intelligence for Precision Agriculture (pp. 159-182). Auerbach Publications.

Raghunath, V., Kunkulagunta, M., & Nadella, G. S. (2023). Enhancing Data Integration Using AI and ML Techniques for Real-Time Analytics. *International Journal of Machine Learning for Sustainable Development*, *5*(3).

Shahi, A., & Mittal, A. (2024). The Impact of Federated Learning on AI-Enhanced Healthcare Delivery. In *Pioneering Smart Healthcare 5.0 with IoT, Federated Learning, and Cloud Security* (pp. 57-66). IGI Global.

Sharanya, S., Vijayalakshmi, V., & Radha, R. (2024). Achieving Green Sustainability in Computing Devices in Machine Learning and Deep Learning Techniques. In *Computational Intelligence for Green Cloud Computing and Digital Waste Management* (pp. 172–186). IGI Global. DOI: 10.4018/979-8-3693-1552-1.ch009

Sreelakshmi, S., Babu, A. A., Lakshmipriya, C., Gracious, L. A., Nalini, M., & Subramanian, R. S. (2024, October). Enhancing Intrusion Detection Systems with Machine Learning. In 2024 2nd International Conference on Self Sustainable Artificial Intelligence Systems (ICSSAS) (pp. 557-564). IEEE. DOI: 10.1109/ICSSAS64001.2024.10760341

Subha, S., Balakrishnan, C., & Anish, T. P. (2024, August). Optimizing Machine Learning Algorithms for Heart Disease Prediction in Healthcare: A Comparative Study. In 2024 5th International Conference on Electronics and Sustainable Communication Systems (ICESC) (pp. 866-872). IEEE. DOI: 10.1109/ICESC60852.2024.10689877

Subramanian, R. S., Yamini, B., Sudha, K., & Sivakumar, S. (2024). Ensemble-based deep learning techniques for customer churn prediction model. *Kybernetes*. Advance online publication. DOI: 10.1108/K-08-2023-1516

Verdecchia, R., Cruz, L., Sallou, J., Lin, M., Wickenden, J., & Hotellier, E. (2022, June). Data-centric green ai an exploratory empirical study. *In 2022 international conference on ICT for sustainability (ICT4S)* (pp. 35-45). IEEE.

Verdecchia, R., Sallou, J., & Cruz, L. (2023). A systematic review of Green AI. *Wiley Interdisciplinary Reviews. Data Mining and Knowledge Discovery*, *13*(4), e1507. DOI: 10.1002/widm.1507

Chapter 15
Sustainable Digital Transformation Through Energy-Efficient Edge and Fog Computing

Venkata Ramana Kaneti
VNR Vignana Jyothi Institute of Engineering and Technology, India

B. Senthilkumaran
https://orcid.org/0000-0002-7111-1950
Vel Tech Rangarajan Dr. Sagunthala R&D Institute of Science and Technology, India

K. Dhivya
SRM Institute of Science and Technology, India

B. Chitra
Panimalar Engineering College, India

T. Nithya
https://orcid.org/0009-0006-8784-1305
Rajalakshmi Institute of Technology, India

B. Yuvasri
R.M.K. College of Engineering and Technology, India

V. Arunkumar
https://orcid.org/0009-0003-7296-145X
Mallareddy College of Engineering, India

ABSTRACT

With the demand for realtime data processing and effective management of resources, edge and fog computing have become the key solutions for sustainable development issues in the digital world. This survey paper provides an overview of edge and fog computing and their application in enabling sustainable practices across sectors with less energy consumption and carbon footprint than cloud computing. In this context, we explore the structures and main elements of edge and fog computing,

DOI: 10.4018/979-8-3373-0766-4.ch015

Copyright © 2025, IGI Global Scientific Publishing. Copying or distributing in print or electronic forms without written permission of IGI Global Scientific Publishing is prohibited.

focusing on energy-related approaches, local data processing benefits, and green hardware solutions. Moreover, we look at other application areas like smart cities, health care, industrial IoT, and agriculture where real-life successful cases with sustainable impact are also illustrated. The paper also discusses issues and drawbacks of the solutions such as security issue and the issue of compatibility between different solutions. This survey has underlined the importance of edge and fog computing to support the sustainable development in the world that becomes more interconnected.

1.INTRODUCTION

The terms Edge and Fog computing are recent trends developed to overcome the shortcomings of cloud computing by providing computational resources nearer to the end user and the data. The two models are designed for minimizing latency, increasing bandwidth utilization, and increasing processing power at the network periphery(Ometov et al 2022). These technologies have the potential of enhancing sustainability in a world that is rapidly going digital through the provision of better resource efficiency and minimized energy consumption, reduced carbon emissions.

1.1 Definition of Edge and Fog Computing

Edge computing is a distributed computing paradigm in which computing and data processing are done near the source of data such as on the IoT devices, the gateway or local servers(Kumar et al 2019). This means that there is little need for large amounts of information to be sent to centralized cloud data centers, which can be a very slow and resource consuming process. In edge computing, edge nodes are responsible for computing, decision making and real time analysis so that response time is faster and dependency on cloud is reduced. In contrast to the fog computing, which is an extension of the edge computing, an additional layer is introduced between the edge devices and cloud. Fog nodes are actually in the middle of the hierarchy, they collect data from edge devices, process it locally and then provide other necessary information to the cloud or other higher tier resources(Jain et al 2016). This intermediate layer is somewhat useful in decisions about load distribution within the network and can assist in preventing overloading of both edge and cloud infrastructures. Combined, edge and fog computing enable the effective distribution of data processing tasks across networks, making it possible to meet the ever increasing demand for IoT gadgets and real time data processing.

1.2 Overview of Sustainability Challenges in the Digital Era

With development of the digital technologies, the environmental factor that comes into play has also evolved. The growing popularity of cloud-computing infrastructure has led to high energy consumption from the large scale operation of data centers. These data centers, however, are highly effective in generating large amounts of carbon emissions that worsen the global climate. Further, the rapid increase of IoT devices and the volume of data being produced has become a problem in resource utilization, largely due to the fact that processing may occur in cloud data centers that may be quite distant from the end user. It also impacts sustainable challenges on the aspect of resource optimization. The original cloud paradigm is characterized by the need for extra hardware, computer equipment with low occupancy rates, and huge amounts of energy consumption for cooling equipment. Smart devices, IoT and connected systems are on the rise meaning more data requires processing in some form. This puts a lot of strain on existing networks, which means that finding more efficient ways of dealing with data is an important challenge.

1.3 Importance of Edge and Fog Computing in Promoting Sustainable Practices

These are realizable through edge and fog computing that provide potential solutions to these challenges owing to local data processing. Edge and fog computing take data processing closer to the source, meaning that there is less reliance on long distance data transfer to central cloud servers, and therefore less energy is consumed for data transfer and storage. In addition, these systems also mean better control of resources such as bandwidth and storage, meaning less demand on data centers and, therefore, less energy use. Edge and fog computing can thus help to decrease the expenses on both operation and environmental impact thanks to the diminished need for significant data centers. For example, in smart city solutions, the edge can process traffic data or energy consumption without frequent interaction with the cloud, which can both increase latency and energy consumption. Furthermore, fog computing's intermediate layer allows for better distribution of computations between devices and locations, and enables the implementation of efficient solutions for particular requirements.

1.4 Scope and Objectives of the Survey Paper

Thus, this survey paper will present a comprehensive understanding of how edge and fog computing support sustainability in the digital world. It will discuss the various architectures, advantages, and disadvantages of these paradigms to address the energy optimization, resources management, and carbon foot printing. Therefore, based on the analysis of the primary application areas and green protocols, the paper aims to demonstrate the pragmatic value of utilizing edge and fog computing for greener solutions. Moreover, the paper will review the current literature on this topic and define potential development directions for improving the sustainability of computing practices.

2. OVERVIEW OF EDGE AND FOG COMPUTING

Edge and fog computing are crucial to managing the productivity issue as a result of the skyrocketing amount of data produced by smart devices, the IoT, and real-time applications(Anusha, S et al . These paradigms tend to centralize computation and data storage to where data is produced in real time, this makes it faster, use less bandwidth and efficient. Edge and fog are two different yet related concepts that help to implement computing closer to the edge and the device.

2.1 Edge Computing

2.1.1 Definition and Architecture

Edge computing on the other hand is a distributed computing model whereby data is processed nearer to their origin, for instance, in IoT devices, sensors, or edge servers. In this model, those computational tasks that were previously handled in large centralized data centers are processed in the networks' periphery, which brings such advantages as faster data processing and lesser data to be sent to the cloud(Murthy et al 2021).

The architecture of edge computing consists of several key components:

Edge Devices: These are the devices that are producing data for instance sensors, IoTs, smart cameras and mobile gadgets.

Edge Nodes: These are the computing resources that are usually placed close to data source. These nodes collect data and perform analytics and decision making on the data without having to forward the data to cloud.

Connectivity: Devices and nodes use local networks or LPWANs so that information can be transferred between devices or nodes and nodes as quickly as possible.

2.1.2 Comparison with Traditional Cloud Computing

Conventional cloud computing assumes that computation takes place in centrally located facilities known as data centers. Data from the end-user devices is sent to the cloud for processing and storage This causes high latency bandwidth consumption and dependence on a continuous connection(Bhandari et al 2021). On the other hand, edge computing minimizes the instances under which data will be transferred across large distances since most of the computation occurs near the source reducing latency and bandwidth consumption. Also, edge computing can be more energy effective since it does not require sending large amount of data to remote servers.

2.2 Fog Computing

2.2.1 Definition and Architecture

Fog computing extends the idea of edge computing but adds a middle layer between the edge devices and the cloud. This intermediate layer known as fog shall be used to gather and filter data in order to simplify the process of analyzing data in the cloud or larger data centers(Bhambri et al 2022). It provides a more distributed and flexible computation to make data processed at various positions between the cloud and the end devices.

Key components of fog computing include:

Fog Nodes: These are middle devices most of which are positioned near the edge devices and are responsible for processing and filtration of data.
Gateway Devices: These devices are used to interconnect edge devices with fog nodes, where it collects information from different sources and forwards it to a specific fog node.
Connectivity: Fog computing needs sound communication interfaces to interconnect edge devices, fog nodes, and cloud services to enable data processing at each level.

2.3 Relationship between Fog and Edge Computing

Even though, edge and fog computing are similar in their objectives, which are to minimize latency, enhance utilization, and become more efficient, they vary in the sense that the former processes data on the edge, while the latter does it in the fog(Priyadarshini et al 2019). Edge computing is the idea of processing data at the device or network edge, while fog computing adds an extra tier of processing between the cloud and the edge. Fog computing is much more scalable and flexible because resources can be distributed among several fog nodes which means that there will be no overload of a certain fog node or cloud data centers(Dhanalakshmi et al 2024).

2.4 Use Cases and Applications

Edge computing and fog computing are used in different fields to bring efficiency and real-time decision-making solutions.

Smart Cities: The providing of infrastructure in smart cities in edge and fog computing such as traffic systems, street lighting and waste management. These systems can form real-time decisions that can help control energy, lessen traffic, and enhance public services because they process data locally.
Healthcare: Real-time health monitoring by wearable devices that gather data and process it on the edge is highly dependent on edge computing. Fog computing can help to aggregate medical data across devices and make faster decisions for improving patient outcomes while lessening the load on health-care central authorities.
Industrial IoT: In manufacturing, edge and fog computing help in the following areas; Predictive maintenance, real-time monitoring, and automation. Processing at the edge enables these machines to diagnose faults and alert operators in real-time and consequently, minimize unnecessary time off work(Ponmalar et al 2024).
Agriculture: In precision agriculture, fog and edge computing help in monitoring soil moisture, weather, and crop health in real-time. It makes it easy for farmers to make real-time decisions about watering, pest control and fertilizing hence making farming sustainable and reducing on the use of resources.

Therefore, edge and fog computing are revolutionizing industries by decentralizing the processing of data and enhancing system interaction. While edge computing deals with computation at the device level, fog computing adds an intermediate layer to enhance resource management making the system more effective and elastic for numerous use cases.

3. SUSTAINABILITY CHALLENGES IN COMPUTING

With every development in digital technologies, the effects on the environment have become more alarming. The original cloud computing paradigm which has been used to facilitate the centralized access and distribution of computing resources on a global scale, has a number of sustainability drawbacks such as high energy consumption, high latency and resource wastage. This is made worse by the growing need for more storage and processing of data in the current and future systems. This section discusses the sustainability challenges of the conventional cloud computing, the challenge of addressing large data and processing requirement sustainably, and data centers as source of emissions.

3.1 Environmental Impact of Traditional Cloud Computing

Conventional cloud computing models use centralized data centers to store server, storage, and network objects. Cloud services are beneficial in terms of convenience and flexibility as well as scalability but come with rather significant environmental impacts such as energy and resource consumption. Computers in data centers consume a lot of energy to run the equipment as well as to facilitate cooling of the hardware because servers produce heat during their operations. Several research works have indicated that data centres around the globe use about one percent of the world's power and this is expected to increase following the increasing use of cloud services. Furthermore, cloud computing services rely on fossil energy in many cases, which in turn raises the carbon cost of data storage and computing. While some of the tech firms have pledged to power their operations with clean energy, most data centers are still hooked on fossil energy. The use of these conventional energies also results in emission of greenhouse gases and climatic change. Another sustainability issue is the issue of latency which is characteristic of cloud computing. Data has to be transmitted large distances between end-users and central data centers, which not only creates a network problem but consumes extra power for the transmission. This is especially true for applications that need real-time processing including autonomous vehicles, industrial IoT, or health care applications where delay can lead to inefficiency, wastage of resources, and sometimes fatal consequences.

3.2 Challenges in Managing Large-Scale Data and Processing Demands

As the number of connected devices continues to grow due to the IoT and other emerging technologies, coupled with the growing amount of data in the world, the challenge of dealing with large volumes of data in a scalable and resource-friendly manner becomes more and more challenging. Cloud computing, however, provides a mechanism for scaling resources, usually at the price of power consumption. Data centers manage huge volumes of information and centralization results in high power consumption and resource demands with minimal focus on the spatial distribution of data.

The use of the cloud to store data also results in data duplication and ineffectiveness, as backup copies of data are placed in various locations for purposes of reliability and accessibility. This is not only a waste of storage space but also increases energy consumption of the storage system. In addition, cloud computing involves frequent transfer of data between data centers, and therefore increases the demand on networking equipment, which in turn, increases the load on the environment.

The continuous expansion of big data, the use of artificial intelligence and machine learning has put more strain on cloud structures. These applications need computational power and more computation power means more energy is consumed. To address this growth, enhancing the capability of the hardware while at the same time maintaining energy efficiency is a challenge that can be met through control of workloads, better design of the hardware, and data compression.

3.3 Role of Data Centers in Contributing to Carbon Emissions

Data centres are central to cloud computing and are one of the worst offenders when it comes to carbon emissions within the technology sector. Based on the reports from environmental organizations, data center industry across the global emits between 2-3% of global carbon emissions, and this is in par with the aviation industry. This figure also includes the cost of power used to run the hardware and the cooling systems that are needed for the equipment to operate at the right temperature. Particularly in the warm climates, high-power cooling systems are used, and this adds to the environmental problems faced by the data centers. These cooling systems use massive amounts of energy and most of this energy comes from renewable resources. Thus, today, many data centers are among the primary focuses of sustainable activities that include energy efficiency, renewable energy sources, and carbon footprint reduction. For some firms, the said goals have been achieved by offsetting costs of purchasing renewable energy sources and energy-efficient technologies; however, the enormity of data processing and storage necessitates continued exploitation of the environment. Consequently, exploring solutions to the sustainability issues arising from data centers is essential in order to lower the environmental impact of cloud computing services. Traditional cloud computing imposes certain environmental effects such as energy usage, latency and wastage of resources. Energy consumption and carbon emissions are areas where data centers have great importance in this impact. The ever growing needs of large scale data processing and management still presents a daunting task. Future development of cloud computing will require solutions to decrease energy consumption and increase resource productivity and environmental responsibility.

4. ENERGY EFFICIENCY IN THE EDGE AND FOG COMPUTING

A major advantage of edge and fog computing is energy efficiency and it is more efficient than traditional cloud computing. As a result, edge and fog computing limit the distance over which data is transmitted and the consumption of resources in cloud data centers. This section examines some of the approaches used in edge and fog settings in the consumption of energy, processing of data, and selection of sustainable hardware.

4.1 Energy Management Strategies

Techniques for Optimizing Energy Consumption

Power consumption is a major challenge in edge and fog computing, and more so as more and more devices are connected and data is generated. Several strategies are employed to optimize energy use in these decentralized environments:

Dynamic Resource Allocation: Another major strategy of controlling energy utilization is the dynamic provisioning of resources, which implies the distribution of computational resources depending on the current need. In edge and fog environment the resource such as processing power, memory, and storage can be dynamically provisioned based on the workload demand. For example, edge nodes may increase or decrease the amount of resources employed depending on real time data processing requirements while using energy optimally. This has mitigated the problem of wasted energy from underutilized resources as witnessed in the conventional cloud data centers.

Load Balancing: In distributed systems, load balancing strategies aim at distributing computational loads across edge and fog nodes. By avoiding the situation where a particular node is overloaded with work and ensuring that an optimal load is assigned to the nodes in a system, load balancing promotes conserving of energy. When nodes are overloaded they consume more power to process the tasks making them less efficient. System load distribution across the available nodes, including fogs, in a dynamic way enables better resource utilization and low energy consumption.

4.2 Data Processing and Storage Optimization

4.2.1 Local Processing Advantages

The most important benefit of edge and fog computing is the local processing. Since most of the computation and data analysis are done close to the source of data, the requirement of transmitting data for long distances to the cloud is minimized. This decreases the amount of energy required for transmittance of networks as well as the power required for cloud data servers. Real-time processing at the local level is possible, which is highly important for applications with low latency, like self-driving cars, smart communities, or health control systems. Since data is processed locally at the edge and fog nodes, the nodes can take a decision without having to wait for the cloud to compute, which saves time and energy. This decentralised approach also eases network load and optimizes the performance of the system since only the most imperative data is transferred to the cloud.

4.2.2 Cache and Data Aggregation Techniques

Data caching and aggregation is another way through which energy can be optimised in edge and fog computing. Data caching means the replication of data that is often used at the edge or fog nodes in order to minimize the frequency of data access from remote sources or cloud. Energy is saved because in most cases, data is not fetched from the central data centers every time, this uses a lot of bandwidth and energy.

Data aggregation is also important for energy efficiency in such places as well. Rather than sending basic, unstructured data to the cloud, edge and fog nodes can perform and filter data at the same time. Since more than one data set is taken in a single shot, there is less need of swapping packets of data thereby making the communication overhead minimal. This not only reduces energy consumption but also conserves bandwidth and also increases the system efficiency of the network.

4.3 Sustainable Hardware Choices

4.3.1 Energy-Efficient Hardware for Edge and Fog Computing

Besides the best utilization of software and resources, hardware selection is a vital factor in sustainability in edge and fog computing(Suárez-Albela et al 2017). The hardware that has to work within these environments has to be optimized for power and thermal considerations. Some of the key components of energy-efficient hardware for edge and fog computing include:

1.Low-Power Processors: Most edge and fog devices like IoT sensors and nodes, have low power processors that are optimized to provide minimum required computational power with least power consumption. These processors are usually designed to be power-efficient in activities such as data gathering and initial sorting – thus saving total processing energy.
2.Solid-State Drives (SSDs): Conventional HDDs are highly power consumptive because they rely on mechanical systems. However, SSDs are much more power efficient as they consume less power and are ideal for use in edge and fog nodes. SSD have faster data access rates and are more reliable, thus making them ideal for places where data has to be processed at the shortest time possible and in the least energy consuming manner.
3.Energy-Efficient Networking Components: Similar to edge and fog computing equipment, networking equipment should also be developed with energy efficiency in mind. Low power Wi-Fi, 5G and LPWAN are other technologies that help use low energy to transmit data over short and long distances in the network communication process.
4.Edge-Aware GPUs: GPUs are widely employed in the edge and fog computing utilization for such purposes as machine learning and AI. The low-power GPUs are used to provide high computation capability while consuming less power that allows for edge computing like image processing and real-time data analysis.

One of the biggest strengths of edge and fog computing is its ability to ensure energy efficiency, as multiple measures and tools operate simultaneously to manage resource utilization. Dynamic resource allocation and load balancing are some of the reasons used to cut down energy wastage in the hope of using available resources optimally. Data processing and caching, as well as data aggregation, reduce the distance data are transported and thus, reduce energy consumption. Last but not least, the use of low-power processors, SSDs, and energy-efficient networking components guarantee that all the physical gear that underpins edge and fog computing is as environmentally friendly as it can be. These strategies combined enhance the sustainability of decentralized computing systems in the modern world(Zou et al 2019).

5. APPLICATION DOMAINS FOR SUSTAINABLE EDGE AND FOG COMPUTING

Edge and fog computing are revolutionizing industries by providing efficient, real-time data processing in the premises of data origin. Such a change not only improves system efficiency and decreases the time delay but is also beneficial for sustainability initiatives as it improves energy consumption and minimizes resource utilization(Chithaluru et al 2024). In this section, we discuss how edge and fog computing is being adopted in different domains to help make sustainable smart cities, healthcare, industrial IoT, and agriculture.

5.1 Smart Cities

With regards to smart cities, edge and fog computing can effectively control the resource of a city and enhance its performance of city functions. These computing models allow handling data produced by numerous sensors, devices, and IoT systems integrated into the urban environment, eliminating the need for complex and potentially slower and less efficient cloud-based systems.

1.Traffic Control: Edge and fog computing make traffic more efficient as real-time data from traffic cameras, sensors and GPS connected cars can be processed. Through the analysis of the traffic flows at the local level, edge and fog nodes can change the traffic signals, suggest changes in the traffic flow, and inform drivers in real time. This also helps in easing traffic jam, saves fuel and thus helps in cutting down carbon di oxide emission.

2.Waste Management: In smart waste management system, use of bin sensors or dumpster level information is used to transmit information about their fill status. It is analyzed in edge and fog computing, which can outline the most suitable routes and time schedules for waste collection. This saves time that would otherwise be spent on moving around to pick wastes that could have at one time been recycled, which therefore should be beneficial economically and environmentally.

As a result of decentralized computing, smart cities can better allocate their resources, minimize energy utilization, and improve sustainability of the urban services(Paul et al 2025).

5.2 Healthcare

Real-time health monitoring and better methods of processing the medical data are introduced by the edge and fog computing. These technologies give real time local processing of patients' data hence results in quicker and improved health decisions.

1.Real-Time Health Monitoring and Telemedicine: Wearable devices and remote health monitoring systems are being used in edge computing to get immediate results of patient's health status including heart rates, blood pressure, and glucose levels. This data is then processed locally in the edge nodes so that alerts can be raised immediately in case of signs of distress or otherwise a deviation from the normal. This helps to decrease the frequency of the cloud communication, conserve energy and make sure that vital health data is processed as soon as possible which is productive in sensitive health related cases(Anita, M. et al 2024).

2.Fog Computing in Medical Data Processing: Fog computing helps medical institution by offering an additional layer that can compute and collect data from different places including hospitals, clinics, and centers for remote care. Fog nodes pre-process the data, in essence, downplaying unimportant data and only forwarding important information to the cloud. This means that the number of data that are being transferred through the network is cut down, the usage of bandwidth is minimized and the effectiveness of the health care delivery system enhanced. They also improve patient management because they provide more localized decisions regarding patients(Siva, S. R et al 2024). Edge and fog computing boost healthcare efficiency, improve patient outcomes, and align with sustainability objectives by minimizing latency, improving data transmission, and offering real-time data(Kaur et al 2024).

5.3 Industrial IoT (IIoT)

Consequently, the edge and fog computing in IIoT applications enhance sustainable manufacturing operations, productivity, predictive maintenance and resource utilization.

1.Predictive Maintenance: In the industrial context, edge devices can be used to continuously supervise the status of the mechanical assets, their temperatures, and vibrations, and other parameters. This data is processed locally at the edge or the fog layer to have the ability to identify anomalies and possibly impending equipment failure. Predictive maintenance helps the manufacturers to eliminate the regular breakdowns and subsequent losses which include; Machine and equipment wastage, energy wastage and raw material wastage.

2.Resource Optimization: It also means that edge and fog computing can be used to improve the efficiency of resources such as energy and water in industries. These systems can control the flow of data by processing it locally and then change production plans and equipment settings as well as resources in real time to decrease energy use and environmental effects. For instance, in fog nodes, the management of energy-progressive tasks such as heating, cooling or lighting is achieved in a way that energy is only consumed in the right time.

Edge and fog computing help industries to make intelligent decisions in real-time and process data and, therefore, reduce waste and enhance sustainability in industries.

5.4 Agriculture

In precision agriculture, edge and fog computing are revolutionising how farmers use resources and/or observe environmental factors for efficient and sustainable farming.

1.Efficient Resource Use: Various sensors installed in agricultural fields capture information on moisture and temperature of the ground, health of the crops and prevailing climate. Edge computing makes it possible to process this data locally, therefore helping the farmers to make decisions on irrigation, fertilization, and pest control at the right time. For instance, should a certain level of moisture in the soil be reached, the edge node can cause water sprinklers to come on and water is used in the right measure without wastage.

2.Environmental Monitoring: Fog computing can collate information from numerous sensors in the field and only send valuable data to the cloud for analysis. The farmers can be able to control the environment factors such as the quality of the soil, the weather conditions, and the status of crops in order to get high yields with little amounts of fertilizers, pesticides and water. This minimizes the effect of farming on the natural environment, enhances soil quality and sustainability of the natural resources. The use of edge and fog computing allows farmers to make better decisions that can increase yield while minimizing loss and negative impact on the environment, so bringing more positive changes to the agriculture industry.

In many industries, edge and fog computing have several benefits, including optimization of resources and time, as well as the minimization of wastage. In smart cities, they enhance the flow of traffic and the disposal of wastes respectively. In the field of healthcare, they enhance real time health monitoring and management of data processing. In industrial IoT, they enhance the performance of maintenance and resource consumption. Last but not the least they allow precision farming that employs the use of limited water and has least effect on the environment. As edge and fog computing innovate these industries by decentralizing computing while enhancing data flow, they are essential for sustainability's sake.

6. GREEN PROTOCOLS AND STANDARDS FOR EDGE AND FOG COMPUTING

It is therefore important for edge and fog computing systems, as they develop to incorporate energy efficient protocols and standards in an effort to minimize the effects of distributed computing on the environment. As the networks are decentralized, the protocols that are set to be energy efficient are crucial in these networks to minimize power used in data transmission, processing and management. This section examines energy efficient communication protocols, standards currently in place that promote sustainability and potential developments in green protocols in edge and fog computing.

6.1 Protocols Designed for Energy Efficiency in Edge and Fog Environments

In edge and fog computing, protocols are vital and used in the reduction of energy consumption of devices, communication networks as well as data processing systems. Many protocols have been developed either from scratch or based on other protocols in order to handle energy efficiency in these settings.

1. **MQTT (Message Queuing Telemetry Transport):** It is a lightweight messaging protocol of the pub/sub pattern, which is widely seen in IoT and edge computing. Its characteristics include simple structure, small message headers, low usage of network bandwidth, and thus can be used in scenarios where the network connection is not very strong and the energy consumption is a concern. MQTT makes communication between devices and edge nodes lightweight and effective which is important in handling many sensors or IoT devices. MQTT is more suitable for smart cities, healthcare and industrial IoT applications since they require real time data exchange with low power usage.
2. **CoAP (Constrained Application Protocol):** CoAP is another REST-full protocol that is resource-constrained friendly and is used in IoT and edge computing. The technology is designed for low energy and bandwidth platforms and is commonly employed in settings where efficiency is vital. CoAP uses the UDP, which consumes less energy than the TCP in situations where connections are intermittent. CoAP is applied in applications that need short messages such as smart homes, environmental monitoring and agricultural systems. Due to the elimination of complexity of the data interchange and discontinuity of connection, CoAP plays a crucial role in conserving energy in edge and fog systems.

3.6LoWPAN (IPv6 over Low-Power Wireless Personal Area Networks): This protocol is intended to facilitate low-energy devices to interconnect seamlessly in IoT networks. Due to the IPV6 header compression and package size optimization, the energy needed for data transfer in IoT devices is minimized by 6LoWPAN. Wireless sensor networks and smart cities are two primary use cases of 6LoWPAN because many devices require low-power wireless connectivity to communicate with edge nodes or gateways.

4.Energy-Efficient Routing Protocols: Energy efficient routing protocols for edge and fog networks are also important. Algorithms like the Energy-Aware Routing Protocol (EARP) and Low-Energy Adaptive Clustering Hierarchy (LEACH) are specifically intended to conserve power in a sensor network by choosing the most power efficient paths for the data to travel. These protocols help in maintaining the energy consumption of the nodes of the network on an average so that the lifetime of the network increases and the energy consumption of the system decreases.

6.2 Current Standards and Frameworks Supporting Sustainable Practices

There are some standards and frameworks that are enabling energy efficient sustainable practices in edge and fog computing domain. These include work towards defining energy-proiling paradigms for devices, protocols, and networks, as well as determining energy-efficient ways in which these networks should be designed.

1.IEEE 802.15.4: This standard outlines the physical layer and media access for low power wireless devices. Zigbee and 6LoWPAN are several IoT protocols that are based on it and energy efficiency in edge and fog networks is also depended on it. In the case of IoT networks, IEEE 802.15.4 is designed to minimize energy consumption when devices communicate with each other hence increasing the battery lifespan of such devices.

2.Green Computing Standards: Today, there are various guidelines for green IT, for example, Green Electronics Council and International Organization for Standardization (ISO). These standards are aimed at the efficient use of energy embodied in hardware, reduction of waste, and recycling. For instance, ISO/IEC 30134 concerns the metrics and frameworks of energy-efficient data center, which are an important part of the fog and edge computing environment.

3.OpenFog Consortium: The OpenFog Consortium has provided a reference architecture of fog computing and recommendations regarding energy consumption. The consortium activities are primarily aimed at developing fog computing environments and the practical application of fog computing solutions for promoting sustainability by improving resource consumption, network architecture, and energy efficiency. Some of the principles of green computing such as local processing, efficient data transfer and minimal energy consumption are part of the OpenFog architecture.

4.Energy Star Certification: For hardware and devices for edge and fog computing the Energy Star certification program assists in identifying the most efficient energy products. This certification is for the networking devices and servers and other equipment that can be used in edge and fog computing. Energy Star plays a role in decreasing the general environmental footprint of edge and fog computing infrastructures by encouraging energy-efficient hardware.

6.3 Future Directions for Developing Green Protocols and Best Practices

Thus, as the edge and fog computing concepts develop, the need for more effective and environmentally friendly protocols and guidelines is increasing. Some key areas of future development include:

1.AI-Driven Energy Optimization: AI and ML have the ability to control the power consumption of the edge and fog systems in a way that would be more efficient constantly. With the help of AI algorithms, the traffic flow in the network can be analyzed, the amount of workload, and the resources required to meet such demands can be predicted dynamically and the resources to be utilized can be managed to reduce energy usage. These algorithms can be incorporated into protocols and the network management systems, which makes them even more flexible to different circumstances and minimizes energy consumption to the last level.

2.Integration of Renewable Energy: Since edge and fog nodes are being placed in hard-to-reach or mobile areas, incorporating solar or wind power to power those nodes will help minimize the use of non-renewable energy. Future protocols could include ways to supervise the energy supply, so that appliances work in an ecological way, using local renewable energy, if any.

3.Decentralized Energy Management: Subsequent green protocols might focus on distributed energy control in the edge fog cloud continuum. Thus, edge and fog systems can support more localized energy harvesting and storage, allowing them to work even with limited connection to the central data centers and, therefore, reducing the dependence on energy-hungry cloud computing services to meet sustainability objectives.

4.Standardization of Green Metrics: It will be important to create a set of standard parameters for assessing the level of energy efficiency of edge and fog systems to maintain the effectiveness of sustainability efforts. These metrics could include energy per transaction, transmission energy cost, energy efficient of the equipments and others. By setting these metrics, further development of green protocols can be informed and it will be easier to compare the environmental impact of various systems.

The sustainability of the edge and fog computing systems is highly dependent on green protocols and standards. MQTT, CoAP, and other energy saving routing schemes reduce energy consumption of devices and networks, and IEEE 802.15.4 and Energy Star certify energy efficient hardware and systems. For the future, AI based optimization, renewable energy integration and standardization of green metrics for edge and fog computing will be the way forward. With such green protocols and practices adopted the industry can guarantee that these technologies will be used to enhance efficiency and reduce the impacts to the environment.

7. CHALLENGES AND LIMITATIONS

These are edge and fog computing that have the potential of increasing sustainability by minimizing energy consumption and the negative effects of conventional cloud computing On the same note, the adoption of edge and fog computing has certain barriers to widespread adoption. These are diverse issues starting from the technical ones, for example, how to achieve compatibility and how to scale up the solution to other, more abstract, problems, for example, how to ensure security and privacy, and how to achieve high performance while maintaining sustainability in practical applications.

7.1 Technical Challenges

1.Interoperability: Interoperability of the systems, devices, and protocols is one of the main issues that has to be resolved in the course of implementing edge and fog computing solutions. In edge and fog contexts, for instance, there are many devices with different characteristics and communication interfaces, and, therefore, it is challenging to achieve end-to-end communication. Lan applications vary depending on the vendors because they employ exclusive technologies and standards. This is mainly due to lack of standard interface and protocol in order to harmonize different edge devices, fog nodes and cloud systems. This lack of interoperability can hamper the scale of edge and fog solutions, and thus the uptake of effective energy-efficient practices.

2.Scalability: The other challenge that affects the scalability of edge and fog computing systems is scalability. With the growing number of IoT devices and edge nodes, there is an even bigger amount of data produced in the networks. The challenge then arises in how to efficiently handle this data across edge and fog devices spread out over a wide network in a sustainable manner. Fog and edge computing systems must be able to grow and expand in order to accommodate vast volumes of data and processing tasks while minimizing power consumption. This may include, for hardware, how to ensure that the energy efficient devices being deployed are able to cope with increased work load, and for software, how to properly distribute and manage data as the network grows in size. The need to achieve scalability without impacting energy efficiency is best determined by planning the network architecture and resource management appropriately.

3.Resource Management and Optimization: Resource management is a key ingredient in sustainability, especially in edge and fog computing. Edge and fog environments may have dynamic workloads and are resource constrained and, thus, resource allocation is not always easy. Just as it is impossible to turn on a heater and have it instantly warm up a room, computing power, storage and energy resources cannot be allocated in a linear manner, but need complex algorithms that can predict demand, and distribute computing power and energy efficiently while adapting to changing environmental conditions. Managing energy efficiency for resources in distributed systems and use of resources in large scale can sometimes be a daunting task.

7.2 Security and Privacy Concerns

As edge and fog computing are inherently distributed computing systems, these architectures pose several security and privacy challenges. In conventional cloud computing, user data is stored in well protected and monitored central data centers hence security measures can be easily installed. Nevertheless, in edge and fog computing the data is processed at the nodes which can be located in rather unconstrained and potentially hostile environments including public spaces, industrial zones or remote areas.

1.Data Privacy: The most important problem of the decentralized computing is how to protect the privacy of the data. Since edge and fog nodes perform data computations before forwarding them to the cloud, it is imperative to apply encryption, access control, and anonymization mechanisms to avoid unauthorized data access and ensure that privacy-sensitive data are safeguarded. This is especially crucial in cases of healthcare, smart city, and industrial IoT where data protection laws (e.g., GDPR, HIPAA) apply.

2.Security of Edge Nodes: Due to the nature of edge devices where they are placed in uncontrolled environments, are more susceptible to physical interference and cyber threats. Providing protection to these edge nodes therefore needs efficient and light-weight security solutions that enable protection against intrusion while at the same time consuming minimal resources that may affect the performance and energy usage of the system. Techniques like secure boot, programmable hardware security module, and secure communication protocols are necessary but they must be implemented for low energy IoT devices.

3.Vulnerability to Distributed Attacks: Edge and fog computing also have another problem called the distributed denial-of-service (DDoS) attack because of the decentralization of nodes. The deployment of a massive, decentralized system of fogs and edge nodes also entails a constant identification of threats and proactive, real-time mitigation techniques that may introduce additional levels of complication and energy consumption.

7.3 Balancing Performance and Sustainability

1.Latency and Real-Time Processing: Most edge and fog computing applications, including remote monitoring of health conditions and self-driving vehicles, need fast processing and fast decisions. Energy-efficient may introduce longer processing time or delay in data transmission hence may be disadvantageous in applications that require a shorter data processing timc. For example, in order to decrease energy consumption in fog nodes and place them into low power mode, the time it takes to process data or communicate data across nodes may be significantly longer than if the nodes were constantly active.

2.Energy-Efficient Algorithms vs. System Responsiveness: Sometimes, algorithms that consume the least amount of energy to run may cause delays or slow down a system. For instance, some algorithms used for resource allocation and load balancing put a lot of emphasis on energy efficiency, and this means that the processes involved will take longer time to complete than is desirable. The major challenge is to strike a balance between achieving sustainable energy management and maximizing system performance in order to guarantee the efficiency and reliability of edge and fog systems in practical use.

3.Sustainability vs. Overhead: Applying energy-efficient protocols and managing resources may add extra load to the processors, and the resultant effect maybe the opposite of energy conservation. For instance, the application of advanced mathematical models for energy efficiency, data accumulation or load distribution might require more power, and thus weaken the beneficial effects of these methods. This is an important trade-off between energy efficiency and system overhead that is very important to solve in order to prevent sustainability from causing poor performance.

Both edge and fog computing present a great opportunity of improving sustainability, through efficient use of resources, real-time analysis, and low energy effects. However, the successful implementation of these systems faces issues concerning integration, extension, protection, privacy, and optimization between system performance and cost. All these issues call for constant research and development of the technological and policy-related solutions that would provide a seamless interconnection of distributed systems, adequate security measures, and power-saving algorithms of work, while at the same time maintaining a high level of efficiency. The elimination of these barriers will be critical in optimizing the ability of edge and fog computing to foster sustainable, efficient and secure computing environments in the future.

8. FUTURE TRENDS AND RESEARCH DIRECTIONS

With the development of edge and fog computing this trend will only grow stronger in shaping the future of sustainability across industries. New trends, such as integration with 5G, use of Artificial Intelligence for edge computing and possibilities to use quantum computing are considered to change the way of data processing and resource management. Moreover, future studies that focus on creating effective algorithms and frameworks will define how energy and resources are consumed in edge and fog contexts. In the following sections, these trends and areas of research are described in more detail.

8.1. Integration with 5G Networks

The current development of the 5G network is one of the main disruptive technologies for edge and fog computing. 5G has the high-speed and low latency which are essential for real-time applications that are really important for sustainability in smart city, healthcare, industrial IoT. 5G integrated with edge and fog computing makes it possible to perform complex analysis of large volumes of data at the edge with little latency thereby enhancing the ability to control resources and respond quickly to environmental influences. The integration of 5G improves the capacity of a large number of IoT devices to be deployed at the edge. This makes it possible to monitor the infrastructure in the urban environment, energy use and the physical environment with higher resolution in real time. For instance, in smart cities, 5G-enabled edge computing can enhance traffic management, avoid traffic jams, and enhance air quality measurement, which are all ecologically friendly. In addition, the energy per bit of 5G networks is also reduced compared with previous generations, which will help communication infrastructure to reduce carbon emission and contribute to the sustainable development.

8.2. AI-Driven Edge Applications

AI is finding its way at the edge to support intelligent action and minimize energy consumption. There are AI algorithms that work within the device and do not require the sharing of huge amounts of data to the cloud; these include the machine learning (ML) and deep learning(Saravanan K et al 2023). This lowers the amount of data that needs to be transmitted and the energy used in doing so, yet at the same time allows for quicker adaptation to change. Some of the uses include: Predictive maintenance in industrial sectors, real-time energy management in smart grids, and health management through the use of wearables. For example, edge AI could forecast when an industrial tool is more likely to develop a fault and thereby avoid frequent breakdowns. Likewise, in managing energy consumption in buildings or industrial plants, AI algorithms can be used in order to minimize energy consumption and, in effect, decrease costs. Sustainability outcomes are expected to be made more efficient by the integration of AI and edge computing. There is growing interest in reducing the energy consumption of the AI models in the edge environments where data are processed to avoid a balance of the benefits of the edge AI.

8.3. Quantum Computing at the Edge

There is a lot of possibility to improve the computational capability through the integration of quantum computing and edge computing. Despite being relatively a new field, quantum computing provides the capability to solve problems that cannot be solved or would take an immense amount of time on classical machines. The implementation of quantum computing at the edge could change the energy efficiency of the algorithms required for the optimization of the edge environment through the use of fewer resources and time. For instance, quantum computing can revolutionize optimization issues like resource, traffic flow, and electrical-energy grid optimization. In industrial IoT, quantum algorithms may refine the prognosis of equipment failure and enhance the efficiency of the predictive maintenance system. Quantum computing at the edge is a concept that is still largely theoretical in many ways today, but the opportunity for massive energy savings is considerable as quantum hardware gets real and more power efficient. As for the quantum computing for the edge, the research is in the early stage, however, the prospects of the energy-efficient algorithm development especially for such demanding tasks as optimization and simulation can open the door to the sustainability improvement. The problem will be to scale quantum computing to the point where it is usable and energy efficient at the edge where resources are limited.

8.4. Green Algorithm and Framework

With thc increasing complexity and size of the edge and fog computing systems, it is becoming increasingly important to have energy efficient sustainable algorithms. The most common tasks that are being considered in terms of energy efficiency by researchers include data aggregation, load-proportioning, and resource management. Efficient algorithms for processing data are essential for energy conservation in the distributed edge and fog computing systems. These strategies include the task relocation strategy which is a process of moving computational tasks between devices to another depending on the energy levels. Moreover, increased investigations of scheduling algorithms that incorporate the energy utilization of devices will ensure the optimization of performance and energy efficiency. These algorithms' main goal is to reduce the energy consumption of these devices while at the same time being able to satisfy the real time application demands. Moreover, research on energy efficient networking protocols is also under way to minimize communication overhead in fog and edge infrastructures. Thus, MQTT (Message Queuing Telemetry Transport) and CoAP (Constrained Application Protocol), which are lightweight protocols suitable for low-power devices, are frequently applied to improve the efficiency of the interaction and reduce energy consumption in edge and fog networks. New green protocols that reduce the overhead information transfer while at the same time improving reliability and response time will be important to advance sustainability. Another research area is related to the design of the energy-conscious operating systems for the edge nodes. All these operating systems can control the power use of the hardware and this can be done through power management, control of the CPU frequency and even power off of non-active components. In this domain, the goal of the research is to design operating systems that would learn and optimize the energy requirements of edge applications, thus lowering the overall energy consumption.

The development of edge and fog computing to support sustainability is contingent on other trends including 5G integration of edge computing, AI, and the future of quantum computing at the edge. It is shown that these technologies create new opportunities to increase efficiency and decrease losses, as well as increase the responsiveness of systems. The further exploration of sustainable algorithms, energy efficient computing, and green protocols will form a crucial part of the environmental gains of the systems. The two technologies of edge and fog computing will continue to grow in importance for reaching sustainability goals as new research and developments are made to address current issues.

9. CONCLUSION

Edge and fog computing are crucial for making sustainability goals achievable through energy efficiency and reduction of resource usage in different sectors. These paradigms of computing decentralization allow localized data processing and, therefore, minimize the data transfer to the cloud, decreasing power consumption and latency. Edge and fog computing enhance the capability of real-time applications better since it processes data closer to the data source and saves computational resources of the cloud. The development of AI, 5G and other smart technologies make these systems smarter and economical to address such problems. Of all the benefits that edge and fog computing have brought into the society, the most important one is the ability to cut down on carbon emissions. These systems reduce the dependence on computation on central data centres which are big energy consumers and sources of carbon emissions. This results in the development of efficient systems that are in concordance with the global efficiency standards. Nonetheless, the opportunities for edge and fog computing to enable sustainability will only be reached in their next phase of innovation and development. With the development of technologies such as AI, quantum computing, 5G and others, solutions associated with energy efficient algorithms, rational communication protocols and sustainable hardware must be found. Future studies on energy-conscious algorithms and green computing will guarantee that both edge and fog systems are sustainable. The call to action is clear: What comes as crucial is the incorporation of sustainability in the design and deployment of edge and fog computing systems. The development of edge and fog computing solutions must consider sustainable practices by policymakers, industry leaders, and academics to build a future where technology is a force for good on the environment.

REFERENCES

Anita, M., Ambhika, C., & Anish, T. P. (2024). Exploring the Landscape of Artificial Intelligence in Healthcare Applications. In *AI Healthcare Applications and Security, Ethical, and Legal Considerations* (pp. 29-48). IGI Global.

Anusha, S., Ezhilvandan, M., Gayathri, S., Sivaraman, V., & Anish, T. P. (2024). Emerging trends in edge AI for Industry 4.0 and 5.0: Technologies, applications, and challenges. *AI Innovations in Service and Tourism Marketing*, 211-228.

Bhambri, P., Rani, S., Gupta, G., & Khang, A. (Eds.). (2022). *Cloud and fog computing platforms for internet of things*. CRC Press. DOI: 10.1201/9781003213888

Bhandari, G. P., & Gupta, R. (2021). An overview of cloud and edge computing architecture and its current issues and challenges. *Research Anthology on Architectures, Frameworks, and Integration Strategies for Distributed and Cloud Computing*, 2340-2370.

Chithaluru, P., Narsimhulu, P., Yadav, N. S., Chawla, P., & Tiwari, R. (2024). Fog computing: Advancing Sustainable Development Goals (SDGs). In *Cloud and Fog Optimization-based Solutions for Sustainable Developments* (pp. 280-298). CRC Press.

Dhanalakshmi, M., Tamilarasi, K., Saravanan, S., Sujatha, G., & Boopathi, S. (2024). Fog Computing-Based Framework and Solutions for Intelligent Systems: Enabling Autonomy in Vehicles. In *Computational Intelligence for Green Cloud Computing and Digital Waste Management* (pp. 330-356). IGI Global.

Jain, A., & Singhal, P. (2016, November). Fog computing: Driving force behind the emergence of edge computing. In *2016 International Conference System Modeling & Advancement in Research Trends (SMART)* (pp. 294-297). IEEE. DOI: 10.1109/SYSMART.2016.7894538

Kaur, G., Harnal, S., Goyal, A., Tiwari, R., & Cheng, X. (2024). Applications and challenges for sustainable development with cloud/fog/edge computing. *Cloud and Fog Optimization-based Solutions for Sustainable Developments*, 27-47.

Kumar, V., Laghari, A. A., Karim, S., Shakir, M., & Brohi, A. A. (2019). Comparison of fog computing & cloud computing. *Int. J. Math. Sci. Comput*, *1*, 31–41.

Murthy, J. S. (2021). Edgecloud: A distributed management system for resource continuity in edge to cloud computing environment. In *Research Anthology on Architectures, Frameworks, and Integration Strategies for Distributed and Cloud Computing* (pp. 2684-2700). IGI Global. DOI: 10.4018/978-1-7998-5339-8.ch130

Ometov, A., Molua, O. L., Komarov, M., & Nurmi, J. (2022). A survey of security in cloud, edge, and fog computing. *Sensors (Basel)*, *22*(3), 927. DOI: 10.3390/s22030927 PMID: 35161675

Paul, P. (2025). SDG-oriented cloud-fog-edge-blockchain model for sustainable development. In *Artificial Intelligence and Information Technologies* (pp. 460–466). CRC Press.

Ponmalar, A., Vijayakumar, K., Lakshmipriya, C., Karthikeyan, M., & PJ, B. P. (2024). Meta-Heuristics and Machine Learning Applications in Complex Systems. In *Metaheuristic and Machine Learning Optimization Strategies for Complex Systems* (pp. 257-275). IGI Global.

Priyadarshini, R., Malarvizhi, N., & Neeba, E. A. (2019). A study on capabilities and challenges of fog computing. In *Novel Practices and Trends in Grid and Cloud Computing* (pp. 249–273). IGI Global. DOI: 10.4018/978-1-5225-9023-1.ch015

Saravanan, K., Prakash, R. B., Balakrishnan, C., Kumar, G. V. P., Subramanian, R. S., & Anita, M. (2023, December). Support Vector Machines: Unveiling the Power and Versatility of SVMs in Modern Machine Learning. In *2023 3rd International Conference on Innovative Mechanisms for Industry Applications (ICIMIA)* (pp. 680-687). IEEE.

Siva, S. R., Sudha, K., Pooja, E., Maheswari, B., & Girija, P. (2024). Revolutionizing Healthcare Delivery: Applications and Impact of Cutting-Edge Technologies. *AI and IoT Technology and Applications for Smart Healthcare Systems*, 75-91.

Suárez-Albela, M., Fernández-Caramés, T. M., Fraga-Lamas, P., & Castedo, L. (2017). A practical evaluation of a high-security energy-efficient gateway for IoT fog computing applications. *Sensors (Basel)*, *17*(9), 1978. DOI: 10.3390/s17091978 PMID: 28850104

Zou, Z., Jin, Y., Nevalainen, P., Huan, Y., Heikkonen, J., & Westerlund, T. (2019, March). Edge and fog computing enabled AI for IoT-an overview. In *2019 IEEE International Conference on Artificial Intelligence Circuits and Systems (AICAS)* (pp. 51-56). IEEE. DOI: 10.1109/AICAS.2019.8771621

Chapter 16
Federated Learning Frameworks for Energy-Efficient AI in Distributed Data Centres

S. Prabakeran
https://orcid.org/0000-0003-1140-0440
SRM Institute of Science and Technology, India

T. Sethukarasi
RMK Engineering College, India

V. Indumathi
SRM Institute of Science and Technology, India

ABSTRACT

The rising energy demands of large data centers call for energy-efficient AI training methods. Federated Learning (FL), a decentralized paradigm, offers a solution by enabling model training across distributed devices without centralizing sensitive data. This review explores FL's integration with distributed data centers to achieve energy efficiency, analyzing methods like federated averaging and energy-aware protocols to minimize resource use. It highlights techniques such as model compression, quantization, and adaptive FL to reduce on-device computation while maintaining performance. Practical implementation is discussed through tools like TensorFlow Federated and PySyft, with case studies from healthcare, finance, and IoT showcasing cost reductions and sustainability. Future research directions include combining FL with edge computing and low-power AI hardware, emphasizing FL's potential for scalable, sustainable AI.

DOI: 10.4018/979-8-3373-0766-4.ch016

Copyright © 2025, IGI Global Scientific Publishing. Copying or distributing in print or electronic forms without written permission of IGI Global Scientific Publishing is prohibited.

1. INTRODUCTION

1.1 Overview of Federated Learning

Federated Learning (FL) represents a paradigm shift in artificial intelligence (AI) training methodologies, addressing challenges posed by traditional centralized learning approaches. Unlike centralized models, where data is aggregated into a single repository for training, FL enables distributed training directly at data sources such as edge devices, servers, or data centers. This decentralized training process is orchestrated by periodically aggregating locally computed updates to refine a global model.

Key principles of FL include:

- **Decentralization:** Data remains on local devices, ensuring that sensitive information is not transmitted to a central server.
- **Collaborative Training:** Multiple entities collaboratively train a shared model while retaining control over their data.
- **Privacy Preservation:** By design, FL minimizes the risk of data breaches, enhancing user privacy and compliance with regulations such as GDPR and CCPA.

Compared to traditional centralized learning approaches, FL offers distinct advantages. First, it reduces the risk of data exposure, making it suitable for domains like healthcare and finance, where data privacy is paramount. Second, FL reduces the need for large-scale data transmission, which can be costly and time-intensive. Finally, FL supports collaborative learning across diverse datasets, enabling more generalized and robust models.

FL's benefits extend beyond privacy and security, providing a foundation for sustainable and scalable AI systems. As AI continues to permeate diverse industries, its adoption in frameworks like FL is crucial for addressing pressing challenges in computational efficiency, energy consumption, and data governance.

Federated Learning (FL) represents a paradigm shift in artificial intelligence (AI) training methodologies, addressing challenges posed by traditional centralized learning approaches. Unlike centralized models, where data is aggregated into a single repository for training, FL enables distributed training directly at data sources such as edge devices, servers, or data centers. This decentralized training process is orchestrated by periodically aggregating locally computed updates to refine a global model.

1.2 Importance of Energy Efficiency in AI Model Training

The energy requirements for AI training have escalated dramatically due to the advancement of more intricate models. Training advanced deep neural networks (DNNs) like GPT and Vision Transformers (ViTs) necessitates substantial processing resources, frequently resulting in considerable electricity consumption. Research indicates that the training of a single large-scale language model can produce carbon emissions comparable to those emitted by many automobiles throughout their operational lifespan.

The environmental consequences of energy-intensive AI activities are significant. Data centres, essential to AI infrastructure, represent approximately 1% of worldwide power usage and are anticipated to expand as AI use intensifies. These facilities release substantial amounts of greenhouse gases, exacerbating global warming. Confronting these energy concerns is not merely an operational requirement but a moral obligation for the AI research community.

Consequently, energy efficiency is becoming a fundamental component of sustainable AI techniques. Methods like model pruning, quantisation, and distributed training architectures seek to minimise the energy consumption of AI while maintaining performance integrity. In this scenario, FL provides distinct advantages. By utilising local processing and minimising inter-device transmission, federated learning inherently supports energy conservation goals, rendering it an attractive option for artificial intelligence applications in remote data centres.

1.3 Addressing Real-World Challenges in Federated Learning

While FL offers numerous benefits, its real-world implementation presents significant challenges. Key concerns include:

- **Communication Overhead**: Frequent communication between devices and central servers can lead to high energy costs and latency, particularly in large-scale deployments.
- **Data Heterogeneity**: Devices involved in FL often have diverse data distributions, leading to inconsistencies in model convergence and performance.
- **Security Concerns**: FL is vulnerable to adversarial attacks, poisoning attempts, and privacy threats, necessitating robust security measures like differential privacy and secure aggregation.

A comprehensive approach to mitigating these challenges includes optimizing communication protocols, utilizing adaptive aggregation techniques, and developing energy-aware security frameworks.

1.4 Expanding on Energy Trade-offs in Federated Learning

Although FL reduces data transmission costs by processing data locally, it introduces new energy trade-offs. For example, federated averaging (FedAvg) minimizes transmission frequency but increases local computation load. Balancing communication costs with computation savings is crucial. Comparative analyses have shown that adaptive federated learning algorithms, which dynamically adjust training rounds and client participation, can optimize energy efficiency.

1.5 Relevance and Benefits of Using Federated Learning in Distributed Data Centers

Distributed data centers, characterized by geographically dispersed computational nodes, are integral to modern computing ecosystems. These centers handle diverse workloads, from cloud computing to real-time data processing, requiring efficient resource utilization and operational agility. Federated Learning is well-suited for this environment, offering several benefits:

1. **Reduced Data Movement:** By processing data locally, FL minimizes the need for transferring large datasets across networks, reducing bandwidth costs and associated energy expenditures.
2. **Operational Efficiency:** FL aligns seamlessly with distributed architectures, enabling parallel computations that maximize resource utilization and minimize idle times.
3. **Energy Savings:** Localized computations in FL reduce the energy consumed during data transmission, a significant factor in traditional centralized approaches.
4. **Scalability and Resilience:** FL supports incremental training and dynamic adaptation, making it robust against node failures and network disruptions.

This chapter explores how FL frameworks can optimize energy efficiency in distributed data centers, focusing on the synergies between decentralized learning paradigms and sustainable computing practices. By examining current advancements, challenges, and opportunities, the chapter highlights the transformative potential of FL in shaping the future of energy-conscious AI systems.

2. BACKGROUND AND LITERATURE REVIEW

Federated learning (FL) has gained significant attention in various domains, particularly in enhancing energy efficiency and ensuring data privacy across distributed networks. Recent studies highlight its applications in sustainable AI, network traffic management, healthcare diagnostics, and fraud detection, showcasing its versatility and impact.

2.1 Energy-Efficient Federated Learning

Energy efficiency in federated learning is a critical research area, with various approaches proposed to balance computational performance and sustainability. (Li et al. 2022) emphasize the trade-offs between energy consumption and model accuracy, introducing strategies that optimize FL training while reducing carbon footprints. Similarly, (Savazzi et al. 2022) analyse the environmental impact of FL, demonstrating that optimizing communication overhead and computational efficiency can significantly lower energy consumption in large-scale distributed systems.

A notable implementation in smart infrastructure is highlighted by (A. Kumar et al 2023), where FL optimizes energy usage in smart buildings by leveraging decentralized data while minimizing cloud dependency. (L. Dupont et al. 2023) extend this concept to smart grids, integrating FL with distributed energy systems to enhance efficiency and reduce operational costs. Additionally, (T. Nguyen, et al. 2023) propose a hierarchical dynamic FL model for data centers, significantly improving energy management while maintaining performance across distributed networks.

2.2 Federated Learning in Sustainable AI

The integration of FL with sustainable AI practices has been explored by (J. Thompson et al. 2024) and (S. Lee, et al. 2024), where carbon-aware FL models are deployed in distributed data centres to achieve carbon-neutral computing. These studies focus on leveraging AI-driven optimizations to dynamically adjust computational workloads based on carbon intensity metrics, leading to more sustainable AI operations. Predict the (D. Roberts et al. 2021) also contributes by presenting methodologies for building cloud-based sustainable AI/ML solutions, emphasizing federated training to minimize data transfer and reduce environmental impact.

2.3 Privacy-Preserving and Secure Federated Learning

Security and privacy are paramount in federated learning, especially in sensitive domains such as healthcare and finance. (A. Singh, et al. 2023) explores FL in medical diagnostics, ensuring privacy-preserving training while maintaining high diagnostic accuracy. Similarly, A. Ryffel, et al. 2023 introduces secure computation techniques in FL to enhance privacy guarantees, particularly in distributed healthcare and financial systems.

In fraud detection, (T. Becker, S. et al. 2023) utilizes FL to improve global fraud identification without sharing sensitive customer data, demonstrating the potential of privacy-aware learning in financial applications. (H. Bianchi, et al. 2023) extends this approach by employing FL in mobile keyboard personalization, balancing user experience enhancements with data privacy.

2.4 Federated Learning for Network and System Optimization

FL's role in optimizing network traffic and distributed systems has been extensively studied. (J. Reynolds, M. et al. 2023) presents an FL-based framework for managing network traffic, improving real-time data processing while reducing central server load. Similarly, (D. Beutel, J. et al. 2023) provides a flexible FL framework for heterogeneous systems, addressing challenges in decentralized machine learning applications.

(Konecky et al. 2016) introduce the federated averaging (FedAvg) algorithm, a foundational approach that optimizes FL performance across diverse network conditions. This technique has been widely adopted in later studies, enhancing scalability and efficiency in distributed AI models.

The literature underscores the growing importance of FL in achieving energy-efficient, privacy-preserving, and scalable AI solutions. The integration of FL with sustainable AI practices, secure data handling, and network optimization continues to evolve, paving the way for innovative applications across multiple domains. Future research should focus on further refining energy-efficient FL models while addressing emerging challenges in data security and model robustness.

3. METHODOLOGIES AND TECHNOLOGIES

3.1 Detailed Explanation of Federated Learning Algorithms and Protocols

Federated Learning (FL) algorithms constitute the foundation of distributed model training, facilitating collaborative learning while safeguarding data privacy. Federated Averaging (FedAvg), introduced by (McMahan et al. 2017), is a fundamental algorithm. FedAvg functions by consolidating locally trained model updates from distributed clients and average them to revise the global model. Although FedAvg effectively reduces data transmission and safeguards privacy, it is not intrinsically optimised for energy efficiency, prompting the development of more advanced variants.

Energy-efficient versions of FedAvg comprise algorithms that dynamically regulate client involvement and communication frequency. Adaptive sampling algorithms, for instance, dynamically choose clients according to their computational and energy resources. Asynchronous federated learning techniques mitigate straggler effects—where slower devices hinder overall training—by updating the global model using available clients, thus conserving energy and computational resources.

Protocols designed to improve communication efficiency are essential for energy-efficient federated learning. Quantisation methods, including the reduction of model update precision, decrease the volume of data transmitted between clients and the central server. Compression strategies, like sparsification, diminish communication cost by conveying just essential gradients or model parameters. Gradient sparsification has demonstrated the potential to decrease bandwidth utilisation by as much as 90% in certain applications, hence substantially reducing energy consumption. Moreover, error feedback systems guarantee the preservation of the global model's accuracy despite these rigorous optimisations.

3.2 Techniques for Reducing Energy Consumption in Distributed Environments

Energy efficiency in distributed systems is attained by optimising computing and communication operations. Data processing methodologies, like pre-filtering and dimensionality reduction, diminish the quantity of data that must be processed and disseminated, hence lowering energy consumption. Feature selection approaches can discern pertinent features at the data source, hence minimising superfluous computation during local model training.

Computation offloading is a crucial method that involves transferring resource-intensive operations from low-powered edge devices to more powerful servers or edge nodes. This method is very efficacious in federated learning environments with heterogeneous devices exhibiting diverse energy capacity. Delegating workloads to high-performance edge nodes decreases total energy consumption and prolongs the battery life of edge devices.

Bandwidth optimisation methods additionally aid energy conservation. Coordinating training intervals with times of minimal network traffic mitigates contention and energy expenditure. Moreover, batch training, which involves aggregating several local updates prior to communication, reduces the frequency of contacts between clients and the server.

Energy-aware federated learning algorithms dynamically modify model training parameters according to resource availability. Algorithms can prioritise clients with greater residual energy or modify learning rates to diminish computational demands. These adaptive methods guarantee that energy consumption within the FL system is equitably distributed across participating devices, hence improving the framework's overall sustainability.

3.3 Tools and Platforms for Implementing Federated Learning in Data Centers

Numerous tools and systems facilitate the deployment of federated learning in dispersed data centres, providing functionalities aimed at simplifying integration, improving performance, and maximising energy efficiency. TensorFlow Federated (TFF) is a prominent framework that offers comprehensive APIs for emulating federated learning processes and deploying models in distributed settings. TFF possesses inherent customisation features, rendering it appropriate for both research and practical applications.

PySyft, a further open-source tool, emphasises safe and private federated learning deployments. It interacts effortlessly with deep learning frameworks like PyTorch and TensorFlow, enabling developers to deploy FL models with sophisticated privacy-preserving techniques, like differential privacy and safe multi-party computation. Likewise, Flower (Federated Learning Framework) offers a versatile architecture that accommodates different FL conFigureurations, facilitating energy-efficient training across many devices.

Cloud and edge computing platforms are essential for facilitating federated learning in data centres. AWS IoT Greengrass and Microsoft Azure IoT Edge provide integration functionalities for the deployment of federated learning models at the edge, hence minimising latency and energy usage. These platforms utilise the nearness of edge nodes to data sources, facilitating local computing and model updates. By allocating processing jobs to edge devices, these platforms reduce the energy requirements of centralised data centres while ensuring optimal performance.

Integrating FL technologies with current data centre infrastructure necessitates meticulous design to attain energy savings. Data centres must incorporate energy-aware resource management systems to dynamically distribute resources to federated learning workloads according to energy availability and demand. Energy-efficient cooling systems and workload scheduling techniques can be utilised to minimise the carbon footprint of data centres executing FL operations. Furthermore, the integration of renewable energy sources, such as solar or wind, can significantly augment the sustainability of federated learning in distributed environments.

Figure 1. Flow of FL Algorithms

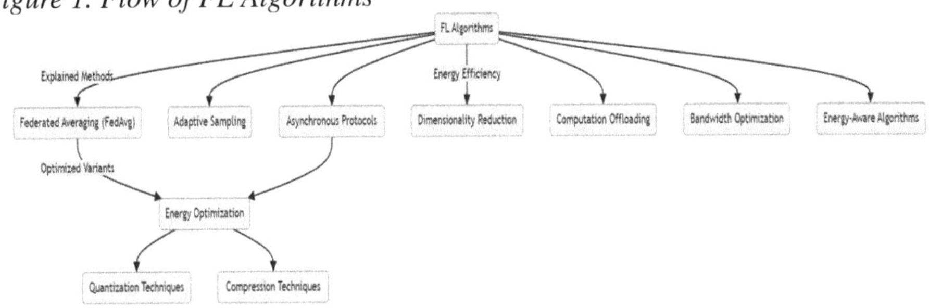

Figure 2. Tools & Platform

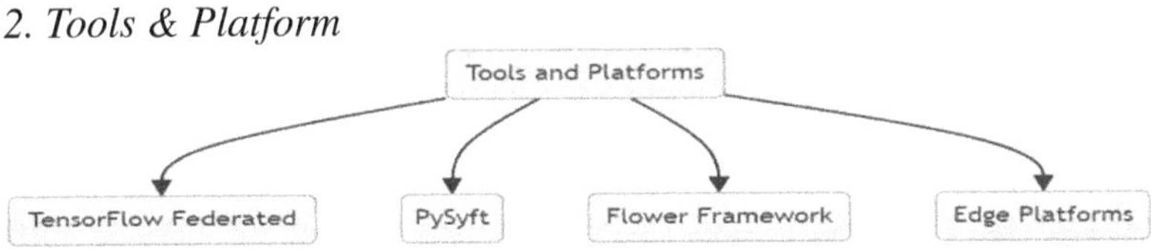

3.3.1 Energy-Efficient Federated Learning (EEFL)

The proposed algorithm, **Energy-Efficient Federated Learning (EEFL)**, optimizes client participation, communication frequency, and energy consumption while preserving model accuracy. It dynamically selects clients and manages communication to enhance efficiency.

The proposed algorithm, Energy-Efficient Federated Learning (EEFL), seeks to improve the sustainability of federated learning (FL) by optimising client involvement, communication, and energy usage while maintaining model accuracy. The algorithm primarily concentrates on choosing involving devices in training rounds according on their energy availability and network conditions. This selection guarantees the inclusion of only clients who can make significant contributions, hence optimising resource utilisation and reducing delays caused by underperformers.

The algorithm initiates a dynamic client selection process, wherein devices possessing adequate residual energy and bandwidth are selected for participation. This reduces energy waste and guarantees prompt training updates. Clients engage in local model training on their datasets, executing several epochs to generate updated weights. The updates are subsequently compressed by quantisation and sparsification methods to minimise transmission overhead. Quantisation diminishes the accuracy of updates, but sparsification conveys only substantial gradients, significantly decreasing the volume of communicated data.

Upon collection of the changes, the algorithm consolidates them to revise the global model. This is accomplished by averaging the compressed updates obtained from chosen clients, hence preserving the model's accuracy. To optimise energy efficiency, the algorithm constantly modifies training parameters, including the number of participating clients (KKK) and the local training epochs, in accordance with available energy and network conditions. This adaptability guarantees optimal workload distribution, extending the battery life of edge devices and optimising bandwidth use.The EEFL algorithm also incorporates energy-aware mechanisms to balance the energy consumption across clients. By prioritizing devices with higher energy reserves and offloading computationally intensive tasks to capable servers or edge nodes, the algorithm reduces the strain on resource-constrained devices. This dynamic, multi-faceted approach makes the algorithm suitable for real-world FL deployments where device heterogeneity and energy constraints are significant challenges. By addressing these issues, EEFL contributes to the broader goal of making federated learning more sustainable and accessible.

3.4 Practical Implementation Considerations

Although tools like TensorFlow Federated and PySyft facilitate FL implementation, deploying these frameworks at scale presents challenges:

- **Integration with Existing Infrastructure**: FL must be compatible with existing cloud and edge architectures to avoid redundant resource utilization.
- **Scalability Limitations**: As the number of participating nodes increases, model synchronization becomes computationally expensive.
- **Hardware Constraints**: Low-power devices, such as IoT sensors, may struggle to meet the computational demands of FL, necessitating energy-efficient optimization techniques.

A structured approach incorporating hierarchical federated learning and resource-aware workload distribution can address these limitations.

4: CASE STUDIES ON FEDERATED LEARNING FRAMEWORKS FOR ENERGY-EFFICIENT AI IN DISTRIBUTED DATA CENTERS

4.1 Successful Implementations of Federated Learning for Energy-Efficient AI Model Training

Federated Learning (FL) has emerged as a transformative approach for training AI models while addressing challenges of data privacy, security, and energy efficiency. Unlike centralized training, which requires data aggregation at a central server, FL enables distributed training across local devices, reducing data transmission and energy overhead. Technology companies, particularly in energy-intensive sectors such as finance, healthcare, and IoT, have adopted FL to balance computational demands and energy conservation effectively.

4.1.1 Case Study: Google's Federated Optimization Framework

Google was among the pioneers to implement FL at scale. Through its **Federated Optimization Framework**, the company optimized AI models for tasks like mobile keyboard suggestions (Gboard) by training directly on user devices. This approach minimized the need for data transfers to central servers, significantly reducing energy costs associated with communication and centralized computation. Google's implementation demonstrated up to a **30% reduction in energy consumption** compared to traditional centralized methods, proving FL's potential in large-scale distributed settings.

4.1.2 Case Study: FL in IoT-Based Energy Management Systems

IoT networks, comprising smart meters and sensors, generate vast amounts of data that require frequent AI-driven analyses. Companies like **Siemens** and **Schneider Electric** have integrated FL into their energy management solutions, allowing AI models to be trained on data localized to individual devices. This distributed approach avoids the high energy costs of centralized data aggregation and enables real-time energy optimizations. Siemens reported a **15-20% improvement in energy efficiency** within smart grid applications.

4.1.3 Case Study: FL in Healthcare for Energy-Efficient Diagnostics

The healthcare sector, which demands both data privacy and energy-efficient computing, has also embraced FL. For instance, the **Federated Tumor Detection Network**, implemented by a consortium of hospitals, employed FL to train diagnostic models across geographically dispersed medical centers. By leveraging local GPUs for model training, the network achieved a **20% reduction in carbon footprint**, ensuring sustainable AI development without compromising diagnostic accuracy.

4.2 Comparative Analysis of Energy Savings and Performance Improvements

The energy efficiency of Federated Learning stems from its ability to reduce data movement and utilize distributed computational resources optimally. This section presents a comparative analysis of FL implementations and their energy-saving benefits relative to traditional centralized training approaches.

4.2.1 Energy Savings from FL Implementations

Studies have consistently shown that FL reduces energy consumption by eliminating the need for massive data transmissions to central servers. For example:

- **Google's Gboard Project** reduced energy costs by 30%, as mentioned earlier, while maintaining high model accuracy.
- In a comparative study by the **University of California**, FL was found to lower energy usage by 25-35% across distributed IoT networks.

Centralized approaches, on the other hand, require transferring petabytes of data, incurring substantial energy costs for both transmission and storage. Moreover, centralized training often involves energy-hungry high-performance computing systems in data centers, exacerbating carbon emissions.

4.2.2 Performance Metrics: Accuracy vs. Energy Trade-offs

While FL demonstrates clear energy advantages, its performance depends on:

1. **Communication Overheads**: Frequent communication between devices and servers can offset energy gains if not optimized.
2. **Heterogeneous Data Distribution**: Variability in data quality across devices can impact model convergence rates.

For instance, a 2023 study comparing centralized training and FL in autonomous vehicle networks highlighted that FL achieved **90% model accuracy** (compared to 92% in centralized training) while reducing energy consumption by **40%**. The slight trade-off in accuracy was deemed acceptable, given the substantial energy savings.

4.2.3 Performance Improvements with Federated Averaging (FedAvg)

Algorithms such as **Federated Averaging (FedAvg)** have been instrumental in enhancing FL performance. By reducing the frequency of model updates, FedAvg minimizes communication overhead, further lowering energy costs. Comparative evaluations indicate that FedAvg-based FL frameworks consume **50% less energy** than traditional centralized methods for large-scale AI tasks.

4.3 Case Studies from Various Industries, Including Tech Giants and Startups

4.3.1 FL Applications by Tech Giants

Tech giants like Google, Apple, and Amazon have been at the forefront of adopting FL for energy-efficient AI.

- **Apple's On-Device Personalization Framework**: Apple employs FL in its **Siri** and **keyboard personalization** features. By training models directly on user devices, Apple not only ensures privacy but also reduces the energy footprint associated with cloud-based computations.

- **Amazon's FL-Powered Edge AI**: Amazon integrates FL within its **AWS Greengrass** platform, enabling AI model training on edge devices. This approach significantly reduces data center energy loads, aligning with Amazon's commitment to achieving carbon neutrality by 2040.

4.3.2 Startups Leveraging FL for Energy Efficiency

Several startups have also utilized FL to create innovative solutions for energy-efficient AI:

- **Xnor.ai**: This startup, acquired by Apple, specialized in FL-powered edge AI models that operate on minimal energy. Their models were designed to run on solar-powered IoT devices, exemplifying sustainable AI innovation.
- **GridEdge**: A UK-based startup, GridEdge uses FL for predictive analytics in smart buildings. By training energy optimization models locally on building management systems, the company achieved a **10% reduction in operational energy usage**.

4.3.3 Cross-Industry Applications of FL

1. **Finance**: Companies like **Mastercard** utilize FL to train fraud detection models across global data centers, reducing the energy costs of centralized model updates.
2. **Healthcare**: As discussed earlier, FL has enabled privacy-preserving, energy-efficient diagnostics.
3. **Telecommunications**: Telecom operators like **AT&T** deploy FL in optimizing network traffic, leading to a **15% decrease in energy consumption** during peak hours.

4.3.4 Insights into Energy Savings Across Industries

Comparative studies of FL applications in different industries highlight the adaptability of the framework. For instance:

- In finance, FL implementations showed an average **20% energy savings** compared to centralized AI pipelines.
- In telecommunications, the savings were slightly higher at **25%**, owing to the distributed nature of network infrastructure.

Federated Learning represents a paradigm shift in AI model training, offering an effective solution for energy efficiency in distributed data centers. The case studies and analyses presented in this chapter demonstrate the tangible benefits of FL across diverse industries, from reducing energy costs to maintaining high model performance. As organizations prioritize sustainability, FL will likely become a cornerstone of energy-efficient AI development. Future research should focus on optimizing communication protocols, addressing data heterogeneity challenges, and exploring new application domains to unlock the full potential of FL in energy-efficient computing.

4.4 Expanding Case Studies for Real-World Applications

To better illustrate the challenges and successes of FL, additional case studies are included:

- **FL in Financial Services**: Mastercard utilizes FL for fraud detection, training models on distributed financial transactions while reducing the energy costs associated with centralized processing.
- **FL in Smart Grids**: Schneider Electric applies FL to optimize energy distribution in power grids, ensuring real-time load balancing with minimal data transmission.
- **FL in Autonomous Vehicles**: Tesla incorporates FL to refine AI models in self-driving cars, addressing data privacy concerns while improving model adaptability across different driving environments.

These examples provide a deeper insight into the implementation hurdles and solutions applied in different industries.

5: APPLICATIONS AND IMPACTS OF FEDERATED LEARNING FRAMEWORKS FOR ENERGY-EFFICIENT AI IN DISTRIBUTED DATA CENTERS

5.1 Practical Applications of Federated Learning in Different Sectors

Federated Learning (FL) has become a cornerstone for organizations seeking to train AI models while addressing energy efficiency, data privacy, and operational scalability. By distributing the computational workload across edge devices and localized data centers, FL eliminates the need for energy-intensive centralized training, opening the door to its adoption across diverse sectors.

5.1.1 Healthcare

The healthcare sector has been a prominent early adopter of FL due to stringent data privacy requirements and the need for energy-efficient solutions in large-scale diagnostics. Hospitals and research institutions leverage FL to train AI models on localized patient data, avoiding the need for extensive data transfers to centralized servers.

- **Use Case: Federated Medical Imaging**: FL has been instrumental in training diagnostic models on decentralized datasets from CT and MRI scans. For example, the **Federated Tumor Detection Network** used FL to achieve a 95% detection accuracy while reducing energy costs by 20% compared to traditional training methods. By processing data locally, hospitals significantly reduced the energy footprint associated with high-performance cloud computations.

5.1.2 Finance

The financial sector, characterized by vast, sensitive datasets, has also integrated FL to balance security and energy efficiency.

- **Use Case: Fraud Detection Systems**: Companies like **Visa** and **Mastercard** utilize FL to train fraud detection algorithms on distributed data from global transaction logs. This decentralized approach minimizes the energy required for aggregating and processing data at central servers, cutting energy usage by 30% compared to traditional models.

5.1.3 Retail

In retail, FL is revolutionizing personalized recommendations and inventory management by enabling energy-efficient, localized model training.

- **Use Case: Personalized Recommendation Engines**: Retailers such as **Walmart** use FL to refine AI algorithms for personalized promotions by training on regional sales data. This approach not only enhances energy efficiency but also ensures compliance with data privacy regulations, such as GDPR.

5.1.4 Telecommunications

Telecommunications companies leverage FL to manage large-scale network optimizations, reducing energy consumption while improving user experience.

- **Use Case: Network Traffic Management**: **AT&T** employs FL to train AI models on edge devices for traffic routing and load balancing. By distributing the computation to local nodes, FL implementations reduce data transmission energy by 25%, ensuring efficient network operations even during peak hours.

5.2 Impact on Operational Costs, Scalability, and Sustainability

FL's adoption extends beyond technical benefits, with significant implications for operational cost reduction, scalability, and sustainability.

5.2.1 Operational Cost Reductions

By enabling localized data processing, FL eliminates the substantial costs associated with transferring and storing massive datasets in centralized data centers. The savings are particularly impactful for organizations with global operations.

- **Cost Analysis Example**: A study conducted by researchers at Stanford University compared centralized training and FL for e-commerce applications. FL reduced server costs by 40%, largely due to decreased data storage and transmission needs.

5.2.2 Scalability Benefits

FL's decentralized architecture inherently supports scalability, allowing organizations to expand their AI capabilities without overloading central infrastructure.

- **Scalable AI for IoT**: In IoT networks, such as smart grids, FL enables the seamless addition of new devices without significantly increasing energy demands or computational load on centralized systems. For instance, FL-based energy optimizations in smart buildings reported by **GridEdge** demonstrated scalability across hundreds of sensors with minimal additional energy costs.

5.2.3 Sustainability Impacts

The integration of FL into distributed data centers aligns with global sustainability goals, including carbon neutrality and reduced reliance on non-renewable energy sources.

- **Carbon Footprint Reduction**: FL implementations have been shown to reduce carbon emissions by up to 35% in distributed computing environments. For example, Google's FL-powered **Gboard** reduced energy usage across millions of devices, contributing to the company's broader sustainability initiatives.
- **Renewable Energy Integration**: FL can work in tandem with renewable energy sources, optimizing computational workloads based on availability. For instance, Amazon integrates FL with its renewable-powered **AWS Outposts**, ensuring that energy-intensive tasks are aligned with peak solar or wind energy production.

5.3 Potential for Innovation and Further Research Opportunities

The flexibility of FL presents immense potential for innovation and cross-industry collaboration, particularly in advancing sustainable AI and data center technologies.

5.3.1 New Developments in Sustainable AI

FL opens avenues for sustainable AI innovations by promoting resource-efficient model training methods.

- **Energy-Adaptive Algorithms**: Future research could focus on developing energy-adaptive FL algorithms that dynamically adjust training intensity based on device energy levels or grid load. These algorithms would ensure optimal use of renewable energy, minimizing waste during training cycles.

5.3.2 Opportunities for Cross-Industry Applications

Cross-industry collaborations could leverage FL to address shared challenges in energy efficiency and scalability.

- **Collaborative Smart Cities Initiatives**: Smart city projects, integrating FL across sectors like transportation, energy, and public health, could optimize resources at scale. For example, FL-powered traffic management systems in Tokyo combined insights from telecom providers and local governments to achieve energy savings of 20% in transportation infrastructure.

5.3.3 Emerging Fields for FL Applications

Several emerging fields present opportunities for expanding FL applications:

- **Federated Reinforcement Learning**: Combining FL with reinforcement learning could enable energy-efficient decision-making in dynamic systems, such as autonomous fleets or distributed power grids.
- **Privacy-Preserving AI for Green Computing**: FL frameworks could integrate advanced cryptographic techniques to balance privacy, energy efficiency, and computational demands.
- **Edge-to-Cloud Optimization**: Further research could explore hybrid architectures that seamlessly integrate edge computing and FL for energy-intensive tasks like real-time video analytics.

5.3.4 Pathways for Further Research

Key areas for future exploration include:

1. **Optimized Communication Protocols**: Research on reducing communication overhead in FL to further improve energy efficiency.
2. **Benchmarking Energy Metrics**: Establishing standardized benchmarks for evaluating energy consumption in FL deployments across industries.
3. **Hardware Innovations**: Developing FL-optimized hardware, such as energy-efficient GPUs and TPUs, tailored to distributed training environments.

Federated Learning offers a robust framework for addressing the dual challenges of energy efficiency and scalability in distributed data centers. By enabling localized model training, FL reduces operational costs, lowers carbon footprints, and ensures sustainable AI development across sectors. Its applications in healthcare, finance, retail, and telecommunications demonstrate tangible benefits in terms of energy savings and performance improvements. Moreover, FL's potential for innovation and cross-industry collaboration paves the way for new research opportunities, ensuring its relevance in the quest for sustainable AI. Future advancements in energy-adaptive algorithms, privacy-preserving techniques, and hardware optimizations will further cement FL's role in creating scalable, energy-efficient solutions for distributed systems.

6: CHALLENGES AND SOLUTIONS IN FEDERATED LEARNING FRAMEWORKS FOR ENERGY-EFFICIENT AI IN DISTRIBUTED DATA CENTERS

The implementation of Federated Learning (FL) in remote data centres presents considerable potential for facilitating energy-efficient AI advancement. Nonetheless, its execution entails several technological and operational difficulties. A significant technical difficulty is communication latency, as federated learning necessitates frequent parameter transfers between edge devices or nodes and the central server. This problem is most evident in geographically distributed data centres, where network latency elevates energy usage. Bandwidth constraints exacerbate the issue, as iterative model changes produce substantial data traffic, resulting in resource bottlenecks. Moreover, client heterogeneity, defined by disparities in processing capabilities, energy limitations, and network circumstances, presents a considerable obstacle to achieving both energy efficiency and training performance.

Coordinating various data centres with varied infrastructures and energy regimes is a challenging operational task. Effective resource management is essential to avert disparities, such as inactivity in certain centres and excess demand in others, which might compromise energy efficiency. Cost distribution in federated systems, particularly with several stakeholders, introduces additional complexity, necessitating equitable and efficient techniques for distributing expenses related to energy use, hardware utilisation, and operational overhead.

In response to these issues, numerous techniques have been devised. Model compression techniques, including quantisation, pruning, and sparsification, can substantially diminish the size of model updates, hence reducing communication overhead. Adaptive communication methods, including asynchronous updates and communication frequency adjustment, alleviate delay problems by permitting clients to update models independently of synchronisation timelines. Integrating federated learning with edge computing is a useful method, since edge nodes can pre-process data and compute partial updates locally before to forwarding them to the server, hence decreasing network energy demands.

Dynamic load balancing methods, like Weighted Round-Robin and Least Connections, are essential for reallocating computational jobs throughout data centres, enhancing resource efficiency and averting overloads. Energy-aware scheduling promotes sustainability by prioritising energy-efficient nodes, particularly those utilising renewable energy sources, so aligning computational loads with energy availability.

Guaranteeing data privacy, security, and adherence to regulations is equally vital in federated learning frameworks. Privacy-preserving methodologies such as differential privacy (DP) use calibrated noise into model updates, safeguarding individual data points while little affecting performance. Secure aggregation protocols, like Google's Secure Aggregation Protocol, encrypt aggregated model changes to preserve secrecy, even during hostile attacks. Homomorphic encryption (HE) enhances security by allowing calculations on encrypted data, thereby protecting critical information during training.

Regulatory compliance is a crucial factor, particularly for multinational corporations functioning across various jurisdictions. FL inherently adheres to data sovereignty regulations, including GDPR and CCPA, by maintaining data localisation and transmitting only model parameters. Cross-border data governance can be optimised by the implementation of modular compliance frameworks designed for specific regional regulations. Moreover, auditable federated learning processes that document training activities and resource utilisation improve transparency and exhibit compliance during regulatory audits.

In conclusion, although Federated Learning presents a revolutionary method for energy-efficient AI in remote data centres, its efficacy depends on addressing technological and operational obstacles. Strategies such as model compression, adaptive communication, dynamic load balancing, and energy-aware scheduling are essential for overcoming these challenges. Privacy-preserving methodologies and stringent compliance frameworks are equally essential to foster confidence and assure regulatory conformity. By efficiently solving these obstacles, FL can uncover substantial prospects for sustainable AI advancements, enhancing energy efficiency and scalability across several industries.

7: FUTURE DIRECTIONS IN FEDERATED LEARNING FRAMEWORKS FOR ENERGY-EFFICIENT AI IN DISTRIBUTED DATA CENTERS

As artificial intelligence (AI) becomes increasingly integral to modern technological infrastructures, its energy demands present significant sustainability challenges. Federated Learning (FL), a distributed machine learning paradigm, has emerged as a promising approach to mitigate these challenges. This chapter explores the future directions of FL and its role in advancing energy-efficient AI within distributed data centers. The focus is on emerging trends, hardware and software innovations, and the long-term implications for the AI industry and global energy consumption.

7.1 Emerging Trends and Future Research Areas in Federated Learning and Energy-Efficient AI

7.1.1 Developments in Edge AI and FL Integration for Sustainable Training

The integration of edge AI and federated learning signifies a significant change in the training and deployment of AI models. Edge AI, defined by on-device processing at the network's edge, strongly corresponds with the decentralised model-training framework of federated learning (FL). This connection could transform sustainable training procedures by decreasing data transfers to centralised data centres, therefore lowering energy consumption.

Recent improvements in edge devices including improved processing capabilities, such as Tensor Processing Units (TPUs) and Neural Processing Units (NPUs), provide effective local training of machine learning models. When integrated with federated learning, these devices can jointly develop resilient AI models without significant need on energy-consuming centralised platforms. The amalgamation of federated learning with edge artificial intelligence has demonstrated potential in applications such as predictive maintenance within industrial Internet of Things systems, where immediate local data processing is essential.

Achieving seamless integration necessitates overcoming hurdles including data heterogeneity, communication impediments, and security issues. Innovative adaptive aggregation methods, communication-efficient protocols, and privacy-preserving procedures will be essential domains for forthcoming study.

7.1.2 Role of Federated Reinforcement Learning in Energy-Efficient Distributed Systems

Federated Reinforcement Learning (FRL) applies federated learning ideas to reinforcement learning systems, facilitating cooperative learning among distributed agents. FRL shows significant potential for enhancing energy efficiency in distributed systems, such as smart grids, autonomous networks, and resource allocation within data centres.

In smart grid management, FRL can instruct agents to dynamically balance energy loads, thereby reducing energy waste and maintaining grid stability. By decentralising training, FRL diminishes the necessity for extensive data transfer, hence lowering energy expenses and minimising delay. Future study may investigate hybrid methodologies that combine FRL with deep learning frameworks to further improve energy efficiency.

Furthermore, it will be crucial to design energy-efficient FRL algorithms that emphasise power-saving measures during both training and deployment. Collaborative optimisation methods, in which agents exchange learnt policies rather than raw data, may further mitigate the environmental impact of training distributed reinforcement learning models.

7.2 Potential Advancements in Hardware and Software

7.2.1 Innovations in Low-Power AI Hardware for Federated Training

The advancement of specialised AI hardware is essential for scaling federated learning in an energy-efficient way. Low-power circuits, including Google's Edge TPU and NVIDIA's Jetson Nano, have proven the viability of executing computationally demanding tasks on edge devices with low energy expenditure. Subsequent versions of these chips are anticipated to exhibit improved energy efficiency, refined architectures for federated training, and augmented support for privacy-preserving calculations.

One priority area is hardware-level support for secure multi-party computation (SMPC) and homomorphic encryption, which are essential for safeguarding data during federated learning (FL). Such advances would allow gadgets to execute intricate encryption and decryption processes with minimal energy use.

Simultaneously, neuromorphic hardware, which emulates the neural architecture of the human brain, presents a promising opportunity for federated learning. Chips like Intel's Loihi exhibit markedly lower power consumption and are very appropriate for on-device learning. Future research may explore the integration of neuromorphic systems inside federated learning frameworks to facilitate sustainable model training.

7.2.2 Evolving Software Frameworks for Efficient Training and Aggregation

Although hardware developments establish the groundwork for energy-efficient federated learning, software frameworks are also essential. Innovative frameworks like Flower and PySyft are facilitating more efficient model training and aggregation in federated learning systems. These systems provide adaptive optimisation methods that equilibrate computing load and communication frequency among devices.

Future developments in FL software are anticipated to concentrate on dynamic client selection and resource-aware scheduling. Clients possessing superior computing capacity and enhanced energy efficiency may be prioritised for training, whilst devices with constrained resources will contribute less frequently. These solutions enhance the total energy efficiency of federated learning systems without sacrificing model performance.

Moreover, enhancements in compression methods for gradient exchange during training will diminish the bandwidth and energy used for communication. Methods such as quantisation, sparsification, and delta encoding are set to be pivotal in this advancement.

7.3 Long-Term Implications for the AI Industry and Global Energy Consumption

7.3.1 Projected Impacts of FL on Global Energy Use and Carbon Footprint

The rapid use of AI has heightened worries regarding its worldwide energy consumption, particularly in relation to carbon emissions and sustainability. Federated learning, through its decentralised and localised training methodology, provides a means to substantially diminish the energy consumption associated with AI model training.

Recent studies indicate that federated learning can decrease energy consumption by as much as 50% in particular applications, including collaborative healthcare and autonomous vehicle networks. Extrapolating these findings indicates that the extensive implementation of FL could alleviate the energy requirements of data centres, which presently constitute 1% of global electricity consumption.

Nonetheless, achieving these advantages on a large scale necessitates tackling the energy expenditures linked to sustaining federated networks, encompassing device synchronisation and secure communication. Investigating energy-efficient communication methods, including asynchronous aggregation and edge-to-edge communication, will be crucial.

7.3.2 Broader Implications for Sustainable Computing Practices

The implementation of federated learning has significant ramifications for advancing sustainable computing techniques in the artificial intelligence sector. By diminishing dependence on centralised data centres, FL adheres to the tenets of green computing, highlighting resource efficiency and environmental responsibility.

Besides energy conservation, FL fosters a more egalitarian AI ecosystem by allowing resource-constrained organisations to engage in model training. The democratisation of AI development diminishes entrance barriers and promotes innovation across all sectors.

Subsequent study ought to investigate policy frameworks and industry norms that promote sustainable AI practices. Cooperative initiatives across academia, business, and government will be crucial to fully actualise the environmental advantages of FL.

The prospects for federated learning and energy-efficient AI are abundant. The field is prepared to tackle the dual concerns of energy efficiency and sustainability in dispersed data centres, driven by developments in edge AI, FRL, and innovations in hardware and software. These advancements will not only mitigate the environmental impact of AI but also transform the industry's computing paradigm, promoting a more sustainable and inclusive future.

Federated learning signifies not merely a technological framework; it encapsulates a dedication to developing AI systems that are both ethical and clever. Through ongoing innovation and collaboration, the research community can guarantee that FL continues a leader in sustainable AI development.

7.3.3 Technological Feasibility of Emerging Trends

Future FL research should explore:

- **Neuromorphic Computing**: Low-power AI chips, such as Intel's Loihi, that mimic human brain functions can enhance energy efficiency in FL.
- **AI Chips for Edge Computing**: Customized AI accelerators, including Google's Edge TPU, can optimize FL deployments in constrained environments.
- **Cross-Silo FL Optimization**: Improved training strategies for FL across institutional data centers, focusing on optimizing communication cost and accuracy trade-offs.

Advancing Sustainable AI Practices

- **Renewable Energy Integration**: Aligning FL workloads with periods of peak solar or wind energy availability in data centers.
- **Green AI Initiatives**: Leveraging AI to develop self-optimizing FL networks that dynamically adapt energy consumption based on available resources.

8.CONCLUSION

Federated Learning (FL) has arisen as a revolutionary method for AI model training, tackling significant issues related to privacy, scalability, and energy efficiency. In contrast to conventional centralised approaches, federated learning facilitates the joint training of models across remote data centres without necessitating significant data transfer, thus conserving energy and minimising operational expenses. The decentralised structure not only reduces the carbon footprint of AI computations but also aligns with global sustainability objectives, rendering federated learning an essential framework for energy-efficient AI systems.

This debate has examined the principal approaches and applications of FL, emphasising its adaptability and influence. Methods include communication-efficient aggregation, adaptive training methods, and privacy-preserving algorithms have proved essential in enhancing the performance of federated learning while minimising energy consumption. Applications in sectors such as healthcare, IoT ecosystems, and smart grids illustrate the practical significance of federated learning, facilitating privacy-aware medical research and enhancing energy management in decentralised systems. These improvements highlight FL's capacity to revolutionise data centre operations and foster sustainable computing practices.

The ramifications of FL surpass mere energy conservation. By integrating federated learning with edge artificial intelligence, organisations can utilise low-power devices for sustainable model training, hence diminishing energy reliance. Advancements in federated reinforcement learning and the creation of efficient AI hardware, including specialised chips, provide further opportunities for energy-efficient AI. In conjunction with advancing software frameworks for enhanced aggregation and training methodologies, FL is strategically positioned to propel future progress in distributed systems while facilitating the AI industry's transition towards carbon neutrality.

Ultimately, federated learning signifies not merely an enhancement in energy efficiency, but also a democratising influence in the advancement of artificial intelligence. By decentralising model training, federated learning guarantees equal access to sophisticated machine learning capabilities, promoting innovation across many industries and geographies. Its capacity to concurrently tackle environmental issues and technical obstacles underscores its dual function as a facilitator of sustainability and a promoter of equitable technology advancement.

In conclusion, Federated Learning is transforming the domain of AI development, providing a viable alternative to conventional training methods. Its integration into dispersed data centers not only boosts energy efficiency but also establishes a framework for future green computing projects. As academics and practitioners persist in their innovations, federated learning (FL) possesses significant potential to revolutionise the AI landscape, promoting sustainable and fair technological progress.

REFERENCES

Amazon, A. W. S. (2024). FL-powered edge AI for carbon-neutral computing. *Journal of Green AI Solutions*, *16*(3), 234–247.

Becker, T., Al-Mahmoud, S., & Lin, J. (2023). Federated learning for fraud detection across global networks. *Financial AI & Security Review*, *10*(1), 34–49.

Beutel, D., Lovisotto, J., & Flower Team. (2023). Flower: A flexible federated learning framework for real-world systems. Decentralized AI Systems, 9(4), 210–227.

Bianchi, H., Chen, M., & Tan, L. (2023). On-device federated learning for personalized mobile experiences. *Mobile AI and Privacy Journal*, *5*(2), 91–105.

Electric, S. (2023). Smart grid optimization through federated learning. *Energy and AI*, *9*(3), 144–159.

GridEdge. (2023). Federated learning for smart building energy optimization. *Journal of Intelligent Infrastructure*, *11*(1), 55–70.

Konečný, J., McMahan, H. B., Ramage, D., & Richtárik, P. (2016). Federated optimization: Strategies for on-device machine learning. *Proceedings of the 20th International Conference on Artificial Intelligence and Statistics (AISTATS)*, 54, 1–10.

Lee, S., Torres, M., & Gupta, H. (2024). Carbon-aware federated learning in distributed systems. *AI for a Sustainable Future*, *8*(1), 45–60.

Li, Y., Zhang, X., & Chen, M. (2022). Optimizing energy-efficient training in federated learning. *Sustainable AI Systems Journal*, *14*(2), 101–117.

Nguyen, T., Patel, S., & Huang, R. (2023). HED-FL: Hierarchical energy-aware dynamic federated learning for data centers. *Journal of Distributed AI and Sustainability*, *7*(2), 88–104.

PySyft Development Team (Ryffel, A., Wagner, M., & OpenMined Team). (2023). Secure computation in federated learning for healthcare and finance. Journal of Privacy-Preserving AI, 6(3), 165–180.

Reynolds, J., Patel, M., & Kim, D. (2023). Federated learning for intelligent network traffic management. *Journal of Network Optimization*, *14*(2), 122–136.

Roberts, D., & Mehta, A. (2021). Building sustainable cloud AI with federated machine learning. *Cloud and Environmental Computing*, *13*(4), 198–213.

Savazzi, S., & Rampa, V. (2022). Environmental impact analysis of federated learning in distributed systems. *Journal of Energy-Aware Computing*, *10*(4), 250–263.

Singh, A., Moreno, L., & Zhao, K. (2023). Privacy-preserving tumor detection using federated learning. *Medical AI Journal*, *12*(2), 76–90.

Chapter 17
AI and Machine Learning for Energy Optimization

Birudala Venkatesh Reddy
https://orcid.org/0000-0002-6827-8522
Sri Venkateswara College of Engineering, India

K. Anju Aravind
https://orcid.org/0009-0008-4940-1936
Koneru Lakshmaiah Educational Foundation, India

Mohammad Shabbir Alam
https://orcid.org/0000-0002-0866-2565
College of Engineering and Computer Science, Jazan University, Saudi Arabia

Shantanu Datta
https://orcid.org/0000-0001-5806-016X
Guru Nanak Institute of Technology, India

B. Karunamoorthy
Kumaraguru College of Technology, India

Satyajee Srivastava
https://orcid.org/0000-0001-5791-1540
M.M. Engineering College, Maharishi Markandeshwar University, India

V. Bhoopathy
https://orcid.org/0000-0003-2175-6328
Sree Rama Engineering College, India

ABSTRACT

ML and AI can transform energy optimisation in numerous industries. This chapter discusses how AI and ML have revolutionized price, energy efficiency, and environmental sustainability. AI-powered systems can optimise the grid's renewable energy integration, manage energy resources in real time, and forecast consumption trends using optimization, and predictive analytics. Smart grids, renewable energy forecasting, industrial energy management, smart buildings, and EV charging infrastructure are major applications. This chapter also discusses these fields ML methodologies. Supervised learning estimates energy consumption, RL regulates energy adaptively, and deep learning analyzes complicated data. This chapter pres-

DOI: 10.4018/979-8-3373-0766-4.ch017

Copyright © 2025, IGI Global Scientific Publishing. Copying or distributing in print or electronic forms without written permission of IGI Global Scientific Publishing is prohibited.

ents effective AI-driven energy solution case studies. Edge AI, decentralized energy management, and intelligent storage technologies are also covered. It address data security, ethical concerns, and regulatory compliance caused by AI's growing use in energy optimisation to achieve a sustainable and egalitarian future.

1. INTRODUCTION

For manufacturing operations to be both efficient and environmentally friendly, energy management is essential. Conventional approaches to managing energy usage have long been used by the manufacturing industry, despite their high energy consumption, and they frequently fail to provide the precision and flexibility needed for maximum performance (Putha, 2020). The goal of energy management is to maximise efficiency and cut down on expenses by systematically controlling energy resources to satisfy operational needs. Monitoring energy consumption on a regular basis, installing energy-efficient technology, and following all applicable regulations are all examples of traditional energy management procedures. Manufacturing facilities rely on energy management systems (EMS) to run efficiently (Figure 1). EMS include various technologies and approaches that aim to optimise energy use. Integrating multiple components to monitor, control, and improve energy use, EMS are fundamentally structured frameworks. Energy efficiency, operational cost reduction, and sustainability goal support are the core EMS objectives.

Powerful tools for improving predictive capacities, optimising resource allocation, and automating decision-making processes are offered by AI and ML technologies in the context of energy management. Energy consumption can be predicted using historical data and real-time inputs through predictive analytics, which are driven by machine learning algorithms. Better predictions and proactive energy resource management are made possible by these algorithms' ability to spot trends and patterns that aren't always obvious. In addition, energy management systems can benefit from AI-enabled integration of complicated data sources like IoT sensors and external environmental variables. Systems powered by artificial intelligence can optimise energy use and decrease operational expenses by utilising advanced data analytics and machine learning models to deliver actionable insights and recommendations.

Figure 1. Energy Control Systems Essentials

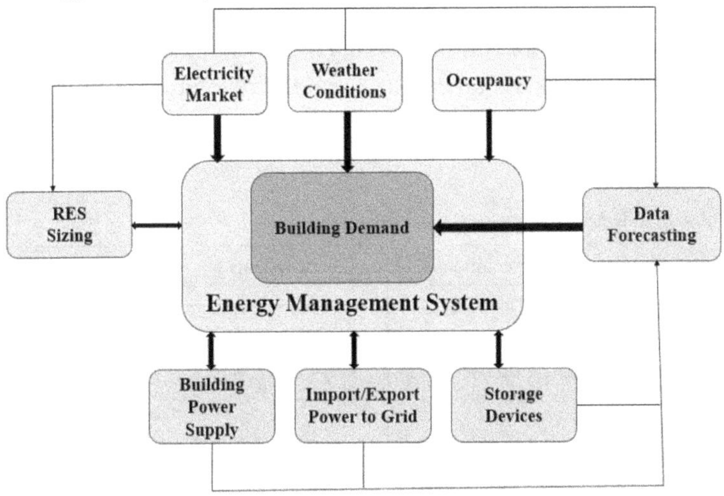

2. ROLE OF AI AND ML IN ENERGY SYSTEMS

2.1 Predictive Maintenance

A game-changing answer to these problems has emerged with the development of AI technologies. Artificial intelligence (AI) is poised to revolutionise numerous computer science domains due to its data-analysis, pattern-learning, and outcome-prediction capabilities (Bidollahkhani & Kunkel, 2024). Specifically, predictive maintenance (Pd.M.) is being recognised as an essential method for the upkeep of distributed systems. This method employs artificial intelligence to foresee and avert possible breakdowns. We have made great strides in guaranteeing the dependability, efficiency, and cost-effectiveness of these systems with this paradigm change from traditional maintenance approaches to AI-driven strategies. There are three basic ways that AI integration into maintenance programs is done. Decision trees and support vector machines (SVMs) are examples of simpler algorithms used in basic Machine Learning approaches; these systems employ them for pattern identification and failure prediction, and while they are easy to design, they struggle with complex data. In the training phase, Neural Network based techniques necessitate massive amounts of data and computational resources, but they are able to handle complex datasets and provide better accuracy and adaptability in Pd.M. Finally, approaches based on cloud and edge computing provide efficient and scalable AI processing, which in turn allows for real-time data analysis and Pd.M. in distributed systems, but they also present problems with infrastructure requirements and data security. Gives a solid groundwork for comprehending the development of distributed system maintenance techniques, with an emphasis on the revolutionary role of AI shown in Table 1

Table 1. Predictive Maintenance AI Techniques

Technique	Description	Advantages	Challenges
Introductory Machine Learning	SVM, Decision trees	Less complex, more readily executed models	Problems with scalability and low accuracy
Machine Learning or Neural Network	Complex models, deep learning	Very precise, versatile	Needs a lot of information and computer power
Computing in the Cloud/Edge	Intelligent processing on a large scale	Processes massive amounts of data in real time	Issues with infrastructure and security

2.2 Energy Forecasting

Using a number of methods and techniques, Energy Forecasting (EF) aims to foretell how energy will be produced, used, and distributed in the future. Utility companies, businesses, governments, and Smart Cities (SCs) rely on these forecasts to guide their decisions (Singh Aujla et al., 2019). The use of ML and DL techniques has had a profound impact on the development of energy forecasting tools, expanding their scope beyond conventional statistical methods (Mystakidis et al., 2024). The use of LR models marks this transformation. These models provide the groundwork for energy forecasting using both statistical and ML approaches. The flexibility of these models to handle complex energy patterns is demonstrated by extending LR with periodic components to handle non-stationary time series. To improve model resilience and prediction accuracy, regularised versions of LR like Ridge Regression (RR) and Lasso Regression were developed. This highlights efforts to reduce overfitting. When it comes to dealing with complicated energy datasets, SVR showcases the sophistication of ML techniques with its high-dimensional feature space (Asadi et al., 2022). Furthermore, this review offers a broad overview of the ways in which the field of EF research is evolving.

2.3 Demand-Side Management

Numerous power systems applications have made use of Artificial Intelligence (AI) techniques, but demand-side response research has only just begun to take an interest in them (Kalam et al., 2024). Since DSM has shown to be a viable way for providing power system demand adaptability, many system operators are adamant on expanding its size and breadth. To make DSM schemes more effective, an autonomous design that can learn from its surroundings and incorporate new data, such as consumer preferences, is required. Predictions of energy prices and demand in DSM have relied heavily on supervised learning methods based on kernels and trees. It's also used for making predictions. Unsupervised learning methods rely solely on input from the user to determine significant relevance patterns. There are no unique matrices because no structure has been defined. Thus, there is less clarity regarding the method of learning. Due of the scarcity of labelled data, this is useful in DSM. Unsupervised algorithms have mostly been used in DSM for clustering, which is the process of grouping things like load profiles such that individuals in one cluster have traits similar to one neighbouring it but distinct from those in other clusters. Among the many fascinating methods for teaching computers new skills, Reinforcement Learning (RL) stands out. RL accounts for the issue of an agent learning to achieve a certain objective in an unfamiliar environment. Two key features that distinguish reinforcement learning from other methods are the availability of an overdue incentive and the use of a trial-and-error search methodology shown in Figure 2.

Figure 2. Techniques of DSM

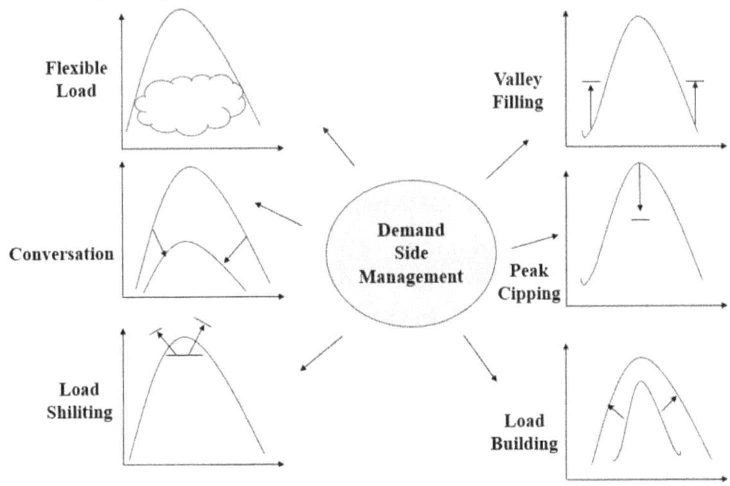

3. AI in Renewable Energy Optimization

Conventional energy sources contribute to urban pollution, although every developing nation relies on them for development. Management in Smart Cities consistently suggests renewable energy systems as a means to lessen urban pollution (Panchal & Patel, 2018),(Panchal & Thakkar, 2016). It is now more important than ever to develop smarter city strategies to deal with massive urbanisation, increase living standards, and enhance energy management without negatively impacting city environments (Kanase-Patil et al., 2020). Researchers are aiming to enhance service performance while making the most of renewable energy sources. Energy management's decision-making abilities are crucial for improving maximum utilisation and efficiency. Optimal decision-making in a variety of contexts is essential for energy planning.

Figure 3. Energy Management of Smart Cities

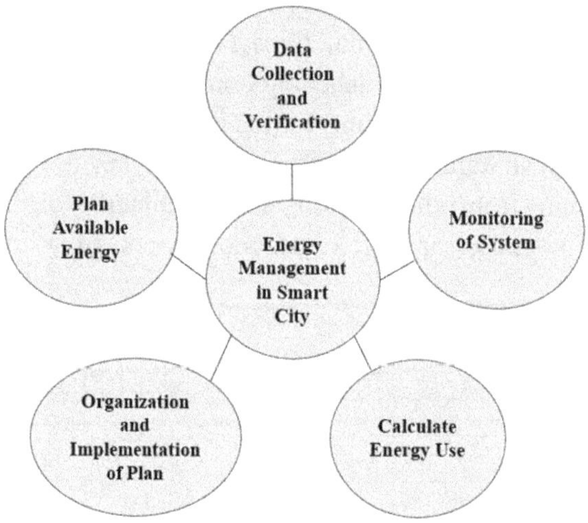

Figure 3 is an overarching diagram of the Smart City's energy management system that incorporates components from all areas of action. Energy planning and operation procedures make use of a number of methods, including optimisation, data collecting, and power system monitoring. An intelligent system is necessary for the planning and control of the electricity system in a smart city. An energy management system is essential for a smart city because it can gather and verify data from the supply and demand sides of the energy equation. Constant monitoring of the energy system and consumption calculations are made possible by this data collecting. Planning available energy and plan execution are both assisted by the energy management system. It is also possible to mimic the features of various energy conversion systems, such as those involving solar and wind power, as well as diesel generators and storage. Preliminary system sizing has also looked at iterative optimisation and energy flow optimisation. To optimise operations, real-time weather forecasting and receding horizon optimisation have been implemented.

3.1 Solar Energy

Solar power is undeniably a leading energy source, but its reliability is questionable. Similarly, weather and other environmental factors affect the accessibility of alternative energy sources. Researchers are being incentivised to discover additional renewable energy sources and explore ways to integrate them in order to extract more energy (Kanase-Patil et al., 2020). This is in response to the growing demand for energy in specific regions (Suresh et al., 2022),(X. Zhao et al., 2020). There are limitations to the usage of renewable energy resources because of their intermediary character. Installing large-scale renewable energy projects, energy storage and reconversion facilities, or IRES could help with the problem of improving the performance of these resources.

3.2 Wind Energy

The decision-making process in the renewable energy company is impacted by several external circumstances. There is more room for error in the output characteristics of wind-powered renewable generators compared to traditional generators powered by fossil fuels (Kang et al., 2009). Determining which energy resources are suitable for a particular situation requires careful consideration of a number of important factors. Energy and economic efficiency, the return on investment for producing energy from renewable sources, and the price of energy on the market are the representative variables. In contrast to energy efficiency, which refers more narrowly to maximising the benefit from energy resources, economic efficiency seeks to maximise the benefit from the same productive resources or to acquire the same benefit at the lowest possible cost. Production costs and market prices are the signals that direct resource allocation in a market environment. One key aspect influencing the production and allocation of renewable energy is the price of electricity on the market, since this is the primary product of renewable energy's transformation. Renewable energy is now prohibitively expensive to produce compared to fossil fuel energy, making a level playing field between the two sources of power highly unlikely. One of the biggest challenges in creating renewable energy sources is determining the precise amount of renewable energy resources. Wind energy, for instance, varies greatly with respect to both time and location, adding another layer of operational complexity and commercial uncertainty. Since the quantity of resources has a direct impact on both energy and economic efficiency, the outcomes of resource assessments form the basis for making decisions about the construction of wind capacity.

3.3 Energy Storage

The need for energy systems in human society has been steadily rising in recent years, due to rising demands from both energy use and environmental governance (Items et al., 2020),(Ali Kadhem et al., 2017). The keys to this energy revolution are maintaining stable power prices, updating outdated infrastructure, making power systems more adaptable and dependable, decreasing emissions of carbon dioxide, adapting to changes in the atmosphere, and supplying dependable power to outlying areas with growing power demands [1,3]. An energy storage system (ESS) has been developed with great vigour in recent years to fulfil the demands for energy savings and carbon reductions. It uses sustainable energy (Abdalla et al., 2021). A stable power grid and effective integration of renewable power sources like wind and solar are both compromised by the intermittent and unpredictable nature of renewable energy supply. Renewable energy and distributed energy storage capacity has, nevertheless, kept growing. An efficient solution to the aforementioned issues is energy storage technology, which allows for the rapid and flexible adjustment of system power and the application of various energy storage devices to the power system. Dependability of renewable energy networks such as wind, solar, storage, and distribution has been studied (Abdukhakimov et al., 2019),(Azizivahed et al., 2020). Distributing energy peaks, modulating frequency, smoothing fluctuations, and producing high-quality electrical energy are all possible with the use of energy storage technologies. Furthermore, there are substantial economic benefits and energy storage technology can offer a short-term, easily switched off energy source (Sekhar & Tupakula, 2019),(Nazir et al., 2020). The purpose of this study is to introduce energy storage technologies and to detail the current states of energy storage applications in an effort to persuade the AI energy sector to enhance and vigorously back the development of renewable energy sources. The development of renewable energy absorption, the enhancement of power grid control capacities, and the assurance of safe and cost-effective grid services are all greatly aided by energy storage, an important and regulated tool in the grid.

4. SMART GRID MANAGEMENT WITH AI

Transforming the conventional electrical power grid from a mechanically regulated system to a network controlled by computers is the idea behind the smart grid. These smart grid technologies have revolutionised grid planning and operation in three key areas (Omitaomu & Niu, 2021). Firstly, they can now automatically respond to process adjustments based on data communicated back to operation centres. Secondly, data can be shared among various devices and systems. Lastly, operators can access and apply data processed and analysed from digital technologies throughout the grid. The smart grid opens the door to both virtual and real AI systems. Grid operators can be assisted in their work by informatics included in virtual AI systems. With or without human input, physical AI systems may optimise and control particular grid processes. These systems can even learn from their own mistakes. Artificial general intelligence (AGI) and artificial narrow intelligence (ANI) are the two main subsets of smart grid AI systems. An AI system that does load forecasting using several datasets is an example of an ANI; these systems are created for specific tasks with relevant criteria and limits.AI systems designed to learn and evolve independently, similar to humans, are called AGI. True smart grid systems may be possible in the future with the development of AGI systems. Over the last decade, there has been a surge in artificial intelligence research aimed at smart grid applications. Similarly, a number of articles published during the past four years have reviewed some of these research (Venayagamoorthy, 2009). This survey paper presents some present AI applications in some of the areas not covered by these existing reviews. It also discusses some challenges of applying AI to smart grid problems and highlights some future potential applications of AI techniques to the smart grid. The authors recognise that one article cannot provide a comprehensive review of all the AI techniques for smart grid applications in load forecasting, power grid stability assessment, faults detection, and security problems. In general, the following categories best describe the smart grid's artificial intelligence techniques:

Supervised learning: Supervised learning is a technique in artificial intelligence that uses previously researched input-output mappings to forecast the outcomes of new input.

Unsupervised learning: Unsupervised learning is a subfield of machine learning that makes use of unlabelled data to identify patterns of similarity and difference.

ES: The ES is a human specialist in loop techniques that are applied to specific issues.

Reinforcement learning (RL): A technique for intelligent creatures that seeks to maximise the notion of cumulative reward is at the heart of reinforcement learning (RL), which sets it apart from supervised and unsupervised learning.

Ensemble methods: To improve overall performance and circumvent an algorithm's constraints, ensemble approaches combine the output of multiple AI systems.

4.1 Real-Time Grid Monitoring

Efficient monitoring is key for hybrid energy systems to ensure optimal performance. These systems integrate several energy sources and storage technologies (Nishtar & Afzal, 2023). Anomaly detection, control, and real-time data analysis are all made possible with AI and the Internet of Things working together. Internet of Things (IoT) devices allow for seamless data gathering and communication, while AI algorithms analyse data for insights. As a result of this integration, adaptive control strategies are made possible in hybrid energy systems, and monitoring is made easier. Efficiency is also improved. It comes to collecting details about different energy sources, several studies have demonstrated that IoT devices are better than conventional data collection approaches. A study that demonstrated the efficient usage of IoT-enabled sensors in a hybrid microgrid, showing how these devices effectively monitored variables like power consumption, battery life, wind speed, and solar irradiance. In a similar vein, (Nathali Silva et al., 2017)looked explored how home energy usage in a hybrid configuration may be measured using IoT-based smart metres, giving people the ability to see their energy use in real-time and make informed choices about how to lower their carbon impact. Hybrid power systems are made more efficient and reliable with the use of Internet of Things monitoring, which offers many advantages. To start, optimising energy use and making suitable alterations to maintain system stability are made possible by the real-time data collected by IoT devices (Alahakoon & Yu, 2016). Operators and AI algorithms can accurately evaluate the system's performance because data is constantly collected from various energy sources (Afzal, 2015). The advantages of enhanced controllability in terms of system stability and efficiency were highlighted in a study that investigated the integration of IoT devices into a hybrid renewable energy system (De Benedetti et al., 2018). The benefits of using the Internet of Things (IoT) for real-time data monitoring are displayed in Table 2 below.

Table 2. Real Time Data Monitoring Benefits in IoT

Gathering Data in Real Time	**Improving energy efficiency and maintaining system stability are two of the most important goals of the Internet of Things (IoT)**
Communicating Effortlessly	Through dependable connectivity made possible by IoT devices, various components are able to coordinate the flow of energy and minimise losses
Control Strategies that are Dynamic	Internet of Things (IoT) monitoring provides data-driven adaptive control solutions with real-time insights into system states
Enhanced Responsiveness and Resilience	The incorporation of the IoT improves the responsiveness of the system, enabling it to better manage fluctuating energy demands

4.2 Dynamic Pricing Models

One major mechanism for enhancing smart grid dependability is Demand-Side Management (DSM). This involves customers dynamically modifying or moving their electricity consumption (Bu et al., 2011). One of the most significant DSM tactics to encourage customers to utilise electricity wisely and efficiently is smart pricing, which has recently garnered a lot of attention (Xin Song & Jiayu Qu, 2014). Inclining block rates, essential peak pricing, and real-time pricing are three important smart pricing models. Since wholesale prices can change by an order of magnitude over time, real-time pricing is crucial in the smart grid since it allows retailers to routinely adjust their prices to reflect variations in the cost of the energy supply. On the topic of smart grid real-time pricing, there is some published work. In (Holland & Mansur, 2007), the authors talked about how real-time pricing could lower emissions of then there is no as well as in the USA. Combining real-time pricing with inclining block rates, (Mohsenian-Rad et al., 2010) CO 2 offered a computationally feasible and automated optimization-based strategy for residential load regulation in a retail energy market. They also took into account the user-side real-time price forecast. In order to keep overall power usage below generating capacity, maximise aggregate user utility, minimise cost to the energy provider, and implement real-time pricing, an algorithm was suggested in (Xin Song & Jiayu Qu, 2014). In order to achieve an ideal aggregate load profile at the equilibrium of an energy consumption scheduling game, the authors of (Mohsenian-Rad et al., 2010) suggested a smart pricing tariff that would take into account user interactions.

4.3 Decentralized Energy Systems

The high expense of delivered power is a result of our reliance on centralised energy systems, which run largely on fossil fuels and necessitate substantial investments to build transmission and distribution networks that reach outlying areas (Kaundinya et al., 2009) . Alternative power generating and distribution systems are urgently needed to address these issues. In contrast to centralised energy systems, decentralised energy systems rely on renewable energy sources, run on smaller scales (a few kWh scale) whether the grid is present or not, and can reach remote areas easily due to power generation being close to demand sites. The degree of decentralisation determines the feasibility of implementing decentralised energy systems. With village decentralisation, residents have a say in system management, and power is distributed according to demand. Very rarely is it possible to feed the grid with surplus power. In contrast, decentralisation at the industrial level is also an option; in this setup, power produced as a waste product of a process (such bagasse co-generation) is primarily utilised to meet the demands of the company, with any excess being fed into the grid. Whether the system runs in grid-connected (GC) or stand-alone (SA) mode is also dependent on the level of decentralisation.

Autonomous Platforms: One definition of a stand-alone system is one that generates electricity apart from the power grid. These work well in outlying areas without access to the grid and other energy sources. Because they are frequently the most cost-effective option for applications far from the utility grid, stand-alone systems make up the bulk of solar installations in remote regions of the world. Lighthouses and other outlying stations, supplemental power units (UPSs) for use in emergencies or the military, and factories that deal with sensitive electronics are also good examples. Disadvantages inherent to SA systems include a poor capacity factor, high battery costs, and a limited ability to store electricity, which forces the waste of excess energy.

Grid-connected systems: Tell the difference between two kinds of grid-connected systems. In the first, meeting local electrical demands is the top focus of the GC system; excess generation is sent into the grid, and when there is a deficit, power is taken from the grid. Utility scale is an alternative that allows utilities to oversee decentralised stations in the same manner as big power facilities. The central utility grid receives all of the GC systems' outputs regardless of the local demands.

5. MODEL DEVELOPMENT AND AI TECHNIQUES

To account for the complexity and unpredictability of renewable energy systems, this study makes use of artificial intelligence models such as optimisation techniques, deep learning models, and machine learning algorithms. Methods employed in the research included:

- **Genetic Algorithms for Grid Management:** Utilising a Genetic Algorithm (GA) allowed for the optimisation of grid performance and the management of renewable energy integration into the system (Mukaddim & Hider, 2023). By balancing renewable energy generation with demand and storage capacities, the GA was employed to ascertain the best grid load distribution strategies. Taking into account gearbox losses and overloading concerns, the overall energy loss in the system defined the GA's fitness function. By comparing the results of each generation, the algorithm iterated to find the optimal load distribution technique.
- **Artificial Intelligence for Energy Prediction:** Machine learning models such as k-Nearest Neighbours (k-NN), Random Forest (RF), and Support Vector Regression (SVR) were employed to forecast energy generation from solar and wind sources using weather data. Models were assessed using Mean Absolute Error (MAE) and Root Mean Squared Error (RMSE), two metrics used to train models to detect patterns in the historical data. We optimised and integrated the top-performing model into our renewable energy system.
- **Applying Deep Learning to Forecast Time Series:** It used Long Short-Term Memory (LSTM) networks to record the patterns and dependencies in energy generation over time. Time-series prediction applications, including predicting wind and solar power generation, are ideal for LSTM networks. Predicting future energy generation for certain time intervals was done using past energy data and meteorological variables in the training of the LSTM model using a sliding window technique.
- **Making the Most of Reinforcement Learning for Energy Storage:** Using Deep Reinforcement Learning (DRL), a model was created to optimise energy storage by altering the charging and discharging cycles of systems. The DRL agent was programmed to improve the efficiency of energy storage by reducing energy waste and making sure that power was sent out when demand was high and stored when generation was surplus. To train the agent, we employed a reward function that penalised overcharging or draining the battery above certain limitations, with the goal of minimising the difference between the expected and actual states of the battery.

6. CHALLENGES AND LIMITATIONS

The potential of Artificial Intelligence (AI) to transform energy efficiency optimisation is enormous, but it is not without its limitations and obstacles (Fan et al., 2023); (Rane, 2023);(Stecuła et al., 2023), This section delves into the main obstacles that come with examining AI's function in optimising energy efficiency (Tosin Michael Olatunde et al., 2024). These include worries about data privacy and security, the difficulty of integrating and implementing AI, and problems with regulations and policies. Information on energy use, particularly in the context of smart buildings and manufacturing processes, may be very private and delicate. The potential breach of privacy and confidentiality due to unapproved access, misuse, or exploitation of sensitive data is a cause for concern. Unauthorised parties might gain access to energy systems, alter data, or halt operations if cyberattacks and data breaches were to affect AI systems. Protecting AI systems and data from cyber threats requires strong cybersecurity measures, which can be difficult to implement (Farzaneh et al., 2021). Artificial intelligence (AI) integration into energy systems is already complicated enough without having to contend with data privacy legislation like the EU's General Data Protection Regulation (GDPR) or California's Consumer Privacy Act (CCPA). Data management and privacy regulations must be carefully considered to ensure compliance while utilising AI to optimise energy efficiency. Expertise in artificial intelligence algorithms, data analytics, and energy systems is necessary to implement AI solutions for optimising energy efficiency. In complex environments like smart cities or industrial facilities, integrating AI with existing infrastructure and systems can be a technical challenge. In order to train and make decisions, AI algorithms need trustworthy data. Data availability and quality assurance, particularly in real-time and on a large scale, can be difficult to achieve. Poor AI performance could be the result of missing data, incorrect information, or inconsistent results (Y. Zhao et al., 2019).It usually takes a lot of time, money, and computing power to implement AI solutions. Particularly when it comes to optimising energy efficiency, small and medium-sized organisations may struggle to embrace and incorporate AI due to resource restrictions. Uncertainty and ambiguity surround regulatory regulations and compliance obligations for artificial intelligence in energy systems, as the regulatory landscape is continually growing. Artificial intelligence (AI) technologies for optimising energy efficiency may face obstacles in adoption and implementation due to a lack of clarity on legal frameworks and standards. The broad use of artificial intelligence (AI) for optimising energy efficiency could be hindered by policy obstacles, such as subsidies or incentives that favour conventional energy sources over renewable energy or efficiency measures. It is crucial to remove legislative obstacles and establish a favourable legislative climate in order to encourage investment and innovation in energy solutions powered by artificial intelligence (Liu et al., 2023),(Gajdzik et al., 2023). Seamless integration and collaboration might be impeded by a lack of standardisation and interoperability among energy infrastructure and AI technologies. To guarantee interoperability, compatibility, and scalability, it is essential to establish common standards and protocols for energy systems that are enabled by AI. Ultimately, to fully harness the power of AI in the energy sector, we must overcome the obstacles and limitations linked to data privacy and security, technical complexity, resource constraints, regulatory and policy uncertainties, and more. Only then can we reap the rewards of AI in energy efficiency optimisation. To conquer these obstacles and propel the implementation of energy solutions driven by artificial intelligence, players from the public sector, private sector, academic institutions, and civil society must work together.

7. FUTURE TRENDS AND INNOVATIONS

Energy optimisation is constantly changing, and the way energy systems work will be changed by incorporating sophisticated technologies like quantum computing, AI-driven policymaking, and edge AI. These advancements hold great potential for making energy networks more resilient and adaptable, in addition to improving their efficiency and dependability. We delve into these trends below.

7.1 Cutting-Edge AI for Efficient Power Use

Edge AI is the practice of deploying AI close to or at the point of data generation, as opposed to using centralised cloud systems. Edge AI has the ability to revolutionise energy optimisation by lowering latency and facilitating decision-making in real-time.

How It Works: Data is collected from energy sources, consumption sites, and grid systems by devices like smart meters and sensors that are Internet of Things enabled. The data is processed locally by Edge AI rather than sent to a central server, enabling fast answers.

Applications:

Systems for Renewable Energy: Solar panels and wind turbines can optimise their energy output by adjusting to changing environmental circumstances with the help of edge AI.

Advanced Power Grids: By analysing data on energy demand and supply in real-time, edge AI enables dynamic grid balancing, which improves grid dependability and prevents outages.

IoT Appliances: Autonomous energy optimisation based on real-time environmental data and human behaviour is possible with intelligent home equipment, such as HVAC systems controlled by AI.

Benefits:

Enhanced Security: There is less risk of cyberattacks on sensitive energy data processed locally.

Faster Processing: Because it reduces delays, local processing is perfect for apps that need to respond quickly.

Less Consumption of Bandwidth: Edge AI lowers costs and energy consumption by processing data locally, reducing the quantity of data transferred to central systems.

Artificial intelligence at the network's periphery is opening the door to a new model of distributed energy management that will improve system resilience and efficiency.

7.2 AI-Driven Policy Making

Sustainable practices rely on energy policies, which must often strike a balance between complex, interconnected issues. To optimise energy systems, AI-driven policymaking provides a data-driven approach to regulatory design and implementation.

How It Works: Models in artificial intelligence, which include simulation algorithms and machine learning, sift through mountains of data that include things like energy use, economic indicators, environmental effects, and consumer habits. This information is valuable for policymakers as they consider different scenarios and the implications of different regulatory actions.

Applications:

Carbon Emission Regulations: Artificial intelligence aids lawmakers in foreseeing how carbon taxes and emission limits would affect business operations and GDP development, allowing for more well-rounded and fruitful policymaking.

Energy Pricing Models: To aid in the development of tariffs that encourage energy efficiency, AI can model the impact of dynamic pricing strategies on customer behaviour and grid stability.

Renewable Energy Incentives: By examining trends of past and future adoption, machine learning models determine how successful renewable energy subsidy programs have been.

Benefits:

Adaptive Regulations: The ability to analyse data in real-time enables policies to be adjusted in response to changing conditions.

Decisions of Data-Driven: AI reduces the impact of bias and guarantees that policies are grounded in factual evidence.
Scenario Analysis: By conducting virtual tests of different situations, policy-makers can save both time and resources.

AI-driven policymaking is a game-changer, opening the door for organisations and governments to develop long-term, financially sound energy plans.

7.3 Quantum Computing in Energy

The exciting new area of quantum computing in computational science has great potential to address the challenging optimisation issues plaguing energy systems. Unprecedented processing power is made possible by quantum computers, which use the laws of quantum mechanics to process enormous datasets and numerous variables concurrently.

How It Works: With its usage of qubits which, thanks to superposition, can represent both 0 and 1 at the same time quantum computers are able to process information in a way that classical computers cannot. The ability to simultaneously investigate several solutions to a problem is a key feature of quantum computers.

Applications in Energy
Grid Stability: By simulating and preventing energy grid cascading failures, quantum models guarantee a constant supply of power.
Balance of Multiple Variables: Optimal distribution of energy across vast grids subject to fluctuating demand and supply can be studied and optimised by quantum algorithms.
Maximising the Life of Batteries: By improving the efficiency of charge-discharge cycles, optimising battery performance, and anticipating degradation, quantum AI improves energy storage.

Sustainable Distribution of Resources: By taking grid restrictions, weather patterns, and energy storage into account, quantum computing can determine the best methods for integrating renewable energy sources into the grid.

Benefits:
Scalability:
As the world's energy systems expand and diversify, their complexity will rise. However, quantum computing is up to the challenge.
Speeding Up the Resolution of Issues: Jobs that used to take years on traditional computers now take just minutes.

Accuracy Raised: Optimisation methods and forecasts for complicated systems are both improved by quantum models.

Despite its relative youth, quantum computing has the potential to completely transform energy optimisation by solving problems that classical approaches failed to.

New developments like quantum computing, AI-driven governance, and Edge AI show how cutting-edge innovation might revolutionise power grids. These advancements have great potential for a more environmentally friendly future by making energy optimisation smarter, more efficient, and more sustainable as they develop further.

8. CASE STUDIES

Several prominent case studies have emerged from the industrial sector's use of AI-driven energy management systems, demonstrating the revolutionary possibilities of these tools (Putha, 2020). These examples show how artificial intelligence (AI) may optimise energy use, improve operational efficiency, and cut costs without sacrificing quality or throughput in production.

- A worldwide automaker is a good example because it integrated an AI-driven energy management system into all of its production facilities. The main goal was to lower the hefty energy bills that come with operating high-power equipment, HVAC systems, and lights in massive manufacturing plants. A more precise prediction of energy demand based on production schedules, weather conditions, and real-time sensor data was achieved by the company by employing powerful AI algorithms for real-time optimisation and predictive analytics. At peak load times, the AI system intelligently turned down non-essential systems and optimised the operation of key machinery to run at the most energy-efficient levels without affecting production output. This allowed for dynamic energy consumption adjustment. This resulted in yearly savings for the manufacturing in the millions of dollars, as well as a 15% decrease in total energy usage and a substantial decrease in peak energy demand prices.
- An additional convincing example is a huge chemical processing factory that struggled to keep its energy efficiency consistent throughout all of its complicated, energy-intensive processes. Because the chemical processes involved necessitated exact control over pressures, temperatures, and flow rates, the patterns of energy use at the plant were extremely varied. Machine learning

models built on historical process data were utilised to accurately anticipate energy usage by the plant when an AI-driven energy management system was integrated. In real time, the AI system suggested tweaks to process settings that would maximise energy efficiency without sacrificing product safety or quality. The plant reduced its energy usage by 12% over a two-year period, enhanced the reliability of its processes, and reduced operational disruptions caused by poorly managed energy resources.

- In the third case study, we look at what happened to an electronics company that used AI-driven energy management systems throughout their whole plant. The manufacturer encountered substantial energy expenses as a result of the heavy reliance on precise machinery and cleanrooms, which necessitate meticulous regulation of surrounding circumstances. In order to track and optimise energy use across several manufacturing lines and environmental control systems, this facility's AI system used a mix of deep learning algorithms and IoT enabled sensors. We were able to cut our energy use by 20% thanks to the AI system's ability to forecast our energy needs and make real-time adjustments to the functioning of our HVAC, lighting, and production equipment. The facility was also able to take advantage of cheaper energy during off-peak hours because to the system's improved management of energy procurement. In addition to cutting costs significantly, the firm also improved sustainability by decreasing its carbon footprint.

All sorts of industrial settings can benefit from energy management systems powered by artificial intelligence, as shown in these case studies. Whether it's the chemical, electronics, or automotive industries, they all show how AI can tailor its solutions to meet unique demands while delivering real savings in energy and money. To ensure the technology works well with current processes and provides the most value, they also stress the significance of tailoring AI solutions to the specific operational needs of each manufacturing plant.

9. CONCLUSION

More and more individuals are paying attention to how the environment is changing. Research in fundamental engineering is now focused on ensuring the long-term viability of economies, societies, and environments. Producing goods and carrying out operations in an eco-conscious manner are becoming more and more demands placed on manufacturers (Bi & Wang, 2012). Some examples of emerging sustainability-related system paradigms in the manufacturing sector include environmentally conscious manufacturing, green manufacturing, and sustainable manufacturing (SM). By improving efficiency, dependability, and sustainability, artificial intelligence and machine learning present revolutionary possibilities for optimising energy use. In order to achieve energy security and address climate change, it will be vital to integrate AI and ML as global energy systems advance. An even more efficient and sustainable future is promised by the ongoing developments in computing power, algorithms, and energy data analytics.

REFERENCES

Abdalla, A. N., Nazir, M. S., Tao, H., Cao, S., Ji, R., Jiang, M., & Yao, L. (2021). Integration of energy storage system and renewable energy sources based on artificial intelligence: An overview. *Journal of Energy Storage, 40*(July 2020), 102811. DOI: 10.1016/j.est.2021.102811

Abdukhakimov, A., Bhardwaj, S., Gashema, G., & Kim, D.-S. (2019). Reliability Analysis in Smart Grid Networks Considering Distributed Energy Resources and Storage Devices. *International Journal of Electrical and Electronic Engineering & Telecommunications*, *8*(5), 233–237. DOI: 10.18178/ijeetc.8.5.233-237

Afzal, J. (2015). Towards Protocols for Vehicular Ad Hoc Networks (VANETs). *International Journal of Computer Science and Software Engineering*, *4*(8), 204–208. DOI: 10.6084/m9.figshare.23771313

Al Mukaddim, A., & Hider, M. A. (2023). Optimizing Renewable Energy Systems Using Artificial Intelligence: Enhancing Efficiency and Sustainability. *International Journal of Machine Learning Research in Cybersecurity and Artificial Intelligence*, *01*, 846–881.

Alahakoon, D., & Yu, X. (2016). Smart Electricity Meter Data Intelligence for Future Energy Systems: A Survey. *IEEE Transactions on Industrial Informatics*, *12*(1), 425–436. DOI: 10.1109/TII.2015.2414355

Ali Kadhem, A., Abdul Wahab, N. I., Aris, I., Jasni, J., & Abdalla, N., A., & Matsukawa, Y. (. (2017). Reliability Assessment of Generating Systems with Wind Power Penetration via BPSO. *International Journal on Advanced Science, Engineering and Information Technology*, *7*(4), 1248. DOI: 10.18517/ijaseit.7.4.2311

Asadi, M., TaghaviGhalesari, A., & Kumar, S. (2022). Machine learning techniques for estimation of Los Angeles abrasion value of rock aggregates. *European Journal of Environmental and Civil Engineering*, *26*(3), 964–977. DOI: 10.1080/19648189.2019.1690585

Azizivahed, A., Arefi, A., Ghavidel, S., Shafie-khah, M., Li, L., Zhang, J., & Catalao, J. P. S. (2020). Energy Management Strategy in Dynamic Distribution Network Reconfiguration Considering Renewable Energy Resources and Storage. *IEEE Transactions on Sustainable Energy*, *11*(2), 662–673. DOI: 10.1109/TSTE.2019.2901429

Bi, Z. M., & Wang, L. (2012). Optimization of machining processes from the perspective of energy consumption: A case study. *Journal of Manufacturing Systems*, *31*(4), 420–428. DOI: 10.1016/j.jmsy.2012.07.002

Bidollahkhani, M., & Kunkel, J. M. (2024). Revolutionizing System Reliability. *The Role of AI in Predictive Maintenance Strategies, c*, 49–57. http://arxiv.org/abs/2404.13454

Bu, S., Yu, F. R., & Liu, P. X. (2011). Dynamic pricing for demand-side management in the smart grid. *2011 IEEE Online Conference on Green Communications*, 47–51. DOI: 10.1109/GreenCom.2011.6082506

De Benedetti, M., Leonardi, F., Messina, F., Santoro, C., & Vasilakos, A. (2018). Anomaly detection and predictive maintenance for photovoltaic systems. *Neurocomputing*, *310*, 59–68. DOI: 10.1016/j.neucom.2018.05.017

Fan, Z., Yan, Z., & Wen, S. (2023). Deep Learning and Artificial Intelligence in Sustainability: A Review of SDGs, Renewable Energy, and Environmental Health. *Sustainability (Basel)*, *15*(18), 13493. DOI: 10.3390/su151813493

Farzaneh, H., Malehmirchegini, L., Bejan, A., Afolabi, T., Mulumba, A., & Daka, P. P. (2021). Artificial Intelligence Evolution in Smart Buildings for Energy Efficiency. *Applied Sciences (Basel, Switzerland)*, *11*(2), 763. DOI: 10.3390/app11020763

Gajdzik, B., Wolniak, R., Nagaj, R., Grebski, W. W., & Romanyshyn, T. (2023). Barriers to Renewable Energy Source (RES) Installations as Determinants of Energy Consumption in EU Countries. *Energies*, *16*(21), 7364. DOI: 10.3390/en16217364

Holland, S. P., & Mansur, E. T. (2007). Is real-time pricing green? The environmental impacts of electricity demand variance. *The Review of Economics and Statistics*.

Items, R., Rose, W., Rose, W., If, T., & Rose, W. (2020). The importance of social relations in shaping energy demand. *Nature Energy*, *5*, 3.

Kalam, M. A., Saxena, A., Hassnain, M. Z., Dash, A. K., Singh, J., & Singh, G. K. (2024). An explicit investigation in demand side management based on artificial intelligence techniques. *IEEE Access*, *PP*, 1–1. DOI: 10.1109/ACCESS.2024.3432805

Kanase-Patil, A. B., Kaldate, A. P., Lokhande, S. D., Panchal, H., Suresh, M., & Priya, V. (2020). A review of artificial intelligence-based optimization techniques for the sizing of integrated renewable energy systems in smart cities. *Environmental Technology Reviews*, *9*(1), 111–136. DOI: 10.1080/21622515.2020.1836035

Kang, D.-J., Park, J., & Yeo, S.-S. (2009). Intelligent Decision-Making System with Green Pervasive Computing for Renewable Energy Business in Electricity Markets on Smart Grid. *EURASIP Journal on Wireless Communications and Networking*, *2009*(1), 247483. DOI: 10.1155/2009/247483

Kaundinya, D. P., Balachandra, P., & Ravindranath, N. H. (2009). Grid-connected versus stand-alone energy systems for decentralized power—A review of literature. *Renewable & Sustainable Energy Reviews*, *13*(8), 2041–2050. DOI: 10.1016/j.rser.2009.02.002

Liu, Z., Yu, C., Qian, Q. K., Huang, R., You, K., Visscher, H., & Zhang, G. (2023). Incentive initiatives on energy-efficient renovation of existing buildings towards carbon–neutral blueprints in China: Advancements, challenges and prospects. *Energy and Building*, *296*, 113343. DOI: 10.1016/j.enbuild.2023.113343

Mohsenian-Rad, A.-H., Wong, V. W. S., Jatskevich, J., Schober, R., & Leon-Garcia, A. (2010). Autonomous Demand-Side Management Based on Game-Theoretic Energy Consumption Scheduling for the Future Smart Grid. *IEEE Transactions on Smart Grid*, *1*(3), 320–331. DOI: 10.1109/TSG.2010.2089069

Mystakidis, A., Koukaras, P., Tsalikidis, N., Ioannidis, D., & Tjortjis, C. (2024). Energy Forecasting: A Comprehensive Review of Techniques and Technologies. *Energies*, *17*(7), 1662. DOI: 10.3390/en17071662

Nathali Silva, B., Khan, M., & Han, K. (2017). Big Data Analytics Embedded Smart City Architecture for Performance Enhancement through Real-Time Data Processing and Decision-Making. *Wireless Communications and Mobile Computing*, *2017*, 1–12. DOI: 10.1155/2017/9429676

Nazir, M. S., Wang, Y., Bilal, M., Sohail, H. M., Kadhem, A. A., Nazir, H. M. R., Abdalla, A. N., & Ma, Y. (2020). Comparison of Small-Scale Wind Energy Conversion Systems: Economic Indexes. *Cleanroom Technology*, *2*(2), 144–155. DOI: 10.3390/cleantechnol2020010

Nishtar, Z., & Afzal, J. (2023). A Review of Real-Time Monitoring of Hybrid Energy Systems by Using Artificial Intelligence and IoT. *Pakistan Journal of Engineering and Technology*, *6*(3), 8–15. DOI: 10.51846/vol6iss3pp8-15

Olatunde, T. M., Okwandu, A. C., Akande, D. O., & Sikhakhane, Z. Q. (2024). REVIEWING THE ROLE OF ARTIFICIAL INTELLIGENCE IN ENERGY EFFICIENCY OPTIMIZATION. *Engineering Science & Technology Journal*, *5*(4), 1243–1256. DOI: 10.51594/estj.v5i4.1015

Omitaomu, O. A., & Niu, H. (2021). Artificial Intelligence Techniques in Smart Grid: A Survey. *Smart Cities*, *4*(2), 548–568. DOI: 10.3390/smartcities4020029

Panchal, H. N., & Patel, N. (2018). ANSYS CFD and experimental comparison of various parameters of a solar still. *International Journal of Ambient Energy*, *39*(6), 551–557. DOI: 10.1080/01430750.2017.1318785

Panchal, H. N., & Thakkar, H. (2016). Theoretical and experimental validation of evacuated tubes directly coupled with solar still. *Thermal Engineering*, *63*(11), 825–831. DOI: 10.1134/S0040601516110045

Putha, S. (2020). AI-Driven Energy Management in Manufacturing: Optimizing Energy Consumption and Reducing Operational Costs. *Distributed Learning and Broad Applications in Scientific Research*, *6*, 313–353.

Rane, N. L. (2023). Integrating Leading-Edge Artificial Intelligence (AI), Internet of Things (IoT), and Big Data Technologies for Smart and Sustainable Architecture, Engineering and Construction (AEC) Industry: Challenges and Future Directions. *International Journal of Data Science and Big Data Analytics*, *3*(2), 73–95. DOI: 10.51483/IJDSBDA.3.2.2023.73-95

Sekhar, P. C., & Tupakula, R. R. (2019). Model predictive controller for single-phase distributed generator with seamless transition between grid and off-grid modes. *IET Generation, Transmission & Distribution*, *13*(10), 1829–1837. DOI: 10.1049/iet-gtd.2018.6345

Singh Aujla, G., Garg, S., Batra, S., Kumar, N., You, I., & Sharma, V. (2019). DROpS: A demand response optimization scheme in SDN-enabled smart energy ecosystem. *Information Sciences*, *476*, 453–473. DOI: 10.1016/j.ins.2018.09.047

Song, X., & Qu, J. (2014). An improved real-time pricing algorithm based on utility maximization for smart grid. *Proceeding of the 11th World Congress on Intelligent Control and Automation, 2015-March*(March), 2509–2513. DOI: 10.1109/WCICA.2014.7053118

Stecuła, K., Wolniak, R., & Grebski, W. W. (2023). AI-Driven Urban Energy Solutions—From Individuals to Society: A Review. *Energies*, *16*(24), 7988. DOI: 10.3390/en16247988

Suresh, M., Meenakumari, R., Panchal, H., Priya, V., El Agouz, E. S., & Israr, M. (2022). An enhanced multiobjective particle swarm optimisation algorithm for optimum utilisation of hybrid renewable energy systems. *International Journal of Ambient Energy*, *43*(1), 2540–2548. DOI: 10.1080/01430750.2020.1737837

Venayagamoorthy, G. K. (2009). Potentials and promises of computational intelligence for smart grids. *2009 IEEE Power & Energy Society General Meeting, August 2009*, 1–6. DOI: 10.1109/PES.2009.5275224

Zhao, X., Jiang, N., Liu, J., Yu, D., & Chang, J. (2020). Short-term average wind speed and turbulent standard deviation forecasts based on one-dimensional convolutional neural network and the integrate method for probabilistic framework. *Energy Conversion and Management, 203*(October), 112239. DOI: 10.1016/j.enconman.2019.112239

Zhao, Y., Li, T., Zhang, X., & Zhang, C. (2019). Artificial intelligence-based fault detection and diagnosis methods for building energy systems: Advantages, challenges and the future. *Renewable and Sustainable Energy Reviews, 109*(November 2018), 85–101. DOI: 10.1016/j.rser.2019.04.021

Compilation of References

Aazam, M., Zeadally, S., & Harras, K. A. (2020, March 1). Health Fog for Smart Healthcare. *IEEE Consumer Electronics Magazine*, *9*(2), 96–102. DOI: 10.1109/MCE.2019.2953749

Abdalla, A. N., Nazir, M. S., Tao, H., Cao, S., Ji, R., Jiang, M., & Yao, L. (2021). Integration of energy storage system and renewable energy sources based on artificial intelligence: An overview. *Journal of Energy Storage, 40*(July 2020), 102811. DOI: 10.1016/j.est.2021.102811

Abdel-Nasser, M., & Mahmoud, K. (2019). Accurate photovoltaic power forecasting models using deep LSTM-RNN. *Neural Computing & Applications*, *31*(7), 2727–2740. DOI: 10.1007/s00521-017-3225-z

Abdukhakimov, A., Bhardwaj, S., Gashema, G., & Kim, D.-S. (2019). Reliability Analysis in Smart Grid Networks Considering Distributed Energy Resources and Storage Devices. *International Journal of Electrical and Electronic Engineering & Telecommunications*, *8*(5), 233–237. DOI: 10.18178/ijeetc.8.5.233-237

Abdul-Qawy, A. S., Pramod, P. J., Magesh, E., & Srinivasulu, T. (2015). The internet of things (iot): An overview. *International Journal of Engineering Research and Applications*, *5*(12), 71–82.

Abeydeera, L. H. U. W., Mesthrige, J. W., & Samarasinghalage, T. I. (2019). Global research on carbon emissions: A scientometric review. In *Sustainability (Switzerland)* (Vol. 11). MDPI. DOI: 10.3390/su11143972

ACM Digital Library. (2021). *A survey on artificial intelligence and machine learning*. https://dl.acm.org/doi/pdf/10.1145/3483410

Afzal, J. (2015). Towards Protocols for Vehicular Ad Hoc Networks (VANETs). *International Journal of Computer Science and Software Engineering*, *4*(8), 204–208. DOI: 10.6084/m9.figshare.23771313

Agarwal, S., Nath, A., & Chowdhury, D. (2012). Sustainable approaches and good practices in green software engineering. *International Journal of Research and Reviews in Computer Science, 3*(1), 1425.

Ahmed, R., Sreeram, V., Mishra, Y., & Arif, M. (2020). A review and evaluation of the state-of-the-art in PV solar power forecasting: Techniques and optimization. *Renewable & Sustainable Energy Reviews, 124*, 109792. DOI: 10.1016/j.rser.2020.109792

Akil, B., Zhou, Y., & Röhm, U. (2017, December). On the usability of Hadoop MapReduce, Apache Spark & Apache flink for data science. In *2017 IEEE International Conference on Big Data (Big Data)* (pp. 303-310). IEEE. DOI: 10.1109/BigData.2017.8257938

Akyildiz, I. F.. (2020). 6G and beyond: The future of wireless networks. *IEEE Communications Magazine, 58*(3), 62–69.

Al Mukaddim, A., & Hider, M. A. (2023). Optimizing Renewable Energy Systems Using Artificial Intelligence: Enhancing Efficiency and Sustainability. *International Journal of Machine Learning Research in Cybersecurity and Artificial Intelligence, 01*, 846–881.

Alahakoon, D., & Yu, X. (2016). Smart Electricity Meter Data Intelligence for Future Energy Systems: A Survey. *IEEE Transactions on Industrial Informatics, 12*(1), 425–436. DOI: 10.1109/TII.2015.2414355

Al-Emran, M., & Griffy-Brown, C. (2023). The role of technology adoption in sustainable development: Overview, opportunities, challenges, and future research agendas. *Technology in Society, 73*, 102240. DOI: 10.1016/j.techsoc.2023.102240

Ali Kadhem, A., Abdul Wahab, N. I., Aris, I., Jasni, J., & Abdalla, N., A., & Matsukawa, Y. (. (2017). Reliability Assessment of Generating Systems with Wind Power Penetration via BPSO. *International Journal on Advanced Science, Engineering and Information Technology, 7*(4), 1248. DOI: 10.18517/ijaseit.7.4.2311

Al-Sarawi, S., Anbar, M., Alieyan, K., & Alzubaidi, M. (2017, May). Internet of Things (IoT) communication protocols. In *2017 8th International conference on information technology (ICIT)* (pp. 685-690). IEEE.

Alsharif, M. H., Kelechi, A. H., Jahid, A., Kannadasan, R., Singla, M. K., Gupta, J., & Geem, Z. W. (2024). A comprehensive survey of energy-efficient computing to enable sustainable massive IoT networks. *Alexandria Engineering Journal, 91*, 12–29. DOI: 10.1016/j.aej.2024.01.067

Amazon, A. W. S. (2024). FL-powered edge AI for carbon-neutral computing. *Journal of Green AI Solutions*, *16*(3), 234–247.

Amodei, D., & Hernandez, D. (2018). AI and compute. Retrieved from https://openai.com/blog/ai-and-compute/

Amodei, D., & Clark, J. (2021). Measuring the environmental impact of machine learning. *Nature Sustainability*, *4*(7), 567–576. DOI: 10.1038/s41893-021-00782-7

Amshavalli, R. S., & Kalaivani, J. (2023, May). A Comprehensive Survey on Role of Fog Computing and Need for Semantic Technology in Modern Computing Platform. In *2023 7th International Conference on Intelligent Computing and Control Systems (ICICCS)* (pp. 719-725). IEEE. DOI: 10.1109/ICICCS56967.2023.10142888

Anita, M., Ambhika, C., & Anish, T. P. (2024). Exploring the Landscape of Artificial Intelligence in Healthcare Applications. In AI Healthcare Applications and Security, Ethical, and Legal Considerations (pp. 29-48). IGI Global.

Anita, M., Ambhika, C., & Anish, T. P. (2024). Exploring the Landscape of Artificial Intelligence in Healthcare Applications. In *AI Healthcare Applications and Security, Ethical, and Legal Considerations* (pp. 29–48). IGI Global.

Anthony, L. F. W., Kanding, B., & Selvan, R. (2020). CarbonTracker: Tracking and predicting the carbon footprint of training deep learning models. arXiv preprint arXiv:2007.03051. https://arxiv.org/abs/2007.03051

Anusha, S., Ezhilvandan, M., Gayathri, S., Sivaraman, V., & Anish, T. P. (2024). Emerging trends in edge AI for Industry 4.0 and 5.0: Technologies, applications, and challenges. *AI Innovations in Service and Tourism Marketing*, 211-228.

Ardito, L.. (2018). Towards sustainable innovation: A systematic review of the literature. *Journal of Cleaner Production*, *172*, 2157–2174.

Arroba, P., Buyya, R., Cárdenas, R., Risco-Martín, J. L., & Moya, J. M. (2024). Sustainable edge computing: Challenges and future directions. *Software, Practice & Experience*, *54*(11), 2272–2296. DOI: 10.1002/spe.3340

Asadi, M., TaghaviGhalesari, A., & Kumar, S. (2022). Machine learning techniques for estimation of Los Angeles abrasion value of rock aggregates. *European Journal of Environmental and Civil Engineering*, *26*(3), 964–977. DOI: 10.1080/19648189.2019.1690585

Aslam, S., Herodotou, H., Mohsin, S. M., Javaid, N., Ashraf, N., & Aslam, S. (2021). A survey on deep learning methods for power load and renewable energy forecasting in smart microgrids. *Renewable & Sustainable Energy Reviews*, *144*, 110992. DOI: 10.1016/j.rser.2021.110992

Aswini, J., Sudha, K., Ganesh, G., Subramanian, S., & Ghinea, G. (2024). AI-powered parallel computing architecture and its applications. In *The convergence of self-sustaining systems with AI and IoT* (pp. 23–39). IGI Global. DOI: 10.4018/979-8-3693-1702-0.ch002

Avent, B., Kairouz, P., & McMahan, H. B. (2019). Advances and open problems in federated learning. *Foundations and Trends in Machine Learning*, *14*(1–2), 1–210. DOI: 10.1561/2200000073

Azizivahed, A., Arefi, A., Ghavidel, S., Shafie-khah, M., Li, L., Zhang, J., & Catalao, J. P. S. (2020). Energy Management Strategy in Dynamic Distribution Network Reconfiguration Considering Renewable Energy Resources and Storage. *IEEE Transactions on Sustainable Energy*, *11*(2), 662–673. DOI: 10.1109/TSTE.2019.2901429

Bajaj, S., & Kumar, R. (2021). Environmental benchmarks for AI systems. *Sustainable AI*, *1*, 15–22. DOI: 10.1016/j.susai.2021.100001

Bajaj, S., Paritosh, P., & Singh, R. (2021). Sustainable AI: Methods and trends. *Energy and AI*, *3*, 200–212. DOI: 10.1016/j.eneai.2021.100015

Baliga, J., Ayre, R., Hinton, K., & Tucker, R. (2019). Energy consumption in wired and wireless networks. *IEEE Communications Magazine*, *49*(6), 70–77. DOI: 10.1109/MCOM.2011.5783987

Bannour, N., Ghannay, S., Névéol, A., & Ligozat, A.-L. (2021). Evaluating the carbon footprint of NLP methods: A survey and analysis of existing tools. In Proceedings of the Second Workshop on Simple and Efficient Natural Language Processing (pp. 11–21). https://aclanthology.org/2021.si-1.2/

Batko, K., & Ślęzak, A. (2022). The use of Big Data Analytics in healthcare. *Journal of Big Data*, *9*(1), 3. DOI: 10.1186/s40537-021-00553-4 PMID: 35013701

Batmunkh, A. (2022). Carbon Footprint of The Most Popular Social Media Platforms. *Sustainability (Basel)*, *14*(4), 2195. Advance online publication. DOI: 10.3390/su14042195

Becker, T., Al-Mahmoud, S., & Lin, J. (2023). Federated learning for fraud detection across global networks. *Financial AI & Security Review*, *10*(1), 34–49.

Begum, A., Naim, A., & Sabahath, A. (2024). The Impact of AI on Sustainability. In *Harnessing High-Performance Computing and AI for Environmental Sustainability* (pp. 99–113). IGI Global. DOI: 10.4018/979-8-3693-1794-5.ch005

Bergstra, J., & Bengio, Y. (2012). Random search for hyper-parameter optimization. *Journal of Machine Learning Research, 13*(2), 281–305. https://www.jmlr.org/papers/volume13/bergstra12a/bergstra12a.pdf

Berkaya, S. K., Ergin, S., Gulmezoglu, M. B., Gunal, E. S., Gunal, S., & Uysal, A. K. (2018). A survey on ECG analysis. *Biomedical Signal Processing and Control, 43*, 216–235. DOI: 10.1016/j.bspc.2018.03.003

Beutel, D., Lovisotto, J., & Flower Team. (2023). Flower: A flexible federated learning framework for real-world systems. Decentralized AI Systems, 9(4), 210–227.

Bhambri, P., Rani, S., Gupta, G., & Khang, A. (Eds.). (2022). *Cloud and fog computing platforms for internet of things*. CRC Press. DOI: 10.1201/9781003213888

Bhandari, G. P., & Gupta, R. (2021). An overview of cloud and edge computing architecture and its current issues and challenges. *Research Anthology on Architectures, Frameworks, and Integration Strategies for Distributed and Cloud Computing*, 2340-2370.

Bharany, S., Sharma, S., Khalaf, O. I., Abdulsahib, G. M., Al Humaimeedy, A. S., Aldhyani, T. H., Maashi, M., & Alkahtani, H. (2022). A systematic survey on energy-efficient techniques in sustainable cloud computing. *Sustainability (Basel), 14*(10), 6256. DOI: 10.3390/su14106256

Bhuie, A. K.. (2020). Circular economy and e-waste management: Review and perspectives. *Environmental Science & Technology, 54*(18), 11316–11333.

Bianchi, H., Chen, M., & Tan, L. (2023). On-device federated learning for personalized mobile experiences. *Mobile AI and Privacy Journal, 5*(2), 91–105.

Bibikar, S., Vikalo, H., Wang, Z., & Chen, X. (2022). Federated dynamic sparse training: Computing less, communicating less, yet learning better. In *Proceedings of the AAAI Conference on Artificial Intelligence* (Vol. 36, Issue 6, pp. 6080–6088). DOI: 10.1609/aaai.v36i6.20555

Bidollahkhani, M., & Kunkel, J. M. (2024). Revolutionizing System Reliability. *The Role of AI in Predictive Maintenance Strategies, c*, 49–57. http://arxiv.org/abs/2404.13454

Bi, Z. M., & Wang, L. (2012). Optimization of machining processes from the perspective of energy consumption: A case study. *Journal of Manufacturing Systems*, *31*(4), 420–428. DOI: 10.1016/j.jmsy.2012.07.002

Bojarski, M., Del Testa, D., Dworakowski, D., Firner, B., Flepp, B., Goyal, P., Jackel, L. D., Monfort, M., Muller, U., Zhang, J., ... (2016). End to end learning for self-driving cars. arXiv preprint arXiv:1604.07316. https://arxiv.org/abs/1604.07316

Bonnardel, N., Piolat, A., & Le Bigot, L. (2011). The impact of colour on Website appeal and users' cognitive processes. *Displays*, *32*(2), 69–80. DOI: 10.1016/j.displa.2010.12.002

Boopathi, S. (2024). Advancements in Optimizing Smart Energy Systems Through Smart Grid Integration, Machine Learning, and IoT. In *Optimization Techniques for Hybrid Power Systems: Renewable Energy, Electric Vehicles, and Smart Grid* (pp. 33-61). IGI Global.

Boopathi, S. (2024). Energy Cascade Conversion System and Energy-Efficient Infrastructure. In *Sustainable Development in AI, Blockchain, and E-Governance Applications* (pp. 47-71). IGI Global. DOI: 10.4018/979-8-3693-1722-8.ch004

Boscovic, D., Vakil, F., Dautovi, S. and Toši, Milenko. (2011). Pervasive wireless CDN for greening video streaming to mobile devices. MIPRO, 629-236.

Bu, S., Yu, F. R., & Liu, P. X. (2011). Dynamic pricing for demand-side management in the smart grid. *2011 IEEE Online Conference on Green Communications*, 47–51. DOI: 10.1109/GreenCom.2011.6082506

Cao, Z., Zhou, X., Hu, H., Wang, Z., & Wen, Y. (2022). Toward a systematic survey for carbon neutral data centers. *IEEE Communications Surveys and Tutorials*, *24*(2), 895–936. DOI: 10.1109/COMST.2022.3161275

Castillo-García, G., Morán-Fernández, L., & Bolón-Canedo, V. (2023). Efficient feature selection for domain adaptation using mutual information maximization. In *European Symposium on Artificial Neural Networks, Computational Intelligence and Machine Learning*. DOI: 10.14428/esann/2023.ES2023-61

Chen, B., Wan, J., Celesti, A., Li, D., Abbas, H., & Zhang, Q. (2018, September). Edge Computing in IoT-Based Manufacturing. *IEEE Communications Magazine*, *56*(9), 103–109. DOI: 10.1109/MCOM.2018.1701231

Cheng, Y., Wang, D., Zhou, P., & Zhang, T. (2022). Model compression: Techniques and applications. *IEEE Signal Processing Magazine*, *35*(1), 32–41. DOI: 10.1109/MSP.2022.00198

Chen, J., Zeng, G.-Q., Zhou, W., Du, W., & Lu, K.-D. (2018). Wind speed forecasting using nonlinear-learning ensemble of deep learning time series prediction and extremal optimization. *Energy Conversion and Management, 165*, 681–695. DOI: 10.1016/j.enconman.2018.03.098

Chen, T., Gao, X., & Chen, G. (2016). The features, hardware, and architectures of data center networks: A survey. *Journal of Parallel and Distributed Computing, 96*, 45–74. DOI: 10.1016/j.jpdc.2016.05.009

Chen, Z.-G., Zhan, Z.-H., Kwong, S., & Zhang, J. (2022). Evolutionary computation for intelligent transportation in smart cities: A survey. *IEEE Computational Intelligence Magazine, 17*(2), 83–102. DOI: 10.1109/MCI.2022.3155330

Chithaluru, P., Narsimhulu, P., Yadav, N. S., Chawla, P., & Tiwari, R. (2024). Fog computing: Advancing Sustainable Development Goals (SDGs). In *Cloud and Fog Optimization-based Solutions for Sustainable Developments* (pp. 280-298). CRC Press.

Cocaña-Fernández, A., Sánchez, L., & Ranilla, J. (2015, August). A software tool to efficiently manage the energy consumption of HPC clusters. In *2015 IEEE International Conference on Fuzzy Systems (FUZZ-IEEE)* (pp. 1-8). IEEE. DOI: 10.1109/FUZZ-IEEE.2015.7338079

Das, A., Debnath, B., Modak, N., Das, A., & De, D. (2020, December). E-waste inventorisation for sustainable smart cities in India: A cloud-based framework. In *2020 IEEE International Women in Engineering (WIE)Conference on Electrical and Computer Engineering (WIECON-ECE)* (pp. 332-335). IEEE. DOI: 10.1109/WIECON-ECE52138.2020.9397960

De Benedetti, M., Leonardi, F., Messina, F., Santoro, C., & Vasilakos, A. (2018). Anomaly detection and predictive maintenance for photovoltaic systems. *Neurocomputing, 310*, 59–68. DOI: 10.1016/j.neucom.2018.05.017

Deng, R.. (2016). Green energy source powered base stations: Opportunities and challenges. *IEEE Communications Magazine, 54*(5), 36–42.

Dhanalakshmi, M., Tamilarasi, K., Saravanan, S., Sujatha, G., & Boopathi, S. (2024). Fog Computing-Based Framework and Solutions for Intelligent Systems: Enabling Autonomy in Vehicles. In *Computational Intelligence for Green Cloud Computing and Digital Waste Management* (pp. 330-356). IGI Global.

Dhar, P. (2020). The carbon impact of artificial intelligence. *Nature Machine Intelligence, 2*(8), 423–425. DOI: 10.1038/s42256-020-0219-9

Dhatterwal, J. S., Malik, K., Kaswan, K. S., & Elngar, A. A. (2025). Federated Learning: Overview, Challenges, and Ethical Considerations. *Artificial Intelligence Using Federated Learning*, 1-15.

Díaz-Vico, D., Torres-Barrán, A., Omari, A., & Dorronsoro, J. R. (2017). Deep neural networks for wind and solar energy prediction. *Neural Processing Letters*, *46*(3), 829–844. DOI: 10.1007/s11063-017-9613-7

Directive Studies, W. E. E. E. (2021). *E-waste management: Policies and practices*. European Commission Reports.

Dodge, J., Schwartz, R., & Smith, N. A. (2020). Green AI: Reducing the carbon footprint of AI research. *Communications of the ACM*, *63*(7), 54–63. DOI: 10.1145/3408039

Dong, H., Munir, A., Tout, H., & Ganjali, Y. (2021). Next-generation data center network enabled by machine learning: Review, challenges, and opportunities. *IEEE Access : Practical Innovations, Open Solutions*, *9*, 136459–136475. DOI: 10.1109/ACCESS.2021.3117763

Duan, P., Mao, G., Liang, W., & Zhang, D. (2018). A unified spatio-temporal model for short-term traffic flow prediction. *IEEE Transactions on Intelligent Transportation Systems*, *20*(9), 3212–3223. DOI: 10.1109/TITS.2018.2873137

ecoiron (2007). http://ecoiron.blogspot.com/2007/01/black-google-would-save-3000-megawatts.html, accessed 13/02/2025

Electric, S. (2023). Smart grid optimization through federated learning. *Energy and AI*, *9*(3), 144–159.

Elgabli, A., Park, J., Bedi, A. S., Issaid, C. B., Bennis, M., & Aggarwal, V. (2020). Q-GADMM: Quantized group ADMM for communication-efficient decentralized machine learning. *IEEE Transactions on Communications*, *69*(1), 164–181. DOI: 10.1109/TCOMM.2020.3026398

Energy efficiency 101. (n.d.). *Resources for the Future*. Retrieved January 01, 2025, https://www.rff.org/publications/explainers/energy-efficiency-101/

European Union. (2024). Artificial intelligence act: European parliament legislative resolution of 13 March 2024 on the proposal for a regulation of the European Parliament and of the Council on laying down harmonised rules on artificial intelligence (Artificial Intelligence Act) and amending certain Union legislative acts (COM(2021)0206 – C9-0146/2021 – 2021/0106(COD)). Retrieved from [URL].

Fang, X.. (2020). AI-enabled energy efficiency in wireless networks. *IEEE Communications Magazine*, *58*(6), 28–34.

Fan, Z., Yan, Z., & Wen, S. (2023). Deep Learning and Artificial Intelligence in Sustainability: A Review of SDGs, Renewable Energy, and Environmental Health. *Sustainability (Basel)*, *15*(18), 13493. DOI: 10.3390/su151813493

Farzaneh, H., Malehmirchegini, L., Bejan, A., Afolabi, T., Mulumba, A., & Daka, P. P. (2021). Artificial Intelligence Evolution in Smart Buildings for Energy Efficiency. *Applied Sciences (Basel, Switzerland)*, *11*(2), 763. DOI: 10.3390/app11020763

Fayyazi, M., Sardar, P., Thomas, S. I., Daghigh, R., Jamali, A., Esch, T., Kemper, H., Langari, R., & Khayyam, H. (2023). Artificial intelligence/machine learning in energy management systems, control, and optimization of hydrogen fuel cell vehicles. *Sustainability (Basel)*, *15*(6), 5249. DOI: 10.3390/su15065249

Feng, X., Zhang, Y., & Zhou, W. (2021). Life-cycle assessment of AI models. *Journal of Cleaner Production*, *305*, 127–140. DOI: 10.1016/j.jclepro.2021.127832

Gajdzik, B., Wolniak, R., Nagaj, R., Grebski, W. W., & Romanyshyn, T. (2023). Barriers to Renewable Energy Source (RES) Installations as Determinants of Energy Consumption in EU Countries. *Energies*, *16*(21), 7364. DOI: 10.3390/en16217364

Ganesh, A., McCallum, A., & Strubell, E. (2019). Energy and policy considerations for NLP. *Proceedings of ACL 2019*, 3645–3650. DOI: 10.18653/v1/P19-1355

Gao, T., Shao, H., & Wang, Y. (2021). Renewable energy for AI computations. *Energy*, *219*, 105–115. DOI: 10.1016/j.energy.2021.105837

García-Mira, R., Dumitru, A., Alonso-Betanzos, A., Sánchez-Maroño, N., Fontenla-Romero, O., Craig, T., & Polhil, J. (2017). Testing scenarios to achieve workplace sustainability goals using backcasting and agent-based modeling. *Environment and Behavior*, *49*(9), 1007–1027. DOI: 10.1177/0013916516673869

Garg, S., Kumar, N., & Sharma, P. (2022). Green AI: Trends and challenges. *Sustainable Computing : Informatics and Systems*, *34*, 100624. DOI: 10.1016/j.suscom.2022.100624

Gaur, A. S., Raghuvanshi, C. S., & Sharan, H. O. (2024). Smart Prediction Farming Using Deep Learning and AI Techniques. In *Sustainable Development in AI, Blockchain, and E-Governance Applications* (pp. 152-170). IGI Global. DOI: 10.4018/979-8-3693-1722-8.ch009

Genemo, M. (2023). Quantum convolutional neural network for agricultural mechanization and plant disease detection. In *Proceedings of the International Conference on Image Processing and Capsule Networks* (pp. 225–237). Springer. DOI: 10.1007/978-981-99-7093-3_15

George, D. A., & Murthy, G. R. (Eds.). (2024). *Towards Wireless Heterogeneity in 6G Networks*. CRC Press. DOI: 10.1201/9781003369028

Ghasemi, A., & Toroghi Haghighat, A. (2020). A multi-objective load balancing algorithm for virtual machine placement in cloud data centers based on machine learning. *Computing*, *102*(9), 2049–2072. DOI: 10.1007/s00607-020-00813-w

Ghazal, T. M., Hasan, M. K., Ahmad, M., Alzoubi, H. M., & Alshurideh, M. (2023). Machine learning approaches for sustainable cities using the Internet of Things. In *The effect of information technology on business and marketing intelligence systems* (pp. 1969–1986). Springer., DOI: 10.1007/978-3-031-12382-5_108

Giebel, G., & Kariniotakis, G. (2017). Wind power forecasting – A review of the state of the art. *Renewable Energy Forecasting*, *59*, 59–109. DOI: 10.1016/B978-0-08-100504-0.00003-2

Gonzalez, J. E., Le, Q., & Patterson, D. (2022). Carbon efficiency of ML systems. *Communications of the ACM*, *65*(5), 85–93. DOI: 10.1145/3465810

Goundar, S., Avanija, J., Sunitha, G., Madhavi, K. R., & Bhushan, S. B. (Eds.). (2021). *Innovations in the industrial Internet of Things (IIoT) and smart factory*. IGI Global. DOI: 10.4018/978-1-7998-3375-8

Greening, I. C. T. (2012). Survey on conflict minerals due diligence initiatives.

GridEdge. (2023). Federated learning for smart building energy optimization. *Journal of Intelligent Infrastructure*, *11*(1), 55–70.

Gupta, A.. (2014). Energy-efficient mobile devices: Review of techniques and research directions. *Journal of Network and Computer Applications*, *39*, 213–228.

Gupta, B. B., & Quamara, M. (2020). An overview of Internet of Things (IoT): Architectural aspects, challenges, and protocols. *Concurrency and Computation*, *32*(21), e4946. DOI: 10.1002/cpe.4946

Gupta, V., Singh, A., & Tiwari, M. K. (2020). Efficient data centers for AI training. *IEEE Access : Practical Innovations, Open Solutions*, *9*, 8123–8132. DOI: 10.1109/ACCESS.2020.3045178

Harnal, S., Tiwari, R., Garg, L., & Mathur, A. (Eds.). (2024). *Cloud and Fog Optimization-based Solutions for Sustainable Developments* (1st ed.). CRC Press., DOI: 10.1201/9781003494430

Hassan, N., Gillani, S., Ahmed, E., Yaqoob, I., & Imran, M. (2018, November). The Role of Edge Computing in Internet of Things. *IEEE Communications Magazine*, *56*(11), 110–115. DOI: 10.1109/MCOM.2018.1700906

Heeks, R. (2020). ICT4D 3.0: Poverty reduction with equitable and sustainable ICT. *Third World Quarterly*, *41*(5), 779–797.

Henderson, P., Hu, J., & Morgenstern, J. (2020). Towards environmentally sustainable machine learning. *NeurIPS Workshop on Green AI,* 1–8. Retrieved from https://arxiv.org/abs/1907.10597

Henderson, P., Hu, J., Romoff, J., Brunskill, E., Jurafsky, D., & Pineau, J. (2020). Towards the systematic reporting of the energy and carbon footprints of machine learning. *Journal of Machine Learning Research*, *21*(248), 1–43. https://www.jmlr.org/papers/volume21/20-226/20-226.pdf

Hoffmann, F., Lorenz, M., & Schuler, J. (2021). Carbon offsets for AI technologies. *Environmental Research Letters*, *16*(5), 015003. DOI: 10.1088/1748-9326/abcde1

Holland, S. P., & Mansur, E. T. (2007). Is real-time pricing green? The environmental impacts of electricity demand variance. *The Review of Economics and Statistics*.

Hong, S., Park, S., Youn, H., Lee, J., & Kwon, S. (2024). Implementation of Smart Farm Systems Based on Fog Computing in Artificial Intelligence of Things Environments. *Sensors (Basel)*, *24*(20), 6689. DOI: 10.3390/s24206689 PMID: 39460169

Hong, T., & Fan, S. (2016). Probabilistic electric load forecasting: A tutorial review. *International Journal of Forecasting*, *32*(3), 914–938. DOI: 10.1016/j.ijforecast.2015.11.011

IBM. (2022, April 19). *What is green computing?* Retrieved January 01, 2025, https://www.ibm.com/think/topics/green-computing

Inacio, E. C., & Dantas, M. A. (2014). A survey into performance and energy efficiency in HPC, cloud and big data environments. *International Journal of Networking and Virtual Organisations*, *14*(4), 299–318. DOI: 10.1504/IJNVO.2014.067878

Interdigital. (n.d.). *How sustainable are our mobile networks?* InterDigital.com. https://www.interdigital.com/white_papers/how-sustainable-are-our-mobile-networks

Intergovernmental Panel on Climate Change (IPCC). (2014). Mitigation of climate change. In *Contribution of Working Group III to the Fifth Assessment Report of the Intergovernmental Panel on Climate Change* (p. 1454). Cambridge University Press.

Items, R., Rose, W., Rose, W., If, T., & Rose, W. (2020). The importance of social relations in shaping energy demand. *Nature Energy*, *5*, 3.

Jafri, S. (2025, February 6). *What is Network Function Virtualization (NFV)?* WWT. https://www.wwt.com/article/what-is-network-function-virtualization

Jager, W., Guijarro-Berdiñas, B., Bouman, L., Antosz, P., Alonso-Betanzos, A., Salt, D., Polhill, J. G., Rodríguez Arias, A., & Sánchez-Maroño, N. (2024). Simulating the role of norms in processes of social innovation: Three case studies. *Journal of Artificial Societies and Social Simulation*, *27*(1), 6. DOI: 10.18564/jasss.5168

Jain, A., & Singhal, P. (2016, November). Fog computing: Driving force behind the emergence of edge computing. In *2016 International Conference System Modeling & Advancement in Research Trends (SMART)* (pp. 294-297). IEEE. DOI: 10.1109/SYSMART.2016.7894538

Jalasri, M., Panchal, S. M., Mahalingam, K., Venkatasubramanian, R., Hemalatha, R., & Boopathi, S. (2025). AI-Powered Smart Energy Management for Optimizing Energy Efficiency in High-Performance Computing Systems. In *Future of Digital Technology and AI in Social Sectors* (pp. 329–366). IGI Global.

Javaid, S., Fahim, H., Zeadally, S., & He, B. (2024). From sensing to energy savings: A comprehensive survey on integrating emerging technologies for energy efficiency in WBANs. *Digital Communications and Networks*. Advance online publication. DOI: 10.1016/j.dcan.2024.11.012

Jayasutha, D., Prabhu, R. V., Sassirekha, S. M., Maithili, K., Girija, P., & Subramanian, R. S. (2024). Exploring the Intersection of Sustainable Energy, AI, and Ethical Considerations. In AI Applications for Clean Energy and Sustainability (pp. 139-160). IGI Global.

Jayasutha, D., Prabhu, R. V., Sassirekha, S. M., Maithili, K., Girija, P., & Subramanian, R. S. (2024). Exploring the Intersection of Sustainable Energy, AI, and Ethical Considerations. In *AI Applications for Clean Energy and Sustainability* (pp. 139–160). IGI Global. DOI: 10.4018/979-8-3693-6567-0.ch008

Jeong, Y. S., & Park, J. H. (2020). Security, privacy, and efficiency of sustainable computing for future smart cities. *Journal of Information Processing Systems*, *16*(1), 1–5. DOI: 10.3745/JIPS.2006.2.1.001

Jeyaraman, N., Jeyaraman, M., Yadav, S., Ramasubramanian, S., Balaji, S., Muthu, S., Lekha, P. C., & Patro, B. P. (2024, July 10). Applications of Fog Computing in Healthcare. *Cureus*, *16*(7), e64263. DOI: 10.7759/cureus.64263 PMID: 39130982

Jeyaranjani, J., Rangaswamy, K., Ashwitha, A., Gandi, R., Roopa, R., & Anjaiah, P. (2024). Navigating Green Computing Challenges and Strategies for Sustainable Solutions. In *Computational Intelligence for Green Cloud Computing and Digital Waste Management* (pp. 42–59). IGI Global. DOI: 10.4018/979-8-3693-1552-1.ch003

Jiang, C., Fan, T., Gao, H., Shi, W., Liu, L., Cérin, C., & Wan, J. (2020). Energy aware edge computing: A survey. *Computer Communications*, *151*, 556–580. DOI: 10.1016/j.comcom.2020.01.004

Jouppi, N. P., Patil, N., & Young, C. (2017). In-datacenter performance analysis of a Tensor Processing Unit. *Proceedings of ISCA*, *2017*, 1–12. DOI: 10.1145/3079856.3080246

Jouppi, N., Kurian, G., Li, S., Ma, P., Nagarajan, R., Nai, L., Patil, N., Subramanian, S., Swing, A., & Towles, B.. (2023). TPU v4: An optically reconfigurable supercomputer for machine learning with hardware support for embeddings. In *Proceedings of the 50th Annual International Symposium on Computer Architecture* (pp. 1–14). IEEE. DOI: 10.1145/3579371.3589350

Kalam, M. A., Saxena, A., Hassnain, M. Z., Dash, A. K., Singh, J., & Singh, G. K. (2024). An explicit investigation in demand side management based on artificial intelligence techniques. *IEEE Access*, *PP*, 1–1. DOI: 10.1109/ACCESS.2024.3432805

Kalyani, Y., & Collier, R. (2021). A systematic survey on the role of cloud, fog, and edge computing combination in smart agriculture. *Sensors (Basel)*, *21*(17), 5922. DOI: 10.3390/s21175922 PMID: 34502813

Kanase-Patil, A. B., Kaldate, A. P., Lokhande, S. D., Panchal, H., Suresh, M., & Priya, V. (2020). A review of artificial intelligence-based optimization techniques for the sizing of integrated renewable energy systems in smart cities. *Environmental Technology Reviews*, *9*(1), 111–136. DOI: 10.1080/21622515.2020.1836035

Kang, D.-J., Park, J., & Yeo, S.-S. (2009). Intelligent Decision-Making System with Green Pervasive Computing for Renewable Energy Business in Electricity Markets on Smart Grid. *EURASIP Journal on Wireless Communications and Networking*, *2009*(1), 247483. DOI: 10.1155/2009/247483

Karaboga, D.. (2019). Swarm intelligence: Nature-inspired algorithms for energy-efficient computing. *Swarm and Evolutionary Computation*, *48*, 84–96.

Kaundinya, D. P., Balachandra, P., & Ravindranath, N. H. (2009). Grid-connected versus stand-alone energy systems for decentralized power—A review of literature. *Renewable & Sustainable Energy Reviews*, *13*(8), 2041–2050. DOI: 10.1016/j.rser.2009.02.002

Kaur, G., Harnal, S., Goyal, A., Tiwari, R., & Cheng, X. (2024). Applications and challenges for sustainable development with cloud/fog/edge computing. *Cloud and Fog Optimization-based Solutions for Sustainable Developments*, 27-47.

Kavitha, T., Hemalatha, S., Saravanan, T. M., Singh, A. K., Alam, M. I., & Warshi, S. (2022, January). Survey on cloud computing security and scheduling. In *2022 International Conference on Computer Communication and Informatics (ICCCI)* (pp. 1-4). Ieee. DOI: 10.1109/ICCCI54379.2022.9740932

Kazi, R. H., Grossman, T., Cheong, H., Hashemi, A., & Fitzmaurice, G. W. (2017). DreamSketch: Early stage 3D design explorations with sketching and generative design. In *Proceedings of the 30th Annual ACM Symposium on User Interface Software and Technology* (pp. 401–414). ACM. DOI: 10.1145/3126594.3126662

Khan, W. Z., Ahmed, E., Hakak, S., Yaqoob, I., & Ahmed, A. (2019). Edge computing: A survey. *Future Generation Computer Systems*, *97*, 219–235. DOI: 10.1016/j.future.2019.02.050

Khirirat, S., Magnússon, S., Aytekin, A., & Johansson, M. (2021). A flexible framework for communication-efficient machine learning. In *Proceedings of the AAAI Conference on Artificial Intelligence* (Vol. 35, Issue 9, pp. 8101–8109). DOI: 10.1609/aaai.v35i9.16987

Kim, I. H., Liu, Y.-H., Pallister, S., Pol, W., Roberts, S., & Lee, E. (2022). Fault-tolerant resource estimate for quantum chemical simulations: Case study on Li-ion battery electrolyte molecules. *Physical Review Research*, *4*(2), 023019. DOI: 10.1103/PhysRevResearch.4.023019

Kim, I., Kim, B., & Sidorov, D. (2022). Machine learning for energy systems optimization. *Energies*, *15*(11), 4116. DOI: 10.3390/en15114116

Konečnỳ, J., McMahan, H. B., Ramage, D., & Richtárik, P. (2016). Federated optimization: Strategies for on-device machine learning. *Proceedings of the 20th International Conference on Artificial Intelligence and Statistics (AISTATS)*, 54, 1–10.

Kong, X., Wu, Y., Wang, H., & Xia, F. "Edge Computing for Internet of Everything: A Survey," in *IEEE Internet of Things Journal*, vol. 9, no. 23, pp. 23472-23485, 1 Dec.1, 2022, DOI: 10.1109/JIOT.2022.3200431

Koomey, J. (2011). *Growth in data center electricity use 2005 to 2010*. Analytics Press.

Koseleva, N., & Ropaite, G. (2017). Big data in building energy efficiency: Understanding of big data and main challenges. *Procedia Engineering*, *172*, 544–549. DOI: 10.1016/j.proeng.2017.02.064

Kubiak, K., Dec, G., & Stadnicka, D. (2022). Possible Applications of Edge Computing in the Manufacturing Industry—Systematic Literature Review. *Sensors (Basel)*, *22*(7), 2445. DOI: 10.3390/s22072445 PMID: 35408059

Kumar, P., Ali, I., & Thanki, D. V. (2018). Demand-side management: energy efficiency and demand response. In *Handbook of Research on Power and Energy System Optimization* (pp. 453–479). IGI Global. DOI: 10.4018/978-1-5225-3935-3.ch013

Kumar, P., Pandey, D., Srivastav, R. K., & Pandey, P. K. (2023, August). Network Traffic Analysis and Prediction Using Machine Learning. *International Journal of Research Publication and Reviews*, *4*(8), 2071–2075.

Kumar, V., Laghari, A. A., Karim, S., Shakir, M., & Brohi, A. A. (2019). Comparison of fog computing & cloud computing. *Int. J. Math. Sci. Comput*, *1*, 31–41.

Lakumarapu, S., Nithyanandhan, R., Bhargavi, V. S., Anish, T. P., & Nalini, M. (2024, August). Machine Learning Approaches for Liver Disease Prediction: A Comparative Analysis. *In 2024 5th International Conference on Electronics and Sustainable Communication Systems (ICESC)* (pp. 159-164). IEEE.

Lakumarapu, S., Nithyanandhan, R., Bhargavi, V. S., Anish, T. P., & Nalini, M. (2024, August). Machine Learning Approaches for Liver Disease Prediction: A Comparative Analysis. In *2024 5th International Conference on Electronics and Sustainable Communication Systems (ICESC)* (pp. 159-164). IEEE. DOI: 10.1109/ICESC60852.2024.10689974

Landset, S., Khoshgoftaar, T. M., Richter, A. N., & Hasanin, T. (2015). A survey of open source tools for machine learning with big data in the Hadoop ecosystem. *Journal of Big Data*, *2*(1), 1–36. DOI: 10.1186/s40537-015-0032-1

Lannelongue, L., Grealey, J., & Inouye, M. (2021). Green algorithms: Quantifying the carbon footprint of computation. *Advancement of Science*, *8*(12), 2100707. DOI: 10.1002/advs.202100707 PMID: 34194954

Le, Q. V., & Tan, M. (2019). EfficientNet: Rethinking model scaling. Proceedings of ICML 2019, 6105–6114. Retrieved from https://proceedings.mlr.press

Lee, S., Torres, M., & Gupta, H. (2024). Carbon-aware federated learning in distributed systems. *AI for a Sustainable Future*, *8*(1), 45–60.

Lee, Y., & Song, M. (2020). Adaptive Color Selection to Limit Power Consumption for Multi-Object GUI Applications in OLED-Based Mobile Devices. *Energies*, *13*(10), 2425. Advance online publication. DOI: 10.3390/en13102425

Leong, J., May Yee, K., Baitsegi, O., Palanisamy, L., & Ramasamy, R. K. (2023). Hybrid project management between traditional software development lifecycle and agile based product development for future sustainability. *Sustainability (Basel)*, *15*(2), 1121. DOI: 10.3390/su15021121

Li, L., Jamieson, K., DeSalvo, G., Rostamizadeh, A., & Talwalkar, A. (2017). Hyperband: A novel bandit-based approach to hyperparameter optimization. *Journal of Machine Learning Research*, *18*(1), 6765–6816. http://jmlr.org/papers/volume18/17-555/17-555.pdf

Lin, K.-P., Pai, P.-F., & Ting, Y.-J. (2019). Deep belief networks with genetic algorithms in forecasting wind speed. *IEEE Access : Practical Innovations, Open Solutions*, *7*, 99244–99253. DOI: 10.1109/ACCESS.2019.2929542

Liu, Z., Wang, Y., Han, K., Zhang, W., Ma, S., & Gao, W. (2021). *Post-training quantization for vision transformer* (Vol. 34). Advances in Neural Information Processing Systems, https://arxiv.org/abs/2110.02280

Liu, Z., Yu, C., Qian, Q. K., Huang, R., You, K., Visscher, H., & Zhang, G. (2023). Incentive initiatives on energy-efficient renovation of existing buildings towards carbon–neutral blueprints in China: Advancements, challenges and prospects. *Energy and Building*, *296*, 113343. DOI: 10.1016/j.enbuild.2023.113343

Li, W., Cao, J., Guan, J., Zhou, S., Liang, G., So, W. K., & Szczecinski, M. (2018). A general framework for unmet demand prediction in on-demand transport services. *IEEE Transactions on Intelligent Transportation Systems*, *20*(8), 2820–2830. DOI: 10.1109/TITS.2018.2873092

Li, Y., Wen, Y., Tao, D., & Guan, K. (2019). Transforming cooling optimization for green data center via deep reinforcement learning. *IEEE Transactions on Cybernetics*, *50*(5), 2002–2013. DOI: 10.1109/TCYB.2019.2927410 PMID: 31352360

Li, Y., Zhang, X., & Chen, M. (2022). Optimizing energy-efficient training in federated learning. *Sustainable AI Systems Journal*, *14*(2), 101–117.

Lombardi, M., Pascale, F., & Santaniello, D. (2021). Internet of things: A general overview between architectures, protocols and applications. *Information (Basel)*, *12*(2), 87. DOI: 10.3390/info12020087

Lottick, K., Susai, S., Friedler, S. A., & Wilson, J. P. (2019). Energy usage reports: Environmental awareness as part of algorithmic accountability. arXiv preprint arXiv:1911.08354. https://arxiv.org/abs/1911.08354

Lourenço, A., Ferraz, C., Meira, J., Marreiros, G., Bolón-Canedo, V., & Alonso-Betanzos, A. (2023). Automated green machine learning for condition-based maintenance. In *European Symposium on Artificial Neural Networks, Computational Intelligence and Machine Learning*. DOI: 10.14428/esann/2023.ES2023-85

Luccioni, A. S., & Hernandez-Garcia, A. (2023). Counting carbon: A survey of factors influencing the emissions of machine learning. arXiv preprint arXiv:2302.08476. https://arxiv.org/abs/2302.08476

Madakam, S., Ramaswamy, R., & Tripathi, S. (2015). Internet of Things (IoT): A literature review. *Journal of Computer and Communications*, *3*(5), 164–173. DOI: 10.4236/jcc.2015.35021

Magubane, Z., Tarwireyi, P., & Adigun, M. O. (2019, November). Evaluating the energy efficiency of IoT routing protocols. In *2019 International Multidisciplinary Information Technology and Engineering Conference (IMITEC)* (pp. 1-7). IEEE. DOI: 10.1109/IMITEC45504.2019.9015904

Mahesh, B. (2020). Machine learning algorithms-a review. *International Journal of Science and Research (IJSR).(Internet)*, *9*(1), 381-386.

Maheshwaran, T., Muthumarilakshmi, S., Vinoth, N. A. S., Suganya, K., Maheswari, B., & Girija, P. (2024). Securing E-Commerce Strategies With Cloud, Blockchain, AI, and ML. In *Strategies for E-Commerce Data Security: Cloud, Blockchain, AI, and Machine Learning* (pp. 470–500). IGI Global. DOI: 10.4018/979-8-3693-6557-1.ch019

Mahmoud, R., Yousuf, T., Aloul, F., & Zualkernan, I. (2015, December). Internet of things (IoT) security: Current status, challenges and prospective measures. In *2015 10th international conference for internet technology and secured transactions (ICITST)* (pp. 336-341). IEEE.

Maithili, K., Ponmalar, A., Yamini, B., Karthikeyan, M., Anish, T. P., Maheswari, B., & Subramanian, R. S. (2024). Advances in AI and Machine Learning for Healthcare Informatics. In *Machine Learning and Generative AI in Smart Healthcare* (pp. 1–22). IGI Global. DOI: 10.4018/979-8-3693-3719-6.ch001

Mallek, M., Euchi, J., & Jerbi, Y. (2021). A review on optimization modeling of hybrid energy systems. *Research Anthology on Clean Energy Management and Solutions*, 71-95.

Malmodin, J., & Lundén, D. (2018). The Energy and Carbon Footprint of the Global ICT and E&M Sectors 2010-2015. *Sustainability (Basel), 10*(9), 3027. DOI: 10.3390/su10093027

Marinakis, V. (2020). Big data for energy management and energy-efficient buildings. *Energies, 13*(7), 1555. DOI: 10.3390/en13071555

Marsan, M. A.. (2013). A simple analytical model for the energy-efficient design of cellular networks. *IEEE Transactions on Communications, 61*(8), 3366–3378.

Matthew, U. O., Asuni, O., & Fatai, L. O. (2024). Green Software Engineering Development Paradigm: An Approach to a Sustainable Renewable Energy Future. In *Advancing Software Engineering Through AI, Federated Learning, and Large Language Models* (pp. 281-294). IGI Global.

Milojevic-Dupont, N., & Creutzig, F. (2021). Machine learning for geographically differentiated climate change mitigation in urban areas. *Sustainable Cities and Society, 64*, 102526. DOI: 10.1016/j.scs.2020.102526

Mobile Industry Impact Report Sustainable Development Goals. (2024, October 2). External Affairs. https://www.gsma.com/solutions-and-impact/connectivity-for-good/external-affairs/2024-mobile-industry-impact-report-sustainable-development-goals

Mohamed, N., Almazrouei, S. K., Oubelaid, A., Bajaj, M., Jurado, F., & Kamel, S. (2023, June). Artificial intelligence (AI) and machine learning (ML)-based Information security in electric vehicles: A review. In *2023 5th Global Power,Energy and Communication Conference (GPECOM)* (pp. 108-113). IEEE.

Mohsenian-Rad, A.-H., Wong, V. W. S., Jatskevich, J., Schober, R., & Leon-Garcia, A. (2010). Autonomous Demand-Side Management Based on Game-Theoretic Energy Consumption Scheduling for the Future Smart Grid. *IEEE Transactions on Smart Grid, 1*(3), 320–331. DOI: 10.1109/TSG.2010.2089069

Moore, G. E. (1998). Cramming more components onto integrated circuits. *Proceedings of the IEEE, 86*(1), 82–85. DOI: 10.1109/JPROC.1998.658762

Moreno-Vozmediano, R., Montero, R. S., Huedo, E., & Llorente, I. M. (2019). Efficient resource provisioning for elastic cloud services based on machine learning techniques. *Journal of Cloud Computing (Heidelberg, Germany), 8*(1), 1–18. DOI: 10.1186/s13677-019-0128-9

Mouha, R. A. R. A. (2021). Internet of things (IoT). *Journal of Data Analysis and Information Processing, 9*(02), 77–101. DOI: 10.4236/jdaip.2021.92006

Murthy, J. S. (2021). Edgecloud: A distributed management system for resource continuity in edge to cloud computing environment. In *Research Anthology on Architectures, Frameworks, and Integration Strategies for Distributed and Cloud Computing* (pp. 2684-2700). IGI Global. DOI: 10.4018/978-1-7998-5339-8.ch130

Murugesan, S. (2008). Harnessing Green IT: Principles and Practices. *IT Professional, 10*(1), 24–33. DOI: 10.1109/MITP.2008.10

Mystakidis, A., Koukaras, P., Tsalikidis, N., Ioannidis, D., & Tjortjis, C. (2024). Energy Forecasting: A Comprehensive Review of Techniques and Technologies. *Energies, 17*(7), 1662. DOI: 10.3390/en17071662

Nadella, G. S., Satish, S., Meduri, K., & Meduri, S. S. (2023). A Systematic Literature Review of Advancements, Challenges and Future Directions of AI And ML in Healthcare. *International Journal of Machine Learning for Sustainable Development, 5*(3), 115–130.

Nafiz, M. S., Das, S. S., Morol, M. K., Juabir, A. A., & Nandi, D. (2023, February 6). *ConvoWaste: an automatic waste segregation machine using deep learning*. arXiv.org. https://arxiv.org/abs/2302.02976 DOI: 10.1109/ICREST57604.2023.10070078

Nair, R., Sharma, P., Bhagat, A., & Dwivedi, V. K. (2018). A survey on IoT (Internet of Things) emerging technologies and its application. [IJEUCD]. *International Journal of End-User Computing and Development, 7*(2), 1–20. DOI: 10.4018/IJEUCD.2018070101

Naseer, M., Zhang, W., & Zhu, W. (2020). Early prediction of a team performance in the initial assessment phases of a software project for sustainable software engineering education. *Sustainability (Basel), 12*(11), 4663. DOI: 10.3390/su12114663

Nathali Silva, B., Khan, M., & Han, K. (2017). Big Data Analytics Embedded Smart City Architecture for Performance Enhancement through Real-Time Data Processing and Decision-Making. *Wireless Communications and Mobile Computing, 2017*, 1–12. DOI: 10.1155/2017/9429676

Nazir, M. S., Wang, Y., Bilal, M., Sohail, H. M., Kadhem, A. A., Nazir, H. M. R., Abdalla, A. N., & Ma, Y. (2020). Comparison of Small-Scale Wind Energy Conversion Systems: Economic Indexes. *Cleanroom Technology, 2*(2), 144–155. DOI: 10.3390/cleantechnol2020010

Nevavuori, P., Narra, N., & Lipping, T. (2019). Crop yield prediction with deep convolutional neural networks. *Computers and Electronics in Agriculture, 163*, 104859. DOI: 10.1016/j.compag.2019.104859

Nguyen, T., Patel, S., & Huang, R. (2023). HED-FL: Hierarchical energy-aware dynamic federated learning for data centers. *Journal of Distributed AI and Sustainability*, *7*(2), 88–104.

Nishanth, J. R., Deshmukh, M. A., Kushwah, R., Kushwaha, K. K., Balaji, S., & Sampath, B. (2023). Particle swarm optimization of hybrid renewable energy systems. In *Intelligent Engineering Applications and Applied Sciences for Sustainability* (pp. 291–308). IGI Global. DOI: 10.4018/979-8-3693-0044-2.ch016

Nishtar, Z., & Afzal, J. (2023). A Review of Real-Time Monitoring of Hybrid Energy Systems by Using Artificial Intelligence and IoT. *Pakistan Journal of Engineering and Technology*, *6*(3), 8–15. DOI: 10.51846/vol6iss3pp8-15

Nithya, T., Kumar, V. N., Gayathri, S., Deepa, S., Varun, C. M., & Subramanian, R. S. (2023, August). A comprehensive survey of machine learning: Advancements, applications, and challenges. In *2023 Second International Conference on Augmented Intelligence and Sustainable Systems (ICAISS)* (pp. 354-361). IEEE. DOI: 10.1109/ICAISS58487.2023.10250547

Novoa-Paradela, D., Fontenla-Romero, O., & Guijarro-Berdiñas, B. (2023). Fast deep autoencoder for federated learning. *Pattern Recognition*, *143*, 109805. DOI: 10.1016/j.patcog.2023.109805

Olatunde, T. M., Okwandu, A. C., Akande, D. O., & Sikhakhane, Z. Q. (2024). REVIEWING THE ROLE OF ARTIFICIAL INTELLIGENCE IN ENERGY EFFICIENCY OPTIMIZATION. *Engineering Science & Technology Journal*, *5*(4), 1243–1256. DOI: 10.51594/estj.v5i4.1015

Ometov, A., Molua, O. L., Komarov, M., & Nurmi, J. (2022). A survey of security in cloud, edge, and fog computing. *Sensors (Basel)*, *22*(3), 927. DOI: 10.3390/s22030927 PMID: 35161675

Omitaomu, O. A., & Niu, H. (2021). Artificial Intelligence Techniques in Smart Grid: A Survey. *Smart Cities*, *4*(2), 548–568. DOI: 10.3390/smartcities4020029

Osta, M., Alameh, M., Younes, H., Ibrahim, A., & Valle, M. (2019). Energy efficient implementation of machine learning algorithms on hardware platforms. In 2019 26th IEEE International Conference on Electronics, Circuits and Systems (ICECS) (pp. 21–24). IEEE. DOI: 10.1109/ICECS46596.2019.8965157

Panchal, H. N., & Patel, N. (2018). ANSYS CFD and experimental comparison of various parameters of a solar still. *International Journal of Ambient Energy*, *39*(6), 551–557. DOI: 10.1080/01430750.2017.1318785

Panchal, H. N., & Thakkar, H. (2016). Theoretical and experimental validation of evacuated tubes directly coupled with solar still. *Thermal Engineering*, *63*(11), 825–831. DOI: 10.1134/S0040601516110045

Patel, A.B. (2021) "Wireless and Mobile Computing: Build Secure and Maintain Wireless Solutions" Published in *International Journal of Trend in Scientific Research and Development (ijtsrd),* ISSN: 2456- 6470, Volume-5 | Issue-5, August 2021, pp.346-351.

Patel, Y. S., Mehrotra, N., & Soner, S. (2015, February). Green cloud computing: A review on Green IT areas for cloud computing environment. In *2015 International Conference on Futuristic Trends on Computational Analysis and Knowledge Management (ABLAZE)* (pp. 327-332). IEEE. DOI: 10.1109/ABLAZE.2015.7155006

Patterson, D., Gonzalez, J., Le, Q., Liang, C., Munguia, L.-M., Rothchild, D., So, D., Texier, M., & Dean, J. (2021). Carbon emissions and large neural network training. arXiv:2104.10350.

Paul, P. (2025). SDG-oriented cloud-fog-edge-blockchain model for sustainable development. In *Artificial Intelligence and Information Technologies* (pp. 460–466). CRC Press.

Periyasamy, A. G., Singh, A., & Ravindra, K. (2022). Carbon Emissions from Virtual and Physical Modes of Conference and Prospects for Carbon Neutrality: An Analysis From India. *Air, Soil and Water Research*, *15*, 11786221221093298. Advance online publication. DOI: 10.1177/11786221221093298

Pham, A.-D., Ngo, N.-T., Truong, T. T. H., Huynh, N.-T., & Truong, N.-S. (2020). Predicting energy consumption in multiple buildings using machine learning for improving energy efficiency and sustainability. *Journal of Cleaner Production*, *260*, 121082. DOI: 10.1016/j.jclepro.2020.121082

Pham, Q. B., Kumar, M., Di Nunno, F., Elbeltagi, A., Granata, F., Islam, A. R. M. T., Talukdar, S., Nguyen, X. C., Ahmed, A. N., & Anh, D. T. (2022). Groundwater level prediction using machine learning algorithms in a drought-prone area. *Neural Computing & Applications*, *34*(13), 10751–10773. DOI: 10.1007/s00521-022-07009-7

Pitchai, R., Tiwari, S., Viji, C., Kistan, A., Puviarasi, R., & Gokul, S. (2024). Green Technologies, Reducing Carbon Footprints, and Maximizing Energy Efficiency with Emerging Innovations: Green Computing. In *Convergence Strategies for Green Computing and Sustainable Development* (pp. 86-110). IGI Global.

Ponmalar, A., Vijayakumar, K., Lakshmipriya, C., Karthikeyan, M., & PJ, B. P. (2024). Meta-Heuristics and Machine Learning Applications in Complex Systems. *In Metaheuristic and Machine Learning Optimization Strategies for Complex Systems (pp. 257-275).* IGI Global.

Ponnusamy, V., Sharma, B., & Lee, G. M. (2021). Green energy in data centers using internet of things. In *Role of IoT in green energy systems* (pp. 225–246). IGI Global. DOI: 10.4018/978-1-7998-6709-8.ch010

Prabha, D., Subramanian, R. S., Balakrishnan, S., & Karpagam, M. (2019). Performance evaluation of Naive Bayes classifier with and without filter based feature selection. *International Journal of Innovative Technology and Exploring Engineering (IJITEE) ISSN*, 2278-3075.

Prabha, D., Subramanian, R. S., Dinesh, M. G., & Girija, P. (2024). Sustainable Farming Through AI-Enabled Precision Agriculture. In Artificial Intelligence for Precision Agriculture (pp. 159-182). Auerbach Publications.

Pramanik, P. K. D., Pal, S., & Choudhury, P. (2019). Smartphone Crowd Computing: A rational approach for sustainable computing by curbing the environmental externalities of the growing computing demands. In *Chapman and Hall/CRC eBooks* (pp. 45–80). DOI: 10.1201/9780429298288-3

Priyadarshini, R., Malarvizhi, N., & Neeba, E. A. (2019). A study on capabilities and challenges of fog computing. In *Novel Practices and Trends in Grid and Cloud Computing* (pp. 249–273). IGI Global. DOI: 10.4018/978-1-5225-9023-1.ch015

Putha, S. (2020). AI-Driven Energy Management in Manufacturing: Optimizing Energy Consumption and Reducing Operational Costs. *Distributed Learning and Broad Applications in Scientific Research*, *6*, 313–353.

PySyft Development Team (Ryffel, A., Wagner, M., & OpenMined Team). (2023). Secure computation in federated learning for healthcare and finance. Journal of Privacy-Preserving AI, 6(3), 165–180.

Qolomany, B., Al-Fuqaha, A., Gupta, A., Benhaddou, D., Alwajidi, S., Qadir, J., & Fong, A. C. (2019). Leveraging machine learning and big data for smart buildings: A comprehensive survey. *IEEE Access : Practical Innovations, Open Solutions*, *7*, 90316–90356. DOI: 10.1109/ACCESS.2019.2926642

Radu, L. D. (2017). Green cloud computing: A literature survey. *Symmetry*, *9*(12), 295. DOI: 10.3390/sym9120295

Raghunath, V., Kunkulagunta, M., & Nadella, G. S. (2023). Enhancing Data Integration Using AI and ML Techniques for Real-Time Analytics. *International Journal of Machine Learning for Sustainable Development*, *5*(3).

Rahnamay Bonab, S., Haseli, G., & Jafarzadeh Ghoushchi, S. (2024). Digital technology and information and communication technology on the carbon footprint. In *Decision Support Systems for Sustainable Computing* (pp. 101–122). Elsevier., DOI: 10.1016/B978-0-443-23597-9.00005-6

Raihan, A. (2023). A comprehensive review of artificial intelligence and machine learning applications in energy sector. *Journal of Technology Innovations and Energy*, *2*(4), 1–26. DOI: 10.56556/jtie.v2i4.608

Rane, N. L. (2023). Integrating Leading-Edge Artificial Intelligence (AI), Internet of Things (IoT), and Big Data Technologies for Smart and Sustainable Architecture, Engineering and Construction (AEC) Industry: Challenges and Future Directions. *International Journal of Data Science and Big Data Analytics*, *3*(2), 73–95. DOI: 10.51483/IJDSBDA.3.2.2023.73-95

Rani, S., Bhambri, P., Kataria, A., Khang, A., & Sivaraman, A. K. (Eds.). (2023). *Big Data, Cloud Computing and IoT: Tools and Applications*. CRC Press. DOI: 10.1201/9781003298335

Renggli, C., Ashkboos, S., Aghagolzadeh, M., Alistarh, D., & Hoefler, T. (2019). SparCML: High-performance sparse communication for machine learning. In *Proceedings of the International Conference for High Performance Computing, Networking, Storage and Analysis* (pp. 1–15). DOI: 10.1145/3295500.3356222

Reynolds, J., Patel, M., & Kim, D. (2023). Federated learning for intelligent network traffic management. *Journal of Network Optimization*, *14*(2), 122–136.

Roberts, D., & Mehta, A. (2021). Building sustainable cloud AI with federated machine learning. *Cloud and Environmental Computing*, *13*(4), 198–213.

Robillard, M. P. (2016, November). Sustainable software design. In *Proceedings of the 2016 24th ACM SIGSOFT international symposium on foundations of software engineering* (pp. 920-923). DOI: 10.1145/2950290.2983983

Rolnick, D., Donti, P. L., Kaack, L. H., Kochanski, K., Lacoste, A., Sankaran, K., Ross, A. S., Milojevic-Dupont, N., Jaques, N., Waldman-Brown, A., Luccioni, A. S., Maharaj, T., Sherwin, E. D., Mukkavilli, S. K., Kording, K. P., Gomes, C. P., Ng, A. Y., Hassabis, D., Platt, J. C., & Bengio, Y. (2022). Tackling climate change with machine learning. *ACM Computing Surveys*, *55*(2), 1–96. DOI: 10.1145/3485128

Rong, H., Zhang, H., Xiao, S., Li, C., & Hu, C. (2016). Optimizing energy consumption for data centers. In *Renewable and Sustainable Energy Reviews* (Vol. 58, pp. 674–691). Elsevier Ltd., DOI: 10.1016/j.rser.2015.12.283

Saeed, M. M., Saeed, R. A., Azim, M. A., Ali, E. S., Mokhtar, R. A., & Khalifa, O. (2022, May). Green machine learning approach for QoS improvement in cellular communications. In *2022 IEEE 2nd International Maghreb Meeting of the Conference on Sciences and Techniques of Automatic Control and Computer Engineering (MI-STA)* (pp. 523-528). IEEE. DOI: 10.1109/MI-STA54861.2022.9837585

Sagiroglu, S., & Sinanc, D. (2013, May). Big data: A review. In *2013 international conference on collaboration technologies and systems (CTS)* (pp. 42-47). IEEE. DOI: 10.1109/CTS.2013.6567202

Salinas, D., Bohlke-Schneider, M., Callot, L., Medico, R., & Gasthaus, J. (2019). *High-dimensional multivariate forecasting with low-rank Gaussian copula processes* (Vol. 32). Advances in Neural Information Processing Systems, https://arxiv.org/abs/1812.02417

Sami, K. N., Amin, Z. M. A., & Hassan, R. (2020). Waste management using machine learning and deep learning algorithms. *International Journal on Perceptive and Cognitive Computing*, *6*(2), 97–106. DOI: 10.31436/ijpcc.v6i2.165

Sánchez-Maroño, N., Alonso-Betanzos, A., Fontenla-Romero, O., Brinquis-Núñez, C., Polhill, J. G., Craig, T., Dumitru, A., & García-Mira, R. (2015). An agent-based model for simulating environmental behavior in an educational organization. *Neural Processing Letters*, *42*(1), 89–118. DOI: 10.1007/s11063-014-9390-5

Sánchez-Maroño, N., Rodríguez Arias, A., Lema-Lago, I., Guijarro-Berdiñas, B., Dumitru, A., & Alonso-Betanzos, A. (2022). How agent-based modeling can help to foster sustainability projects. In *Proceedings of the 26th International Conference on Knowledge-Based and Intelligent Information and Engineering Systems (KES 2022)*. DOI: 10.1016/j.procs.2022.09.313

Saravanan, K., Prakash, R. B., Balakrishnan, C., Kumar, G. V. P., Subramanian, R. S., & Anita, M. (2023, December). Support Vector Machines: Unveiling the Power and Versatility of SVMs in Modern Machine Learning. In *2023 3rd International Conference on Innovative Mechanisms for Industry Applications (ICIMIA)* (pp. 680-687). IEEE.

Saravanan, S., Khare, R., Umamaheswari, K., Khare, S., Gowda, B. K., & Boopathi, S. (2024). AI and ML Adaptive Smart-Grid Energy Management Systems: Exploring Advanced Innovations. In *Principles and Applications in Speed Sensing and Energy Harvesting for Smart Roads* (pp. 166-196). IGI Global.

Saravanan, K. P., Carpenter, P. M., & Ramirez, A. (2014, June). A performance perspective on energy efficient HPC links. In *Proceedings of the 28th ACM international conference on Supercomputing* (pp. 313-322). DOI: 10.1145/2597652.2597671

Sasubilli, M. K., & Venkateswarlu, R. (2021, January). Cloud computing security challenges, threats and vulnerabilities. In *2021 6th international conference on inventive computation technologies (ICICT)* (pp. 476-480). IEEE. DOI: 10.1109/ICICT50816.2021.9358709

Savazzi, S., & Rampa, V. (2022). Environmental impact analysis of federated learning in distributed systems. *Journal of Energy-Aware Computing, 10*(4), 250–263.

Saxena, A., Gupta, K., & Pala, S. (2024). Convergence Strategies for Green Computing and Sustainable Development. In *Convergence Strategies for Green Computing and Sustainable Development* (pp. 62–85). IGI Global.

Schwartz, R., Dodge, J., Smith, N. A., & Etzioni, O. (2020). Green AI. *Communications of the ACM, 63*(12), 54–63. DOI: 10.1145/3381831

Seifi, A., & Moshayeri, A. (2024). *The Influence of Color Schemes and Aesthetics on User Satisfaction in Web Design: An Empirical Study*. Https://Www.Ijahci.Com/Index.Php/Ijahci/Article/View/21

Sekhar, P. C., & Tupakula, R. R. (2019). Model predictive controller for single-phase distributed generator with seamless transition between grid and off-grid modes. *IET Generation, Transmission & Distribution, 13*(10), 1829–1837. DOI: 10.1049/iet-gtd.2018.6345

Semerikov, S., Striuk, A., Striuk, L., Striuk, M., & Shalatska, H. (2020). Sustainability in Software Engineering Education: a case of general professional competencies. In *E3S Web of Conferences* (Vol. 166, p. 10036). EDP Sciences. DOI: 10.1051/e3sconf/202016610036

Shahi, A., & Mittal, A. (2024). The Impact of Federated Learning on AI-Enhanced Healthcare Delivery. In *Pioneering Smart Healthcare 5.0 with IoT, Federated Learning, and Cloud Security* (pp. 57-66). IGI Global.

Sharma, R., Kamble, S. S., Gunasekaran, A., Kumar, V., & Kumar, A. (2020). A systematic literature review on machine learning applications for sustainable agriculture supply chain performance. *Computers & Operations Research, 119*, 104926. DOI: 10.1016/j.cor.2020.104926

Shor, P. W., & Preskill, J. (2021). Quantum computing and its implications for energy efficiency. *Nature Physics, 17*, 757–764.

Shumska, M., & Bunte, K. (2023). Multispectral texture classification in agriculture. In Proceedings of the European Symposium on Artificial Neural Networks, Computational Intelligence and Machine Learning. https://www.esann.org/sites/default/files/proceedings/2023/ESANN2023_65.pdf

Singh Aujla, G., Garg, S., Batra, S., Kumar, N., You, I., & Sharma, V. (2019). DROpS: A demand response optimization scheme in SDN-enabled smart energy ecosystem. *Information Sciences*, *476*, 453–473. DOI: 10.1016/j.ins.2018.09.047

Singh, J., Chugh, A., & Singh, A. K. (2024). Sustainability in the Age of AI: Exploring Challenges and Innovative Solutions. In *Convergence Strategies for Green Computing and Sustainable Development* (pp. 1-16). IGI Global.

Singh, A., Moreno, L., & Zhao, K. (2023). Privacy-preserving tumor detection using federated learning. *Medical AI Journal*, *12*(2), 76–90.

Singh, R., & Gill, S. S. (2023). Next generation edge computing: A roadmap to net zero emissions. *Journal of Economy and Technology*, *1*, 208–221. DOI: 10.1016/j.ject.2023.12.001

Singh, S., Sulthana, R., Shewale, T., Chamola, V., Benslimane, A., & Sikdar, B. (2021). Machine-learning-assisted security and privacy provisioning for edge computing: A survey. *IEEE Internet of Things Journal*, *9*(1), 236–260. DOI: 10.1109/JIOT.2021.3098051

Siva, S. R., Sudha, K., Pooja, E., Maheswari, B., & Girija, P. (2024). Revolutionizing Healthcare Delivery: Applications and Impact of Cutting-Edge Technologies. *AI and IoT Technology and Applications for Smart Healthcare Systems*, 75-91.

Smith, T., Yu, X., & Zhang, R. (2020). Distributed learning for AI sustainability. *Proceedings of ICML 2020*, 1024–1031. Retrieved from https://proceedings.mlr.press/

Snoek, J., Larochelle, H., & Adams, R. P. (2012). Practical Bayesian optimization of machine learning algorithms. Advances in Neural Information Processing Systems, 25, 1–9. https://proceedings.neurips.cc/paper/2012/hash/82ebf97e5b3496b60f2b70443a890351-Abstract.html

Sobin, C. C. (2020). A survey on architecture, protocols and challenges in IoT. *Wireless Personal Communications*, *112*(3), 1383–1429. DOI: 10.1007/s11277-020-07108-5

Solanki, A., & Nayyar, A. (2019). Green internet of things (G-IoT): ICT technologies, principles, applications, projects, and challenges. In *Handbook of research on big data and the IoT* (pp. 379-405). IGI Global.

Song, X., & Qu, J. (2014). An improved real-time pricing algorithm based on utility maximization for smart grid. *Proceeding of the 11th World Congress on Intelligent Control and Automation, 2015-March*(March), 2509–2513. DOI: 10.1109/WCICA.2014.7053118

Songhorabadi, M., Rahimi, M., MoghadamFarid, A. M., & Haghi Kashani, M. (2023). Fog computing approaches in IoT-enabled smart cities. *Journal of Network and Computer Applications*, *211*, 103557. DOI: 10.1016/j.jnca.2022.103557

Sorkun, M. C., Paoli, C., & Incel, Ö. D. (2017). Time series forecasting on solar irradiation using deep learning. In 2017 10th International Conference on Electrical and Electronics Engineering (ELECO) (pp. 151–155). IEEE.

Sreelakshmi, S., Babu, A. A., Lakshmipriya, C., Gracious, L. A., Nalini, M., & Subramanian, R. S. (2024, October). Enhancing Intrusion Detection Systems with Machine Learning. *In 2024 2nd International Conference on Self Sustainable Artificial Intelligence Systems (ICSSAS)* (pp. 557-564). IEEE.

Sreelakshmi, S., Babu, A. A., Lakshmipriya, C., Gracious, L. A., Nalini, M., & Subramanian, R. S. (2024, October). Enhancing Intrusion Detection Systems with Machine Learning. In *2024 2nd International Conference on Self Sustainable Artificial Intelligence Systems (ICSSAS)* (pp. 557-564). IEEE. DOI: 10.1109/ICSSAS64001.2024.10760341

Stamoulis, D., Ding, R., Wang, D., Lymberopoulos, D., Priyantha, B., Liu, J., & Marculescu, D. (2019). Single-path NAS: Designing hardware-efficient convnets in less than 4 hours. In *Joint European Conference on Machine Learning and Knowledge Discovery in Databases* (pp. 481–497). Springer. https://doi.org/DOI: 10.1007/978-3-030-30494-3_30

Stecuła, K., Wolniak, R., & Grebski, W. W. (2023). AI-Driven Urban Energy Solutions—From Individuals to Society: A Review. *Energies*, *16*(24), 7988. DOI: 10.3390/en16247988

Suárez-Albela, M., Fernández-Caramés, T. M., Fraga-Lamas, P., & Castedo, L. (2017). A practical evaluation of a high-security energy-efficient gateway for IoT fog computing applications. *Sensors (Basel)*, *17*(9), 1978. DOI: 10.3390/s17091978 PMID: 28850104

Suárez-Marcote, S., Morán-Fernández, L., & Bolón-Canedo, V. (2023). Logarithmic division for green feature selection: An information-theoretic approach. In *European Symposium on Artificial Neural Networks, Computational Intelligence and Machine Learning*. DOI: 10.14428/esann/2023.ES2023-77

Subha, S., Balakrishnan, C., & Anish, T. P. (2024, August). Optimizing Machine Learning Algorithms for Heart Disease Prediction in Healthcare: A Comparative Study. In *2024 5th International Conference on Electronics and Sustainable Communication Systems (ICESC)* (pp. 866-872). IEEE. DOI: 10.1109/ICESC60852.2024.10689877

Subramaniam, B., & Feng, W. C. (2012, May). The green index: A metric for evaluating system-wide energy efficiency in hpc systems. In *2012 IEEE 26th International Parallel and Distributed Processing Symposium Workshops & PhD Forum* (pp. 1007-1013). IEEE. DOI: 10.1109/IPDPSW.2012.123

Subramanian, R. S., Girija, P., Sudha, K., & Aswini, J. SivaKumar, S., & Nattesan, N. V. S. (2023, January). Alleviating the naive bayes assumption using filter approaches. In 2023 5th International Conference on Smart Systems and Inventive Technology (ICSSIT) (pp. 1430-1436). IEEE.

Subramanian, R. S., Sudha, K., & Ramana, K. V. SivaKumar, S., Nithyanandhan, R., & Nalini, M. (2023, February). Hybrid Variable Selection Approach to Analyse High Dimensional Dataset. In 2023 7th International Conference on Computing Methodologies and Communication (ICCMC) (pp. 1489-1495). IEEE.

Subramanian, R. S., Yamini, B., Sudha, K., & Sivakumar, S. (2024). Ensemble-based deep learning techniques for customer churn prediction model. *Kybernetes*. Advance online publication. DOI: 10.1108/K-08-2023-1516

Sudha, K., Balakrishnan, C., Anish, T. P., Nithya, T., Yamini, B., Subramanian, R. S., & Nalini, M. (2024). Data Insight Unveiled: Navigating Critical Approaches and Challenges in Diverse Domains Through Advanced Data Analysis. *Critical Approaches to Data Engineering Systems and Analysis*, 90-114.

Sudha, K., Nithyanandhan, R., Anish, T. P., Girija, P., & Nalini, M. (2024, July). Enhancing Healthcare Data Security in the Cloud: Integrating ML-Based Intrusion Detection Systems. *In 2024 2nd World Conference on Communication & Computing (WCONF)* (pp. 1-7). IEEE.

Sudha, K., Ambhika, C., Maheswari, B., Girija, P., & Nalini, M. (2023). AI and IoT applications in medical domain enhancing healthcare through technology integration. In *AI and IoT-Based Technologies for Precision Medicine* (pp. 280–294). IGI Global.

Sung, Y., Sharma, P. K., Lopez, E. M., & Park, J. H. (2016). FS-OpenSecurity: A taxonomic modeling of security threats in SDN for future sustainable computing. *Sustainability (Basel)*, *8*(9), 919. DOI: 10.3390/su8090919

Sun, Z., Liu, J., & Zhou, P. (2021). Quantization-aware training for efficient AI models. *Neural Networks*, *150*, 25–37. DOI: 10.1016/j.neunet.2021.03.005

Suresh, M., Meenakumari, R., Panchal, H., Priya, V., El Agouz, E. S., & Israr, M. (2022). An enhanced multiobjective particle swarm optimisation algorithm for optimum utilisation of hybrid renewable energy systems. *International Journal of Ambient Energy*, *43*(1), 2540–2548. DOI: 10.1080/01430750.2020.1737837

Surya, P., Pachauri, P., Pachauri, A., Chaturvedi, P., Yadav, S. A., & Singh, D. (2021, November). Virtualization Risks and associated Issues in Cloud Environment. In *2021 International Conference on Technological Advancements and Innovations (ICTAI)* (pp. 521-525). IEEE. DOI: 10.1109/ICTAI53825.2021.9673424

Sustainable networks: Ericsson Intelligent Operations Guide. (n.d.). https://www.ericsson.com/en/reports-and-papers/further-insights/sustainable-networks-the-intelligent-operations-guide

Svorobej, S., Endo, P. T., Bendechache, M., Filelis-Papadopoulos, C., Giannoutakis, K. M., Gravvanis, G. A., Tzovaras, D., Byrne, J., & Lynn, T. (2019). Simulating fog and edge computing scenarios: An overview and research challenges. *Future Internet*, *11*(3), 55. DOI: 10.3390/fi11030055

Swasty, W., & Adriyanto, A. R. (2017). Does Color Matter on Web User Interface Design. *CommIT (Communication and Information Technology). Journal*, *11*(1), 17. DOI: 10.21512/commit.v11i1.2088

Szostak, D., Włodarczyk, A., & Walkowiak, K. (2021). Machine learning classification and regression approaches for optical network traffic prediction. *Electronics (Basel)*, *10*(13), 1578. DOI: 10.3390/electronics10131578

Tank, B., & Gandhi, V. (2023). A Comparative Study on Cloud Computing, Edge Computing and Fog Computing. In *Recent Developments in Electronics and Communication Systems* (pp. 665–670). IOS Press. DOI: 10.3233/ATDE221329

Tay, Y., Bahri, D., Yang, L., Metzler, D., & Juan, D.-C. (2020). Sparse Sinkhorn attention. In International Conference on Machine Learning (pp. 9438–9447). PMLR. https://proceedings.mlr.press/v119/tay20a.html

TechTarget. (2023, March 14). *What is green computing?* Data Center. Retrieved January 01, 2025, from https://www.techtarget.com/searchdatacenter/definition/green-computing

The Impact of Typography on Web Design: A Comprehensive Guide to Aesthetics and Readability. (n.d.). Https://Guidelines.India.Gov.in/Activity/the-Impact-of-Typography-on-Web-Design-a-Comprehensive-Guide-to-Aesthetics-and-Readability/

ichindelean, M., ichindelean, M. T., Cetină, I., & Orzan, G. (2021). A comparative eye tracking study of usability—Towards sustainable web design. *Sustainability (Basel), 13*(18), 10415. Advance online publication. DOI: 10.3390/su131810415

Tiwari, N., Sarkar, S., Bellur, U., & Indrawan, M. (2014). An empirical study of hadoop's energy efficiency on a HPC cluster. *Procedia Computer Science, 29*, 62–72. DOI: 10.1016/j.procs.2014.05.006

Trébaol, T. (2020). CUMULATOR - a tool to quantify and report the carbon footprint of machine learning computations and communication in academia and healthcare. https://doi.org/DOI: 10.13140/RG.2.2.32835.20009

UL Environment, Green Electronics Council unveil UL ECOLOGO/EPEAT Joint-Certification for Mobile Phones | UL Solutions. (n.d.). UL Solutions. https://www.ul.com/news/ul-environment-green-electronics-council-unveil-ul-ecologoepeat-joint-certification-mobile

Ummah, M. S. (2019). Understanding and Implementing User Interface Laws: Differentiating UI Laws from UX Laws in the UI/UX Design Process. *Sustainability (Switzerland), 11*(1), 1–14. http://scioteca.caf.com/bitstream/handle/123456789/1091/RED2017-Eng-8ene.pdf?sequence=12&isAllowed=y%0Ahttp://dx.doi.org/10.1016/j.regsciurbeco.2008.06.005%0Ahttps://www.researchgate.net/publication/305320484_SISTEM_PEMBETUNGAN_TERPUSAT_STRATEGI_MELESTARI

United Nations. (2023, August). *What is sustainable development?* United Nations. https://www.un.org/sustainabledevelopment/blog/2023/08/what-is-sustainable-development/

United Nations. (n.d.). *Sustainable development goals.* United Nations. https://sdgs.un.org/goals

Varrette, S., Plugaru, V., Guzek, M., Besseron, X., & Bouvry, P. (2014, September). HPC performance and energy-efficiency of the OpenStack cloud middleware. In *2014 43rd International Conference on Parallel Processing Workshops* (pp. 419-428). IEEE. DOI: 10.1109/ICPPW.2014.62

Veerachamy, R., & Ramar, R. (2022). Agricultural irrigation recommendation and alert (AIRA) system using optimization and machine learning in Hadoop for sustainable agriculture. *Environmental Science and Pollution Research International, 29*(14), 19955–19974. DOI: 10.1007/s11356-021-13248-3 PMID: 33788091

Venayagamoorthy, G. K. (2009). Potentials and promises of computational intelligence for smart grids. *2009 IEEE Power & Energy Society General Meeting, August 2009*, 1–6. DOI: 10.1109/PES.2009.5275224

Verdecchia, R., Cruz, L., Sallou, J., Lin, M., Wickenden, J., & Hotellier, E. (2022, June). Data-centric green ai an exploratory empirical study. *In 2022 international conference on ICT for sustainability (ICT4S)* (pp. 35-45). IEEE.

Verdecchia, R., Sallou, J., & Cruz, L. (2023). A systematic review of Green AI. *Wiley Interdisciplinary Reviews. Data Mining and Knowledge Discovery, 13*(4), e1507. DOI: 10.1002/widm.1507

Verma, J., & Sharma, Y. (2024). Achieving Sustainability Through Green Technology: The Need of the Nations. In *Convergence Strategies for Green Computing and Sustainable Development* (pp. 52-61). IGI Global.

View of Color Psychology in Marketing. (n.d.). Https://Www.Jbt.Org.Pk/Index.Php/Jbt/Article/View/99/85.

Vinoth, S., Vemula, H. L., Haralayya, B., Mamgain, P., Hasan, M. F., & Naved, M. (2022). Application of cloud computing in banking and e-commerce and related security threats. *Materials Today: Proceedings, 51*, 2172–2175. DOI: 10.1016/j.matpr.2021.11.121

Vinuesa, R., Azizpour, H., Leite, I., Balaam, M., Dignum, V., Domisch, S., Felländer, A., Langhans, S. D., Tegmark, M., & Fuso Nerini, F. (2020). The role of artificial intelligence in achieving the sustainable development goals. *Nature Communications, 11*(1), 1–10. DOI: 10.1038/s41467-019-14108-y PMID: 31932590

Vishwakarma, M., & Nigam, A. (2024), Comparative Analysis of 4G and 5G Networks: A Review Study, *International Journal for Multidisciplinary Research*, Volume 6, Issue 3, May-June 2024.

Vroom, R. (n.d.). Styling influence to the loyalty for knowledge sharing on WikID. Https://Www.Academia.Edu/16724582/Styling_influence_to_the_loyalty_for_knowledge_sharing_on_WikID

Wang, H., Qin, C., Bai, Y., Zhang, Y., & Fu, Y. (2021). Recent advances on neural network pruning at initialization. *arXiv preprint arXiv:2103.06460.*

Wang, H., Li, G., Wang, G., Peng, J., Jiang, H., & Liu, Y. (2017). Deep learning-based ensemble approach for probabilistic wind power forecasting. *Applied Energy, 188*, 56–70. DOI: 10.1016/j.apenergy.2016.11.111

Wang, J., Tchapmi, L. P., Ravikumar, A. P., McGuire, M., Bell, C. S., Zimmerle, D., Savarese, S., & Brandt, A. R. (2020). Machine vision for natural gas methane emissions detection using an infrared camera. *Applied Energy, 257*, 113998. DOI: 10.1016/j.apenergy.2019.113998

Wang, S., & Guo, W. (2014). Sustainable Growth for Cellular Wireless Networks. In *Handbook of Research on Progressive Trends in Wireless Communications and Networking* (pp. 18–43). IGI Global. DOI: 10.4018/978-1-4666-5170-8.ch002

Wan, Y., Qu, Y., Gao, L., & Xiang, Y. (2022). Privacy-preserving blockchain-enabled federated learning for B5G-driven edge computing. *Computer Networks, 204*, 108671. DOI: 10.1016/j.comnet.2021.108671

Wu, C., Kreidieh, A., Vinitsky, E., & Bayen, A. M. (2017). Emergent behaviors in mixed-autonomy traffic. In Proceedings of the Conference on Robot Learning (pp. 398–407). PMLR. https://proceedings.mlr.press/v78/wu17a.html

Xiao, G., Lin, J., Seznec, M., Wu, H., Demouth, J., & Han, S. (2023). SmoothQuant: Accurate and efficient post-training quantization for large language models. In International Conference on Machine Learning (pp. 38087–38099). PMLR. https://proceedings.mlr.press/v202/xiao23a.html

Xu, N., Yang, J., Needham, M., Boscovic, D., & Vakil, F. (2010). Toward the Green Video CDN. *2010 IEEE/ACM International Conference on Green Computing and Communications*, 430-435.

Yadav, P., Singh, B., Bhaskar, A., Srivastava, S., & Singh, S. K. (2024). Role of Artificial Intelligence in Renewable Energy Management for Sustainable Development. In *Methodologies, Frameworks, and Applications of Machine Learning* (pp. 108-124). IGI Global. DOI: 10.4018/979-8-3693-1062-5.ch006

Yadav, A. (2024). Leveraging Artificial Intelligence for Sustainable Development and Environmental Resilience. In *Exploring Ethical Dimensions of Environmental Sustainability and Use of AI* (pp. 140–165). IGI Global.

Yamini, B., Beslin, P. P., Anish, T. P., Gracelin, S. B., Dinesh, M. G., Nalini, M., & Siva, S. R. (2024). Advancements in Cognitive Radio Networks: Protocols, Architectures, Challenges, and Future Perspectives. In Spectrum and Power Allocation in Cognitive Radio Systems (pp. 1-17). IGI Global.

Yamini, B., Prasanna, V., Ambhika, C., Anuradha, M., Maheswari, B., Subramanian, S. R., & Nalini, M. (2023). A comprehensive survey of deep learning: Advancements, applications, and challenges. *International Journal on Recent and Innovation Trends in Computing and Communication, 11*(8s), 445–453. DOI: 10.17762/ijritcc.v11i8s.7225

Yamini, B., Ramana, K. V., Nalini, M., Devi, D. C., Maheswari, B., & Siva, S. R. (2024). Customer churn prediction model in enterprises using machine learning. *International Journal of Advanced Technology and Engineering Exploration, 11*(110), 94.

Yang, T.-J., Chen, Y.-H., & Sze, V. (2017). Designing energy-efficient convolutional neural networks using energy-aware pruning. In *Proceedings of the IEEE Conference on Computer Vision and Pattern Recognition* (pp. 5687–5695). IEEE. DOI: 10.1109/CVPR.2017.643

Yang, Y., & Ma, M. (2014). Sustainable mobile computing. *Computing*, *96*(2), 85–86. DOI: 10.1007/s00607-013-0309-1

Yin, X., Wu, G., Wei, J., Shen, Y., Qi, H., & Yin, B. (2021). Deep learning on traffic prediction: Methods, analysis, and future directions. *IEEE Transactions on Intelligent Transportation Systems*, *23*(6), 4927–4943. DOI: 10.1109/TITS.2021.3054840

Zafrir, O., Boudoukh, G., Izsak, P., & Wasserblat, M. (2019). Q8BERT: Quantized 8-bit BERT. In 2019 Fifth Workshop on Energy Efficient Machine Learning and Cognitive Computing—NeurIPS Edition (EMC2-NIPS) (pp. 36–39). IEEE. https://doi.org/DOI: 10.1109/EMC2-NIPS48266.2019.00012

Zekić-Sušac, M., Mitrović, S., & Has, A. (2021). Machine learning based system for managing energy efficiency of the public sector as an approach towards smart cities. *International Journal of Information Management*, *58*, 102074. DOI: 10.1016/j.ijinfomgt.2020.102074

Zhang, H.. (2021). Energy-efficient IoT networks: Challenges and opportunities. *IEEE Network*, *35*(2), 15–21.

Zhang, M., Kafy, A.-A., Xiao, P., Han, S., Zou, S., Saha, M., Zhang, C., & Tan, S. (2023). Impact of urban expansion on land surface temperature and carbon emissions using machine learning algorithms in Wuhan, China. *Urban Climate*, *47*, 101347. DOI: 10.1016/j.uclim.2022.101347

Zhang, Y., & Feng, J. (2024). *Towards a Smart and Sustainable Future with Edge Computing-Powered Internet of Things: Fundamentals, Applications, Challenges, and Future Research Directions. Journal of The Institution of Engineers*. Series B.

Zhao, Y., Li, T., Zhang, X., & Zhang, C. (2019). Artificial intelligence-based fault detection and diagnosis methods for building energy systems: Advantages, challenges and the future. *Renewable and Sustainable Energy Reviews, 109*(November 2018), 85–101. DOI: 10.1016/j.rser.2019.04.021

Zhao, X., Jiang, N., Liu, J., Yu, D., & Chang, J. (2020). Short-term average wind speed and turbulent standard deviation forecasts based on one-dimensional convolutional neural network and the integrate method for probabilistic framework. *Energy Conversion and Management*, *203*(October), 112239. DOI: 10.1016/j.enconman.2019.112239

Zheng, Z., Zhu, J., & Lyu, M. R. (2013, June). *Service-generated big data and big data-as-a-service: an overview. In 2013 IEEE international congress on Big Data.* IEEE. DOI: 10.1109/BigData.Congress.2013.60

Zhu, C., Zhang, W., Chiang, Y.-H., Ye, N., Du, L., & An, J. (2022, March/April). Software-Defined Maritime Fog Computing: Architecture, Advantages, and Feasibility. *IEEE Network*, *36*(2), 26–33. DOI: 10.1109/MNET.003.2100433

Zou, Z., Jin, Y., Nevalainen, P., Huan, Y., Heikkonen, J., & Westerlund, T. (2019, March). Edge and fog computing enabled AI for IoT-an overview. In *2019 IEEE International Conference on Artificial Intelligence Circuits and Systems (AICAS)* (pp. 51-56). IEEE. DOI: 10.1109/AICAS.2019.8771621

About the Contributors

P. J. Beslin Pajila is an accomplished academic and researcher with over 12 years of experience in teaching and research, specializing in Wireless Sensor Networks. She completed her Ph.D. in Computer Science and Engineering from Anna University in 2022. She has published two SCI papers, two Scopus-indexed papers, and contributed to several book chapters. Dr. Pajila has taught at esteemed institutions such as Vel Tech Rangarajan Dr. Sagunthala R&D Institute of Science and Technology and Francis Xavier Engineering College, contributing significantly to the academic community. Her areas of expertise include Python, Data Structures, and Machine Learning. In addition to her teaching career, she has industry experience as a Business Analyst at CentizenInc, Tirunelveli. Dr. Pajila has participated in numerous conferences and delivered expert lectures, covering topics such as Artificial Intelligence, Cybersecurity, and Data Science. She is also an active reviewer for prominent journals including Soft Computing and Journal of Intelligent & Fuzzy Systems. Throughout her career, Dr. Pajila has been recognized for her academic contributions and active involvement in department activities, holding positions such as Department Placement Coordinator and GATE Coordinator. She is passionate about programming, gardening, and art, and continues to contribute to advancements in AI, IoT, and sustainable technologies.

Belfin Robinson Vimala is a Postdoctoral Research Associate at the Department of Neurology, University of North Carolina, specializing in fMRI and neuroinformatics. With a Ph.D. in Computer Science and Engineering from Karunya Institute of Technology and Sciences, she focuses on data science, network science, and graph theory. Her research on Alzheimer's and chronic pain diagnostics, leveraging machine learning and deep learning models, has contributed significantly to biomarker identification with high accuracy. Dr. Vimala has also worked extensively in developing diagnostic models for epilepsy and facial pain using advanced imaging techniques. Her professional journey includes roles as an

Assistant Professor at Karunya University, where she developed algorithms for community detection and COVID-19 prediction, widely cited across the globe. In addition to her academic achievements, Dr. Vimala has industry experience as a software engineer at Wipro Technologies and Robert Bosch. She has authored several journal articles and presented at international conferences, focusing on social networks, health informatics, and machine learning applications. Dr. Vimala has also been recognized for her leadership roles, including organizing technical events and serving on program committees for prominent international conferences. Her contributions to both academia and industry reflect her expertise in data-driven research and healthcare innovation, making her a well-regarded professional in her field.

Y. Harold Robinson is a distinguished academic and researcher with over 17 years of teaching experience and 2 years of industrial experience. He is currently a Professor at Francis Xavier Engineering College, Tirunelveli, and a recognized Ph.D. supervisor at Anna University. He earned his Ph.D. in Information and Communication Engineering from Anna University, Chennai, in 2016. Dr. Robinson has published 145 research papers in Scopus/SCI indexed journals and has authored several books on topics ranging from cloud computing to IoT and blockchain technology. His research interests include wireless sensor networks, mobile ad-hoc networks, and machine learning. He has also been recognized as one of the world's top 2% scientists by Stanford University. Dr. Robinson has completed postdoctoral research at Vellore Institute of Technology and holds multiple technical certifications. His work in the academic field has earned him significant recognition in both teaching and research, contributing to advancements in computer science.

C. Gopala Krishnan is a seasoned academic professional with over 19 years of experience, currently serving as an Associate Professor in the Department of Computer Science and Engineering at GITAM School of Technology, Bengaluru. He earned his Ph.D. from St. Peter's Institute of Higher Education and Research in 2018, with earlier degrees from Anna University and Madurai Kamaraj University. His teaching expertise spans across a variety of subjects including Computer Networks, Mobile Computing, and Wireless Sensor Networks. Dr. Gopala Krishnan has participated in numerous faculty development programs and delivered guest lectures on emerging technologies. His research contributions include several papers published in prestigious journals, focusing on areas such as ad-hoc networks, cloud computing, and wireless sensor networks. He has also been actively involved in funded projects, co-leading initiatives aimed at preserving Indian heritage through deep learning and promoting technology awareness among rural students. A member of the ISTE, Dr. Gopala Krishnan is known for his strong technical, communication, and analytical skills. Fluent in Tamil, English, and Hindi, he also enjoys playing shuttle badminton during his free time.

***

A. Mathankumar is an Assistant Professor in the Department of Artificial Intelligence and Data Science at Vel Tech Multi Tech Dr. Rangarajan Dr. Sakunthala Engineering College, Avadi, Chennai. He is passionate about teaching, research, and guiding students in AI and data-driven technologies. His academic interests include machine learning, data analytics, and innovative problem-solving.

Mathan Kumar is working as assistant professor in artificial intelligence.

A. Rajasekar is an Associate Professor in the Department of Artificial Intelligence and Data Science at Sri Sai Ram Institute of Technology. He is dedicated to research and teaching in AI and data science. His work focuses on mentoring students and driving innovations in intelligent systems.

A Rizwanbasha is a faculty member at Panimalar Engineering College, committed to excellence in teaching and student development.He focuses on enhancing learning through innovative teaching methods and research. His dedication extends to guiding students in academics and projects.

VenkateshanA is a faculty member at Sri Muthukumaran Institute of Technology, Chennai. He is dedicated to teaching and mentoring students in core engineering subjects. His academic interests include innovative teaching methodologies and student development.

Farooq Ahmad is currently working as Assistant Professor and Training Coordinator (IUCAT) in the Department of Computer Application, Integral University, Lucknow, INDIA. Dr. Farooq holds a bachelor's degree in Science from DDU University, a Master's degree from Harcourt Butler Technological Institute, Kanpur and achieved his PhD degree in Computer Application from Integral University, Lucknow. He has diverse background of 24+ Years of total experience in IT software development industry and education with over 7 years of project management, 4 years of Database Architect, 4 years of Programmer Analyst and 9 years of Academic/Research, Teaching, Technical Training and coordination of the Technical Trainings. He has published quality research papers in Journals, National and International Conferences of repute. He is contributing his knowledge and experience as speaker and member of technical committee in various international Journals/Conferences of repute. His areas of interest are Web

Technologies, RDBMS, SQL, PLSQL, C, C++, Python, Java, R Programming, DSA, MERN & MEAN Stack, Artificial Intelligence, Machine Learning, Data Warehousing and Mining.

Mohammad Shabbir Alam received the M.C.A degree in computer science and application from Aligarh Muslim University, Aligarh in 2007. Mohammad Shabbir Alam is currently a senior lecturer in College of Computer Science and Information Technology at Jazan University, Jazan Kingdom of Saudi Arabia. His research interest includes Deep Learning,IoT, Image Processing and Machine Learning. He has published over 10 papers in peer reviewed journal, 5 Australian and 3 Indian Patents.

B. Senthilkumaran is an Assistant Professor in the Department of Computer Science and Engineering at the School of Computing, Vel Tech Rangarajan Dr. Sagunthala R&D Institute of Science and Technology (Deemed to be University), located in Vel Nagar, Chennai, Tamil Nadu. He contributes significantly to the academic and research activities within the institution, fostering growth and innovation in the field of computer science.

B. Yamini (Yamini Bhavani Shankar) is an Associate Professor in the Department of Networking and Communications, School of Computing, at SRM Institute of Science and Technology (SRMIST), Kattankulathur. She is passionate about teaching, research, and mentoring students in advanced networking and communication technologies. Her contributions to academia are reflected through her publications and active involvement in innovative projects.

Yuvasri B is an faculty member in the Department of Computer Science and Engineering at R.M.K. College of Engineering and Technology. She is actively involved in research and academic development, contributing to advancements in computer science. With a strong commitment to teaching, she mentors students and fosters innovation in emerging technologies. Ms. Yuvasri continues to engage in scholarly activities to enhance knowledge in her field.

B. Chitra is an Assistant Professor at Panimalar Engineering College, specializing in computer science and engineering. With a strong academic background, she is dedicated to teaching and research in emerging technologies. She has contributed to various publications and actively participates in academic development. Dr. Chitra is committed to mentoring students and fostering innovation

Lekha D is an author and researcher in Computer Science and Engineering at R.M.K. College of Engineering and Technology, India. She actively contributes to research in her field, focusing on emerging technologies and advancements. Based in Puduvoyal, Tamil Nadu, she is dedicated to academic excellence and innovation.

D. Poornima., Assistant professor in the Department of Computer Science and Engineering in Sathyabama Institute of Science and Technology, Chennai. She has 13 years of teaching experience. Her publication includes 17 articles from various journals. Her research interests include,, Digital Image Processing and Digital Signal Processing.

D. Prabhu is a faculty member in the Department of Computer Science and Engineering at the School of Computing, Vel Tech Rangarajan Dr. Sagunthala R&D Institute of Science and Technology, Avadi, Chennai. He is dedicated to teaching, research, and mentoring in computer science. With a passion for academic excellence, he contributes to innovative learning and technological advancements.

D. Vijayakumar is an Assistant Professor in the Department of Mechanical Engineering at Vel Tech Multi Tech Dr. Rangarajan Dr. Sakunthala Engineering College, Chennai. He is committed to excellence in teaching and research in mechanical engineering. His focus is on mentoring students and fostering innovation in the field.

Shantanu Datta did his Ph.D (Mechanical Engineering) from IIT(ISM) Dhanbad. He did M.Tech from NIT Agartala, Tripura and did his Bachelor of Engineering in Mechanical Engineering from Amravati University, Maharashtra. Dr. Shantanu Datta has 12 years of teaching and industrial experience. Dr. Datta is life time member of Indian Society for Technical Education. He had published various technical articles in the reputed Scopus indexed journals and published four patents. His area of interest is Applied Fluid Mechanics, Renewable Energy Sources and application of Artificial Intelligence in the pipeline fault detection system. He had worked on Genetic Algorithm based pipe line fault detection technique. He is now faculty of Guru Nanak Institute of Technology, Sodepur, Kolkata.

Anita Devare has completed PhD in Mathematics. Her area of research addresses the solutions to the problems in the Applied Mathematics.

Manoj Devare received BSc & MSc degree from North Maharashtra University and PhD in Computer Science from Bharati Vidyapeeth University, India. He is working as Associate Professor at Amity Institute of Information Technology, Amity University Mumbai. He has 17 years of teaching and research experience in Computer Science. His PhD thesis was based on the Congestion Controlling in Homogeneous and Heterogeneous Computer Networks. Dr. Manoj won the "Best

Paper Award", in ICSCI 2008. He has served as Post Doctorate Fellow at Centre of Excellence on HPC, Uni. of Calabria, Italy under young researcher scheme. He has been developed Desktop Cloud system. His research deals with IoT, Cloud, Machine Learning and innovative applications of those technologies to scientific problems. He has 02 Patents pending; he edited 05 book chapters, 09 Int. Journal papers, 15 conference Papers. He has delivered 08 national and international keynote speeches. He is connected with review process of reputed international journal papers, edited chapters from the reputed journals like Elsevier's FGCS, Springer's review system, Symbiosis International Journal.

K. Dhivya is an Assistant Professor in the Department of Electronics and Communication Engineering at SRM Institute of Science and Technology, Kattankulathur, Chengelpet. With a strong academic background, she is dedicated to teaching and research in the field of ECE.

Shweta Dwivedi is an Assistant Professor in the Department of Computer Application at Integral University, Lucknow. She earned her Ph.D. from Maharishi University in 2022. Her research interests include image processing and machine learning, and she has published extensively in these areas. Dr. Shweta has also been involved in coordinating MOOCs and value-added courses, such as "Green Computing." Her administrative roles include various committee memberships at Integral University. She has received multiple patents for innovative technologies and has participated in numerous national seminars and workshops. Dr. Shweta contributions span both academic and practical applications in her field.

Indra E is a faculty member at Mailam Engineering College, committed to excellence in teaching and student development. She focuses on enhancing learning through innovative teaching methods and research. Her dedication extends to guiding students in academics and projects.

G. Mariammal is an Assistant Professor in the Department of Computer Science and Engineering at Vel Tech Rangarajan Dr. Sagunthala R&D Institute of Science and Technology, Avadi. She specializes in computer science education and research, contributing to advancements in areas like data science and software development. Mariammal is committed to fostering innovation and academic growth in her students and research community.

Priyam Ganguly is an accomplished data engineer, analyst, and academic contributor with a career spanning various industries and roles. Currently working as a Data Analyst at Hanwha QCells America, Priyam specializes in leveraging tools like Tableau, Snowflake, and SQL to drive business intelligence and operational efficiency. His work has significantly impacted the energy, fulfillment, and financial sectors by developing data-driven solutions and optimizing decision-making processes. Priyam is also a recognized IEEE researcher and peer reviewer, contributing to high-impact AI and computational intelligence research. His scholarly contributions include several published papers on topics like deep learning in healthcare and advanced AI architectures for predictive analytics. As a program committee member, he has played an instrumental role in curating and enhancing the quality of research for various events. Beyond academia, Priyam has judged globally prestigious awards like the Globee Awards and Brandon Hall Excellence Awards, assessing innovations across technology and business domains. He is actively involved in judging hackathons, aimed at fostering STEM education among students and professionals. As a keynote speaker, Priyam has delivered thought leadership on topics like ethical data visualization, AI transformation, and advancements in analytics. His multidisciplinary expertise and commitment to advancing AI scholarship make him a prominent figure at the intersection of academia and industry.

Ranita Ganguly, I am an IEEE member and work as a Quality Consultant at 3D Technologies LLC for my prestigious client Charles Schwab (a Financial services company that operates in the capital markets industry), with substantial contributions to the field of Mobile computing and with profound commitment to Mobile Learning and Mobile Technology. I consistently try to exhibit technical excellence, creativity, and leadership throughout my career. I am committed to advancing my profession and supporting fellow engineers. I am a Fellow of Hackathon Raptors, IICSPA, and the Royal Society of Arts (RSA) due to my qualities and professional achievements. I am recognized due to my technical expertise, contributions to the field, and active involvement in the community. I have done my Doctorate from Delaware State University and my Master's from Pune University. I have 12 years of rich experience in validating mobile apps for mobile computing and 5 years of mentoring experience.

I Vasudevan is an Assistant Professor in the Department of Computer Science and Engineering at Vel Tech Rangarajan Dr. Sagunthala R&D Institute of Science and Technology. With expertise in CSE, he is dedicated to research and academic excellence. He actively contributes to teaching, mentoring, and innovative advancements in his field.

Rajeshkumar J is an Assistant Professor in the School of Computing and Information Technology at REVA University. He is dedicated to teaching and research in computing and information technology. His work focuses on mentoring students and fostering innovation in the field.

J. Refonaa has graduated from Anna University with Bachelor's Degree in information Technology . she has received her M. E degree in Computer Science and Engineering from Anna University, Chennai in 2013, she has graduated with her Ph.D. in Computer Science in 2021 from Sathyabama Institute Of Science and Technology. She is currently an Assistant Professor at Sathyabama Institute of Science & Technology in Chennai. She has over eleven years of teaching experience .Her research interests are Spatial Data Mining, Big Data, Soft Engineering, Database Management System etc. She has presented her research findings in various reputed journals and has published more than 53 articles in various journals and conferences, as well as published books and monographs in various publications. She has also published three patents in IPR.

Sudha K is a faculty member at R.M.D Engineering College. She is committed to teaching and research, focusing on advancing scientific knowledge and innovation.

Anbumaheshwari K. is studying Master Degree in Computer science and Engineering From Sethu Institute Technology.

Anju Aravind K, Received the Master of Engineering in Anna University, TamilNadu, India in 2015 and Received the Bachelor of Engineering in Anna University, TamilNadu, India in 2011and worked as Java Programmer in private company, TamilNadu, India in 2011 – 2015. Am worked as an Assistant Professor in Mother Teresa Institute of Science and Technology, Telangana, India in 2019 – 2023. Currently am working as an Assistant Professor in Koneru Lakshmaiah Education Foundation, Guntur, India in 2023 – present.

Aravindaraj K is an Assistant Professor in the Faculty of Management at SRM Institute of Science and Technology, Kattankulathur. His areas of interest are data science, supply chain, and logistics.

Hemakumar K is an Assistant Professor in the Department of Information Technology at Adhiparasakthi Engineering College. He is dedicated to teaching, research, and mentoring students in IT. With a passion for academic excellence, he contributes to innovative learning and technological advancements.

R. Kennady is an Assistant Professor in the Department of Artificial Intelligence and Data Science at Rajalakshmi Institute of Technology. He is committed to teaching, research, and mentoring in AI and data science. With a passion for academic excellence, he contributes to innovative learning and technological advancements.

K. Vijayakumar is an Assistant Professor in the Department of Artificial Intelligence and Data Science at Panimalar Engineering College. He specializes in AI, machine learning, and data analytics. With a passion for research and teaching, he actively contributes to the academic and technological growth of students. His interests include deep learning, big data, and innovative AI applications.

B.Karunamoorthy did his Ph.D (Electrical Engineering) from Anna University Chennai. He did M.E from Anna University, Chennai and did his Bachelor of Engineering in Electrical and Electronics Engineering from Madras University, Tamilnadu. Dr.B.Karunamoorthy has 18 years of teaching and 4 years of industrial experience. Dr.B.Karunamoorthy is life time member of Indian Society for Technical Education. He had published various technical articles in the reputed Scopus indexed journals and published 30 patents. His area of interest is Embedded system, Embedded controller for Power Electronics, Renewable Energy Sources and application of Artificial Intelligence . He had worked on Design and developement of Electric Vehicle. He is now faculty of Kumaraguru College of Technology, Coimbatore, Tamilnadu.

Dhivya Kesavan is an Assistant Professor in the Department of Electronics and Communication Engineering at SRM Institute of Science and Technology, Kattankulathur. She specializes in advanced communication technologies and actively contributes to research and academic development. With a strong commitment to teaching, she mentors students and fosters innovation in electronics and communication engineering. Dr. Dhivya Kesavan continues to engage in scholarly activities, enhancing knowledge in her field.

Zohaib Hasan Khan, Assistant Professor, ECE Department, Integral University, Lucknow. I have received the B. Tech, M. Tech, P.hD and LLB degree. My research interests include AI, CyberLaw and security, Ethical Hacking, Digital Electronics, Electronics Devices & circuits, Mixers, Wireless communication, Solar Energy and Entrepreneurship, Data Communication Networks.

Arthy M is an Assistant Professor in the Department of Data Science and Business Systems at the School of Computing, SRM Institute of Science and Technology (SRMIST). She is committed to teaching and research in data science and business systems. Based at SRM Nagar, Kattankulathur, she actively contributes to academic excellence and innovation.

Ezhilvendan M. is an Assistant Professor in the Department of Artificial Intelligence and Machine Learning at Panimalar Engineering College, Poonamalle, Chennai-600123, Tamil Nadu, India. He obtained his B.Tech in Information

Technology from IFET College of Engineering, Villupuram, his M.E in Network Engineering from Veltech Multitech Dr. Rangarajan Dr. Sakunthala Engineering College, Avadi, Chennai, and is currently pursuing a Ph.D. in Information and Communication Engineering as a part-time research scholar at Anna University. His study domain encompasses Artificial Intelligence, Machine Learning, and Deep Learning. He has around 12 years of Academic Experience. He has authored several publications in international and national journals, as well as books,book Chapters and conferences.

M. Maheswari received the Ph.D. Degree in Computer Science and engineering from Anna University, India, in November 2019. She is currently working as a Associate Professor, School of Computing, Sathyabama University, Chennai, India. She has rich teaching and research experience. She has published papers in reputed Inter- national Conferences and refereed Journals. She has organized many technical events and symposiums. Her research interests include machine learning, Recommender Systems, Computer Networks and Data Mining. She serves as a Life Member in CSI and ISTE Computer Society.

Mercy Theresa M is an Assistant Professor in the Department of Data Science and Business Systems at the School of Computing, SRM Institute of Science and Technology, Kattankulathur. She specializes in data science, business systems, and emerging computing technologies. With a strong academic and research background, she is dedicated to mentoring students and advancing technological innovations. Her areas of interest include machine learning, big data analytics, and AI-driven business solutions.

Thrushna Matharasi, I am the Director Engineering, Data & AI at Solera Holdings based in Dallas, Texas,USA with over 12+ years of industry experience. I have completed the prestigious CORE Program from Harvard Business School and hold a Master's degree in Engineering from the University of Bridgeport. I have a proven track record of integrating generative AI and machine learning solutions to solve complex business problems in finance, healthcare, and mobile advertising. At Solera, I lead a 20+ member team of engineers, data analysts, and scientists, driving initiatives that blend advanced analytics with real-time data solutions, strategies that I have implemented of machine learning models have resulted in significant revenue gains, while projects like integrating Looker and Snowflake have saved over $1 million annually with a passion for solving complex data challenges, I continuously seek innovative solutions that improve data workflows, enhance performance, and save costs.

Nupur Mittal holds a PhD in Electronics and serves as an Assistant Professor in the Department of Electronics & Communication Engineering at Integral University, Lucknow. Her research interests encompass digital electronics, RF (Transceiver) IC design, filters, current conveyors, solar energy, and related Devices, Artificial Intelligence, Machine Learning. She can be reached at mittalnupur2004@gmail .com or mittal@iul.ac.in. ORCID ID: 0000-0002-3765-8813

GokuldhevM Mony is a faculty member at Vel Tech Rangarajan Dr. Sagunthala R&D Institute of Science and Technology. He is committed to teaching and research, focusing on advancing scientific knowledge and innovation.

Pavithra N is an Assistant Professor in the Department of Information Technology at Jeppiaar Institute of Technology. She is dedicated to teaching, research, and mentoring in computer science. With a strong academic background, she contributes to technological advancements and innovative learning.

GajalakshmiP is a faculty member at Adhiparasakthi Engineering College, committed to excellence in teaching and student development. She focuses on enhancing learning through innovative teaching methods and research. Her dedication extends to guiding students in academics and projects.

Girija P is a faculty member in the Computer Science and Engineering department at Vel Tech Rangarajan Dr. Sagunthala R&D Institute of Science and Technology in Avadi, Chennai. She plays a crucial role in advancing academic and research efforts at the institution.

Aniket Gangadharrao Patil is an Assistant Professor at MGMU's Jawaharlal Nehru Engineering College in Chhatrapati Sambhajinagar (Aurangabad), Maharashtra. He plays a pivotal role in advancing the academic and research initiatives at the college, shaping the next generation of engineers. Prof. Patil is dedicated to providing top-notch education and promoting innovation among his students. His commitment to academic excellence is evident in his efforts to enhance the learning experience.

Daisy Merina R. is a dedicated academic and researcher with a strong background in Computer Science and Engineering. She holds a Master of Engineering (M.E.) from Sethu Institute of Technology, Virudunagar, and is currently pursuing a Ph.D. at Anna University. As an Assistant Professor and Program Coordinator, she has contributed significantly to both academia and practical applications in her field. Her areas of expertise include Algorithms, Data Structures, Python programming, and Machine Learning Algorithms. Daisy is a published author, with notable works including books on Basics of Algorithms, Data Structures, and Embedded System Design. Her research contributions include papers on IoT-based solutions for agriculture and water quality analysis, as well as innovative projects like intelligent systems for healthcare and visually impaired aid systems.

R. Nithyanandhan is an Assistant Professor in the Department of Computer Science and Engineering at S A Engineering College. He is dedicated to teaching, research, and guiding students in cutting-edge areas of computer science. His academic interests include software development, data structures, and emerging technologies.

Prem Kumar R is a faculty member at R.M.K. College of Engineering and Technology in Puduvoyal, Tamil Nadu. Known for his dedication to advancing academic and technical knowledge, he plays a pivotal role at the institution

Siva Subramanian R is a distinguished member of R.M.K. College of Engineering and Technology in Puduvoyal, Tamil Nadu. Known for his dedication to advancing academic and technical knowledge, he plays a pivotal role at the institution

Vidhya Muthulakshmi R is an Assistant Professor in the field of Artificial Intelligence and Data Science at Panimalar Engineering College. With a strong commitment to academic excellence, she plays a vital role in shaping the next generation of AI and Data Science professionals. Her work focuses on innovative teaching methods and cutting-edge research, contributing to the advancement of these rapidly evolving fields. Vidhya is dedicated to fostering a deep understanding of AI and Data Science among her students.

Vinoth R is an Associate Professor in the Department of CSE at R.M.K College of Engineering and Technology. He is dedicated to teaching, research, and mentoring in computer science. With a strong academic background, she contributes to technological advancements and innovative learning.

Amshavalli R.S. is an Assistant professor in the Department of Computer Science and Engineering in, Sathyabama Institute of Science and Technology,Chennai. She received her M.Tech in Information Technology from Crescent B.S.Abdur Rahman University, Chennai, India. She has 11 years of teaching experience. Her publication includes 15 articles from various journals. Her research interests include networking, image processing..

D. Ravindran is an Associate Professor at the School of Management, Kristu Jayanti College, Autonomous, Bengaluru. He has extensive experience in management education, with a focus on research and teaching in areas such as marketing and business strategy. Dr. Ravindran is dedicated to academic excellence and contributes actively to both teaching and research in the management field.

B. Venkatesh Reddy has got his B.tech degree in Electrical and Electronics from SVU College of Engineering, Tirupati, AP in 2012. He got his M.Tech degree in power electronics from JNTU Hyderabadin 2014. He got his Ph.D from Sri Venkateswara University in 2024. His area of interests are Power Electronics, Renewable energy sources, Artificial Intelligence Applications,DC-DC converters. Presently he is working as Assistant Professor in Department of EEE, S.V College of Engineering, Tirupati, AP, India. Email: venkateshreddy.b@svce.edu.in

Anusha S is an Assistant Professor in the Department of Information Technology at Easwari Engineering College. She is passionate about teaching and research, focusing on advancements in IT and computer science. Anusha actively mentors students while contributing to academic growth through publications and projects.

Balapriya S is an Assistant Professor in the Department of Computer Science and Engineering at Sathyabama Institute of Science and Technology, Chennai, Tamil Nadu. She is committed to advancing the field of computer science through her research and teaching, contributing to the academic excellence of the institution. Dr. Balapriya is known for her dedication to student development and her innovative approach to education. Her work plays a crucial role in preparing students for successful careers in technology

DeepaS. is an Assistant Professor in the Department of Computer Science and Business Systems at R.M.D. Engineering College. She is dedicated to teaching, research, and mentoring students in CSBS. With a passion for academic excellence, she contributes to innovative learning and technological advancements.

Gayathri S is an Assistant Professor in the Department of Computer Science and Engineering at S A Engineering College. She is committed to excellence in teaching and research in computer science. Her focus is on mentoring students and fostering innovation in technology.

KerthyS. is an Assistant Professor in the Department of Information Technology at Jeppiaar Institute of Technology. He is committed to excellence in teaching and research in IT. Her focus is on mentoring students and fostering innovation in technology.

Nagarajan S is an Assistant Professor in the Department of Computer Science and Engineering at R.M.K. Engineering College. He is dedicated to teaching and research, contributing to advancements in computer science. His academic interests include emerging technologies and innovation in the field.

PrabakeranS. is an Associate Professor in the Department of Networking and Communications at SRM Institute of Science and Technology, Kattankulathur, Chennai, with over 14 years of experience. His research interests include Network Security, Information Security, Cloud Computing, Wireless Sensor Networks, Machine Learning Techniques, Natural Language Processing, and Data Analytics.

PraveenS. graduated from thiruvalluvar university with a bachelor's degree in computer science and application. He got a master's degree in computer science from thiruvalluvar university, vellore. He has more than 2 years of teaching experience in the department of computer science and engineering at sathyabama institute of science and technology. His area of research is database management system, networking, and cloud computing. He has also presented his paper work in various journals and conferences.

UdhayashankarS is a distinguished member of Vel Tech Multi Tech Dr.Rangarajan Dr.Sakunthala Engineering College. Known for his dedication to advancing academic and technical knowledge, he plays a pivotal role at the institution

Nandha Gopal S M is a faculty member at Thejus Engineering College. He is dedicated to teaching and research in engineering and technology. His work focuses on mentoring students and fostering innovation in his field.

SassirekhaS. M. is a faculty member at Mailam Engineering College, committed to excellence in teaching and student development. She focuses on enhancing learning through innovative teaching methods and research. Her dedication extends to guiding students in academics and projects.

S.L. Jany Shabu received her Bachelor of Science in Mathematics in 2000 and MS(Information Technology & Ecommerce) in 2003 from Manonmanium Sundaranar University, Tirunelveli, Tamilnadu. In 2009, she graduated from Sathyabama University, Jeppiaar Nagar, Chennai, Tamil Nadu with a Master of Technology in Information Technology, and in 2021, she completed a Ph.D. in Computer Science. She worked as a System trainee at Universal Technology Park, Trivandrum. She is currently an Associate Professor at Sathyabama Institute of Science & Technology in Chennai. She has over nineteen years of teaching experience as research, student development activities & administrative work. Her area of interest in research is in Data Science, Machine Learning, Image Processing, Database Management System & Web Technology etc. She serves as a reviewer for reputed journals and has published more than 60 articles in various journals and conferences, as well as books and monographs in various publications. She has also published three patents in IPR. . Dr.S.L.Jany Shabu Associate Professor Computer Science Sathyabama Institute of Science & Technology, Chennai-600119

Satyajee Srivastava has over 22 years of teaching and industry experience. He received his Ph.D. in Computer Science and is an Artificial Intelligence developer, researcher, practitioner and educator. He has Publication of 12 Books and 100 Articles in Journals of repute He is presently serving as Professor, CSE Department, M.M. Engineering College, Maharishi Markandeshwar (Deemed To Be University), Mullana, Ambala, Haryana.He is an active machine learning researcher and regularly teaches courses and maintains resources for the data scientist. His research has pioneered developments in deep learning, outlier detection and profile discovery A.I., Data Science Machine Learning, Big DATA and Green Computing.

L. Sudha is an Assistant Professor in the Faculty of Management at SRM Institute of Science and Technology (SRMIST), Kattankulathur. She is dedicated to teaching, research, and mentoring in management studies. With a strong academic background, she contributes to business education and innovative research.

MaheshwaranT. is an Assistant Professor in the Department of Information Technology at Sri Manakula Vinayagar Engineering College, Puducherry. He contributes to the academic and technological advancements of the institution through his expertise and dedication. His work significantly enhances the educational environment and fosters innovation in the field of information technology.

NithyaT. is an Assistant Professor in the Department of Computer Science and Engineering at Rajalakshmi Institute of Technology. She specializes in advanced computing technologies and actively contributes to research and academia. With a passion for teaching, she mentors students and fosters innovation in computer science. Dr. Nithya has participated in various academic and research activities, enhancing knowledge in her field.

SethukarasiT. is the Professor and Head of the Department of Computer Science and Engineering at R.M.K. Engineering College, with 27 years of experience. She earned her Ph.D. in Information & Communication Engineering from Anna University, Chennai, in 2013. Her research interests include Machine Learning, Data Mining, and Soft Computing. Dr. Sethukarasi has published over 70 research papers and supervised seven Ph.D. scholars.

Uma MageswariT. is an Assistant Professor in the Department of Artificial Intelligence and Data Science at Sri Sai Ram Institute of Technology, Chennai. She is passionate about AI research and innovative teaching methodologies. Her work focuses on mentoring students and advancing technology in data science.

VeeramaniT. is an Associate Professor in the Department of Artificial Intelligence and Data Science at Panimalar Engineering College. He is committed to teaching, research, and mentoring in AI and data science. With a focus on academic excellence, he contributes to innovative learning and technological advancements.

Venkata RamanaT. is an Associate Professor in the Department of CSE - AIML at CVR College of Engineering. He is dedicated to teaching and research in artificial intelligence and machine learning. His work focuses on mentoring students and advancing innovations in AI and computing.

AnishT. P. received his M.E. Degree from the Department of Computer Science and Engineering at Saveetha Engineering College (Affiliated to Anna University), Chennai, India, in 2011. He is currently an Assistant Professor at R.M.K. College of Engineering and Technology, Puduvoyal, India. He is pursuing his Ph.D. degree in Information and Communication Engineering from Anna University. His current research interest includes Machine Learning, Deep Learning and Big Data analytics.

Arunkumar V is a faculty member at Malla Reddy College of Engineering, specializing in computer science and engineering. With a strong academic background, he is dedicated to teaching and research in emerging technologies. He actively engages in mentoring students and contributing to academic development. Mr. Arunkumar is committed to fostering innovation and advancing knowledge in his field.

BhoopathyVaradharajan is a Professor at Sree Rama Engineering College. He holds a Ph.D. in Information and Communication Engineering from Anna University and has over 16 years of academic experience. Specializing in wireless sensor networks and IoT, he has published numerous research papers and holds several international patents. Dr. Bhoopathy is a recipient of prestigious awards for his contributions to education and research. His commitment to academia continues to drive innovation and excellence in the field of computer science.

Indumathi V is in the Department of Computational Intelligence at SRM Institute of Science and Technology. She holds a B.E. from Anna University (2006) and an M.Tech from Sastra University (2009). Her expertise includes analytical skills, data analysis, deep learning, machine learning, AWS, R, and Tableau.

KalpanaV. is an Associate Professor in the Department of Computer Science and Engineering at Vel Tech Rangarajan Dr. Sagunthala R&D Institute of Science and Technology, Chennai. She is dedicated to teaching, research, and guiding students in advanced areas of computer science. Her academic contributions include publications, projects, and active participation in innovative research.

V. Sameswari is an Assistant Professor at Rajiv Gandhi National Institute of Youth Development, Sriperumbudur. She has a strong academic background with M.Sc, M.Phil, and Ph.D. qualifications. Her work focuses on research, teaching, and mentoring students in youth development and related fields.

SathyaV. is a dedicated faculty member in the Department of Computer Science and Engineering at Vel Tech Rangarajan Dr. Sagunthala R&D Institute of Science and Technology, Chennai. With a focus on advancing research and education in computer science, she plays a crucial role in guiding students and contributing to academic growth. Her expertise and commitment to teaching help shape future technology professionals. Dr. Sathya is known for her innovative approach to education and research.

Ramya BharathiV.K. is an Assistant Professor at Sathyabama Institute of Science and Technology in Chennai. She contributes to the academic and research environment at the institution.

KanetiVenkata Ramana is an Assistant Professor in the Department of Computer Science and Engineering at VNR Vignana Jyothi Institute of Engineering and Technology, Hyderabad. With extensive experience in academia, he specializes in advanced computing technologies and research. He has contributed to various publications and conferences, showcasing expertise in computer science. Dr. Kaneti actively engages in mentoring students and advancing research in emerging technological domains.

Nirali Verma is pursuing PhD from Amity Institute of Information Technology at Amity University Mumbai. Her interest lies in the application of the data structures and design of efficient algorithms.

Index

Symbols

A

B

C

D

E

R

S

U

W

www.ingramcontent.com/pod-product-compliance
Lightning Source LLC
LaVergne TN
LVHW080613300926
849162LV00005B/1141
9798337307664